Also by Philip Larkin

THE COMPLETE POEMS

The Complete Poems

PHILIP LARKIN

Edited and with an introduction and

commentary by Archie Burnett

FARRAR, STRAUS AND GIROUX   NEW YORK

Farrar, Straus and Giroux
18 West 18th Street, New York 10011

Library of Congress Control Number: 2011945978
Paperback ISBN: 978-0-374-53366-3

www.fsgbooks.com
www.twitter.com/fsgbooks • www.facebook.com/fsgbooks

10 9 8 7

Contents

Contents

Acknowledgements

For help of various kinds I am grateful to: Professor James Booth; Bill and Mairi Burnett; my son William; Brian and Catherine Chaney; Amit Davé; Alex B. Effgen; Katy Evans Pritchard; my colleague Marilyn Gaull; Charlotte Graves-Taylor; the late Jean Hartley; Paul Keegan; Professor John Kelly; Joe McCann (Maggs Bros. Ltd.); my wife Janet; Mary Morris; Leon and Paul Naiditch; James L. Orwin; Dr John Osborne; David and Shirley Popham; my colleague Christopher Ricks; Donald Sommerville; Matt Tantony; Ann Thwaite; the late Jeff Vent (to whom I owe most of the notes on King Henry VIII School, Coventry); Simon Westmancoat; Frances Whistler; and Edward P. Wilson.

The staffs of several libraries have greatly facilitated research: the Bodleian Library (Dr Christopher Fletcher; Oliver House; Colin Harris; Dr Judith Priestman, who kindly arranged access to restricted papers, provided expert guidance through the Bodleian archives of Larkin papers and checked several references; Julia Wagner; Rebecca Wall); the British Library (Michael Boggan); the Brynmor Jones Library, University of Hull (Judy Burg, Kate Butler, Nicola Herbert, Helen E. Roberts, Laura Wilson, Simon Wilson); the Huntington Library; Queen's University, Belfast (Ursula Mitchel); and the Poetry Collection, University of Buffalo, The State University of New York (Dr James Maynard).

I am very grateful to the National Endowment for the Humanities for awarding me a Research Fellowship that freed me from teaching and administrative responsibilities for two semesters and thus enabled me to advance the work substantially towards publication. For covering the cost of research trips I am grateful to Boston University, and also to Christopher Ricks, who generously made available funds from his Andrew W. Mellon Foundation Distinguished Achievement Award. Boston University also funded research assistance from Jay Vithalani, a PhD student at the Editorial Institute, who expertly unearthed copies of early printings in periodicals as well as books and articles on the poetry. Another of the Institute's PhD students, Silvia Glick, proofread the final typescript.

Special thanks must go to Anthony Thwaite, who over the years has done more than anyone for Larkin. Even when making corrections to his text in *Collected Poems*, or taking a different editorial view, I have been aware of building on the foundation he laid down. At typescript stage, he generously offered numerous corrections and suggestions that have resulted in significant improvements.

Abbreviations Used

AGIW	Philip Larkin, *A Girl in Winter* (1947)
AL	*About Larkin*: Journal of the Philip Larkin Society
Amis, *Letters*	*The Letters of Kingsley Amis*, ed. Zachary Leader (2000)
AT	Anthony Thwaite (b. 1930)
AWJ	Philip Larkin, *All What Jazz: A Record Diary, 1961–71*, revised edition (1985)
BL	The British Library
Bloomfield (2002)	B. C. Bloomfield, *Philip Larkin: A Bibliography 1933–1994*, revised and enlarged edition (2002)
Bodleian	The Bodleian Library, Oxford
Booth (1992)	James Booth, *Philip Larkin: Writer* (1992)
Booth (2000)	James Booth, ed., *New Larkins for Old: Critical Essays* (2000)
Booth (2005)	James Booth, *Philip Larkin: The Poet's Plight* (2005)
BP	Barbara Pym (1913–80)
Bradford (2005)	Richard Bradford, *First Boredom, Then Fear: The Life of Philip Larkin* (2005)
Brennan (2002)	Maeve Brennan, *The Philip Larkin I Knew* (2002)
ChP	*Chosen Poems*, thirty-five poems in typescript collected by Larkin in April 1941
CM	Charles Monteith (1921–95)
Cooper (2004)	Stephen Cooper, *Philip Larkin: Subversive Writer* (2004)
CP (1988)	*Philip Larkin: Collected Poems*, ed. Anthony Thwaite (1988)
CP (2003)	*Philip Larkin: Collected Poems*, ed. Anthony Thwaite (2003)
Day (1987)	Roger Day, *Larkin* (1987)
EIC	*Essays in Criticism*
1st Coll	Untitled collection by Larkin of seven poems in typescript dating from June to September 1939 (Hull DPL 2/1/1)

FP	*Further Poems*, 'Nine poems of depression and dismay' in typescript, collected by Larkin in June 1940
FR	*Philip Larkin: Further Requirements: Interviews, Broadcasts, Statements and Book Reviews*, second edition, ed. Anthony Thwaite (2002)
Hartley (1988)	*Philip Larkin 1922–1985: A Tribute*, ed. George Hartley (1988)
Hull	Hull History Centre, Hull
HW	Philip Larkin, *High Windows* (1974)
ITGOL	*In the Grip of Light*, a collection of twenty-five poems in typescript made by Larkin by early 1948
JB	John Betjeman (1906–84)
JBS	James Ballard Sutton (1921–97)
JE	Judy Egerton (b. 1928)
Jean Hartley (1989)	Jean Hartley, *Philip Larkin, The Marvell Press and Me* (1989)
KA	Kingsley Amis (1922–95)
L	Philip Larkin (1922–85)
Leader (2009)	*The Movement Reconsidered: Essays on Larkin, Amis, Gunn, Davie, and Their Contemporaries*, ed. Zachary Leader (2009)
Leggett (1999)	B. J. Leggett, *Larkin's Blues: Jazz, Popular Music, and Poetry* (1999)
LTM	*Philip Larkin: Letters to Monica*, ed. Anthony Thwaite (2010)
MB	Maeve Brennan (1929–2003)
MJ	Monica [Margaret Beale] Jones (1922–2001)
Morrison (1980)	Blake Morrison, *The Movement: English Poetry and Fiction of the 1950s* (1980)
Motion (1993)	Andrew Motion, *Philip Larkin: A Writer's Life* (1993)
N&Q, NS	*Notes and Queries*, New Series
OBTCEV	*The Oxford Book of Twentieth-Century English Verse*, chosen by Philip Larkin (1973)
OED	*The Oxford English Dictionary*, online edition
Osborne (2008)	John Osborne, *Larkin, Ideology and Critical Violence: A Case of Wrongful Conviction* (2008)

Palmer (2008)   Richard Palmer, *Such Deliberate Disguises: The Art of Philip Larkin* (2008)

PAug40   *Poems August 1940*, seventeen poems in typescript collected by Larkin and dated August 1940

p.c.   postcard

Petch (1981)   Simon Petch, *The Art of Philip Larkin* (1981)

POW   *Poetry from Oxford in Wartime*, ed. William Bell (February 1945)

PS   Patricia ['Patsy'] Strang [née Avis], later Murphy (1928–77)

RB   *Reference Back: Philip Larkin's Uncollected Jazz Writings 1940–84*, ed. Richard Palmer and John White (1999)

RC   Robert Conquest (b. 1917)

Regan (1992)   Stephen Regan, *Philip Larkin* (1992)

Regan (1997)   *Philip Larkin*, New Casebooks series, ed. Stephen Regan (1997)

RW   Philip Larkin, *Required Writing: Miscellaneous Pieces 1955–1982* (1983)

Salwak (1989)   *Philip Larkin: The Man and his Work*, ed. Dale Salwak (1989)

SL   *Selected Letters of Philip Larkin, 1940–1985*, ed. Anthony Thwaite (1992)

7P   *Seven Poems*, in typescript, collected by Larkin and dated January 1942

7th Coll   *The Seventh Collection*, thirteen poems in typescript collected by Larkin and dated July 1942

TAWG   Philip Larkin, *Trouble at Willow Gables and Other Fictions*, ed. James Booth (2002)

Thwaite (1982)   *Larkin at Sixty*, ed. Anthony Thwaite (1982)

Timms (1973)   David Timms, *Philip Larkin* (1973)

TLD   Philip Larkin, *The Less Deceived* (1955)

TLS   *The Times Literary Supplement*, London

TNS   Philip Larkin, *The North Ship* (1945)

Tolley (1997)   *Larkin At Work: A Study of Larkin's Mode of Composition as seen in his Workbooks* (1997)

Tolley (2005)   *Philip Larkin: Early Poems and Juvenilia*, ed. A. T. Tolley (2005)

t.s.   typescript

TWW   Philip Larkin, *The Whitsun Weddings* (1964)

Introduction

This edition includes all of Larkin's poems whose texts are accessible.[1] In all but a few cases, the poems were completed by Larkin, or, viewed in their context, are self-contained. By this latter criterion, verses from letters, mainly short, and by turns sentimental, affectionate, satirical and scurrilous, are included.[2] These were omitted from *Philip Larkin: Collected Poems* (1988) 'a little regretfully' (p. xxi) by the editor, Anthony Thwaite, who in any case printed many of them in *Selected Letters of Philip Larkin 1940–1985* (1992), where they could be seen in context. In the present edition, in order to present texts from letters as verse, lineation and punctuation have sometimes been regularised. Some unfinished poems preserved in typescript by the poet are also included, as in *Collected Poems* (1988). Typescripts were made by him subsequent to drafting in his workbooks, and, though he sometimes altered their wording by hand, they represent a substantiated stage of composition.[3] A number of these have not been published before. Excluded, however, are mere scraps of verse such as those he mentions in early letters to James Sutton as having flitted into his head as a possible poem or (more usually) part of one. Some pieces from the workbooks that contain no uncancelled alternative readings and may be complete are incorporated, but not fragments, or drafts with uncancelled alternative readings.[4]

In *Collected Poems* (1988), Anthony Thwaite announced that he had enlarged the poetic corpus by printing for the first time sixty-one poems dating from 1946 to 1983, and another twenty-two from 1938 to 1945.[5] In *Philip Larkin: Early Poems and Juvenilia* (2005), A. T. Tolley added many more:

> Almost all the poems that Larkin completed after 1950 were published by him; and they were included in the original *Collected Poems*. However, while Larkin completed about a hundred and sixty poems between 1950 and his death in 1985, he wrote over two hundred and fifty poems between 1938 and 1946.[6]

Why, then, given the existence of *Collected Poems* and Tolley's volume, a new edition? An accurate text is, and always must be, the chief justification. *Collected Poems* (1988) contains a scattering of errors, some of which were subsequently corrected.[7] Tolley's edition is another matter altogether: its text of the poems contains 72 errors of wording, 47 of punctuation, 8 of letter-case, 5 of word-division, 4 of font and 3 of format.[8] (For details see the notes in the commentary of the present edition on the texts of individual poems.) No review picked up on this, but that is because reviewers on the whole do not have time, or take time, to investigate the sources of the texts: this is one reason why editors must bear large responsibilities. Some of the other shortcomings of the volume involve inconsistent editorial practice: sometimes clear errors (often the result of Larkin's typing) are cumbersomely reproduced, with '[*sic*]' (or sometimes '[sic]') inserted intrusively in the main body of the text of the poems; but at other times errors go uncorrected, or are corrected silently.[9] In the present edition, Larkin's errors in the texts of poems are identified in the notes, and corrected. Minor errors in letters are corrected silently.

In the case of poems printed in *Collected Poems* (1988), Tolley routinely proves an uncritical follower of the text, dates and bibliographical information supplied. But when there are errors, it serves the interests of neither poet nor reader to reproduce them. In the present edition, the primary sources have been examined independently with a view to correcting errors of any kind.

Bibliographical information on the sources of the texts is given in more detail than in previous editions. The record of sources in *Collected Poems* (1988) and Tolley (2005) is often unhelpfully rudimentary (as in 'TS'), or lacking altogether. When archives are large, or when more than one version of a text exists, it is necessary to specify sources explicitly.[10] Also given is an approximate indication of the extent of drafts in Larkin's eight workbooks, in order to convey some sense of what the process of composition entailed. (Famous poems like *Church Going* and *The Whitsun Weddings*, for instance, did not come easily.[11]) 'Nine pages of drafts' should not be taken to mean that drafts may be found on nine pages, but rather that the drafts amount in bulk to nine workbook pages.

Dates are supplied for the various versions of poems as they evolved. One advantage of doing this is that the process of composition is charted more faithfully than in an overall chronological arrangement based on a single date for each poem. Larkin wrote dates throughout his workbooks, and this makes it possible to be precise about the points at which, or between which, drafting of a poem began and ended. It was his practice to type up a poem as soon as drafting in the workbooks had been completed, and though he sometimes made subsequent alterations by hand,[12] the date of the typescript can usually be calculated from the point when composition in the workbook ceased. Evidence outside the workbooks for dates comes from typescript collections of early poems that Larkin made, from correspondence, from independent witnesses and from publications.

In *Collected Poems* (1988), it was the editor's policy to give the completion date for each poem, wherever possible.[13] However, the phrase 'completion date' is ambiguous: it turns out to mean the date by which all of the poem is represented in some form – a complete draft; not, as one might surmise, the date on which Larkin stopped working on the poem. This often results in a misleading account of the workbook evidence alone. A 'completion date' of 12 October 1944 is given for *Night-Music* (poem XI in *TNS*) in both editions of *Collected Poems* and in Tolley's edition of *Early Poems and Juvenilia* (2005), and one of the drafts in *Workbook 1* does indeed bear the date '12. x. 44'. But the drafts, beginning after '8. x. 44', continue substantially after 12 October 1944 and before the next date in the workbook, 23 October 1944. The drafts fall, therefore, between 8 and 23 October 1944, the latter being the date by which the poet stopped drafting the poem in the workbook. The completion date for *Reasons for Attendance* is given as 30 December 1953 in *Collected Poems* (1988), 80. But the complete draft dated '30 xii 53' is preceded by another draft, complete inasmuch as all of the poem is represented in it, and it is dated '29 xii 53'. The completion date of 16 January 1951 given in *Collected Poems* (1988), 52, for *Next, Please*, is corrected in *Collected Poems* (2003), 203, to 10 January 1961. However, the draft dated '10. 1. 61' lacks lines 15–20, and the whole poem was not represented in some form until a draft of lines 1–20 was completed on the next page before '6 Feb'. 'Unfinished Poem' is dated '1951' in *Collected Poems* (1988), 61. There are eight pages of drafts after 22 August 1951 in *Workbook 2*, but only of six stanzas: the ten stanzas printed from a typescript Larkin made are not represented until five pages of drafts before 22 January 1953 in *Workbook 3*. The date 1 February 1976 given in *Collected Poems* (1988), 206, for 'Morning at last: there in the snow' cannot be a completion date: it applies only to a draft of the first three lines. Nor can 12 October 1944 be the completion date for 'Within the dream you said' (*TNS* X): that date is written in *Workbook 1* below a draft of the first verse only.

But this is to consider only the workbook evidence: when a poem had been substantially drafted, Larkin would make revisions at typescript stage, or when he made typescript collections, or prior to publication or republication. The evidence of the workbooks and typescripts is in fact hardly ever the whole of the story of composition: all the versions of the text must be collated with the text as finally printed in order to establish the point at which he stopped making changes. A fuller account in the commentary of the bibliographical evidence and dates is less likely to mislead, and should in any case give a more vivid sense of the poet at work. The dates given in the present edition are therefore more precise than those previously available, and in quite a number of cases wrong dates have been silently corrected.[14] The earliest and latest dates of composition are given in a chronological list at the end of the volume.

Also recorded, for the first time, are variant wordings from typescripts and manuscripts late in the composition process, and from printings that precede, or, in cases like some of the poems in *In the Grip of Light* and *XX Poems*, succeed, the published versions. In order to preserve the published versions as they were constituted originally (apart from errors and misprints), versions of the text that postdate them are placed among variant wordings. Variants in punctuation, word-division, letter-case or font are not recorded. To record even only variants in wording from the extensive drafts in the eight large workbooks, and from other manuscripts bearing early drafts, would require a large and complex *apparatus criticus*, and would be an altogether more elaborate and ambitious undertaking than is appropriate to this edition.

In the record of variants, cancellation – whether by scoring out, writing through, or, occasionally, by a reordering of words signalled by loops, brackets or arrows – is represented in all cases by a single strikethrough. Where most of a line undergoes change, the whole line is represented. Where a minor portion of a line is involved, the change is represented by the relevant portion from the copy-text (the 'lemma'), a single square bracket, and the variant text. Thus,

21 Watched] ~~She saw~~ Watched *Hull DPL 2/3/15*

records that where in line 21 of the poem the copy-text has 'Watched', in the version in the typescript designated Hull DPL 2/3/15 'She saw' is cancelled and replaced by 'Watched'.

A major justification for a new edition is to provide, for the first time, a commentary on the poems. It covers: Larkin's many comments on his work; closely relevant historical contexts; persons and places; echoes and allusions; and linguistic usage. The commentary will often outline the circumstances that gave rise to a poem, which should not, of course, be confused with what the poem explicitly says: John Osborne's 2008 book *Larkin, Ideology and Critical Violence: A Case of Wrongful Conviction* repeatedly demonstrates how critics have sometimes unjustifiably or riskily tied the meaning of the poems to a biographical context rather than to the text itself. However, Osborne himself is rightly careful not to deny the importance of the biographical circumstances, which were in most cases outlined by Larkin himself. 'An April Sunday brings the snow', for instance, was occasioned by, and relates with tender intimacy to, the death of Larkin's father, right down to the detail of the jars containing a hundred or so pounds of jam that he left behind. Many such instances could be given. Osborne correctly insists that 'An April Sunday brings the snow' does not specify the sex of the 'you' addressed, the relationship of the speaker to that person, or indeed details of skin colour or ethnicity.[15] But though the poem's vagueness may transcend in some respects the particularities of the context that gave rise to it, that does not mean to say that all adducible alternative contexts are equally plausible, or equally relevant to what the poem may be about.

Here, however, is not the place to argue about the variable relation of biography to text: the editor's duty ends with providing the reader with information that has some bearing on the poems, and it is for the reader to assess the pressure of that bearing. It may be helpful to call to mind a distinction made by Christopher Ricks between what went into the making of the poem and what went into the meaning of the poem;[16] but in Larkin's case there is often significant overlap.

As to echo and allusion, Larkin stated in 1955, somewhat sensationally, that he had 'no belief in "tradition" or a common myth-kitty or casual allusions in poems to other poems or poets', which he found 'unpleasantly like the talk of literary understrappers letting you see they know the right people'.[17] It is not clear whether in saying this he is dismissing literary allusiveness *tout court*: his whole statement is so flatly dismissive – really, *no* belief in tradition? – that it is difficult to feel confident that in the phrase 'casual allusions' he is distinguishing those that parade literariness from those that bring literary enrichment. Maybe he is, however: according to his friend Jean Hartley, he relished the thought of his readers trying to locate the phrase 'the less deceived' in *Hamlet*, and felt that if readers picked up the context 'it would give them an insight into his basic passivity as regards poetry and life'.[18] And when the reviewer Anthony Cronin quoted the verse from *Toads* containing '*Stuff your pension!*' and 'the stuff | That dreams are made on', Larkin wondered whether or not he had noticed 'the concealed Shakespeare quotation'.[19] In a letter of 21 November 1971 to Monica Jones, he acknowledges a source for the phraseology at the end of his poem *Days*:

Did I tell you about my discovery in Larkin Studies? I was rereading *The Wind in the Willows*, & found within a few pages of each other 'long coats' and 'running' and 'over the fields'. Isn't that odd? It's where Toad crashes the car & is chased. I'm sure I got the words from there – hiding places thirty years deep, at least.[20]

It is also now common knowledge – he made no secret of it – that Larkin was influenced at different times by Yeats, Auden, D. H. Lawrence, Dylan Thomas, Hardy, T. S. Eliot and others. In his poems, consciously or unconsciously, he echoes and alludes to other literature, and to jazz and adverts too, and he is sensitive to the nuances of slang and cliché. His letters are also highly allusive. So great was his capacity when young for mimicry and pastiche that a number of poems are thoroughly Yeatsian or Audenesque without being indebted to any particular passage in Yeats or Auden. In the commentary, only specific points of influence are recorded. When rejecting alleged sources and allusions and parallels, I have been guided by the same principle that I applied in my edition of *The Poems of A. E. Housman* (1997): that 'the parallels are too general, commonplace, or conventional, or too lacking in verbal specificity, to convince'.[21] It is my conviction, nevertheless, that many more traces of allusiveness remain to be uncovered in Larkin's poetry.

ARCHIVES AND TEXTS

The principal archives containing Larkin's poems are at Hull, London and Oxford. The largest, now housed in the History Centre at Hull, holds all but the first of the eight workbooks in which poems were drafted, various typescript collections and other typescripts the poet made, and poems tucked away in correspondence. The first workbook is in the British Library.[22] The Bodleian Library has a copy of *Sugar and Spice: A Sheaf of Poems by Brunette Colman* (MS Eng. c. 2356), six poems written in August and September 1943, which Larkin sent to Bruce Montgomery;[23] a typescript corrected in ink and pencil of forty-five other early poems (MS Eng. c. 2357), twenty-nine of which were published in *The North Ship*; and Larkin's reworking of Bruce Montgomery's poem *Crewe* (MS Eng. c. 2762).[24] It also has poems Larkin included in letters, most notably in the extensive and invaluable correspondence with Monica Jones (MSS Eng. c. 7403–48, 7553–5), which the library acquired in 2006.

The workbooks contain much that is uncontroversially incomplete. Sometimes drafts of poems are extensive, but inconclusive, leaving either versions that are cancelled but not further revised or uncancelled alternative versions. Unfinished in these ways are such projected poems as *Single to Belfast*, of which there are just over fourteen pages of drafts in *Workbook 2*, or *The Duration* (alternatively titled *Life*), of which there are fourteen pages of drafts in *Workbook 7*, or *Letters to My Mind*, of which there are just over four pages of drafts in *Workbook 8*. The only way to present such material faithfully is in a complete transcription, with layout and cancellations correctly represented: anything else distorts what is there. This, however, would be an entirely different (and much more costly) undertaking from that of the present edition.

It is on grounds that the poet left only cancelled and incomplete versions of lines 3–4 of *The Winter Palace* that – not without regret – the poem has been removed from the canon in the present edition. The basis of the text printed in *Collected Poems* (1988), 211, Hull DPL [1/8/50],[25] is a typescript with holograph corrections in pencil. Lines 3–4 are represented in *Collected Poems* as: 'I spent my second quarter-century | Losing what I had learnt at university'. The problem is that Larkin cancelled 'Losing' at the start of line 4 and provided no alternative, and that he also cancelled lines 3–4 with a wavy line. Further, he drafted alternative versions of the lines below the type-script text, but, unfortunately, these drafts achieve neither a final version without uncancelled alternative versions nor a couplet that, like the rest of the poem, rhymes or half rhymes. Line 3 is left in two versions: 'For something inside me is trying to wash [*alternative* shrug] off' and as 'For some time now my mind has been struggling'; line 4, as 'Stuff that has stuck to my mind'. Given this state of affairs, it seems best to acknowledge that Larkin did not finish work on the poem, and leave it at that.

Great caution must always be exercised with manuscript (and especially workbook) materials. It is not possible in many cases for an editor to judge how (or even whether) pieces of text relate to each other, or when a poem is complete. Only the author has authority in such matters. However, it is often demonstrably an error to regard disparate pieces of text as belonging together just because they appear on the same page. A case in point is Hull DPL (2) 1/4/4. On this sheet are written: a title, underlined, with two lines of verse; an asterisk in the middle of the next line; five lines of verse after a blank line; and four lines of verse after another blank line. The title and two lines do not obviously relate to what follows them: they are in a different metre and a totally different register, with no shared vocabulary, and it has been established[26] that they are a parody of the opening of Sidney Keyes's *Elegy* (*In memoriam S. K. K.*). The groups of five and four lines that follow are not a continuation of the parody. In them, the only sign of internal coherence is that in the four-line section 'the sandwiches they are cutting for me to take | – For they love me' refers back to the parents mentioned in the previous section. To describe all this, as Susannah Tarbush does,[27] as 'the second poem which Larkin addressed to Penelope' and as an 'abandoned 11-line draft' (implying a draft of the poem), is without warrant.

THE POET AND HIS POEMS

Larkin took practical steps to make sure his own manuscripts survived, as James Booth points out:

> From an early age he carefully preserved his poetic manuscripts and, from 5 October 1944 to November 1980, he wrote (and carefully dated) virtually all his complete and incomplete drafts in a series of eight workbooks. The first of these he presented to the British Library as early as 1964. Moreover he gave Maeve Brennan a copy of the unfinished 'The Dance', and left a tape-recording of himself reading it. In 1975 he suggested to Betty Mackereth that she might make some money by selling her typescript of the unpublished poem 'When first we faced, and touching showed': 'Flog it to Texas if it seems embarrassing.'[28] He inserted typed fair copies of 'When first we faced', 'Morning at last: there in the snow' and 'Love Again' in the final workbook. His signals to posterity could scarcely be clearer. Thwaite records that Larkin 'often referred . . . to work which would have to be left for the "posthumous volume" of his poems'.[29] It is true that, at the very end of his life he suffered a loss of creative nerve. In his notoriously 'repugnant' (self-contradictory) will, his purist super-ego inserted a clause requiring his executors to destroy his unpublished work 'unread'. Fortunately, in another clause, his poetic ego gave them full permission to publish what they wished (Motion xvi).[30]

However, the preservation of unpublished verse is not the only indication that he thought more of his poems would, or should, see the light: as James Booth again reminds us, numerous poems remained unpublished during his lifetime that he had tried to get published.[31]

Larkin's keen interest in the preservation and publication of his poems is further evidenced by his habit, from the beginning, of making collections. There were eleven, in typescript, before the publication of *The North Ship* in July 1945. An account of these is given in Appendix

1, where it will be seen that the accoutrements of title pages and prefaces show the young Larkin fantasising about being a published writer. By early 1948,[32] he had gathered together twenty-five poems under the title *In the Grip of Light* (Hull DPL 2/1/8). The collection contained:

'The wind blew all my wedding-day' [later in *XX Poems*, *TLD*, entitled *Wedding-Wind*]
'Heaviest of flowers, the head' [from *TNS*]
Plymouth: 'A box of teak, a box of sandalwood' [from *Mandrake*, May 1946]
'At the chiming of light upon sleep'
'Who whistled for the wind, that it should break'
'Come then to prayers'
'Coming at last to night's most thankful springs'
'Lift through the breaking day'
'Past days of gales'
'I put my mouth ' [from *TNS*]
The Quiet One: 'Her hands intend no harm' [from *Mandrake*, May 1946]
Getaway: 'One man walking a deserted platform' [from *TNS*, where it was untitled]
'Many famous feet have trod'
Night-Music: 'At one the wind rose' [from *TNS*]
To a Very Slow Air: 'The golden sheep are feeding, and'
Träumerei: 'In this dream that dogs me I am part'
'Within a dream, you said' [from *TNS*]
'Some must employ the scythe'
Winter: 'In the field, two horses' [from *TNS*]
Deep Analysis: 'I am a woman lying on a leaf'
Thaw: 'Tiny immortal streams are on the move'
Dying Day: 'There is an evening coming in'
Two Guitar Pieces:
(i) 'The tin-roofed shack by the railroad'
(ii) 'I roll a cigarette, and light'
'And the wave sings because it is moving'[33]

In the Grip of Light was a title that seemed to Larkin 'to sum up the state of being alive'.[34] He informed B. C. Bloomfield on 6 December 1976 that he had told Jenny Stratford that it was previously going to be called 'Canto', 'and this explains the word "Canto" scribbled against a number of the poems in the manuscript book'. He continues:

I found that in fact the poems so indicated had been sent to a man called Arthur Ley who was proposing to start a poetry magazine called *Canto*. I think this was in 1947, but I can check if you want. As far as I know, *Canto* never appeared, and so the story ended more or less before it began. I am much relieved, however, to know that I didn't contemplate such a corny title for any collection of mine.[35]

In a 1964 interview with Ian Hamilton, Larkin described the title *In the Grip of Light* as 'portentous', and expressed relief that nobody accepted the collection.[36] It remained in typescript.

Another early collection he made was *XX Poems,* in which the poems were numbered in roman:

Wedding-Wind: 'The wind blew all my wedding-day' [from *ITGOL,* later in *TLD,* again entitled *Wedding-Wind*]
Modesties: 'Words as plain as hen-birds' wings'
'Always too eager for the future, we' [later in *TLD,* entitled *Next, Please*]
'Even so distant, I can taste the grief' [later in *TLD,* entitled *Deceptions*]
'Latest face, so effortless' [later in *TLD,* entitled *Latest Face*]
Arrival: 'Morning, a glass door, flashes'
'Since the majority of me'
Spring: 'Green-shadowed people sit, or walk in rings' [later in *TLD*]
'Waiting for breakfast, while she brushed her hair' [added to *TNS,* 1966]
Two Portraits of Sex:
(1) *Oils*: 'Sun. Tree. Beginning. God in a thicket. Crown'
(2) *Etching*: 'Endlessly, time-honoured irritant' [later in *TLD,* entitled *Dry-Point*]
'On longer evenings' [later in *TLD,* entitled *Coming*]
'Since we agreed to let the road between us' [later in *TLD,* entitled *No Road*]
'If my darling were once to decide' [later in *TLD,* entitled *If, My Darling*]
'Who called love conquering'
'The widest prairies have electric fences' [later in *TLD,* entitled *Wires*]
The Dedicated: 'Some must employ the scythe'
Wants: 'Beyond all this, the wish to be alone' [later in *TLD*]
'There is an evening coming in' [later in *TLD,* entitled *Going*]

At Grass: 'The eye can hardly pick them out' [later in *TLD*]

XX Poems, unlike *In the Grip of Light*, did reach print, in the form of 100 copies of a booklet produced privately by Carswells of Belfast. Larkin tells Monica Jones in a letter of 17 October 1950 that he is thinking of having a pamphlet privately printed.[37] He is characteristically scathing about the 'shouting mediocrity' of three quarters of the poems,[38] and he dismisses all of them as 'old friends, hopeless old friends whom you know will never get a job,'[39] as '20 snivelling, not-very-interesting cerebrations',[40] and, when he has corrected the proofs, as 'very *bitty*, scraps, motley' lacking 'cohesion or wealth.'[41] In a letter of 20 February 1951 he tells James Sutton: 'I have sent a typescript of 20 poems to the printers to be made into what I feel sure will be an ugly little booklet of ugly little poems. As far as possible I have excluded all the psalm smiting stuff: very many poems are left to moulder in my file.'[42]

Looking back in 1951, he confesses ruefully:

This has been a scrappy & troubled time with me, 1945–50, and very little grip or purpose is really likely to be reflected in its poems. I feel that there's a high proportion of *personal maunder*, & here and there a putting-in of the foot – they aren't at all the brilliant highpowered squad of dialectical descriptions that I'd *like* to pass round my friends – but there we are, the rejected ones are worse, so there's no help.[43]

The title of the collection involved protracted deliberation:

Originally I'd thought of 20 *poems for nothing*, but Kingsley shuddered at it: said it was like Roy Campbell.

Apart from all the impossible kinds of title, I don't like the drab kind (*Poems*), or the self-denigrating kind (*Stammerings*), or the clever kind (*Stasis*).

I want something unaffected & unpretentious – for Lord knows there are few to pretend anything about. *Speaking from Experience?* – sounds like 'Twelve broadcast talks by the Radio Padre'.

I'll get my booklet done, even if I have to call it *Poetical Pieces*.[44]

He flirts with the idea of a clever literary title from Flaubert:

The only other title recently happened on is *A heart sample*, *Heart sample*, or simply *Samples*. With a reference to Flo Bear's story, you know.

I'm not sure I really like it all the same – it sounds a bit American. And *heart* is one of the unusable words, too.

Today I like 'A heart sample' rather better.

I mean it's no use pretending that there's anything original or massive about the poems, or even anything consistent in them. They are simply samples: a cutting, a cross-section, a series of overflows.

As for Flo Bear, you know the story (*Un coeur simple*) but it probably wouldn't have occurred to you to make such a silly pun.[45]

On 11 February he is typing out final versions, and on 14 February the collection has gone to the printers with the plain title *XX Poems*:[46]

In the end I abandoned the *Heart sample* line, & despairing of ever choosing anything I could endure I fell back on 'XX POEMS', wch is about as free from offence as I can manage, & with a slight undercurrent of Guinness double X and Ezra Pound's Cantos.

If you'd really liked *Heart &c* I might have had it, but really the word 'heart' does stick in my gullet.[47]

He expresses no great regard for the poems, but hopes their publication marks a change for the better:

As they stand now there is something about each one I like, though few I like in entirety. It seems funny to be without them – like having one's hair cut. I should like to believe I shall now move on to a better era – less of Misery Inc., fewer easy-ways-out-via-Pessimist Drains, Ltd., more infrequent references to the Joy-through-Weakness movement.[48]

The collection was dedicated to Kingsley Amis: 'because he inscribed *The legacy* to me, even if it never arrived at print'.[49] The copies were delivered to Larkin on 27 April 1951,[50] and the next day he enclosed a copy with his letter to Monica Jones. Looking back on 6 January 1955, he told Alan Brownjohn:

XX POEMS is not really a publication. In 1951 I thought the poems I had written look well in type, so I had a local printer make a hundred copies of the enclosed collection for me privately. These I sent to various friends, and by now most have appeared in print elsewhere.[51]

Though he did not hold the collection in high regard, he did have favourites among individual poems. On 8 May 1951 he told James

Sutton: 'I think my favourite poems at present are I, V, XIV and XX, but I don't mind any of them, except perhaps XIII which is included as being "very important" to show how my mind works.'[52] On 10 July 1951 he declared:

> The favourites seem to be I, V, XIII, XIV, and XX (if those are the right numbers): I like II and XII: in fact, I like them all except perhaps IX & X. Charles Madge was very nice about them: can't think what he sees in them: his stuff is 1,000 times cleverer. My few friends have all been kind. I sent them round to a lot of big names – Eliot, Spender, MacNeice & co., but without any address, so they can't answer even if they wanted to. And as I only put 1d stamps on (the rate has gone up to 1½d, they tell me) that's perhaps as well. None of these has burst into print exclaiming that a new poet has arisen – at least, not so far as I know.[53]

In the Grip of Light was never published as a collection, and *XX Poems* was, in the poet's own estimation, 'not really a publication'. These might alone seem sufficient grounds for not preserving them as collections. A further, decisive reason, however, is that to do so would involve substantial duplication. Three poems appear in both collections, and two of those were included in *The Less Deceived*. Six more from *In the Grip of Light* and one from *XX Poems* were published in *The North Ship*; and a further eleven poems from *XX Poems* were chosen for *The Less Deceived*. Had Larkin regarded *In the Grip of Light* and *XX Poems* as having the integrity of published volumes in which the choice of poems and their order were sacrosanct, he would not have included so many of the poems in volumes published later.

Given his practice of collecting his poems, it is no surprise that Larkin was in favour of a collected edition of his poetry. On 7 July 1977 he told Charles Monteith of Faber and Faber: 'there is nothing I should like more than a *Collected Poems* under your imprint'.[54] And more than that? He was certainly far from hostile to the idea of unpublished material being made available. As a librarian giving a talk on the importance of preserving contemporary literary manuscripts, he once said that 'Unpublished work, unfinished work, even notes towards unwritten work all contribute to our knowledge of a writer's intentions.'[55] In his introduction to *Poetry in the Making*, the catalogue of an exhibition of manuscripts of poems by British poets in the British Museum (1967), he spoke warmly about the attention scholars pay to manuscripts, and lamented the fact that, as manuscripts of British writers frequently ended up in American libraries, 'definitive editions of such British writers will in all probability be American'.[56]

Publication and preservation are also editorial concerns. In the present edition the four main volumes published in Philip Larkin's lifetime, *The North Ship* (1945), *The Less Deceived* (1955), *The Whitsun Weddings* (1964) and *High Windows* (1974) are preserved as collections and printed in order of publication. This was the arrangement favoured in the revised edition of *Collected Poems* (2003), but not in the earlier, larger *Collected Poems* (1988) where the editor, Anthony Thwaite, opted for a chronological arrangement of poems 'completed by Larkin between 1946 and the end of his life together with a few unpublished poems which Larkin preserved in typescript', followed by 'a substantial selection of his earlier poems, from 1938 until the end of 1945'.[57] To the four published volumes are appended two collections: of verse published in the poet's lifetime but not collected by him, and of verse not published in his lifetime. In these two categories, the poems are arranged in a chronological sequence: in the first, according to publication date, in the second according to the date on which Larkin stopped working on each poem. At the end is a handful of undated poems.

There are always gains and losses in editorial choices. Coleridge advocated a thoroughgoing chronological arrangement on grounds that it enables the reader readily to follow a development (or a deterioration) from early to late.[58] But such an arrangement is not without problems and disadvantages,[59] and they are sufficiently weighty in Larkin's case to have prevented its adoption in the present edition. The main reservations concern the representation of the corpus of published poems: Larkin was severe on himself in choosing to publish only a fraction of what he wrote; he was aware of the fact that published volumes would come to constitute the authorial identity; and, clinchingly, his choice of poems and arrangement of them within the published volumes – creative and critical acts both – were decisions he did not take lightly. Asked in 1981 whether he took great care in ordering the poems in a collection, he replied:

> Yes, great care. I treat them like a music-hall bill: you know, contrast, difference in length, the comic, the Irish tenor, bring on the girls.[60] I think 'Lines on a Young Lady's Photograph Album' is a good opener, for instance: easy to understand, variety of mood, pretty end. The last one is chosen for its uplift quality, to leave the impression that you're more serious than the reader had thought.[61]

This turns characteristically self-deprecatory;[62] but before it does so, the prompt candour of 'Yes, great care' is unmistakable. In terse gravity the phrase resembles his answer to a question about another concern of his: '*Do you think much about growing older. Is it something that worries you?* Yes, dreadfully.'[63]

The only loss incurred in respecting the integrity of the published volumes is a sense of the chronology of the composition of their contents, and of the relation in time, too, of poems chosen for inclusion to those excluded. Accordingly, at the end of the commentary a list of composition dates of all the poems is provided. Some dates (particularly of early poems) can only be approximate, but in most cases fairly precise dates can be given: those on which, or between which, Larkin began and stopped working on a poem. Still more precise dates, of the various stages of composition, are given in the notes on individual poems in the commentary.

NOTES TO THE INTRODUCTION

1 In 'Philip Larkin and the Bodleian Library', *Bodleian Library Record*, 14. 1 (Oct. 1991), 54, 55, Judith Priestman announced that, under the stipulation of Mrs Ann Montgomery, widow of Bruce Montgomery, the letters from L to her husband are closed to readers until 2035, and that among Montgomery's papers (not necessarily letters) are twenty-one early unpublished poems. Those she quotes from have now all been published, either in Tolley (2005) – though not from the Bodleian MSS – or in the present edition.

2 Anthony Thwaite's selected edition of *Philip Larkin: Letters to Monica* appeared in 2010. In the commentary I draw upon the entire correspondence, most of it not included in Thwaite's selection, citing the Bodleian classification numbers of the MSS, and providing cross-references to Thwaite's edition when verse is published in it for the first time.

3 L in a 1982 interview with *Paris Review* (RW, 70): 'I write – or used to – in notebooks in pencil, trying to complete each stanza before going on to the next. Then when the poem is finished I type it out, and sometimes make small alterations.' This is confirmed in a letter to A. T. Tolley dated 30 Sept. 1982: 'It was always my practice to transfer a poem from manuscript to the typewriter, usually at the point at which a coherent and consecutive version had emerged; this did not mean that that version was final': Tolley (1997), 26.

4 I have made three exceptions to this principle: *Compline*, 'Sting in the shell' and 'The poet has a straight face'. These poems have already been published, but without acknowledgement that the first two each contain one uncancelled alternative reading, and the third contains two. I record the alternatives in the variants.

5 CP (1988), xv. Some of the poems appeared only in XX *Poems*, which, given the limited private circulation of the collection, would extend the corpus of poems in CP (1988) still further.

6 Tolley (2005) xv.

7 On p. 16 there should be a comma after 'sleep'; p. 21, there should be a comma after 'snow'; p. 23, 'blocks' should be 'block'; p. 28, 'You have been here some time.' should be in parentheses; p. 31, '*will*' should be '*Will*', 'notes' should be 'rites', and 'the wish' should be 'one wish'; p. 36, 'abdicated' should be 'abdicating' (not

corrected in *CP*, 2003); p. 45, there should be a comma after 'o'clock' (not corrected in *CP*, 2003); p. 62, 'stationary' should be in italics; p. 69, punctuation after 'earth . . .?)' should be a semicolon, not a colon; p. 76, 'tiny first' should be 'first tiny' (not corrected in *CP*, 2003); p. 105, 'last' should be 'lost', "Wrinkling' should be 'Wincing', 'waves' should be 'vanes', and there should be a comma after 'away'; p. 113, as noted by R. J. C. Watt in *A Concordance to the Poetry of Philip Larkin* (1995), xv, 'brillance' is of course a misprint for 'brilliance', corrected in the rev. edn (1990); p. 124, the comma at the end of l. 2 should be a full stop; p. 139, 'windows' should be 'window', 'buses' should be ''buses', the full stop after 'morning' should be a dash, 'goes down,' at the end of l. 8 should be before 'in fields' in l. 9, and there should be a comma after 'squares'; p. 141, 'brides' should be 'bribes', corrected in 1988 reprint; p. 171, L's date '1969' below *Homage to a Government*, omitted in 1988, is reinstated in 2003; p. 216, the misprint 'Teachers' for 'Teachests', which was taken from the text printed in *The Observer*, was corrected in 1990, though the punctuation at the end of l. 2 remained a comma instead of a semicolon; p. 219, the comma at the end of l. 6 should be a semicolon. In the poems from 1938 to 1945 (pp. 225–311) there are three errors of wording: p. 245, 'shows' should be 'showers'; p. 259, 'These' should be 'Those'; p. 271, 'dimmed' should be 'dim'. There are also six errors of punctuation, of which I give details in the notes on the poems concerned. In *CP* (2003), p. 111, 'Negroes' should be 'negroes'; p. 114, there should be a comma after 'bash'; p. 125, 'worthwhile' should be 'worth while'; p. 128, 'cicatrised' should be 'cicatrized'; p. 134, there should be a comma after 'lanes'.

8 This applies only to the texts of the poems. There are many other errors. See, for instance, the account of L's early typescript collections in Appendix 1 to the present edition.

9 For a sample of the range of the editorial shortcomings, see the notes in the Commentary in the present edition on: *Coventria*, 'The poet has a straight face', 'There are moments like music, minutes', 'At school, the acquaintance', 'O what ails thee, bloody sod', 'The doublehanded kiss and the brainwet hatred' and *Fourth Former Loquitur*.

10 For the confusion that results when the source of the text is not clearly identified, see, for instance, the note in the Commentary on the text of 'As a war in years of peace'.

11 As the accounts in Tolley (1997), 73–99, demonstrate.

12 See fn. 3 (above).

13 Introduction, xx.

14 This applies to dates in Motion (1993), as well as to those in *CP* and Tolley (2005).

15 Osborne (2008), 181.

16 *Inventions of the March Hare. Poems 1909–1917 by T. S. Eliot*, ed. Christopher Ricks (1996), xxv.

17 *RW*, 79. L later stated that he assumed that D. J. Enright, who solicited the statement, would use the replies he received as raw material for an introduction to *Poets of the 1950s*, and that he was 'rather dashed to find them printed *verbatim*': *RW*, 79 n. John Skinner remarks: 'and yet, after almost thirty years of writing poetry which subverts or even refutes the view expressed in this passage, Larkin then publishes the same lines *verbatim* himself': 'Philip Larkin by Philip Larkin', *Ariel*, 20. 1 (Jan. 1989), 79.

18 Hartley (1989), 74.

19 To MJ, 28 July 1956: Bodl. MS Eng. c. 7414/16. RC in Thwaite (1982), 34, remarks justly that L 'is by no means as rigorous in avoiding quotation from others as might be thought to follow from his deprecation . . . of "casual allusions in poems to other poems or poets"'.

20 Bodl. MS Eng. c. 7443/128.

21 Introduction, lx.

22 L gave it as a gift. When he tells MJ about the donation in a letter dated 22 May 1964 (Bodl. MS Eng. c. 7428/38), he describes the notebook as 'jammed with unpublished poems etc. [. . .] all fearfully dull, stodgy humorless (?) thin Yeats-&-catpiss. Still.' On 31 July 1964 he tells her: 'Actually it's a most interesting book, showing poems worth printing after years and years of crap': Bodl. MS Eng. c. 7428/95.

23 A seventh poem, *Fourth Former Loquitur*, is absent, but a corrected pencil draft is loosely tipped in between the final page and the cover of the Hull copy, DPL (2) 1/11, as James Booth notes (*TAWG*, 242).

24 None of these Bodleian MSS of early poems receives so much as a mention in A. T. Tolley's volume of *Early Poems and Juvenilia* (2005).

25 The reference is missing from the Hull catalogue.

26 By Tim Kendall in *AL*, 2 (Oct. 2008), 10, and 28 (Oct. 2009), 17–18; and by Geoff Weston in *AL*, 30 (Oct. 2010), 15.

27 *AL*, 25 (Apr. 2008), 10.

28 'Written in a Kate Greenaway Valentine's Day card, sent to Betty Mackereth on 30.xii.1975 (unpublished)': Booth (2005), 205.

29 *CP* (1988), xxii.

30 Booth (2005), 18–19.

31 Booth (2005), 19.

32 A. T. Tolley in Hartley (1988), 168, and *CP* (1988), 217, both give 1947, when the collection may have been put together, but the date '1948' is written in L's hand on the front cover of the collection.

33 I have italicised titles and regularised their capitalisation in L's typescript. A. T. Tolley's account, 'Philip Larkin's Unpublished Book: "In the Grip of Light"', *Agenda*, 22. 2 (Summer 1984), 76–86, is deeply flawed. From the list of contents (77) he omits *Winter*, *Getaway* and 'At the chiming of light upon sleep'; he lists two poems, 'If hands could free you, heart' and 'Kick up the fire, and let the flames break loose', that are not in the collection; he gives the title *To a Very Slow Air* as *Slow Song*; he adds the title *The Dedicated* to 'Some must employ the scythe', which is untitled in *ITGOL*; and he omits the titles from 'Her hands intend no harm' and 'There is an evening coming in'. The account in *CP* (1988), 317–18, contains only one error: in *ITGOL*, the opening of 'Within the dream, you said' (from *TNS*) is 'Within a dream'.

34 To JBS, 28 Jan. 1948: *SL*, 144.

35 *SL*, 553.

36 *FR*, 26.

37 Bodl. MS Eng. c. 7403/78.

38 To MJ, 1 Nov. 1950: Bodl. MS Eng. c. 7403/100.

39 To MJ, 5 Nov. 1950: Bodl. MS Eng. c. 7403/109.

40 To MJ, 11 Nov. 1950: Bodl. MS Eng. c. 7403/118.

41 To MJ, 13 Apr. 1951: Bodl. MS Eng. c. 7405/34.

42 Hull DP 174/2/210.

43 To MJ, 28 Apr. 1951: Bodl. MS Eng. c. 7405/40.

44 To MJ, 16 Jan. 1951: Bodl. MS Eng. c. 7404/77, 78.

45 To MJ, 16 Jan., 31 Jan., 6 Feb. 1951: Bodl. MSS Eng. c. 7404/77, 78, 95, 96, 101.

46 To MJ, 11 Feb., 14 Feb. 1951: Bodl. MSS Eng. c. 7404/109, 112.

47 To MJ, 14 Feb. 1951: Bodl. MSS Eng. c. 7404/113.

48 To MJ, 11 Feb. 1951: Bodl. MS Eng. c. 7404/113.

49 To MJ, 28 Apr. 1951: Bodl. MS Eng. c. 7405/40. *The Legacy* was Amis's first novel, unpublished.

50 Bloomfield (2002), 17.

51 *SL*, 234.

52 *SL*, 171. I (*Wedding-Wind*), V ('Latest face, so effortless'), XIV ('If my darling were once to decide'), XX (*At Grass*), XIII ('Since we agreed to let the road between us').

53 *SL*, 173–4. I (*Wedding-Wind*), V ('Latest face, so effortless'), XIII ('Since we agreed to let the road between us'), XIV ('If my darling were once to decide'), XX (*At Grass*), II (*Modesties*), XII ('On longer evenings'), IX ('Waiting for breakfast while she brushed her hair'), X (*Two Portraits of Sex*).

54 *SL*, 568. See also Jean Hartley (1989), 173.

55 *RW*, 99.

56 'Operation Manuscript', *FR*, 122.

57 Introduction, xv.

58 *The Collected Works of Samuel Taylor Coleridge, Table Talk*, ed. Carl Woodring (1990), 1. 453 (1 Jan. 1834).

59 See Ian Jack, 'A Choice of Orders: The Arrangement of "The Poetical Works"', in *Textual Criticism and Literary Interpretation*, ed. Jerome J. McGann (1985), 127–43. ('Poetical' was misprinted as 'Political', one of too many errors in the volume.)

60 The principle of arrangement is confirmed by Jean Hartley (1989), 68: 'his aim was to make the tone as various as possible . . . by alternating poems with different atmospheres and styles rather than keeping the mood level and grouping similar poems together'. She notes that L did this not only for *TLD*, but for *TWW* and *HW* as well.

61 *FR*, 55.

62 Booth (2005), 16, notes L's 'affectation of casualness', and Palmer (2008), 95, catches the subversive facetiousness of his reply, suggesting as it does 'something of a party turn' instead of great care. On grounds that L often says what his audience wants to hear, Gillian Steinberg, *Philip Larkin and His Audiences* (2010), 47, wishes to allow for L's 'Yes, great care' being 'equally disingenuous'. But it cannot be equally so if L is giving two different accounts of his practice and the second makes light of the first. Further, it is hardly plausible that L would immediately say he took little or no care. Steinberg's allowance here sits oddly with her perceptions of L's self-mockery elsewhere.

63 1979 interview with *The Observer*: *RW*, 55.

THE POEMS

THE POEMS

THE NORTH SHIP

I

to Bruce Montgomery

All catches alight
At the spread of spring:
Birds crazed with flight
Branches that fling
Leaves up to the light –   5
Every one thing,
Shape, colour and voice,
Cries out, Rejoice!
    A drum taps: a wintry drum.

Gull, grass and girl   10
In air, earth and bed
Join the long whirl
Of all the resurrected,
Gather up and hurl
Far out beyond the dead   15
What life they can control –
All runs back to the whole.
    A drum taps: a wintry drum.

What beasts now hesitate
Clothed in cloudless air,   20
In whom desire stands straight?
What ploughman halts his pair
To kick a broken plate
Or coin turned up by the share?
What lovers worry much   25
That a ghost bids them touch?
    A drum taps: a wintry drum.

Let the wheel spin out,
Till all created things
With shout and answering shout   30
Cast off rememberings;
Let it all come about
Till centuries of springs
And all their buried men
Stand on the earth again.   35
    A drum taps: a wintry drum.

II

This was your place of birth, this daytime palace,
This miracle of glass, whose every hall
The light as music fills, and on your face
Shines petal-soft; sunbeams are prodigal
5   To show you pausing at a picture's edge
To puzzle out the name, or with a hand
Resting a second on a random page –

The clouds cast moving shadows on the land.

Are you prepared for what the night will bring?
10   The stranger who will never show his face,
But asks admittance; will you greet your doom
As final; set him loaves and wine; knowing
The game is finished when he plays his ace,
And overturn the table and go into the next room?

III

The moon is full tonight
And hurts the eyes,
It is so definite and bright.
What if it has drawn up
5   All quietness and certitude of worth
Wherewith to fill its cup,
Or mint a second moon, a paradise? –
For they are gone from earth.

IV
Dawn

To wake, and hear a cock
Out of the distance crying,
To pull the curtains back
And see the clouds flying –
5   How strange it is
For the heart to be loveless, and as cold as these.

V
Conscript
for James Ballard Sutton

The ego's county he inherited
From those who tended it like farmers; had
All knowledge that the study merited,
The requisite contempt of good and bad;

But one Spring day his land was violated;   5
A bunch of horsemen curtly asked his name,
Their leader in a different dialect stated
A war was on for which he was to blame,

And he must help them. The assent he gave
Was founded on desire for self-effacement   10
In order not to lose his birthright; brave,
For nothing would be easier than replacement,

Which would not give him time to follow further
The details of his own defeat and murder.

VI

Kick up the fire, and let the flames break loose
To drive the shadows back;
Prolong the talk on this or that excuse,
Till the night comes to rest
While some high bell is beating two o'clock.   5
Yet when the guest
Has stepped into the windy street, and gone,
Who can confront
The instantaneous grief of being alone?
Or watch the sad increase   10
Across the mind of this prolific plant,
Dumb idleness?

VII

The horns of the morning
Are blowing, are shining,
The meadows are bright
    With the coldest dew;
5   The dawn reassembles.
Like the clash of gold cymbals
The sky spreads its vans out
    The sun hangs in view.

Here, where no love is,
10   All that was hopeless
And kept me from sleeping
    Is frail and unsure;
For never so brilliant,
Neither so silent
15   Nor so unearthly, has
    Earth grown before.

VIII
Winter

In the field, two horses,
Two swans on the river,
While a wind blows over
A waste of thistles
5   Crowded like men;
And now again
My thoughts are children
With uneasy faces
That awake and rise
10   Beneath running skies
From buried places.

For the line of a swan
Diagonal on water
Is the cold of winter,
15   And each horse like a passion
Long since defeated

Lowers its head,
And oh, they invade
My cloaked-up mind
Till memory unlooses   20
Its brooch of faces –
Streams far behind.

Then the whole heath whistles
In the leaping wind,
And shrivelled men stand   25
Crowding like thistles
To one fruitless place;
Yet still the miracles
Exhume in each face
Strong silken seed,   30
That to the static
Gold winter sun throws back
Endless and cloudless pride.

IX

Climbing the hill within the deafening wind
The blood unfurled itself, was proudly borne
High over meadows where white horses stood;
Up the steep woods it echoed like a horn
Till at the summit under shining trees   5
It cried: Submission is the only good;
Let me become an instrument sharply stringed
For all things to strike music as they please.

How to recall such music, when the street
Darkens? Among the rain and stone places   10
I find only an ancient sadness falling,
Only hurrying and troubled faces,
The walking of girls' vulnerable feet,
The heart in its own endless silence kneeling.

X

Within the dream you said:
Let us kiss then,

In this room, in this bed,
But when all's done
5   We must not meet again.

Hearing this last word,
There was no lambing-night,
No gale-driven bird
Nor frost-encircled root
10   As cold as my heart.

XI
Night-Music

At one the wind rose,
And with it the noise
Of the black poplars.

Long since had the living
5   By a thin twine
Been led into their dreams
Where lanterns shine
Under a still veil
Of falling streams;
10   Long since had the dead
Become untroubled
In the light soil.
There were no mouths
To drink of the wind,
15   Nor any eyes
To sharpen on the stars'
Wide heaven-holding,
Only the sound
Long sibilant-muscled trees
20   Were lifting up, the black poplars.

And in their blazing solitude
The stars sang in their sockets through the night:
'Blow bright, blow bright
The coal of this unquickened world.'

XII

Like the train's beat
Swift language flutters the lips
Of the Polish airgirl in the corner seat.
The swinging and narrowing sun
Lights her eyelashes, shapes 5
Her sharp vivacity of bone.
Hair, wild and controlled, runs back:
And gestures like these English oaks
Flash past the windows of her foreign talk.

The train runs on through wilderness 10
Of cities. Still the hammered miles
Diversify behind her face.
And all humanity of interest
Before her angled beauty falls,
As whorling notes are pressed 15
In a bird's throat, issuing meaningless
Through written skies; a voice
Watering a stony place.

XIII

I put my mouth
Close to running water:
Flow north, flow south,
It will not matter,
It is not love you will find. 5

I told the wind:
It took away my words:
It is not love you will find,
Only the bright-tongued birds,
Only a moon with no home. 10

It is not love you will find:
You have no limbs
Crying for stillness, you have no mind
Trembling with seraphim,
You have no death to come. 15

XIV
Nursery Tale

All I remember is
The horseman, the moonlit hedges,
The hoofbeats shut suddenly in the yard,
The hand finding the door unbarred:
5   And I recall the room where he was brought,
Hung black and candlelit; a sort
Of meal laid out in mockery; for though
His place was set, there was no more
Than one unpolished pewter dish, that bore
10   The battered carcase of a carrion crow.

So every journey that I make
Leads me, as in the story he was led,
To some new ambush, to some fresh mistake:
So every journey I begin foretells
15   A weariness of daybreak, spread
With carrion kisses, carrion farewells.

XV
The Dancer

Butterfly
Or falling leaf,
Which ought I to imitate
In my dancing?

And if she were to admit
The world weaved by her feet
Is leafless, is incomplete?
And if she abandoned it,
5   Broke the pivoted dance,
Set loose the audience?
Then would the moon go raving,
The moon, the anchorless
Moon go swerving
10   Down at the earth for a catastrophic kiss.

XVI

The bottle is drunk out by one;
At two, the book is shut;
At three, the lovers lie apart,
Love and its commerce done;
And now the luminous watch-hands   5
Show after four o'clock,
Time of night when straying winds
Trouble the dark.

And I am sick for want of sleep;
So sick, that I can half-believe   10
The soundless river pouring from the cave
Is neither strong, nor deep;
Only an image fancied in conceit.
I lie and wait for morning, and the birds,
The first steps going down the unswept street,   15
Voices of girls with scarves around their heads.

XVII

To write one song, I said,
As sad as the sad wind
That walks around my bed,
Having one simple fall
As a candle-flame swells, and is thinned,   5
As a curtain stirs by the wall
– For this I must visit the dead.
Headstone and wet cross,
Paths where the mourners tread,
A solitary bird,   10
These call up the shade of loss,
Shape word to word.

That stones would shine like gold
Above each sodden grave,
This, I had not foretold,   15
Nor the birds' clamour, nor
The image morning gave
Of more and ever more,

As some vast seven-piled wave,
20   Mane-flinging, manifold,
Streams at an endless shore.

XVIII

If grief could burn out
Like a sunken coal,
The heart would rest quiet,
The unrent soul
5   Be still as a veil;
But I have watched all night

The fire grow silent,
The grey ash soft:
And I stir the stubborn flint
10   The flames have left,
And grief stirs, and the deft
Heart lies impotent.

XIX
Ugly Sister

I will climb thirty steps to my room,
Lie on my bed;
Let the music, the violin, cornet and drum
Drowse from my head.

5   Since I was not bewitched in adolescence
And brought to love,
I will attend to the trees and their gracious silence,
To winds that move.

XX

I see a girl dragged by the wrists
Across a dazzling field of snow,
And there is nothing in me that resists.
Once it would not be so;
Once I should choke with powerless jealousies;   5
But now I seem devoid of subtlety,
As simple as the things I see,
Being no more, no less, than two weak eyes.

There is snow everywhere,
Snow in one blinding light.   10
Even snow smudged in her hair
As she laughs and struggles, and pretends to fight;
And still I have no regret;
Nothing so wild, nothing so glad as she
Rears up in me,   15
And would not, though I watched an hour yet.

So I walk on. Perhaps what I desired
– That long and sickly hope, someday to be
As she is – gave a flicker and expired;
For the first time I'm content to see   20
What poor mortar and bricks
I have to build with, knowing that I can
Never in seventy years be more a man
Than now – a sack of meal upon two sticks.

So I walk on. And yet the first brick's laid.   25
Else how should two old ragged men
Clearing the drifts with shovels and a spade
Bring up my mind to fever-pitch again?
How should they sweep the girl clean from my heart,
With no more done   30
Than to stand coughing in the sun,
Then stoop and shovel snow onto a cart?

The beauty dries my throat.
Now they express
All that's content to wear a worn-out coat,   35
All actions done in patient hopelessness,
All that ignores the silences of death,

Thinking no further than the hand can hold,
All that grows old,
40 Yet works on uselessly with shortened breath.

Damn all explanatory rhymes!
To be that girl! – but that's impossible;
For me the task's to learn the many times
When I must stoop, and throw a shovelful:
45 I must repeat until I live the fact
That everything's remade
With shovel and spade;
That each dull day and each despairing act

Builds up the crags from which the spirit leaps
50 – The beast most innocent
That is so fabulous it never sleeps;
If I can keep against all argument
Such image of a snow-white unicorn,
Then as I pray it may for sanctuary
55 Descend at last to me,
And put into my hand its golden horn.

XXI

I dreamed of an out-thrust arm of land
Where gulls blew over a wave
That fell along miles of sand;
And the wind climbed up the caves
5 To tear at a dark-faced garden
Whose black flowers were dead,
And broke round a house we slept in,
A drawn blind and a bed.

I was sleeping, and you woke me
10 To walk on the chilled shore
Of a night with no memory,
Till your voice forsook my ear
Till your two hands withdrew
And I was empty of tears,
15 On the edge of a bricked and streeted sea
And a cold hill of stars.

XXII

One man walking a deserted platform;
Dawn coming, and rain
Driving across a darkening autumn;
One man restlessly waiting a train
While round the streets the wind runs wild,   5
Beating each shuttered house, that seems
Folded full of the dark silk of dreams,
A shell of sleep cradling a wife or child.

Who can this ambition trace,
To be each dawn perpetually journeying?   10
To trick this hour when lovers re-embrace
With the unguessed-at heart riding
The winds as gulls do? What lips said
Starset and cockcrow call the dispossessed
On to the next desert, lest   15
Love sink a grave round the still-sleeping head?

XXIII

If hands could free you, heart,
        Where would you fly?
Far, beyond every part
Of earth this running sky
Makes desolate? Would you cross   5
City and hill and sea,
        If hands could set you free?

I would not lift the latch;
        For I could run
Through fields, pit-valleys, catch   10
All beauty under the sun –
Still end in loss:
I should find no bent arm, no bed
        To rest my head.

XXIV

Love, we must part now: do not let it be
Calamitous and bitter. In the past
There has been too much moonlight and self-pity:
Let us have done with it: for now at last
Never has sun more boldly paced the sky,
Never were hearts more eager to be free,
To kick down worlds, lash forests; you and I
No longer hold them; we are husks, that see
The grain going forward to a different use.

There is regret. Always, there is regret.
But it is better that our lives unloose,
As two tall ships, wind-mastered, wet with light,
Break from an estuary with their courses set,
And waving part, and waving drop from sight.

XXV

Morning has spread again
Through every street,
And we are strange again;
For should we meet
How can I tell you that
Last night you came
Unbidden, in a dream?
And how forget
That we had worn down love good-humouredly,
Talking in fits and starts
As friends, as they will be
Who have let passion die within their hearts.
Now, watching the red east expand,
I wonder love can have already set
In dreams, when we've not met
More times than I can number on one hand.

XXVI

This is the first thing
I have understood:
Time is the echo of an axe
Within a wood.

XXVII

Heaviest of flowers, the head
Forever hangs above a stormless bed;
Hands that the heart can govern
Shall be at last by darker hands unwoven;
Every exultant sense   5
Unstrung to silence –
The sun drift away.

And all the memories that best
Run back beyond this season of unrest
Shall lie upon the earth   10
That gave them birth.
Like fallen apples, they will lose
Their sweetness at the bruise,
And then decay.

XXVIII

Is it for now or for always,
The world hangs on a stalk?
Is it a trick or a trysting-place,
The woods we have found to walk?

Is it a mirage or miracle,   5
Your lips that lift at mine:
And the suns like a juggler's juggling-balls,
Are they a sham or a sign?

Shine out, my sudden angel,
Break fear with breast and brow,   10

I take you now and for always,
For always is always now.

XXIX

Pour away that youth
That overflows the heart
Into hair and mouth;
Take the grave's part,
5   Tell the bone's truth.

Throw away that youth
That jewel in the head
That bronze in the breath;
Walk with the dead
10   For fear of death.

XXX

So through that unripe day you bore your head,
And the day was plucked and tasted bitter,
As if still cold among the leaves. Instead,
It was your severed image that grew sweeter,
5   That floated, wing-stiff, focused in the sun
Along uncertainty and gales of shame
Blown out before I slept. Now you are one
I dare not think alive: only a name
That chimes occasionally, as a belief
10   Long since embedded in the static past.

Summer broke and drained. Now we are safe.
The days lose confidence, and can be faced
Indoors. This is your last, meticulous hour,
Cut, gummed; pastime of a provincial winter.

XXXI
The North Ship

Legend

I saw three ships go sailing by,
Over the sea, the lifting sea,
And the wind rose in the morning sky,
And one was rigged for a long journey.

The first ship turned towards the west,   5
Over the sea, the running sea,
And by the wind was all possessed
And carried to a rich country.

The second turned towards the east,
Over the sea, the quaking sea,   10
And the wind hunted it like a beast
To anchor in captivity.

The third ship drove towards the north,
Over the sea, the darkening sea,
But no breath of wind came forth,   15
And the decks shone frostily.

The northern sky rose high and black
Over the proud unfruitful sea,
East and west the ships came back
Happily or unhappily: 20

But the third went wide and far
Into an unforgiving sea
Under a fire-spilling star,
And it was rigged for a long journey.

Songs
65° N

My sleep is made cold
By a recurrent dream
Where all things seem
Sickeningly to poise
5   On emptiness, on stars
Drifting under the world.

When waves fling loudly
And fall at the stern,
I am wakened each dawn
10   Increasingly to fear
Sail-stiffening air,
The birdless sea.

Light strikes from the ice:
Like one who near death
15   Savours the serene breath,
I grow afraid,
Now the bargain is made,
That dream draws close.

70° N
Fortunetelling

'You will go a long journey,
In a strange bed take rest,
And a dark girl will kiss you
As softly as the breast
5   Of an evening bird comes down
Covering its own nest.

'She will cover your mouth
Lest memory exclaim
At her bending face,
10   Knowing it is the same
As one who long since died
Under a different name.'

75° N
Blizzard

Suddenly clouds of snow
Begin assaulting the air,
As falling, as tangled
As a girl's thick hair.

Some see a flock of swans,   5
Some a fleet of ships
Or a spread winding-sheet,
But the snow touches my lips

And beyond all doubt I know
A girl is standing there   10
Who will take no lovers
Till she winds me in her hair.

Above 80° N

'A woman has ten claws,'
Sang the drunken boatswain;
Farther than Betelgeuse,
More brilliant than Orion
Or the planets Venus and Mars,   5
The star flames on the ocean;
'A woman has ten claws,'
Sang the drunken boatswain.

XXXII

Waiting for breakfast, while she brushed her hair,
I looked down at the empty hotel yard
Once meant for coaches. Cobblestones were wet,
But sent no light back to the loaded sky,
Sunk as it was with mist down to the roofs.   5
Drainpipes and fire-escape climbed up
Past rooms still burning their electric light:
I thought: Featureless morning, featureless night.

Misjudgment: for the stones slept, and the mist
Wandered absolvingly past all it touched,   10

Yet hung like a stayed breath; the lights burnt on,
Pin-points of undisturbed excitement; beyond the glass
The colourless vial of day painlessly spilled
My world back after a year, my lost lost world
15   Like a cropping deer strayed near my path again,
Bewaring the mind's least clutch. Turning, I kissed her,
Easily for sheer joy tipping the balance to love.

But, tender visiting,
Fallow as a deer or an unforced field,
20   How would you have me? Towards your grace
My promises meet and lock and race like rivers,
But only when you choose. Are you jealous of her?
Will you refuse to come till I have sent
Her terribly away, importantly live
25   Part invalid, part baby, and part saint?

THE LESS DECEIVED

Lines on a Young Lady's Photograph Album

At last you yielded up the album, which,
Once open, sent me distracted. All your ages
Matt and glossy on the thick black pages!
Too much confectionery, too rich:
I choke on such nutritious images.   5

My swivel eye hungers from pose to pose –
In pigtails, clutching a reluctant cat;
Or furred yourself, a sweet girl-graduate;
Or lifting a heavy-headed rose
Beneath a trellis, or in a trilby hat   10

(Faintly disturbing, that, in several ways) –
From every side you strike at my control,
Not least through these disquieting chaps who loll
At ease about your earlier days:
Not quite your class, I'd say, dear, on the whole.   15

But o, photography! as no art is,
Faithful and disappointing! that records
Dull days as dull, and hold-it smiles as frauds,
And will not censor blemishes
Like washing-lines, and Hall's-Distemper boards,   20

But shows the cat as disinclined, and shades
A chin as doubled when it is, what grace
Your candour thus confers upon her face!
How overwhelmingly persuades
That this is a real girl in a real place,   25

In every sense empirically true!
Or is it just *the past*? Those flowers, that gate,
These misty parks and motors, lacerate
Simply by being over; you
Contract my heart by looking out of date.   30

Yes, true; but in the end, surely, we cry
Not only at exclusion, but because
It leaves us free to cry. We know *what was*

Won't call on us to justify
35   Our grief, however hard we yowl across

The gap from eye to page. So I am left
To mourn (without a chance of consequence)
You, balanced on a bike against a fence;
To wonder if you'd spot the theft
40   Of this one of you bathing; to condense,

In short, a past that no one now can share,
No matter whose your future; calm and dry,
It holds you like a heaven, and you lie
Unvariably lovely there,
45   Smaller and clearer as the years go by.

Wedding-Wind

The wind blew all my wedding-day,
And my wedding-night was the night of the high wind;
And a stable door was banging, again and again,
That he must go and shut it, leaving me
5   Stupid in candlelight, hearing rain,
Seeing my face in the twisted candlestick,
Yet seeing nothing. When he came back
He said the horses were restless, and I was sad
That any man or beast that night should lack
10   The happiness I had.

                    Now in the day
All's ravelled under the sun by the wind's blowing.
He has gone to look at the floods, and I
Carry a chipped pail to the chicken-run,
Set it down, and stare. All is the wind
15   Hunting through clouds and forests, thrashing
My apron and the hanging cloths on the line.
Can it be borne, this bodying-forth by wind
Of joy my actions turn on, like a thread
Carrying beads? Shall I be let to sleep
20   Now this perpetual morning shares my bed?
Can even death dry up
These new delighted lakes, conclude
Our kneeling as cattle by all-generous waters?

Places, Loved Ones

No, I have never found
The place where I could say
This is my proper ground,
Here I shall stay;
Nor met that special one   5
Who has an instant claim
On everything I own
Down to my name;

To find such seems to prove
You want no choice in where   10
To build, or whom to love;
You ask them to bear
You off irrevocably,
So that it's not your fault
Should the town turn dreary,   15
The girl a dolt.

Yet, having missed them, you're
Bound, none the less, to act
As if what you settled for
Mashed you, in fact;   20
And wiser to keep away
From thinking you still might trace
Uncalled-for to this day
Your person, your place.

Coming

On longer evenings,
Light, chill and yellow,
Bathes the serene
Foreheads of houses.
A thrush sings,   5
Laurel-surrounded
In the deep bare garden,
Its fresh-peeled voice
Astonishing the brickwork.
It will be spring soon,   10

It will be spring soon –
And I, whose childhood
Is a forgotten boredom,
Feel like a child
15   Who comes on a scene
Of adult reconciling,
And can understand nothing
But the unusual laughter,
And starts to be happy.

Reasons for Attendance

The trumpet's voice, loud and authoritative,
Draws me a moment to the lighted glass
To watch the dancers – all under twenty-five –
Shifting intently, face to flushed face,
5   Solemnly on the beat of happiness.

– Or so I fancy, sensing the smoke and sweat,
The wonderful feel of girls. Why be out here?
But then, why be in there? Sex, yes, but what
Is sex? Surely, to think the lion's share
10   Of happiness is found by couples – sheer

Inaccuracy, as far as I'm concerned.
What calls me is that lifted, rough-tongued bell
(Art, if you like) whose individual sound
Insists I too am individual.
15   It speaks; I hear; others may hear as well,

But not for me, nor I for them; and so
With happiness. Therefore I stay outside,
Believing this; and they maul to and fro,
Believing that; and both are satisfied,
20   If no one has misjudged himself. Or lied.

Dry-Point

Endlessly, time-honoured irritant,
A bubble is restively forming at your tip.
Burst it as fast as we can –
It will grow again, until we begin dying.

Silently it inflates, till we're enclosed   5
And forced to start the struggle to get out:
Bestial, intent, real.
The wet spark comes, the bright blown walls collapse,

But what sad scapes we cannot turn from then:
What ashen hills! what salted, shrunken lakes!   10
How leaden the ring looks,
Birmingham magic all discredited,

And how remote that bare and sunscrubbed room,
Intensely far, that padlocked cube of light
We neither define nor prove,   15
Where you, we dream, obtain no right of entry.

Next, Please

Always too eager for the future, we
Pick up bad habits of expectancy.
Something is always approaching; every day
Till then we say,

Watching from a bluff the tiny, clear,   5
Sparkling armada of promises draw near.
How slow they are! And how much time they waste,
Refusing to make haste!

Yet still they leave us holding wretched stalks
Of disappointment, for, though nothing balks   10
Each big approach, leaning with brasswork prinked,
Each rope distinct,

Flagged, and the figurehead with golden tits
Arching our way, it never anchors; it's

15   No sooner present than it turns to past.
        Right to the last

        We think each one will heave to and unload
        All good into our lives, all we are owed
        For waiting so devoutly and so long.
20   But we are wrong:

        Only one ship is seeking us, a black-
        Sailed unfamiliar, towing at her back
        A huge and birdless silence. In her wake
        No waters breed or break.

Going

        There is an evening coming in
        Across the fields, one never seen before,
        That lights no lamps.

        Silken it seems at a distance, yet
5   When it is drawn up over the knees and breast
        It brings no comfort.

        Where has the tree gone, that locked
        Earth to the sky? What is under my hands,
        That I cannot feel?

10   What loads my hands down?

Wants

        Beyond all this, the wish to be alone:
        However the sky grows dark with invitation-cards
        However we follow the printed directions of sex
        However the family is photographed under the flagstaff –
5   Beyond all this, the wish to be alone.

        Beneath it all, desire of oblivion runs:
        Despite the artful tensions of the calendar,
        The life insurance, the tabled fertility rites,
        The costly aversion of the eyes from death –
10   Beneath it all, desire of oblivion runs.

Maiden Name

Marrying left your maiden name disused.
Its five light sounds no longer mean your face,
Your voice, and all your variants of grace;
For since you were so thankfully confused
By law with someone else, you cannot be 5
Semantically the same as that young beauty:
It was of her that these two words were used.

Now it's a phrase applicable to no one,
Lying just where you left it, scattered through
Old lists, old programmes, a school prize or two, 10
Packets of letters tied with tartan ribbon –
Then is it scentless, weightless, strengthless, wholly
Untruthful? Try whispering it slowly.
No, it means you. Or, since you're past and gone,

It means what we feel now about you then: 15
How beautiful you were, and near, and young,
So vivid, you might still be there among
Those first few days, unfingermarked again.
So your old name shelters our faithfulness,
Instead of losing shape and meaning less 20
With your depreciating luggage laden.

Born Yesterday
for Sally Amis

Tightly-folded bud,
I have wished you something
None of the others would:
Not the usual stuff
About being beautiful, 5
Or running off a spring
Of innocence and love –
They will all wish you that,
And should it prove possible,
Well, you're a lucky girl. 10

But if it shouldn't, then

May you be ordinary;
Have, like other women,
An average of talents:
15   Not ugly, not good-looking,
Nothing uncustomary
To pull you off your balance,
That, unworkable itself,
Stops all the rest from working.
20   In fact, may you be dull –
If that is what a skilled,
Vigilant, flexible,
Unemphasised, enthralled
Catching of happiness is called.

Whatever Happened?

At once whatever happened starts receding.
Panting, and back on board, we line the rail
With trousers ripped, light wallets, and lips bleeding.

Yes, gone, thank God! Remembering each detail
5   We toss for half the night, but find next day
All's kodak-distant. Easily, then (though pale),

'Perspective brings significance,' we say,
Unhooding our photometers, and, snap!
What can't be printed can be thrown away.

10   Later, it's just a latitude: the map
Points out how unavoidable it was:
'Such coastal bedding always means mishap.'

Curses? The dark? Struggling? Where's the source
Of these yarns now (except in nightmares, of course)?

No Road

Since we agreed to let the road between us
Fall to disuse,
And bricked our gates up, planted trees to screen us,
And turned all time's eroding agents loose,
5   Silence, and space, and strangers – our neglect

Has not had much effect.

Leaves drift unswept, perhaps; grass creeps unmown;
No other change.
So clear it stands, so little overgrown,
Walking that way tonight would not seem strange,   10
And still would be allowed. A little longer,
And time will be the stronger,

Drafting a world where no such road will run
From you to me;
To watch that world come up like a cold sun,   15
Rewarding others, is my liberty.
Not to prevent it is my will's fulfilment.
Willing it, my ailment.

Wires

The widest prairies have electric fences,
For though old cattle know they must not stray
Young steers are always scenting purer water
Not here but anywhere. Beyond the wires

Leads them to blunder up against the wires   5
Whose muscle-shredding violence gives no quarter.
Young steers become old cattle from that day,
Electric limits to their widest senses.

Church Going

Once I am sure there's nothing going on
I step inside, letting the door thud shut.
Another church: matting, seats, and stone,
And little books; sprawlings of flowers, cut
For Sunday, brownish now; some brass and stuff   5
Up at the holy end; the small neat organ;
And a tense, musty, unignorable silence,
Brewed God knows how long. Hatless, I take off
My cycle-clips in awkward reverence,

Move forward, run my hand around the font.   10
From where I stand, the roof looks almost new —

Cleaned, or restored? Someone would know: I don't.
Mounting the lectern, I peruse a few
Hectoring large-scale verses, and pronounce
'Here endeth' much more loudly than I'd meant.
The echoes snigger briefly. Back at the door
I sign the book, donate an Irish sixpence,
Reflect the place was not worth stopping for.

Yet stop I did: in fact I often do,
And always end much at a loss like this,
Wondering what to look for; wondering, too,
When churches fall completely out of use
What we shall turn them into, if we shall keep
A few cathedrals chronically on show,
Their parchment, plate and pyx in locked cases,
And let the rest rent-free to rain and sheep.
Shall we avoid them as unlucky places?

Or, after dark, will dubious women come
To make their children touch a particular stone;
Pick simples for a cancer; or on some
Advised night see walking a dead one?
Power of some sort or other will go on
In games, in riddles, seemingly at random;
But superstition, like belief, must die,
And what remains when disbelief has gone?
Grass, weedy pavement, brambles, buttress, sky,

A shape less recognisable each week,
A purpose more obscure. I wonder who
Will be the last, the very last, to seek
This place for what it was; one of the crew
That tap and jot and know what rood-lofts were?
Some ruin-bibber, randy for antique,
Or Christmas-addict, counting on a whiff
Of gown-and-bands and organ-pipes and myrrh?
Or will he be my representative,

Bored, uninformed, knowing the ghostly silt
Dispersed, yet tending to this cross of ground
Through suburb scrub because it held unspilt
So long and equably what since is found
Only in separation – marriage, and birth,
And death, and thoughts of these – for which was built

This special shell? For, though I've no idea
What this accoutred frowsty barn is worth,
It pleases me to stand in silence here;

A serious house on serious earth it is,   55
In whose blent air all our compulsions meet,
Are recognised, and robed as destinies.
And that much never can be obsolete,
Since someone will forever be surprising
A hunger in himself to be more serious,   60
And gravitating with it to this ground,
Which, he once heard, was proper to grow wise in,
If only that so many dead lie round.

Age

My age fallen away like white swaddling
Floats in the middle distance, becomes
An inhabited cloud. I bend closer, discern
A lighted tenement scuttling with voices.
O you tall game I tired myself with joining!   5
Now I wade through you like knee-level weeds,

And they attend me, dear translucent bergs:
Silence and space. By now so much has flown
From the nest here of my head that I needs must turn
To know what prints I leave, whether of feet,   10
Or spoor of pads, or a bird's adept splay.

Myxomatosis

Caught in the centre of a soundless field
While hot inexplicable hours go by
What trap is this? Where were its teeth concealed?
You seem to ask.
            I make a sharp reply,
Then clean my stick. I'm glad I can't explain   5
Just in what jaws you were to suppurate:
You may have thought things would come right again
If you could only keep quite still and wait.

37

Toads

Why should I let the toad *work*
  Squat on my life?
Can't I use my wit as a pitchfork
  And drive the brute off?

5 Six days of the week it soils
  With its sickening poison –
Just for paying a few bills!
  That's out of proportion.

Lots of folk live on their wits:
10   Lecturers, lispers,
Losels, loblolly-men, louts –
  They don't end as paupers;

Lots of folk live up lanes
  With fires in a bucket,
15 Eat windfalls and tinned sardines –
  They seem to like it.

Their nippers have got bare feet,
  Their unspeakable wives
Are skinny as whippets – and yet
20   No one actually *starves*.

Ah, were I courageous enough
  To shout *Stuff your pension!*
But I know, all too well, that's the stuff
  That dreams are made on:

25 For something sufficiently toad-like
  Squats in me, too;
Its hunkers are heavy as hard luck,
  And cold as snow,

And will never allow me to blarney
30   My way to getting
The fame and the girl and the money
  All at one sitting.

I don't say, one bodies the other
  One's spiritual truth;

But I do say it's hard to lose either,
    When you have both.   35

Poetry of Departures

Sometimes you hear, fifth-hand,
As epitaph:
He chucked up everything
And just cleared off,
And always the voice will sound   5
Certain you approve
This audacious, purifying,
Elemental move.

And they are right, I think.
We all hate home   10
And having to be there:
I detest my room,
Its specially-chosen junk,
The good books, the good bed,
And my life, in perfect order: 15
So to hear it said

He walked out on the whole crowd
Leaves me flushed and stirred,
Like *Then she undid her dress*
Or *Take that you bastard*;   20
Surely I can, if he did?
And that helps me stay
Sober and industrious.
But I'd go today,

Yes, swagger the nut-strewn roads,   25
Crouch in the fo'c'sle
Stubbly with goodness, if
It weren't so artificial,
Such a deliberate step backwards
To create an object: 30
Books; china; a life
Reprehensibly perfect.

Triple Time

This empty street, this sky to blandness scoured,
This air, a little indistinct with autumn
Like a reflection, constitute the present –
A time traditionally soured,
5 A time unrecommended by event.

But equally they make up something else:
This is the future furthest childhood saw
Between long houses, under travelling skies,
Heard in contending bells –
10 An air lambent with adult enterprise,

And on another day will be the past,
A valley cropped by fat neglected chances
That we insensately forbore to fleece.
On this we blame our last
15 Threadbare perspectives, seasonal decrease.

Spring

Green-shadowed people sit, or walk in rings,
Their children finger the awakened grass,
Calmly a cloud stands, calmly a bird sings,
And, flashing like a dangled looking-glass,
5 Sun lights the balls that bounce, the dogs that bark,
The branch-arrested mist of leaf, and me,
Threading my pursed-up way across the park,
An indigestible sterility.

Spring, of all seasons most gratuitous,
10 Is fold of untaught flower, is race of water,
Is earth's most multiple, excited daughter;

And those she has least use for see her best,
Their paths grown craven and circuitous,
Their visions mountain-clear, their needs immodest.

Deceptions

'Of course I was drugged, and so heavily I did not regain my
consciousness till the next morning. I was horrified to discover
that I had been ruined, and for some days I was inconsolable, and
cried like a child to be killed or sent back to my aunt.'
  Mayhew, *London Labour and the London Poor*

Even so distant, I can taste the grief,
Bitter and sharp with stalks, he made you gulp.
The sun's occasional print, the brisk brief
Worry of wheels along the street outside
Where bridal London bows the other way,   5
And light, unanswerable and tall and wide,
Forbids the scar to heal, and drives
Shame out of hiding. All the unhurried day
Your mind lay open like a drawer of knives.

Slums, years, have buried you. I would not dare   10
Console you if I could. What can be said,
Except that suffering is exact, but where
Desire takes charge, readings will grow erratic?
For you would hardly care
That you were less deceived, out on that bed,   15
Than he was, stumbling up the breathless stair
To burst into fulfilment's desolate attic.

I Remember, I Remember

Coming up England by a different line
For once, early in the cold new year,
We stopped, and, watching men with number-plates
Sprint down the platform to familiar gates,
'Why, Coventry!' I exclaimed. 'I was born here.'   5

I leant far out, and squinnied for a sign
That this was still the town that had been 'mine'
So long, but found I wasn't even clear
Which side was which. From where those cycle-crates
Were standing, had we annually departed   10

For all those family hols? . . . A whistle went:
Things moved. I sat back, staring at my boots.

'Was that,' my friend smiled, 'where you "have your roots"?'
No, only where my childhood was unspent,
I wanted to retort, just where I started:

By now I've got the whole place clearly charted.
Our garden, first: where I did not invent
Blinding theologies of flowers and fruits,
And wasn't spoken to by an old hat.
And here we have that splendid family

I never ran to when I got depressed,
The boys all biceps and the girls all chest,
Their comic Ford, their farm where I could be
'Really myself'. I'll show you, come to that,
The bracken where I never trembling sat,

Determined to go through with it; where she
Lay back, and 'all became a burning mist'.
And, in those offices, my doggerel
Was not set up in blunt ten-point, nor read
By a distinguished cousin of the mayor,

Who didn't call and tell my father *There
Before us, had we the gift to see ahead* –
'You look as if you wished the place in Hell,'
My friend said, 'judging from your face.' 'Oh well,
I suppose it's not the place's fault,' I said.

'Nothing, like something, happens anywhere.'

Absences

Rain patters on a sea that tilts and sighs.
Fast-running floors, collapsing into hollows,
Tower suddenly, spray-haired. Contrariwise,
A wave drops like a wall: another follows,
Wilting and scrambling, tirelessly at play
Where there are no ships and no shallows.

Above the sea, the yet more shoreless day,
Riddled by wind, trails lit-up galleries:
They shift to giant ribbing, sift away.

Such attics cleared of me! Such absences!

Latest Face

Latest face, so effortless
Your great arrival at my eyes,
No one standing near could guess
Your beauty had no home till then;
Precious vagrant, recognise   5
My look, and do not turn again.

Admirer and admired embrace
On a useless level, where
I contain your current grace,
You my judgment; yet to move   10
Into real untidy air
Brings no lasting attribute –
Bargains, suffering, and love,
Not this always-planned salute.

Lies grow dark around us: will   15
The statue of your beauty walk?
Must I wade behind it, till
Something's found – or is not found –
Far too late for turning back?
Or, if I will not shift my ground,   20
Is your power actual – can
Denial of you duck and run,
Stay out of sight and double round,
Leap from the sun with mask and brand
And murder and not understand?   25

If, My Darling

If my darling were once to decide
Not to stop at my eyes,
But to jump, like Alice, with floating skirt into my head,

She would find no tables and chairs,
No mahogany claw-footed sideboards,   5
No undisturbed embers;

The tantalus would not be filled, nor the fender-seat cosy,
Nor the shelves stuffed with small-printed books for the Sabbath,

Nor the butler bibulous, the housemaids lazy:

10   She would find herself looped with the creep of varying light,
Monkey-brown, fish-grey, a string of infected circles
Loitering like bullies, about to coagulate;

Delusions that shrink to the size of a woman's glove,
Then sicken inclusively outwards. She would also remark
15   The unwholesome floor, as it might be the skin of a grave,

From which ascends an adhesive sense of betrayal,
A Grecian statue kicked in the privates, money,
A swill-tub of finer feelings. But most of all

She'd be stopping her ears against the incessant recital
20   Intoned by reality, larded with technical terms,
Each one double-yolked with meaning and meaning's rebuttal:

For the skirl of that bulletin unpicks the world like a knot,
And to hear how the past is past and the future neuter
Might knock my darling off her unpriceable pivot.

Skin

Obedient daily dress,
You cannot always keep
That unfakable young surface.
You must learn your lines –
5   Anger, amusement, sleep;
Those few forbidding signs

Of the continuous coarse
Sand-laden wind, time;
You must thicken, work loose
10   Into an old bag
Carrying a soiled name.
Parch then; be roughened; sag;

And pardon me, that I
Could find, when you were new,
15   No brash festivity
To wear you at, such as
Clothes are entitled to
Till the fashion changes.

Arrivals, Departures

This town has docks where channel boats come sidling;
Tame water lanes, tall sheds, the traveller sees
(His bag of samples knocking at his knees),
And hears, still under slackened engines gliding,
His advent blurted to the morning shore.   5

And we, barely recalled from sleep there, sense
Arrivals lowing in a doleful distance –
Horny dilemmas at the gate once more.
Come and choose wrong, they cry, *come and choose wrong*;
And so we rise. At night again they sound,   10

Calling the traveller now, the outward bound:
O *not for long*, they cry, O *not for long* –
And we are nudged from comfort, never knowing
How safely we may disregard their blowing,
Or if, this night, happiness too is going.   15

At Grass

The eye can hardly pick them out
From the cold shade they shelter in,
Till wind distresses tail and mane;
Then one crops grass, and moves about
– The other seeming to look on –   5
And stands anonymous again.

Yet fifteen years ago, perhaps
Two dozen distances sufficed
To fable them: faint afternoons
Of Cups and Stakes and Handicaps,   10
Whereby their names were artificed
To inlay faded, classic Junes –

Silks at the start: against the sky
Numbers and parasols: outside,
Squadrons of empty cars, and heat,   15
And littered grass: then the long cry

Hanging unhushed till it subside
To stop-press columns on the street.

Do memories plague their ears like flies?
20 They shake their heads. Dusk brims the shadows.
Summer by summer all stole away,
The starting-gates, the crowds and cries –
All but the unmolesting meadows.
Almanacked, their names live; they

25 Have slipped their names, and stand at ease,
Or gallop for what must be joy,
And not a fieldglass sees them home,
Or curious stop-watch prophesies:
Only the groom, and the groom's boy,
30 With bridles in the evening come.

THE WHITSUN WEDDINGS

Here

Swerving east, from rich industrial shadows
And traffic all night north; swerving through fields
Too thin and thistled to be called meadows,
And now and then a harsh-named halt, that shields
Workmen at dawn; swerving to solitude   5
Of skies and scarecrows, haystacks, hares and pheasants,
And the widening river's slow presence,
The piled gold clouds, the shining gull-marked mud,

Gathers to the surprise of a large town:
Here domes and statues, spires and cranes cluster   10
Beside grain-scattered streets, barge-crowded water,
And residents from raw estates, brought down
The dead straight miles by stealing flat-faced trolleys,
Push through plate-glass swing doors to their desires –
Cheap suits, red kitchen-ware, sharp shoes, iced lollies,   15
Electric mixers, toasters, washers, driers –

A cut-price crowd, urban yet simple, dwelling
Where only salesmen and relations come
Within a terminate and fishy-smelling
Pastoral of ships up streets, the slave museum,   20
Tattoo-shops, consulates, grim head-scarfed wives;
And out beyond its mortgaged half-built edges
Fast-shadowed wheat-fields, running high as hedges,
Isolate villages, where removed lives

Loneliness clarifies. Here silence stands   25
Like heat. Here leaves unnoticed thicken,
Hidden weeds flower, neglected waters quicken,
Luminously-peopled air ascends;
And past the poppies bluish neutral distance
Ends the land suddenly beyond a beach   30
Of shapes and shingle. Here is unfenced existence:
Facing the sun, untalkative, out of reach.

Mr Bleaney

'This was Mr Bleaney's room. He stayed
The whole time he was at the Bodies, till
They moved him.' Flowered curtains, thin and frayed,
Fall to within five inches of the sill,

5   Whose window shows a strip of building land,
Tussocky, littered. 'Mr Bleaney took
My bit of garden properly in hand.'
Bed, upright chair, sixty-watt bulb, no hook

Behind the door, no room for books or bags –
10   'I'll take it.' So it happens that I lie
Where Mr Bleaney lay, and stub my fags
On the same saucer-souvenir, and try

Stuffing my ears with cotton-wool, to drown
The jabbering set he egged her on to buy.
15   I know his habits – what time he came down,
His preference for sauce to gravy, why

He kept on plugging at the four aways –
Likewise their yearly frame: the Frinton folk
Who put him up for summer holidays,
20   And Christmas at his sister's house in Stoke.

But if he stood and watched the frigid wind
Tousling the clouds, lay on the fusty bed
Telling himself that this was home, and grinned,
And shivered, without shaking off the dread

25   That how we live measures our own nature,
And at his age having no more to show
Than one hired box should make him pretty sure
He warranted no better, I don't know.

Nothing To Be Said

For nations vague as weed,
For nomads among stones,
Small-statured cross-faced tribes
And cobble-close families

In mill-towns on dark mornings   5
Life is slow dying.

So are their separate ways
Of building, benediction,
Measuring love and money
Ways of slow dying.   10
The day spent hunting pig
Or holding a garden-party,

Hours giving evidence
Or birth, advance
On death equally slowly.   15
And saying so to some
Means nothing; others it leaves
Nothing to be said.

Love Songs in Age

She kept her songs, they took so little space,
      The covers pleased her:
One bleached from lying in a sunny place,
One marked in circles by a vase of water,
One mended, when a tidy fit had seized her,   5
      And coloured, by her daughter –
So they had waited, till in widowhood
She found them, looking for something else, and stood

Relearning how each frank submissive chord
      Had ushered in   10
Word after sprawling hyphenated word,
And the unfailing sense of being young
Spread out like a spring-woken tree, wherein
      That hidden freshness sung,
That certainty of time laid up in store   15
As when she played them first. But, even more,

The glare of that much-mentioned brilliance, love,
      Broke out, to show
Its bright incipience sailing above,
Still promising to solve, and satisfy,   20
And set unchangeably in order. So
      To pile them back, to cry,

Was hard, without lamely admitting how
It had not done so then, and could not now.

Naturally the Foundation will Bear Your Expenses

Hurrying to catch my Comet
    One dark November day,
Which soon would snatch me from it
    To the sunshine of Bombay,
5   I pondered pages Berkeley
    Not three weeks since had heard,
Perceiving Chatto darkly
    Through the mirror of the Third.

Crowds, colourless and careworn,
10   Had made my taxi late,
Yet not till I was airborne
    Did I recall the date –
That day when Queen and Minister
    And Band of Guards and all
15   Still act their solemn-sinister
    Wreath-rubbish in Whitehall.

It used to make me throw up,
    These mawkish nursery games:
O when will England grow up?
20   – But I outsoar the Thames,
And dwindle off down Auster
    To greet Professor Lal
(He once met Morgan Forster),
    My contact and my pal.

Broadcast

Giant whispering and coughing from
Vast Sunday-full and organ-frowned-on spaces
Precede a sudden scuttle on the drum,
'The Queen', and huge resettling. Then begins

A snivel on the violins: 5
I think of your face among all those faces,

Beautiful and devout before
Cascades of monumental slithering,
One of your gloves unnoticed on the floor
Beside those new, slightly-outmoded shoes.   10
Here it goes quickly dark. I lose
All but the outline of the still and withering

Leaves on half-emptied trees. Behind
The glowing wavebands, rabid storms of chording
By being distant overpower my mind   15
All the more shamelessly, their cut-off shout
Leaving me desperate to pick out
Your hands, tiny in all that air, applauding.

Faith Healing

Slowly the women file to where he stands
Upright in rimless glasses, silver hair,
Dark suit, white collar. Stewards tirelessly
Persuade them onwards to his voice and hands,
Within whose warm spring rain of loving care   5
Each dwells some twenty seconds. *Now, dear child,
What's wrong*, the deep American voice demands,
And, scarcely pausing, goes into a prayer
Directing God about this eye, that knee.
Their heads are clasped abruptly; then, exiled   10

Like losing thoughts, they go in silence; some
Sheepishly stray, not back into their lives
Just yet; but some stay stiff, twitching and loud
With deep hoarse tears, as if a kind of dumb
And idiot child within them still survives   15
To re-awake at kindness, thinking a voice
At last calls them alone, that hands have come
To lift and lighten; and such joy arrives
Their thick tongues blort, their eyes squeeze grief, a crowd
Of huge unheard answers jam and rejoice –   20

What's wrong! Moustached in flowered frocks they shake:
By now, all's wrong. In everyone there sleeps

A sense of life lived according to love.
To some it means the difference they could make
25 By loving others, but across most it sweeps
As all they might have done had they been loved.
That nothing cures. An immense slackening ache,
As when, thawing, the rigid landscape weeps,
Spreads slowly through them – that, and the voice above
30 Saying *Dear child*, and all time has disproved.

For Sidney Bechet

That note you hold, narrowing and rising, shakes
Like New Orleans reflected on the water,
And in all ears appropriate falsehood wakes,

Building for some a legendary Quarter
5 Of balconies, flower-baskets and quadrilles,
Everyone making love and going shares –

Oh, play that thing! Mute glorious Storyvilles
Others may license, grouping round their chairs
Sporting-house girls like circus tigers (priced

10 Far above rubies) to pretend their fads,
While scholars *manqués* nod around unnoticed
Wrapped up in personnels like old plaids.

On me your voice falls as they say love should,
Like an enormous yes. My Crescent City
15 Is where your speech alone is understood,

And greeted as the natural noise of good,
Scattering long-haired grief and scored pity.

Home is so Sad

Home is so sad. It stays as it was left,
Shaped to the comfort of the last to go
As if to win them back. Instead, bereft
Of anyone to please, it withers so,
5 Having no heart to put aside the theft

And turn again to what it started as,

A joyous shot at how things ought to be,
Long fallen wide. You can see how it was:
Look at the pictures and the cutlery.
The music in the piano stool. That vase.   10

Toads Revisited

Walking around in the park
Should feel better than work:
The lake, the sunshine,
The grass to lie on,

Blurred playground noises   5
Beyond black-stockinged nurses –
Not a bad place to be.
Yet it doesn't suit me,

Being one of the men
You meet of an afternoon: 10
Palsied old step-takers,
Hare-eyed clerks with the jitters,

Waxed-fleshed out-patients
Still vague from accidents,
And characters in long coats   15
Deep in the litter-baskets –

All dodging the toad work
By being stupid or weak.
Think of being them!
Hearing the hours chime,   20

Watching the bread delivered,
The sun by clouds covered,
The children going home;
Think of being them,

Turning over their failures   25
By some bed of lobelias,
Nowhere to go but indoors,
No friends but empty chairs –

No, give me my in-tray,
My loaf-haired secretary,   30

My shall-I-keep-the-call-in-Sir:
What else can I answer,

When the lights come on at four
At the end of another year?
35 Give me your arm, old toad;
Help me down Cemetery Road.

Water

If I were called in
To construct a religion
I should make use of water.

Going to church
5 Would entail a fording
To dry, different clothes;

My liturgy would employ
Images of sousing,
A furious devout drench,

10 And I should raise in the east
A glass of water
Where any-angled light
Would congregate endlessly.

The Whitsun Weddings

That Whitsun, I was late getting away:
    Not till about
One-twenty on the sunlit Saturday
Did my three-quarters-empty train pull out,
5 All windows down, all cushions hot, all sense
Of being in a hurry gone. We ran
Behind the backs of houses, crossed a street
Of blinding windscreens, smelt the fish-dock; thence
The river's level drifting breadth began,
10 Where sky and Lincolnshire and water meet.

All afternoon, through the tall heat that slept
    For miles inland,

A slow and stopping curve southwards we kept.
Wide farms went by, short-shadowed cattle, and
Canals with floatings of industrial froth;   15
A hothouse flashed uniquely: hedges dipped
And rose: and now and then a smell of grass
Displaced the reek of buttoned carriage-cloth
Until the next town, new and nondescript,
Approached with acres of dismantled cars.   20

At first, I didn't notice what a noise
      The weddings made
Each station that we stopped at: sun destroys
The interest of what's happening in the shade,
And down the long cool platforms whoops and skirls   25
I took for porters larking with the mails,
And went on reading. Once we started, though,
We passed them, grinning and pomaded, girls
In parodies of fashion, heels and veils,
All posed irresolutely, watching us go,   30

As if out on the end of an event
      Waving goodbye
To something that survived it. Struck, I leant
More promptly out next time, more curiously,
And saw it all again in different terms: 35
The fathers with broad belts under their suits
And seamy foreheads; mothers loud and fat;
An uncle shouting smut; and then the perms,
The nylon gloves and jewellery-substitutes,
The lemons, mauves, and olive-ochres that   40

Marked off the girls unreally from the rest.
      Yes, from cafés
And banquet-halls up yards, and bunting-dressed
Coach-party annexes, the wedding-days
Were coming to an end. All down the line   45
Fresh couples climbed aboard: the rest stood round;
The last confetti and advice were thrown,
And, as we moved, each face seemed to define
Just what it saw departing: children frowned
At something dull; fathers had never known   50

Success so huge and wholly farcical;
      The women shared

The secret like a happy funeral;
While girls, gripping their handbags tighter, stared
55   At a religious wounding. Free at last,
And loaded with the sum of all they saw,
We hurried towards London, shuffling gouts of steam.
Now fields were building-plots, and poplars cast
Long shadows over major roads, and for
60   Some fifty minutes, that in time would seem

Just long enough to settle hats and say
    I nearly died,
A dozen marriages got under way.
They watched the landscape, sitting side by side
65   – An Odeon went past, a cooling tower,
And someone running up to bowl – and none
Thought of the others they would never meet
Or how their lives would all contain this hour.
I thought of London spread out in the sun,
70   Its postal districts packed like squares of wheat:

There we were aimed. And as we raced across
    Bright knots of rail
Past standing Pullmans, walls of blackened moss
Came close, and it was nearly done, this frail
75   Travelling coincidence; and what it held
Stood ready to be loosed with all the power
That being changed can give. We slowed again,
And as the tightened brakes took hold, there swelled
A sense of falling, like an arrow-shower
80   Sent out of sight, somewhere becoming rain.

Self's the Man

Oh, no one can deny
That Arnold is less selfish than I.
He married a woman to stop her getting away
Now she's there all day,

5   And the money he gets for wasting his life on work
She takes as her perk

To pay for the kiddies' clobber and the drier
And the electric fire,

And when he finishes supper
Planning to have a read at the evening paper   10
It's *Put a screw in this wall* –
He has no time at all,

With the nippers to wheel round the houses
And the hall to paint in his old trousers
And that letter to her mother   15
Saying *Won't you come for the summer.*

To compare his life and mine
Makes me feel a swine:
Oh, no one can deny
That Arnold is less selfish than I.   20

But wait, not so fast:
Is there such a contrast?
He was out for his own ends
Not just pleasing his friends;

And if it was such a mistake   25
He still did it for his own sake,
Playing his own game.
So he and I are the same,

Only I'm a better hand
At knowing what I can stand   30
Without them sending a van –
Or I suppose I can.

Take One Home for the Kiddies

On shallow straw, in shadeless glass,
Huddled by empty bowls, they sleep:
No dark, no dam, no earth, no grass –
Mam, get us one of them to keep.

Living toys are something novel,   5
But it soon wears off somehow.
Fetch the shoebox, fetch the shovel –
Mam, we're playing funerals now.

Days

What are days for?
Days are where we live.
They come, they wake us
Time and time over.
5   They are to be happy in:
Where can we live but days?

Ah, solving that question
Brings the priest and the doctor
In their long coats
10 Running over the fields.

MCMXIV

Those long uneven lines
Standing as patiently
As if they were stretched outside
The Oval or Villa Park,
5   The crowns of hats, the sun
On moustached archaic faces
Grinning as if it were all
An August Bank Holiday lark;

And the shut shops, the bleached
10 Established names on the sunblinds,
The farthings and sovereigns,
And dark-clothed children at play
Called after kings and queens,
The tin advertisements
15 For cocoa and twist, and the pubs
Wide open all day;

And the countryside not caring:
The place-names all hazed over
With flowering grasses, and fields
20 Shadowing Domesday lines
Under wheat's restless silence;
The differently-dressed servants

With tiny rooms in huge houses,
The dust behind limousines;

Never such innocence,   25
Never before or since,
As changed itself to past
Without a word – the men
Leaving the gardens tidy,
The thousands of marriages   30
Lasting a little while longer:
Never such innocence again.

Talking in Bed

Talking in bed ought to be easiest,
Lying together there goes back so far,
An emblem of two people being honest.

Yet more and more time passes silently.
Outside, the wind's incomplete unrest   5
Builds and disperses clouds about the sky,

And dark towns heap up on the horizon.
None of this cares for us. Nothing shows why
At this unique distance from isolation

It becomes still more difficult to find   10
Words at once true and kind,
Or not untrue and not unkind.

The Large Cool Store

The large cool store selling cheap clothes
Set out in simple sizes plainly
(Knitwear, Summer Casuals, Hose,
In browns and greys, maroon and navy)
Conjures the weekday world of those   5

Who leave at dawn low terraced houses
Timed for factory, yard and site.
But past the heaps of shirts and trousers

Spread the stands of Modes For Night:
10   Machine-embroidered, thin as blouses,

Lemon, sapphire, moss-green, rose
Bri-Nylon Baby-Dolls and Shorties
Flounce in clusters. To suppose
They share that world, to think their sort is
15   Matched by something in it, shows

How separate and unearthly love is,
Or women are, or what they do,
Or in our young unreal wishes
Seem to be: synthetic, new,
20   And natureless in ecstasies.

A Study of Reading Habits

When getting my nose in a book
Cured most things short of school,
It was worth ruining my eyes
To know I could still keep cool,
5   And deal out the old right hook
To dirty dogs twice my size.

Later, with inch-thick specs,
Evil was just my lark:
Me and my cloak and fangs
10   Had ripping times in the dark.
The women I clubbed with sex!
I broke them up like meringues.

Don't read much now: the dude
Who lets the girl down before
15   The hero arrives, the chap
Who's yellow and keeps the store,
Seem far too familiar. Get stewed:
Books are a load of crap.

As Bad as a Mile

Watching the shied core
Striking the basket, skidding across the floor,
Shows less and less of luck, and more and more

Of failure spreading back up the arm
Earlier and earlier, the unraised hand calm,   5
The apple unbitten in the palm.

Ambulances

Closed like confessionals, they thread
Loud noons of cities, giving back
None of the glances they absorb.
Light glossy grey, arms on a plaque,
They come to rest at any kerb: 5
All streets in time are visited.

Then children strewn on steps or road,
Or women coming from the shops
Past smells of different dinners, see
A wild white face that overtops   10
Red stretcher-blankets momently
As it is carried in and stowed,

And sense the solving emptiness
That lies just under all we do,
And for a second get it whole,   15
So permanent and blank and true.
The fastened doors recede. *Poor soul,*
They whisper at their own distress;

For borne away in deadened air
May go the sudden shut of loss   20
Round something nearly at an end,
And what cohered in it across
The years, the unique random blend
Of families and fashions, there

At last begin to loosen. Far   25
From the exchange of love to lie

Unreachable inside a room
The traffic parts to let go by
Brings closer what is left to come,
30   And dulls to distance all we are.

The Importance of Elsewhere

Lonely in Ireland, since it was not home,
Strangeness made sense. The salt rebuff of speech,
Insisting so on difference, made me welcome:
Once that was recognised, we were in touch.

5   Their draughty streets, end-on to hills, the faint
Archaic smell of dockland, like a stable,
The herring-hawker's cry, dwindling, went
To prove me separate, not unworkable.

Living in England has no such excuse:
10   These are my customs and establishments
It would be much more serious to refuse.
Here no elsewhere underwrites my existence.

Sunny Prestatyn

Come To Sunny Prestatyn
Laughed the girl on the poster,
Kneeling up on the sand
In tautened white satin.
5   Behind her, a hunk of coast, a
Hotel with palms
Seemed to expand from her thighs and
Spread breast-lifting arms.

She was slapped up one day in March.
10   A couple of weeks, and her face
Was snaggle-toothed and boss-eyed;
Huge tits and a fissured crotch
Were scored well in, and the space
Between her legs held scrawls

That set her fairly astride
A tuberous cock and balls

Autographed *Titch Thomas*, while
Someone had used a knife
Or something to stab right through
The moustached lips of her smile.
She was too good for this life.
Very soon, a great transverse tear
Left only a hand and some blue.
Now *Fight Cancer* is there.

First Sight

Lambs that learn to walk in snow
When their bleating clouds the air
Meet a vast unwelcome, know
Nothing but a sunless glare.
Newly stumbling to and fro   5
All they find, outside the fold,
Is a wretched width of cold.

As they wait beside the ewe,
Her fleeces wetly caked, there lies
Hidden round them, waiting too, 10
Earth's immeasurable surprise.
They could not grasp it if they knew,
What so soon will wake and grow
Utterly unlike the snow.

Dockery and Son

'Dockery was junior to you,
Wasn't he?' said the Dean. 'His son's here now.'
Death-suited, visitant, I nod. 'And do
You keep in touch with —' Or remember how
Black-gowned, unbreakfasted, and still half-tight 5
We used to stand before that desk, to give

'Our version' of 'these incidents last night'?
I try the door of where I used to live:

Locked. The lawn spreads dazzlingly wide.
A known bell chimes. I catch my train, ignored.
Canal and clouds and colleges subside
Slowly from view. But Dockery, good Lord,
Anyone up today must have been born
In '43, when I was twenty-one.
If he was younger, did he get this son
At nineteen, twenty? Was he that withdrawn

High-collared public-schoolboy, sharing rooms
With Cartwright who was killed? Well, it just shows
How much . . . How little . . .Yawning, I suppose
I fell asleep, waking at the fumes
And furnace-glares of Sheffield, where I changed,
And ate an awful pie, and walked along
The platform to its end to see the ranged
Joining and parting lines reflect a strong

Unhindered moon. To have no son, no wife,
No house or land still seemed quite natural.
Only a numbness registered the shock
Of finding out how much had gone of life,
How widely from the others. Dockery, now:
Only nineteen, he must have taken stock
Of what he wanted, and been capable
Of . . . No, that's not the difference: rather, how

Convinced he was he should be added to!
Why did he think adding meant increase?
To me it was dilution. Where do these
Innate assumptions come from? Not from what
We think truest, or most want to do:
Those warp tight-shut, like doors. They're more a style
Our lives bring with them: habit for a while,
Suddenly they harden into all we've got

And how we got it; looked back on, they rear
Like sand-clouds, thick and close, embodying
For Dockery a son, for me nothing,
Nothing with all a son's harsh patronage.
Life is first boredom, then fear.

Whether or not we use it, it goes,
And leaves what something hidden from us chose,
And age, and then the only end of age.

Ignorance

Strange to know nothing, never to be sure
Of what is true or right or real,
But forced to qualify *or so I feel*,
Or *Well, it does seem so:*
Someone must know.   5

Strange to be ignorant of the way things work:
Their skill at finding what they need,
Their sense of shape, and punctual spread of seed,
And willingness to change;
Yes, it is strange,   10

Even to wear such knowledge – for our flesh
Surrounds us with its own decisions –
And yet spend all our life on imprecisions,
That when we start to die
Have no idea why.   15

Reference Back

That was a pretty one, I heard you call
From the unsatisfactory hall
To the unsatisfactory room where I
Played record after record, idly,
Wasting my time at home, that you   5
Looked so much forward to.

Oliver's *Riverside Blues*, it was. And now
I shall, I suppose, always remember how
The flock of notes those antique negroes blew
Out of Chicago air into   10
A huge remembering pre-electric horn
The year after I was born
Three decades later made this sudden bridge

From your unsatisfactory age
15   To my unsatisfactory prime.

Truly, though our element is time,
We are not suited to the long perspectives
Open at each instant of our lives.
They link us to our losses: worse,
20   They show us what we have as it once was,
Blindingly undiminished, just as though
By acting differently we could have kept it so.

Wild Oats

About twenty years ago
Two girls came in where I worked –
A bosomy English rose
And her friend in specs I could talk to.
5   Faces in those days sparked
The whole shooting-match off, and I doubt
If ever one had like hers:
But it was the friend I took out,

And in seven years after that
10   Wrote over four hundred letters,
Gave a ten-guinea ring
I got back in the end, and met
At numerous cathedral cities
Unknown to the clergy. I believe
15   I met beautiful twice. She was trying
Both times (so I thought) not to laugh.

Parting, after about five
Rehearsals, was an agreement
That I was too selfish, withdrawn,
20   And easily bored to love.
Well, useful to get that learnt.
In my wallet are still two snaps
Of bosomy rose with fur gloves on.
Unlucky charms, perhaps.

Essential Beauty

In frames as large as rooms that face all ways
And block the ends of streets with giant loaves,
Screen graves with custard, cover slums with praise
Of motor-oil and cuts of salmon, shine
Perpetually these sharply-pictured groves   5
Of how life should be. High above the gutter
A silver knife sinks into golden butter,
A glass of milk stands in a meadow, and
Well-balanced families, in fine
Midsummer weather, owe their smiles, their cars,   10
Even their youth, to that small cube each hand
Stretches towards. These, and the deep armchairs
Aligned to cups at bedtime, radiant bars
(Gas or electric), quarter-profile cats
By slippers on warm mats,   15
Reflect none of the rained-on streets and squares

They dominate outdoors. Rather, they rise
Serenely to proclaim pure crust, pure foam,
Pure coldness to our live imperfect eyes
That stare beyond this world, where nothing's made   20
As new or washed quite clean, seeking the home
All such inhabit. There, dark raftered pubs
Are filled with white-clothed ones from tennis-clubs,
And the boy puking his heart out in the Gents
Just missed them, as the pensioner paid   25
A halfpenny more for Granny Graveclothes' Tea
To taste old age, and dying smokers sense
Walking towards them through some dappled park
As if on water that unfocused she
No match lit up, nor drag ever brought near,   30
Who now stands newly clear,
Smiling, and recognising, and going dark.

Send No Money

Standing under the fobbed
Impendent belly of Time
Tell me the truth, I said,
Teach me the way things go.
5   All the other lads there
Were itching to have a bash,
But I thought wanting unfair:
It and finding out clash.

So he patted my head, booming *Boy,*
10   *There's no green in your eye:*
Sit here, and watch the hail
Of occurrence clobber life out
To a shape no one sees –
Dare you look at that straight?
15   *Oh thank you*, I said, *Oh yes please,*
And sat down to wait.

Half life is over now,
And I meet full face on dark mornings
The bestial visor, bent in
20   By the blows of what happened to happen.
What does it prove? Sod all.
In this way I spent youth,
Tracing the trite untransferable
Truss-advertisement, truth.

Afternoons

Summer is fading:
The leaves fall in ones and twos
From trees bordering
The new recreation ground.
5   In the hollows of afternoons
Young mothers assemble
At swing and sandpit
Setting free their children.

Behind them, at intervals,

Stand husbands in skilled trades,   10
An estateful of washing,
And the albums, lettered
Our Wedding, lying
Near the television:
Before them, the wind   15
Is ruining their courting-places

That are still courting-places
(But the lovers are all in school),
And their children, so intent on
Finding more unripe acorns,   20
Expect to be taken home.
Their beauty has thickened.
Something is pushing them
To the side of their own lives.

An Arundel Tomb

Side by side, their faces blurred,
The earl and countess lie in stone,
Their proper habits vaguely shown
As jointed armour, stiffened pleat,
And that faint hint of the absurd –   5
The little dogs under their feet.

Such plainness of the pre-baroque
Hardly involves the eye, until
It meets his left-hand gauntlet, still
Clasped empty in the other; and   10
One sees, with a sharp tender shock,
His hand withdrawn, holding her hand.

They would not think to lie so long.
Such faithfulness in effigy
Was just a detail friends would see: 15
A sculptor's sweet commissioned grace
Thrown off in helping to prolong
The Latin names around the base.

They would not guess how early in
Their supine stationary voyage   20
The air would change to soundless damage,

Turn the old tenantry away;
How soon succeeding eyes begin
To look, not read. Rigidly they

25   Persisted, linked, through lengths and breadths
Of time. Snow fell, undated. Light
Each summer thronged the glass. A bright
Litter of birdcalls strewed the same
Bone-riddled ground. And up the paths
30   The endless altered people came,

Washing at their identity.
Now, helpless in the hollow of
An unarmorial age, a trough
Of smoke in slow suspended skeins
35   Above their scrap of history,
Only an attitude remains:

Time has transfigured them into
Untruth. The stone fidelity
They hardly meant has come to be
40   Their final blazon, and to prove
Our almost-instinct almost true:
What will survive of us is love.

HIGH WINDOWS

HIGH WINDOWS

To the Sea

To step over the low wall that divides
Road from concrete walk above the shore
Brings sharply back something known long before –
The miniature gaiety of seasides.
Everything crowds under the low horizon: 5
Steep beach, blue water, towels, red bathing caps,
The small hushed waves' repeated fresh collapse
Up the warm yellow sand, and further off
A white steamer stuck in the afternoon –

Still going on, all of it, still going on!   10
To lie, eat, sleep in hearing of the surf
(Ears to transistors, that sound tame enough
Under the sky), or gently up and down
Lead the uncertain children, frilled in white
And grasping at enormous air, or wheel   15
The rigid old along for them to feel
A final summer, plainly still occurs
As half an annual pleasure, half a rite,

As when, happy at being on my own,
I searched the sand for Famous Cricketers,   20
Or, farther back, my parents, listeners
To the same seaside quack, first became known.
Strange to it now, I watch the cloudless scene:
The same clear water over smoothed pebbles,
The distant bathers' weak protesting trebles   25
Down at its edge, and then the cheap cigars,
The chocolate-papers, tea-leaves, and, between

The rocks, the rusting soup-tins, till the first
Few families start the trek back to the cars.
The white steamer has gone. Like breathed-on glass   30
The sunlight has turned milky. If the worst
Of flawless weather is our falling short,
It may be that through habit these do best,
Coming to water clumsily undressed
Yearly; teaching their children by a sort   35
Of clowning; helping the old, too, as they ought.

Sympathy in White Major

When I drop four cubes of ice
Chimingly in a glass, and add
Three goes of gin, a lemon slice,
And let a ten-ounce tonic void
In foaming gulps until it smothers
Everything else up to the edge,
I lift the lot in private pledge:
He devoted his life to others.

While other people wore like clothes
The human beings in their days
I set myself to bring to those
Who thought I could the lost displays;
It didn't work for them or me,
But all concerned were nearer thus
(Or so we thought) to all the fuss
Than if we'd missed it separately.

A decent chap, a real good sort,
Straight as a die, one of the best,
A brick, a trump, a proper sport,
Head and shoulders above the rest;
How many lives would have been duller
Had he not been here below?
Here's to the whitest man I know —
Though white is not my favourite colour.

The Trees

The trees are coming into leaf
Like something almost being said;
The recent buds relax and spread,
Their greenness is a kind of grief.

Is it that they are born again
And we grow old? No, they die too.
Their yearly trick of looking new
Is written down in rings of grain.

Yet still the unresting castles thresh

In fullgrown thickness every May.   10
Last year is dead, they seem to say,
Begin afresh, afresh, afresh.

Livings

I

I deal with farmers, things like dips and feed.
Every third month I book myself in at
The ------ Hotel in ----ton for three days.
The boots carries my lean old leather case
Up to a single, where I hang my hat.   5
One beer, and then 'the dinner', at which I read
The ----*shire Times* from soup to stewed pears.
Births, deaths. For sale. Police court. Motor spares.

Afterwards, whisky in the Smoke Room: Clough,
Margetts, the Captain, Dr. Watterson;   10
Who makes ends meet, who's taking the knock,
Government tariffs, wages, price of stock.
Smoke hangs under the light. The pictures on
The walls are comic – hunting, the trenches, stuff
Nobody minds or notices. A sound   15
Of dominoes from the Bar. I stand a round.

Later, the square is empty: a big sky
Drains down the estuary like the bed
Of a gold river, and the Customs House
Still has its office lit. I drowse   20
Between ex-Army sheets, wondering why
I think it's worth while coming. Father's dead:
He used to, but the business now is mine.
It's time for change, in nineteen twenty-nine.

II

Seventy feet down
The sea explodes upwards,
Relapsing, to slaver
Off landing-stage steps –

77

5   Running suds, rejoice!

Rocks writhe back to sight.
Mussels, limpets,
Husband their tenacity
In the freezing slither –
10   Creatures, I cherish you!

By day, sky builds
Grape-dark over the salt
Unsown stirring fields.
Radio rubs its legs,
15   Telling me of elsewhere:

Barometers falling,
Ports wind-shuttered,
Fleets pent like hounds,
Fires in humped inns
20   Kippering sea-pictures –

Keep it all off!
By night, snow swerves
(O loose moth world)
Through the stare travelling
25   Leather-black waters.

Guarded by brilliance
I set plate and spoon,
And after, divining-cards.
Lit shelved liners
30   Grope like mad worlds westward.

III

Tonight we dine without the Master
(Nocturnal vapours do not please);
The port goes round so much the faster,
Topics are raised with no less ease –
5   Which advowson looks the fairest,
What the wood from Snape will fetch,
Names for *pudendum mulieris*,
Why is Judas like Jack Ketch?

The candleflames grow thin, then broaden:
10   Our butler Starveling piles the logs

And sets behind the screen a jordan
(Quicker than going to the bogs).
The wine heats temper and complexion:
Oath-enforced assertions fly
On rheumy fevers, resurrection,   15
Regicide and rabbit pie.

The fields around are cold and muddy,
The cobbled streets close by are still,
A sizar shivers at his study,
The kitchen cat has made a kill;   20
The bells discuss the hour's gradations,
Dusty shelves hold prayers and proofs:
Above, Chaldean constellations
Sparkle over crowded roofs.

Forget What Did

Stopping the diary
Was a stun to memory,
Was a blank starting,

One no longer cicatrized
By such words, such actions   5
As bleakened waking.

I wanted them over,
Hurried to burial
And looked back on

Like the wars and winters   10
Missing behind the windows
Of an opaque childhood.

And the empty pages?
Should they ever be filled
Let it be with observed   15

Celestial recurrences,
The day the flowers come,
And when the birds go.

High Windows

When I see a couple of kids
And guess he's fucking her and she's
Taking pills or wearing a diaphragm,
I know this is paradise

5 Everyone old has dreamed of all their lives –
Bonds and gestures pushed to one side
Like an outdated combine harvester,
And everyone young going down the long slide

To happiness, endlessly. I wonder if
10 Anyone looked at me, forty years back,
And thought, *That'll be the life;*
No God any more, or sweating in the dark

About hell and that, or having to hide
What you think of the priest. He
15 *And his lot will all go down the long slide*
Like free bloody birds. And immediately

Rather than words comes the thought of high windows:
The sun-comprehending glass,
And beyond it, the deep blue air, that shows
20 Nothing, and is nowhere, and is endless.

Friday Night in the Royal Station Hotel

Light spreads darkly downwards from the high
Clusters of lights over empty chairs
That face each other, coloured differently.
Through open doors, the dining-room declares
5 A larger loneliness of knives and glass
And silence laid like carpet. A porter reads
An unsold evening paper. Hours pass,
And all the salesmen have gone back to Leeds,
Leaving full ashtrays in the Conference Room.

10 In shoeless corridors, the lights burn. How
Isolated, like a fort, it is –
The headed paper, made for writing home

(If home existed) letters of exile: *Now*
Night comes on. Waves fold behind villages.

The Old Fools

What do they think has happened, the old fools,
To make them like this? Do they somehow suppose
It's more grown-up when your mouth hangs open and drools,
And you keep on pissing yourself, and can't remember
Who called this morning? Or that, if they only chose,   5
They could alter things back to when they danced all night,
Or went to their wedding, or sloped arms some September?
Or do they fancy there's really been no change,
And they've always behaved as if they were crippled or tight,
Or sat through days of thin continuous dreaming   10
Watching light move? If they don't (and they can't), it's strange:
      Why aren't they screaming?

At death, you break up: the bits that were you
Start speeding away from each other for ever
With no one to see. It's only oblivion, true: 15
We had it before, but then it was going to end,
And was all the time merging with a unique endeavour
To bring to bloom the million-petalled flower
Of being here. Next time you can't pretend
There'll be anything else. And these are the first signs: 20
Not knowing how, not hearing who, the power
Of choosing gone. Their looks show that they're for it:
Ash hair, toad hands, prune face dried into lines –
      How can they ignore it?

Perhaps being old is having lighted rooms   25
Inside your head, and people in them, acting.
People you know, yet can't quite name; each looms
Like a deep loss restored, from known doors turning,
Setting down a lamp, smiling from a stair, extracting
A known book from the shelves; or sometimes only   30
The rooms themselves, chairs and a fire burning,
The blown bush at the window, or the sun's
Faint friendliness on the wall some lonely
Rain-ceased midsummer evening. That is where they live:

35   Not here and now, but where all happened once.
          This is why they give

An air of baffled absence, trying to be there
Yet being here. For the rooms grow farther, leaving
Incompetent cold, the constant wear and tear
40   Of taken breath, and them crouching below
Extinction's alp, the old fools, never perceiving
How near it is. This must be what keeps them quiet:
The peak that stays in view wherever we go
For them is rising ground. Can they never tell
45   What is dragging them back, and how it will end? Not at night?
Not when the strangers come? Never, throughout
The whole hideous inverted childhood? Well,
          We shall find out.

Going, Going

I thought it would last my time –
The sense that, beyond the town,
There would always be fields and farms,
Where the village louts could climb
5   Such trees as were not cut down;
I knew there'd be false alarms

In the papers about old streets
And split-level shopping, but some
Have always been left so far;
10   And when the old part retreats
As the bleak high-risers come
We can always escape in the car.

Things are tougher than we are, just
As earth will always respond
15   However we mess it about;
Chuck filth in the sea, if you must:
The tides will be clean beyond.
– But what do I feel now? Doubt?

Or age, simply? The crowd
20   Is young in the M1 café;
Their kids are screaming for more –
More houses, more parking allowed,

More caravan sites, more pay.
On the Business Page, a score

Of spectacled grins approve   25
Some takeover bid that entails
Five per cent profit (and ten
Per cent more in the estuaries): move
Your works to the unspoilt dales
(Grey area grants)! And when   30

You try to get near the sea
In summer . . .
                    It seems, just now,
To be happening so very fast;
Despite all the land left free
For the first time I feel somehow   35
That it isn't going to last,

That before I snuff it, the whole
Boiling will be bricked in
Except for the tourist parts –
First slum of Europe: a role   40
It won't be so hard to win,
With a cast of crooks and tarts.

And that will be England gone,
The shadows, the meadows, the lanes,
The guildhalls, the carved choirs.
There'll be books; it will linger on   45
In galleries; but all that remains
For us will be concrete and tyres.

Most things are never meant.
This won't be, most likely: but greeds   50
And garbage are too thick-strewn
To be swept up now, or invent
Excuses that make them all needs.
I just think it will happen, soon.

The Card-Players

Jan van Hogspeuw staggers to the door
And pisses at the dark. Outside, the rain
Courses in cart-ruts down the deep mud lane.
Inside, Dirk Dogstoerd pours himself some more,
5   And holds a cinder to his clay with tongs,
Belching out smoke. Old Prijck snores with the gale,
His skull face firelit; someone behind drinks ale,
And opens mussels, and croaks scraps of songs
Towards the ham-hung rafters about love.
10   Dirk deals the cards. Wet century-wide trees
Clash in surrounding starlessness above
This lamplit cave, where Jan turns back and farts,
Gobs at the grate, and hits the queen of hearts.

Rain, wind and fire! The secret, bestial peace!

The Building

Higher than the handsomest hotel
The lucent comb shows up for miles, but see,
All round it close-ribbed streets rise and fall
Like a great sigh out of the last century.
5   The porters are scruffy; what keep drawing up
At the entrance are not taxis; and in the hall
As well as creepers hangs a frightening smell.

There are paperbacks, and tea at so much a cup,
Like an airport lounge, but those who tamely sit
10   On rows of steel chairs turning the ripped mags
Haven't come far. More like a local bus,
These outdoor clothes and half-filled shopping bags
And faces restless and resigned, although
Every few minutes comes a kind of nurse

15   To fetch someone away: the rest refit
Cups back to saucers, cough, or glance below
Seats for dropped gloves or cards. Humans, caught
On ground curiously neutral, homes and names
Suddenly in abeyance; some are young,

Some old, but most at that vague age that claims 20
The end of choice, the last of hope; and all

Here to confess that something has gone wrong.
It must be error of a serious sort,
For see how many floors it needs, how tall
It's grown by now, and how much money goes 25
In trying to correct it. See the time,
Half-past eleven on a working day,
And these picked out of it; see, as they climb

To their appointed levels, how their eyes
Go to each other, guessing; on the way 30
Someone's wheeled past, in washed-to-rags ward clothes:
They see him, too. They're quiet. To realise
This new thing held in common makes them quiet,
For past these doors are rooms, and rooms past those,
And more rooms yet, each one further off 35

And harder to return from; and who knows
Which he will see, and when? For the moment, wait,
Look down at the yard. Outside seems old enough:
Red brick, lagged pipes, and someone walking by it
Out to the car park, free. Then, past the gate, 40
Traffic; a locked church; short terraced streets
Where kids chalk games, and girls with hair-dos fetch

Their separates from the cleaners – O world,
Your loves, your chances, are beyond the stretch
Of any hand from here! And so, unreal, 45
A touching dream to which we all are lulled
But wake from separately. In it, conceits
And self-protecting ignorance congeal
To carry life, collapsing only when

Called to these corridors (for now once more 50
The nurse beckons –). Each gets up and goes
At last. Some will be out by lunch, or four;
Others, not knowing it, have come to join
The unseen congregations whose white rows
Lie set apart above – women, men; 55
Old, young; crude facets of the only coin

This place accepts. All know they are going to die.
Not yet, perhaps not here, but in the end,

And somewhere like this. That is what it means,
60 This clean-sliced cliff; a struggle to transcend
The thought of dying, for unless its powers
Outbuild cathedrals nothing contravenes
The coming dark, though crowds each evening try

With wasteful, weak, propitiatory flowers.

Posterity

Jake Balokowsky, my biographer,
Has this page microfilmed. Sitting inside
His air-conditioned cell at Kennedy
In jeans and sneakers, he's no call to hide
5 Some slight impatience with his destiny:
'I'm stuck with this old fart at least a year;

I wanted to teach school in Tel Aviv,
But Myra's folks' – he makes the money sign –
'Insisted I got tenure. When there's kids – '
10 He shrugs. 'It's stinking dead, the research line;
Just let me put this bastard on the skids,
I'll get a couple of semesters leave

To work on Protest Theater.' They both rise,
Make for the Coke dispenser. 'What's he like?
15 Christ, I just told you. Oh, you know the thing,
That crummy textbook stuff from Freshman Psych,
Not out of kicks or something happening –
One of those old-type *natural* fouled-up guys.'

Dublinesque

Down stucco sidestreets,
Where light is pewter
And afternoon mist
Brings lights on in shops
5 Above race-guides and rosaries,
A funeral passes.

The hearse is ahead,
But after there follows

A troop of streetwalkers
In wide flowered hats,
Leg-of-mutton sleeves,
And ankle-length dresses.

There is an air of great friendliness,
As if they were honouring
One they were fond of;
Some caper a few steps,
Skirts held skilfully
(Someone claps time),

And of great sadness also.
As they wend away
A voice is heard singing
Of Kitty, or Katy,
As if the name meant once
All love, all beauty.

Homage to a Government

Next year we are to bring the soldiers home
For lack of money, and it is all right.
Places they guarded, or kept orderly,
Must guard themselves, and keep themselves orderly.
We want the money for ourselves at home
Instead of working. And this is all right.

It's hard to say who wanted it to happen,
But now it's been decided nobody minds.
The places are a long way off, not here,
Which is all right, and from what we hear
The soldiers there only made trouble happen.
Next year we shall be easier in our minds.

Next year we shall be living in a country
That brought its soldiers home for lack of money.
The statues will be standing in the same
Tree-muffled squares, and look nearly the same.
Our children will not know it's a different country.
All we can hope to leave them now is money.

1969

This Be The Verse

They fuck you up, your mum and dad.
They may not mean to, but they do.
They fill you with the faults they had
And add some extra, just for you.

5   But they were fucked up in their turn
By fools in old-style hats and coats,
Who half the time were soppy-stern
And half at one another's throats.

Man hands on misery to man.
10   It deepens like a coastal shelf.
Get out as early as you can,
And don't have any kids yourself.

How Distant

How distant, the departure of young men
Down valleys, or watching
The green shore past the salt-white cordage
Rising and falling,

5   Cattlemen, or carpenters, or keen
Simply to get away
From married villages before morning,
Melodeons play

On tiny decks past fraying cliffs of water
10   Or late at night
Sweet under the differently-swung stars,
When the chance sight

Of a girl doing her laundry in the steerage
Ramifies endlessly.
15   This is being young,
Assumption of the startled century

Like new store clothes,
The huge decisions printed out by feet
Inventing where they tread,
20   The random windows conjuring a street.

Sad Steps

Groping back to bed after a piss
I part thick curtains, and am startled by
The rapid clouds, the moon's cleanliness.

Four o'clock: wedge-shadowed gardens lie
Under a cavernous, a wind-picked sky.   5
There's something laughable about this,

The way the moon dashes through clouds that blow
Loosely as cannon-smoke to stand apart
(Stone-coloured light sharpening the roofs below)

High and preposterous and separate –   10
Lozenge of love! Medallion of art!
O wolves of memory! Immensements! No,

One shivers slightly, looking up there.
The hardness and the brightness and the plain
Far-reaching singleness of that wide stare   15

Is a reminder of the strength and pain
Of being young; that it can't come again,
But is for others undiminished somewhere.

Solar

Suspended lion face
Spilling at the centre
Of an unfurnished sky
How still you stand,
And how unaided   5
Single stalkless flower
You pour unrecompensed.

The eye sees you
Simplified by distance
Into an origin,   10
Your petalled head of flames
Continuously exploding.

Heat is the echo of your
Gold.

15 Coined there among
Lonely horizontals
You exist openly.
Our needs hourly
Climb and return like angels.
20 Unclosing like a hand,
You give for ever.

Annus Mirabilis

Sexual intercourse began
In nineteen sixty-three
(Which was rather late for me) –
Between the end of the *Chatterley* ban
5   And the Beatles' first LP.

Up till then there'd only been
A sort of bargaining,
A wrangle for a ring,
A shame that started at sixteen
10 And spread to everything.

Then all at once the quarrel sank:
Everyone felt the same,
And every life became
A brilliant breaking of the bank,
15 A quite unlosable game.

So life was never better than
In nineteen sixty-three
(Though just too late for me) –
Between the end of the *Chatterley* ban
20 And the Beatles' first LP.

Vers de Société

My wife and I have asked a crowd of craps
To come and waste their time and ours: perhaps
You'd care to join us? In a pig's arse, friend.
Day comes to an end.
The gas fire breathes, the trees are darkly swayed.   5
And so *Dear Warlock-Williams: I'm afraid –*

Funny how hard it is to be alone.
I could spend half my evenings, if I wanted,
Holding a glass of washing sherry, canted
Over to catch the drivel of some bitch   10
Who's read nothing but *Which*;
Just think of all the spare time that has flown

Straight into nothingness by being filled
With forks and faces, rather than repaid
Under a lamp, hearing the noise of wind,   15
And looking out to see the moon thinned
To an air-sharpened blade.
A life, and yet how sternly it's instilled

All solitude is selfish. No one now
Believes the hermit with his gown and dish   20
Talking to God (who's gone too); the big wish
Is to have people nice to you, which means
Doing it back somehow.
Virtue is social. Are, then, these routines

Playing at goodness, like going to church?   25
Something that bores us, something we don't do well
(Asking that ass about his fool research)
But try to feel, because, however crudely,
It shows us what should be?
Too subtle, that. Too decent, too. Oh hell,   30

Only the young can be alone freely.
The time is shorter now for company,
And sitting by a lamp more often brings
Not peace, but other things.
Beyond the light stand failure and remorse   35
Whispering *Dear Warlock-Williams: Why, of course –*

Show Saturday

Grey day for the Show, but cars jam the narrow lanes.
Inside, on the field, judging has started: dogs
(Set their legs back, hold out their tails) and ponies (manes
Repeatedly smoothed, to calm heads); over there, sheep
(Cheviot and Blackface); by the hedge, squealing logs
(Chain Saw Competition). Each has its own keen crowd.
In the main arena, more judges meet by a jeep:
The jumping's on next. Announcements, splutteringly loud,

Clash with the quack of a man with pound notes round his hat
And a lit-up board. There's more than just animals:
Bead-stalls, balloon-men, a Bank; a beer-marquee that
Half-screens a canvas Gents; a tent selling tweed,
And another, jackets. Folks sit about on bales
Like great straw dice. For each scene is linked by spaces
Not given to anything much, where kids scrap, freed,
While their owners stare different ways with incurious faces.

The wrestling starts, late; a wide ring of people; then cars;
Then trees; then pale sky. Two young men in acrobats' tights
And embroidered trunks hug each other; rock over the grass,
Stiff-legged, in a two-man scrum. One falls: they shake hands.
Two more start, one grey-haired: he wins, though. They're not so
  much fights
As long immobile strainings that end in unbalance
With one on his back, unharmed, while the other stands
Smoothing his hair. But there are other talents –

The long high tent of growing and making, wired-off
Wood tables past which crowds shuffle, eyeing the scrubbed spaced
Extrusions of earth: blanch leeks like church candles, six pods of
Broad beans (one split open), dark shining-leafed cabbages – rows
Of single supreme versions, followed (on laced
Paper mats) by dairy and kitchen; four brown eggs, four white eggs,
Four plain scones, four dropped scones, pure excellences that
  enclose
A recession of skills. And, after them, lambing-sticks, rugs,

Needlework, knitted caps, baskets, all worthy, all well done,
But less than the honeycombs. Outside, the jumping's over.
The young ones thunder their ponies in competition

Twice round the ring; then trick races, Musical Stalls,
Sliding off, riding bareback, the ponies dragged to and fro for
Bewildering requirements, not minding. But now, in the
    background,
Like shifting scenery, horse-boxes move; each crawls
Towards the stock entrance, tilting and swaying, bound   40

For far-off farms. The pound-note man decamps.
The car park has thinned. They're loading jumps on a truck.
Back now to private addresses, gates and lamps
In high stone one-street villages, empty at dusk,
And side roads of small towns (sports finals stuck   45
In front doors, allotments reaching down to the railway);
Back now to autumn, leaving the ended husk
Of summer that brought them here for Show Saturday –

The men with hunters, dog-breeding wool-defined women,
Children all saddle-swank, mugfaced middleaged wives   50
Glaring at jellies, husbands on leave from the garden
Watchful as weasels, car-tuning curt-haired sons –
Back now, all of them, to their local lives:
To names on vans, and business calendars
Hung up in kitchens; back to loud occasions   55
In the Corn Exchange, to market days in bars,

To winter coming, as the dismantled Show
Itself dies back into the area of work.
Let it stay hidden there like strength, below
Sale-bills and swindling; something people do,   60
Not noticing how time's rolling smithy-smoke
Shadows much greater gestures; something they share
That breaks ancestrally each year into
Regenerate union. Let it always be there.

Money

Quarterly, is it, money reproaches me:
    'Why do you let me lie here wastefully?
I am all you never had of goods and sex.
    You could get them still by writing a few cheques.'

5   So I look at others, what they do with theirs:
    They certainly don't keep it upstairs.
By now they've a second house and car and wife:
    Clearly money has something to do with life

– In fact, they've a lot in common, if you enquire:
10   You can't put off being young until you retire,
And however you bank your screw, the money you save
    Won't in the end buy you more than a shave.

I listen to money singing. It's like looking down
    From long french windows at a provincial town,
15   The slums, the canal, the churches ornate and mad
    In the evening sun. It is intensely sad.

Cut Grass

Cut grass lies frail:
Brief is the breath
Mown stalks exhale.
Long, long the death

5   It dies in the white hours
Of young-leafed June
With chestnut flowers,
With hedges snowlike strewn,

White lilac bowed,
10   Lost lanes of Queen Anne's lace,
And that high-builded cloud
Moving at summer's pace.

The Explosion

On the day of the explosion
Shadows pointed towards the pithead:
In the sun the slagheap slept.

Down the lane came men in pitboots
Coughing oath-edged talk and pipe-smoke,   5
Shouldering off the freshened silence.

One chased after rabbits; lost them;
Came back with a nest of lark's eggs;
Showed them; lodged them in the grasses.

So they passed in beards and moleskins,   10
Fathers, brothers, nicknames, laughter,
Through the tall gates standing open.

At noon, there came a tremor; cows
Stopped chewing for a second; sun,
Scarfed as in a heat-haze, dimmed.   15

The dead go on before us, they
Are sitting in God's house in comfort,
We shall see them face to face –

Plain as lettering in the chapels
It was said, and for a second   20
Wives saw men of the explosion

Larger than in life they managed –
Gold as on a coin, or walking
Somehow from the sun towards them,

One showing the eggs unbroken.   25

OTHER POEMS PUBLISHED
IN THE POET'S LIFETIME

Winter Nocturne

Mantled in grey, the dusk steals slowly in,
Crossing the dead, dull fields with footsteps cold.
The rain drips drearily; night's fingers spin
A web of drifting mist o'er wood and wold,
As quiet as death. The sky is silent too,   5
Hard as granite and as fixed as fate.
The pale pond stands; ringed round with rushes few
And draped with leaning trees, it seems to wait
But for the coming of the winter night
Of deep December; blowing o'er the graves   10
Of faded summers, swift the wind in flight
Ripples its silent face with lapping waves.
The rain falls still: bowing, the woods bemoan;
Dark night creeps in, and leaves the world alone.

Fragment from May

Stands the Spring! – heralded by its bright-clothed
        Trumpeters, of bough and bush and branch;
Pale Winter draws away his white hands, loathed,
        And creeps, a leper, to the cave of time.
Spring the flowers! – a host of nodding gold,   5
        Leaping and laughing in the boist'rous wind,
Tinged with a yellow as yet not grown old,
        Green and yellow set against the soil.
Flowers the blossom! – loaded, swaying arms
        Of sated stalks, heaped with pink and white   10
Of fresh youth's cheek; they lightly throw their charms
        Into the fragrance of the deep, wet grass.

Summer Nocturne

Now night perfumes lie upon the air,
As rests the blossom on the loaded bough;
And each deep-drawn breath is redolent
Of all the folded flowers' mingled scent
That rises in confused rapture now,   5

As from some cool vase filled with petals rare;
And from the silver goblet of the moon
A ghostly light spills down on arched trees,
And filters through their lace to touch the flowers
10 Among the grass; the silent, dark moon-hours
Flow past, born on the wayward breeze
That wanders through the quiet night of June.
Now time should stop; the web of charm is spun
By the moon's fingers over lawns and flowers;
15 All pleasures I would give, if this sweet night
Would ever stay, cooled by the pale moonlight;
But no! for in a few white-misted hours
The East must yellow with to-morrow's sun.

Street Lamps

When night slinks, like a puma, down the sky,
    And the bare, windy streets echo with silence,
Street lamps come out, and lean at corners, awry,
    Casting black shadows, oblique and intense;
5   So they burn on, impersonal, through the night,
    Hearing the hours slowly topple past
Like cold drops from a glistening stalactite,
    Until grey planes splinter the gloom at last;
Then they go out.
                    I think I noticed once
10   – 'Twas morning – one sole street-lamp still bright-lit,
Which, with a senile grin, like an old dunce,
    Vied the blue sky, and tried to rival it;
And, leering pallid though its use was done,
Tried to cast shadows contrary to the sun.

Spring Warning

And the walker sees the sunlit battlefield
Where winter was fought: the broken sticks in the sun;
    Allotments fresh spaded: here are seen
    The builders on their high scaffold,
5   And the red clubhouse flag.
The light, the turf, and all that grows now urge

The uncertain dweller blinking to emerge,
To learn the simpler movements of the jig
And free his gladder impulses from gag.

But there are some who mutter: 'Joy   10
Is for the simple or the great to feel,
    Neither of which we are.' They file
      The easy chain that bound us, jeer
        At our ancestral forge:
Refuse the sun that flashes from their high   15
Attic windows, and follow with their eye
The muffled boy, with his compelling badge,
On his serious errand riding to the gorge.

Last Will and Testament

Anxious to publicise and pay our dues
Contracted here, we, Bernard Noel Hughes
And Philip Arthur Larkin, do desire

To requite and to reward those whom we choose;
To thank our friends, before our time expire,   5
And those whom, if not friends, we yet admire.

First, our corporeal remains we give
Unto the Science Sixth – demonstrative
Of physical fitness – for minute dissection;

Trusting that they will generously forgive   10
Any trifling lapses from perfection,
And give our viscera their close attention.

– With one exception: we bequeath our ears
To the Musical Society, and hope
It finds out why they loathed the panatrope –   15

(And, however pointed it appears,
We leave the wash-bowls twenty cakes of soap)
Item, herewith to future pioneers

In realms of knowledge, we bequeath our books,
And woe pursue who to a master quotes   20
The funnier of our witty marginal notes.

Likewise, we leave the Modern Sixth the jokes

This year has fostered, and to him who croaks
Of Higher School Certificates, ten sore throats.

25   Item, our school reports we leave the Staff,
To give them, as we hope, a hearty laugh;
And Kipling's 'If' to hang upon their wall.

Sympathy for the impossible task
Of teaching us to swim the six-beat crawl
30   We leave our swimming master. Item, all

Our *Magnets* and our *Wizards* we consign
To the Librarian in the cause of Culture
And may his Library flourish well in future;

Next (now the troops have taken their departure)
35   With ever-grateful hearts we do assign
To our French master, all the Maginot Line.

Essays, and our notes on style and diction,
We leave our English master, confident
He won't consider them as an infliction.

40   Our German master, for the sore affliction
Of teaching us, we humbly present
With an Iron Cross (First Class, but slightly bent);

To the Art Master, as the only one
Appreciative (and, Philistines to thwart)
45   We leave a blue cap and four ties that stun:

And all the Scholarships we never won
We give to those who want things of that sort:
And to the Savings Groups . . . our full support.

Our Games Master we leave some high-jump stands
50   – The reason why we know he understands –
And to the Carpenter the grass he's mown.

To Paul Montgomery, a sturdy comb
To discipline his rough and ruddy strands;
And Mr H. B. Gould we leave . . . alone.

55   We leave our Latin cribs to William Rider,
And may his shadow never disappear;
To the Zoologists, a common spider;

And, for their services throughout the year,

To the Air Defence Cadets a model glider;
And to the First XV a cask of beer.   60

Item, to Percy Slater we now send
A candle he can burn at either end,
And hours of toil without the ill-effects;

Our badges we resign to future Prefects,
The lines-book, too; to F. G. Smith, our friend,   65
We leave a compact and a bottle of Cutex;

And all the paper that we never needed
For this *Coventrian*, to Ian Fraser,
And may he triumph where we've not succeeded:

To his subordinates, an ink eraser . . .   70
And this Magazine itself? Well, there's always a
Lot of people queer enough to read it.

> Herewith we close, with Time's apology
> For the ephemeral injury,
> On this 26th of July, 1940.   75

Ultimatum

But we must build our walls, for what we are
Necessitates it, and we must construct
The ship to navigate behind them, there.
Hopeless to ignore, helpless instruct
For any term of time beyond the years   5
That warn us of the need for emigration:
Exploded the ancient saying: Life is yours.

For on our island is no railway station,
There are no tickets for the Vale of Peace,
No docks where trading ships and seagulls pass.   10

Remember stories you read when a boy
– The shipwrecked sailor gaining safety by
His knife, treetrunk, and lianas – for now
You must escape, or perish saying no.

Story

Tired of a landscape known too well when young:
The deliberate shallow hills, the boring birds
Flying past rocks; tired of remembering
The village children and their naughty words,
5   He abandoned his small holding and went South,
Recognised at once his wished-for lie
In the inhabitants' attractive mouth,
The church beside the marsh, the hot blue sky.

Settled. And in this mirage lived his dreams,
10   The friendly bully, saint, or lovely chum
According to his moods. Yet he at times
Would think about his village, and would wonder
If the children and the rocks were still the same.

But he forgot all this as he grew older.

A Writer

'Interesting, but futile,' said his diary
Where day by day his movements were recorded
And nothing but his loves received inquiry;
He knew, of course, no actions were rewarded,
5   There were no prizes: though the eye could see
Wide beauty in a motion or a pause,
It need expect no lasting salary
Beyond the bowels' momentary applause.

He lived for years and never was surprised:
10   A member of his foolish, lying race
Explained away their vices: realised
It was a gift that he possessed alone:
To look the world directly in the face;
The face he did not see to be his own.

May Weather

A month ago in fields
Rehearsals were begun;
The stage that summer builds
And confidently holds
Was floodlit by the sun   5
And habited by men.

But parts were not correct:
The gestures of the crowd
Invented to attract
Need practice to perfect,   10
And balancing of cloud
With sunlight must be made;

So awkward was this May
Then training to prepare
Summer's impressive lie –   15
Upon whose every day
So many ruined are
May could not make aware.

Observation

Only in books the flat and final happens,
Only in dreams we meet and interlock,
The hand impervious to nervous shock,
The future proofed against our vain suspense;

But since the tideline of the incoming past   5
Is where we walk, and it is air we breathe,
Remember then our only shape is death
When mask and face are nailed apart at last.

Range-finding laughter, and ambush of tears,
Machine-gun practice on the heart's desires   10
Speak of a government of medalled fears.

Shake, wind, the branches of their crooked wood,
Where much is picturesque but nothing good,
And nothing can be found for poor men's fires.

Disintegration

Time running beneath the pillow wakes
Lovers entrained who in the name of love
Were promised the steeples and fanlights of a dream;
Joins the renters of each single room
5   Across the tables to observe a life
Dissolving in the acid of their sex;

Time that scatters hair upon a head
Spreads the ice sheet on the shaven lawn;
Signing an annual permit for the frost
10   Ploughs the stubble in the land at last
To introduce the unknown to the known
And only by politeness make them breed;

Time over the roofs of what has nearly been
Circling, a migratory, static bird,
15   Predicts no change in future's lancing shape,
And daylight shows the streets still tangled up;
Time points the simian camera in the head
Upon confusion to be seen and seen.

Mythological Introduction

A white girl lay on the grass
With her arms held out for love;
Her goldbrown hair fell down her face,
And her two lips move:

5   See, I am the whitest cloud that strays
       Through a deep sky:
       I am your senses' crossroads,
       Where the four seasons lie.

She rose up in the middle of the lawn
10   And spread her arms wide;
And the webbed earth where she had lain
Had eaten away her side.

A Stone Church Damaged by a Bomb

Planted deeper than roots,
This chiselled, flung-up faith
Runs and leaps against the sky,
A prayer killed into stone
Among the always-dying trees;   5
Windows throw back the sun
And hands are folded in their work at peace,
Though where they lie
The dead are shapeless in the shapeless earth.

Because, though taller the elms,   10
It forever rejects the soil,
Because its suspended bells
Beat when the birds are dumb,
And men are buried, and leaves burnt
Every indifferent autumn,   15
I have looked on that proud front
And the calm locked into walls,
I have worshipped that whispering shell.

Yet the wound, O see the wound
This petrified heart has taken,   20
Because, created deathless,
Nothing but death remained
To scatter magnificence;
And now what scaffolded mind
Can rebuild experience   25
As coral is set budding under seas,
Though none, O none sees what pattern it is making?

Plymouth

A box of teak, a box of sandalwood,
A brass-ringed spyglass in a case,
A coin, leaf-thin with many polishings,
Last kingdom of a gold forgotten face,

5 These lie about the room, and daily shine
 When new-built ships set out towards the sun.

 If they had any roughness, any flaw,
 An unfamiliar scent, all this has gone;
 They are no more than ornaments, or eyes,
10 No longer knowing what they looked upon,
 Turned sightless; rivers of Eden, rivers of blood
 Once blinded them, and were not understood.

 The hands that chose them rest upon a stick.
 Let my hands find such symbols, that can be
15 Unnoticed in the casual light of day,
 Lying in wait for half a century
 To split chance lives across, that had not dreamed
 Such coasts had echoed, or such seabirds screamed.

Portrait

 Her hands intend no harm:
 Her hands devote themselves
 To sheltering a flame;
 Winds are her enemies,
5 And everything that strives
 To bring her cold and darkness.

 But wax and wick grow short:
 These she so dearly guards
 Despite her care die out;
10 Her hands are not strong enough
 Her hands will fall to her sides
 And no wind will trouble to break her grief.

Fiction and the Reading Public

 Give me a thrill, says the reader,
 Give me a kick;
 I don't care how you succeed, or
 What subject you pick.
5 Choose something you know all about
 That'll sound like real life:

Your childhood, your Dad pegging out,
How you sleep with your wife.

But that's not sufficient, unless
You make me feel good –   10
Whatever you're 'trying to express'
Let it be understood
That 'somehow' God plaits up the threads,
Makes 'all for the best',
That we may lie quiet in our beds   15
And not be 'depressed'.

For I call the tune in this racket:
I pay your screw,
Write reviews and the bull on the jacket –
So stop looking blue   20
And start serving up your sensations
Before it's too late;
Just please me for two generations –
You'll be 'truly great'.

Pigeons

On shallow slates the pigeons shift together,
Backing against a thin rain from the west
Blown across each sunk head and settled feather.
Huddling round the warm stack suits them best,
Till winter daylight weakens, and they grow   5
Hardly defined against the brickwork. Soon,
Light from a small intense lopsided moon
Shows them, black as their shadows, sleeping so.

Tops

Tops heel and yaw,
Sent newly spinning:
Squirm round the floor
At the beginning,
Then draw gravely up   5
Like candle-flames, till
They are soundless, asleep,

Moving, yet still.
So they run on,
10 Until, with a falter,
A flicker – soon gone –
Their pace starts to alter:
Heeling again
As if hopelessly tired
15 They wobble, and then
The poise we admired
Reels, clatters and sprawls,
Pathetically over.
– And what most appals
20 Is that first tiny shiver,
That stumble, whereby
We know beyond doubt
They have almost run out
And are starting to die.

Success Story

To fail (transitive and intransitive)
I find to mean *be missing, disappoint,*
Or *not succeed in the attainment of*
(As in this case, *f. to do what I want*);
5 They trace it from the Latin *to deceive* . . .

Yes. But it wasn't that I played unfair:
Under fourteen, I sent in six words
My Chief Ambition to the Editor
With the signed promise about afterwards –
10 *I undertake rigidly to forswear*

The diet of this world, all rich game
And fat forbidding fruit, go by the board
Until – But that *until* has never come,
And I am starving where I always did.
15 Time to fall to, I fancy: long past time.

The explanation goes like this, in daylight:
To be ambitious is to fall in love
With a particular life you haven't got

And (since love picks your opposite) won't achieve.
That's clear as day. But come back late at night,   20

You'll hear a curious counter-whispering:
Success, it says, you've scored a great success.
Your wish has flowered, you've dodged the dirty feeding,
Clean past it now at hardly any price –
Just some pretence about the other thing.   25

Modesties

Words as plain as hen-birds' wings
Do not lie,
Do not over-broider things –
Are too shy.

Thoughts that shuffle round like pence
Through each reign,   5
Wear down to their simplest sense,
Yet remain.

Weeds are not supposed to grow,
But by degrees
Some achieve a flower, although   10
No one sees.

Breadfruit

Boys dream of native girls who bring breadfruit,
          Whatever they are,
As bribes to teach them how to execute
Sixteen sexual positions on the sand;
This makes them join (the boys) the tennis club,   5
Jive at the Mecca, use deodorants, and
On Saturdays squire ex-schoolgirls to the pub
          By private car.

Such uncorrected visions end in church
          Or registrar: 10
A mortgaged semi- with a silver birch;
Nippers; the widowed mum; having to scheme
With money; illness; age. So absolute

Maturity falls, when old men sit and dream
15 Of naked native girls who bring breadfruit
　　　　Whatever they are.

Love

The difficult part of love
Is being selfish enough,
Is having the blind persistence
To upset an existence
5 Just for your own sake.
What a cheek it must take.

And then the unselfish side –
How can you be satisfied,
Putting someone else first
10 So that you come off worst?
My life is for me.
As well ignore gravity.

Still, vicious or virtuous,
Love suits most of us.
15 Only the bleeder found
Selfish this wrong way round
Is ever wholly rebuffed,
And he can get stuffed.

When the Russian tanks roll westward, what defence for you and me?
Colonel Sloman's Essex Rifles? The Light Horse of L.S.E.?

How

How high they build hospitals!
Lighted cliffs, against dawns
Of days people will die on.
I can see one from here.

5 How cold winter keeps
And long, ignoring

Our need now for kindness.
Spring has got into the wrong year.

How few people are,
Held apart by acres   10
Of housing, and children
With their shallow violent eyes.

Heads in the Women's Ward

On pillow after pillow lies
The wild white hair and staring eyes;
Jaws stand open; necks are stretched
With every tendon sharply sketched;
A bearded mouth talks silently   5
To someone no one else can see.

Sixty years ago they smiled
At lover, husband, first-born child.

Smiles are for youth. For old age come
Death's terror and delirium.   10

Continuing to Live

Continuing to live – that is, repeat
A habit formed to get necessaries –
Is nearly always losing, or going without.
     It varies.

This loss of interest, hair, and enterprise –   5
Ah, if the game were poker, yes,
You might discard them, draw a full house!
     But it's chess.

And once you have walked the length of your mind, what
You command is clear as a lading-list.   10
Anything else must not, for you, be thought
     To exist.

And what's the profit? Only that, in time,
We half-identify the blind impress

15   All our behavings bear, may trace it home.
             But to confess,

On that green evening when our death begins,
Just what it was, is hardly satisfying,
Since it applied only to one man once,
20   And that one dying.

The Life with a Hole in it

When I throw back my head and howl
People (women mostly) say
But you've always done what you want,
You always get your own way
5   – A perfectly vile and foul
Inversion of all that's been.
What the old ratbags mean
Is I've never done what I don't.

So the shit in the shuttered château
10   Who does his five hundred words
Then parts out the rest of the day
Between bathing and booze and birds
Is far off as ever, but so
Is that spectacled schoolteaching sod
15   (Six kids, and the wife in pod,
And her parents coming to stay) . . .

Life is an immobile, locked,
Three-handed struggle between
Your wants, the world's for you, and (worse)
20   The unbeatable slow machine
That brings what you'll get. Blocked,
They strain round a hollow stasis
Of havings-to, fear, faces.
Days sift down it constantly. Years.

I hope games like tossing the caber
Are never indulged in at Faber;
To balance a column
Of cash is more solemn
And much more rewarding a labour!   5

Aubade

I work all day, and get half-drunk at night.
Waking at four to soundless dark, I stare.
In time the curtain-edges will grow light.
Till then I see what's really always there:
Unresting death, a whole day nearer now,   5
Making all thought impossible but how
And where and when I shall myself die.
Arid interrogation: yet the dread
Of dying, and being dead,
Flashes afresh to hold and horrify.   10

The mind blanks at the glare. Not in remorse
– The good not done, the love not given, time
Torn off unused – nor wretchedly because
An only life can take so long to climb
Clear of its wrong beginnings, and may never;   15
But at the total emptiness for ever,
The sure extinction that we travel to
And shall be lost in always. Not to be here,
Not to be anywhere,
And soon; nothing more terrible, nothing more true.   20

This is a special way of being afraid
No trick dispels. Religion used to try,
That vast, moth-eaten musical brocade
Created to pretend we never die,
And specious stuff that says *No rational being*   25
Can fear a thing it will not feel, not seeing
That this is what we fear – no sight, no sound,
No touch or taste or smell, nothing to think with,

Nothing to love or link with,
30   The anaesthetic from which none come round.

And so it stays just on the edge of vision,
A small unfocused blur, a standing chill
That slows each impulse down to indecision.
Most things may never happen: this one will,
35   And realisation of it rages out
In furnace-fear when we are caught without
People or drink. Courage is no good:
It means not scaring others. Being brave
Lets no one off the grave.
40   Death is no different whined at than withstood.

Slowly light strengthens, and the room takes shape.
It stands plain as a wardrobe, what we know,
Have always known, know that we can't escape,
Yet can't accept. One side will have to go.
45   Meanwhile telephones crouch, getting ready to ring
In locked-up offices, and all the uncaring
Intricate rented world begins to rouse.
The sky is white as clay, with no sun.
Work has to be done.
50   Postmen like doctors go from house to house.

1952–1977

In times when nothing stood
But worsened, or grew strange,
There was one constant good:
She did not change.

Femmes Damnées

The fire is ash: the early morning sun
Outlines the patterns on the curtains, drawn
The night before. The milk's been on the step,
The *Guardian* in the letter-box, since dawn.

Upstairs, the beds have not been touched, and thence   5
Builders' estates and the main road are seen,
With labourers, petrol-pumps, a Green Line 'bus,
And plots of cabbages set in between.

But the living-room is ruby: there upon
Cushions from Harrods, strewn in tumbled heaps   10
Around the floor, smelling of smoke and wine,
Rosemary sits. Her hands are clasped. She weeps.

She stares about her: round the decent walls
(The ribbon lost, her pale gold hair falls down)
Sees books and photos: 'Dance'; 'The Rhythmic Life';   15
Miss Rachel Wilson in a cap and gown.

Stretched out before her, Rachel curls and curves,
Eyelids and lips apart, her glances filled
With satisfied ferocity; she smiles,
As beasts smile on the prey they have just killed.   20

The marble clock has stopped. The curtained sun
Burns on: the room grows hot. There, it appears,
A vase of flowers has spilt, and soaked away.
The only sound heard is the sound of tears.

New eyes each year
Find old books here,
And new books, too,
Old eyes renew;
So youth and age   5
Like ink and page
In this house join,
Minting new coin.

The Mower

The mower stalled, twice; kneeling, I found
A hedgehog jammed up against the blades,
Killed. It had been in the long grass.

I had seen it before, and even fed it, once.
5   Now I had mauled its unobtrusive world
Unmendably. Burial was no help:

Next morning I got up and it did not.
The first day after a death, the new absence
Is always the same; we should be careful

10   Of each other, we should be kind
While there is still time.

Bridge for the Living

The words of a cantata composed by Anthony Hedges to celebrate the
opening of the Humber Bridge, first performed at the City Hall in Hull
on 11 April 1981.

Isolate city spread alongside water,
Posted with white towers, she keeps her face
Half-turned to Europe, lonely northern daughter,
Holding through centuries her separate place.

5   Behind her domes and cranes enormous skies
Of gold and shadows build; a filigree
Of wharves and wires, ricks and refineries,
Her working skyline wanders to the sea.

In her remote three-cornered hinterland
10   Long white-flowered lanes follow the riverside.
The hills bend slowly seaward, plain gulls stand,
Sharp fox and brilliant pheasant walk, and wide

Wind-muscled wheatfields wash round villages,
Their churches half-submerged in leaf. They lie
15   Drowned in high summer, cartways and cottages,
The soft huge haze of ash-blue sea close by.

Snow-thickened winter days are yet more still:
Farms fold in fields, their single lamps come on,

Tall church-towers parley, airily audible,
Howden and Beverley, Hedon and Patrington,   20

While scattered on steep seas, ice-crusted ships
Like errant birds carry her loneliness,
A lighted memory no miles eclipse,
A harbour for the heart against distress.

                    *

And now this stride into our solitude,   25
A swallow-fall and rise of one plain line,
A giant step for ever to include
All our dear landscape in a new design.

The winds play on it like a harp; the song,
Sharp from the east, sun-throated from the west,   30
Will never to one separate shire belong,
But north and south make union manifest.

Lost centuries of local lives that rose
And flowered to fall short where they began
Seem now to reassemble and unclose,   35
All resurrected in this single span,

Reaching for the world, as our lives do,
As all lives do, reaching that we may give
The best of what we are and hold as true:
Always it is by bridges that we live.   40

When Coote roared: 'Mitchell! what about this jazz?'
Don thought, That's just the talent Philip has;
And even if he finds it bad or worse
At least he'll have less time for writing verse . . .

Dear CHARLES, My Muse, asleep or dead,
Offers this doggerel instead
To carry from the frozen North
Warm greetings for the twenty-fourth
Of lucky August, best of months   5
For us, as for that Roman once –
For you're a Leo, same as me
(Isn't it comforting to be

So lordly, selfish, vital, strong?
10   Or do you think they've got it wrong?),
And may its golden hours portend
As many years for you to spend.

One of the sadder things, I think,
Is how our birthdays slowly sink:
15   Presents and parties disappear,
The cards grow fewer year by year,
Till, when one reaches sixty-five,
How many care we're still alive?
Ah, CHARLES, be reassured! For you
20   Make lasting friends with all you do,
And all you write; your truth and sense
We count on as a sure defence
Against the trendy and the mad,
The feeble and the downright bad.
25   I hope you have a splendid day
Acclaimed by wheeling gulls at play
And barking seals, sea-lithe and lazy
(My view of Cornwall's rather hazy),
And humans who don't think it sinful
30   To mark your birthday with a skinful.

Although I'm trying very hard
To sound unlike a birthday card,
That's all this is: so you may find it
Full of all that lies behind it –
35   Admiration; friendship too;
And hope that in the future you
Reap ever richer revenue.

By day, a lifted study-storehouse; night
        Converts it to a flattened cube of light.
Whichever's shown, the symbol is the same:
        Knowledge; a University; a name.

Party Politics

I never remember holding a full drink.
　　　My first look shows the level half-way down.
What next? Ration the rest, and try to think
　　　Of higher things, until mine host comes round?

Some people say, best show an empty glass: 　　　　　　　　　　5
　　　Someone will fill it. Well, I've tried that too.
You may get drunk, or dry half-hours may pass.
　　　It seems to turn on where you are. Or who.

POEMS NOT PUBLISHED
IN THE POET'S LIFETIME

Who's that guy hanging on a rail?
You know, I know, A. B. Sale.

Coventria

We are the school at the top of the hill,
    That Henry the King did will,
If he came back and saw it now
    The sight would make him ill!
The Head's a lout – Hardy's a weed   5
    With his lop-eared, pop-eyed gaze
'Up the scrubbers and kick 'is teeth!'
    Will haunt us to the end of our days!

On field or in room, wherever we may be,
    When the print our eyes do maim,   10
We are bawled at, screeched at, yelled at, too,
    By the scum of the teaching game –
Saint's aggressive jaw – Phip's squeaky voice
    As he elucidates Vergil's lays . . .
'Nah then, Fahve Ell, yew shoot up!'   15
    Will haunt us to the end of our days!

When we look back, in the years yet to be,
    And our days live again in thought,
There's one old figure that atones for all the rest
    Tho' throughout the school you sought –   20
The Grand Old Man, with Bunyan on high,
    It like a banner he does raise . . .
'Oh, well, gud luck to ye all – GUDBYE!!!!'
    Will haunt us to the end of our days!

Thought Somewhere in France 1917

The biggest joke in History, I think,
Was the China War, of 1840 Anno Domini,
For the reason of our aggression
Was a high moral disgust with dope.
Is spiritual dope better than physical dope?   5
If so, the newspapers are safe;

And so is this sergeant who is bringing along
The rum ration; for we must go over the top.
You must dope men before they will murder for you.

What the half-open door said to the empty room when a chance draft ruffled the pages of an old scorebook which happened to be lying on the top of a cupboard when the last blazer had gone home

Waft, waft, thou Summer wind,
No blade is so unkind
Of white ribbed Winter's blast:

Thou blow'st, from day to week
5   Dust upon beauty's cheek
And mak'st them one, at last.

Butterflies

Side-stepping, fluttering, quick-flecking,
     dropping like tops under the blue sky
Skipping white under the sultry pall of green
     summer trees
5   Or side-slipping over rich green hedges
     of cottage gardens, with red and
     yellow flowers
Of the sun, white-robed in linen,
Priests of the golden sun, dancing because
10   the sun says to them: Dance, that ye
     need no other day
Butterflies, tossing their hours away
    Like honey drops.

Darling, when in the evening I am
15   alone on the land
When the low sweep of the sunwarmed country
    returns to me like a forgotten dream
I could wish that we had been born as they
To take our day with the essence of laughter
20   And when the sunset silhouettes the forked elm

To fall apart amongst the flowers
Forgotten, forgetting what we should never have known.

A Meeting – Et Seq. (2)

Together we stood
On the edge of the world
The sun was like a scimitar
In the hands of a dying Sultan
Together we stood.   5

I loved you more than I have ever loved before
Either you, or anyone else.
The way you spoke brought tears to my eyes
And I suddenly felt I had done you a great wrong.

And as the sun fell   10
I left you
And neither of us are dead.

But I still remember
When the torn banners of life were for the moment furled
And we stood, that summer evening,   15
Together, on the edge of the world.

The Ships at Mylae

You are not happy here. Not here,
When the aching wind sweeps
Or when the rain beats upon the empty streets
Or night moans, and trees toss
Like women in labour.   5

Not when the world's strings are muted by snow
Tipping the utmost twigs
Over the dark ice of the pond.

Not when your face is jaded and lined
By electric lights and blotting paper   10
Not when January darkens at four p.m.
        and the fields are sullen and muddy
        and faces are yellow with artificial light

and lost cars
15   hissing through the
            icy dusk
            actual shroud
            of the wormy winter night
            and the trees
20   stand, stuck like
            many strange shapes of iron
            waiting for nothing
            dripping with
            drops of sour rain

25   Stanley!
        You who serene from unsung argosies
        Gazed on the mounting foam!
        Feeling the ship bound forward as the rowers
        Swept with their oars the full breast of the sea!
30   Surely you knelt on many a sunwarmed rock
        To toss torn flowers into a deep pool
        Or let the waves unheeded wash your feet
        As expectant you scanned the line
        Where blues of skies and seas are wed.
35   Surely you looked upon an empty world
        From some new hill
        And the leaping new sun
        Made the gold lights of your hair dance
        In some lost pagan adoration!
40   Ran down to an empty beach
        And saw the first waves break, and
        The first spume fly from the black, unbroken rocks!
        Lived every day to the ultimate second
        And when at last night fell
45   Surely you lay calm – breathing under the stars
        Dreaming of nothing but the unanalysed sweetness of life.

Alvis Victrix

What is this voluptuous monster, painted red,
Silently swimming along the Albany Road
With flabby lecher with a paunch well-fed,
Steering home to some rich-hung abode?

Regard his lips, like fat pink coffin-worms,   5
His padded hands that idly twist the wheel;
His puffy eyes are like malignant germs,
And obscene glances covertly do steal.

But see the rose on the rich, rotting heap;
The golden hair, the close-hugged cricket cap,   10
The folded flannels, and the oiled bat,
Eyes as calm as summer seas in sleep,
White hands neat folded on the docile lap,
Sitting, bolt upright, on the cushions fat.

Stanley en Musique

The dull whole of the drawing room
Is crucified with crystal nails,
Dresden shepherdesses smirk
As Stanley practises his scales;

Maternal corsets creak delight   5
At faultless sequence from beneath;
Brows furrowed at his taxing task
His tongue peeps out between his teeth;

(He tops the uniformity
of natal avenue; his tie   10
is knotted neat, and penny cards
put Sunday wrinkles round his eye)

The rhythm breaks, and then reforms
Into bowel-piercing waltz supreme:
His washed hands trace the melody   15
Of 'When I Grow Too Old to Dream'.

Th'adjusted clock upon the shelf
Tells him of his hour the end;
The lid he closes, and slips off
To   with a friend.   20

Founder's Day, 1939

(1)

I looked for a pearl
And I found but a stone
I hoped for rose-curl
– Save the wind's moan
5 And the rain's whirl
I was alone.

I waited a while
And uttered sun-call
Wet pavements smashed tile
10 Of rose and blue, all;
O, I hoped for your smile
I met a blank wall.

(2)

All day the clouds hung over the cathedral
Like soggy paper bags bursting with water
15 And spilt their water onto the spire
And along its narrow streets.
All day raindrops spattered against stretched umbrellas
All day I bubbled with curses
While the silly, pointless rain trotted down
20 Or fell, like a silver sword,
Avenging some old wrong.

Yes, now you can dimly shine and gild the clouds
Now they have departed, now the pavilion is locked
And the wide field empty;
25 Now no sound breaks the dark whole of the building
As night blocks the tall windows of the silent hall
And the dim eyes of John Hales
Stare into the thickening gloom.

Collected Fragments

(1) Statue in the Rain.
        Rain falling
        Chips of broken melodies
        In darkened rooms where walls are tall
        And corners are cold and dark
        There I sit   5
        A column of dull silence in a cube of dark twilight
        (a hand resting lax upon the paper
            eyes sightless, like those of a blind man,
            sphering his universe within his skull)
        A crushed eggshell   10
        Legs like bags of soot
        Lips like dough
        Waiting for some future day . . .

(2) July Rain.
        Outside wet tyres are on wet roads
        Inside, the electric light casts shadows
        different from those that are buried in the pavements
    Somewhere under this falling sky
    You are . . .   5

(3) . . . waiting under the moon . . .
    Whenever I am not quite sad, waiting, too nervous to be
quiet yet too quiet to move about decisively,
    When rain jerks neurotically outside like a taut fish
taken by a stretched line, hard-arched in the spray   5
    When I am waiting for you between seeing you, yet not
quite sure I shall see you again
    Then I begin to whistle the twelve bar blues
    Stereotyped stagnant recircling stalactited tunes
    Inevitably incomprehensible and encircled variations   10
    Beaten, like lead under a lazy hand,
    Like paving slabs into my brain.

(4) Der tag.
    What can I say, now the slow movement of summer has been
        played to its close?
    Now there is only the frayed thread of the cricket field
    To hold the seeds in the withered pod? . . .

The sun was battling to close our eyes
with his thick hot fingers

Faraway there was the flicker of a hand
a laughing glance
                    All life flowered
5   Under the dusty trees.

Chorus from a Masque

You take our advice
If life isn't nice
The fault's with you;
Points of view
5   Reveal that some
Are happy, handsome,
Rich, and carefree:
You're contrary
You are the misfit
10 All along
Though you don't think it
You are wrong.

Stanley et la Glace

        Three pennies gain a twisted whorl
        Of cold ice-cream, coiled in a wreath;
        I, fascinated, watch your tongue
Curl pink beyond your little ivory teeth.

5   Lap, lap . . . just as, perhaps, a cat
        With planted paws and bended head
        Would flick the surface of its milk
Vibrating purrs when it at last felt fed . . .

        But these Homeric similes
10   Inadequately fail to say
        How, even though you were a tongue

Your eyes watched moving forms, shapes, faraway;

  Although the fibres of your frame
  Were concentrated, pink and small,
  Not even the ice-cream could claim   15
To occupy you, brain and eyes and all.

  We, who adore you, can but serve.
  We lay no claim to be your guide;
  Merely husks of coiled ice-cream
Who have come this far, happy, at your side. 20

Erotic Play

Your summer will sing of this.
  – I know it, (if it sings at all);
Quand vous serez bien vieux . . .
  Memories of sunlit wall;

Golden hours of broken talk   5
  'Neath the crab-backed apple tree;
Friends far scattered, factory-wide;
  Home and sisters – even me?

Do I grudge your wasted hours
  When my own flow like a tide   10
Of ice-grey misery, or else
  Golden, when I'm at your side?

When you enjoy your scattered time
  Who am I to question you?
You are merely doing that   15
  Which is more than I can do.

The Days of thy Youth

  Ah, the rock is crumbling
  And our foothold slipping:
  Near the horizon there are clouds;
  The sun still shines
  But the wind, the wind is rising; 5
  And some have already gone before,

Some will soon go.
But for the second we are safe . . .

Yet under the sun there can be nothing durable,
10   And you will change, and grow,
And flourish, and, then, toppling, decline;
And very shortly be less than a name
Chipped upon stone, washed by November rains;
Far away, I shall be nothing more.

15   And nothing will be left to show
Why I am standing here, twisting this cord,
Watching your calm young eyes as you regard
A scene a long way off, as the cold night
Drops veil on veil across the windy skies.

(À un ami qui aime.)

Disparaging my taste in ties
      Relaxèd warmly on my lap,
I gazed into his lovely eyes
      And saw the snow beyond the gap.

5   I could elaborate this theme
            But think that I shall not;
      If one can accept the dream
            The rest is best forgot.

      For everywhere the traps are laid;
10   We must remember blooms,
      And pianos being played
            In sunlit morning rooms,

For life is not a storm of love,
      Nor a tragedy of sex:
15   It only is a question of
            Deriving joy from shapely necks.

The grinding halt of plant, and clicking stiles,
Releases on the streets a second horde
Cleaned from steel-chipped sweat: cool and new
Yet with an aching in the legs and feet

Which cheats a Grecian holiday. 5
Feet slabbily resound on pavement stones,
Silk mufflers are touched by slanting rays
From the west, where the burnt sun sinks.

The old procession of the sexual march
Leads o'er familiar ways. The urined trees, 10
The horse's oval stain, the canine filth,
The horde of houses under the sapphire sky
Crouching aggressively in their dirt –
We know it. Dabs of black and white
Lead weary feet to littered carpet-tufts 15
Hearsall Common waits, a broken charger.

A young, dishonoured hand seeks iron support
– We have not captured Ratisbon, and so
Naturally, anything in the nature of a death
Is not involved – creeping beneath the blue 20
Of sleeve, the threaded device, the hand; seeking
The opal balloon again, eyes spin: trees, trousers,
Cigarette paper, and the memory
Of soggy sandbags topsy like a spun mirror.

Eight hours . . . the white, thick coffee cup, 25
Descending crumbs like parachutes: the eyes,
Incurious, inquiring . . . for the hundredth time
He straightens the absurd cap, thrilling as
His fingers touch the alien serge and badge.
Even yet, the novelty is fresh unwrapped, 30
And crisp hair palpitates
In biscuit curls.

Minutes hop away like fleas, and as small;
The block-square action of a charted force
Admits no weakness in its mortared bricks; 35
Ankles touch above black polished shoes
Knees, elbows pressing, holding . . .
'Hold, hold, hold . . . Jesus hung in night,
There was mud in the trenches, and strength
In the War Office telegram . . .' 40

'Land of Hope and Glory' on a crackt whistle
Stimulates adrenalin. Perform a duty:
Snap of a salute: the smiles, lined,

The boiled smile,
45 The indifferent corner of a dry moustache.
At last the hand reaches the hour: Withdraw!
Disperse your troops, slacken shoulders, knees
Aching with the promise of cushions and horsehair.

A splintered day reforms under the evening sky;
50 The whistled tune clips a frayed edge as
At the corner of a street (which might be
The edge of the world) one is conscious
Of a fluid body underneath the uniform;
Between the absurd tilt and the stiff collar
55 Moves a book, a poem, a symphony
In creation, not yet formed and finished.

The lamp post fits the shoulders for a minute;
The cavernous depth of a news-seller's mouth
Announces victory (price one penny).
60 Away the opal balloon sways at its cable.
With grass-sweeping roar the bomber's wheels lift
And surge into the sun, away into the west,
Where the last rays glint on the wing,
And the illusive spinning disc, and the snouted bombs.

65 He who has never felt the sunlit wall,
Or the dust kicked by a cricket boot;
Walked husk-like amongst the sunshaded parents
Flowered around the mown grass where the shadows
Lengthen as the sun declines over the pavilion –
70 He longs, in the movement of an eyebrow,
To fly away himself, into the heat of noon
Leaving the dewy grass where he now stands;

The same hand that leant against a wheel
Would seize the gear of life, and crash the cogs,
75 To rise into the upper air, distending
Hair-lined nostrils to the acid stratosphere,
Kept from some eyes by spectacles. Alas!
A cockpit glance shows the warm summer land
Left behind, voluntarily, left, left, never
80 To revisit . . . But impatience stands:

The unblown trumpet wakes the dormant heart:
Hints of pipes, and control

Of bigger and larger and oilier and noisier
Machines: (poison for clear skin, opium for eyes,
Dullness for hair, blotting paper to life's elixir   85
As the years pad over). But enlarge the shoes!
Abolish sub-elevation! Cast the cap
Into the shadow of the motorbike!

Words stumble: stay awhile, could you not
Watch, with us, one hour? We, to whom   90
The quivering sprig, dew-flecked, against blue
And wool-white is life, we urge
That your hand should not shadow the paternal watch
Before your time; let the sunlight weave your hair,
Before it is matted by a hat; let your lips laugh   95
Before they take the shredding cigarette . . .

As shadows of lamp posts tell us time fades
With outstretched hands we leave the retreating back
And hear the echo of the shining feet
Treading the kiss with uncomprehending eyes . . .   100
A body nerved with ambition to suicide.

Smash all the mirrors in your home,
Don't look at blinded shop windows;
Wear wrong clothes, read authors you dislike;
Sleep in the rain, ask twenty different people
The way to your own house; clean your bike;   5
Scrub your scullery; translate eighty Latin
Lines a day; learn Greek;
Brush up your German.

Walking, note light on a factory,
Worn shoes in a window, old records,   10
The great meat, and the poulterer gutting a rabbit,
The shine from new Cornish pasties.
Here coats hang, the Jew blinks in a doorway,
Posters flap victory receding dropping rewards,
And the autumn leaves   15
Sweep driven over the railway.

Talking, watching, see the man's hands,
Woman's head turning, child absorbed in nothing.
Take friends not as extensions, but people.

20   See the dog-pulled, mask biblike, who is he?
The blimpish woman, purple and powdered,
Nature's whore, say you, so what, say I?
And whom you love, make comfortable with cushions,
Make tea, conversation, but don't beg.

25   Love. – Get it, narrow beam to burning dot
White and intense, intensify, then
Spread the focus, see all as they are,
All faces as white, minds as scrolls.
Feed love, fire's intellect, till the cold blaze

30   Splits shell, cracks cocoon, lights the new page
Ready for sharpened pencil; lose life
In the great light of the waiting souls.

    Watch, my dear, the darkness now
Poured around the chimney pots
Velvetly upon your hair
Pale where autumn sunlight sets

5   Softening collisions raw
That are part of day's set pace
Mending now the rend and tear
Of light's brambles. Now remains
Only leaves' whisk over stones

10   And the starlight on your face.

    Maudlin sensuality
Possibly is cause of this
But the unlived life awaits
Falls behind us as we pass

15   Sense's sole reality
Tells me of your lovely mouth
All the various loves and hates
Mingle to a single phrase
'Run the night until its close.

20   Fight before all life is south.'

    Has all History rolled to bring us here?
If so, it needn't interfere;
Further rolling will suit us fine.

(We lit the last fire with the warning sign)
There's nothing to do any more. All the lights are out.   5

    It's not worth the trouble, nor the expense;
    Out in the park, a rotting fence
    Falls to the weeds; in the woods there are spies
    Watching the windows with their great big eyes,
There's nothing to do any more. All the lights are out.   10

    They've blocked the roads to the hills, and now
    We can't get away if we wanted to.
    The servants have gone, I expect, out of a back way;
    We sit here watching the shut of day.
There's nothing to do any more. All the lights are out.   15

    The floor is littered with odds and ends
    Half-smoked cigarettes, photos of friends;
    In the butler's pantry the mice now lurk;
    And the piano keys are stiff and won't work.
There's nothing to do any more. All the lights are out.   20

    The bottle now is nearly done:
    There isn't even enough for one.
    Better leave it for him who will find
    The rumpled sofa and the hand behind.
There's nothing to do any more. All the lights are out.   25

In a second I knew it was your voice speaking
Caught along the wind
For a second I lived through the summer weeks
And others, sometimes finding
What I had hoped for, what I thought   5
With heart and mind.

Yet as I trod on, my feet stamped out the burning
Flame sprung in me
My heart sobbed, cried 'O go back! Return!
What is the use of fleeing?'   10
But on, on: the rain thrust you behind again
Cried: To be.

(A Study in Light and Dark)

The glow, back over the common, comes from the railway:
that's the Church candle, been burning now quite a number of years:
there, that's the light the lover flicks
as he follows the joys of consummation with the joys of a cigarette:
5   that light was the flash as a man shot himself:
that's a searchlight feeling for bombers:
there, the light appears as the squinting wife regards the fuddled
     husband:
these are twin headlights of a capitalist's car:
this, the gaslight of a trodden worker who would tread:
10   that's the light of a cinema:
that's the light of Mars
that's the moon
that's a match.

       Alone now, in my dark room,
15   The pebbles cease to drop into the rocking pool
       And gradually the surface quietens
       Reflecting image of darkest peace and silence.
       No questions catch the clothes
       But only as it were a spreading
20   Draws all threads to their finished pattern
       And you are pieced together bit by bit
       Set against the evening
       Lovely and glowing, like a chain of gold.

Within, a voice said: Cry!
Your sorrow will become
Less, if you fashion some
Half-thought into half-lie.

5   But without, the soiled mesh
Of clouds on sun shines gold
Upon the metal cold
Of leaves, polished afresh.

Without, O, somewhere, you;
10   Not knowing who or where

I am, or how despair
Gnaws at my life anew.

What is the difference between December and January?
Between green December and frosty January
between frosty December and sunny January
What is it?

December is the brick wall bruising apples   5
the final clamp on the aching mist
the deepening of red to black
the last log before the windows pale.

December says: last laughter
last laughter before hail is met   10
last laughter before you shut the door behind you
Feel shapes of dead trees in wind and rain.

January is black
There, frozen out of movement, fingers can't find
fields scalloped in black iron   15
heart held by aching iron.

January says: first aching
first aching when holed bucket is half ice-held
first aching when calendar leaves are crushed
'in remembered dates.   20

The difference lies under the snow
in the black tree boles
what they were, what are, are becoming:
Death has claimed, and the march goes on.

To a Friend's Acquaintance

Are you my innocent? I expect you are:
        Still, it doesn't matter;
Remote as even the nearest star
        That I see flutter
        In the pool, in the gutter.   5

(These aren't my first words to you; I
        Did write many

More, further back, under a quite different sky –
    Words like honey,
      Sickly and sunny.)

But you may as well be accepted as the
    Latest in ideals;
(New model for my troops) a divinity
    Dead as all grails
      When the defence fails.

To a Friend

O let the passing moon delight
To touch the pillow where you lie,
And let her cool hand smooth away
All hint of mortality,
Awareness of a coming fate,
And every other form of stress:
Let the settling night obey.
When at last the windows shine,
Stirred by opal clouds of dawn
May you rise in loveliness.

In the nightmare of the years,
And the torment of the hours,
May the summer rest on you
With a trace of former flowers,
As the evening breeze repairs
Rakings of a year repass;
And the kiss that stays as true
Bring to you instinctive peace,
Something of the careless grace
That rests upon the summer grass.

A Farewell

Take your tomorrow: go, I give you leave
    To turn your face from me;
Yet ask that you should save
One backward look, as at the door you stand,

To sign my love, before your hand   5
    Floods the sun's ecstasy.

That I might think you knew your power
    Which takes you now from me,
And know why as you go I must stay here.
For you are born to triumph; I decay,   10
And as you turn to take your waiting day,
    Remain in atrophy.

Young Woman's Blues

So if you saw him not alone
But living, in that distant land,
Then all my life is overthrown
    All days
    Are vain: 5
Yet if I weep now, who will understand?

O there can be no second love
For me; go, soldier, to your wars;
I shall remain, the hills to rove,
    And stay   10
    Away
Letting the cold night cover me with stars.

Lie there, my tumbled thoughts,
That through th'involuntary year
Have fallen hot without retorts;
    Queer
Medley now, of loves,   5
And daily hate, and yearly fear,
Of the mind taking off its gloves,
    Into nudity, sheer.

So we are encrusted
With the days, bright interlocked,
And learn that only time is trusted.   10
    Pistol cocked
We pass through knotted jungle
Ready to be shot, or shocked,

15   And find, alert for private bungle,
                Coffins, inscribed, unlocked.

        Now the shadows that fall from the hills
        Darken the walls: all the meadows
        Sleep under their trees: and distant the stars
        Stretch far beyond, to spin, to freeze.

5   So the pull of memory only makes me grasp,
        Standing here, where we so often stood,
        How you, and others, are the trees and fields,
        Near; and I, more distant than I ever knew.

        The pistol now again is raised
                The ruler poised to draw the line
        The final letter is ready phrased
                And waits the sign
5   But there's no sign.

        For something scuttles from the shade
                New mood chases mood half gone
        Laugh at scene painstakingly laid
                And pass on
10   Clock ticks on.

        Have you seen for the last time now
                Several times at least. The drums
        Drive the dying army through the snow
                And the laugh comes
15   And spring comes.

        One day darkness will drag us down
                Fall faintly, glad of its powerful blow
        Apart, we are old, a day older, we drown
                And the hours grow
20   And the crops grow.

Autumn has caught us in our summer wear
    Brother, and the day
    Breathes coldly from fields far away
As white air.
We are cold at our feet, and cold at our throats,   5
Crouching, cold, deaf to the morning's half-notes.

See, over the fields are coming the girls from the Church,
    Gathering the fruits
    · For their Harvest Festival; leaves, berries, and roots
– Such is their search.   10
I do not think that we shall be
Troubled by their piety.

Tomorrow we shall hear their old bells ringing
    For another year;
        We shall achingcold be here   15
– Not singing.
Outside, the frost will bite, thaw, then return;
Inside, the candle will burn.

Evensong

'I think I read, or have been told,
    That once there was a thing called love;
(The pages of the manuscripts
    Give lyrics to a lady's glove).

'Today we pace the sexual stones   5
    And coyish shrieks we cutely utter;
Sexual laughter rings along
    The cynic echo of the gutter.

'The empty faces drip delight,
    The scabrous hands grope for a mate,   10
Happy in imbecility
    Our mental age is roughly eight.

'But who am I to curse or carp?
    I, fashioned with a face that's odd?
For every wise man's son doth know,   15
    The people's voice is that of God.'

This is one of those whiteghosted mornings
Of early winter, when the sun is red;
Our side of the pane is coldly wet
And every left leaf trembles
5   With a drop of sun dew,
High, high above
The sky is blue.

The kind of day that burns down to
Bonfires at four o' clock,
10   And rotten apples on the leafclogged lawn;
The blue smoke drifting across the brickdark road
As the boys come running home from school.

We see the spring breaking across rough stone
        And pause to regard the sky;
But we are pledged to work alone,
        To serve, bow, nor ask if or why.

5   Summer shimmers over the fishpond.
        We heed it but do not stop
At the may-flies' cloud of mist,
        But penetrate to skeleton beyond.

Autumn is the slow movement;
10   We gather our harvest and thank the lofty dusk.
Although glad for the grain, we are
        Aware of the husk.

And winter closes on us like a shroud.
        Whether through windows we shall see spring again
15   Or not, we are sure to hear the rain
        Chanting its ancient litany, half-aloud.

Why did I dream of you last night?
Now morning is pushing back hair with grey light
Memories strike home, like slaps in the face:
Raised on elbow, I stare at the pale fog beyond the window.

So many things I had thought forgotten 5
Return to my mind with stranger pain:
– Like letters that arrive addressed to someone
Who left the house so many years ago.

The cycles hiss on the road away from the factory
Bearing their lights through the dark: the old man knows
He will take his leather bag from the handlebars;
The youth swing into the lighted kitchen: the journey
Complete, the boy recognise the childhood doors. 5

In the deeper city, among the thunder of buses,
The laughter of standing youths drowns the cry
Of the news-seller with his eternal today.
And at warm theatre doors some are showing their passes
Ignorant of neurotic schoolgirls in the library. 10

Multiplication of examples is not needed
To show the individual vibrations of the chord
That is this night. Yet only the normal lover's jarred
Mind feels its grief. For other's worth is graded,
And in an hour some will have died. 15

So you have been, despite parental ban
That would not hear the old demand again;
One who through rain to empty station ran
And bought a ticket for the early train.

We heard of all your gain when you had gone, 5
And talked about it when the meal lay done,
The night drawn in, electric light switched on,
Your name breathed round the tealeaves and last bun:

How you had laughed, the night before you left;
All your potentialities, untried, 10

147

Their weakness doffed, became our hero, deft,
    The don, the climber on the mountain side:

We knew all this absurd, yet were not sad.
    Today your journey home is nearly done:
15 That bag above your head, the one you had
    When seventeen, when you were still a son,

Is labelled now with names we do not know;
    The gloved hands hang between the static knees,
And show no glee at closing evening's glow –
20   Are you possessor of the sought-for ease?

That name for which you fought – does it quite fit?
    And is your stubborn silence only tact?
Boys wish to imitate who hear of it –
    But will you tell them to repeat your act?

Through darkness of sowing
And hours of saying
That such is not dead
Or believing in glowing
5 You as a braid,
Bright, run as a thread;
In these moments of seeing
Our eyes meet from turning
You from your leisure
10 I from life's fading
– Meet in the censure
Of the sun's pleasure.

Then all my training
Argues in rising
15 To break down your bluff:
But the great simple singing
Of you as a leaf
Or your personal laugh
Silences question.
20   You are the reason
    From reason unwrapped
    That exists without caution
    Gold none can corrupt
    And all must accept.

Falling of these early flowers
Under winter clouds of rain
Rends the lover's heart;
Yet the wind that wrecks the shrine
And the rotting of the stairs   5
Should be a deeper death.
Pull of mind from form apart
Will for ever sing the seas;
The constant thought, behind the eyes
That change at every breath.   10

Fading of this early flower,
As the turning suns deride,
Whispers now at evening:
'Everything falls to the shade,
Gasping to the withered air,   15
Once was beautiful.'
Impervious to reasoning,
The frantic answer dies alike:
'O what need have you thus to take.
Who is so wonderful?'   20

        Praise to the higher organisms!
                Aristocrats
        Impervious to private prisms
        And the new moon in glass.
O, let us kneel at their cheap pointed feet,   5
And then retreat.

        Those to whom analysis
                Is foreign,
        Such indecency as this
        Silly as D. H. Lawrence;   10
O come, let us drink with sewage of reality
To true morality.

        And, especially, the Kings
                Be remembered;
        To whom life is coloured rings,   15
        Violin's ecstasies, leaves in September.

                                                    149

May their deaths be amusing as old steeples
And other people's.

     (from James Hogg)
Lock the door, Lariston, lock it, I say to you,
Latch it and lock it and look from the pane:
     There, you see, in the bushes?
     The obvious hushes –
5   They are beginning to watch you again.

O, watch the west, Lariston, 'way on the whitening
Road gleams the glitter of gasbomb and gun;
     They have been plotting
     Compulsory rotting,
10   To saw up the moon, and to blow out the sun.

O, lock the door, Lariston, laughing is madness now,
Leap from your ingle-nook, no time to cringe,
     Lock it, don't vacillate –
     No, it is now too late.
15   They are here, and have splintered it straight from the hinge.

Turning from obscene verses to the stars
The bells remind us of the sleeping roofs,
     The coming hostile stares,
     And serried graves.

5   Diversity protests too much, methinks.
Yet others looked, and they found as few keys . . .
     We accept them with some thanks,
     But they don't help the days.

One is tempted strongly to accept
10   The individual reality
     World, in hung flesh lapt,
     The past, a nullity.

But O, diversity is preferable to that!
The ever-vicious circle of green horror,

The filter for the lot   15
And the eternal mirror!

And now the clock has struck the quarter-hour.
I have a feeling that I don't like life;
But life likes me, and draws me near
Her shining teeth.   20

Autumn sees the sun low in the sky;
Leans gently, washing the pale landscape,
With long shadows;
When the berries hang in the hedges
The sun softly freckles the lanes   5
And lights the meadows.

On a late, pale blue afternoon
Thought, as my shadow gesticulated before me
On sunlit tuft,
How like all the evenings in summer it was,   10
When we held the same cup in unrelated hands,
And drank the same draught.

Prologue

Such is our springtime, sprawling its sprouting
Leaves to the laughing of flat gramophones
But it cannot deceive
Or even save
Who sardonically greet   5
The simple and great.

Standing on love's farther shores
He reflects:
Wonders at his memory of tears,
Letters unposted; remembered facts
Forming the pattern of a well-known tale   5
In which he made moves, was checked,
And left the table.

So on the cooler banks

He stands;
10 Through that flood of fire, thinks,
I fought; watches where its rage extends,
Considers who and how he was;
Yet crossing leaves, from other lands,
　　　No mark nor trace.

Epilogue

Will hoped-for rains
Bring our delight
　　　And springing profit?
Or will six sterile Junes
5 Kill; or worse, the bright
　　　Giant obliterate?

Remark

Seconds of tangled love and art,
　　　The mistress-motif, cause the heart
　　　　　　To struggle at its nets;
　　　Conspicuous the urge once more
5 To clarify and to adore
　　　What nature forward sets.

For as the common joke is love,
　　　The April trick sent from above,
　　　　　　And art a troubling visit –
10 　　　Their joining in a heart of oak –
Or even deal – makes nature's joke
　　　Unusually exquisite.

Long Jump

This rectangle cut
From our green field
Has the appearance of a grave,
And we as mourners move
5 Or stand beside

It in a shuffling knot.
Strange, o strange the picture!
From railings where errandboys lean
Below green budding trees
To the scattered entrants with bare arms and knees   10
In everything a unity of line
A momentary perfect structure
Centred on jumper flashing past blurred faces
Scattering flurried earth:
Design extended to the little watching crowds   15
And the cathedrals of bright flying clouds
Across the earth and us, speaking of death.

So strange, that these appreciative gazes
Of the few awkward watchers might provoke
A question as to motives and intent: 20
'Is it a boredom, friendship, love or loyalty
To half-remembered names holds you in fealty
On this high field: by what far worship sent?
Is there a prayer beneath your anxious joke
For a new earth, a sailing life   25
Controlled by swinging tides of blood
This scene a glimpse of green to burst the husk?'
And to the shivering boys I longed to ask:
'Whether your mind approves as good or bad,
Paints different colours love and strife,   30
Tenderness or hate,
Puts reason on desire, your presence here
Might be significant, for, barring fiction,
Is attacking or defence your cause for action?'

Instead, I wandered where   35
Young men with parted hair contested at
The discus-throwing, and thought how
Spontaneity seemed exiled to this corner
Of fenced school field, acted in derision:
And silently, in words of indecision,   40
Confirmed how we were all one sneering mourner
Mourning the past in a decaying now:

What beauty there is here is stroked by rot
Mouths speak with a reek of decay
Eyes stare as through water at   45

The latest circumlocutions of art,
And we, beneath a sky of neutral grey,
Suggest that it is dawn, but fancy not.

But as to the real truth, who knows? The earth
50 May yet bring forth, the past the future
Flowering over walls, a leaping urge
And I, composer of life's dirge,
Be called upon to broadcast and to nurture,
Assist, not at a funeral, but a birth.

Quests are numerous; for the far acid strand
Invites, over the dimpled sea as blue
    As the vast empty sky regarded
    Through hourglass and shifting sand;

5 Easy, the heraldic clouds
Curled like breath from the fiery
    Nostrils of the sun's horses,
    To watch the horizon,

Seeing there the mirage of desires
10 Its minarets and lions, through
    The limited telescope
    Of a prejudice or a love.

But easy to remain inert
Watching the whole scene from the sheltered beach
15   Under the sun, swinging its arc above
    The tall palm trees,

Until the falling of glass waves, the cry
Of birds merge like blurred angry sun
    Beneath the bloodred eyes, and
20   No more is heard, or believed, seen.

For the mind to betray
With its deadly paralytic ray
The unwary body, that is a

Familiar thing. But threnody
Of being sung by shrinking body   5
Is a more peculiar way to die.

Yet in me is combat
Fought like this: the weird bat
Of soul, escapeless, will expire at

Length. Yet who will deny   10
A gaudy universe is nigh?
Not me. Yet who obstructs the seeing? I.

        For who will deny
A gaudy universe is nigh?
Not me. Yet who obstructs the seeing? I.

Poem

Still beauty,
o silent, happy
without change:
a blown bubble
a set tinge   5
no sun can rearrange –
can we, can
this not escape man?
this desperate desire
for relieved pain   10
of dissolution, for
no ash after fire!

No, a deathwish
only, you would cash.
a scudding ripple   15
of living, in the flesh
is only; a momentary apple,
a quick sundapple

frozen, are mute.
20   you also, my quick fruit
of bloom and sense,
eternity would defeat
although your decadence
indicts our scornful chance.

Midsummer Night, 1940

The sun falls behind Wales; the towns and hills
Sculptured on England, wait again for night
As a deserted beach the tide that smoothes

Its rumpled surface flat: as pale as moths
5   Faces from factory pass home, for what respite
Home offers: crowds vacate the public halls:

And everywhere the stifling mass of night
Swamps the bright nervous day, and puts it out.
In other times, when heavy ploughmen snored,

10   And only some among the wealthy sneered,
On such a night as this twilight and doubt
Would mingle, and the night would not

Be day's exhaustion; there would drift about
Strange legends of the bridge across the weir,
15   Rings found in the grass, with undertone

Of darker terror, stories of the tarn,
The horned stranger, a pervading fear
No jolly laugh disperses. But

We, on this midsummer night, can sneer
20   In unison at mind that could confuse
The moon and cheese, or trust in lightfoot images,

And point with conscious pride to our monstrosities
– Gained by no cerebral subterfuge,
Yet more convincing – a compulsory snare,

25   Expending of resources for the use
Of all the batty guardians of pain
– With no acknowledgment of pleasure, even –

The angels yawning in an empty heaven;
Alternate showers of dynamite and rain;
And choosing forced on free will: fire or ice.   30

Two Sonnets

I: The Conscript

So he evolved a saving fiction as
The moving world abraised him: in which he
Obeyed a self-writ charter: 'My soul is
A sacred centre, hid in folds; and who
Would violate its privacy would tear   5
The pleading rosebud to disclose its heart.'
And so he did not pray to his Creator,
Lounging aside, disdaining joy or hurt.

And when the world compelled him to the killing
He heard no inner voices – none was calling,   10
There was no core of life within his bud
To animate his thoughts of good and bad,
And save his frozen heart, for all to see
Immobile in death's lovely tracery.

II: The Conscientious Objector

This was the first fruit of his new resolve –
The old loves sickened, and the starting point
Of one which might have proved as strong grown faint.
The stars that were so friendly now revolve
Without commenting on him; all that was neat,   5
Warm and familiar in the old regime
Pleads his return to their slick, ordered time,
And half of him obeys, welcomes defeat,

Disgrace. For that is all that it would be
Save safety – of a sort. If he persist   10
His northern way, love's lights and murmuring sea
Will drop behind; longer will grow the nights,
Shorter the days, till, lost amongst the mist,
He falls amid cold logic's stalactites.

Further Afterdinner Remarks
(extempore)

I never was much of a one for beauty
    In leaf or life, not one to kindle
A chaste exquisiteness from duty –
    Always regard them somewhat as a swindle.

5   The moments living gives to stop our notions
    Like cook giving a plum to save the larder,
Or as a friendly capitalist gives good conditions
    To make his workers work so much the harder.

Keats and Shakespeare wrote a lot of verse –
10   And very nice too, if you're bent that way –
But will it help when life grows quickly worse,
    Or will it answer when you question why?

This sun that's setting, how it gilds the houses!
    With bank on bank of arched clouds afire –
15   Now every trembling leaf speaks to me: 'Now is
    The time to kiss, to tremble, to expire! . . .'

This face I see before me – it is yours –
    Why must I penetrate its walls of flesh,
Why clairvoyantly see what the years
20   Will do to make it just a wrinkled mesh

Tracing the bone? That has as little point
As any trick you play of ecstasy,
    Life, you stewed-up remainder of the joint:
    In such an argument we shan't agree

25   Not till the stars come down with the angels
    To greet me, and shake my hand in the public square:
Then I shall have a reason for changing
    My views, my life, my love, the style of my hair –

Perhaps, on that day, I shall be one for a spot
30   Of beauty, in living and hoping, in mental prism
See reasons for everything about me, not
    A mere dweller on the other lip of the chasm

Watching the earth at play – I shall join them – the dresses!

'Well played, sir!' from the side of the court at the fiery volley;   35
The beautiful symbolic hours as conversion progresses –
    'You're quite different from the rest' – 'Do you like Shelley?'

Historical
Fact:

Shelley
had a belly.

But as to the real truth, who knows? The earth
May yet bring forth, the past the future
Flowering over walls, a leaping urge –
And I, composer of life's dirge,
Be called upon to broadcast and to nurture: 5
Assist, not at a funeral, but a birth.

It is late: the moon regards the city,
Honeycombs of houses, each
Its nervous cell of light and pity.
Like the sun she cannot teach
The mad who with alacrity   5
Refuse to feel or comprehend;
Burn their nerves at either end.

Despite insane accoutrements,
Their colleges and churches, still
They cannot atrophy their sense   10
Entirely, and their maze of will
With all its taut accomplishments
Cannot prevent the sudden flashes
Of unrelated images

That print upon the brain as clear   15
As mountain's portrait in a lake;
Still for the North they blindly steer
But still their South's imploring ache
That cannot give or domineer

20   Offers it simple evidence
    In unregarded incidents.

    And the painter who can see
    With an integrated eye
    To make these separate shots agree
25   For every mind must try, must try:
    Must in private purity
    Teach all to see and to behave,
    Loosing to hold; by losing, save.

    A birthday, yes, a day without rain
    A cake but no candles, we're born again
    The church cat is ordering cocktail glasses
    The general's arranging the ensemble classes
5   The cissy is going for cross-country runs
    We haven't much time, get ready at once:
    For Jim
    Goal-getter, holer-in-one,
    Hurdler, high-jumper, hope of our side,
10   Our hush-hush engine, our wonder liner,
    Our gadget, our pride,
    Our steel-piercing bullet, our burglarproof safe
    Will
    Save . . .

        Art is not clever
        Art is not willing
        Art is rather silly.

    And for ever
5   Art has been recalcitrant
    To the searcher who meant
    To capture art and glory like a swan.

        Art is the performing
        Of the single act
10   Of love or accepted duty:
        Is sometimes beauty,
        But is always the statement
        Of the simple fact.

O today is everywhere
Summer's warm sincerity
And her landscapes all appear
Ranged in easy poetry;
Shadows dark against the hedges   5
On the further side of fences;
Hot all sloping sides of roofs
And small unconsidered ledges
Near the sky, where sparrows roost.
Flies are buzzing in the privet,   10
Bees are dropping to their coloured
Landing grounds of green and gold.
Now there can be nothing private
The endless roads lead everywhere
The skimming wind caresses all   15
The sun's including stare is equal:
Everything upon this island
Runs from valley up to tor
Drops from cavern down to plain
In a sweep of harvest corn   20
Ending at the farmer's home,
Or among the rocks, alone,
In the sea's rejoicing spume.

Creative Joy

Anything or nothing
Can release his writing
The dream recollection
Of face or anything
From beauty to decay   5
Compels instant attention
At that hour of that day:
Demands immediate attempt
And his full strength.

An hour past, a page   10
Threequarters done
The demand of the sun
Draws him from doors

Returning to rows
Scolding in defeated rage.

The spaniel on the tennis court
Nuzzles his shadow as he runs,
Oblivious of a cooling earth
And various human skeletons;

He does not try to seem sincere
Sincerity is not his job;
Nor beauty, either of himself
Or any other of the mob.

His scraps appear like striking hours;
Doors wait ajar for him at night;
The hands that move above his head
Do not affect his appetite.

He's happy? Good. He's ill? If that,
Unhappy snivels in the warm:
He's confident? Chases a 'bus:
Afraid? There is a thunderstorm.

Nothing is his. The tennis court
To him is Paradise; with reason:
He has a great advantage for
There is no serpent in his Eden.

Schoolmaster

He sighed with relief. He had got the job. He was safe.
Putting on his gown, he prepared for the long years to come
That he saw, stretching like aisles of stone
Before him. He prepared for the unreal life
Of exercises, marks, honour, speech days and games,
And the interesting and pretty animals that inspired it all,
And made him a god. No, he would never fail.

Others, of course, had often spoken of the claims
Of living: they were merely desperate.
His defence of Youth and Service silenced it.

It was acted as he planned: grown old and favourite,

With most Old Boys he was quite intimate –
For though he never realised it, he
Dissolved. (Like sugar in a cup of tea.)

When we broke up, I walked alone
  And walked into the Hall;
And saw long sheets of manuscript
  All nailed up on the wall;

I pulled them down, quite thinking   5
  That they were by some japer,
For they were written in capitals
  Upon some lavatory paper;

However, I don't think this was so
  – Although it may have been –   10
But I will print them here for you,
  And you can learn their theme:

'When I was eight, I came to school
  With large and curious eyes,
Imagining that everyone   15
  Was of enormous size;

'Yes, I was eight years old when I
  Toddled in with Doubt;
And Doubt is still my fellow as
  Eighteen, I saunter out.   20

'O, I am educated
  For I have been told so –
You'd really be surprised, my dear,
  At all the things I know.

'When I was twelve years old, I learnt   25
  How to add a to b,
And how the Romans said "I love"
  And when the French say "thee".

'And I learnt how the tundra
  Behaves up in the North,   30
And all about the prairies,
  And ships in the Firth of Forth.

'And I was taught how Jesus

Had come to save my soul,
35 And all about the Pyramids,
And how to play in goal.

'When I was a sweet fifteen
I learnt about the dead,
I learnt how when an acid's near
40 A litmus paper's red.

'I learnt about the triangles
And their peculiar ways,
I learnt some poetry about
"Lime-blossoms in a haze".

45 'When I was a sweet sixteen
I began to specialise:
I learnt to read the poets
And to write a lot of lies.

'And also read some Molière,
50 And a little Hugo too,
And learnt what Garibaldi said
In 1862.

'And I can give statistics
About Roumania's oil,
55 And talk about the country
(Productivity of soil)

'And I have read the poets
Yes, every bloody one:
From Langland up to Shelley
60 And from Auden back to Donne.

'And O my hair is wavy
And O my eyes are soft
And O my smile is gentle
And my thoughts are up aloft:

65 'O yes my hair is wavy
But it comes out by the roots,
And falls in golden strands about
My neatly-polished boots.

'O yes my eyes are gentle;
70 And yet my mind is quicker,

For I read eleven hours a day
    And my specs are getting thicker.

'And though my smile is kindly
    My teeth are rotting in my head,
And though my thoughts are up aloft
    My lower half is dead.

'O what am I becoming
    Who is so brilliant?
Shall I become quite famous?
    Sometimes I think I shan't.

'Sometimes I think that you, sir,
    Have killed your lovely duck,
And I shall lay no golden eggs
    For you to gloat and cluck;

'I think your education
    Has maimed my better half
And has blown up my other side
    With cubic feet of gas.

'O I wish I wish I wish I were
    Anyone but myself:
For though my mind is in the skies
    My body's on the shelf.

'And there are awful crimes I know
    And men who don't succeed,
But they are at least more interesting
    Than what I can achieve.

'O teach me how to live a life
    And be as all men should,
O teach me what is earth, and fire,
    And what resides in wood.

'O teach me to recognise the false
    And recreate the true:
Make me forget the verb "to know"
    Remember "be" and "do".

'O teach me why the stars, and birds,
    And I myself are one:

For I your victim ask that you
    Undo the harm you've done.'

From the window at sundown
Walking out onto grass
I receive intimation
Of the usual peace.

5   Harvests lie
Resting in sheaves across
The arching fields.
Sounds fall on moss;

Are deadened; die.
10   The village is there
As for years;
Its bells shake gently the air

I breathe; breathing
Try imagining contrast
15   Between this peace
And my veiled holocaust.

But emotion under
Guise of reason says:
You are the motivator; no,
20   You are this peace.

'You've only one life and you'd better not lose it,
No good protesting that you didn't choose it;
Whoever's responsible, you'll have to pay,
And you're only alive for a Year and a Day.

5   'Your spring is so lovely, you don't realise:
You gaze at the world with great big eyes;
These are the days when you will, as a rule,
Feel like a genius and think like a fool.

'Then comes the summer: you think you're mature,
10   And possibly marry, you're so very sure;
Or perhaps you scorn others, and travel among
The sweeping giraffes, in the lands of the sun.

'Autumn perhaps is the greatest of fun:
You lose your belief in the things that you've done;
The bank clerk reflects that his pay isn't large: 15
The professor's had up on a serious charge.

'Winter creeps out of his legendary lair,
But it isn't so bad, 'cos you're only half there,
Just a failing machine that awaits termination,
A pest to yourself and your nearest relation.   20

'That is your Year; on the Day you deny
Your whole way of life; see The Truth; and then die;
You cannot convey and there's noone to hear
So you give up the struggle and just disappear.

'Yes, living is hard, but there were others before;   25
So sit on your hands and hold your jaw;
Make a fool of yourself, for nobody minds;
And soon enough for you they'll pull down the blinds.'

Envoi

Darling, I wrote the preceding review
When you'd done something I hoped you'd do;
So doesn't it shake your simple faith
In the Perfectibility of the Human Race?

The question of poetry, of course,
Is difficult: some say a poet should
Mix with his fellows, be a social force;
Others say he should be simply good;
Others, that he should be a Communist;   5
Perhaps a scholar, even drive a van;
Or spend his waking hours in being kissed;
Or all these, and become a Complete Man.

Myself, I think that poetry is merely
The Ego's protest at the world's contempt,   10
And that there are no normal poets, really.
Therefore, if as tonight, dear, he should move
In motions of spending and the acts of love,
He has lived his poem; all his power is spent.

Rupert Brooke

Give him his due – some liked his poetry;
And certainly he had an influence
While living as a man; his eloquence
Can move; and with friends life passed happily
5   With opening spring-time in a Warwick garden,
Alone in Munich, or in warm Tahiti
Before exploding war returned him quickly
To write five sonnets that the old have taken.

Indeed, he was perfect like an apple – but there were
10   Hints of an unsound core: ophthalmic at Rugby,
Nervous at Cambridge, rarely in good health;
Poisoned by coral and water; sun's enemy;
Brothers and friends all dead, some killed in the war –
Yes, his blood wrote poems; both foretold his death.

Postscript

On Imitating Auden

Imitating you is fairly easy
Because you have but one sincerity,
Whereas most people – I as well – have two:
One to themselves, one to the good and true.
5   As in you they are synonymous
My allegiance to the good is obvious
To lead me to you. Perhaps is beneficial
To adopt the breezy tone, in general,
Of one who's Pure-in-Heart, but there is danger.
10   One's character betrayed may turn to anger,
And fill its tortuous streets with revolution,
Making the resonant hollow, the laughing
Greasy. May have happened. The solution
I do not know, but have been wondering
15   That when walking on your by-pass road,
Straight and clean and windy, shall be amazed
To reach the Other Town of light and action,
Far from all reticence and putrefaction,

And be compelled to face the expectant look
Of thousands, without money, home, or book.   20

The earliest machine was simple:
Could clock the blue revolving days,
    Their single rain and sun
That fell uncensored to their grass;
Easy then with facile grace   5
    An unintentional symbol
That quickly and unnoticed dies,
    Its power done,

Gone from those fields; to where desires
Like icefloes breaking in the Spring   10
    Their crude procession make;
Earnest and, yes, dangerous days
Garish with exciting dyes
    In terms of blood and fires,
And love, that trap of logic, sprung   15
    By silent lake.

But the endless tidal splinter
That the sway of blood contains
    Those desires destroys,
Destroys their images of life,   20
While the fine selfconscious laugh
    Is shrivelled to a whimper
In uncertain, plaintive tones
    Of pervert's joys.

Yes, joy is a long way from here,   25
And the distance far enough
    To veil the primal curse
That planned, will plan, is planning now
For us, and those we shall not know,
    This course that, year by year,   30
Leading from fire to ash will leave
    A Christian; or worse.

Mr. A. J. Wilton
Has not the skill of Milton*;
Though he seems to have mastered
The art of a Bastard+

* (1608–74) + (1566–1618)

There's a high percentage of bastards
                    . . . BASTARDS
                    . . . BASTARDS!!
There's a high percentage of Bastards
5   Not very far from here!

    Yo ho you buggers (pause)
              "   (")
              "   (")
    Let's pee into their beer.

10   There's a large proportion of cuntcorks
                    . . . CUNTCORKS
                    . . . CUNTCORKS!!
    There's a large proportion of cuntcorks
            arsing round about!

15   Yo ho you buggers!
              "
              "
        Let's pull their ballocks out!

Christmas 1940

'High on arched field I stand
Alone: the night is full of stars:
Enormous over tree and farm
        The night extends,
5   And looks down equally to all on earth.

'So I return their look; and laugh
To see as them my living stars
Flung from east to west across
        A windless gulf!

– So much to say that I have never said,
        Or ever could.'

Ghosts

They said this corner of the park was haunted,
At tea today, laughing through windows at
The frozen landscape. One of them recounted
The local tale: easy where he sat
With lifted cup, rocked in the servile flow   5
Of disbelief around, to understand
And bruise. But something touched a few
Like a slim wind with an accusing hand –
Cold as this tree I touch. They knew, as I,
Those living ghosts who cannot leave their dreams,   10
And in years after and before their death
Return as they can, and with ghost's pleasure search
Those several happy acres, or those rooms
Where, like unwilling moth, they collided with
The enormous flame that blinded and hurt too much.   15

Poem

Walking on summer grass beneath the trees
It is only the sprawling lovers that he sees,

And viewed from the embankment, autumn fires
Seem like symbols of many assuaged desires;

Schools interest him deeply, and members of teams,   5
Who possess what he avoids, except in dreams,

So receive his savage fits of gentleness
As befits one of his loneliness.

Prayer of a Plum

I am a ripe plum on a sunny wall;
Oh don't, don't shake me, or I'll fall.

For this great summer, as long as we remember,
Has burned right through, from April to September;

5   And now it's nearly done: yet still there wanders
Music at evening from the tall french windows,

When every dying rose attends, and we
Rest on the richest wall in history.

The violet sunset whispers: You have sinned.
10   But give us till we drop a gentle wind:

Although the anarchy of frost must come
Protect from Autumn gales each lucent plum:

And when the Winter fractures earth and sky
Let us have fallen, and in quietness lie.

A bird sings at the garden's end.

This evening all the backgardens are full of birds,
Past the road and the railway to the woods,
And the park, and the bridge at the river's bend,
5   Calling quietly in a cindered peace,
Where I and my shadow look each other in the face.

Shall I walk, with the mild sun touching
– in my shadow, running before me on the stone?
It hardens, and the clouds roll up for rain,
10   And I am unbrothered again, catching
At my pockets now the sun has gone –

No, it is back again; look at the sun.

This morning, with a swagger in my glance,
Money swording at my thigh, I strode
15   Casually up the forbidden road
To the station hiding in the trees and fence,

Bought a single ticket, saw a train,
Noted the black express was still dawn-due to run.

Shall I link hands with my shadow and stroll
Down the canal and over the railway bridge?   20
Recall the inn's stories: 'The city's rage
Will bite you, son, after the third stile.'
Shall I show myself a haunter of outgoing ways,
A longer, regretful at boundaries?

They are walking in pairs past the shut shops.   25

Through the streets, they and I pass,
And I see a devil shouting in their face,
But no word from either pair of lips
Mitigates the silence we employ . . .

A boy-linked shadow passes a girl and boy.   30

I run behind a tree and scribble notes:
        'The enemy fling into grass on sight;
        Play with cycles, get a pipe alight;
        Go shrieking out in foursomes in the boats;
        They wear greased foreheads. In the dark,   35
        Never leave the main paths in the park.'

I sit on the bank pulling out a letter
And the twelve white swans swim up for bread;
'Nothing for you,' I say, 'I'm going to read'
– Turn and catch a girl amazed in laughter   40
Ready to run and tell dad the very latest.

Shall I tell my shadow who I've missed?
Sit among the captains' tailored talk
Dark-sweatered, in the hotel's mirrored bar,
Gaze like a wizard at my amber beer   45
That winks at me, and froths up when I walk?

Or leave my shadow in the yard
And sit behind french-windows with a word?

Shadow, run before me when we depart,
Run through the morning streets, sit on my side   50
Girder-flickered as we bridge the road
For the last time – how I taste that bit!
Oh, bold bad future, let me run away

And leave our quarrel till another day –
55   Yes, shadow, come and with me say goodbye
To the soldiers and the greengrocer's dog
And the bitch in the Woolpack that sold me a flag,
To the park, and the castle burnished on high,
The river and the racecourse and the canal
60   And the sandbags, falling down as usual;
From the train bursting into the sun
With the steam running rosy under the blue sky
I can throw my handfuls of bustickets away –

            Shadow, when distance is done,
65   Leave us; when we meet
Be a lost shadow in the rest of the night.

I should be glad to be in at the death
Of our loud cities, wet hoardings,
Faces, and trivial assertive breath –
I should like to see the last of these things.

5   When I see the Sunday paper in the old-world cottage,
Main roads, or a fleet of delivery vans,
When I think how people have to earn a wage,
Then I want to lie down, and forget I'm a man,

Wishing the day would come, as it must,
10   When it will all go, all ploughed into line
With fields, and the plough itself stand to rust,
And nothing happen for a long time.

Chant

A trainload of tanks is leaving the town
A ship outside the harbour is going down
The sky's full of aeroplanes overhead
And the streets are full of soldiers that are going to be dead.

5   Down to the factory go dad and mother
They go in one door, shells come out the other,
A letter told my sister she'd got to leave home
With a ticket for a very distant aerodrome.

Bought a paper printed on human skin
That told the living to keep smiling and the dead to grin,   10
Sat in the cinema and saw the News
Thought it was a horror film and looked down at my shoes.

Picked up a revolver and put it down again,
Travelled eighty miles in an express train,
Saw a poster staring with a picture of a bomb   15
Saw it was the station I'd started from.

Dreamed I was walking through a field of corn
And it was all men and women, chained where they were born,
The blades of the reaper turned in the sun
And nothing I could do would help anyone.   20

Went up on a mountain, looked as far as I could see,
The world was as dead as a petrified tree,
Only the sea moved up the shore
And all was winter for evermore.

Hard Lines, or
Mean Old W. H. Thomas Blues

Divided by wet roads the fields are wet
With Brown March sucking at the schoolboy's foot;
And apathetic through this afternoon
Of ivied houses barren in the rain
I sit and send my swan of music out.   5

Barren the lilt of comfort she can salvage
And lost the phrase embroidered on the badge:
The wall-high thinker round the garden shed
Cannot with these go easily to bed
Nor once more melt his year-long thoughts to rage,   10

Lacking the wordy bloodstream at command,
The green selfconscious spurt that drives the hand
Of Dylan in his womb of whiskey rocked,
And lacking too the brilliant-muscled tact
Of Auden riding through his ogreland,   15

Is forced to pause and wonder what it means,
Condemned to blued frenchwindows while it rains,
The slab of garden differing so much

From college lawns mown shaven to the touch
And speaking clock from far friends' conversations.

The same perplexing as the weathers halt
Ready to swamp with summer every fault
That logic winter by a bare gasfire
Has given time and reason to inquire
For every man with fear enough to doubt.

Blank on, dumb river and the bleaching sky,
Cunning behind the trees for all to see,
You show no answers but you keep us taped
With evidence that cannot well be faked
To make each surgeon like a sinner cry:

'Where does the power come from? Who hears it call?
Are all the chosen chosen when at school?
If they neglect their orders, are they marked
With cancer's swiftly-disappearing tact,
Or do they rot like apples where they fall?'

Some hear the answers in a sexy dorm
Or after summer windy on the prom
Or now as I await a letter's flop
To plait my ragged ends to formal shape
All these and others to the listening come;

For flanked though many be with loaves and wine
An orchardbosomed lover soft as skin
The mastering moments never speak to two
But choose them single as diseases do
And make their books and carpets leave them lone . . .

                              *

I miss the bull of truth; a raw recruit
Spatter her regions with my stammered set
Of explorations in her provinces,
And watch, the shadow of the sun advances
The cold that keeps the summer's flood to cut

Ready to wash and revel all the brain,
Showing the hands the way to love again.
Waxed summer shall burn fierce again this year.

Who is the faceless reaper that I fear?
Where have those visions gone I said I'd seen?   55

'O won't it be just posh
When we beat the ruddy Boche?
When the battle we have won
When we've licked the bloomin' 'un,
Then earth's treasure will be mine   5
And the sun forever shine.'

Having grown up in shade of Church and State
        Breathing the air of drawing-rooms and scent,
Following the Test Match, tea unsweet in Lent,
        Been given quite a good bat when aged eight,
With black suit, School House tie, and collar white,   5
        Two hair-brushes and comb, a curl to coax,
He smiles demurely at his uncle's jokes,
        And reads the *Modern Boy* in bed at night.

And when, upon the cricket field, he bats,
        – All perfect strokes – (one sees the dotted line)   10
And with a careful twelve tries not to vex,
        We hear the voice: 'Y'know, he's good! Why, that's
A graceful player!' True? Perhaps. Benign,
        We diagnose a case of good old sex.

When the night puts twenty veils
Over the sun, and the west sky pales
        To black its vast sweep:
        Then all is deep
Save where the street lamp gleams upon the rails.   5

This summertime must be forgot
– It will be, if we would or not –
        Who lost or won?
        Oblivious run:
And sunlight, if it could, would coldly rot.   10

So. Let me accept the role, and call
Myself the circumstances' tennis-ball:

We'll bounce: together
Or not, whether
15   Either, let no tears silent fall.

Nothing significant was really said,
Though all agreed the talk superb, and that
The brilliant freshman with his subtle thought
Deserved the praise he won from every side.
5   All but one declared his future great,
His present sure and happy; they that stayed
Behind, among the ashes, were all stirred
By memory of his words, as sharp as grit.

The one had watched the talk: remembered how
10   He'd found the genius crying when alone;
Recalled his words: 'O what unlucky streak
Twisting inside me, made me break the line?
What was the rock my gliding childhood struck,
And what bright unreal path has led me here?'

Prince, fortune is accepted among these rooms
That have echoes when lit with voices
    Of the unbruised that roam
    Caressive under our shadowing vices:

5   Awaiting when they can assume the coming
Life. In the meantime the names attest
    So many delicious identities skimming
    Each unknown and unloving artist

That parades unconscious to our leprous eyes
10   Loved but forgetful of the claiming hearth,
    Attaining, unsusceptible to ease,
    Like a king his earth.

The hills in their recumbent postures
　　Look into the silent lake;
The bare trees stare across the pastures,
　　Waiting for the wind to wake.

As evening dims these sculptured forms　　　　5
　　The mind demands of mortal eye:
'If one should fall among these farms,
　　Would not the lake reflect the sky?'

At once he realised that the thrilling night
Was changing into beauty, and that where
Had been a laughing and a grotesque sight
Stood now a scene of drama. Stars were near
And implicated: all the leaning trees　　　　5
Shadowed their silent path with drifting air
Blown from the moon across the cloudy seas
Of sundown to him and his darling, there.

But life could not deceive him, for he knew
That moments such as these entailed a price　　　10
That he was marked to pay; and even though
It was so pleasant simply to agree,
He saw the present tense could not suffice
To pay these charges of futurity.

After-Dinner Remarks

I

A good meal can somewhat repair
　　The eatings of slight love;
And now the evening ambles near,
Softly, through the scented air,
Laying by the tautened fear:　　　　5
　　Peace sliding from above.

The trees stand in the setting sun,
　　I in their freckled shade
Regard the cavalcade of sin,
Remorse for foolish action done,　　　　10

That pass like ghosts regardless, in
    A human image made;

And as usual feel rather sad
    At the cathedral spire,
15   The calling birds that call the dead,
The waving grass that warns the glad,
I think of all that has been said
    About this faint desire;

Of where the other beings move
20   Among this evening town,
Innocent of impendent grave,
Happy in their patterned groove,
Who do not need a light to save
    Or cheer when they lie down.

25   The handsome and the happy, cut
      In one piece from the rock;
With living flesh beneath their coat,
Who cannot their emotions glut,
And know not how to sneer or gloat,
30   But only sing or mock,

To these my thoughts swing as a tide
    Turns to its sunny shore;
These I would choose my heart to lead
Instruct and clean, perhaps elide
35   What evil thought was bearing seed,
    And must spring up no more.

II

Pondering reflections as
    Complex and deep as these,
I saw my life as in a glass:
40   Set to music (negro jazz),
Coloured by culture and by gas,
    The idea of a kiss:

Contemptible: I quite agree,
    Now that the evening dies,
45   The sky proceeds from blue to grey
By imperceptible degree

And light and curtains drawn allay
    The vastness of the skies.

Stigmatised the exile who
    Cannot go from his land,   50
I in a dream of sea and hay,
Of kissing wind and merging blue
Think what I could have won today
    By stretching out my hand,

The challenge that I could proclaim   55
    The vows that I could swear;
Equipment to attempt the climb,
Or by straight love the world to tame,
What gesture in the face of time
    Could I have fashioned there.   60

Though living is a dreadful thing
    And a dreadful thing is it –
Life the niggard will not thank,
She will not teach who will not sing,
And what serves, on the final bank,   65
    Our logic and our wit?

III

Who for events to come to him
    May wait until his death:
Life will not violate his home
But leaves him to his evenings dim;
When all the world starts out to roam,   70
    She lets him save his breath.

What does he gain? Alas, relief
    Shrivels with his youth;
He will forget the way to laugh,
Cut off by his mental reef   75
From music hall and tall giraffe –
    He will distort the truth.

Against these facts this can be set –
    We do not make ourselves: 80
There is no point in such deceit,
To introspectively regret

Can never our defect defeat,
       Or mend our broken halves.

85   Those who are born to rot, decay –
       And am I one of these?
A keyhole made without a key,
A poem none can read or say,
A gate none open wide to see
90   The fountains and the trees.

Excuse for doing nothing, yes –
       But I can still point out
That none can will and will for years
Be neither Aaron nor a Tess
95   But only see, through staling tears,
       A quickly-spawning doubt.

IV

Choose what you can: I do remain
       As neuter: and meanwhile
Exploding shrapnel bursts the men
100   Who thought perhaps they would disdain
The world that from its reechy den
       Emerges with a smile;

All the familiar horrors we
       Associate with others
105   Are coming fast along our way:
The wind is warning in our tree
And morning papers still betray
       The shrieking of the mothers.

And so, while summer on this day
110   Enacts her dress rehearsals,
Let us forget who has to die,
Swim in the delicious bay,
Experience emotion by
       The marvellous cathedrals;

115   Sad at our incompetence
       Yet powerless to resist
The eating bane of thought that weans
Us to a serious birthday whence

We realise the sterile 'teens
    And what we shall have missed   120

When all the lovely people that
    Instinct should have obeyed
Have passed us in our tub of thought,
As on this evening when we sat
Devoid of help from simple 'ought'   125
    Or resolution's aid.

Around, the night drops swiftly down
    Its veils; does not condemn
Or praise the different actions done.
The hour that strikes across the town   130
Caresses all and injures none
    As sleep approaches them.

Unexpectedly the scene attained
Traditional aptness. Everything was there:
The stars, the darling, and the pathway, veined
By moonlight through the trees; the drifting air
That, quickened by the water's imminence,   5
Cooled the hot palm and stirred the sticky hair.
All assumed its rightful prominence
To strike the pose.
                  Time rearranged the pair;
And yet there came from life no counterthrust,
No gentle summer sky was overcast,   10
No recompense demanded – only trust,
So that she could prepare her blow to shatter,
Her lianas grow to stifle; as in the past
With others, whose names now no longer matter.

There are moments like music, minutes
Untroubled as notes that hang
Motionless, invisible on air:
Here the individual is eased from his fear,
His knotted life, and everything in it:
For here is no logic or harangue,

Here is simple, pointless existence like art,
Fact plain as a child's demand: Why
Is the sun red? Here are hours
Only shown by the moving shadows of flowers,
Long as poised beats of heart,
Drifting like waters of eternity

And with dignity like chords of an organ
Descending in great flights of stone,
Solid, for ever here. Nothing to do
But look. Day opens into day.
And, certain of ultimate hearing, even the known
Problems may briefly turn their gaze from man.

Could wish to lose hands
And feet, their touching and their being,
    Obstinate with their nails'
    Neat termination. And

Pointing them like conductors of lightning
At clouds, call down energy and fire
    Inwards; or perhaps as
    A dying man lose knowledge

Of them and their doing; or as the Nile,
Splayed in a delta as these fingers are,
    Pours out its individual stream
    Diffusedly, and is lost in the sea.

There is no language of destruction for
The use of the chaotic; silence the only
Path for those hysterical and lonely.
That upright beauty cannot banish fear,
Or wishing help the weak to gain the fair   5
Is reason for it: that the skilled event,
Gaining applause, cannot a death prevent,
Short-circuits impotent who travel far.

And no word can be spoken of which the sense
Does not accuse and contradict at once.   10
And he gets no assistance from the world
Which will not help his looking into words,
Nor will the lovely, gay as any leaf,
Assuage his anguish. And the lions laugh.

Out in the lane I pause: the night
Impenetrable round me stands,
And overhead, where roofline ends,
        The starless sky
Black as a bridge: the only light   5
Gleams from the little railway
        That runs nearby.

From the steep road that travels down
Towards the shops, I hear the feet
Of lonely walkers in the night   10
        Or lingering pairs;
Girls and their soldiers from the town
Who in the shape of future years
        Have equal shares;

But not tonight are questions posed   15
By them; no, nor the bleak escape
Through doubt from endless love and hope
        To hate and terror;
Each in their double Eden closed
They fail to see the gardener there   20
        Has planted Error;

Nor can their wish for quiet days
Be granted; though their motions kiss

This evening, and make happiness

25   Plain as a book,
They must pursue their separate ways
And flushed with puzzled tears, turn back
                Their puzzled look.

And if, as of gipsy at a fair,

30   Sorry, I inquire for them
If things are really what they seem,
                The open sky
And all the gasping, withered air
Can only answer: 'It is so'

35   In brief reply.

So through the dark I walk, and feel
The ending year about me lapse,
Dying, into its formal shapes
                Of field and tree;

40   And think I hear its faint appeal
Addressed to all who seek for joy,
                But mainly me:

'From those constellations turn
Your eyes, and sleep; for every man

45   Is living; and for peace upon
                His life should rest;
This must everybody learn
For mutual happiness; that trust
                Alone is best.'

New Year Poem

The short afternoon ends, and the year is over;
Above trees at the end of the garden the sky is unchanged,
An endless sky; and the wet streets, as ever,
Between standing houses are empty and unchallenged.

5   From roads where men go home I walk apart
– The buses bearing their loads away from works,
Through the dusk the bicycles coming home from bricks –
There evening like a derelict lorry is alone and mute.

These houses are deserted, felt over smashed windows,

10   No milk on the step, a note pinned to the door

Telling of departure: only shadows
Move when in the day the sun is seen for an hour,
Yet to me this decaying landscape has its uses:
To make me remember, who am always inclined to forget,
That there is always a changing at the root,   15
And a real world in which time really passes.

For even together, outside this shattered city
And its obvious message, if we had lived in that peace
Where the enormous years pass over lightly
– Yes, even there, if I looked into your face   20
Expecting a word or a laugh on the old conditions,
It would not be a friend who met my eye,
Only a stranger would smile and turn away,
Not one of the two who first performed these actions.

For sometimes it is shown to me in dreams   25
The Eden that all wish to recreate
Out of their living, from their favourite times;
The miraculous play where all their dead take part,
Once more articulate; or the distant ones
They will never forget because of an autumn talk   30
By a railway, an occasional glimpse in a public park,
Any memory for the most part depending on chance.

And seeing this through that I know that to be wrong,
Knowing by the flower the root that seemed so harmless
Dangerous; and all must take their warning   35
From these brief dreams of unsuccessful charms,
Their aloof visions of delight, where Desire
And Fear work hand-in-glove like medicals
To produce the same results. The bells
That we used to await will not be rung this year,   40

So it is better to sleep and leave the bottle unopened:
Tomorrow in the offices the year on the stamps will be altered;
Tomorrow new diaries consulted, new calendars stand;
With such small adjustments life will again move forward
Implicating us all; and the voice of the living be heard: 45
'It is to us that you should turn your straying attention;
Us who need you, and are affected by your fortune;
Us you should love and to whom you should give your word.'

Evening, and I, young,
Watch the single star beyond
The quiet road and trees;
Move in time and know
5   The evenings of the tired who died
Under their guardian hill:
Move in space and realise
The ones I love in lighted rooms
Their movements and their peace.

10   But who can tell the many myriad stars?
Not I, not I, though soon I must face them and feel
The light night wind singing against my eyes.
Stand on a hill, or lean from dark window –
The stars in their intricate patterns will daze
15   Any who stare; useless to try to order their mass,
Their number, they are balanced in system
Which you cannot better. What was simple
And moving, a note on a single string,
Now it flings jagged colours, rehearses
20   Orchestras of sound and rhythm to your dazzled ears,
Eyes, nor can see, grasp with mazed mind.
If you must, as I must, gaze at their whirling
Miraculous display, nothing can save
From the cascading mind, the rocks that receive
25   The final crashing turrets of the brain.

From this chaos, what result? Watch:
Night wears through its hours at last, and
Again we stand where we stood, watching a single star,
By the stark tree on the hill, and think
30   Of faces, webbed with decay, that once
Pulled us protesting through sunlight on water,
Rain on grass: the rusted hands rest on a stick.
O love then, for there is little time for them,
For then east sky is white and the star will fade,
35   The last stronghold will fall, day pass, defence vanish,
And we depart as we came, with a pale star,
Shading our eyes before death's imminent sun.

Stranger, do not linger
Though you feel stronger
Their darling languor;
Balloons in evening swaying
Cast on this meadow   5
Their moving shadow,
And tall grass saying
'Always remain', may seem
Happy to some,
Happy and unafraid.   10
Be not deceived
Believing them saved;
Only their weakness calls,
Captures, and then kills
Who wrong choice has made;   15
With unconscious terror
Has run to hide in mirror;
Now, trusting no singer,
Commits the fatal error,
Can sight no anger   20
Can sate no hunger.

The Poet's Last Poem

Several eagles crossed my page
I put down my pen
Returning from a pilgrimage
So many separate men
Lifted their hands in the air   5
Pointed at heaven
Sun flashed on rings there
Seven times seven
'Pass by,' I told them
'Reckers of rocks,   10
Here is no golden,
Dreamed-of box.'

Ponds of agate and crystal,
Apples of rubies,
Diamonded inkwells,   15

Wait for my hand;
Desmond in diamonds
Lawrence in laurels
David in garnets
20   Wait for me there, là-bas, there . . .

The world in its flowing is various; as tides,
Or stars arrayed, has rules imposed
By others on it as their personal guides.
To dig, divert, mark out, and to enclose
5   The plot of life bequeathed to each, or
File and order all diverse reports
Sent in from outposts of the hand and ear
– Simple their language that the brain distorts –
That is the mind's natural destructiveness
10   Aiding its plea for reason; even so
Its charts and plans are made in readiness.

And yet, as tides in winter when
The glass is sunk, incalculable flow
Of life can break down mortared walls, drown men.

Time and Space were only their disguises
Under which their hatred chose its shapes
From swords in bushes, flowers like periscopes,
And mirrors that revealed themselves as faces.

5   And later, clouds flew past me as I sat;
Stations like ships swam up to meet the train
And bowed; all time was equal like the sun;
Each landscape was elaborately set.

But now this blackened city in the snow
10   Argues a will that cannot be my own,
And one not wished for: points to show

Time in his little cinema of the heart
Giving a première to Hate and Pain;
And Space urbanely keeping us apart.

The house on the edge of the serious wood
    Was aware, was aware
    Of why he came there,
And the reticent toad never told what it knew
When from the wet bracken it saw him pass through;   5
And round the next corner a tree poked its head:
'He's coming; be careful; pretend to be dead.'

Down on the river the swans sailed on,
    And on flowed the river
    For ever and ever   10
Over the interlocked counties and shires,
But never revealed that they knew his desires;
Reflected him walking alone in the sun,
And smiled at each other when he had gone.

On the school field at the edge of the town   15
    Where surely the secret
    Would not be so sacred
And might any moment materialise
He looked at the juniors with hopeful eyes
– But none of them moved until he had gone,   20
Then the game went on, the game went on.

No, neither the wood nor river nor child
    Showed as they should
    The True and the Good
Like a valley in blossom or plain as snow,   25
For they rather resented what he wished them to do;
Imagined he wished them to mirror his mind
That grew like a sapling and orchid combined;

But for once they were wrong: for the motives of acts
    Are rarely the same   30
    As their name, as their name;
And they were not aware of his previous tours
Upon southern Alps, across northern moors,
Seeking in one place always another,
And travelling further from mother, from mother: 35

No, they were not told of the willing lanes,
    The black mill-pond

Of which he was fond;
The warm and the narrow, the shadowed, the queer
As opposed to the open, the broad and the clear,
Those strange dark patterns of his heart's designs
That would only respond to secret signs

That signalled in attics and gardens like Hope,
    And ever would pass
      From address to address,
As he watched from windows in the failing light
For his world that was always just out of sight
Where weakness was part of the ordinary landscape
And the friendly road knew his footstep, his footstep.

Out of this came danger
    And sudden anger
For grace is stronger
    Than any singer
And every place
    Reveals its face
Till sunlit grass
    Shall flower and pass.
In ancient years
    Where childhood's tears
Like mended tears
    Prevent the seers
A falling rock
    A fading rick
Across the rake
    Where cattle reek
These too will show
    Where sinks the snow
And on their shore
    Where love is shy
But till this come
    As others came
The mental comb
    Shall irk and scream
Shall in its place
    Shatter the splice

Attack the grace
    Wither grass
    In paradise.

The Dead City: A Vision

The firing slowly ceased from the ragged walls;
At last, the besiegers
Scaled the fortifications
And dropped, knives ready, in the inner dark.

Nothing moved; no shot, no sound of talk;   5
The starry towers gave no intimations
Of the heirs of the ages
Where they were, their given answers to what calls.

Diverging, they spread through the city. Pails
Were unspilt, taps dripping, books open at pages;   10
External signs of inward emotions;
Yet any living heart could no one stalk,

For they lay dead, in the midst of all their work,
Lying quite peacefully, in unstudied motions,
No vein twisted, hand torn in final orgies,   15
All of them, quite still. They lay in gaols,

Locked in: death had laid his seals
On all, in device no human forges;
In restaurants, bedrooms, and railway stations;
Lovers lay dead together in the park.   20

The soldiers kept guns cocked for any lurk-
ing figure: nothing moved: suddenly they saw fortifications
Lit by red glow, burning roofs, bridges, barges,
All the north of the city was ablaze: eyes it reveals.

At school, the acquaintance
May come from daily glance
Or willing circumstance;

Or later, a letter
5   Reveals a mild hater
And a wish to know better.

The occasional meeting
Shows time defeating
The need of mating;

10   Shows stronger need,
A narrower greed,
But be afraid

Of closer look,
To smiling speak
15   Of leaf and rock;

For this is likeness
Not of greatness
But weakness and weakness.

The wind at creep of dawn
Through arches and spires
Swells, and on the lawn
Manoeuvres, alone;

5   Who kept planes like desires
Back in alien shires
Last night, this daybreak pass
Where misery has signed

Every unhappy face,
10   And, wind, in meetingplace
Of wish and fear, be kind
In dreams to each unconsummated mind.

Those who are born to rot, decay –
      And am I one of these?
A keyhole cast without a key
A poem none can read or say
A gate none open wide to see   5
      The fountains and the trees?

O what ails thee, bloody sod,
Alone and palely loitering,
The leaves are blowing in the quad
      And no birds sing:

Along the lines of windows spring   5
The orange lights of cosy fun
The radiogram is whispering,
      The day is done:

Why do you wander at the edge
Of the flat weedless gardens' lawn,   10
Down by the river blows the sedge,
      With none to warm,

Though through the evening comes the cry
Of yearly massacres perform'd
Amid the clash of where on why;   15
      The question formed

Upon the lips that, kissing, choke;
Sprawling amid the chestnut leaves
That circle lightly for a joke
      Around who grieves.   20

And this is why I shag alone
Ere half my creeping days are done
The wind coughs sharply in the stone,
      There is no sun

To light my way to bed: the leaves   25
Are brown upon the icy tree;
The swallows all have left the eaves
      Silently, silently.

After the casual growing-up
Between rick and room, the learning of tricks
To startle and amuse, which, it was told
In the safety of the home, would satisfy the world,
5   Came the sudden invasion: came the avenging dragon.
In a dozen days the landscape had been shattered:
Most of the family fled beyond recall
From the great shudders that shook birds dead from trees
And snakes that came advancing up the lawn:
10   Then with strange satisfaction the mallet sank in the clock,
Flames woke in the bookcase with a strangled yelp;
Riding warily through that county, the handful of horsemen
Heard all too often the warning to turn back
And scattered: one was slain by alighting eagle,
15   Others by falling.
                     They did not reach the house
Where like a horse he stood among the flowers
Forcing through floorboard: movement not made there.
Only behind the shut eyes in occasional integration
Came the brief portraits from the private album
20   With a conjurer's impudence, showing how it happened;
Yet knowing none other than these careless lies
In sunlit accent, thither nosed his wish:
Thither where at least it all was hidden
In clouds of days: the penalty of change,
25   Whose explosion even then was half expected.

There behind the intricate carving
A great conqueror is living,
Who in choice of book can prove
Scholarship's impersonal love,
5   Can in touch of hand imply
The sport's familiarity,
In movement of an eyebrow show
That all can pardon when all know.

Yet certain cruder literature
10   Or illegible signature
Or a voice singing, can arouse
A spirit from its ancient house,

Can send him wishing on a journey
Camouflaged among the many
Whose tangible and mountain ranges
Hide his microscopic changes.

Sailors brought back strange stories of those lands
To thrill professors, who in turn retold
The legend to their sons, until their minds
Could mirror every detail: how the gold
Of sunset spread a path across the sea   5
To point the traveller's way; the single palm
Guarding the bay that promised ecstasy
On the sand's softness where could tread no harm . . .

Yes, all the maps deceived them: they who raised
The sails of Pity on the sea of Need   10
Exploring, foundered in a gale of woe:
Splintered their vessels under horror's rock
Amid the tides that savaged to and fro
That generation's wreck.

Dances in Doggerel

(i)

How can the sunlight entertain
Except upon your window pane?
Or what else can the sky effect
Without the colour you reflect?
Each star would powerdive to the grave   5
Without the title that you gave,
And birds would leave an empty wood
If you forgot their names for good;
So even more, who justifies
The lamp that never lit your eyes,   10
The door that never let you in,
The book that you did not begin?
Who can extend a word of grace
To films that do not show your face,
Loudspeakers that your voice distort,   15
Or gramophones that cut you short?

What value has a word or scene
Except to show where you have been,
And take its formal place upon
20   The landscape of illusion?

For who by railway leaves behind
Your praising scenery, will find
The sun without a word to say,
The sky to face another way;
25   The stars will talk together, and
The birds will never be at hand;
The lamp will wonder who you are,
The door will always be ajar,
The book predict an age of woe,
30   The film a real murder show,
The blind loudspeaker threaten pain,
The gramophone not sing again,
For they become, outside your rule,
A painting by a different school,
35   A poem in a different tongue,
A song too ghastly to be sung,
Or most of all, a freakish play,
Enacted in broad light of day,
With me upon the blinding stage
40   At whom the hostile audience rage . . .

(ii)

The longest-running hit of Summer
Lacked a leading character;
Though the settings on the river seemed
Far better than was ever dreamed,
45   And minor players knew their parts
With songs like arrows to our hearts,
Something still was missing – not
That one could quarrel with the plot –
But it seemed no character would enter
50   And speak directly from the centre,
Charming all the play's applause,
And being both result and cause
Of every flower and bridge and tree
In their expensive pageantry.
55   No presence vitalised the cast

That all their normal best surpassed,
Or sung an idiotic verse
With more than usual personal force,
And so production slowly ceased;
The theatre was to Autumn leased,   60
The wind tore tatters in the wood,
The flowers blew down and lay for good,
Clouds proceeded down the river,
Raindrops made its surface quiver,
The sun charred to a smouldering heap,   65
Garden turned over in their sleep,
And Autumn's tragic, slight romance
Played to a thinning audience.

Now the old year lies behind
In ashes, and at last I find   70
One who in slapstick Spring's revue
With beauty could astonish too,
Would star in Summer's loaded masque
As regally as I could ask,
Capture Autumn's slipping grace   75
By a shadow on the face,
And Winter's classic speech recite
Beneath the moon's frostbitten light;
But now the players have moved on
And happiness has come and gone,   80
And in a different land I live,
The part no longer mine to give.

Lines after Blake

Skies by Time are threaded through,·
Not stopping to admire the view,
But any scene described can be
A paradise of sympathy;

Do literary memories   5
Serve to pay the Devil's fees?
And Falsehood's memorable face
Evanescent Truth displace?

If the flower forgets the earth

10 And the eldest son his birth
There is no place in daylight thought
For what myopic darkness taught.

I don't like March!
It's stiff like starch,
And the fucking snow
Doth blow, doth blow;
5   The wind's fingers
Fasten on strangers
And the heart's dangers
Come and go.

The iron tree
10   Threatens at me,
And the sky is low
And warns of woe;
Out of a cloud
A voice is heard
15   Saying aloud:
'Have you killed the snow?'

The doublehanded kiss and the brainwet hatred
At noontide marry, and are happy mated;
But the unwarm eye and wish of luck
Bear tears at midnight and come unstuck.

5   The flesh of love bears both the nail and hammer
Fenced in its brave armour;
But alone I spawn the thin sweat on the rose
And the rotten lip and fingers in the salt nose.

A day has fallen past
     A light flared through my eyes
And sunk; the windy skies
     Show no forecast;
5   There was sun and wind
     Flowers here and there

Some gardens bare
   Some ruined;

And did I care
   Walking among it?   10
Was my heart lit
   By the new air?

No, I did as I do
   Every day and night
Drink up the light   15
   Until I see you.

If days were matches I would strike the lot
   Till we met again;
Or if like apples, shake and let them rot,
   The whole crop down;

If hours were poems I would write a book   5
   To mark our meeting;
Or each a black and crying rook –
   I'd go out shooting;

If minutes were miles between us I would run
   Faster than horses;   10
Or like dead leaves? The bonfire I would burn
   Would join our faces;

But since all days and hours and minutes grow
   As slow as wheat,
What can my words do, but show   15
   Them summer heat?

Harry their greenness upward without resting,
   And be the weather
To end this absence with a harvesting
   To reap together?   20

I walk at random through the evening park
The river flows, the tennis courts resound
The children loud upon the playground sing
And in stricter training for the sexual act
5 Girls and their soldiers pace between the trees.

I walk beneath the sunlit castle walls
The timbered street tilts beautifully down
To reach the taming moat where skiff and punt
Circle giggling from the waterfall
10 And a professor in the sunset rapes a flower.

I walk among the shut and Sunday shops
See my bent height reflected in a blind
Avoid the pitying curious glances of
The soldiers clattering abreast, and stare
15 Past the misshapen men and boys in suits.

Along the railinged path between the plots
Of friendly cabbages I hear the trains
See standing all the unconnected trucks
Note the signals down and welcoming
20 And pause and shiver in the railway arch.

I watch the smoke cough golden in the air
And feel the track curve shining out of sight
And like a swallow cry to travel south
With suitcase packed and one-way ticket punched
25 Breathless to hear you shouted by the guard
And see your name slide painted into view.

At the flicker of a letter
Brought from smashed city under frozen sky
In late November, at the year's sombre ending –
I at a tall window standing
5 Watch the tumultuous clouds go by,
Go by over field and street, college and river.

What they must not say
At this letter is awaking,
Is skimming like leaves that scatter,
10 As these few leaves that loiter

On the wet bough shaking –
Is awake, and can a hearing justify:

'Admit your detection, ostentatiously understanding,
But sad in a corner at arrival of your letter;
Confess that no man can deny   15
His ultimate reliance on his silly way;
May seek another but shall find no better,
No better to love, and none so unending.'

Where should we lie, green heart,
But drowned at summer's foot,
As our arms embroider
Each tall tree shut
In the heat's soundless armour?   5

How should I speak, but with
Love's many-rooted breath
As a blank bird, or a song
Shaped in the sprung faith
Of this year's southern tongue?   10

Heart and heart, to nakedness
Unlayered and sewn close,
In this new and blind hour
Sleep defenceless;
Tongues of the year   15

Unfold through kiss-damp lips
The wound spring shapes;
And the hearts repeat
Every tide's push and lapse
From finish to start.   20

I am the latest son
Of an ancient family;
In me have crossed again
Their argument and pride,
And all the quality   5
Of men left better dead;

From one I take my stride

A second wore my smile
My loving from a third
Comes to his bitter end
And stubborn through my will
Another works his mind;

I hold the land they left
Watching as I walk
The robin on the shaft
The spade drawn bright from soil
– Oddments the mind brings back
During the evening stroll

That leads me back to home,
Knowing all the time
That I shall dream their dream,
Tell the lies they told,
And at the end like them
Die as they have died.

This triumph ended in the curtained head:
The walls blew out and spring remained outside,
Flaring through thick of trees;

Love blew a fuse and saw us in the sun
Nailing the writer's dust against the breeze,
A season and nothing done;

The modern wind runs steady past my ear,
As broken from a broken land I come
Into the furious year

Where hot grass parts the rivers and the roads,
The petrol throne of hoardings and the drum
Of the drought-giving birds.

Here childhood ends, and days again become
The real spread country forcing through my dream.

The sun swings near the earth,
And in his noon-hot breath
Green things break blind and thick
Between the tar and brick.

The railing is tangled in the hedge,
The lawn loses its edge,   5
And faceless through the hours
Move the stiff shadows of flowers.

Only man feels the sun
As thumbs pressed on his neck; man   10
Sweats, a bit contemptuous
Of the whole thing, and sleeps in his house.

Leave

There was to be dancing
In the cretonned lounge;
Three kinds of blancmange,
And a cake with icing;

The barrel by the radiogram   5
Held seven gallons
As a balance
To the seven-pound ham;

They had eggs and butter
Whiskey and chicken   10
– There wasn't a tradesman
They could have known better.

Hilda was setting the things
In the rose-coloured light;
All the napkins were white   15
In their silver rings;

She looked at the clock,
Thought his train might be late;
Took a sticky date
Tugged at her frock.   20

All the family sat round

– Even the dog as well
Thought it was the bell
At every sound:

25 Father read the leader
Again and again
Queenie and Cousin Pen
Study the carpet border:

Till at last the bell went
30 At six thirty-four;
Auntie Bee was at the door
Smelling of scent.

Oh what a chatter
As he stood in the hall,
35 Hung his greatcoat on the wall
And his respirator;

All the months after
His day of service
Fell like grass
40 At the scythe of their laughter.

Mother got up the dinner
Father forgot the leader
Gave him scotch and soda
And a cheap Corona.

45 And all they wanted to know –
If an offensive was brewing
All he's been doing
How fast he can go;

Billy asked about
50 The latest designs:
Auntie Bee: 'How many Huns'
Lights have you put out?'

Uncle Joe: 'Is the pay steady?'
Queenie was intent
55 On his badge and what it meant –
Then dinner was ready.

They ate till eight;
Course after course

Trifle and tinned asparagus
Piled on his plate;

They drank lime juice and cider
Port and beer
Smoked another cigar
Had another whiskey and soda:

Then Dad got the Rover
An old four-seater
And drove to the theatre
Nine, or over.

Oh how they laughed
At every joke the comic could make
Although Uncle Joe had belly-ache
And hurriedly left.

Then they danced till two-thirty
After a cold supper
Uncle Joe's humour
Approaching the dirty;

Auntie Bee got tight
In dropped Mrs Horner
Got him in a corner
Said it was splendid to fight.

At last, after hours and hours,
Too tired to think
They piled the plates in the sink
And straggled upstairs.

Hilda combed her hair
In their pink double room;
He heard the doom
Of 'Alone at last, dear.'

He had momentary schemes
Of pretending sleep
Then gave up hope –
She lay in his arms.

   . . .

The next day dawned fine
But soon filled with clouds
95 Like dirty great birds:
It began to rain.

He lay all morning in bed
With a hard face;
She did odd jobs in the house
100 Sullenly, as she always did.

As the pool hits the diver, or the white cloud
Gathers the plane scudding through the sky,
You met and married all my weeping world,
And far beyond the harbours where the child
5 Had played at kissing, all a giant day
Swung me on the logic of your tide.

Calm and burnished, past the year we swam,
Parting the doors of warning soft as grass,
For it was apathy, not love, we feared
10 Might chain the entrance to the sacred wood,
And separation was a country dance,
A condition of rejoining, when it came.

But on my own in exile all my fears
Watch the landscape in between us grow,
15 The spawning hills and chimneys thrusting up
Among the roads that tangle off the map
To cheat me if I make a bolt for you,
And lead and lose me through the faceless flowers.

Flesh to flesh was loving from the start,
But only to itself, and could not calm
My skeleton of glass that sits and starves,
Nor my marsh hand that sets my music out:

5 It is not kissing at the acid root
Where my bald spirit found a crying home,
Nor my starved blood that your excitement loves,
And wears all brilliant badged upon your coat:

Yet hand will praise, and skeleton delight,

And root will kiss, and spirit hold you warm,   10
And blood will call you blood and wear your lives
All red and blue and golden on its heart.

. . .

But you are far away and I have grown
A sack of fever hanging from the sun.

July Miniatures

The days, torn single from a sketching-block,
With all their scribbles are discarded;
So a mouth went, but for a mistake –
So a face looked, till the day it died –
So, if I could draw it, would be shown   5
This wind that blows the sky across the field,
And how today the town kneels in the rain.

. . .

If I look till the clouds crack
I shall still see a wet street
And the wet trees along it;
If I think till my heart break
It won't stop the rain   5
Or my bad life alone.

. . .

Summer has broken up
Fiercely between the hard, defended roads.

Near one of the farms, sunk in the sloping fields,
A bunch of soldiers (on tactical exercise)
Lounge smoking at a gate: they are very still;   5
Watching two men in shirtsleeves stacking the hay crop;
Above, unnoticed in the sunless skies,
A plane banks in a long descending circle
Preparing to land at the aerodrome, over the hill.

Blind through the shouting sun
On the oiled grooves of windy April I run
Crossing the young brink of Spring and Summer's union.

Birds are preaching to the walking pylons
5 Trying to drown the planes and spraying sirens
And buds preach too, but form their phrase in silence.

The hedge's eager hands stretch green towards me
And I am free
To snap a spray, twist it, gaily or cruelly,

10 Mock Autumn's collapsing haystacks, as the flowers
Yellow in the graveyard mock the hours
Of the printed dead the downstairs worm devours:

For what pretty thing will come to pass
Is nowhere written in the traceless grass
15 Nor who lies shot and rotten in the hourglass.

The Returning

They who are slow to forget death's face
Darken our maps like hills, or show
As old stains on the future's laundered cloth;
Another voice speaks under their breath,
5 Another heart, harder and more slow,
Drives their dry blood; they have lost grace
By sharpened gestures.
                            They avoid some words;
The strident young enthrall and anger them;
For our surface of things
10 They have a different, shocking set of meanings;
In a recurrent dream
They gather on old battlefields like birds.

Now

O now, as any other spot in time,
Its victims has: the blindly bold, the tame,
The aged – all are ticked off on the list.
The wheel was spun, and these our years have lost;
So we, convicted by the sundial's ban   5
Of the connived-at sin of being born,
Must by this order pack to travel light
Without the map that always comes too late.

Some say, that only this event will cure
Our tainted plant which needs a drastic care   10
To bring it to maturity. While some
– Whose ends, perhaps, are even just the same –
Abandon with regret what they were doing
So as to learn the rudiments of dying.

The poet has a straight face
Otherwise he would be out of place.
Nothing like comedy
Can ever be admitted as poetry.

I

When so many dropped on the harsh   5
Morning between our century's two nights
Having died like a rag on a nail, with uncrossed hands,
Which of the death-saddened ears will note
A single body's achievement of nineteen years?

The tale is a country one,   10
Slow as a root for the telling,
How, hatched and thatched,
One difficult day a sleep-walking child
Woke in the house of mirrors,

Saw its name signed   15
As receiving a load of years; saw the new oil
In the new engines getting greater power;

Saw with a start
Its interesting face and the faces of all the others.

20   And in wondering evening walks
The world flew past, and was caught
And catalogued under glass:
And some faces were so beautiful
That their simple images grew wet with tears.

25   But the mirrors broke and slid
Silver like scales to the ground
And the wind threw the fences down
And the path all eaten with flowers
Strayed into the wood and was lost;

30   And vanishing into the hill
The columns of marching men
Are thicker and brighter than wheat,
While under the spread of the moon
The cities lie ruined and mad.

II

35   Now every promise is withdrawn,
And every spring runs underground;
Here are the paths no longer worn
And not a signpost can be found;
          In body and in mind
40   The hero stands alone.

The twisted jumbled with the straight,
The years are telescoped and burnt;
Much will never be retaught
Now, that we have never learnt:
45   All unprepared are sent
               Against the failing light.

Dumb among the rocks and sand
Prayers are waiting to be said;
Prayers will never understand
50   What's left of the prayerless dead –
               Blood beating in my hand
               Words climbing in my head.

III

Yet I do not want to end
With a night falling and the wind and no stars
And, faintly, the high-flying bombers: 55
The years push each other away
And rooms and their faces recede,
And I will build no tomb on your day
Any more than travellers consecrate a house
Where they were warm and happy for a night.   60

I will blow these words through no trumpet,
Coil after coil of metal praise;
Unfurl no figured banner to the wind
To be saluted by the grave cadets
And sold on ashtrays at a monument;   65
Tonight, hands in my pockets,
I face the window to Wales, and merely stare
In your wet direction.

For the time of heroics is past,
Farther than our forgotten childhoods,   70
Those acid summers of the twenties
When Lawrence still saw hope for some of us,
But died before the thirties stamped it out;
Now there is nothing left to swear or promise,
No everlasting past or future;   75
Only this day in a nameless town,

And my thoughts tracking the empty roads
To your nameless town, where you
Will be sitting with your hands across your knees
Smiling at another sealed-up year   80
Dropped like a sun behind suburban houses;
Flushed and timid are the kindnesses
And wanting the old unnoticed life again,
The clocks put back and winter coming on.

So I lift a dark glass   85
Fluent against the light,
And over the wine of memory and hoping,
Soft as a licking candle say my wish,
Soft as the flame
Licking the bud of blood and wine, repeat   90

A rote of prayer for you and yours
On this, your day in the year;

May out of the clouds of chance
A calm wind blow, a bird be sighted and steer
95   Straight for your bough, and its pursuing love
Break in the air, a scarlet target afloat
For the strength of your striking arrow;
The length of your heart
Be furrowed under your hand,
100   And the summer's end fall heavy in your arms.

IV

The land in sun and shadow
And the horns of morning
    Blowing, shining,
Waken the drowned girl
105   Frosted under the soil
In a dazzling meadow.

For today the flag is flown
From the castle of leaves
    That lives, that lives;
110   Now will the heir regain
Ten valleys curving in
The chest of the sun;

And loud in the lighted ear
A human year of life
115   Is beating in a laugh,
And the sound of silver blood
Bursts in a wave, to flood
A human shore.

To James Sutton

Poem

I hear you are at sea, and at once
In my head the anonymous ship
    Swings like a lamp;
I think of equipment and meals, and the long
Sane hours of a funnel   5
Against the birdless, interleaving plain.

I stand at the kerb, and hear
The day of shops break over my feet
    In scum the colour of eyes;
I man the helm of the clocks,   10
Under the cave of my hand the crowd
Wave in the cinema like weed.

Yet I stand in a shell's porch, wound
On a salting wind that blows
    Sand on the wheels and faces,   15
And the landless moon lifts over the street,
Calling my loosened fingers from the bay
And long beach of loving.

The land parts and falls. O in my slack heart
The slant of your ship is resurrected,   20
    The singing and lubbers' jokes;
For the seabed of Time is deeper than ten cathedrals,
The route is unridden, and the navigating worm
Hauls me to fear at last.

Llandovery
Is responsible for the discovery
That semen
Can be produced without wemen.

Fuel Form Blues

Oh see that Fuel Form comin' through the post
Oh *see* that Fuel Form comin' through the post
It's five weeks late and worse filled up than most.

If your house burns a fire, Lord, you gotta say how long,
5   You gotta put down the merchant that you get it from,
You gotta put it down, and put it down all wrong.

I'd rather be a commando, or drive a railway train,
I'd rather be a commando, Lord! drive a railway train,
Than sort dem Fuel Forms into streets again.

10   They're large about the blots, the writing's kinda small,
They can spell their own name but that's just all,
Fuckin' Fuel Forms, only thing that I crave,
Fuckin' Fuel Forms, they just won't have,
Fuckin' Fuel Forms, gonna carry me to my grave, carry me to my grave.

Poem

I met an idiot at a bend in the lane
Who said: I told you not to come here again.
     How tall you're getting. Do you still
     Roll each day away like an iron wheel,
5   Making four spokes of food? And I expect the windows
     Want cleaning again, while the mind wanders
     Helpless over the locked hills of others,
     The beautiful rats, farmers, dockyards, mothers,
     Who wear cruelty and kindnesses like rings –
10   Or have you put away these things?
     I don't blame you. Someday you'll find all lines
     Lead to a vanished point within the loins;
     (Do you remember the acid used at birth?)
     Time's getting on. Somewhere upon this earth,
15   Time's drunken star, the moles have dug your grave;
     One day they'll leave the top off – then who'll save
     The coupons you were cutting out for Life?
     Today death has the last and only laugh.
     But you could change that. Why don't you try?

On each leaf balanced a lighted eye: 20
Rooks called his words: his body seemed to be
The angle of a strange and single tree.

The canal stands through the fields; another
Year bends in propped-up rows.
The sky is a bird's breast, shielding
Blue shadows in the copse: I see
The burnt moon hanging: feel   5
The first and faintest premonition:
Autumn, finger on the breath,
A vapoured death.
And yet the novelty I find in death
Is my coincidence; scores   10
Shiver already in his shaded areas,
Queue for his canteen lunches, live
His ugly camp-life near the villages.
Treat my logic casually, he cries;
And some fall to the trap, hearing   15
His numbing voice on the ancestral wavelength.
It has all happened so quickly.

Down the other bank, children lie fishing;
Their voices scrape the silence of their hands,
Living unguardedly. What were we doing then?   20
We walked at evening, tracing
The landscape of ourselves – but this
Had been done for years; we argued, yes;
And yet it seems each sentence threw
A spade of earth, around our lives   25
Had crept the unforgiving barrenness
That brought the knocking from the bolted door.
– I cannot think what we were doing then:
I cannot fit the broken edge of letters,
The young unfinished days, the faces,   30
I cannot join them to this Now.
Facts hang a bridle. History.
Ports. Inflation. Even now I shy.
It is not reason, that those kisses
Design a bombsite, those coloured poems   35
Burn among papers of an enemy consulate.

Yet orders are given, brittle, monstrous:
When did the climate of their utterance
Begin to grow?
                    Into lucidity
40 The moon is focussed, hurtful and important,
    Turning already our scene into
    A problem of art, and later, pedantry.
    The clarified illusion prepares
    To invade and colonise. But
45 It was less simple than that: living
    An hour after this sunset meant
    More than the fish blipping in the water,
    The beauty fractured to suffering, the moths,
    The fear, the bewildered gap
50 Where hope should be; was
    A simultaneous exertion on all scales
    To grip harmoniously the forward impulse,
    Yet still to be aware
    Of falling, of mist; the element that lies
55 Even at the heart of the perceiving instrument.

Planes Passing

    The guns
    Tap the slack drumhead of the sky
    Where separate bombers crawl,
    Leaving soft trails of sound.
5   Time has run into the ground,
    And the past squats upon the earth
    Searching its fur for fleas.

    Is life drinking, will it ever lift
    Its head from drinking, and move
10 Delicately in an undreamt direction?
    Or have these threads
    Drawn and redrawn in the flesh of night
    Sewn a dead parcel to be stuffed and stink
    Under history's stairs?

15 The guns give an immediate answer.

As a war in years of peace
Or in war an armistice
Or a father's death, just so
I could not visualise us parted:
From the other side regarded   5
It did not seem a likely sorrow.

But parting is no simple act
Making way for what comes next:
Parting is a trailing streamer
Lingering like leaves in autumn   10
Thinning at the winter's comb –
Fading like a marching drummer.

And the throbbing disappears
And I have no gracious tears
To ponder on the consequence   15
Of having seen you drown and die
In my personal history:
And can this be indifference?

A Member of the 1922 Class Looks to the Future

After the war
We shan't fight any more
We shall stop making arms
And live on farms

Because when it all ends   5
We shall all be friends
(Erasing from the memory
Cologne, Coventry)

And it will come to pass
There shall be no lower class   10
We shall all do what we like
And no one will strike

And Nazi Germany
Shall be set free

15 And every subject land
    Will lick our hand.

    – Really, when I foresee
    How lovely it will be
    In these afteryears,
20 My eyes fill with tears.

A Member of the 1922 Class Reads the 1942 Newspapers

    After this war
    It won't be like it was before:
    The word 'enemy'
    Will just vanish from our memory.

5   First of all, Germany
    Will be set free,
    And every subject land
    Will lick our gracious hand.

    Then we shall restart work:
10 No one will shirk
    And no one will strike
    Because we shall all do what we like.

    We shall all become Christians
    And ask no questions
15 For the Church will dispense
    'Birth Control and Common Sense.'

    Then the miner's eldest son
    Will study at Eton
    And lounge on French beaches
20 Sounding his aitches.

    We shall be short
    Of nothing that can be bought,
    So of course we shall be
    Perfectly happy.

25 Indeed, the Millennium
    May come,
    Though, considering the facts,
    As rather an anti-climax.

A Democrat to Others

Fear not, ye conquered hills and plains,
England will remove your chains,
And we shall all live happily
If someone will set England free.

After a particularly good game of rugger
A man called me a bugger
Merely because in a loose scrum
I had my cock up his bum.

Poem

The camera of the eye
Spools out twelve months; the memory
Spells underneath, how this was snow,
And this was drowned in heat, and this
Derelict, among gulls.   5
And every tree has told
Death of the drowsed year,
But none of you, or me,
Aleaf, we, living still.

A year of us. And true words cannot speak   10
Except by accident stuck round the brain,
Chucked from unfinished weeks,
For days can grow
Softly from a stem, and glow,
And fall at last behind a wall   15
Loosening their sweetness on the earth.
The branch lifts up:
And it is all as though they had not been.
And lives can choose a moment to be born,
Put forth their quickened leaves   20
Under the light, and live;
And they can draw some sweetness from the earth
Before the month fall down
And bury them as though they had not been.

25 Words have no lips to kiss them back to life.
Words have no hands to hold their spilled sweetness.

(from the back)
We're Middleton Murry & Somerset Maugham
        Vive la compagnie!
We both try to write in a 'spiritual form',
5   Vive la compagnie!
Lawrence, of course, wrote some quite decent stuff
Although he didn't quite *suffer* enough
– But any-given-one-of-my-short-stories-kicks-him-right-up-the-
    duff . . .
10   VIVE LA COMPAGNIE!

Songs of Innocence and Inexperience

Soul

Onward went the ferry,
The oarsman bold in fear's coin:
Nor more was Man mere Man
But twin spirits of dubious worth;
5 One born still;
The other, whose only birthpangs
Had been the grave of his parent,
Felt Life flow small and novel through his veins;
But set off from the stage,
10 Unafraid, into death.

Birth

Swarming and creeping they made me,
And I stirred in my mother's womb,
Where my body was welded with slowness
And prepared for the death in the tomb.

My body was christened with tear drops   5
And my slumbers were cradled in sighs;
In sadness my bowels were moulded
With the unseeing knowledge that cries.

Fate rested his hand on my forehead
And his agonies raced in my skull;   10
With the death beats of time I was branded,
The rollings that nothing can lull.

So when all was finished and fashioned,
And my body had suffered its shape,
While time its last torment was howling   15
I was born in a land without hope.

The Death of Life

How slowly moves the acrobat
His limbs and lungs are dumb,
For from the circus days of life
The night of death has come.

The giant mountains' shadows move   5
To join the solemn hearse,
The towers and the trees descend
To see the funeral pass.

And all the woods of animals
Look down at the black ground,   10
And only raise their fear stained eyes
To see the death that groaned.

And on the bier with blackness
The god of death is crowned,

15   The symbol of our sadness
      To which the world is bound.

                    – o –

      A broken down chair sprawls in the corner;
              Brother I'm coming.
      The legs – the one that is left –
      Is as useful as a broken matchstick;
5   Brother I'm hurrying.
      No more romantic symbol
      Of happiness alone or in company,
      But a hulk of rotting upholstery:
              Brother I'm nearly there.
10   It no longer has a place
      In the glare of the imprisoned fire,
      But in a cage with a wilder thing –
      A cremation:
              My brother is dead.

To Ursula

      What sex-life is there in an English prison?
      Such a cacophony of warders, bars and locks
      I had never seen;
      Though I have felt (and not with a sense of touch)
5   What convict life must mean:
      Disillusion, frustration and abused relief
      Without the chance of normal success.
      But now – what joy and sanity –
      I am in jail in Mexico!

Spoonerism

      Ugly, horrid, foul, I am;
      I met the virgin at tea:
      Angel, sweetness, divinity,
      Dare I smile?
5   I love you, dearest, let me;
      My filthy hope is strong.

I'll show you my poems, the little charm
That I unworthy . . .
She spat on the ground where she had stood.

I rode all the way . . .   10

I rode all the way on the top of a London bus:
When we reached the terminus I rode back again.
I sat in the front like a driver
And turned the people this way and that
In and out of the traffic;   15
Stopping in time, and ignoring them when the bus was full:
Then I went home and played like God with my toys.

If approached by Sir Cyril Norwood,
Any respectable whore would
Charge double
For her trouble.

Letters

I wrote these letters through a year
And then one day I get them back
And for an hour I drop them in the fire
And in a minute each is burnt and black.

Blues

Sometimes I feel like an eagle in the sky,
Sometimes I feel like an eagle in the sky,
Sometimes I feel I'm gonna lay me down & die.

You can't love a woman, if that woman don't love you,
You can't love a woman, if that woman don't love you,   5
You can't love a woman that don't care what you do.

She gotta want you like whiskey, she gotta need you like rain,
She gotta want you like whiskey, she gotta need you like rain,
She gotta cry when you leave her, and cry till you come back again.
(enter Pee Wee Russell)   10

The – er – university of Stockholm – er –
Presented Jung with a diploma,
Er – I would present Jung
With – ah – DUNG.

The False Friend

It's no good standing there and looking haughty:
I'm very cross: I think you've been a beast,
An utter crawling worm, for nearly all the term –
I think you might apologise, at least.
5   It might interest you to know I heard from Audrey
That Kathleen said that you told Miss LeQuesne
That my liking for French prose was nothing but a pose –
Elspeth, I'll never speak to you again.

Joan always said, she wondered how I stuck you,
10 And now I see that she was jolly right;
Oh, I know we did our Maths strolling round the garden paths
Until the moon came up, and it was night . . .
But Wenda said that you told her last Christmas,
When we'd promised to send *cards* to Miss LeQuesne,
15 That the vow you made was broken, 'cos you sent her a BOOK
    TOKEN
– Elspeth, I'll never *speak* to you again.

Bliss

In the pocket of my blazer
    Is a purse of silken brown
With ten shillings (from my birthday)
    And my weekly half-a-crown.

5   In the toolshed by the stable
    Stands my junior B.S.A.,
See, I leap, I mount, I pedal! –
    And the wind bears me away.

On the left side of the High Street
10   W. H. Smith & Son

Have their local branch, and there I'll
    Stop, and lock my bike, and run

Right up to the glass-topped counter:
    'Have you Colonel Stewart's book
Called "Handling Horses"? . . . Yes – behind you –   15
    It's twelve and six – you needn't look – '

Ballade des Dames du Temps Jadis

Tell me, into what far lands   With a sense of
They are all gone, whom I once knew   'old, unhappy,
With tennis-racquets in their hands,   far-off things'.
And gym-shoes, dabbled with the dew?
Many a one danced like a star,   5
And many a one was proud and gay
Throughout those happy years, that are
So many summer terms away.

Where is Valerie, who led   Lingeringly.
Every tom-boy prank and rag –   10
Is her hair still golden-red?
Can she still dash like a stag
As she did at hide-and-seek?
And would she still refuse to play
With a rotter or a sneak,   15
As many summer terms away?

And Julia, with violet eyes,   Wistfully.
Her cool white skin, and sable hair –
Does she still extemporise
On 'The Londonderry Air'?   20
Does she still want to take the veil
And clothe herself in white and grey?
And be as exquisite and pale
As many summer terms away?

And when we camped on Priory Hill   With a trace of   25
(That year when Beth was nearly gored)   sad humour.
Brenda and Wenda and brown-legged Jill –
Do they remember how it poured?
And how the lamp had got no wick?

And how we tried to sleep on hay
When Sue ate mushrooms and was sick,
So many summer terms away?

How many names cry on the wind!
Ann, who wore an Aertex shirt,
35 Patricia, who played Rosalind,
Jean and her little tartan skirt:
How many crushes, chums, and cliques
Recall in this sad roundelay
Those many golden, golden weeks,
40 So many summer terms away!

With something of
'the monstrous
crying of wind' –
Yeats, of course.

Now the ponies all are dead,
The summer frocks have been outgrown,
The books are changed, beside the bed,
And all the stitches that were sewn
45 Have been unpicked, and in disgust
The diaries have been thrown away,
And hockey-sticks are thick with dust –
Those summer terms have flown away.

More slowly, but
gathering feeling
for the end.

Ah, tell me, in what fairy-land
50 Can I meet Jacqueline or June,
Eat lemon-caley from my hand? –
But no: it has all gone too soon,
And Christine, Barbara, and Madge,
Elspeth, Elizabeth, Esme
55 Are with my blazer and my badge,
So many summer terms away.

Rising to, and
falling from, an
ecstasy of
nostalgia.

Holidays

(To all schoolgirls who visit the Shakespeare Memorial Theatre at Stratford-on-Avon, during the season.)

Let's go to Stratford-on-Avon, and see a play!
    Let's pull Pam and Barbara out of their double bed,
Snatch a breakfast, wheel the four bicycles out of the shed,
    And with lunch in the saddlebags, mount and pedal away!

5 For September is here, and the summer is nearly past;
    There's dew on the blackberries; mist, and the watery sun

Of autumn draw close, the season is almost done . . .
    Ah, pedal, brown legs, for this matinee may be the last!

Who cares what we see? I have been all of them,
    Rosalind, Viola, Portia, Beatrice too,   10
I have laughed as they laughed, Jessica, Imogen,
    And, like Miranda, have woken in worlds brave and new:

Cleopatra and Juliet – yes, I have loved and died,
    Or, like Desdemona, been slain by a passionate hand;
Ah, pedal, brown legs! on to the magic land,   15
    To the queue, and the stools, and the shilling to get inside.

September is here, but the leaves still hang and are green,
    The sun still shines, the bees surround the flowers –
For today, then, we can be happy; for these few hours
    Let the curtain go up once more, and the play be seen: 20

For winter will come, when the wind endlessly grieves
    For all it has lost, the youth, the joy, the pain,
When the last term is over, the theorems forgotten again,
    And we no more to each other than fallen leaves.

The School in August

The cloakroom pegs are empty now,
And locked the classroom door,
The hollow desks are dim with dust,
And slow across the floor
A sunbeam creeps between the chairs   5
Till the sun shines no more.

Who did their hair before this glass?
Who scratched 'Elaine loves Jill'
One drowsy summer sewing-class
With scissors on the sill?   10
Who practised this piano
Whose notes are now so still?

Ah, notices are taken down,
And scorebooks stowed away,
And seniors grow tomorrow   15
From the juniors today,

And even swimming groups can fade,
Games mistresses turn grey.

Fourth Former Loquitur

A group of us have flattened the long grass
Where through the day we watched the wickets fall
Far from the pav. Wenda has left her hat,
And only I remain, now they are gone,
5   To notice how the evening sun can show
The unsuspected hollows in the field,
When it is all deserted.
                Here they lay,
Wenda and Brenda, Kathleen, and Elaine,
And Jill, shock-headed and the pockets of
10   Her blazer full of crumbs, while over all
The sunlight lay like amber wine, matured
By every minute. Here we sprawled, barelegged,
And talked of mistresses and poetry,
Shelley and Miss LeQuesne, and heard the tale
15   Once more of Gwyneth and the garden-rake,
Grass between clear-cut lips, that never yet
Thrilled to the rouge: a schoolbag full of books,
(Todhunter's Algebra – for end of term
Does not mean you can slack) and dusty feet
20   Bare-toed in sandals – thus we lay, and thus
The filmy clouds drew out like marble veins,
The sun burned on, the great, old whispering trees
Lengthened their shadows over half the pitch:
Deckchairs that the governors had filled
25   Grew empty, and the final score was hung,
To show for once the Old Girls had been licked.
Ah what remains but night-time and the bats,
This flattened grass, and all the scores to be
Put in the magazine?
                Be not afraid,
30   Brenda and Wenda, Kathleen and Elaine
And brown-legged Jill – three years lie at your back
And at your feet, three more: in just a week

The end of term will part us, to the pale
And stuccoed houses we loved so much.

Wenda, Brenda, Kathleen and Elaine   35
Have flattened down the long grass where they've lain,
And brownlegged Jill has left her hat,
For they have gone to laugh and talk with those
Who've played the Old Girls' match out to its close.

I would give all I possess
(money, keep, wallet, personal effects, and articles of dress)
To stick my tool
Up the prettiest girl in Warwick King's High School.

'Sent you a letter, but it had to go by boat,
I said I sent you a letter, but it had to go by boat,
Er – pardon me a moment while I pour
whiskey down the inside of my throat . . .'

The wind that blows from Morpeth
Is an old and a young thing,
And its song in the eaves
Of love and of death
Thrills my heart like a harp-string . . .   5
Morpeth, Morpeth . . .

Morpeth doth murder sleepe, therefore my duff
Shall sleepe namoore . . .

Address to Life, by a Young Man Seeking a Career

Freckling summers have crossed my brow
    To the number of just eighteen;
And I know that I should be deciding now
    To what profession I lean;
All others with whom I have spent my youth   5
    Have chosen their own avenue,

Yet (though I'm ashamed to tell you the truth)
      There's nothing that *I* want to do.

Life, you are busy, I appreciate that,
10   Arranging for everyone;
But I really think we should have a chat
      About what I am going to become;
I've really tried to discover your aims
      Whatever their nature and kind,
15 But, although not the sort of a fellow who blames
      – I think I've slipped out of your mind.

Do you want me to work and to gain a degree
      And to live in the shade of the spires?
Do you want me to study philosophy
20   Or catalogue human desires?
Do you want me to be the authority
      On Milton and Dryden and Pope?
If this is the future you've mapped out for me,
      Then why don't you give me some hope?

25 (You don't, I suppose, really propose
      To make me a student of science:
If that is your wish, I'm afraid I oppose
      With a gently stubborn defiance;
For everyone knows that I fall in a doze
30   When faced with a real microscope;
And if you chose this, the facts interpose,
      And thus there is really no hope.)

And Classics as well can all go to hell
      For I've acted upon your advice;
35 I've again and again thrown them all down the drain
      For I never supposed they were nice.
Thus it is clear that a scholar's career
      Doesn't seem to be your little plan;
But why won't you speak? For every week
40   Is pushing me nearer the Pan.

Or do you intend I should regally spend
      A fortune, and live like a king?
To live between Greece and Paris and Nice?
      I don't think I should like such a thing:
45 – And first you must give the means thus to live,

Before I can safely smirk;
For at present you see it does look to me
    As if I shall have to work.

Life, what is your aim? I say it again:
    Direct and control my inquiries;   50
I've poured out my woes in poems and prose
    And even in several diaries;
See, I invite you to teach me to write
    On my psychological squalls;
You will not comply, and, although I do try,   55
    The result is invariably · · · · ·

Therefore I am not a don or a swot
    Or a dandy who grinds down the poor;
I'm not such a blighter to think I'm a writer
    When others so obviously are.   60
Do you think, perhaps, I'm one of the chaps
    Who is either a Bull or a Bear?
Although it is funny, when it comes to money
    I'm really no earthly good there.

Although not an Eric, shall I be a cleric   65
    And sermonise every Sunday?
That would be a trick that would make me quite sick
    From Saturday right through to Monday;
I've tried being good, and I don't think I could,
    And I never get very excited,   70
So I let fall a tear for the Bishop's career
    To which I was never invited.

And similarly, I shan't be an M.P.
    Although I could burble quite well;
If you think of the Army – well, Life, you're just barmy   75
    – Though of course one can never quite tell –
I belong to no faction of people of action
    Whether pacifist, fascist or red,
In actual fact, I never could act,
    Because I am more than half dead.   80

This long catalogue is a wearisome job
    And it's one that you, Life, ought to do:
My predestined fate I quietly await,
    The choosing is all up to you.

85 Whatever proposal, if at my disposal,
　　　I'll follow with loyalty blind;
But the earth's getting colder, and I'm growing older –
　　　So please won't you make up your mind?

Postscript 1943

I'm sorry to say, that as life looks today,
90　　　I'm going to reside out in Wellington,
Where everyone's rude, and ashamed of a nude,
　　　And nobody's heard of Duke Ellington;
Life, you aren't a god, you're a bloody old sod
　　　For giving me such an employment
95 'Cos in such a bad job only pulling my knob
　　　Will bring me the slightest enjoyment.

What ant crawls behind the picture?
Some dull cavalier monotony
Shone with obsolete rust;
Woman and man, two dogs and a horse:
5 But oh, the fly, and oh, the centipede.
Grin at me, you sheep and cows.
Why are you together on that silly hill?
Where is the cowherd and where the shepherd?
And where the important worm?
10 Give gold Grand Guignol,
Shout your largesse to the poor;
Ignoring the bat that flies in your ear.
Black ships sail, moving nowhere,
On an unknown sea,
15 Spurning the albatross –
Stop it you maniacs, you will die!
The landgirl is riding her piebald bicycle:
No car will run over her dog.

Someone stole a march on the composer
And substituted dirt for genius;
He was blind and so unwitting –
Non compos till they played it to him.
This was his death-shriek of Infamy: 5
'Oh, to treat an old man so!'
The thief merely laughed, and whistled an air –
The very tune he had stolen;
But the old chap never smiled:
He didn't see the joke: he was blind.   10

Did you hear his prayer, God?
Did you sympathise with this poor braggart?
Did you know his shame
In trampling on his pride to petition aid?
You know you did, you monstrous thing;   5
Your kindness and gentility gave extra ears,
And you kicked him in the teeth to help him on.

Leap Year

I saw it smell; I heard it stink.
Whose book review rejuvenated Asia?
A black cat stalking along the sky
With an old man, a lampshade for a hat,
With a brassière hung from one ear   5
This was all he had. In place of the other
Grinned a sunken peanut's skull;
Machinegun belts served for his hair,
Two torpedoes for his eyes:
The book he wrote reverberated over Europe.   10
Marching feet, and a toboggan under his arse,
Two-pennyworth of chips for a brain;
A fivepenny fish dangled before his knees
And the motive power was a tart.
We spat on a pillarbox, ran in a vertical street   15
And vomited along a shop-front;
We hit a bull in the eye, and the Old Man died:
But the book enjoyed a prodigious success.

Some large man had a pendulous eyeball
That socketed under his ear,
That looked backwards and forwards alike,
And published anything secreted or virginal we had
5   With imponderable impunity.
How were we safe, we dared not ask;
The fly-paper had us all.
By what unknown effort some brave fellow staggered free
And rushed at the eye with a pin:
10   Onward David, rush onwards with our bouquet of Hope,
But what avails a flower against a flame?

End

My train draws out, and the last thing I see
Is my three friends turning from the light,
And I am left to travel through the night
With this one thought for company:
5   Even a king will find himself alone,
Calling for songs one night, old songs, will find
The guests departed, nothing left behind
Except the silence, and a clean-picked bone.

On Poetry

What have these years brought
But flakes of life?
Sodden ways and thought,
And now, the worst of all,
5   Love slashed with a knife,
The singing-voice grown gutteral.

Cheapening, worthlessness –
All can be borne
While that voice is dauntless;
10   But let it once fail
And the hair will be shorn,
The very heart grow pale.

Inscription on a Clockface

For this as it is,
Not beautiful or strong,
In every detail less
Than in its former days –
Let us rejoice, as long   5
As we have breath to praise.

Wall up the day in words;
Let no quarrelsome branch break loose
Or petalled ignorance be dropped,
And you will have built a statue of bread
To be pecked to death by the birds.   5

What is it a bird sings?
The encarmining of piebald agonies?
Or none of these things?

There is snow in the sky.
When will it fall down,
That the grey clouds that weigh
Immoveable across the town
Can break and blow away?   5
And I accept afresh
This tattered coat of flesh,
These crossed sticks of bone.

If I saw the sky in flames
The sky being charred like paper
Each constellation crackling like a thornbush,
I should wish to have lain with women,
Ridden horses to the sea.   5

When my body fills with death
Like a jar of smoke, like a ship
Lying at last on the seabed –
I shall wish to have lain with women,
Ridden horses to the sea.   10

When this face was younger,
    One man and I
Heaped love on each other
    Till love ran dry;
5   Since mine was the stronger
       Mine is the more pain:
He loves no longer:
      I love not again.

Honour William Yeats for this success:
Attaining to such lyric wildness
That shouts of bawdy insult, joke, and curse
Never transgressed an inch outside his verse.

Poem

Summer extravagances shrink:
And now memories drop
Forsakenly, I used to think,
A finite and shapely crop,
5   Nothing was more mistaken:
At the fierce unfinished centre
Everything grows and is broken,
Spring, summer, and winter.

If gulls rose in the wind
10   Crying, and fell away
From the climbed headland
One similar day
To this, we were lucky but
Can claim no credit,
15   For nothing consolate
Ever was granted;

And the eye must descend
Through the sparse field of years
To this empty land,
20   This desert of houses
Where the aristocratic
And to-be-denied

Gold sun throws back
Endless and cloudless pride.

If I wrote like D. H. Lawrence, I wouldn't need to drink no beer,
I said, if I wrote like D. H. Lawrence, I wouldn't need to drink no
   beer,
I wouldn't need to move another inch from here, no, not from
   here . . .

Poem

Last night, by a restless bed
In one of five empty rooms
Round which the nightwinds creep,
The electric fire burnt red,
And I lay, drained of dreams,   5
A prey of all but sleep.

It had all happened again,
Every card gone from my hand
And not a trick taken;
Everything lost in vain   10
At the tables where lovers stand
And the dicebox is shaken.

For morning to come,
For the light to rouse me up
It seemed would be consummate grief –   15
And yet it did come,
The grey light did take shape,
Grief surpassed itself.

And so I learned at last
Things run beyond despair   20
To find joy moving about
Like stags through morning mist;
Find that last plateau, where
Regrets are cancelled out,

Where terrible, terrible   25
Springs that baseless joy
Careless of everything;

A joy it's possible
To tear apart like a toy
30   Yet hear the pieces sing:

A joy that has no use
For me or anyone
Unless when, stripped of hope
Of love, of all excuse
35   For gladness, we go on
And dance at the end of the rope.

For this, the bag's repacked,
The train that is the train
For everywhere is caught,
40   And wheels cry out the fact
It will all happen again,
The same battles be fought,

And all for no reason – all
Because in that last field
45   Light has defeated dark,
Grief wrestles, and must fall
Yielding as night must yield
To the awakening lark.

Girl Saying Goodbye

How she must feel the frailty
Of mouth on mouth!
How all she knew at night
Is lost in the light!

5   Starstrong, the wheels begin to move:
And this is all the loyalty
Earth can show earth.
She can show no more love.

Mary Cox in tennis socks
    Mary Cox in shorts
Teacups tinkling in the breeze
Tables underneath the trees
And Mary Cox with suntanned knees   5
    In tennis socks and shorts.

White lines drawn across the lawn
    And Mary Cox in shorts
Jug and glasses in the shade
Lilac trees and lemonade   10
Racquet-presses carefully laid
    Beside the tennis-courts.

But summer dies and summer skies
    Grow cloudy in my thoughts
Yet still as in a crystal creeps   15
The shadow of a rose that sleeps
And Mary Cox's shadow leaps
    In tennis socks and shorts.

Small paths lead away
From the fence round the wood,
Small animals prey
Where no foot ever trod;
Smoke leans from unseen fires   5
In many villages,
Where wet leaves and briars
Burn behind cottages.

There are more fruits, more flowers
Than one hand can pick,   10
More trembling hours,
More eyes, more music
Than one slow traveller
Ever can meet,
Though bright illusion spur   15
His credulous feet.

Sheaves under the moon in ghostly fruitfulness
Cold berries in the hedge, flowers rank with seed,
The many leaves that die, but find no rest,
All journey down towards forgetfulness,
5   Towards death, ages of deathly autumns spread
Across the land, seeming a white mist,

I see them as a robe the year puts on
Against the sharpening stars, the incarnate year
Displayed, as if in evidence winter demands
10 Of life filled up to brimming. And the sun
Draws off from autumn in a kind of fear:
I am ashamed to face death with empty hands.

[CREWE]

The corruption of his eye
Reflects her images of death
That crowd like branches in the sky,
And yet wheels part them on a breath
5   And on the platform only I
Remember roses root in earth,
Earth that gathers, earth where all
The golden leaves must fall, must fall.

Why should I be out walking
On the night of a high wind?
Why should I understand
The trees in their talking?
5   Because I have had no lover
Since love ran dry
When this face was younger
This wind was high.

We are the night-shite shifters shifting the shite by night and shouting
BALLOCKS
They make a lovely stew
BALLOCKS
They're very good for you   5
ARSEHOLES
Wrapped up in parcels
And labelled 'Arseholes
In parcels
For you'.   10

Snow has brought the winter to my door:
Walking among its scraps I try to fix
Afresh what symbols I have used before
But find them shrunk like snowdrifts in a thaw
Of less account than heaps of broken sticks.   5

Time runs like water underneath the ice,
Runs on above high cloud, until it bring
Ruin onto winter's ceremonies
Disordering the frost no less than these
Past emblems, split and buried in last spring.   10

They with their going leave no power at all,
Or I would summon up new imagery
As supple as the rooks that rise and fall
Over these northern fields: but I can call
No mortal birds down to a barren tree.   15

To S. L.

Because there is no housing from the wind,
No health in winter, and no permanence
Except in the inclement grave,
Among the littering alien snow I crave
The gift of your courage and indifference.   5

243

Because the images would not fit
Of silent instrument, unplenteous horn,
Alone in the deserted street
I walked, till suddenly on the wind
5   A chill heresy was borne:
'No wishing of your starveling heart
Nor choice of inharmonious mind
Brought you in these great riches any part.'

Days like a handful of grey pearls
Go past me, savourless and cold;
Among the many hours and miles,
Among the many faces, only one
5   Was happy – that, a woman, old,
Witless, counting her fingers in the sun.

The winter seems too great a load to move,
And fantasies of spring to house
Deeply in caverns with outmoded love;

10   Dreams before daybreak cannot keep
Their essences, or surely I should rouse
Into a dáwn where all that's past seems sleep.

Numberless blades of grass
And only one thin blade
That is the moon.
          I have made
As many promises
5   As there are grasses frightened by the wind
In lonely fields, promises enough
Till eyes applauded, yet turned farther off,
Unsatisfied with words. In this I was blind.
Such promises have not proved durable:
10   Breath is as well spent praying to the moon.

Blade of the moon, drop down:
Harvest my spent grasses. Come to the fall.

'Draw close around you
Your courage and love,
Lest the winter find you
Helpless, lest you have
No coals nor kindling sticks 5
Built up against what time
The iron cloud breaks,
Winter attacks one room.'

Was I so scant of these
That, for a word of love 10
Said among lengthening days,
I have nothing to give?
Did winter so envenom
Its barren grappling
That love dare not assume 15
The racing approach of spring?

I have despatched so many words
Against the sun, that now, like homing birds
Each carrying its separate branch of pain,
Heavily they gather at my heart again.

Where was this silence learned,
Heart, whose one care it was
To wall each day up in words?
Wind does not rage the less
Over the hillside grass, 5
Nor are the common birds
Plumed with less delicate feather
Than when their least could rouse
You quickly to counterpart.
Can it be that, whether 10
Solicited or not,
The cold face never turned?

Ride with me down into the spring
For the long secret roots have woven
Everything into a ritual,
And you, whose face throughout the months has grown
5   To something nearly tangible,
Can mingle with it like a living thing.

All beauty that the winter bears
Was laid like shadows on your brow
That your gentleness should not be
10   Shamed by this meeting:
I would bring you to the ceremony.
Why do you stand so, letting fall these tears?

Safely evening behind the window
Falls, and the fresh trees have aroused,
Trees which at noonday stood amazed
At a loud bird breaking from a furrow,
5   Wheeling, falling, crying above its nest
So dark-earth-cradled; lost with its own shadow.

Yet your beauty, startled from my heart,
Went to no exile. This I had not loved
Till I had seen it laugh and be unmoved
10   At my praises – having no part in it.

Song with a Spoken Refrain

'Do not tie my love,
And yours shall go free,
When I am disfavoured,
Do not love me,
5   Above all else I hate
Love out of charity.'
And this was said in a confident voice.

'I love you well enough,
But being cold
10   I have no need of love –

And I am told
Love does distress the young
And plague the old.'
And this was said in a confident voice.

Happiness is a flame
Balanced upon the tip
Of the flight of moving days.
Where does its strength come?
It is drawn out of sleep,   5
From loyalty of friends,
Or out of drunkenness,
Dreams and long-spun pretence?
Is it a faith that burns?
Or is it no more than sense   10
Of outlays and returns,
Work of our many hands?

These compass, at the best,
As much as an idiot could,
Who, at the height of June,   15
Sets out to reach the sun,
Taking the first road
That promises the West.
Friends feel and speak disgust
When all else has felt and spoken;   20
Sleep gives more ground to death;
And can it be called faith,
Proud every bone is broken?
While years in that leprous bed,
Pillowed with fantasy, must   25
Lay sickness upon the mouth.

All these man loses, yet
The flame does not lose its height:
Bankrupt in front of death
Dreams, friends and sleep blow free,   30
Free generation's thread,
And all the rational joys
Fall broken-winged; and he
Who sought for the mystery

35   Finds at the finish this:
         'Happiness rests upon
         Devoutness of the blood,
         Rich oil of youth and strength
         Soon passes, and at length
40   Has nothing of what it would;
         Then, when its power is gone,
         It learns to fall and rise
         As the sun, as the sea of grass,
         As the ocean of whispering leaves,
45   Through numberless births and graves.'

Lie with me, though the night return outside.
Wind changes weathercocks: would it could change
Me to a bridegroom, you into a bride,
And this our world, painful and dull and strange,
5   Back to its innocence.
                 But now the rain
Falls steadily on young, half-ripened corn,
And we have missed our summer. Not again
Can love cast storms back in the teeth of storms.

When trees are quiet, there will be no more weeping,
But their distress is long; and when the wind
Dies out, all the now-wakeful will be sleeping:
Let that hour come, when silent clocks turn blind
5   The speculating stars, when the strings' quest
Strives to a halt, and all this pain makes end,
And all my thoughts an unpredicted rest.

The dead are lost, unravelled; but if a voice
Could shake them back, reshape each sunless bone
To cage a mind, and offer them a choice
Of painful walking on the earth again,
Or, once more, death – how their sad eagerness   5
Would beat against this life! Even that breath
They fought to catch an hour before their death
Would fire their lungs with too much happiness.

Cries in the street, the slam of a broken door,
Windows of fog, black wheeltracks in the snow –   10
All would enchant them. But what can the dead give?
Such knowledge has no words: it comes before
The second when life drops them, and they know
The golden quality of things that live.

Lift through the breaking day,
        Wind that pursues the dawn:
Under night's heedless stone
Houses and river lay –
        Now to the east they shine.   5

Climb the long summer hills
        Where the wide trees are spread,
Drown the cold-shadowed wood
With noise of waterfalls;
        And under chains of cloud   10

Fly on towards the sea:
        Sing there upon the beach
Till all's beyond death's reach,
And empty shells reply
        That all things flourish.   15

Past days of gales
When skies are colourless
The acorn falls,
Dies; so for this space
5 Autumn is motionless.

Because the sun
So hesitates in this decay,
I think we still could turn,
Speak to each other in a different way;
10 For ways of speaking die,

And yet the sun pardons our voices still,
And berries in the hedge
Through all the nights of rain have come to the full,
And death seems like long hills, a range
15 We ride each day towards, and never reach.

The cry I would hear
Is not in the wind,
Is not of birds,
Nor the dry sound
5 Sadness can strike
Off the fruitful air.
In a trap's teeth
What are the words
That break in a shriek,
10 That break against death?

Who whistled for the wind, that it should break
Gently, on this air?
On what ground was it gathered, where
For the carrying, for its own sake,
5 Is night so gifted?
              Mind never met
Image of death like this, and yet
(All winds crying for that unbroken field,
Day having lifted)
10 Black flowers burst out wherever the night has knelt.

Sky tumbles, the sea
    Exhausts its tides:
All that they bring
    Is a salt living.

Why do you think love
    Washes up diamonds?   5
What does a kiss put
    Into empty hands?

Would you wear a shell necklace,
    Sleep under a boat,   10
Wait winter after winter,
    Nothing but wait?

Sting in the shell
By a blade beaten
To milk-white excitement
Resign torment
And into a pattern   5
Come still, still.

Your ringing, rage
Up the stinging track,
Outraces my carried
Argument – that married   10
All faces back
Unsiring age.

A stick's-point, drawn
Down a pool's clear bed,
Conjures a sand-cloud
Boiling without sound,
And yet defined   5
Sharply as the desire your parts have sown.

There is no clearer speaking
Than a bird places on the light
This level evening.
The building of thick tongues
5   Is stilled, and I am called
To hesitate again towards the unbuilt
Mansions. Beyond the tenderest songs,
What proud undominating flock
Of graces chose this one unspelling beak?

THE MAYOR OF BRISTOL WAS DRINKING GIN,
HE OPENED HIS MOUTH AND THE FART ROLLED IN.

Beggars

The mangers are all chaff:
Wind claps about the fields
Frightening thin birds –
There is not corn enough;
5   The black cowl and the white cowl
        Never show us their faces.

Rats scuttle in the barn,
Sheep crowd beneath the hedge:
Soldiers are on the march
10   And the dogs off the chain;
        The black cowl and the white cowl
        Never show us their faces.

Though we beg for hours
Where the high-roads cross,
15   No living thing will pass:
All are within doors;
        The black cowl and the white cowl
        Never show us their faces.

I have loaded my soul
20   With a maledictus,
For beef and a big house
Would help it on to Hell –

The black cowl and the white cowl
Never show us their faces.

When the tide draws out
The wreck emerges;
A seabird drifts about,
And sometimes perches
There on the shapeless hull   5
To make unsettling cries –
Voice of a drowned soul in disguise,
Come nightly to lament like a grey gull.

All day the hull bisects
The waves that travel at the shore,   10
Until the eye accepts
Illusion that it moves once more:
Filled with the desperation of the dead
It seems to press
Out to the west, out towards loneliness –   15
Till I grow sickened, and must turn my head.

I had thought life would move,
Above the years incredibly take wing;
All by a sudden flight to prove
Slack folded hands bring everything,   20
Bring sails, that in the morning come to the full,
The wind transfiguring the endless waters
Out of all knowledge: but no minute stirs,
No day mounts up to follow the grey gull.

Blues Shouter

There ain't no music
East side of this city
That's mellow like mine is,
That's mellow like mine.

5   Wooden guitar, light cavern
Where the strings pound:
Hideout, haven,
Romping walk of sound.

Innocent beat
10   No one can imprison,
No one can rob or cheat,
Bully or argue down.

Honour the shaking
Chamber under a hand:
15   Untouchable, talking,
Coherent diamond,

Here making a heaven –
Hive of sound,
Of joy, driven
20   All wild and underground.

That girl is lame: look at my rough
Hands. Can there be skill enough
On earth to ease the bone back to its place?
Is human patience wise enough to trace
5   Wandering pain? And were I allowed to find
Grief's mainspring, could as sick a mind
Give comfort?
               Among such roots to intercede,
What flawless fingers I should need,
Hands I have not, hands I could only gain
10   By an apprenticeship so free from pain
All would have been made new. But at that spring,
She would not look to me for anything.

Voices round a light
Search through the cold,
From house to house
Carrying precious news
Of feet, that on this night   5
Leave prints of gold.

Hour by hour their breath
Dissolves against the frost
That they deny with singing;
A climbing ladder of song   10
From barns of death
Against the ungentle stars is gently lost.

New hands hold up the light
They are so certain of,
That lays their faith   15
On darkness like a wreath,
A crowning. Voices that melt the night,
Unfearing voices, can you have strength enough?

Laforgue

You stuck words into us like pins: the great Papa,
Childless with weeping, went on making money;
But the animals were friendly, etc. etc. crip
cropper, crup crup, CRAP CRAP CRAP.

And did you once see Russell plain?
And did he start at Condon's nod,
Ten choruses of 'Da-da Strain'?
        You lucky fucking sod!

From this day forward, may you find
All things more easy and more kind:
May happiness invade each day
And all contentment come to stay.
5   Remember, by this almanac,
You started giving long ago
Your unconsidered goodness: so
May the world now pay you back.

Coming at last to night's most thankful springs,
I meet a runner's image, sharply kept
Ambered in memory from mythology;
A man who never turned aside and slept,
5   Nor put on masks of love; to whom all things
Were shadowlike against the news he bore,
Pale as the sky: one who for certainty
Had not my hesitations, lest he see
The loud and precious scroll of sounding shields
10   Not worth the carrying, when held before
The full moon travelling through her shepherdless fields.

Deep Analysis

I am a woman lying on a leaf;
    Leaf is silver, my flesh is golden,
Comely at all points, but I became your grief
    When you would not listen.

5   Through your one youth, whatever you pursued
      So singly, that I would be,
Desiring to kiss your arms and your straight side
      – Why would you not let me?

Why would you never relax, except for sleep,
10   Face turned at the wall,
Denying the downlands, wheat, and the white sheep?
      And why was all

Your body sharpened against me, vigilant,
      Watchful, when all I meant

Was to make it bright, that it might stand 15
    Burnished before my tent?

I could not follow your wishes, but I know
    If they assuaged you
It would not be crying in this dark, your sorrow,
    It would not be crying, so 20

That my own heart drifts and cries, having no death
    Because of the darkness,
Having only your grief under my mouth
    Because of the darkness.

Come then to prayers
And kneel upon the stone,
For we have tried
All courages on these despairs,
And are required lastly to give up pride, 5
And the last difficult pride in being humble.

Draw down the window-frame
That we may be unparted from the darkness,
Inviting to this house
Air from a field, air from a salt grave, 10
That questions if we have
Concealed no flaw in this confessional,
And, being satisfied,
Lingers, and troubles, and is lightless,
And so grows darker, as if clapped on a flame, 15
Whose great extinguishing still makes it tremble.

Only our hearts go beating towards the east.
Out of this darkness, let the unmeasured sword
Rising from sleep to execute or crown
Rest on our shoulders, as we then can rest 20
On the outdistancing, all-capable flood
Whose brim touches the morning. Down
The long shadows where undriven the dawn
Hunts light into nobility, arouse us noble.

And the wave sings because it is moving;
Caught in its clear side, we also sing.

We are borne across graves, together, apart, together,
In the lifting wall imprisoned and protected,
5   And so devised to make ourselves unhappy.
Apart, we think we wish ourselves together,
Yet sue for solitude upon our meetings,
Till the unhindered turning of the sea
Changes our comforts into griefs greater
10   Than they were raised to cancel, breaking them.

Such are the sorrows that we search for meaning,
Such are the cries of birds across the waters,
Such are the mists the sun attacks at morning,
Laments, tears, wreaths, rocks, all ridden down
15   By the shout of the heart continually at work
To break with beating all our false devices;
Silver-tongued like a share it ploughs up failure,
Carries the night and day, fetches
Profit from sleep, from skies, driven or star-slung,
20   From all but death takes tithes,
Finds marrow in all but death to feed
And frame to us, but death it cannot invoke.

Death is a cloud alone in the sky with the sun.
Our hearts, turning like fish in the green wave,
25   Grow quiet in its shadow. For in the word death
There is nothing to grasp; nothing to catch or claim;
Nothing to adapt the skill of the heart to, skill
In surviving, for death it cannot survive,
Only resign the irrecoverable keys.
30   The wave falters and drowns. The coulter of joy
Breaks. The harrow of death
Deepens. And there are thrown up waves.

And the waves sing because they are moving.
And the waves sing above a cemetery of waters.

Two Guitar Pieces

I

The tin-roofed shack by the railroad
Casts a shadow. Wheatstraws in the white dust
And a wagon standing. Stretched out into the sun
A dozen legs are idle in dungarees,
Dark hands and heads shaded from sun and working.   5
One frowns above a guitar: the notes, random
From tuning, wander into the heat
Like a new insect chirping in the scrub,
Untired at noon. A chord gathers and spills,
And a southern voice tails out around one note   10
Contentedly discontent.
                    Though the tracks
Burn to steel cities, they are taking
No one from these parts. Anyone could tell
Not even the wagon aims to go anywhere.

II

I roll a cigarette, and light
A spill at the stove. With a lungful of smoke
I join you at the window that has no curtain;
There we lean on the frame, and look
Below at the platz. A man is walking along   5
A path between the wreckage. And we stare at the dusk,
Sharing the cigarette.
                    Behind us, our friend
Yawns, and collects the cards. The pack is short,
And dealing from now till morning would not bring
The highest hands. Besides, it's too dark to see.   10
So he kicks the stove, and lifts the guitar to his lap,
Strikes this note, that note.
                    I am trembling:
I am suddenly charged with their language, these six strings,
Suddenly made to see they can declare
Nothing but harmony, and may not move   15
Without a happy stirring of the air
That builds within this room a second room;
And the accustomed harnessing of grief

259

Tightens, because together or alone
20 We cannot trace that room; and then again
Because it is not a room, nor a world, but only
A figure spun on stirring of the air,
And so, untrue.
                            And so, I watch the square,
Empty again, like hunger after a meal.
25 You offer the cigarette and I say, Keep it,
Liking to see the glimmer come and go
Upon your face. What poor hands we hold,
When we face each other honestly! And now the guitar again,
Spreading me over the evening like a cloud,
30 Drifting, darkening: unable to bring rain.

Träumerei

In this dream that dogs me I am part
Of a silent crowd walking under a wall,
Leaving a football match, perhaps, or a pit,
All moving the same way. After a while
5 A second wall closes on our right,
Pressing us tighter. We are now shut in
Like pigs down a concrete passage. When I lift
My head, I see the walls have killed the sun,
And light is cold. Now a giant whitewashed D
10 Comes on the second wall, but much too high
For them to recognise: I await the E,
Watch it approach and pass. By now
We have ceased walking and travel
Like water through sewers, steeply, despite
15 The tread that goes on ringing like an anvil
Under the striding A. I crook
My arm to shield my face, for we must pass
Beneath the huge, decapitated cross,
White on the wall, the T, and I cannot halt
20 The tread, the beat of it, it is my own heart,
The walls of my room rise, it is still night,
I have woken again before the word was spelt.

To a Very Slow Air

The golden sheep are feeding, and
Their mouths harbour contentment;
Gladly my tongue praises
This hour scourged of dissension
By weight of their joyous fleeces.   5

The cloven hills are kneeling,
The sun such an anointment
Upon the forehead, on the hands and feet,
That all air is appointed
Our candid clothing, our elapsing state.   10

At the chiming of light upon sleep
A picture relapsed into the deep
Tarn, the hardly-stirring spring
Where memory changes to prefiguring.
Was it myself walking across that grass?   5
Was it myself, in a rank Michaelmas,
Closed among laurels? It was a green world,
Unchanging holly with the curled
Points, cypress and conifers,
All that through the winter bears   10
Coarsened fertility against the frost.
Nothing in such a sanctuary could be lost.
And yet, there were no flowers.
                          Morning, and more
Than morning, crosses the floor.
Have I been wrong, to think the breath   15
That sharpens life is life itself, not death?
Never to see, if death were killed,
No desperation, perpetually unfulfilled,
Would ever go fracturing down in ecstasy?
Death quarrels, and shakes the tree,   20
And fears are flowers, and flowers are generation,
And the founding, foundering, beast-instructed mansion
Of love called into being by this same death
Hangs everywhere its light. Unsheath
The life you carry and die, cries the cock   25

261

On the crest of the sun: unlock
The words and seeds that drove
Adam out of his undeciduous grove.

Many famous feet have trod
Sublunary paths, and famous hands have weighed
The strength they have against the strength they need;
And famous lips interrogated God
5   Concerning franchise in eternity;
And in many differing times and places
Truth was attained (a moment's harmony);
Yet endless mornings break on endless faces:

Gold surf of the sun, each day
10   Exhausted through the world, gathers and whips
Irrevocably from eclipse;
The trodden way becomes the untrodden way,
We are born each morning, shelled upon
A sheet of light that paves
15   The palaces of sight, and brings again
The river shining through the field of graves.

Such renewal argues down
Our unsuccessful legacies of thought,
Annals of men who fought
20   Untiringly to change their hearts to stone,
Or to a wafer's poverty,
Or to a flower, but never tried to learn
The difficult triple sanity
Of being wafer, stone, and flower in turn.

25   Turn out your pockets on the tablecloth:
Consider what we know. A silver piece:
That's life; and, dealing in dichotomies,
This old discoloured copper coin is death.
Turn it about: it is impenetrable.
30   Reverse and obverse, neither bear
A sign or word remotely legible:
But spin the silver to a sphere,

Look in, and testify. Our mortal state
In turn is twisted in a double warp:
35   The light is waking and the dark is sleep,

And twice a day before their gate
We kneel between them. There is more
Knowledge of sleep than death, and yet
Who knows the nature of our casting there,
Trawled inaccessible pool, or set   40

A line to haul its logic into speech?
Easier to balance on the hand
The waking that our senses can command,
For jewels are pebbles on a beach
Before this weaving, scattering, winged-and-footed   45
Privilege, this first, untold
And unrecurring luck that is never completed
Even in distance out of our hands' hold,

That makes, this waking traffic, this one last,
One paramount division. I declare   50
Two lineages electrify the air,
That will like pennons from a mast
Fly over sleep and life and death
Till sun is powerless to decoy
A single seed above the earth: 55
Lineage of sorrow: lineage of joy;

No longer think them aspects of the same;
Beyond each figured shield I trace
A different ancestry, a different face,
And sorrow must be held to blame   60
Because I follow it to my own heart
To find it feeding there on all that's bad:
It is sanctionable and right
Always to be ashamed of being sad.

Ashamed that sorrow's beckoned in   65
By each foiled weakness in the almanac
Engendered by the instinct-to-turn-back
– Which, if there are sins, should be called a sin –
Instinct that so worships my own face
It would halt time herewith   70
And put my wishes in its place:
And for this reason has great fear of death.

Because tides wound it;
The scuttling sand; the noose

75   Of what I have and shall lose,
        Or have not and cannot get;
        Partings in time or space
        Wound it; it weeps sorely;
        Holds sorrow before its face,
80   And all to pretend it is not part of me,

        The blind part. I know what it will not know:
        All stopping-up of cracks
        Against dissolution builds a house of wax,
        While years in wingspans go
85   Across and over our heads. Watch them:
        They are flying east. They are flying to the ebb
        Of dark. They are making sorrow seem
        A spider busy on a forgotten web.

        They are calling every fibre of the world
90   Into rejoicing, a mile-long silken cloth
        Of wings moving lightwards out of death:
        Lineage of joy into mortality hurled,
        Endowing every actual bone
        With motionless excitement. If quick feet
95   Must tread sublunary paths, attest this one:
        Perpetual study to defeat

        Each slovenly grief; the patience to expose
        Untrue desire; assurance that, in sum,
        Nothing's to reach, but something's to become,
100   That must be pitched upon the luminous,
        Denying rest. Joy has no cause:
        Though cut to pieces with a knife,
        Cannot keep silence. What else should magnetize
        Our drudging, hypocritical, ecstatic life?

Thaw

        Tiny immortal streams are on the move:
        The sun its hand uncloses like a statue,
        Distantly: thereby such light is freed
        That all the dingy hospital of snow
5   Dies back to ditches. Chalkbeds of heaven bear
        These nameless tributaries, but they run

To earth. For here their pouring river reigns;
Here, busy with resurrection, sovereign waters
Confer among the roots, causing to fall
From memory forestfuls of six-days' grief.   10

How easily they fall, how easily I let drift
On the surface of morning feathers of self-reproach:
How easily I forget the scolding of snow.

An April Sunday brings the snow,
Making the blossom on the plum trees green,
Not white. An hour or two, and it will go.
Strange that I spend that hour moving between

Cupboard and cupboard, shifting the store   5
Of jam you made of fruit from these same trees:
Five loads – a hundred pounds or more –
More than enough for all next summer's teas,

Which now you will not sit and eat.
Behind the glass, under the cellophane,   10
Remains your final summer – sweet
And meaningless, and not to come again.

And yet – but after death there's no 'and yet'.
Now we have seen you die; and had you burned,
I cannot aphorise 'what I have learned'
As neatly as I sort your desk, and set
The calendar for days you will not see.   5

'Death doesn't do you harm,' you chanced to say
One morning on the lawn, and straightaway
Fear, young and furtive, took its roots in me
Which in these empty days now comes of age.
And yet – because in life there is 'and yet' –   10
What can I hope, except that you were right?

I am washed upon a rock
In an endless girding sea.
The sun is figured like a clock;
It turns and hangs at me.

5 My heart is ticking like the sun:
A lonely cloud drifts in the sky.
I dread its indecision.
If once it block the light, I die.

If I could make a single wish,
10 A bird might hover on the wing,
Within its beak a living fish,
And in the fish a wedding ring;

And when the ring was on my hand
The water would go down, and shrink
15 To harmless mirrors on the sand.
But to wish is first to think,

And to think is to be dumb,
And barren of a word to drop
That to a milder shore might come
20 And, years ahead, erect a crop.

Neurotics

No one gives you a thought, as day by day
You drag your feet, clay-thick with misery.
None think how stalemate in you grinds away,
Holding your spinning wheels an inch too high
5 To bite on earth. The mind, it's said, is free:
But not your minds. They, rusted stiff, admit
Only what will accuse or horrify,
Like slot-machines only bent pennies fit.

So year by year your tense unfinished faces
10 Sink further from the light. No one pretends
To want to help you now. For interest passes
Always towards the young and more insistent,
And skirts locked rooms where a hired darkness ends
Your long defence against the non-existent.

On Being Twenty-six

I feared these present years,
    The middle twenties,
When deftness disappears,
And each event is
Freighted with a source-encrusting doubt,
    And turned to drought.   5

I thought: this pristine drive
    Is sure to flag
At twenty-four or -five;
And now the slag
Of burnt-out childhood proves that I was right.   10
    What caught alight

Quickly consumed in me,
    As I foresaw.
Talent, felicity –
These things withdraw,   15
And are succeeded by a dingier crop
    That come to stop;

Or else, certainty gone,
    Perhaps the rest,   20
Tarnishing, linger on
As second-best.
Fabric of fallen minarets is trash.
    And in the ash

Of what has pleased and passed   25
    Is now no more
Than struts of greed, a last
Charred smile, a clawed
Crustacean hatred, blackened pride – of such
    I once made much.   30

And so, if I were sure
    I have no chance
To catch again that pure
Unnoticed stance,

35   I would calcine the outworn properties,
        Live on what is.

But it dies hard, that world;
        Or, being dead,
Putrescently is pearled,
40   For I, misled,
Make on my mind the deepest wound of all:
        Think to recall

At any moment, states
        Long since dispersed;
45   That if chance dissipates
The best, the worst
May scatter equally upon a touch.
        I kiss, I clutch,

Like a daft mother, putrid
50   Infancy,
That can and will forbid
All grist to me
Except devaluing dichotomies:
        Nothing, and paradise.

Sinking like sediment through the day
To leave it clearer, onto the floor of the flask
(Vast summer vessel) settles a bitter carpet –
        Horror of life.

5   Huge awareness, elbowing vacancy,
Empty inside and out, replaces day.
(Like a fuse an impulse busily disintegrates
        Right back to its root.)

Out of the afternoon leans the indescribable woman:
10   'Embrace me, and I shall be beautiful' –
'Be beautiful, and I will embrace you' –
        We argue for hours.

In our family
Love was disgusting as lavatory.
And not as necessary.

To Failure

You do not come dramatically, with dragons
That rear up with my life between their paws
And dash me butchered down beside the wagons,
The horses panicking; nor as a clause
Clearly set out to warn what can be lost,   5
What out-of-pocket charges must be borne,
Expenses met; nor as a draughty ghost
That's seen, some mornings, running down a lawn.

It is these sunless afternoons, I find,
Instal you at my elbow like a bore.   10
The chestnut trees are caked with silence. I'm
Aware the days pass quicker than before,
Smell staler too. And once they fall behind
They look like ruin. (You have been here some time.)

Epigram on an Academic Marriage

You see that man? He has a month-old wife
He married from emotional cupidity,
Hoping she'd 'put him into touch with Life' –
Now finds all she's in touch with is stupidity.

My Home

Uninteresting land, it must have been,
        A city field –
Coarse bunches of unbitten grass, a lane,
Hedges and paper bags. But it *was* green,
        And now all is concealed   5

By lumpy unadopted avenues,
        By clay-filled scars,
Soft creosoted wood, vases, veneers,
Red and black gates (in front of which the Jews
        Polish their post-war cars) . . .   10

Compline

Behind the radio's altarlight
The hurried talk to God goes on:
Thy Kingdom come, Thy Will be done,
Produce our lives beyond this night,
5   *Open our eyes again to sun.*

Unhindered in the dingy wards
Lives flicker out, one here, one there,
To send some weeping down the stair
With love unused, in unsaid words:
10   For this I would have quenched the prayer,

But for the thought that nature spawns
A million eggs to make one fish.
Better that endless rites beseech
As many nights, as many dawns,
15   If finally God grants one wish.

How to Sleep

Child in the womb,
Or saint on a tomb –
Which way shall I lie
To fall asleep?
5   The keen moon stares
From the back of the sky,
The clouds are all home
Like driven sheep.

Bright drops of time,
10   One and two chime,
I turn and lie straight
With folded hands;
Convent-child, Pope,
They choose this state,
15   And their minds are wiped calm
As sea-levelled sands.

So my thoughts are:
But sleep stays as far,

Till I crouch on one side
Like a foetus again –
For sleeping, like death, 20
Must be won without pride,
With a nod from nature,
With a lack of strain,
And a loss of stature. 25

The Literary World

I

'Finally, after five months of my life during which I could write nothing that
would have satisfied me, and for which no power will compensate me . . .'

My dear Kafka,
When you've had five years of it, not five months,
Five years of an irresistible force meeting an
      immoveable object right in your belly,
Then you'll know about depression. 5

II

Mrs Alfred Tennyson
Answered
    begging letters
    admiring letters
    insulting letters
    enquiring letters 5
    business letters
    and publishers' letters.
She also
    looked after his clothes
    saw to his food and drink 10
    entertained visitors
    protected him from gossip and criticism
And finally
    (apart from running the household) 15
    Brought up and educated the children.

While all this was going on
Mister Alfred Tennyson sat like a baby
Doing his poetic business.

Strangers

The eyes of strangers
Are cold as snowdrops,
Downcast, folded,
And seldom visited.

5   And strangers' acts
Cry but vaguely, drift
Across our attention's
Smoke-sieged afternoons.

And to live there, among strangers,
10   Calls for teashop behaviours:
Setting down the cup,
Leaving the right tip,

Keeping the soul unjostled,
The pocket unpicked,
15   The fancies lurid,
And the treasure buried.

Under a splendid chestnut tree
The rector clenched his fists
And swore that God exists,
Clamping his features stiff with certainty.
5   Twenty-five steps to the pond and ten to the hedge,
And his resolution had wilted round the edge,
Leaving him tilting a blind face to the sky,
Asking to die:
'To die, dear God, before a scum of doubt
10   Smear the whole universe and smudge it out.'
Meanwhile the bees fumbled among the flowers,
The gardener smoked, the children poked about,
The cat lay on the baker's roof for hours.

Just then (but miles away) there knelt
15   A corpse-faced undergrad
Convinced that he was bad:
His soul was just a sink of filth, he felt.
Hare's eyes, staring across his prayer-locked hands,
Saw, not a washstand-set, but mammary glands;

All boyhood's treasure-trove, a *hortus siccus*   20
      Of tits and knickers,
Baited his unused sex like tsetse flies,
Till, maddened, it charged out without disguise
And made the headlines. But the Gothic view
Was pricked with lamps and boys' street-distant cries,   25
Where chestnut-burrs dropped, bounced, and split in two.

      Thus at the end of Shady Lane
      A spinster eyed a fir
      That meant to fall on her.
      Watching it crouch and straighten and crouch again,   30
Her bright and childless eyes screwed up with dread.
And in the north a workman hugged his bed,
Hating the clouds, the stained unsightly breath
      Of carious death.
Down centuries of streets they sit and listen   35
Where children chalk out games and gas lights glisten,
Taking both voices in old arguments,
One plate, one cup laid in the same position
For the departed lodger, innocence.

Westminster's crown has gained a special jewel –
A fat, deceitful, vulgar, Irish fool:
'The heart of Churchill & the wit of Wilde?' –
Teevan touched pitch: the latter was defiled.

Teevan touched pitch: the pitch was very wild.
You can't touch Teevan & be undefiled.

The Spirit Wooed

Once I believed in you,
      And then you came,
      Unquestionably new, as fame
Had said you were. But that was long ago.

You launched no argument,   5
      Yet I obeyed,

Straightway, the instrument you played
Distant down sidestreets, keeping different time.

And never questioned what
     You fascinate
     In me; if good or not, the state
You pressed towards. There was no need to know.

Grave pristine absolutes
     Walked in my mind:
     So that I was not mute, or blind,
As years before or since. My only crime

Was holding you too dear.
     Was that the cause
     You daily came less near – a pause
Longer than life, if you decide it so?

To My Wife

Choice of you shuts up that peacock-fan
The future was, in which temptingly spread
All that elaborative nature can.
Matchless potential! but unlimited
Only so long as I elected nothing;
Simply to choose stopped all ways up but one,
And sent the tease-birds from the bushes flapping.
No future now. I and you now, alone.

So for your face I have exchanged all faces,
For your few properties bargained the brisk
Baggage, the mask-and-magic-man's regalia.
Now you become my boredom and my failure,
Another way of suffering, a risk,
A heavier-than-air hypostasis.

The Dedicated

Some must employ the scythe
Upon the grasses,
That the walks be smooth
For the feet of the angel.
Some keep in repair   5
The locks, that the visitor
Unhindered passes
To the innermost chamber.

Some have for endeavour
To sign away life   10
As lover to lover,
Or a bird using its wings
To fly to the fowler's compass,
Not out of willingness,
But being aware of   15
Eternal requirings.

And if they have leave
To pray, it is for contentment
If the feet of the dove
Perch on the scythe's handle,   20
Perch once, and then depart
Their knowledge. After, they wait
Only the colder advent,
The quenching of candles.

Oils

Sun. Tree. Beginning. God in a thicket. Crown.
Never-abdicating constellation. Blood.
Barn-clutch of life. Trigger of the future.
Magic weed the doctor shakes in the dance.
Many rains and many rivers, making one river.   5
Password. Installation. Root of tongues.

Working-place to which the small seed is guided,
Inlet unvisited by marine biologist,
Entire alternative in man and woman

10 Opening at a touch like a water-flower,
New voice saying new words at a new speed
From which the future erupts like struck oil,

No one can migrate across your boundaries.
No one can exist without a habit for you.
15 No one can tear your thread out of himself.
No one can tie you down or set you free.
Apart from your tribe, there is only the dead,
And even them you grip and begin to use.

Who called love conquering,
When its sweet flower
So easily dries among the sour
Lanes of the living?

5 Flowerless demonstrative weeds
Selfishly spread,
The white bride drowns in her bed
And tiny curled greeds

Grapple the sun down
10 By three o'clock,
When the dire cloak of dark
Stiffens the town.

Arrival

Morning, a glass door, flashes
Gold names off the new city,
Whose white shelves and domes travel
The slow sky all day.
5 I land to stay here;
And the windows flock open
And the curtains fly out like doves
And the past dries in a wind.

Now let me lie down, under
10 A wide-branched indifference,
Shovel faces like pennies
Down the back of mind,
Find voices coined to

An argot of motor-horns,
And let the cluttered-up houses   15
Keep their thick lives to themselves.

For this ignorance of me
Seems a kind of innocence.
Fast enough I shall wound it:
Let me breathe till then   20
Its milk-aired Eden,
Till my own life impound it –
Slow-falling; grey-veil-hung; a theft,
A style of dying only.

Since the majority of me
Rejects the majority of you,
Debating ends forthwith, and we
Divide. And sure of what to do

We disinfect new blocks of days   5
For our majorities to rent
With unshared friends and unwalked ways.
But silence too is eloquent:

A silence of minorities
That, unopposed at last, return   10
Each night with cancelled promises
They want renewed. They never learn.

March Past

The march interrupted the light afternoon.
Cars stopped dead, children began to run,
As out of the street-shadow into the sun

Discipline strode, music bullying aside
The credulous, prettily-coloured crowd,   5
Evoking an over-confident, over-loud

Holiday where the flags lisped and beckoned,
And all was focused, larger than we reckoned,
Into a consequence of thirty seconds.

10   The stamp and dash of surface sound cut short
Memory, intention, thought;
The vague heart sharpened to a candid court

Where exercised a sudden flock of visions:
Pure meetings, pure separations,
15   Honeycombs of heroic apparitions,

Until the crowd closed in behind.
Then music drooped. And what came back to mind
Was not its previous habit, but a blind

Astonishing remorse for things now ended
20   That of themselves were also rich and splendid
But, unsupported, broke, and were not mended –

Astonishing, for such things should be deep,
Rarely exhumable, not in a sleep
So light they can awake and occupy
25   An absent mind when any march goes by.

Marriages

When those of us who seem
Immodestly-accurate
Transcriptions of a dream
Are tired of singleness,
5   Their confidence will mate
Only with confidence –
With an equal candescence,
With a pregnant selfishness.

Not so with the remainder:
10   Frogmarched by old need
They chaffer for a partner –
Some undesirable,
With whom it is agreed
That words such as liberty,
15   Impulse, or beauty
Shall be unmentionable

Scarecrows of chivalry
They strike strange bargains –
Adder-faced singularity

Espouses a nailed-up childhood,
Skin-disease pardons
Soft horror of living,
A gabble is forgiven
By chronic solitude.

So are they gathered in;   25
So they are not wasted,
As they would have been
By intelligent rancour,
An integrity of self-hatred.
Whether they forget   30
What they wanted first or not
They tarnish at quiet anchor.

To put one brick upon another,
Add a third, and then a fourth,
Leaves no time to wonder whether
What you do has any worth.

But to sit with bricks around you   5
While the winds of heaven bawl
Weighing what you should or can do
Leaves no doubt of it at all.

Maturity

A *stationary* sense . . . as, I suppose,
I shall have, till my single body grows
    Inaccurate, tired;
Then I shall start to feel the backward pull
Take over, sickening and masterful –   5
    Some say, desired.

And this must be *the prime of life* . . . I blink,
As if at pain; for it is pain, to think
    This pantomime
Of compensating act and counter-act,   10
Defeat and counterfeit, makes up, in fact,
    My ablest time.

You think yourself no end of fun
Going out with anyone;
Drinks & smokes & late nights too –
It makes us wonder WHAT ELSE YOU DO!!!

Somewhere on the Isle of Mull
Dreiser is talking to a gull
Trying to sell the gull a nest –
Why should that bird look depressed?

When she came on, you couldn't keep your seat;
Fighting your way up through the orchestra,
Tup-heavy bumpkin, you confused your feet,
Fell in the drum – how we went ha ha ha!
5   But once you gained her side and started waltzing
We all began to cheer; the way she leant
Her cheek on yours and laughed was so exalting
We thought you stooging for the management.

But no. What you did, any of us might.
10   And saying so I see our difference:
Not your aplomb (I used mine to sit tight),
But *fancying you improve her*. Where's the sense
In saying love, but meaning interference?
You'll only *change* her. Still, I'm sure you're right.

At thirty-one, when some are rich
And others dead,
I, being neither, have a job instead,
But come each evening back to a high room
5   Above deep gardenfuls of air, on which
Already has been laid an autumn bloom.

And here, instead of planning how
I can best thrive,
How best win fame and money while alive,
10   I sit down, supper over, and begin
One of the letters of a kind I now
Feel most of my spare time is going in:

I mean, letters to women – no,
Not of the sort
The papers tell us get read out in court,   15
Leading directly to or from the bed.
Love-letters only in a sense: they owe
Too much elsewhere to come under that head.

Too much to kindness, for a start;
I know, none better,   20
The eyelessness of days without a letter;
Too much to habit ('Stop? But why on earth . . .?');
Too much to an unwillingness to part
With people wise enough to see my worth.

I'm kind, but not kinetic – don't   25
Enlist a word
Simply because its deed has been deferred;
Ends in themselves, my letters plot no change;
They carry nothing dutiable; they won't
Aspire, astound, establish or estrange.   30

Why write them, then? Are they in fact
Just compromise,
Amiable residue when each denies
The other's want? Or are they not so nice,
Stand-ins in each case simply for an act?   35
Mushrooms of virtue? or, toadstools of vice?

They taste the same. So summer ends,
And nights draw in.
Another evening wasted! I begin
Writing the envelope, and a bitter smoke   40
Of self-contempt, of boredom too, ascends.
What use is an endearment and a joke?

Mother, Summer, I

My mother, who hates thunderstorms,
Holds up each summer day and shakes
It out suspiciously, lest swarms
Of grape-dark clouds are lurking there;
5 But when the August weather breaks
And rains begin, and brittle frost
Sharpens the bird-abandoned air,
Her worried summer look is lost.

And I her son, though summer-born
10 And summer-loving, none the less
Am easier when the leaves are gone;
Too often summer days appear
Emblems of perfect happiness
I can't confront: I must await
15 A time less bold, less rich, less clear:
An autumn more appropriate.

Autumn

The air deals blows: surely too hard, too often?
No: it is bent on bringing summer down.
Dead leaves desert in thousands, outwards, upwards,
Numerous as birds; but the birds fly away,

5 And the blows sound on, like distant collapsing water,
Or empty hospitals falling room by room
Down in the west, perhaps, where the angry light is.
Then rain starts; the year grows suddenly slack.

O rain, o frost, so much has still to be cleared:
10 All this ripeness, all this reproachful flesh,
And summer, that keeps returning like a ghost
Of something death has merely made beautiful,

And night skies so brilliantly spread-eagled
With their sharp hint of a journey – all must disperse
15 Before the season is lost and anonymous,
Like a London court one is never sure of finding

But none the less exists, at the back of the fog,
Bare earth, a lamp, scrapers. Then it will be time
To seek there that ill-favoured, curious house,
Bar up the door, mantle the fat flame,   20

And sit once more alone with sprawling papers,
Bitten-up letters, boxes of photographs,
And the case of butterflies so rich it looks
As if all summer settled there and died.

Best Society

When I was a child, I thought,
Casually, that solitude
Never needed to be sought.
Something everybody had,
Like nakedness, it lay at hand,   5
Not specially right or specially wrong,
A plentiful and obvious thing
Not at all hard to understand.

Then, after twenty, it became
At once more difficult to get   10
And more desired – though all the same
More undesirable; for what
You are alone has, to achieve
The rank of fact, to be expressed
In terms of others, or it's just   15
A compensating make-believe.

Much better stay in company!
To love you must have someone else,
Giving requires a legatee,
Good neighbours need whole parishfuls   20
Of folk to do it on – in short,
Our virtues are all social; if,
Deprived of solitude, you chafe,
It's clear you're not the virtuous sort.

Viciously, then, I lock my door.   25
The gas-fire breathes. The wind outside
Ushers in evening rain. Once more
Uncontradicting solitude

Supports me on its giant palm;
30 And like a sea-anemone
Or simple snail, there cautiously
Unfolds, emerges, what I am.

Unfinished Poem

I squeezed up the last stair to the room in the roof
And lay on the bed there with my jacket off.
Seeds of light were sown on the failure of evening.
The dew came down. I lay in the quiet, smoking.

5 That was a way to live – newspaper for sheets,
A candle and spirit stove, and a trouble of shouts
From below somewhere, a town smudgy with traffic!
That was a place to go, that emaciate attic!

For (as you will guess) it was death I had I mind,
10 Who covets our breath, who seeks and will always find;
To keep out of his thought was my whole care,
Yet down among sunlit courts, yes, he was there,

Taking his rents; yes, I had only to look
To see the shape of his head and the shine of his book,
15 And the creep of the world under his sparrow-trap sky,
To know how little slips his immortal memory.

So it was stale time then, day in, day out,
Blue fug in the room, nothing to do but wait
The start of his feet on the stair, that sad sound
20 Climbing to cut me from his restless mind

With a sign that the air should stick in my nose like bread,
The light swell up and turn black – so I shammed dead,
Still as a stuck pig, hoping he'd keep concerned
With boys who were making the fig when his back was turned;

25 And the sun and the stove and the mice and the gnawed paper
Made up the days and nights when I missed supper,
Paring my nails, looking over the farbelow street
Of tramways and bells. But one night I heard the feet.

Step after step they mounted with confidence.
30 Time shrank. They paused at the top. There was no defence.

I sprawled to my knees. Now they came straight at my door.
This, then, the famous eclipse? The crack in the floor

Widening for one long plunge? In a sharp trice,
The world, lifted and wrung, dripped with remorse.
The fact of breathing tightened into a shroud.   35
Light cringed. The door swung inwards. Over the threshold

Nothing like death stepped, nothing like death paused,
Nothing like death has such hair, arms so raised.
Why are your feet bare? Was not death to come?
Why is he not here? What summer have you broken from?   40

Hospital Visits

At length to hospital
This man was limited,
Where screens leant on the wall
And idle headphones hung.
Since he would soon be dead   5
They let his wife come along
And pour out tea, each day.

I don't know what was said;
Just hospital-talk,
As the bed was a hospital bed.   10
Then one day she fell
Outside on the sad walk
And her wrist broke – curable
At Outpatients, naturally.

Thereafter night and day   15
She came both for the sight
Of his slowing-down body
And for her own attending,
And there by day and night
With her blithe bone mending   20
Watched him in decay.

Winter had nearly ended
When he died (the screen was for that).
To make sure her wrist mended
They had her in again   25

To finish a raffia mat –
This meant (since it was begun
Weeks back) he died again as she came away.

Autobiography at an Air-Station

Delay, well, travellers must expect
Delay. For how long? No one seems to know.
With all the luggage weighed, the tickets checked,
It can't be *long* . . . We amble to and fro,
5   Sit in steel chairs, buy cigarettes and sweets
And tea, unfold the papers. Ought we to smile,
Perhaps make friends? No: in the race for seats
You're best alone. Friendship is not worth while.

Six hours pass: if I'd gone by boat last night
10 I'd be there now. Well, it's too late for that.
The kiosk girl is yawning. I feel staled,
Stupefied, by inaction – and, as light
Begins to ebb outside, by fear; I set
So much on this Assumption. Now it's failed.

Negative Indicative

Never to walk from the station's lamps and laurels
Carrying my father's lean old leather case
Crumbling like the register at the hotel;
Never to be shown upstairs.

5   To a plain room smelling of soap, a towel
Neatly hung on the back of a rush chair,
The floor uneven, the grate choked with a frill,
Muslin curtains hiding the market square;

Never to visit the lame girl who lives three doors
10 Down Meeting-House Lane – 'This pile is ready; these
I shall finish tonight, with luck' – to watch, as she pours
Tea from a gold-lined jubilee pot, her eyes,

Her intelligent face; never, walking away
As light fails, to notice the first star

Pulsing alone in a long shell-coloured sky,
And remember the year has turned, and feel the air

Alive with the emblematic sound of water –

Love

Not love you? Dear, I'd pay ten quid for you:
Five down, and five when I got rid of you.

Marriage

'My wife and I – we're pals. Marriage is fun.'
Yes: two can live as stupidly as one.

Midwinter Waking

Paws there. Snout there as well. Mustiness. Mould.
Darkness; a desire to stretch, to scratch.
Then has the – ? Then is it – ? Nudge the thatch,
Displace the stiffened leaves: look out. How cold,
How dried a stillness. Like a blade on stone,
A wind is scraping, first this way, then that.
Morning, perhaps; but not a proper one.
Turn. Sleep will unshell us, but not yet.

Those who give all for love, or art, or duty,
Mustn't complain when the return is small;
Stop, now; be honest: doesn't the chief beauty
Really consist in getting rid of all?

Gathering Wood

On short, still days
    At the shut of the year
We search the pathways
    Where the coverts were.

5   For kindling-wood we come,
    And make up bundles,
Carrying them home
    Down long low tunnels.

Soon air-frosts haze
10   Snow-thickened shires;
O short, still days!
    O burrow fires!

Long roots moor summer to our side of earth.
I wake: already taller than the green
River-fresh castles of unresting leaf
Where loud birds dash,
5   It unfolds upward a long breadth, a shine

Wherein all seeds and clouds and winged things
Employ the many-levelled acreage.
Absence with absence makes a travelling angle,
And pressure of the sun
10   In silence sleeps like equiloaded scales.

Where can I turn except away, knowing
Myself outdistanced, out-invented? what
Reply can the vast flowering strike from us,
Unless it be the one
15   You make today in London: to be married?

What have I done to be thirty-two?
    It isn't fair!
I've pressed my trousers, banked my screw,
    And brushed my hair –
Yet now they say: 'Move over, you: 5
    You've had your share!'
What *have* I done to be thirty-two
    It *isn't* fair! . . .

'Is your field sunny?
Is your bank green?
Do you remember, dear bunny,
The walks we have been?
The gardens we've seen?'   5

'Dear rabbit, although
You live over the hill
Where our warren don't go,
I remember them still,
And always will.'   10

Boars Hill

Whispering leaves over Boars Hill stables, –
Whispering tongues round Boars Hill tables:
'Professor Finger, they say, has been
Living with a mummy from the Ashmolean';
'The Bolls have too many bills to pay   5
(Heals took the chairs back yesterday)';
'And have you seen the Komansky twins?
One has a tail and one has fins' –
But clipper-clop-clap; under the conifers
Jilly and Guinivere jog in their jodhpurs,   10
Clearing the Matthew Arnold air
Simply by cantering costlily there . . .

Christmas

No traps are set that day; there are no guns;
    Dogs do not bark.
Even our oldest, even our youngest ones
    Hop out by dark.

5   Yet none can tell why such a respite should
    Each year come round,
As if, that day, some mighty Rabbithood
    Peered above ground.

A Sense of Shape

How we behave, I find increasingly,
Depends on something like a sense of shape,
Not on ambition or ability.

What shape's our comfort? That's what it decides,
5   Long before policy has woken up.
The manly square, the lucky seven-sides?

Quarrelsome diamond? dangerous triangle?
Designs more intricate and twice as sharp
Direct us: we adroitly disentangle

10   Person and place and impulse that will best
Illude us we are there (safe in the loop,
Bright in the star) and chuck away the rest.

I shouldn't grumble if we really were.
Most life is wastage: if the chased gold cup
15   Were handed in return, that would be fair.

But these fantasies of dimension sprout

Long Sight in Age

They say eyes clear with age,
As dew clarifies air
To sharpen evenings,
As if time put an edge
Round the lost shape of things   5
To show them there;
The many-levelled trees,
The long soft tides of grass
Wincing away, the gold
Wind-ridden vanes – all these,   10
They say, come back to focus
As we grow old.

Counting

Thinking in terms of one
Is easily done –
One room, one bed, one chair,
One person there,
Makes perfect sense; one set   5
Of wishes can be met,
One coffin filled.

But counting up to two
Is harder to do;
For one must be denied   10
Before it's tried.

Back to this dreary dump,
East Riding's dirty rump,
Enough to make one jump
        Into the Humber –
God! What a place to be: 5
How it depresses me;
Must I stay on, and see
        Years without number?

The local snivels through the fields:
I sit between felt-hatted mums
Whose weekly day-excursion yields
Baby-sized parcels, bags of plums,
5 And bones of gossip good to clack
Past all the seven stations back.

Strange that my own elaborate spree
Should after fourteen days run out
In torpid rural company
10 Ignoring what my labels shout.
Death will be such another thing,
All we have done not mattering.

Getting Somewhere

When next you take the 2.19
To somewhere that you've read about
And find it's worse than where you've been –

No five-star feeds, no concert-hall,
5 No capering *Three-Cornered Hat*,
Just Sandy's Caff and the Police Ball –

Before you start to blow your top,
Look at the chaps who've brought the train
Two hundred bloody miles non-stop

10 While you were sitting on your seat:
They've gone to make themselves at home
In the first boozer down the street.

To Hart Crane

The victrola talked to him all day.
At night
A thin mist blurred the Hudson, and he sought
Bell-bottomed sex, and the saloons like birds.
Only his famous bridge seemed to connect
Landfalls of concrete, Lucifer's graduate.   5

The ape's face ripples and reforms, like verse.

And so in a light train I take the El,
This poem in my pocket like a hole,
Since art and incompleteness are the same,
Seeking the point where an American moon   10
Thrusts northern waters to the Mexique Bay.

A Midland Syllogism

He waited for the train at Coventry,
Peeping at truth like Tom against the rules,
At shameless grace astride brute modesty
(A paradox unanswered by the schools).

So, blinded into sighting an event   5
Towards which, he thought, the whole creation moves,
Tennyson flowered the track with ornament
(His iron horses ran in velvet grooves).

George Whitefield would have called this a conceit
(Something conceited, to be sure, is there):   10
He saw no gorgon in creation's street
Where grace goes naked under Nature's hair.

Outcome of a Conversation

Paying off my rickshaw, I salute Mr. Hakagawa
Who, in his capacity as station-master, bows-in the train.
We discourse gravely on the fall of the yen
And I promise to be here at cherry-time again.

5   Crammed in the corridor, on Birmingham boxes, the Japanese
Chatter with the confidence of singing-birds
Or spontaneous as Austin workers going home.
When I reach the land where only dividends expand and blossom
May my words come as naturally as leaves or their words.

The Wild Ones

He watched the brutal boys pile off the truck
– Fresh meat the bully sun had handled raw –
Shouldering innocence with rifle and pack:
For them the troop-train on the departure-track
5   Steamed and vibrated like a two-bit whore.

He guessed how soon these would be taught to weep,
To value white-towered Argos, to understand
Battle is more than shooting from the hip –
Patroclus frying in the bloodsoaked jeep
10   And crew-cut Achilles two-timed on the sand.

Travellers

In trains we need not choose our company
For all the logic of departure is
That recognition is suspended; we
Are islanded in unawareness, as
5   Our minds reach out to where we want to be.

But carried thus impersonally on,
We hardly see that person opposite
Who, if we only knew it, might be one
Who, far more than the other waiting at
10   Some distant place, knows our true destination.

Behind Time

It seems that Bradshaw made a bad mistake:
He tells you where you go but never why,
Leaving you lonely where your journeys break.

You miss connections when you say good-bye,
And find your cheap excursion into bliss   5
Has no return, however hard you try.

I reached your junction ignorant of this,
Anxious to yield my ticket at your gate,
But travellers need more luggage than a kiss,

Trains behind time are almost always late.   10

You'll do anything for money,
Sonny,
Now they've given you the chuck:
You must find new cocks to suck
– Bloody funny!   5

To +++++ ++++++ and Others

Why don't you have a go,
If you're so bloody clever?
Just to show us, you know.
Why don't you have a go
At *In Homage to Poe*,   5
Death of Pan, or whatever?
Why don't you have a go,
If you're so bloody clever?

Get Kingsley Amis to sleep with your wife,
You'll find it will give you a bunk up in life.

Oh who is this feeling my prick?
Is it Tom, is it Harry, or Dick?

Her birthday always has
    Real rabbit weather,
With tea laid on the grass
    To munch together.

5   Always she wakes and blinks,
    And licks her paws,
And sees the sun, and thinks
    'Tea out of doors!'

My name it is Benjamin Bunny,
I do *nothing at all* when it's sunny,
But when the wind's high,
And the broken sticks dry,
5   I gather and sell them, *for money*.

'Snow has covered up our track,
    Night is coming on;
It will stop us getting back –
    Would we had not gone!'

5   'The fire we made will soon be out
    And the kettle cold
Rabbits living roundabout
    Will think our burrow sold!

'Do stop scratching at the ground!
10   All is safe, I pledge.
We'll go home the long way round
    By *following the hedge*.'

Far Out

Beyond the bright cartoons
Are darker spaces where
Small cloudy nests of stars
Seem to float on the air.

These have no proper names: 5
Men out alone at night
Never look up at them
For guidance or delight,

For such evasive dust
Can make so little clear: 10
Much less is known than not,
More far than near.

'Not to worry, Len's having a dip;
So wash down your 'burger with char
And fasten your tie in its clip
While I take the pots back.' 'Oh, ta.'

Let there be an empty space where *Rabbit* used to stand,
And bundle *Fraser* in to fill it, whiskey eye and shaking hand;
Let the *Dean of Arts* be burdened with crushing teaching load,
He who now may ride so dainty should not quite forget the road . . .

Let the classroom dais be empty where the rabbit used to thump,
Fraser must come in for niners, shaky, blinking, on the jump.

They are all gone into the world of light,
        Kingsley and John and Bob;
I suppose in some way I can't be as bright,
        Not getting myself a job.

5   For me the shops marked BOOKS & MAGAZINES,
        For me the gassy beer,
The trolley-bus at ten past nine, the Deans –
        I'm staying here.

Homeward, rabbit, homeward go
Leave your track across the snow
Winter evening settles round
Homeward go without a sound.

'Living for others,' (others say) 'is best.'
It might pay better than self interest:
For when you bitch things, as you're bound to do,
It's they who don't get what they want, not you.

A *Lecturer* in drip-dry shirt arrayed
Rode with us, his expenses fully paid
To teach creative writing in the States
(Plus a few summer schools and lecture dates).
5   Literature students knew his critics' *argot*
From Tokyo to Cairo and Chicago
For he was good at getting fees and perks
Mythologising-up a few main works
Like *Middlemarch, Lord Jim, Hard Times*, and *Emma*;
10 Each had its pattern and a new dilemma,
And by the time he'd finished it was plain
No-one should read without his help again.
Further, he had some cronies on the Third
Who'd squeeze him in with Brecht & Wm Byrd
15 To talk on *Yeats: the Language of the Will*
or *Myth and Image: Wordsworth's Daffodil*.

Letter to a Friend about Girls

After comparing lives with you for years
I see how I've been losing: all the while
I've met a different gauge of girl from yours.
Grant that, and all the rest makes sense as well:
My mortification at your pushovers,   5
Your mystification at my fecklessness –
Everything proves we play in separate leagues.
Before, I couldn't credit your intrigues
Because I thought all girls the same, but yes,
You bag real birds, though they're from alien covers.   10

Now I believe your staggering skirmishes
In train, tutorial and telephone booth,
The wife whose husband watched away matches
While she behaved so badly in a bath,
And all the rest who beckon from that world   15
Described on Sundays only, where to want
Is straightway to be wanted, seek to find,
And no one gets upset or seems to mind
At what you say to them, or what you don't:
A world where all the nonsense is annulled,   20

And beauty is accepted slang for yes.
But equally, haven't you noticed mine?
They have their world, not much compared with yours,
But where they work, and age, and put off men
By being unattractive, or too shy,   25
Or having morals – anyhow, none give in:
Some of them go quite rigid with disgust
At anything but marriage: that's all lust
And so not worth considering; they begin
Fetching your hat, so that you have to lie   30

Till everything's confused: you mine away
For months, both of you, till the collapse comes
Into remorse, tears, and wondering why
You ever start such boring barren games
– But there, don't mind my *saeva indignatio*:   35
I'm happier now I've got things clear, although
It's strange we never meet each other's sort:

There should be equal chances, I'd've thought.
Must finish now. One day perhaps I'll know
40   What makes you be so lucky in your ratio

– One of those 'more things', could it be? *Horatio.*

None of the books have time
To say how being selfless feels.
They make it sound a superior way
Of getting what you want. It isn't at all.

5   Selflessness is like waiting in a hospital
In a badly-fitting suit on a cold wet morning.
Selfishness is like listening to good jazz
With drinks for further orders and a huge fire.

Goodnight World

Goodnight World
Your toils I flee
Send no importunate
Messengers after me
5   Days I resign
Nights leave to you
You will come too
Too true, too true!

Great baying groans burst from my lips
Looking at women's breasts and hips.

A sit-on-the-fence old gull,
A use-your-own-sense old gull,
A don't-like-that-paprika
Go-back-to-Africa
5   Terribly dense old gull.

BJ's the man in charge,
He shouldn't be at large,
I'm butter, he's marge.

Hotter shorter days arrive, like happiness
Late in life; the sky still deeply blue,
Trees undiminished, municipal roses
Budding repeatedly though drenched with dew,
And the white cricketers at festivals   5
Casting long shadows, while waves tirelessly
Sunder themselves on disused littorals,
Just as if summer were still strong and early.

But to children sitting in fresh rows
And the typist looking out across   10
Baking chimney pots, the unhindered sun
Pouring through window glass deceives, because
No-one can use it. So perhaps none
Enjoys old age, however fine it shows.

And now the leaves suddenly lose strength.
Decaying towers stand still, lurid, lanes-long,
And seen from landing window, or the length
Of gardens, rubricate afternoons. New strong
Rain-bearing night-winds come: then   5
Leaves chase warm 'buses, speckle statued air,
Pile up in corners, fetch out vague broomed men
Through mists at morning –
                                And no matter where
The sallow lapsing drift goes down, in fields
Or squares, behind hoardings, all men hesitate   10
Separately, always, seeing another year gone –
Frockcoated gentleman, farmer at his gate,
Villein with mattock, soldiers on their shields,
All silent, watching the winter coming on.

January

A slight relax of air where cold was
And water trickles; dark ruinous light,
Scratched like old film, above wet slates withdraws.
At garden-ends, on railway banks, sad white
Shrinkage of snow shows cleaner than the net
Stiffened like ectoplasm in front windows.

Shielded, what sorts of life are stirring yet:
Legs lagged like drains, slippers soft as fungus,
The gas and grate, the old cold sour grey bed.
Some ajar face, corpse-stubbled, bends round
To see the sky over the aerials –
Sky, absent paleness across which the gulls
Wing to the Corporation rubbish ground.
A slight relax of air. All is not dead.

Sir George Grouse to Sir Wᵐ Gull:
'Books today are very dull';
Sir Wᵐ Gull to Sir Geo. Grouse
'I never have them in the house.'
Ogh ogh! Hagh!
Ogh ogh! Hagh!

Sir George Grouse to Sir Wᵐ Gull:
'Films today are very dull';
Sir Wᵐ Gull to Sir Geo. Grouse
'Sooner stop in me own house.'

Chaps who live in California
's Books get cornier & cornier.

Praise God from whom all blessings flow,
And shuts the buggers up below.

Sitting across the aisle
Was a delegate from Prestatyn
She was certainly dressed in style
High heels, silk hose, pink satin
'Wish I was the chair she sat in'   5
Evans muttered, turning his file
To hold it across his flies
For now came his cue to rise etc. etc.

Long Last

Suddenly, not long before
Her eighty-first birthday,
The younger sister died.
Next morning, the elder lay
Asking the open door   5
Why it was light outside,

Since nobody had put on
The kettle, or raked the ashes,
Or come to help her find
The dark way through her dress.   10
This went on till nearly one.
Later, she hid behind

The gas stove. 'Amy's gone,
Isn't she,' they remember her saying,
And 'No' when the married niece   15
Told her the van was coming.
Her neck was leaf-brown.
She left cake on the mantelpiece.

This long last childhood
Nothing provides for.   20
What can it do each day
But hunt that imminent door
Through which all that understood
Has hidden away?

Castle, Park, Dean and Hook
Gave the Universities a look.
What racket to take part in
All my eye and Leslie Martin.

I would I were where Russell plays
Through a foul tobacco haze
I would I were where Russell plays
    And Condon calls the key.

Laboratory Monkeys

Buried among white rooms
Whose lights in clusters beam
Like suddenly-caused pain,
And where behind rows of mesh
5   Uneasy shifting resumes
As sterilisers steam
And the routine begins again
Of putting questions to flesh

That no one would think to ask
10   But a Ph.D. with a beard
And nympho wife who –
                But
There, I was saying, are found
The bushy T-shaped mask,
And below, the smaller, eared
15   Head like a grave nut,
And the arms folded round.

O wha will o'er the downs with me
    O wha will with me ride
To a lectureship in Psychology
    In the University of Strathclyde?

Welcome 1966!
Just produce more pricks
Than 1965
And I'll stay alive.

Lowell, Lowell, Lowell, Lowell,
Corn is the thing he does so well . . .

Scratch on the scratch pad
Rabbit *memoranda* –
Handkerchiefs and horoscopes,
Holland gowns and grander;
Scratch on the scratch pad   5
Rabbit *memorabilia* –
Spectacles and spirit lamps,
Steeple hats and sillier;
Much we buy each market day,
More still obtain: 10
All, all is carried home
By slow evening train.

Then the students cursing and grumbling
And running away, and wanting their liquor and women,
And the vice chancellor going to Africa, and the lack of decisions,
And the Senate hostile and the Council unfriendly
And the Refectory dirty and charging high prices: 5
    A hard time we had of it.

Fill up the glasses, since we're here for life,
And flatter Dr Gamme & his wife,
For looking in the mirror tells you true
It's Dr Gamme who looks back at you.

'Here's a health to the Squire,
And also his Lady,
May he brighten the shire
Though his London is shady' &c.

The Dance

'Drink, sex and jazz – all sweet things, brother: far
Too sweet to be diluted to "a dance",
That muddled middle-class pretence at each
No one who really . . .' But contemptuous speech
5   Fades at my equally-contemptuous glance,
That in the darkening mirror sees
The shame of evening trousers, evening tie.
White candles stir within the chestnut trees.
The sun is low. The pavements are half-dry.
10   Cigarettes, matches, keys –
All this, simply to be where you are.

Half willing, half abandoning the will,
I let myself by specious steps be haled
Across the wide circumference of my scorn.
15   No escape now. Large cars parked round the lawn
Scan my approach. The light has almost failed,
And the faint thudding stridency
Some band we have been 'fortunate to secure'
Proclaims from lit-up windows comes to me
20   More as a final warning than a lure:
Alien territory . . .
And once I gain the upstairs hall, that's still

Our same familiar barn ballooned and chained,
The floor reverberates as with alarm:
25   *Not you, not here.* I edge along the noise
Towards a trestled bar, lacking the poise
To look about me; served, maturer calm
Permits a leaning-back, to view
The whole harmoniously-shifting crowd,
30   And with some people at some table, you.
Why gulp? The scene is normal and allowed:
Professional colleagues do

Assemble socially, are entertained

By sitting dressed like this, in rooms like these,
Saying I can't guess what – just fancy, when   35
They could be really drinking, or in bed,
Or listening to records – so, instead
Of waiting till you look my way, and then
Grinning my hopes, I stalk your chair
Beside the deafening band, where raised faces   40
Sag into silence at my standing there,
And your eyes greet me over commonplaces,
And your arms are bare,
And I wish desperately for qualities

Moments like this demand, and which I lack.   45
I face you on the floor, clumsily, as
Something starts up. Your look is challenging
And not especially friendly: everything
I look to for protection – the mock jazz,
The gilt-edged Founder, through the door   50
The 'running buffet supper' – grows less real.
Suddenly it strikes me you are acting more
Than ever you would put in words; I feel
The impact, open, raw,
Of a tremendous answer banging back   55

As if I'd asked a question. In the slug
And snarl of music, under cover of
A few permitted movements, you suggest
A whole consenting language, that my chest
Quickens and tightens at, descrying love –   60
Something acutely local, me
As I am now, and you as you are now,
And now; something acutely transitory
The slightest impulse could deflect to how
We act eternally.   65
Why not snatch it? Your fingers tighten, tug,

Then slacken altogether. I am caught
By some shoptalking shit who leads me off
To supper and his bearded wife, to stand
Bemused and coffee-holding while the band   70
Restarts off-stage, and they in tempo scoff
Small things I couldn't look at, rent

By wondering who has got you now, and whether
That serious restlessness was what you meant,
75   Or was it all those things mixed up together?
(Drink, sex and jazz.) Content
To let it seem I've just been taken short,

I eel back to the bar, where they're surprised
That anyone still wants to drink, and find
80   You and a weed from Plant Psychology
Loose to the music. So you looked at me,
As if about to whistle; so outlined
Sharp sensual truisms, so yearned –
I breathe in, deeply. It's pathetic how
85   So much most people half my age have learned
Consumes me only as I watch you now,
The tense elation turned
To something snapped off short, and localised

Half-way between the gullet and the tongue.
90   The evening falters. Couples in their coats
Are leaving gaps already, and the rest
Move tables closer. I lean forward, lest
I go on seeing you, and souse my throat's
Imminent block with gin. How right
95   I should have been able to keep away, and let
You have your innocent-guilty-innocent night
Of switching partners in your own sad set:
How useless to invite
The sickened breathlessness of being young

100   Into my life again! I ought to go,
If going would do any good; instead,
I let the barman tell me how it was
Before the war, when there were sheep and grass
In place of Social Pathics; then I tread
105   Heavily to the Gents, and see
My coat patiently hanging, and the chains
And taps and basins that would also be
There when the sheep were. Chuckles from the drains
Decide me suddenly:
110   *Ring for a car right now.* But doing so

Needs pennies, and in making for the bar
For change I see your lot are waving, till

I have to cross and smile and stay and share
Instead of walking out, and so from there
The evening starts again; its first dark chill   115
And omen-laden music seem
No more than rain round a conservatory
Oafishly warm inside. I sit and beam
At everyone, even the weed, and he
Unfolds some crazy scheme   120
He's got for making wine from beetroot, far

Too incoherent to survive the band;
Then there's a *Which*-fed argument – but why
Enumerate? For now we take the floor
Quite unremarked-on, and I feel once more   125
That silent beckoning from you verify
All I remember – weaker, but
Something in me starts toppling. I can sense
By staring at your eyes (hazel, half-shut)
Endless receding Saturdays, their dense   130
And spot-light-fingered glut
Of never-resting hair-dos; understand
How the flash palaces fill up like caves
With tidal hush of dresses, and the sharp
And secretive excitement running through   135
Their open ritual, that can alter to
Anguish so easily against the carp
Of an explicit music; then

High o'er the fence leaps Soldier Jim,
Housman the bugger chasing him.

In Xanadu did Kubla Khan
A stately pleasure dome decree:
He would have had to change his plan
If subject to the UGC.

At the sign of The Old Farting Arse
I drink glass after glass after glass;
    All the regulars there
    Think we ought to ban *Hair*
5 And kick Ali's fat Khyber Pass.
We throw darts at a portrait of Mao,
We think Jackie's a posturing cow,
    We say Younger's is piss
    – Yes it is, yes it is –
10 At the sign of The Old Farting Arse.

After drinking Glenfiddich
I say good rubbance to bad riddich.

Morning, noon & bloody night,
Seven sodding days a week,
I slave at filthy *work*, that might
Be done by any book-drunk freak.
5 This goes on till I kick the bucket:
FUCKITFUCKITFUCKITFUCKIT.

The world's great age begins anew,
I'm perning in a gyre,
There's nothing fresh to listen to,
You'd better pull your wire.

See the Pope of Ulster stand,
Spiked shillelagh in each hand,
Vowing to uphold the Border,
Father, Son, and Orange Order.

I dreamed I saw a commie rally,
And put my boot up Tariq Ali;
Then I shagged Vanessa Redgrave,
Waking only when the bed gave.

Holiday

Clouds merge, the coast darkens,
Sunless barley stirs.
The sloping field alters
To weed-ribboned rock,
Waders and lichens. 5
The sea collapses, freshly.

A vacant park inland
Is roughened by wind.
Trees throng the light-oak chapel.
Storm-spots quicken round 10
A railed tomb of sailors.
The house is shuttered.

Embedded in the horizon
A tiny sunlit ship
Seems not to be moving. 15

O things going away!

The polyp comes & goes,
I can't breave frew my effin nose.

How to Win the Next Election

Prison for Strikers,
Bring back the cat,
Kick out the niggers,
How about that?

Trade with the Empire, 5
Ban the Obscene,
Lock up the Commies,
God Save the Queen.

The flag you fly for us is furled,
Your history speaks when ours is dumb,
You have not welcomed in the scum
First of Europe, then the world . . .

The Manciple's Tale

Whilom there was dwelling in this toune
A MANCIPLE, well used to doing doune
Visiting felawes in their owene righte
Especially *cars* he liked left out all nighte . . .
5   Yet curteislye he spak and seyde that eke
Al sholde be sorted oute within an weke
Garaugen wyde, & fyr, shal al be sene;
Lat hit be so, I count hym nat a bene
Larkin sits by the fyr withouten beid
10   *And drinketh of hys bugle-horn the wyn.*

Sod the lower classes,
Kick them up their arses,
And we'll raise our glasses
When they've all caved in.

Poem about Oxford

for Monica

City we shared without knowing
In blacked-out and butterless days,
Till we left, and were glad to be going
(Unlike the arselicker who stays),
5   Does it stick in our minds as a touchstone
Of learning and *la politesse*?
For while the old place hadn't much tone,
Two others we know have got less.

Perhaps not. And yet so much is certain:
10   Aside from more durable things,
I'm glad you don't say you're from Girton,

You'd sooner I wasn't at King's;
To all that it meant – a full notecase,
Dull Bodley, draught beer, and dark blue,
And most often losing the Boat Race –   15
You're added, as I am for you.

So thirty years on, when the cake-queues
And coffees have gone by the board,
And new men in new labs make break-throughs,
Old buildings are cleaned and restored,   20
And students live up to what's said about
Their like in Black Papers and more,
It holds us, like that *Fleae* we read about
In the depths of the Second World War.

Light, Clouds, Dwelling-places

Light from the east, displacing grape-dark sky
Behind illuminated wings of hospitals,
Humped districts of the poor, a high
Money-discerning architectured comb,
Hardens to cloud, a strewn-with-nothing shore   5
Above condensers and canals,
A stretching-out of miles of monochrome
Lightened in patches by
Soft breakages into an upper, paler floor,

As if outside the dullness of our day   10
Boredom renews, recedes. A wintry time-grained air
Rests upon roofs. It wears away
Edges of brickwork, ironwork, woodwork, stone;
Hangs like a mist over the hard bald ground
Past ends of terraced houses, where   15
Goal-chalked half-ruined shelters full of thrown
Chip-sodden paper, stray
Upholstery, concrete, wheels and a hat survive. All round

Ribbed streets in close formation rise and fall
Like a great sigh out of the last century.   20
Groves of interiors, each wall
Papered with decades, tirelessly exhale
Meals, childhoods, coronations, interspersed

With spaces tethered separately

25 Above inscribed foundation-stones, stale
Hollow meeting-hall
And prayer-distempered chapel, while among seats and dust

In unsold cinemas the kisses and
Riding down into the blinding gulch are one.

I have started to say
'A quarter of a century'
Or 'thirty years back'
About my own life.

5 It makes me breathless.
It's like falling and recovering
In huge gesturing loops
Through an empty sky.

All that's left to happen
10 Is some deaths (my own included).
Their order, and their manner,
Remain to be learnt.

When the lead says goonight to the copper,
And Sheppard is cycling unchecked,
I take out a spatulaful of graphite,
And notice the greasy effect.

Sherry does more than Bovril can,
To stop you feeling like puking in the lavatory pan.

This was Mr Bleaney's bungalow,
Standing in the concrete jungle, o-
ver-looking an arterial road –
Here I live with old Toad.

It's plain that Marleen and Patricia would
Be small use to Christopher Isherwood;
But, steady The Buffs!
The Green Howards, Green Cuffs,
And Her Majesty's Household Militia would!   5

Have a little more
At Christmas '74 –
We may not be alive
At Christmas '75.

When first we faced, and touching showed
How well we knew the early moves,
Behind the moonlight and the frost,
The excitement and the gratitude,
There stood how much our meeting owed   5
To other meetings, other loves.

The decades of a different life
That opened past your inch-close eyes
Belonged to others, lavished, lost;
Nor could I hold you hard enough   10
To call my years of hunger-strife
Back for your mouth to colonise.

Admitted: and the pain is real.
But when did love not try to change
The world back to itself – no cost,   15
No past, no people else at all –
Only what meeting made us feel,
So new, and gentle-sharp, and strange?

Dear Jake

And when you write: 'The substance of this section
Is the last singular comic episode
In which four lives were fractured by affection
Our subject tried so lately to unload

5   On one already mentioned (see page thirty),
Whom we can guess not fitted in the least
To cope with all that love and pain and duty,
And so must have been thankful when it ceased',
Dear Jake, I know you really mean 'Hey, Mac,
10   This old goat was so crazy for a fuck he –
No doubt the UP wouldn't print that page.

Well, it was singular; but, looking back,
Only what men do get, if they are lucky.
And when it came there was no thought of age.

Be my Valentine this Monday,
Even though we're miles apart!
Time will separate us one day –
Till then, hyphen with my heart.

5   You are fine as summer weather,
May to August all in one,
And the clocks, when we're together,
Count no shadows. Only sun.

Morning at last: there in the snow
Your small blunt footprints come and go.
Night has left no more to show.

Not the candle, half-drunk wine,
5   Or touching joy; only this sign
Of your life walking into mine.

But when they vanish with the rain
What morning woke to will remain,
Whether as happiness or pain.

We met at the end of the party,
When most of the drinks were dead
And all the glasses dirty:
'Have this that's left,' you said.

5   We walked through the last of summer,
When shadows reached long and blue

Across days that were growing shorter:
You said: 'There's autumn too.'

Always for you what's finished
Is nothing, and what survives   10
Cancels the failed, the famished,
As if we had fresh lives

From that night on, and just living
Could make me unaware
Of June, and the guests arriving,   15
And I not there.

Once more upon the village green
The village cricketers are seen.
The sweet sound of bat on ball
Echoes back from rick and wall,
As the bun-stealers flicker to and fro,   5
[?As] to and fro, my Peter and my Benje long ago!

I want to see them starving,
        The so-called working class,
Their wages weekly halving,
        Their women stewing grass,
When I drive out each morning   5
        In one of my new suits
I want to find them fawning
        To clean my car and boots.

Davie, Davie,
Give me a bad review;
That's your gravy,
Telling chaps what to do.
Forget about style and passion,   5
As long as it's in the fashion –
But let's be fair, it's got you a chair,
Which was all it was meant to do.

Well, I must arise and go now, and go to Innisfree,
Where I have heard it rumoured you can get Guinness free –

After Healey's trading figures,
        After Wilson's squalid crew,
And the rising tide of niggers –
        What a treat to look at you!

California, here I come,
Watching out for drink and bum;
My thesis
On faeces
5   In *Ulysses*
Has knocked –'em
From Stockton
Grammar School to Los Angeles –
California, you're my perk,
10   Help me to indulge my quirk,
Otherwise I'll have to work –
California, here I come!

The little lives of earth and form,
Of finding food, and keeping warm,
        Are not like ours, and yet
A kinship lingers nonetheless:
5   We hanker for the homeliness
        Of den, and hole, and set.

And this identity we feel
– Perhaps not right, perhaps not real –
        Will link us constantly;
10   I see the rock, the clay, the chalk,
The flattened grass, the swaying stalk,
        And it is you I see.

Administration

As day by day shrewd estimation clocks up
Who deserves a smile, and who a frown,
I find the girls I tell to pull their socks up
Are those whose pants I most want to pull down.

Haymakers and reapers by Stubbs
Are better than arses and bubs,
And plume-hatted ninnies,
And children in pinnies,
And even drunk Dutchmen in pubs.   5

The sky split apart in malice
Stars rattled like pans on a shelf
Crow shat on Buckingham Palace
God pissed Himself –

Thought you might welcome a dekko
At this pre-distortion El Greco . . .

Walt Whitman
Was certainly no titman
Leaves of Grass
. . .

If I could talk, I'd be a worthless prof
Every other year off
Just a jetset egghead, *TLS* toff
Not old toad: Frank Kermode.

The daily things we do
For money or for fun
Can disappear like dew
Or harden and live on.
5 Strange reciprocity:
The circumstance we cause
In time gives rise to us,
Becomes our memory.

New brooms sweep clean,
They say, and mean
Change and decay,
Things brushed away;
5 But for old rooms
Where life has been
And love seen,
Keep the old brooms.

Love Again

Love again: wanking at ten past three
(Surely he's taken her home by now?),
The bedroom hot as a bakery,
The drink gone dead, without showing how
5 To meet tomorrow, and afterwards,
And the usual pain, like dysentery.

Someone else feeling her breasts and cunt,
Someone else drowned in that lash-wide stare,
And me supposed to be ignorant,
10 Or find it funny, or not to care,
Even . . . but why put it into words?
Isolate rather this element

That spreads through other lives like a tree
And sways them on in a sort of sense
15 And say why it never worked for me.
Something to do with violence
A long way back, and wrong rewards,
And arrogant eternity.

After eating in honour of Chichele
We stood round and talked rather bichele.

Apples on a Christmas tree!
Or are they tomatoes?
Such teasing ambiguity
No sensible art owes.
We sing the annual mystery   5
In churches and chapels
– But tomatoes on a Christmas tree!
Or are they apples?

The one thing I'd say about A. Thwaite
Is that I prefer him to Braithwaite
But the one who surpasses
Them both up Parnassus
Is Douglas Dunn shouting "Ye baith wait!".   5

The View

The view is fine from fifty,
    Experienced climbers say;
So, overweight and shifty,
    I turn to face the way
    That led me to this day.   5

Instead of fields and snowcaps
    And flowered lanes that twist,
The track breaks at my toe-caps
    And drops away in mist.
    The view does not exist.   10

Where has it gone, the lifetime?
    Search me. What's left is drear.
Unchilded and unwifed, I'm
    Able to view that clear:
    So final. And so near.   15

All work & no wassail
Fait l'existence pas facile.

Good for You, Gavin

It's easy to write when you've nothing to write about
    (That is, when you are young);
The heart-shaped hypnotics the press is polite about
    Rise from an unriven tongue.

5   Later on, attic'd with all-too-familiar
    Teachests of truth-sodden grief,
The pages you scrap sound like school songs, or sillier,
    Banal beyond belief.

So good for you, Gavin, for having stayed sprightly
10   While keeping your eye on the ball;
Your riotous road-show's like Glenlivet nightly,
    A warming to us all.

Beware the travelogue, my son,
The palms that wave, the pigs that grunt,
Beware the Kirkup bird, and shun
The local name for cunt.

'When one door shuts, another opens.' Cock!
When once it's shut, the key turns in its lock.

The chances are certainly slim
Of finding in Barbara Pym
    (I speak with all deference)
    The faintest of reference
5 To what in our youth we called quim –

1982

Long lion days
Start with white haze.
By midday you meet
A hammer of heat –
Whatever was sown   5
Now fully grown;
Whatever conceived
Now fully leaved,
Abounding, ablaze –
O long lion days!   10

My feet are clay, my brains are sodden,
But my secretary's modern,
And if she uses signs like 'K'
Who am I to say her nay?
Kilometre? Kangaroo?   5
I am more at sea than you.

This collection of various scraps
Will be torn into shreds by the craps
'Poetry's Priestley!'
They'll say. 'Oh, how beastly!'
But old Bob will like it, perhaps.   5

Outside, a dog barks
Swinging from your prick, I muse
On Wang-Lei's lyrics.

Last night we put the clocks on
This morning I am late
And as I pull my socks on
I try to calculate

Bun's Outing

Saturday morning
I go for the meat,
Body all aching
Likewise the feet,
5   Fools at my elbow
Gormlessly greet,
Shopping is hell
In Stupidity Street.

After reading the works of MacCaig
I find myself numb, dumb and vague;
As I put it behind me,
Why does it remind me
5   Of latterday wind and Raine (Craig)?

UNDATED
OR APPROXIMATELY DATED POEMS

There was an old fellow of Kaber,
Who published a volume with Faber:
When they said 'Join the club?'
He ran off to the pub –
But Charles called, 'You must *love* your neighbour.'   5

The Way We Live Now

(to be recited in a clear Welsh voice)

I let a fart in the street and a woman looked round;
I pissed on the fire, and got myself covered with ash;
I had half an hour with a whore and came out in a rash,
So I let my sperm fall in the brim of an old hat I found.

I vomited over my shoes in the bogs at the Pheasant;   5
I slipped in the road, and came down with my hand on some slime;
Life is performing these actions time after time
Till Death makes our body smell worse than it does at present.

What is booze for?
Booze is what we drink.
They come, they shake us,
Time and time over.
Beer, whisky, schnapps and gin.   5
What can we drink but booze?
Ah, solving that question, etc.
Brings the priest and the doctor
(And a few pink rats)
Running over the fields.   10

When the night is hoar
And an owl hoots,
Put this on the door
Where you have your roots:
Keep them underground   5
Where they won't be found.

On the shortest day
When the air is cold
Keep visitors away:
What you have you hold.
5   That's what this is for.
Put it on your door

Roses, roses all the way?
Lettuces, lettuces, rabbits say –
So I send my love in troth
To Monica, whose life is both.

No power cuts here –
Lots of good cheer!

Those long thin steeds,
And natural downs
So near at hand,
We cannot see,
5   Nor that tiny
Excitement share
In the delicate stand:
We cannot be

Elsewhere than here –
10 And yet, just so
May others stare
On our casual scene,
And cry for pleasure
At the out-of-reach
15 Enchantment there
Where we have been.

Though there's less at wch to purr,
Be my Valentine this year!
In this single life of mine
You're much more dear than if I'd nine.

Snow on Valentine's Day!
But it will go away.
My love is not like snow:
It will not go.

· COMMENTARY

· COMMENTARY ·

The volume was published by The Fortune Press, London, in July 1945. From the outset, Larkin (hereafter L) did not greatly like the poems. In letters to JBS dated 22 July and 19 Nov. 1944, he remarks that they 'do not greatly please me' and are 'of varying value' (Hull DPL 174/2/96, 106). In another dated 10 Dec. 1944 (174/2/108), he tries to say what's wrong: 'I detect in them a certain impurity, a certain writing for writing's sake, and lack of real inspiration. I felt like making a vow not to write anything until it is really forcing the hat off'n my head, at least in the poetry line.' It is no token of high esteem, therefore, when he tells Vernon Watkins in a letter of 14 Sept. 1945, 'XXVII and XXII are my favourites': Hull DPL (2) 2/18/75. Some twenty years later, he sounds far from having any favourites. He tells CM of Faber and Faber on 16 June 1965 (SL, 374): 'With regard to republication of the poems, I am still undecided about this. They are such complete rubbish, for the most part, that I am just twice as unwilling to have two editions in print as I am to have one, and the only positive reasons for a second edition by you would be if this was necessary in order to secure the copyright, and to correct a few misprints.' When the proofs arrived on 12 Jan. 1966, L remarked to MJ that day in a letter: 'The collection contains some pretty frightful clangers [. . .] The intro seems duller & more egotistic than that to Jill': Bodl. MS Eng. c. 7432/25. The first Faber edition was published on 15 Sept. 1966, and for it L added 'Waiting for breakfast, while she brushed her hair'.

CM in Thwaite (1982), 43: 'Philip had earlier rejected out of hand a suggestion of mine that he should include [. . .] those poems in XX Poems [. . .] which had not been subsequently included in The Less Deceived.' L interviewed by Mary Holland in Queen, 426. 5594 (25 May 1966), 47: 'I'm working on a new edition of my early poetry at the moment, and I was surprised that I didn't want to change anything. I think it's ghastly but I don't want to change it.' L to MJ, 6 Sept. 1966 (Bodl. MS Eng. c. 7433/116): 'Some of the poems don't displease me: others do. There's a kind of early James Joyce atmosphere about some, rather than Yeats, or so I fancy.' Asked at a reading of his poems in November 1974 why he had read nothing from TNS, L replied, 'because I think it's awful': Watt (1989), 174. In

1981: 'I can't really go back to *The North Ship*: it was so very young, born of reading Yeats and so on. Remember Yeats's early poems were wan and droopy, very unlike the later Yeats. I can't explain *The North Ship* at all. It's not very good [. . .] It's popular with musicians, they like setting it. Musicians like things that don't mean too much [. . .] There are some pieces in the book I hate very much indeed': *FR*, 50.

L's Introduction to the Faber edition:

THE NORTH SHIP would probably not have been published if the late William Bell, then an undergraduate at Merton College, had not set about making up a collection which he eventually called *Poetry from Oxford in Wartime*. Oxford poetry was reputedly in the ascendant again following the scarlet and yellow *Eight Oxford Poets* in 1941 (Keith Douglas, Sidney Keyes, John Heath-Stubbs, Drummond Allison, *et al.*), and Bell no doubt thought it was time for another round-up. When his anthology came out in 1944 it had Allison, Heath-Stubbs and Roy Porter from the earlier collection, and the new names of Bell himself, Francis King, myself, Christopher Middleton and David Wright. How many of the second group had been in hard covers before I don't know: certainly I hadn't.

Before it appeared, however, the proprietor of the small but then well-known house that was producing the book wrote to some of its contributors enquiring if they would care to submit collections of their own work. The letter I received was on good-quality paper and signed with an illegible broad-nibbed squiggle: I was enormously flattered, and typed out some thirty pieces on my father's old portable Underwood. The publisher seemed to like them, saying that he could undertake publication early next year 'and perhaps have the book ready in February'. Since this was already the end of November, my excitement ran high, but I must (with memories of *The Writers' and Artists' Year Book*) have parried with some enquiry about terms, for another letter a month later (two days before Christmas) assured me that no agreement was necessary.

Looking at the collection today, it seems amazing that anyone should have offered to publish it without a cheque in advance and a certain amount of bullying. This, however, was not how I saw it at the time. As February turned to March, and March to April, my anticipation of the promised six copies curdled through exasperation to fury and finally to indifference; my astonishment to find now, on looking up the records, that in fact they arrived almost exactly nine months after despatch of typescript (on 31st July 1945) shows how completely I subsequently came to believe my own fantasy of eighteen months or even two years. I inspected them sulkily.

It may not have been the best introduction to publication: my Oxford friend, Bruce Montgomery, was writing Edmund Crispin novels for Gollancz, while Routledge had taken up Keyes and Heath-Stubbs. Still, I was on the same list as Dylan Thomas, Roy Fuller, Nicholas Moore and other luminaries, and the book was nicely enough produced, with hardly any misprints; above all, it was indubitably *there*, an ambition tangibly satisfied. Yet was it? Then, as now, I could never contemplate it without a twinge, faint or powerful, of shame compounded with disappointment. Some of this was caused by the contents but not all: I felt in some ways cheated. I can't exactly say how. It was a pity they had ever mentioned February.

ii

Looking back, I find in the poems not one abandoned self but several – the ex-schoolboy, for whom Auden was the only alternative to 'old-fashioned' poetry; the undergraduate, whose work a friend affably characterized as 'Dylan Thomas, but you've a sentimentality that's all your own'; and the immediately post-Oxford self, isolated in Shropshire with a complete Yeats stolen from the local girls' school. This search for a style was merely one aspect of a general immaturity. It might be pleaded that the war years were a bad time to start writing poetry, but in fact the principal poets of the day – Eliot, Auden, Dylan Thomas, Betjeman – were all speaking out loud and clear, and there was no reason to become entangled in the undergrowth of *Poetry Quarterly* and *Poetry London* except by a failure of judgment. Nor were my contemporaries similarly afflicted. I remember looking through an issue of *The Cherwell*, one day in Blackwell's, and coming across John Heath-Stubbs's 'Leporello': I was profoundly bewildered. I had never heard of Leporello, and what sort of poetry was this – who was he copying? And his friend Sidney Keyes was no more comforting: he could talk to history as some people talk to porters, and the mention of names like Schiller and Rilke and Gilles de Retz made me wish I were reading something more demanding than English Language and Literature. He had most remarkable brown and piercing eyes:

I met him one day in Turl Street, when there was snow on the ground, and he was wearing a Russian-style fur hat. He stopped, so I suppose we must have known each other to talk to – that is, if we had had anything to say. As far as I remember, we hadn't.

The predominance of Yeats in this volume deserves some explanation. In 1943 the English Club was visited by Vernon Watkins, then stationed at an Air Force camp nearby; impassioned and imperative, he swamped us with Yeats until, despite the fact that he had not nearly come to the end of his typescript, the chairman had forcibly to apply the closure. As a final gesture Vernon distributed the volumes he had been quoting from among those of us who were nearest to him, and disappeared, exalted, into the black-out. I had been tremendously impressed by the evening and in the following weeks made it my business to collect his books up again – many of them were limited Cuala Press editions, and later Yeats was scarce at that time – and take them to him at Bradwell, where he was staying with some people called Blackburn who kept a goat. This time Vernon read me Lorca.

As a result I spent the next three years trying to write like Yeats, not because I liked his personality or understood his ideas but out of infatuation with his music (to use the word I think Vernon used). In fairness to myself it must be admitted that it is a particularly potent music, pervasive as garlic, and has ruined many a better talent. Others found it boring. I remember Bruce Montgomery snapping, as I droned for the third or fourth time that evening *When such as I cast off remorse, So great a sweetness flows into the breast . . .* , 'It's not his job to cast off remorse, but to earn forgiveness.' But then Bruce had known Charles Williams. Every night after supper before opening my large dark green manuscript book I used to limber up by turning the pages of the 1933 plum-coloured Macmillan edition, which stopped at 'Words for Music Perhaps', and which meant in fact that I never absorbed the harsher last poems. This may be discernible in what I wrote.

When reaction came, it was undramatic, complete and permanent. In early 1946 I had some new digs in which the bedroom faced east, so that the sun woke me inconveniently early. I used to read. One book I had at my bedside was the little blue *Chosen Poems of Thomas Hardy*: Hardy I knew as a novelist, but as regards his verse I shared Lytton Strachey's verdict that 'the gloom is not even relieved by a little elegance of diction'. This opinion did not last long; if I were asked to date its disappearance, I should guess it was the morning I first read 'Thoughts of Phena At News of Her Death'. Many years later, Vernon surprised me by saying that Dylan Thomas had admired Hardy above all poets of this century. 'He thought Yeats was the greatest by miles', he said. 'But Hardy was his favourite.'

iii

'F/Sgt. Watkins, V.' was the book's kindest and almost only critic. Writing from the Sergeants' Mess, he was generously encouraging (did I recall his Yeats anecdote: 'Always I encourage, always'?), reserving for only one or two pieces his sharpest term of condemnation, 'not a final statement'. 'Yesterday', he added, 'I destroyed about two thousand poems that mean nothing to me now.' Despite this hint, although with considerable hesitation, the book is now republished, as there seems to be still some demand for it. I have corrected two misprints and one solecism. As a coda I have added a poem, written a year or so later, which, though not noticeably better than the rest, shows the Celtic fever abated and the patient sleeping soundly.

P. L.
October 1965.

I

DATE AND TEXT
L included it in a letter to JBS dated 21 Apr. 1944 (Hull DP 174/2/91). It appears on p. 21 of Bodl. MS Eng. c. 2357, a t.s. with L's corrections in ink and pencil which dates from 1943–4. Published in POW, 75–6. The dedication to Bruce Montgomery first appeared in TNS.

9 Yeats favours such refrains in numerous poems, from which Timms (1973), 27–8, singles out Her Anxiety with its 'short dancing lines and portentous refrains'. Note in particular L's second line and Her Anxiety, 2 ('Awaits returning spring'); L's sixth line and Yeats's fifth ('Into some lesser thing'); and 'lovers' (L, 25; Yeats, 7). 10–11 John Skinner compares Yeats, Sailing to Byzantium, 5–6: 'Fish, flesh, or fowl, commend all summer long | Whatever is begotten, born, and dies': Ariel, 20. 1 (Jan. 1989), 80. 27–36 Timms (1973), 28: 'he borrows Yeats's view of time, of evolution and the second coming, his wheel another version of the Yeatsian gyre'.

II

DATE AND TEXT
There exist an undated holograph MS (Hull DLN 3/12) and t.s.
(Hull DPL 2/2/7), both with the heading 'Sonnet'. Published in
Cherwell, 63. 7 (28 Feb. 1942), 76, signed 'R. L.' L to JBS, 5 Mar.
1942 (Hull DP 174/2/40): 'Cherwell printed another sonnet this
week – signed "R. L.". The turds! Why reduce me to P. L. in the
first place? Bleeding sods!' L corrected the error to 'PAL' (i.e. Philip
Arthur Larkin) on a photocopy now in Hull DPL 3/1. He did not
correct the variant wordings in the text.

VARIANTS
4 Shines] Falls *Hull DLN 3/12, Hull DPL 2/2/7*
6 a] your *Hull DLN 3/12*
7 a random] the random *Hull DLN 3/12*
11 greet] ~~see~~ meet *Hull DLN 3/12*
12 final] triumph *Hull DLN 3/12, Hull DPL 2/2/7*
knowing] ~~see~~ seeing ~~knowing~~ *Hull DLN 3/12*; seeing *Cherwell, 1942*
13 is] as *Hull DLN 3/12, Hull DPL 2/2/7, Cherwell, 1942*
finished] final *Hull DPL 2/2/7*

III

DATE AND TEXT
It appears, numbered 'ii.', on p. 11 of Bodl. MS Eng. c. 2357, which
dates from 1943–4. Published in *POW*, 76.

1 Cf. Arnold, *Dover Beach* (another poem about loss), 1–2: 'The sea
is calm to-night . . . the moon lies fair'. 5 *certitude*: *Dover Beach*,
34: 'Nor certitude . . .' Both echoes are noted in Morrison (1980),
17–18.

IV Dawn

DATE AND TEXT
?1943–4. On Hull DPL 2/2/15 (t.s.), it is numbered '6' (encircled),
and ticked in the left margin.

VARIANTS
3 curtains] curtain *Hull t.s.*

V Conscript

DATE AND TEXT
Published in *Phoenix* [Ayton], 3. 1 (Oct.–Nov. 1941), 14. On a photocopy now in Hull DPL 3/1, L corrected the misprinted full stop (for a comma) after 'blame' at the end of l. 8. He also wrote 'June 5th 1941' on the cutting. Included in 7P (Jan. 1942). The dedication to JBS first appeared in TNS.

VARIANTS
Title [No title] 7P

Critics have highlighted debts to Auden, and in particular to the sonnets *In Time of War* (*Sonnets from China*), which share: the 'untypical allegory' (Alan Brownjohn, *Philip Larkin*, 1975, 7); the uncomplicated abstractions like 'good' and 'bad' and the geographical metaphor for the psyche (Day, 1987, 26); and the splitting up of the sonnet into groups of lines (Timms, 1973, 23). To which may be added the mystery-laden narrative set in the past, the vague identities preserved by pronouns ('he', 'they'), and the matter-of-fact reporting of portentous events.

Dedication L to JBS, 19 Nov. 1944 (Hull DP 174/2/106): 'I was rather at a loss to choose a poem to dedicate to you, because only a few of the old ones seemed worth including, but I chose one called "Conscript", a sonnet, do you remember? It had to be something I wrote when we were in fairly close contact, and I believe you said you liked it, once. Anyway, please accept it (again, if it is printed) as a token of high regard.' To JBS, 28 Mar. 1945 (Hull DP 174/2/116): 'Remorse still gnaws me over "Conscript: to James Ballard Sutton", because it is – though by no means the worst poem in the book – a relic of a style I have discarded, before I had begun to "sing". But as I explained before, I wanted to give you a poem written in your company which at the time you liked, and that one, born of conscription and the general hovering vultures of 1940, seemed most suitable.'

Title Sassoon has a poem entitled *Conscripts* in *The Old Huntsman and Other Poems* (1918).

VI

DATE AND TEXT
?1943–4. It appears on p. 11 of Bodl. MS Eng. c. 2357, numbered 'iii'.

VII

DATE AND TEXT

?1943–4. It appears on p. 14 of Bodl. MS Eng. c. 2357, numbered 'xii.'. Published in *POW*, 75. Published in *CP* (1988), 275, with a comma after 'reassembles'; corrected in *CP* (2003), 10.

VARIANTS

2 are] and *POW*

Metrically, the poem is similar to Housman, *More Poems* VI ('I to my perils of cheat and charmer').

1–2 Cf. 'The poet has a straight face', 102–3. 5 Cf. Housman, *Last Poems* XIX ('In midnights of November'), 19: 'Hues in the east assemble'. 7 *vans*: wings ('Chiefly *poet*.', *OED*).

VIII Winter

DATE AND TEXT

?1943–4. Included in *ITGOL*.

VARIANTS (from *ITGOL*)

28 Yet still the] Miracles,
29 Exhume] Exhumed
31 static] thick

3–5 Cf. Housman, *A Shropshire Lad* XVI, 5–6: 'The nettle nods, the wind blows over, | The man . . .'

IX

DATE AND TEXT

There are two and a half pages of drafts in *Wkbk 1* (1/1/11) after '12. x. 44', and the last one, complete, is dated '23. x. 44' at the end. A complete draft, numbered '(ix)', also appears on p. 10 of Bodl. MS Eng. c. 2357.

VARIANTS

11 falling,] ~~straying,~~ stealing, *Bodl. MS*
13 of girls'] ~~of~~ small *Bodl. MS*
14 ~~And the heart kneeling alone in silence praying.~~ Of girls; the heart in its own silence kneeling. *Bodl. MS*

14 Cf. L to JBS, 16 Aug. 1945 (*SL*, 106): 'someone who consciously accepts mystery at the bottom of things, a person who devotes themself to listening for this mystery – an artist – the kind of artist who is perpetually *kneeling* in his heart'. See the note on *Wedding-Wind*, 23.

X

DATE AND TEXT
A draft of the first verse cancelled by a diagonal line dates from between '5. 10. 44' and '12. x. 44' in *Wkbk 1* (1/1/7). The poem appears on p. 7 of Bodl. MS Eng. c. 2537. Included in *ITGOL*.

VARIANTS
1 the] a *ITGOL*

It is one of three poems L selected from *TNS* for a tape-recording for America in 1981, on grounds that they were 'fairly acceptable as poems' though 'not meant to be what I think good nowadays': *FR*, 50. The other two were *TNS* XIII and XXX.

XI Night-Music

DATE AND TEXT
There is a page of drafts, none of which is complete, in *Wkbk 1* (1/1/8) between '5. 10. 44' and '12. x. 44'. The whole poem appears on p. 8 of Bodl. MS Eng. c. 2357, numbered '(vii)'. Included in *ITGOL*.

VARIANTS
Title Night-Music] Nachtmusik *Bodl. MS*
19 trees] boughs *ITGOL*
22 through] ~~all~~ through *Bodl. MS*

14 Salem K. Hassan, *Philip Larkin and his Contemporaries: An Air of Authenticity* (1988), 16, compares Yeats, *Among School Children*, 27: 'Hollow of cheek as though it drank the wind'. 19 Cf. L's 1943 prose piece *Ante Meridian* (*TAWG*, 235): 'I recognise the sound as only the sibilance of the trees'.

XII

DATE AND TEXT

?1943–4. No MS found.

XIII

DATE AND TEXT

?1943–4. It appears on p. 16 of Bodl. MS Eng. c. 2357, numbered 'xvii'. Published in *POW*, 77. Included in *ITGOL*.

VARIANTS

14 seraphim] seraphims *Bodl. MS, POW*; seraphim's *ITGOL*

It is one of three poems selected from *TNS* by L in 1981 for a tape-recording for America, on grounds that they were 'fairly acceptable as poems' though 'not meant to be what I think good nowadays': *FR*, 50. The other two were *TNS* X and XXX.

XIV Nursery Tale

DATE AND TEXT

Aug. 1944. It appears on p. 5 of Bodl. MS Eng. c. 2357, numbered 'i.'. Hull DPL 2/2/14 (t.s.) is headed 'Wellington poems. second series' in L's hand in pencil; the poem is numbered 'i', and it is dated '8. 44' in L's hand in pencil. L was appointed Librarian at Wellington, Shropshire, in Dec. 1943.

VARIANTS

Title [No title] *Bodl. MS and Hull t.s.*

7–10, 16 Cf. Hopkins, 'No I'll not, carrion comfort, Despair, not feed on thee' (opening line).

XV The Dancer

DATE AND TEXT

?1943–4. It appears on p. 16 of Bodl. MS Eng. c. 2357, numbered 'xix'.

VARIANTS

[No prefatory lines in italic] *Bodl. MS*

XVI

DATE AND TEXT
?1943–4. It appears on p. 13 of Bodl. MS Eng. c. 2357. Published in *POW*, 74.

1, 2, 3, 6 Cf. *Sad Steps*, 4 (and note): 'Four o'clock.' 14–16 L quotes the passage in a letter of 28 Oct. 1952 to MJ (Bodl. MS Eng. c. 7407/118), and remarks that he has been marvelling at 'what I thought of as its *definite* quality, precise: a life is rapped: it rings'.

XVII

DATE AND TEXT
?1943–4. It appears on p. 15 of Bodl. MS Eng. c. 2357, numbered 'xiv.'.

VARIANTS
6 stirs] ~~hangs~~ stirs *Bodl. MS*

Booth (1992), 65, notes the general influence of Yeats, *The Fisherman*. In addition to the parallel in Yeats's opening lines, compare in particular Yeats's 'simple' (8), 'write' (11), 'dead' (14), 'stone' (32), and 'stream' (34) with L, ll. 4, 1, 7, 13, 21.
1–3 Yeats, *The Fisherman*, 38–40: 'I shall have written him one | Poem maybe as cold | And passionate as the dawn'.

XVIII

DATE AND TEXT
Two drafts of the whole poem are dated respectively 'October 5th 1944' and '5. 10. 44' in *Wkbk 1* (1/1/3), and L included the poem in a letter of 8 Oct. 1944 to JBS (Hull DPL 174/2/103; *SL*, 91–2). It appears on p. 7 of Bodl. MS Eng. c. 2357, numbered '(v)'.

VARIANTS
9 stubborn] bits of *Bodl. MS, Hull letter*

Day (1987), 26–7, notes that the poem 'bears a certain resemblance to Dylan Thomas's "In my craft or sullen art": in both poems the speaker describes a solitary nocturnal struggle with feelings or poetry, using similar vocabulary – "night", "grief", "heart" – words both abstract and emotive.'

4–5 *unrent . . . veil*: Timms (1973), 24, notes 'the veil of the temple was rent': Matt. 27: 51, Mark 15: 38, Luke 23: 45.

XIX Ugly Sister

DATE AND TEXT
?1943–4. No MS found.

Title As in the fairytale of Cinderella: 'the ugly sisters'.

XX

DATE AND TEXT
A draft appears on pp. 3–4 of Bodl. MS Eng. c. 2357, and the poem is included in a letter to JBS dated 21 Apr. 1944 (Hull DP 174/2/91). Published in *POW*, 72–3.

VARIANTS
24 sack] ~~bag~~ sack *Bodl. MS*
44 stoop] ~~stop~~ stoop *Bodl. MS*

Timms (1973), 27–8, detects a borrowing of narrative technique and metrical and stanzaic form from Yeats's *The Tower*. He notes (28) that Yeats uses the eight-line stanza again in *A Dialogue of Self and Soul*, from which L borrows 'its self-questioning manner and rhyme scheme', and in *Sailing to Byzantium*, which provides L's poem with 'its property-basket of metaphors, and its central idea that a poet makes up for the disappointments of his life through his art'. Timms also detects the influence of Yeats's view of the poet: 'the man struggling with intractable materials, forced to choose "perfection of the life or of the work", and not both, forced into isolation in his tower, or on the crags he builds, for only there may his "spirit leap"'.

21–3 Cooper (2004), 100, notes that Yeats in several poems uses construction metaphors for personal identity. 24, 35 Cf. Yeats, *Sailing to Byzantium*, 9–10: 'An aged man is but a paltry thing, | A tattered coat upon a stick', noted by Timms (1973), 28; also *Among School Children*, 48:'Old clothes upon old sticks'. L included both poems in *OBTCEV*. 56 Katy Aisenberg, 'Ravishing Images.

Ekphrasis in the Poetry and Prose of William Wordsworth, W. H. Auden and Philip Larkin', *American University Studies*, series 4, vol. 158 (1995), 164, notes the legend of the unicorn as 'an animal so pure that it only would approach virgins'.

XXI

DATE AND TEXT

It appears on p. 22 of Bodl. MS Eng. c. 2357, with the heading 'Poem'. Published in *Arabesque* [2], (Hilary Term 1943), 5: this was the publication of the Oxford University Ballet Club, ed. Denis Frankel (St John's, L's college). In a letter dated 16 Mar. 1943 (*SL*, 55), L tells JBS: 'I am trying to gatecrash another anthology, or have I told you? Nothing exciting, "Oxford Poetry" 1942–3'. Published in *Oxford Poetry 1942–3*, ed. Ian Davie (June 1943), 43, together with *Mythological Introduction* and *A Stone Church Damaged by a Bomb*. Reprinted in *CP* (1988), 267, and in Tolley (2005), 198.

VARIANTS

1 out-thrust] outstretched *Oxford Poetry 1942–3*
4 the wind] a wind *Oxford Poetry 1942–3*
7 a] the *Arabesque*; *Oxford Poetry 1942–3*
14 And I was empty] To leave me dry *Oxford Poetry 1942–3*

Don Lee in *AL*, 28 (Oct. 2009), 12: 'In the summer of 1942 Larkin and Philip Brown took an idyllic holiday in Borva House Cottage on the Gower Peninsula, recollected in Poem XXXI [for XXI] in *The North Ship*, "I dreamed of an out-thrust arm of land".'
    In a letter to JBS dated 14 May 1943 (Hull DP 174/2/64) L judged the poem to be 'rather stupid and bad'; in another of 15 June 1943 (Hull DP 174/2/67), 'rather gutless'.

XXII

DATE AND TEXT

Included in a letter to JBS dated 8 Oct. 1944 (*SL*, 92). It appears on p. 6 of Bodl. MS Eng. c. 2357, numbered 'iii.', in a text identical to that in *TNS*. Included in *ITGOL*.

VARIANTS

Title Getaway *ITGOL*

5 round] in *ITGOL*
   wind] bitter wind 1944 *letter*
11 trick] cheat 1944 *letter*
13 winds] wind 1944 *letter*; *ITGOL*

The influence of Auden's *Lullaby* is most noticeable in l. 16 (see below). Further, L refers to the dawn (2, 10), wind(s) (5, 13), dreams (7), the grave (16), and to lovers and love (11, 16); Auden, to 'lovers' (12) and 'the winds of dawn that blow I Softly round your dreaming head' (32–3).

   4 *waiting*: 'Now *rare*. Superseded by *wait for*' (OED). 12 *the unguessed-at heart*: Arnold, *Shakespeare*, 11: 'Did'st tread on earth unguessed-at'; Housman, *A Shropshire Lad* XXIII ('The lads in their hundreds to Ludlow come in for the fair'), 14: 'brushing your elbow unguessed-at'. 16 *Still-sleeping head*: Milton, *At a Vacation Exercise in the College*, 64: 'Strew all their blessings on thy sleeping head'; Auden, *Lullaby*, 1: 'Lay your sleeping head, my love'.

XXIII

DATE AND TEXT
?1943–4. It appears on p. 15 of Bodl. MS Eng. c. 2357.

11 *All . . . under the sun*: reminiscent of *Ecclesiastes* (1: 14, 2: 20, 4: 15, 9: 3).

XXIV

DATE AND TEXT
?1943–4. It appears on p. 16 of Bodl. MS Eng. c. 2357, numbered 'xviii.'. Published in *POW*, 73.

VARIANTS (from Bodl. MS)
 2 bitter] barren
10 regret] remorse
13 with their courses set] set each their course

5–6 Cf. Wordsworth, 'Earth has not anything to show more fair', 9, 11: 'Never did sun more beautifully steep . . . Ne'er saw I, never felt, a calm so deep!'

XXV

DATE AND TEXT
?1943–4. It appears on p. 11 of Bodl. MS Eng. c. 2357, numbered 'i.'. Published in *POW*, 78.

In 1981 adjudged 'not very sharp' by L, who added, 'I distinctly remember the dream and what it was about, but it's quite unimportant': *FR*, 50.

XXVI

DATE AND TEXT
?1943–4. It appears on p. 12 of Bodl. MS Eng. c. 2357, numbered 'vii'.

3–4 Cf. Auden, *Paid on Both Sides* (*CP*, 22): 'death seems | An axe's echo'. Timms (1973), 33, thinks L may be remembering the stage direction at the end of Chekov's *The Cherry Orchard*: '*only the sound is heard, some way away in the orchard of the axe falling on the trees*'.

XXVII

DATE AND TEXT
?1943–4. Two versions appear in Bodl. MS Eng. c. 2357. The first, on p. 12, is numbered 'vi', and differs markedly in ll. 8–14; the second, on p. 13, is numbered 'ix'. Published in *POW*, 74. Included in *ITGOL*.

VARIANTS
8 all the] all ITGOL
8–14 And also shall be laid to rest | Those images that best | Beat out a path along the days | Like the sun through haze. | No other feet but mine will tread | Across them, and when I am dead | What use are they? *Bodl. MS 1st version*

XXVIII

DATE AND TEXT
?1943–4. It appears on p. 14 of Bodl. MS Eng. c. 2357, numbered 'xiii.'.

Leggett (1999), 132–3, detects the influence of Cole Porter's lyric *At Long Last Love*, with its catalogue of questions formulated as 'Is it x or is it y?' Such a catalogue is also present in Auden, *Twelve Songs*, XII ('Some say that love's a little boy'), also influenced by Porter: Leggett (1999), 138–9.
    5 Leggett, 133, cites Porter, l. 19: 'Is it the rainbow or just a mirage?' 7 Salem K. Hassan, *Philip Larkin and his Contemporaries: An Air of Authenticity* (1988), 17, notes that Emily Dickinson describes the sun as 'the Juggler of Day' in 'Blazing in Gold and quenching in Purple', 8. Cooper (2004), 88, compares 'the juggled balls | Hang in the air' in MacNeice, *Letter to Graham and Anne Shepard*, 123–4, in ch. 3 of MacNeice and Auden's *Letters from Iceland*.

XXIX

DATE AND TEXT
?1943–4. No MS found.

7 Cf. *As You Like It*, 2. 1. 14: 'Wears yet a precious jewel in his head'.

XXX

DATE AND TEXT
The earliest version, Hull DPL 2/2/39, is entitled 'Sonnet: Penelope, August, 1942' = Hull t.s. 1. In 1943–4 it appears on p. 22 of Bodl. MS Eng. c. 2357, with the heading 'Poem'. Hull DPL (2) 1/2/5 = Hull t.s. 2 dates from the same period. Published in *POW*, 77. The first version was published in *The Times*, 1 Oct. 2005.

VARIANTS
Title Sonnet: Penelope, August, 1942 *Hull t.s. 1*
  1 that] the *Hull t.s. 2*
  3 cold] green *Bodl. MS*

6 uncertainty] uncertainness *Hull t.s. 1*
10 embedded] abandoned *Hull t.s. 1, Hull t.s. 2*
11–14 Now, when this intricate and shining grief | Breaks next
before your face, how shall I twist | These crooked branches
straight? and how ensure | The day that falls drop riper than before?
Hull t.s. 1

L to Penelope Scott Stokes, 2 Nov. 1965: 'Recently I looked at my
early poems, preparatory to writing a preface to them – did you
know one was "about" you? Insofar as anything was about anything
in those days!' To Penelope Scott Stokes, 16 Nov. 1965: 'it was XXX
in *The North Ship*, only the last word but one was misprinted – it
should have been "provincial".' These letters are reproduced by
Penelope Scott Stokes's daughter Susannah Tarbush in *AL*, 25 (Apr.
2008), 7. L in Hull DPL 4/3, a memoir of his Oxford days: 'I soon
found out that Penelope Scott Stokes, a girl resembling an Eton boy
and whom I had been gently attracted to the term previously had
left Somerville and been married.' On this basis he states that the
sonnet 'So through that unripe day' was 'proved correct': published
by James Booth in *AL*, 24 (Oct. 2007), 5, with 'greatly' for 'gently'.
Penelope Scott Stokes states in a letter dated 28 Apr. 1967 that L did
not really know her: *AL*, 26 (Oct. 2008), 6.

The poem was one of three from *TNS* selected by L in 1981
for a tape-recording for America, on grounds that they were
'fairly acceptable as poems' though 'not meant to be what I think
good nowadays': *FR*, 50. The other two were *TNS* X and XIII.
L remarked further, 'I don't particularly like "XXX" except for
the last quatrain.'

Steve Clark detects a 'discreet series of Medusa references' in 'the
"head" that has been "severed", now "cold", floating "wing-stiff"
in mid-air': 1988, 1994, then Regan (1997), 114–15.

XXXI The North Ship

DATE AND TEXT
Legend Included in a letter to JBS dated 8 Oct. 1944 (*SL*, 90–1):
'I shall be interested to see how the three ships one looks in print, as
I only did it today.' There are two complete drafts amounting to two
and a half pages in *Wkbk 1* (1/1/5, 9), the first, entitled 'Song: The
Three Ships', dated '8. x. 44' at the end, the other, entitled 'Ballad
of the North Ship', after '12. x. 44', dated '23. x. 44' at the end.

An 'improved' version of the last stanza, identical to that in *TNS*, was included in a letter to JBS dated 17 Oct. 1944 (*SL*, 94). The poem appears on p. 9 of Bodl. MS Eng. c. 2357, numbered 'viii'. This version is much closer to that in *TNS* and therefore post-dates the letters to JBS.

Songs 65° N: In *Wkbk 1* (1/1/13) there are two drafts amounting to three pages after '23. x. 44', both complete except for the title, the second dated '27. x. 44' at the end. The poem appears on p. 17 of Bodl. MS Eng. c. 2357.

70° N *Fortunetelling*: There are two drafts in *Wkbk 1* (1/1/13), amounting to just over a page, dated '1-xi-44.' and '2. xi. 44' respectively. The second draft is complete except for the title. The poem appears below the previous poem on p. 17 of Bodl. MS Eng. c. 2357.

75° N *Blizzard*: There is a draft on half a page after '27. x. 44' in *Wkbk 1* (1/1/13), complete except for the title, dated '29. x. 44'. The poem appears after the previous poem on p. 18 of Bodl. MS Eng. c. 2357.

Above 80° N: There is a draft after '29. x. 44' on half a page in *Wkbk 1* (1/1/13), complete except for the title, dated '31. x. 44'. The poem appears below the previous poem on p. 18 of Bodl. MS Eng. c. 2357.

VARIANTS
Legend
Title Song: the Three Ships *8 Oct. 1944 letter*
Subtitle [No subtitle] *Bodl. MS*
   4 one was] they were *8 Oct. 1944 letter*
   6 running] smiling *8 Oct. 1944 letter*
   8 And it was rigged for a long journey *8 Oct. 1944 letter*
   10 quaking] fawning *8 Oct. 1944 letter*
   12 And it was rigged for a long journey *8 Oct. 1944 letter*
   15 But no breath of wind] And a wind of snow *8 Oct. 1944 letter*
   16 And it was rigged for a long journey *8 Oct. 1944 letter*
   17 rose high] lay low *8 Oct. 1944 letter*
   18 proud] sad *8 Oct. 1944 letter*
   20 Both came back from their long journey. *8 Oct. 1944 letter*
   21 went wide and far] drove further on *8 Oct. 1944 letter*
   22 Into an] ~~Over the~~ Into an *8 Oct. 1944 letter*
   23 Where a strange light shone, *8 Oct. 1944 letter*
Songs
Songs] *North Ship Songs Bodl. MS*

Titles 65° N] (1) *Bodl. MS*
70° N | Fortunetelling] (2) | Fortunetelling *Bodl. MS*
75° N | Blizzard] (3) *Bodl. MS*
Above 80° N] (4) *Bodl. MS*

Legend L told JBS (*SL*, 91): 'The last line of each verse is a formal refrain and should be in italics.' (It was not printed thus in *TNS*.) From the outset, L expressed reservations about the poem. To JBS (*SL*, 90, 92): 'I may change words here and there later. It is rather mechanical [. . .] I have just read the three ships in print and think it should be called the three shits. Don't pay much attention to it, it's bloody terrible.' Similarly, on the poem and the sequence it inaugurates, L to JBS, 17 Oct. 1944 (*SL*, 93–4): 'I have just been rewriting The North Ship, the ballad I sent you some days ago. It took a great hold on my imagination, and I planned some more poems to make it into a loosely-linked long poem. But I have tried hard at them without success, and I know why it is. Every now and then I am impelled to try to declare a faith in complete severance from life: and I can never quite do it. Perhaps it is as well, because who knows the consequences? and I always say that no one can write well if he does not believe what he is writing [. . .] In consequence the subsequent poems, planned as analysis and celebration of this faith, have come to nothing. Though I am not surprised I am disappointed, as one always is at any kind of failure.'
    1 Cf. the opening line of the traditional English carol: 'I saw three ships come sailing in'. L to MJ, 20 Dec. 1951 (Bodl. MS Eng. c. 7406/98): 'I hope the three ships of Christmas bring you much happiness and contentment.' **4** 'You understand "journey" is pronounced naturally, to make a little hesitation in the rhythm, not in the godawful prizeday-recitation "journee" manner': L to JBS (*SL*, 91). **11** *the wind hunted it*: Cf. Hopkins, 'See how Spring opens with disabling cold', 2: 'hunting winds'.
    65° N 12 *birdless*: As also in *Next, Please*, 23, and *To James Sutton* | *Poem*, 6.
    Above 80° N 3–4 *Betelgeuse . . . Orion*: Betelgeuse is a yellowish-red variable star of the first magnitude, the brightest in the constellation Orion. Cooper (2004), 106 notes that 'Betelgeuse' derives from the Arabic 'yad al jauza', which means 'Central One' or 'Mysterious Woman'.

XXXII

In *Wkbk 1* (1/1/70) there is a draft of the whole poem dated '15. xii. 47'. (At this stage the title was 'Sunday morning'.) Poem IX in *XX Poems*. George Hartley, Hartley (1988), 301, records that he failed to persuade L to include the poem in the second edition of *TLD*. Published in *Poetry Book Society Bulletin*, 10 (July 1956), [1]. It was added to the first Faber edition of *TNS* (Sept. 1966).

See L's comment on the poem at the end of his Introduction to the Faber edition (above). L to MJ, 22 Oct. 1954 (Bodl. MS Eng. c. 7409/82), when the poem was no. IX in *XX Poems*: 'People never say anything complimentary about IX, but I don't think it's so bad as I used to & [it] certainly says more about me than anything else (except *To fail*). The last line is "exactly me".' In a letter to MJ dated 26 Jan. 1956 (Bodl. MS Eng. c. 7412/131), L lists the poem among 'dregs & throwouts'.
    14–16 Andrew Swarbrick, *Out of Reach: The Poetry of Philip Larkin* (1995), 33, notes the gap of almost one year between *Thaw* and this poem, and takes the lines to refer to 'the rediscovery of a poetic impulse after a year's silence'. **16–17** Andrew Motion, *Philip Larkin* (1982), 33, compares Hardy, *At The Word "Farewell"*, 29–32: 'Even then the scale might have been turned | Against love by a feather, | – But crimson one cheek of hers burned | When we came in together'. **25** L to MJ, 26 Feb. 1956 (Bodl. MS Eng. c. 7413/19): 'obviously people who think themselves the most important person in the world are "immature" – part invalid, part baby & part saint, as I wrote'.

The collection was originally entitled *Various Poems*: Jean Hartley (1989), 68. In 1954 it was rejected by the Dolmen Press, Dublin – 'by the two Irish members of the triumvirate selection board – too self pitying and sexy': L to PS, 9 Oct. 1954 (*SL*, 229). Donald Davie, then a lecturer in English at Trinity College, Dublin, had urged L to try the press, which was run by Liam Miller (1923–87). Zachary Leader identifies the two members of the selection board as the poet, translator, civil servant and academic Thomas Kinsella (b. 1928) and Sean White (1927–77), editor of the Irish literary magazine *Irish Writing*: Amis, *Letters*, 411–12 n. 4. In a letter dated 10 Oct. 1954 to MJ (Bodl. MS Eng. c. 7409/68–9), L gave an account of the rejection of the poems:

> Davie was for them (he said) & the two Irish (young fellows,
> they were) against. They thought them 'too self pitying' (I offered
> Davie this phrase & he gladly accepted it) and 'too sexy' (his own
> words) [. . .] He did tell me 4 (out of 12) they all liked, but I can't
> remember them now, except *Triple Time*. The one he praised was
> *Latest face* (classes in T.C.D. have been analysing this); the one
> he liked least *Wires* – in fact he thought it 'very feeble'! [. . .] O,
> another one that aroused general displeasure was *To fail*, but I
> think perhaps I made an error of judgment in including it. It really
> is very personal indeed.

In a letter of 15 December 1954 to her, he added: '*Reasons for att.* earned the censure of the Dolmen Press boys – too sexy, I suppose, for the priest-ridden crooked little lice. It's not up to much': Bodl. MS Eng. c. 7410/13.

The prospect of having the poems published by George Hartley, editor of the magazine *Listen*, presented itself in 1954. In a letter dated 8 Jan. 1955 L tells MJ that he has found '23 suitable ones' if he assumes 'a standard that disqualifies *Poetry of departures*, & *To fail*, & *Spring*': Bodl. MS Eng. c. 7410/24. Eight days later, he tells her by letter (Bodl. MS Eng. c. 7410/29) that he has 'left everything *in* except *Spring* & *To fail* (now called *Success story*)', and on 29 January, that 'Hartley wants to include *Spring* and *Since we agreed*': Bodl. MS Eng. c. 7410/46. On 2 Oct. 1955 he announces to her: 'Page proofs from Hartley, doing nothing to cheer me up, as his letter refuses to look at Watt's amendments': Bodl. MS Eng. c. 7412/45, referring to Peter Watt of A. P. Watt & Son, literary agents. The volume was published on 24 Nov. 1955 under the imprint of the Marvell Press, Hull, with finance provided by subscription. (Further bibliographical information is in Bloomfield [2002], 21–2.) It contained thirteen poems from *XX Poems*: *Wedding-Wind*; *Next, Please*; *Deceptions*; *Latest Face*; *Spring*; *Dry-Point*; *Coming*; *No Road*; *If, My Darling*; *Wires*; *Wants*; *Going* and *At Grass*.

TEXT

The original subscription edn. contained the misprint 'floor' for 'sea' on p. 38: *FR*, 13; L to MJ, 24 Nov. 1955 (Bodl. MS Eng. c. 7412/98): 'there *is* an absurd misprint! I've just this moment checked it, & am furious with myself: in *Absences* it sh^d be *Rain patters on a sea* . . . How "floor" got in I don't know. I should never use the same word twice in two lines like that.' L told CM on 7 July 1977 (*SL*, 568) that George Hartley was planning 'a new edition free of the myriad misprints of the previous one'.

Jean Hartley (1989), 74, records that 'By the middle of April [1955] Philip had almost completed the titling of poems, which had originally only borne numbers.'

TITLE

Cf. *Hamlet*, 3. 1. 121–2: Hamlet: 'I loved you not.' Ophelia: 'I was the more deceived.' Noted by George Hartley in Thwaite (1982), 88. Cf. also Swift's definition of happiness in 'A Digression on Madness' in section IX of *A Tale of a Tub* as '*a perpetual Possession of being well Deceived*': noted by Laurence Lerner, *Philip Larkin* (1997), 12. L to MJ, 8 Jan. 1955 (Bodl. MS Eng. c. 7410/24): 'I am always at a loss about a title. I'd *like* to call it *Such absences*, to draw attention to my favourite poem! only it doesn't make sense, since my poems aren't *really* "attics cleared of me", far from it, in any way that makes sense.' L to MJ, 16 Jan. 1955 (Bodl. MS Eng. c. 7410/29): 'Provisionally I've called it *Various poems*'. He tells MJ in a letter dated 8 Apr. 1955 (Bodl. MS Eng. c. 7410/92–3) that 'Hartley wants me to give titles to *all* my poems', and that he (L) is thinking of '*Less deceived*' or '*The less deceived*' for 'the Mayhew one'. 'Hartley disliked the title *Various Poems*, so Larkin gave one poem a new title, "Deceptions", and took its old one, "The Less Deceived", for the book: sleevenote from the LP of *TLD* (1959); *FR*, 12. See *Deceptions*, 25. L expressed his views on the title in a letter of Apr. 1955 to Hartley: 'I especially didn't want an "ambiguous" title, or one that made any claims to policy or belief: this (*The Less Deceived*) would however give a certain amount of sad-eyed (and clear-eyed) realism, and if they [i.e. readers] did pick up the context they might grasp my fundamentally passive attitude to poetry (and life too, I suppose) which believes that the agent is always more deceived than the patient, because action comes from desire, and we all know that desire comes from wanting something we haven't got, which may not make us any happier when we have it. On the other hand suffering – well, there is positively no deception about that. No one *imagines* their suffering': Hartley in Thwaite (1982), 88.

In 1981 L replied to the statement that in *TLD* he was saved from the limitations of the Movement by his transcendence of the commonplace (*FR*, 57): 'I never thought the Movement commonplace, if that's what's implied. Not like *Lyrical Ballads*. It was much wittier and more cerebral. I don't want to transcend the commonplace, I love the commonplace, I lead a very commonplace life. Everyday things are lovely to me.'

Lines on a Young Lady's Photograph Album

DATE AND TEXT
L to WA, 17 Aug. 1953 (Bodl. MS Res. c. 616; *SL*, 209): 'I've also begun a poem about your photograph album, wch can't make up its mind whether it's going to be serious or not, as I understand the columns of *The Spectator* are open to me [. . .] no, that sounds commercial: I'd have written it anyway.' To WA, 22 Aug. 1953 (Bodl. MS Res. c. 616): 'I've finished the poem about your album, but haven't sent it to the *Spectator* as it's too long, & in any case I like to give poems a period of quarantine, during which time I take them out & read them fairly often & try to sense any faults not apparent in the first flush of excitement. It's not *particularly* embarrassing – nor particularly *intelligent*, if it comes to that.'

Wkbk 3 contains: just over five pages of drafts of the first five and ninth stanzas dated '17. 8. 53', and another draft of the ninth dated '18. 8. 53' (1/3/8); two pages of drafts of the last four stanzas after '18. 8. 53' (sixteen pages before), dated '18. 9. 53' at the end (1/3/14); and a page of drafts of ll. 33–40 between '6. xii. 53' and '28 xii 53' (1/3/28). Published in *The Fantasy Poets*, no. 21 (Mar. 1954), and in *Q*, a publication of the Students' Representative Council of Queen's University, Belfast, 11 (Hilary [Winter] 1955), 30–1.

The poem relates to WA (b. 1929), whom L met in Belfast in 1950 after his appointment as Sub-Librarian at Queen's University. They corresponded with each other when she left in the autumn of 1950 to study for a Postgraduate Diploma in Librarianship in London, and they became easy friends and companions on her return to Queen's, Belfast. She left when she married Geoff Bradshaw in 1954. In a letter of 26 Nov. 1986, she reports on the changes L made for the poem: 'there were in fact two albums not one, there's not a picture of me wearing a trilby hat (though there is one of me in a beret and moustache for Rag Week). On the other hand, I'm afraid to say, there's definitely my double chin, he got that right. And there's also one of me bathing': Motion (1993), 233–4. The 'reluctant cat' (l. 7) was in reality a dog: WA, reported in *AL*, 24 (Oct. 2007), 15. See also *Maiden Name* and 'When she came on, you couldn't keep your seat', and the notes on *Latest Face*.

In a letter to WA of 28 Oct. 1953 (Bodl. MS Res. c. 616), L refers to the poem as 'your album'; in another of 10 Aug. 1972 (*SL*, 461), as 'your poem – or *one* of your poems'. L to WA, 14 Mar. 1958 (*SL*, 284): 'I won't voluntarily bring your photograph album into the light if you're tired of it: it's having a repeat on Monday (the day you get this, I hope), and later in the month I'm having a shot at recording it (among the rest) for the Poetry Room at Harvard.' AT (*SL*, 284 n.) identifies the recording as the one made for the British Council on 25 Mar. 1958, copies of which were for the Poetry Room at Harvard.

L to WA, 7 Apr. 1954 (*SL*, 225): 'The *Album* starts pedestrianly, I'm afraid, but verses 4–6 and the last one satisfy me. Between them, they constitute a sort of *ave-atque-vale*, the two of them.' To WA, 23 Aug. 1979 (*SL*, 603), on Bloomfield's forthcoming bibliography: 'detailing every silly morsel I've ever written – even the "Photograph Album" in *Q* – not that that was so silly'.

To WA, 18 Feb. 1959 (*SL*, 300): 'An American college-boy from Chicago wrote yesterday saying how much better my album poem was than C. Day-Lewis's: aren't you lucky to have known me rather than him! More cowardly, better writer.' Patricia Ball, 'The Photographic Art', *Review of English Literature*, 3 (Apr. 1962), 54–5, compares L's poem with Day-Lewis's *The Album*. Timms (1973), 76, acknowledges Day-Lewis's poem as a 'literary antecedent': 'Both poems start from the experience of looking at snapshots in an album, both poems are addressed to the subject of the photographs, and both lead to a reflection on how the past affects us in the present. There is no other similarity.' L included Day-Lewis's poem in *OBTCEV*.

Title John Wooley, 'Larkin: Romance, Fiction and Myth', *English*, 35. 153 (Autumn 1986), 237, surmises that this is 'a very eighteenth-century way of embarking on the title to a poem'. *The New Oxford Book of Eighteenth Century Verse*, ed. Roger Lonsdale (1984), contains five poems with titles beginning '*Lines* . . .' More specifically, Wordsworth and Coleridge's *Lyrical Ballads* (1798) contains five poems with titles beginning this way, among them *Lines Written a Few Miles above Tintern Abbey*. **8** Cf. Tennyson, *The Princess*, Prologue, 142: 'sweet girl-graduates in their golden hair'. Noted by Christopher Ricks in a 1965 review of *TWW*, repr. in *Phoenix: A Poetry Magazine*, ed. Harry Chambers, Philip Larkin issue, 11/12 (Autumn and Winter, 1973/4), 7. The photograph of WA is reproduced as illustration 32 in Motion (1993). **10** 'Nobody that I ever knew took earlier to the trilby': school friend Noel Hughes on L in Thwaite (1982), 20. John Whitehead, *Hardy to Larkin: Seven English Poets* (1995), 220, notes that Brett Ashley, the heroine in Hemingway's *Fiesta* (*The Sun Also Rises*), wears a trilby hat. Brett, her hair brushed back 'like a boy's' and referring to herself as 'a chap' (i. 3), is irresistibly attractive to Jake Barnes, who is in love with her but unable to consummate the relationship because of a war wound. **15** J. R. Watson notes the cliché of 'Not quite your class': Salwak (1989), 96. **20** An advertisement featuring two white-coated workmen carrying between them on their shoulders a plank bearing the brand-name of the commercial whitewash. Identified (aptly) by John Whitehead, *Hardy to Larkin*, 221. The advert is reproduced in *AL*, 28 (Oct. 2009), 20. **25** Cf. Auden, *Another Time*, 10: 'a proper flag in a proper place'. **39–40** L to WA, 14 Mar. 1958 (*SL*, 285): 'And no, I *didn't* take one of you bathing: this was just an invention of my evil imagination: the one of you up to the neck in water I left where it was.' Confirmed by WA in interview: *AL*, 1 (Apr. 1996), 14. The photograph is reproduced as illustration 33 in Motion (1993).

Wedding-Wind

DATE AND TEXT

In *Wkbk 1* (1/1/59) there is a draft of the whole poem except for the title dated '26 Sept [1946]'. Included in *ITGOL*; poem I in *XX Poems*.

VARIANTS (from *ITGOL*)
Title [No title]
10 day] morning
11 by] with

L to MJ, 26 Nov. 1950 (Bodl. MS Eng. c. 7404/1), concerning six
poems he has sent to her: 'On the whole I think *Wind* is the best.
I wish I could write more like that, fuller, richer in reference: I am
quite pleased with the to-me successful use of the floods & the
wind as fulfillment & joy.' It is probably the poem of which L said
'I wrote my first good poem when I was twenty-six': *Radio Times*,
16 Aug. 1973, 115. Peter Ferguson in Hartley (1988), 156, guesses
At Grass, but the drafts of that poem were not finished until 1 Mar.
1950. When Ms Patricia Sweet told L that the poem reminded her
of certain scenes in Lawrence's *The Rainbow*, and especially of
the marriage between Tom and Anna, L replied on 4 Dec. 1980:
'"Wedding-Wind" dates from the late Forties, by which time I had
certainly read *The Rainbow*. I think the comparison is reasonable
enough': Hull DPL (2) 2/21/2.
    Petch (1981), 47, notes that it is 'Larkin's only poem with a
recognizably female speaker'.
    12–14 Cf. *A Girl in Winter*, p. 120 of 1964 edn.: 'and a bare-
armed woman came out with a pail. She set it down with a clang
and stared at them'. Noted by Alan Brownjohn in Thwaite (1982),
110. **16** '*Cloths* is right. I think it sounds more impressive than
clothes. Anyway it is unlikely that there would have been a heavy
wash on that particular day': L to D. J. Enright, 26 Apr. 1955 (*SL*,
240). Cf. Yeats, *He Wishes For The Cloths of Heaven*, and Dylan
Thomas's short story, *The Visitor*: 'the wind could never penetrate
his cloths'. **23** The kneeling cattle may recall those at worship in
Hardy's poems *The Lost Pyx*, 49–52, and *The Oxen*, 2, 8, 12 (the
latter included by L in *OBTCEV*). The parallel with *The Oxen*
is noted by Timothy Trengove-Jones, 'Philip Larkin's "Wedding-
Wind"', *English Studies in Africa*, 48. 1 (2005), 91. See 'Climbing
the hill within the deafening wind', 14 .

Places, Loved Ones

DATE AND TEXT
L to PS, 9 Oct. 1954 (*SL*, 230): 'Am now turning to one of my self-
pitying sexy poems. Hell, people don't know what self pity is these

days.' *Wkbk* 4 (1/4/8) contains four pages of drafts of the whole poem except for the title after '27. 8. 54', dated '10 October 1954' at the end. In a letter dated 10 Oct. 1954 to MJ (Bodl. MS Eng. c. 7409/68), L announces: '8.45 p.m. – Have just finished and typed a poem, not good: slangy, unprofound.' KA to L, 13 Nov. 1954 (Amis, *Letters*, 413), seems to refer to a draft: 'What's The key that rusts?'; '"When" in line 17 seems to me inferior to "should"'. Published in *The Spectator*, 194. 6602 (7 Jan. 1955), 18.

VARIANTS (from *The Spectator*)
Title Times, Places, Loved Ones
15 Should] When
turn] turns

1 Stan Smith notes that sonnet XXIV in Auden's sequence *In Time of War* opens with a negative ('No, not their names.'), and that there is some similarity of thought between the two poems: 'Something for Nothing: Late Larkins and Early', *English*, 49 (Autumn 2000), 274. 3 *proper ground*: echoes *Church Going*, 61–2 (to which see note). 20 *Mashed*: Lines 6–7 of Bruce Montgomery's poem, *A Song for K. W. A. (on his fiftieth birthday)*, read 'That what mashes | Us most'. L, invited to comment on the t.s. of Montgomery's poems, encircled 'mashes' and remarked: 'don't get the usage – see Oxf. Conc. Dict. 6th ed. p. 670': Bodl. MS Eng. c. 3917. He had got the usage by the time he wrote his own poem. The primary sense ('crushed') comes with an undertone of 'excited amorously' (*OED*, mash, *v.*² 1.a).

Coming

DATE AND TEXT
In *Wkbk* 1 (1/1/95) there is a complete draft dated '25. 2. 50'. (The title at this stage was 'February'.) Poem XII in *XX Poems*.

VARIANTS
Title [No title] *XX Poems*

In a letter to MJ dated 26 Nov. 1950 (Bodl. MS Eng. c. 7404/1) L confessed to liking the poem. To MJ, 31 Jan. 1951 (Bodl. MS Eng. c. 7407/10): '"The most dense of us are liable to experience unexpected sensations during the short weeks of February. It may be that we are hurrying along a city pavement deep sunk in the illusions of the hour, brooding over some mundane transaction, harassed by domestic responsibility, or distracted by poverty; when, suddenly, something in the air will bring us an entire release, an entire purification of the spirit, and we shall be children again playing our games on those lovely evenings when it first began to be light after tea." Am delighted to discover that in *The twelve months*, for it is the sensation I tried to describe in *On longer evenings*.' ('*The twelve months*' has not been traced.) L reports to MJ in letters dated 25 Mar. 1952 and 28 June 1953 being ravished by birdsong (Bodl. MSS Eng. c. 7407/46, 7408/25). L in 1964 (*FR*, 82): 'The most difficult kind of poem to write is the expression of a sharp uncomplicated experience, the vivid emotion you can't wind yourself into slowly but have to take a single shot at, hit or miss. Some fifteen years ago, in February, I heard a bird singing in some garden when I was walking home from work: after tea I tried to describe it, and after supper revised what I had written. That was the poem, and I must say I have always found it successful. It is called "Coming" – what is coming, I suppose, is spring.'

8 Cf. Virginia Woolf, *The Waves* (1931), Harvest edn., 172: 'When the lark peels high his ring of sound and it falls through the air like an apple paring'. 10–11 L on the sleeve note to the *Listen* recording of *TLD*, quoted in Hartley (1988), 50: 'the repeated line is supposed to suggest the bird call'. 12–13 Cf. 'The poet has a straight face', 70: 'our forgotten childhoods'; and *Dockery and Son*, 45: 'Life is first boredom, then fear'.

Reasons for Attendance

DATE AND TEXT
Wkbk 3 (1/3/30) contains three pages of a draft of the whole poem except for the title after '28 xii 53', dated '29 xii 53' at the end, and a single page bearing another draft, complete except for the title, dated '30 xii 53' at the end. Included by L in a letter to PS, 23 Jan. 1954, where he describes it as 'a poem, of a somewhat sombre turn': *SL*, 222. L to PS, 3 Feb. 1954 (*SL*, 223): 'That poem I sent you is now called *Reasons for attendance*.'

Title Osborne (2008), 79, notes 'standard phraseology on official documents such as those issued by the medical profession'. 1–5 Arthur Terry in Hartley (1988), 96, reports that L told him that the opening lines 'describe looking through the windows of the old Students' Union in University Square [Belfast] while a Saturday night hop was in progress'. 4–5 Leggett (1999), 63, notes Irving Berlin's song *Cheek to Cheek* (1935), 2–4: 'and my heart beats so that I can hardly speak. I And I seem to find the happiness I seek I When we're out together dancing cheek to cheek.' Also Laurence Binyon, *The Little Dancers*, 11: 'Dance sedately; face to face they gaze'. L included the poem in *OBTCEV*. 12 'The *bell* is the trumpet-bell, and is naturally lifted when being played': L to PS, 3 Feb. 1954 (*SL*, 223). Confirmed in a letter to C. K. Tirumalai dated 13 Mar. 1979 (Bodl. MS Eng. c. 2724/24). *rough-tongued bell*: By analogy with Dylan Thomas's 'black-tongued bells' and 'dust-tongued bell': *I See the Boys of Summer*, 28; *It Is the Sinner's Dust-Tongued Bell*, 1. John Whitehead notes the latter: *AL*, 5 (Apr. 1998), 29. 16 *But not for me*: Leggett (1999), 67, notes the 1930 Gershwin song *But Not for Me*, 9: 'They're writing songs of love, but not for me'. (The next line is 'A lucky star's above, but not for me'.) He also notes that L reviewed John Coltrane's version of the Gershwin, and in his next review of a Coltrane recording said bluntly, 'The screeching dreariness of John Coltrane is not for me': *AWJ*, 141, 150. Noting 'bell' (l. 12), cf. the anonymous First World War song *The Bells of Hell*, 1–2, 7–8: 'The bells of hell go ting-a-ling-a-ling I For you but not for me'.

Dry-Point

DATE AND TEXT

Wkbk 2 contains drafts of stanzas 2 and 4 between '12. 3. 50' and '17. 3. 50' (1/2/2), and two pages bearing drafts of the whole poem except for the title between '17. 3. 50' and '20 / 3 / 50' (1/2/4). Poem XI in *XX Poems*, where it was poem (2) under the general title *Two portraits of sex*. (The first was *Oils*.) Published in *Listen*, 1. 2 (Summer 1954), 14–15.

VARIANTS

Title Etching *XX Poems*
9 But] And *Listen, 1954*

L told Jean Hartley that it was about how sex dominates our lives: *AL*, 13 (Apr. 2002), 5. L in 1981 (*FR*, 50–1): 'I get endless trouble about "Dry-Point". Schoolgirls write to me about it, and I have to explain that originally it was one of two poems about sex, and that modesty forbids me to say any more'; *Dry-Point* is saying 'how awful sex is and how we want to get away from it'. L in 1981 on the poem *High Windows* (*FR*, 59): 'I think the end shows a desire to get away from it all, not unlike "Dry-Point" in a way, or "Absences".'

Title Engraving on a copper plate by a needle, without acid.
11–12 Birmingham-manufactured jewellery has long been regarded as sham, cheap (hence 'Brummagem'). Cf. L's jocular remark to MJ, 26 Nov. 1959 (*SL*, 310): 'I used a Brummagem screwdriver (hammer)'. **13–15** L to Renato Oliva, 30 Apr. 1968: 'we cannot define the dimensions or position of the "room", nor prove that it exists, but we believe in it all the same': Hull DPL (2) 3/17/1.

Next, Please

DATE AND TEXT
Wkbk 2 contains seven pages of drafts between '1951' (the year written at the top of the page on which drafting begins) and a draft lacking only ll. 15–20 dated '10. 1. 51' (1/2/33). One of the drafts bears the title 'Tenth days'. There follows a draft of the first five stanzas between '10. 1. 51' and '6 Feb [1951]'. L quotes ll. 1–2 in a letter of 6 Jan. 1951 to MJ (Bodl. MS Eng. c. 7404/ 62 = *LTM*, 30), remarking that he has 'spent ages' in producing them, and 14–21 and the first word of 22 in another of 13 Jan. 1951 (Bodl. MS Eng. c. 7404/72–3 = *LTM*, 33–4). Poem III in *XX Poems*. The poem was broadcast on the BBC Third Programme's *First Reading*, and the *Spectator* agreed to print it but demurred on account of 'tits' in l. 13 (as L told Alan Brownjohn, 6 Jan. 1955: *SL*, 234). Published in *Departure*, 3. 7 (Spring 1955), 4–5.

VARIANTS
Title [No title] *XX Poems* or *Departure, 1955*
2 Pick out the festivals ten weeks away *Letter, 6 Jan. 1951*
21 a black-] black- *Letter, 13 Jan. 1951*

L to MJ, 6 and 13 Jan. 1951 (Bodl. MSS Eng. c. 7404/ 62, 72): 'I think it's just another example of the danger of looking forward to things [. . .] an attempt to capture my feeling on returning here [i.e. Belfast]: a sense of amazement that what we wait for so long & therefore seems so long in coming *shouldn't* take a proportionately long time to pass – instead of zipping away at the same speed as everything else.'

Anthony Thwaite detects the cliché 'when my ship comes in' underlying the poem: *Contemporary English Poetry: An Introduction* (1959; 3rd edn., 1964), 147. Leggett (1999), 160, identifies as a general influence Yeats's poem *What Then?*, which deals with the way the future works out inconclusively or frustratingly, noting (160) that L mistakenly referred to *Next, Please* as 'What next?' in a letter of 23 Feb. 1955 to RC (*SL*, 236). Roger Craik, 'Some Unheard Melodies in Philip Larkin's Poetry', *AL*, 12 (Oct. 2001), 13, cites *Someday*, appended to his *Essays* (1899) by minor poet W. W. M. Hunt, as a *point de départ* for L's poem:

Someday

We lightly say
When our ship with full spread wings
Comes home, and our fortune brings,
This will we do or that;
We have got a plan so pat
For a life all ease and joy,
All gold without alloy,
Someday.

But in the womb of fate
Lies a day of certain date.
And while our someday tarries yet afar
This one day's portal may be now ajar.

Title L had cause to dread the words. 'I began life as a bad stammerer [. . .] Up to the age of 21 I was still asking for railway tickets by pushing written notes across the counter': L in 1964 (*FR*, 24). 'I still stammered quite badly up to the age of maybe thirty. I mean stammered to the point of handing over little slips of paper at the railway station saying third-class return to Birmingham instead of actually trying to get it out': L in 1979 (*RW*, 49). L to M. A. Cowley, 21 Jan. 1980: 'I sympathise with you most sincerely over stammering: it is a dreadful handicap. I stammered fairly noticeably until about 1960, or when I was approaching forty': *AL*, 15 (Apr. 2003), 4. L in 1981 (*FR*, 48): 'I wasn't a happy child: I stammered badly, and this tends to shape your life. You can't become a lecturer or anything that involves talking. By the time you cure yourself – which in my case was quite late, about thirty – all the talking things you might have done are lost. If you catch me tired or frightened, I still stammer.'

11 *prinked*: Timms (1973), 20, notes that Hardy uses the word (as a verb) in *Beeny Cliff*, 9. In addition, Hardy has the verb 'prink' (*The Souls of the Slain*, 58) and the gerund 'prinking' (*Wagtail and Baby*, 12). **20** Cf. Auden, 'Stop all the clocks, cut off the telephone', 12: 'I thought that love would last for ever: I was wrong.' **23** *birdless*: As also in *The North Ship, Songs, 65° N*, 12, and *To James Sutton* | *Poem*, 6.

Going

DATE AND TEXT
The draft in *Wkbk 1*, complete except for the title, dates from between 15 Dec. 1945 and 23 Feb. 1946. Included in *ITGOL*; poem XIX in *XX Poems*.

VARIANTS
Title Dying Day *ITGOL*; [No title] *XX Poems*
4 yet] when *ITGOL*
5 When it] It *ITGOL*
7 locked] locks *ITGOL*

Wants

DATE AND TEXT
Wkbk 2 (1/2/15): contains a one-page draft of the whole poem except for the title after '28. 5. 50', dated '1. 6. 50' at the end; a half-page of drafts of the opening lines after '1. 6. 50'; and a half-page draft of the whole poem except for the title dated '2-6-50' at the end. Poem XVIII in *XX Poems*.

KA on 12 May 1951 (Amis, *Letters*, 259) implies that it is too similar to Auden's *Spain 1937*. This would apply to the rhythm and to the noun-phrase syntax of ll. 7–9. Stan Smith notes that death is 'costed like an account, in a periphrasis that recalls cadentially the abstracted lists of Auden's "Spain"': 'Something for Nothing: Late Larkins and Early', *English*, 49 (Autumn 2000), 271. Booth (1992), 160, notes the 'list of dull phrases reminiscent of early Eliot: '"invitation-cards", "the printed directions of sex", "the family . . . under the flagstaff", "The life insurance"'.

1, 5 Cf. MacNeice, *The Libertine*, 18: 'And after the event the wish to be alone – ', and the refrain (ll. 5, 10, 15, 20, 25) 'O leave me easy, leave me alone'.

Maiden Name

DATE AND TEXT
The poem was occasioned by the marriage in London of WA and Geoff Bradshaw in 1954. In a letter dated 7 Apr. 1954 (*SL*, 225), L wishes her well in her marriage. *Wkbk 5* (1/5/7) contains seventeen pages of drafts of the whole poem after '15 / xi / 53', dated '15 / 1 / 55' at the end. Judging from the position in the *Wkbk* of the drafts of *Myxomatosis*, which L sent to MJ on 14 Nov. 1954, these drafts come after that date. In a letter to D. J. Enright, 26 Apr. 1955 (*SL*, 240), L describes it as 'the last thing I wrote'. He describes it to MJ in a letter dated 30 June 1955 as 'another fairly recent one I think quite good': Bodl. MS Eng. c. 7411/89. '*Maiden name*. This alteration is the original version, which, though perhaps inferior in sense, sounds better to me and I have decided to retain it': L to RC, 7 Sept. 1955 (*SL*, 250). Jean Hartley (1989), 68, records that in the months during which *TLD* was in preparation L amended 'early days' (l. 18) to 'first few days' and 'fine clear days', before settling on 'first few days'.

On WA, see notes on *Lines on a Young Lady's Photograph Album*. See also the notes on *Latest Face*. L to WA, 16 Nov. 1976 (*SL*, 551): 'your memory is B—— if you think you weren't beautiful [. . .] I *think* you knew *Maiden Name* was about you, because I remember you said in a slightly chilly voice that you didn't care for the phrase "thankfully confused".' L to PS, 10 Sept. 1955 (*SL*, 251): 'I reread *Maiden name* in proof the other day, & had to confess it felt rather soggy in the middle'. '"Maiden Name", he said, was "about that shock we all feel when we see for the first time the married name of someone we used to know"': Watt (1989), 174. L in 1981 (*FR*, 55): 'I used to be quite original in those days. As far as I know, nobody else has written about maiden names, and yet they are very powerful things. I often wonder how women survive the transition: if you're called something, you can't be called something else.'

2 *five light sounds*: 'Winifred Arnott'.

Born Yesterday

DATE AND TEXT
Wkbk 3 (1/3/35) contains three and a half pages of drafts after 'For Sally Myfanwy, b 2.5 am 17 / 1 / 54': of ll. 1–19 and five additional

lines dated '20 / 1/ 54', and of 20–4 dated '20. 1. 54'. At this stage there was no title. Published in *The Spectator*, 193. 6579 (30 July 1954), 144. L revised or corrected 'Capture' to 'Catching' in l. 24 on a cutting of the printing (Hull DPL 3/1). Jean Hartley (1989), 82, records that the poem was a 'late inclusion' in *TLD*.

VARIANTS
24 Catching] Capture *The Spectator, 1954*

L to PS, 3 Feb. 1954 (*SL*, 223): 'I fudged up a birthday poem for Kingsley's daughter, which was rather mechanical though he seemed to like it – though I suppose he couldn't very well say he didn't like it.' To RC, 7 Sept. 1955 (*SL*, 250): 'No, I admit *Born y.* doesn't sound too bad. I thought it was a bit sentimental, and I had got a little weary of poems "for" other people's nippers or wives or husbands or weddings, and felt the convention "dated".'

The wishes expressed in the poem are along the lines of those in Yeats, *A Prayer for My Daughter*. Cf. ll. 4–5, 15–17 with Yeats, 17–19: 'May she be granted beauty and yet not | Beauty to make a stranger's eye distraught, | Or hers before a looking-glass'. L included Yeats's poem in *OBTCEV*.

Title Cf. 'not born yesterday', meaning not inexperienced or gullible. Osborne (2008), 80, notes that George Cukor's film *Born Yesterday*, which picked up an Oscar and four further Oscar nominations in 1951, made the curtailed title famous. He comments: 'By deftly alluding to this story of a "dumb blonde" outwitting manipulative men and captivating the cinema audience, Larkin underwrites his theme that those taken for "dull" sometimes lead triumphant lives.' Dedication Sally Myfanwy Amis (1954–2000), daughter of Kingsley and Hillary Amis, was born at 2.05 a.m. on 17 Jan. 1954. KA told L the news of her birth in a letter of 18 Jan. 1954: Amis, *Letters*, 359. In a letter composed on 19, 23 and 26 Jan., KA, not entirely seriously, expressed views that L's poem takes on board: 'I hope she has a lovely childhood and has a lovely time at school and makes a lot of lovely chums and brings them home': Amis, *Letters*, 361. 11–19 Cf. the terms of L's advocacy of BP in a letter dated 15 Aug. 1965 to CM: 'I like to read about people who have done nothing spectacular, who aren't beautiful and lucky, who try to behave well in the limited field of activity they command, but who can see, in little autumnal moments of vision, that the so called "big" experiences of life are going to miss them': Thwaite (1982), 42–3; *SL*, 376. 24 '"Catching" because I want to suggest something continuous through life, not just one isolated instance': L to RC, 7 Sept. 1955 (*SL*, 250).

Whatever Happened?

DATE AND TEXT
Wkbk 3 contains two pages of a complete draft except for the title after '24. x. 53', dated '26. x. 53' at the end. L to WA, 28 Oct. 1953 (Bodl. MS Res. c. 616): 'one written the other night about, oh dear, well, how-we-automatically-change-an-event-in-our-minds-until-it's-no-existence-except-in-nightmares'. L included it with a letter of 1 Nov. 1953 to PS (*SL*, 216). Published in *The Fantasy Poets*, no. 21 (Mar. 1954).

VARIANTS (from the letter of 1 Nov. 1953)
Title The story of an occurrence and a disoccurrence
 6 All's] All
Easily, then] So, at ease
12 'This whole formation means complete mishap.'
13–14 Curses? the darkness, fighting – what recourse | Have these tales now? Except to nightmares, of course.

L to PS, 1 Nov. 1953: 'Having typed it out, I think its fault is being just another poem about ships & journeys when we know it all means something different. In case it isn't clear, it treats of the way in which the mind gets to work on any violent involuntary experience & transforms it out of all knowledge. There are one or two verbal alterations that might be made: I have tried to keep the wording ambiguous, so that "whatever happened" could be sexual as well as violent.' To PS, 11 Nov. 1953 (*SL*, 218): 'I altered my poem a bit on the lines you suggested. It's a facile bit of work, though.'

No Road

DATE AND TEXT
Wkbk 2 (1/2/21) contains four pages of drafts of the whole poem except for the title between '5. 8. 50' and '27. x. 50', and a further page of drafts of stanza 3 dated '28 / x / 50' at the end. Poem XIII in *XX Poems*. Published in *Departure*, 3. 8 (Summer 1955), 12.

VARIANTS

Title [No title] *XX Poems* or *Departure*, 1955

Title Commonly found on road signs where a road ends or has been closed off.

Wires

DATE AND TEXT

Wkbk 2 (1/2/23) contains a half-page draft of the whole poem except for the title dated 'Before breakfast 4 / xi / 50'. L to MJ, 26 Nov. 1950 (Bodl. MS Eng. c. 7404/1): 'The *prairie* one' was 'written straight off before breakfast in pyjamas'. Poem XVI in *XX Poems*. Published in *The Spectator*, 191. 6536 (2 Oct. 1953), 367, with a full stop at the end of l. 4 'that made nonsense of it all': L to PS, 3 Oct. 1953 (*SL*, 213). L to WA, 7 Oct. 1953 (*SL*, 213): '*The Spectator* misprinted the cattle poem last Friday.'

VARIANTS

Title [No title] *XX Poems*

L to MJ, 26 Nov. 1950 (Bodl. MS Eng. c. 7404/1): 'the *prairies* – well, just a little verse: no wings'. Leggett (1999) relates the poem to the proverb 'the grass is always greener on the other side of the fence'. **4** *Not here but anywhere*: See the note on *Aubade*, 18–19.

Church Going

DATE AND TEXT

Wkbk 3 (1/3/49) contains nineteen pages of drafts between '24. 4. 54' and 'abandoned 24 / 5 / 54'. Most of the poem except stanza 5 is represented in some form. L to PS, 10 May 1954 (*SL*, 227): 'I have been writing a long poem about churches recently that I hope will be finished tonight – well, long for me, about 54 lines.' *Wkbk* 4 (1/4/4) contains, after '14 June '54' (ten pages before), a version of part of ll. 60–1 followed by seven pages of drafts of the last three stanzas and additional lines dated '28 / 7 / 54' at the end. At this stage it had no title. Published in *The Spectator*, 195. 6647 (18 Nov. 1955), 665, with the misprints 'sprawling' for 'sprawlings' (l. 4) and 'Gross' for 'Grass' (l. 36); and in *New Lines*, ed. Robert Conquest (1956), with the misprint 'rest' for 'meet' in l. 56, as L pointed out to RC,

7 May 1957 (*SL*, 274). In *TLD*, 'whom' replaced 'which' in l. 51. It was probably a misprint: the drafts in *Wkbk 4* twice have 'which'. Tolley (1997), 86, notes that it was not corrected until the edition of January 1962, and that it survived in the paperback edition of 1973 and in anthologies. AT records that when he pointed out 'whom' in *TLD* to L at lunch on 1 Oct. 1963, L corrected it to 'which': *AL*, 30 (Oct. 2010), 20.

VARIANTS
51 for] round *Spectator, 1955; New Lines (1956)*

In a letter to L of 11 Aug. 1954 (Amis, *Letters*, 399), KA objected to the use of the historic present, criticised the inversion of word-order in l. 55, and found 'blent' (l. 56) 'a bit 18th-c'. L ignored these strictures. L referred to it as 'my Betjeman poem', and explained that 'he had asked his mother to send on her copies of the *Church Times* so that he could brush up on pyxes and stuff': Arthur Terry in Hartley (1988), 96. L to MJ, 3 Aug. 1954 (Bodl. MS Eng. c. 7408/115), sending a copy of 'the churches poem': 'I could write plenty of "background" stuff about it, but you had better read it unsupported first: do remember, however, that I write it partly to exhibit an attitude as well as to try to arouse an emotion – the attitude of the "young heathen" of whom there are plenty about these days – the first line, for instance, is designed both as sincere statement of fact & also as heavy irony.' L to MJ, 10 Aug. 1954 (Bodl. MS Eng. c. 7408/126): 'I think you put your paw on the flaw in *Churchgoing*, a lack of strong continuity – it is dangerously like *chat*, 4th leader stuff. The most important emotion – the church as a place where people came to be serious, were *always* serious, & all their different forms of seriousness came to be intermingled, so that a christening reminded of a funeral & a funeral of a wedding: nowadays these things happen in different buildings & the marvellous "blent air" of a church is growing rarer – this emotion I feel does not come out nearly strongly enough. However, I don't know what can be done about it now.' (The 'fourth leader' is the fourth leading article in *The Times*, 1922–66, usually of a light or humorous nature.)

L to PS, 18 June 1955 (*SL*, 244): 'it wasn't conceived in a spirit of "attacking the Church", but arose in part from reading an appeal made by the Archbishop of Canterbury about 14 months ago for money, without which he said about 200 churches were in imminent danger of ruin'. L kept a cutting, identified in his hand, from *Church*

Times, 7 May 1954, headed 'Save Our Churches week' (Hull DPL 3/1). It announced a campaign on behalf of the Historic Churches Preservation Trust, and quoted the Archbishop of Canterbury as saying that 'over two thousand must be helped at once' to be saved from decay and ruin, and that ringing of bells on 15 May would remind people of the 'great heritage which is ours in these ancient churches, so rich in beauty and in history, such a living and lovely part of England. Eight thousand of them were built more than four hundred years ago.'

L in July 1964 (*FR*, 83): 'One Sunday afternoon in Ireland when I had cycled out into the country I came across a ruined church, the first I had seen. It made a deep impression on me. I had seen plenty of bombed churches, but never one that had simply fallen into disuse, and for a few minutes I felt the decline of Christianity in our century as tangibly as gooseflesh. The poem I subsequently wrote, called "Church Going", did not seem altogether successful to me, and indeed the paper I eventually sent it to [*The Spectator*] procrastinated about publishing it and finally lost it. In the end they did publish it, after about a year, and I immediately had a request from a publisher to send him a collection. I also had a letter from one of the paper's subscribers enclosing a copy of the Gospel of Saint John. In fact it has always been well liked. I think this is because it is about religion, and has a serious air that conceals the fact that its tone and argument are entirely secular.' L to MJ, 29 May 1969 (Bodl. MS Eng. c. 7439/67): 'Any church nowadays is liable to be turned into a mosque or a bingo hall. The end of a civilisation.'

Introducing the poem in Nov. 1974, L mentioned a cycling tour he did when working in Belfast, and stated that the church of the poem 'is in a town south-east of the city': Watt (1989), 173. L complained to JE, 7 Sept. 1960 (*SL*, 319), that American poet John Malcolm Brinnin had talked 'a lot of cock about *C. Going*! Religious feelin be damned. I walked avvry Twalfth since 1928. Be damned to religious feelin.' L in Nov. 1964: 'It is of course an entirely secular poem. I was a bit irritated by an American who insisted to me it was a religious poem. It isn't religious at all. Religion surely means that the affairs of this world are under divine surveillance, and so on, and I go to some pains to point out that I don't bother about that kind of thing, that I'm deliberately ignorant of it – "Up at the holy end", for instance. Ah no, it's a great religious poem; he knows better than me – trust the tale and not the teller, and all that stuff. Of course the poem is about going to church, not religion – I tried to suggest this by the title – and the union of the important stages of human life – birth, marriage and death – that going to church represents; and my own feeling that when they are dispersed into the registry office and the crematorium chapel life will become thinner in consequence. I certainly haven't revolted against the poem. It hasn't become a kind of "Innisfree", or anything like that [. . .] The poem starts by saying, you don't really know about all this, you don't believe in it, you don't know what a rood-loft is – Why do you come here, why do you bother to stop and look round? The poem is seeking an answer [. . .] I think one has to dramatize oneself a little. I don't arse about in churches when I'm alone. Not much, anyway. I still don't know what rood-lofts are': *FR*, 22–3. ('Trust the tale and not the teller' is an allusion to D. H. Lawrence's *Studies in Classic American Literature*, 1924, ch. 1: 'Never trust the artist. Trust the tale.')

L interviewed in 1981 (*FR*, 56–7): 'It came from the first time I saw a ruined church in Northern Ireland, and I'd never seen a ruined church before – discarded. It shocked me. Now of course it's commonplace: churches are not so much ruined as turned into bingo-halls, warehouses for refrigerators or split-level houses for architects. *It's not clear in the poem that you began with a ruined church.* No, it wasn't in the poem, but when you go into a church there's a feeling of something . . . well . . . over, derelict [. . .] I'm not someone who's lost faith: I never had it. I was baptized – in Coventry Cathedral, oddly enough: the old one – but not confirmed. Aren't religions shaped in terms of what people want? No one could help hoping Christianity was true, or at least the happy ending – rising from the dead and our sins forgiven. One longs for these miracles, and so in a sense one longs for religion. But "Church Going" isn't that kind of poem: it's a humanist poem, a celebration of the dignity of . . . well, you know what it says.'

Title Conventionally, implies regular attendance (*OED*, Church-going, *vbl. n.*), as indicated in l. 19. Arthur Marwick, *British Society since 1945* (1986), 16, estimates that in 1950 less than ten per cent of the population were churchgoers. Osborne (2008), 96, catches the punning suggestion that the church is going. **8–9** R. L. Brett, 'Philip Larkin in Hull', Hartley (1988), 102, records that L's 'main recreation was cycling at the week-ends on an old-fashioned upright machine into the neighbouring countryside to visit parish churches'. L to MJ, 23 Nov. 1956 (Bodl. MS Eng. c. 7415/2), on taking off cycle clips: 'the point of it *is* to show *in petto* [secretly, reservedly;

or, in a small way] the conventions of religious observance in decay: a chap goes into a Church, hatless, but knows he ought to take *something* off, so he takes his clips off; but it's all unconscious except that he feels he's doing something rather decent as he does it.' L to Mrs M. K. Sampson, 27 Jan. 1984 (Hull DPL (2) 2/24/101): 'since I am hatless, I take off my cycle-clips because I feel I ought to take off something when entering a church'. **15** *'Here endeth'*: L to Renato Oliva, 30 Apr. 1968: '"Here endeth" occurs several times in the order of prayer in the prayer book of the Church of England, as "Here endeth the first lesson"': Hull DPL (2) 3/17/1. L at the end of a letter to Norman Iles, 29 Sept. 1941 (*SL*, 24): 'Here endeth the 101st lesson.' **17** *an Irish sixpence*: 'It is legal tender, but faintly disrespectful in what is probably an Ulster Protestant church': Alan Brownjohn, *Philip Larkin* (1975), 12. Cooper (2004), 143 n., concludes that since the Eire sixpence was in circulation between 1928 and 1969 in the Republic of Ireland, but would not have been legal tender in the United Kingdom, the gesture of donating it is a cynical one. L to MJ, 4 Dec. 1956 (Bodl. MS Eng. c. 7415/14): 'The Irish 6^d was meant as a comic compromise between GIVING NOTHING and giving REAL MONEY – like the Musical Banks.' Morrison (1980), 234, recalls that George Bowling in Orwell's *Coming Up for Air* revisits his old parish church and donates a sixpence [in part 4, ch. 2]. MacNeice, *In The Cathedral*, 34, provides another precedent for the exact donation: 'But I give sixpence'. **21** *Wondering what to look for*: Raphaël Ingelbien, Booth (2000), 137, compares Eliot, *Four Quartets, Little Gidding*, 27 ('not knowing what you came for'), and notes that L's visitor, like Eliot's, has no personal association with the church he is visiting. **22** L to JBS, 17 Aug. 1943 (Hull DP 174/2/75): 'religion – well, nobody gives a darn for that any longer, not in England, anyway. Methodism caught on fine in the 18th century, but it's worn thin now.' **25** *pyx*: box, often made of gold or silver, in which communion wafers are kept. L could have come across the word in Hardy's poem *The Lost Pyx*. **30** *simples*: medicinal plants or herbs. **38** *A purpose more obscure*: Cf. Eliot, *Four Quartets, Little Gidding*, 1. 32–4: 'From which the purpose breaks only when it is fulfilled | If at all. Either you had no purpose | Or the purpose is beyond the end you figured'. **41** *rood-lofts*: galleries forming the head of the carved screens (beneath the chancel-arch, separating the nave, or main hall, from the choir). 'I mentioned to that fool Hoskins that I had been out cycling on Sunday afternoon and had looked at the church in Ashby-de-la-Zouch and he asked me what the *rood loft* was like!': L, reported by Pamela Hanley, in *AL*, 4 (Oct. 1997), 14. **44** 'The vocabulary and cadence are meant to recall the gifts of the Magi, gold and frankincense and myrrh, and so to show that the last antiquarian has indeed lost the substance of the Christmas message in the accidents of its presentation': R. N. Parkinson in *Critical Survey*, 5. 3 (Winter 1971), 228. *bands*: clergymen's collars. **53** *accoutred*: equipped (the latest example in *OED* is from 1858). **54** L to JE, 19 Jan. 1959 (*SL*, 298): 'The graveyard I am in (standing in, I hasten to add) is about a ¼ mile from my flat. A marvellous place.' **55** KA disapproved of the inversion on grounds that it echoes an overtly 'poetic' context, Keats's *The Eve of St Agnes*, 208 ('A casement high and triple-arched there was'): to L, 11 Aug. 1954 (Amis, *Letters*, 399). *serious earth*. Raphaël Ingelbien, Booth (2000), 138, observes that this 'could easily turn into Eliot's "significant soil"' (*Four Quartets*, *The Dry Salvages*, 5. 50). **55–7** Morrison (1980), 236, compares Frost, *Directive*, 48–9: 'a house in earnest. | Your destination and your destiny's'. **56** *blent*: mingled. Only two examples (from George Eliot) are recorded in *OED*. It is a poeticism, found in Keats ('Happy is England! I could be content', 4); in Hardy as an adjective (*A Wasted Illness*, 6; *In A Museum*, 6) and a verb (*The Maid of Keinton Mandeville*, 11); in Yeats (*Among School Children*, 13), as Morrison (1980), 230, notes; and in MacNeice (*Day of Returning*, 7). **58** *that much*: L to MJ, 11 Mar. 1956 (Bodl. MS Eng. c. 7413/35): 'I have been brooding over "that much" again, but have decided not to change it. The crux of the thing is that, to me, "that much" implies a definite amount, "so much" implies a lot. I know you are *right* & I am *wrong*, but there it is. "So much" ought to mean "just so much", but to me it does suggest the other meaning, "so" in the emphatic sense, as if I mean that what will never be obsolete is really quite a lot.' **61–2** *ground . . . proper*: Palmer (2008), 112, notes the echo in *Places, Loved Ones*, 4: '*my proper ground*'. He is mistaken, however, in thinking that the latter poem was 'written immediately after' *Church Going*: the two are four months apart.

Age

DATE AND TEXT
Wkbk 3 (1/3/50) contains a draft, complete except for a title, on a single page after '24 / 5 / 54', dated '26 5 54' at the end. Published in *The Spectator*, 193. 6575 (2 July 1954), 15.

1 swaddling: wrapping or clothing, esp. for a baby. 4 Cf. *The Old Fools*, 25–6.

Myxomatosis

DATE AND TEXT
Wkbk 5 (1/5/6) contains three pages of drafts of the whole poem between '15 / xi / 53' (fifteen pages earlier) and '15 / 1 / 55' (seventeen pages later). At this stage the poem was entitled 'May Quarter'. L tells MJ in a letter dated 28 Sept. 1954 that he was thinking of her when finishing the poem the previous evening (Bodl. MS Eng. c. 7409/58). He included it in a letter to her dated 14 Nov. 1954 (Bodl. MS Eng. c. 7409/104 = *LTM*, 128). Published in *The Spectator*, 193. 6596 (26 Nov. 1954), 682.

VARIANTS
Title [No title] *14 Nov. 1954 letter*
1 Caught] Caught ?Blind
soundless] soundless sightless *14 Nov. 1954 letter* ['?Blind' is in pencil.]
2 While] As *14 Nov. 1954 letter*
3 *Where*] *How Spectator*
4 sharp] brief *14 Nov. 1954 letter, Spectator*

L to MJ, 14 Nov. 1954 (Bodl. MS Eng. c. 7409/104): 'I'm not keeping "the rabbit one" from you: it's only that in it I kill the rabbit, which makes it totally out of character & rather like a piece of journalism [. . .] It's not much of a poem. But of course *I felt* strongly enough about it [. . .] I strove (queer word) to give the essential pathos of the situation without getting involved in argument. Give me your opinion on sightless/soundless. I believe rabbits are both blind & deaf, so either w^d do – a field with no sights or sounds in. Oh dear. Is this "using" the rabbits? Honestly, my motives are really good – better than the poem, I'm afraid.' To MJ, 28 Nov. 1954 (Bodl. MS Eng. c. 7409/108): 'Did you notice the rabbit poem, tucked away in *the Spr* on Friday? Wonder if I shall receive any letters about it. I don't like the broken line: the first half has insufficient carry-on from the first 3 lines; the second is rather stupidly enigmatic, suggesting a farcical interpretation, like a belch or something of the sort. But I like lines 5 & 6, & lines 7 & 8 are vitiated only by the unspoken "Yes, & you may *not*" hanging about them. I should have done better to choose something more incontrovertible for my *finale*, but the thing was written in such a tearing hurry I didn't stop to consider such niceties. I hope you find it respectful to the awful state of y^r nation. I should hate it if you thought I was just earning a couple of guineas from their sufferings.' To MJ, 29 Jan. 1955 (Bodl. MS Eng. c. 7410/43): 'I hear the Myxomatosis Committee says it will rage again this year. If this is so, I don't want a holiday in rural England. It would be *quite dreadful* to be afraid to go out lest we sh^d happen on any pitiful stricken ones. This Christmas was quite enough for me. Do you know, it is absurd – & I mean that – but I keep thinking of them in terms of Owen's *Exposure*. "Is it that we are dying?" And they looked so like a battlefield – some newly dead, some old, all so terribly abandoned. And of course it was so cold, that day!'

Title: highly infectious viral disease of rabbits, originally artificially introduced to reduce rabbit populations. There was an outbreak in Kent and Sussex in Oct. 1953: Regan (1992), 83. In a letter of 24 Aug. 1958 to JE (*SL*, 288), L expresses dislike of the playwright, journalist and librettist Ronald Duncan on grounds that 'his countryside articles in Punch at the time of myxomatosis were full of caddish glee at this novel solution to the rabbit problem'. On 23 Sept. 1954 he tells MJ he finds Duncan's views 'unamusing, disagreeable, & shameful': Bodl. MS Eng. c. 7409/50. On 28 Sept. 1954 he tells her that the poem began 'as a furious diatribe in response to filthy Ronald Duncan, but it finished as a very casual little anecdote': Bodl. MS Eng. c. 7409/58.

Toads

DATE AND TEXT
Wkbk 3 (1/3/43) contains three pages of drafts of the whole poem except for the title after '13. 3. 54', dated '16. 3. 54' at the end. Published in *Listen*, 1. 2 (Summer 1954), 15–16. L to RC, 7 Sept. 1955 (*SL*, 250), referring to l. 19 in *Listen*: 'Some people – Kingsley

among them – objected to the inversion in v. five. This emendation
avoids that.'

VARIANTS (from *Listen*, 1954)
14 fires] a fire
19 Skinny as whippets are – yet

L to MJ, 4 Apr. 1948 (Bodl. MS Eng. c. 7403/11): 'Why don't people
all dislike work as I do? Am I wrong or are they? Is it natural to
like work?' To WA, 16 May 1952 (Bodl. MS Res. c. 616): 'The only
blot on the landscape is *work* – I think I need no longer make any
hypocritical pretence of enjoying *work* – God, I loathe it, eating
away the best hours of the best days.' To MJ, 24 Nov. 1952 (Bodl.
MS Eng. c. 7407/142): 'Work was invented by people who couldn't
amuse themselves. *But I can.*' To PS, 11 Nov. 1953 (*SL*, 217): 'the
continuance of bloody *work*, which I hate with all my heart'. To MJ,
12 Mar. 1957 (Bodl. MS Eng. c. 7415/103): 'As time goes on, I feel
furious about the toad work – how it lumbers enormously over our
lives. I don't mind the time it takes, but I do mind the worry. That
is really serious, because it spoils most of the time it doesn't take.'
To MB, 7 Aug. 1962 (*SL*, 343): '*work* (that vile thing)'. To Colin
Gunner, 13 Oct. 1971 (*SL*, 448): 'I regard work as something you do
in order to have spare time.'

L did not view work only in this light. To JBS, 20 Dec.1949 (Hull
DP 174/2/191): 'There is something unpleasant about a man not
out at work. Even when I am out among the shops I equate myself
with the useless wall-eyed old buggers with their pipes & woollen
scarves & their stumbling awkward-squad's walk – been sent out
"out of the way" or to get some sage for the stuffing or God knows
what. Lawrence no doubt couldn't endure going to the office every
morning – but I'd sooner go to the office every morning than be like
Will Brangwyn [for 'Brangwen'] in the early days of domesticity
with Anna – "shake the mats, then, if you must do something" . . .
Ooooghgh.' (L is referring loosely to Anna saying 'Shake the rug
then, if you must hang around' in ch. 6 of *The Rainbow*.) L in 1976,
replying on *Desert Island Discs* to the question 'What would you
be happiest to have got away from?': 'I don't think I'd be happy to
get away from anything. The instant answer is work – but over the
years I've come to think that I rather like work': *FR*, 103. To WA,
16 Nov. 1976 (*SL*, 551): '*work*, paradoxically enough, *is* a comfort.
One wakes up wanting to cut one's throat; one goes to work, & in
15 minutes one wants to cut someone else's – complete cure!' L in

1979: 'I've always thought that a regular job was no bad thing for a poet': *RW*, 51. The toad as an image of work became a standard form of reference in L's letters: see *SL*, 347, 398, 466, 476, 510.

Barbara Everett, *EIC*, 30 (July 1980), repr. Regan (1997), 63–4, compares L's toads to 'the Chimaeras carried on the shoulders of men in Baudelaire's prose-poem "Chacun sa Chimère"'.

Title Palmer (2008), 130, notes the plural, and while he admits the possibility that it may denote the toad that squats on the speaker and the toad in him (ll. 1–2, 25–6), he relates 'toads' to an anecdote recounted by Graham Landon in 'Toad Tale', *AL*, 9 (Apr. 2000), 21: In 1936, aged 14, Larkin went to Germany with his father, where in Werningerode they met one Herr Niemand. During a discussion with Sydney Larkin about the work ethic, Niemand turned to Philip and said: '"We have an amusing slang word for money in Germany – *Kröten* – toads. If we work hard we can earn *eine Menge Kröten* – a packet of money. And if a lazy worker has only a few coppers in his pocket we would say *er hatte nur noch paar Kröten in der Tasche* [He has nothing but a couple of toads in his pocket]."' (Surprisingly, Landon himself does not make the connection with *Toads*, despite the poem's concern with the need to work in order to pay bills and earn a pension.) **1–2** 'Sheer genius': L's reply in 1982 to the question 'How did you arrive upon the image of a toad for work or labour?': *RW*, 74. Mark Hutchings, 'Larkin's Toad', *N&Q*, NS 49. 1 (Mar. 2002), 94–5, noting 'Squat' (and 'Squats', l. 26), compares Satan 'Squat like a toad, close at the ear of Eve' in *Paradise Lost*, 4. 800. **11** *Losels*: profligates, ragamuffins; included at MJ's suggestion (Booth [1992], 27; *LTM*, 192–3 n. 1). *OED*'s earliest example is from Langland, *Piers Plowman*, 'A' Text, Prologue, 74. *loblolly-men*: bumpkins, rustics, boors; originally, mates to a ship's surgeon. L to Mrs J. Manthorp, 19 Mar. 1979: 'I wrote "lecturers, lispers", and then thought it would be rather funny to add two more alliterating words. I found "losels" and "loblolly-men" in my *Concise Oxford Dictionary*': Hull DPL (2) 2/10/11. **22** L in 1982: 'I was over fifty before I could have "lived by my writing" – and then only because I had edited a big anthology – and by that time you think, Well, I might as well get my pension, since I've gone so far': *RW*, 62. **23–4** *The Tempest*, 4. 1. 156–8: 'We are such stuff as dreams are made on, and our little life | Is rounded with a sleep'. Noted in Petch (1981), 7. *stuff*. 'A good many of the puns you speak of were unintentional. If I do make a pun, it is usually crashingly obvious, like "the stuff

That dreams are made on"': L to Simon Petch, 26 July 1981 (*SL*, 652). **25–8** L to MJ, 7 Aug. 1953 (Bodl. MS Eng. c. 7408/60): 'There's something cold & heavy sitting on me somewhere, & until something budges it I am no good.' **26** Cf. Virginia Woolf, *The Waves* (Harvest edn., p. 289): 'There is the old brute, too, the savage . . . well, he is here. He squats in me.' **33–6** L in a letter dated 30 Apr. 1968 to Renato Oliva, who had identified one toad as work: 'There are two toads. The other is the "something sufficiently toad-like"': Hull DPL (2) 3/17/1.

Poetry of Departures

DATE AND TEXT

Wkbk 3 (1/3/34) contains three and a half pages of drafts of the whole poem after '20. 1. 54', dated '23 Jan 1954' at the end. L to PS, 23 Jan. 1954 (*SL*, 221): 'Anyhow, it's Saturday night & I've eaten & bathed & finished a poem of dubious worth.' Published in *Poetry and Audience*, 21 (10 June 1954), 6, in *Listen*, 1. 3 (Winter 1954), 2, and in *The Listener*, 54. 1384 (8 Sept. 1955), 373–4. On a cutting of the *Poetry and Audience* printing (DPL 3/1), L wrote 'I can do it if he did!' to the right of l. 21.

VARIANTS

21–2 I can always do what he did! | And knowing it, stay *Poetry and Audience, 1954; Listen, 1954; The Listener, 1955*

JBS to MB, 8 Sept. 1988: 'I, desperate and despairing, was certainly one who said perhaps those very words to Philip – "He chucked up everything | And just cleared off". The poem reveals to me now why our friendship then essentially collapsed or died, the clash of our irreconcilable attitudes [. . .] is all in the poem': *AL*, 5 (Apr. 1998), 26.

In a letter to MJ dated 15 Aug. 1955 (Bodl. MS Eng. c. 7412/17), L expresses the view that there should have been 'much more tone-colour & drama in the reported speech, or the direct speech, is it'. He is referring to the actor's reading on Richard Murphy's BBC broadcast 'Three Modern Poets': see *LTM*, 178 n. 1.

Osborne (2008), 55: 'Somerset Maugham's novel *The Moon and Sixpence* provides much of the spirit and certain of the motifs ('*He chucked up everything*', 'Stubbly with goodness') for "Poetry of Departures". In Maugham's novel Charles Strickland leaves his wife and children and his job to become a painter. In ch. 12 his face is described as having 'the red stubble of the unshaved chin'.

Title Barbara Everett, *EIC*, 30 (1980), repr. Regan (1997), 64: 'the title [. . .] refers to a whole phase of French Symbolist verse with [. . .] ironic casualness'. **25, 27** Cooper (2004), 36, notes that the caricature of manliness is anticipated in the description of Chris in *Jill*, 27, with 'a swagger in his bearing' and his 'square, stubbly jaw'. **30** L to MJ, 3 July 1955 (Bodl. MS Eng. c. 7411/92): 'do you think "to provide an object" w^d express the sense better than "to create an object" in the last verse of *P of ds*? It seems that people understand *object* to mean just a thing, an entity, not as an ambition as I intended.'

Triple Time

DATE AND TEXT
Wkbk 2 (1/2/44) contains four and a half pages of drafts of the whole poem except for the title after '12 June 1951', dated '12 Aug 51' at the end. *Wkbk* 3 (1/3/15) contains, after '18. 9. 53', a complete draft (entitled 'Open any minute') on a single page, dated 'rev 3 / x / 53' at the end. Published in *Poetry and Audience*, 8 (28 Jan. 1954), 8, and in *The Spectator*, 192 (30 Apr. 1954), 513.

VARIANTS
10 lambent] fulgent *Poetry and Audience*

L to MJ, 29 Sept. 1962 (Bodl. MS Eng. c. 7425/65): 'Quite a nice poem – "the thought's good." Expression less good.'
  8 *travelling skies*: L to MJ, 28 Oct. 1952 (Bodl. MS Eng. c. 7407/119): 'travelling clouds'. Cf. Hopkins, *The Alchemist in the City*, 1: 'the travelling clouds'. **12** *fat . . . chances*: A 'fat chance' is (ironically) a remote opportunity or possibility. Allusion noted in Booth (1992), 150.

Spring

DATE AND TEXT
Wkbk 2 (1/2/7) contains: two drafts of the opening lines after '20 / 3 / 50'; a draft (only the opening lines of which correspond to the final poem) with the title 'Saturday', dated '12. 5. 50' at the end; and five pages of drafts of the whole poem (with the title 'Spring

<u>and bachelors</u>'), dated '19. 5. 50' at the end. L included the poem in a letter to JBS the next day (*SL*, 163–4). Poem VIII in *XX Poems*. Reprinted in *Listen*, 1. 2 (Summer 1954), 14. George Hartley, Hartley (1988), 215: *Spring* 'was left out of the manuscript of *The Less Deceived*, and I had to argue very strongly for its inclusion'.

VARIANTS (from the letter to JBS)
Title [No title]
13 Their] Our
14 Their] Our

Arthur Terry, Hartley (1988), 96–7, mistakenly relates the poem to the Botanic Gardens in Belfast. L did not go to Belfast until Oct. 1950, and would have walked to work across Victoria Park, Leicester. L to JBS, 20 May 1950, following the poem (*SL*, 164): 'Do you feel like this when you go walking in Hampstead Heath?' To MJ, 26 Nov. 1950 (Bodl. MS Eng. c. 7404/1): '*Spring* is "smart".' L in 1981 (*FR*, 56): 'I don't think that's a particularly good poem, though there are some nice things in it. I like the last few lines.'
  1 *Green-shadowed . . . rings*: Cf. Virginia Woolf, *The Waves*: '*burnt with dark rings and shadowed green by the grass*' (Harvest edn., 74). *people . . . walk in rings*: Cf. Eliot, *The Waste Land*, 56: 'people, walking round in a ring'. L included the poem in *OBTCEV*. 4–5 L to MJ, 23 July 1950 (Bodl. MS Eng. c. 7403/36), referring to a compass she had given him: 'it dangles like a spyglass & looks fine'. The sun 'dangles' in F. W. Harvey's poem *November*, 2, 11, included by L in *OBTCEV*. 6 Christopher Ricks compares Tennyson, *The Brook*, 13–14: 'the leaf, | When all the wood stands in a mist of green': 1965 review of *TWW*, repr. in *Phoenix: A Poetry Magazine*, ed. Harry Chambers, 11/12 (autumn and winter 1973/4), Philip Larkin issue, 7. 10–11 See the note on *Bridge for the Living*, 1, 3. 12–14 L to JBS, 20 May 1950 (*SL*, 164): 'Line 12 strikes me as enormously true.' Asked to explain his feeling about the closing lines, L in 1981 replied (*FR*, 56): 'Isn't it clear? It means that these people, these indigestible sterilities, see rebirth and resurrection most vividly and imaginatively, but it isn't for them; their way through life isn't a gay confident striding. What they *see* is clear and wonderful, but their needs are immodest in the sense that they want more girls and Jaguars than the normal amount other people get, because they get none.' Asked further if he was distinguishing himself from that type of person, L replied: 'No, that's me all right. Or was: you must remember it's all about thirty years ago.'

Deceptions

DATE AND TEXT
In *Wkbk 1* (1/1/89) the quotation from Mayhew is entered between
3 Jan. and 12 Feb. 1950 (1/1/89), and a draft of the whole poem
except for the title (1/1/92) is dated '20 / 2 / 50'. *Wkbk 2* (1/2/24)
contains a further draft of stanza 2 just after '4 / xi / 50' and before
'28 / 11 / 50'. Poem IV in *XX Poems*.

VARIANTS
Title [No title] *XX Poems*

L to MJ, 14 Aug. 1953 (Bodl. MS Eng. c. 7408/69): 'I do love
the past. Anything more than 20 years back begins to breathe a
luminous fascination for me: it starts my imagination working.
Why? Because it *is* past, I suppose, & leaves my feelings free to
get to work on it. Do you think I should trouble my head about
a prostitute down in Amelia Street, and not safely tucked away
in Mayhew?' L in 1981 (*FR*, 52): 'The more sensitive you are to
suffering the nicer person you are and the more accurate notion
of life you have. Hardy had it right from the start: his early poems
are wonderful – "She, to Him", for example. As I tried to say in
"Deceptions", the inflicter of suffering may be fooled, but the
sufferer never is.'
  Title Originally *The Less Deceived*. Changed in 1955. **Headnote**
Henry Mayhew, *London Labour and the London Poor*, 4 (1861),
241. J. Goode in Hartley (1988), 126–7, summarises Mayhew's
account. The woman was originally the daughter of a Dorsetshire
tenant farmer. She had come to London at sixteen to visit an aunt,
visited a seedy area of the city several times after dark on her own,
and been enticed to a nearby house by a man feigning sudden
illness. There he gave her drugged coffee, raped her, and after
several vain attempts at last persuaded her to become his mistress.
After a few months he grew tired of her, and she spent a further
ten years in prostitution. When Mayhew interviews her she is a
shabbily dressed prostitute over the age of forty. She tells Mayhew:
'You folks as has honour, and character, and feelings, and such can't
understand how all that's been beaten out of people like me. I don't
feel. I'M USED TO IT.' 9 Neil Rhodes, *N&Q*, NS 35 (1988),
342, compares George Herbert's *Affliction* ('Broken in pieces all
asunder'), 7–8: 'My thoughts are all a case of knives, | Wounding
my heart'. He notes that both poems are about 'affliction, grief,

and the possibility of consolation', and that whereas sunrise brings
redress in Herbert's poem, in L's it brings no comfort. **15** *less
deceived*: *Hamlet*, 3. 1. 121–2: Hamlet: 'I loved you not.' Ophelia:
'I was the more deceived.' See L's comments above on the title *The
Less Deceived*, especially those on desire and suffering, in a letter
of April 1955 to George Hartley. *out*: L to Renato Oliva, 30 Apr.
1968: 'means unconscious': Hull DPL (2) 3/17/1. **16–17** There
is a similar image in L's *Round Another Point* (1951): 'Compare
a married couple with their children in their own house to your
miserable middleclass bachelor mounting the stairs of his barren
bourgeois buckshee brothel: the intricacy, the delicacy, the variety of
emotion on the one hand simply towers over the alternative sordid
discharge of seed': *TAWG*, 496–7.

I Remember, I Remember

DATE AND TEXT
Wkbk 3 (1/3/33) contains five pages of drafts of the whole poem
after '8. 1. 54', dated '8 / 1 / 54' at the end. Published in *Platform*, 4
(Autumn 1955), 24.

VARIANTS (from *Platform*)
Title Revenant
16 clearly] nicely
31–2 There | Is standing, if we could but see ahead –

L, in 'Not the Place's Fault' (*FR*, 6, 7), records that he wrote
the poem in Jan. 1954 'after stopping unexpectedly in a train
at Coventry, the town where I was born and lived for the first
eighteen years of my life', that the poem 'was not of course meant
to disparage Coventry, or to suggest that it was, or is, a dull place
to live in, or that I now remember it with dislike or indifference, or
even can't remember it at all', and that 'I should have recognized
the outside of the station better, for I passed and repassed it daily
on my way to and from school.' In 1964 he stated that the journey
in the poem 'was the journey up to Liverpool to get the Belfast
boat': *FR*, 80. In 1967: 'I was thinking how very peculiar it was
that I myself never experienced these things, and I thought one
could write a funny poem about it. So I did. It wasn't denying that
other people did have these experiences, though they did tend to
sound rather clichés': *FR*, 31–2. L to Judie Johnson, 13 Apr. 1965

(Hull DPL 5/6): 'The rhyme scheme is just a piece of cleverness, but like all good rhyme schemes is not meant to be intrusive.'

Title The title of poems by Thomas Hood and by Winthrop Mackworth Praed containing sentimental reminiscences of childhood. Noted in Osborne (2008), 137, who also cites part 2, ch. 3, of Aldous Huxley's *Those Barren Leaves* (1925) – a favourite Larkin novel – as a precedent for reversing the conventions of nostalgic remembrancing: '"I remember, I remember . . ." It is a pointless and futile occupation, difficult none the less not to indulge in'. L in the letter to Judie Johnson: 'It does of course glance at Thomas Hood's poem.' **1–2** Osborne (2008), 143, compares the opening of Eliot's *Journey of the Magi*: 'A cold coming we had of it, | Just the worst time of the the year | For a journey'. **3** *men with number-plates*: L to Renato Oliva, 30 Apr. 1968: 'Coventry is the home of the motorcar industry. When motorcars and lorries are finished, they are driven away from Coventry bearing temporary number-plates by drivers. These drivers have to return to Coventry by train carrying the number-plates': Hull DPL (2) 3/17/1. **9** *cycle-crates*: L in the same letter: 'new cycles, crated up in wooden crates – bicycles are made in Coventry too'. **11** *hols*: holidays (colloquial, esp. schoolchildren's, abbreviation). **26–7** L in 1959: 'It now seems strange to me that all the time I lived in Coventry I never knew any girls, but it did not at the time. I had grown up to regard sexual recreation as a socially remote thing, like baccarat or clog dancing, and nothing happened to alter this view': *FR*, 9. **27** *'all became a burning mist'*: A parody of the kind of cliché found in romantic pulp fiction. Osborne (2008), 140, notes that the phrase was a comedy catchphrase from the 1950s radio programme *Bedtime With Braden*. **29** *ten-point*: Type size. **31–2** *'I remember*: I think italics would look better for that piece of reported speech': L to RC, 7 Sept. 1955 (*SL*, 250).

Absences

DATE AND TEXT
Wkbk 2 contains: five pages of drafts of the whole poem except for the title between '4 / xi / 50' and '28 / 11 / 50' (1/2/28); a half-page of drafts of additional lines beginning with the last line of the poem between '28 / 11 / 50' and '5 xii 50' (1/2/30); and a further half-page of drafts of additional lines beginning with the last line of the

poem between '10. 1. 51' and '6 Feb [1951]' (1/2/34). L to Donald
Hall, 9 June 1956 (*SL*, 263): 'read "sea" for "floor" in line 1'.

L to marine biologist Frank Evans, 16 Aug. 1961 (*SL*, 332–3):
'It seems to me I was confusing two kinds of waves, for I was
certainly thinking of "spilling waves in deep water", as you call
them. This makes nonsense of dropping like a wall, if they in fact
never slope more than 1 in 7. I hope not many of my readers are
oceanographers. I suppose the only waves in deep water I have ever
seen have been from boats, which might themselves upset the water's
behaviour, but I certainly had the impression of waves playing
about on their own like porpoises (I've never seen a p. either) and
was trying to reproduce it.' Mr Evans comments: 'it is only waves
coming in to the beach that roll over and drop like a wall; offshore,
no matter how big the waves are, when they break the water just
spills down the front. It is the size and not the shape of deep-water
waves that changes with the wind strength. Whether in storms
or summer breezes makes no difference to the profile of breaking
waves' (*SL*, 332 n.).
  L in 1962, commenting on his choice of the poem for the
anthology *Poet's Choice* (*FR*, 17): 'I suppose I like "Absences" (a)
because of its subject matter – I am always thrilled by the thought
of what places look like when I am not there; (b) because I fancy
it sounds like a different, better poet rather than myself. The last
line, for instance, sounds like a slightly unconvincing translation
from a French symbolist. I wish I could write like this more often.
Incidentally, an oceanographer wrote to me pointing out that I was
confusing two kinds of wave, plunging waves and spilling waves,
which seriously damaged the poem from a technical viewpoint.
I am sorry about this, but do not see how to amend it now.' L in
1981 (*FR*, 59): 'One longs for infinity and absence, the beauty of
somewhere you're not.' L in 1981 on the poem *High Windows*
(*FR*, 59): 'I think the end shows a desire to get away from it all, not
unlike "Dry-Point" in a way, or "Absences".'
  4 Cf. Bernard Spencer, *Aegean Islands 1940–41*, 3: 'Where
sea like a wall falls'. 8 L to MJ, 27 Nov. 1957 (Bodl. MS Eng. c.
7417/47): 'You know how I prize my few lines in *Such absences*:
well, Hopkins is my model there. *Riddled by wind, trails lit-up
galleries* is my shot at *the lovely behaviour Of silk-sack clouds*
game.' 10 John Osborne, Booth (2000), 147, notes that the short
double exclamation is a favourite mannerism of Rimbaud. Graham

Chesters compares the last, isolated line of Gautier's *Terza Rima*: 'Sublime aveuglement! Magnifique défaut!' ['Sublime blindness! Magnificent flaw!']: 'Tireless play: speculations on Larkin's "Absences"', *Challenges of Translation in French Literature: Studies and Poems in Honour of Peter Broome*, ed. Richard Bales (2005), 57–8. He also mentions (58) Baudelaire's *L'Homme et la Mer* 'with its last, split line, "O lutteurs éternels, ô frères implacables!" ['O eternal wrestlers, implacable brothers'] and direct reflections on the relationship between the moods of man and sea'. See *Sad Steps*, 11–12; *The Card-Players*, 14; *Gathering Wood*, 11–12.

Latest Face

DATE AND TEXT
Wkbk 2 (1/2/35) contains four pages of drafts of stanzas 1 and 2 between '10. 1. 51' and '6 Feb [1951]', and three pages of drafts of the whole poem except for the title between '6 Feb' and '19. iii. 51'. L has written the name 'Winifred Arnott' on the latter. Poem V in *XX Poems*. L to WA, 8 Sept. 1953 (Bodl. MS Res. c. 616; *SL*, 210): '*The Spectator* turned up trumps & took 3 poems, including *Latest face*, & I've already had the proofs. For a time I toyed with providing one of those 17th c. titles "For Miſtress W——A——, whom I did first see walking in the courtyard at ye Queen's University in Belfast", but in the end, you'll be relieved to know, I left it as it was, simply calling it *Poem*.' Published in *The Spectator*, 5 Mar. 1954, with the misprint 'vagrants' for 'vagrant' in l. 5. L to WA, 7 Apr. 1954 (*SL*, 225): '"vagrants", indeed. How many people do they think I write about at once?' He corrected both this error and 'you' for 'your' in l. 21 on a photocopy of the printing (Hull DPL 3/1). In a handwritten note on the cutting, he states: 'This was written in February 1951. *Spectator* printed (or misprinted) it on 5th March 1954.'

VARIANTS
Title [No title] *XX Poems*

L to WA, 1 Oct. 1957, with a copy of *TLD*: 'there are three poems only in this collection that arose directly from knowing you – 2 you know already [*Latest Face* and *Lines on a Young Lady's Photograph Album*], but the one on page 21 [*Maiden Name*] may be new to you, I don't know. I hope you don't find it too embarrassing': *SL*, 280.

L to WA, 4 Apr. 1953 (*SL*, 196, misdated 6 Apr.): 'At present I feel a bit embarrassed that you ever read *Latest Face* or any of that bunch.'

24 L to Renato Oliva, 30 Apr. 1968: 'Denial is compared to an armed warrior. It leaps from the sun because attack often comes from the quarter you least expect (the attack from the sun is a familiar tactic in aerial warfare), and ironically because the sun is the great life giving principle': Hull DPL (2) 3/17/1.

If, My Darling

DATE AND TEXT
Wkbk 2 (1/2/9) contains seven pages of drafts of the whole poem except for the title after '20. 5. 50', dated '23. 5. 50' at the end. Poem XIV in *XX Poems*. Published in *The Fantasy Poets*, no. 21 (Mar. 1954), and in the American magazine *Shenandoah*, 6. 2 (Spring 1955), 31.

VARIANTS
Title [No title] *XX Poems*

L to MJ, 9 May 1951 (Bodl. MS Eng. c. 7405/51), when it was no. XIV in *XX Poems*: 'XIV is the best of the new ones, in my view. The boastfulness is supposed to be offset by humour: it is largely a *funny* poem. Or serio-comic. Or comico-serious. Well, anyway.' In 1981 (*FR*, 55): 'I like it very much too. It was the first poem that made Kingsley [Amis] think I was some good: he loved it when I sent it to him.' To the comment 'It's a fantastically self-derogatory poem, telling the girl that if she really knew me she'd know what a terrible person I am', L replied: 'Well, I think we all think that, with girls. It's funny rather than self-derogatory. I'm surprised it hasn't been anthologized more': *FR*, 55.

9 Claude Rawson suggests the possible influence of the closing lines of Eliot's *Aunt Helen* (in which the footman sits on the dining-table with the housemaid on his knee): *Raritan*, 11. 2 (1991), 43. **14** L to MJ, 23 May 1951 (Bodl. MS Eng. c. 7405/63): '"sicken inclusively outwards" means to spread outwards, like a spot of disease growing, taking in more & more of the surrounding surface'. **21** L to MJ, 23 May 1951: '"Meaning's rebuttal" really is clumsy: I mean (in my simple way) that each of the technical terms intoned by reality (terms that seem denotative not connotative, scientific not emotive) in fact for all their seeming precision are Janus faced & mean also the opposite of what they mean [. . .] A wish for instance may be a simple wish – I want bread. Or it may be a cover wish to conceal the wish for chocolate. Or it may be a direct expression of the hatred of bread, which for some reason can't be confessed. [. . .] if you can conceive "wish" treble-yolked with three meanings like that you will see what I "mean".' **24** *unpriceable*: that cannot be priced (*OED*'s only example of this sense). L in 1981 stated that he wanted 'to change "unpriceable" to "unprintable"', but that KA said no: '"unprintable" would just mean cunt, whereas "unpriceable" *probably* meant cunt but could mean all sorts of other things too': *FR*, 55. KA to L, 4 Aug. 1950: 'unprintable pivot sets the reader wondering whether the phrase as a whole may not mean c—t', '"unpriceable" seems to prolong that effect of *justified eccentricity* of diction that to me is ¾ of the point of the poem [. . .] it means something that can't be priced, not because it's so valuable but because you *don't know* how valuable it is, you can't judge': Amis, *Letters*, 241.

Skin

DATE AND TEXT
Wkbk 3 contains: just over a page of drafts of the opening lines between '13. 3. 54' and '16. 3. 54' (1/3/42), and seven and a half pages bearing two complete drafts dated '4. 4. 54' and '5 / 4 / 54' respectively (1/3/45). Published in *The Spectator*, 193. 6575 (2 July 1954), 15.

L to MJ, 4 July 1959 (Bodl, MS Eng. c. 7420/6): 'Davie said that "Skin" was a "personal" poem [. . .] I don't agree. "Skin" could be about anyone.'
  The poem may be seen in relation to Hardy's poem 'I look into my glass, | And view my wasting skin'.

Arrivals, Departures

DATE AND TEXT
There are six pages of drafts in *Wkbk* 3 (1/3/4): of ll. 1–5 and 12–15 dated '22. 1. 53'; of ll. 13–15, dated '24 / 1/ 53'; and a draft of the whole poem except for the title, dated '24 Jan. 53'. Published in *The*

Fantasy Poets, no. 21 (Mar. 1954), and in *Q*, Queen's University, Belfast, 11 (Hilary [Winter] 1955), 29.

Barbara Everett, *EIC*, 30 (July 1980), repr. Regan (1997), 63, regards it as 'a beautiful imitation [. . .] of Baudelaire's prose-poem "Le Port"'.

1 *This town*: Belfast. 2 *traveller*: commercial traveller. 5–15 'It's like the opening of *Bleak House* here today – I knew it was, for when I awoke I could hear the ships hooting on the river, each to each. Come & choose wrong!': L to MJ, 11 Dec. 1957 (Bodl. MS Eng. c. 7417/58).

At Grass

DATE AND TEXT

Below the twelve pages of drafts after '11 May 1949' in *Wkbk 1* (1/1/82), complete except for the title, L has written 'fin 3. 1. 50'. The date '31. 12. 49' is entered below another poem in the middle of the drafts, which suggests that drafting may have begun in Dec. Poem XX in *XX Poems*. Published in *The Fantasy Poets*, no. 21 (Mar. 1954).

VARIANTS

20 brims] links *The Fantasy Poets, 1954*

L in 1981 (*FR*, 58): *At Grass* was a film 'about Brown Jack. You wouldn't remember him, a famous flat-racer and jumper, I think: there he was, completely forgotten and quite happy.' L again in 1981: 'It was a film about, you know, "Where is Brown Jack now?" Where Brown Jack was now was at grass, quite happy, moving about, no harness, no jockey, nobody shouting the odds, simply cropping the grass and having a gallop when he felt like it': Motion (1993), 188. L immediately knew on seeing the film that 'for some reason' it had impressed him 'very strongly': unpublished text of a television interview by Melvyn Bragg, 16 Apr. 1981, quoted in Motion (1993), 188. Brown Jack was both a jumper and a flat-racer. He won twenty-five times from 1929 to 1934, including the Queen Alexandra Stakes at Ascot in each of those six years.

L to MJ, 28 Oct. 1950 (Bodl. MS Eng. c. 7403/96), on his recent poems: 'They're not all like *At grass*, you know. Only *At grass* is like *At grass*. The others are far more modern & less polished.'

To MJ, 14 Jan. 1956 (Bodl. MS Eng. c. 7412/128): 'Looking at *At grass* I'm struck by the terrific *speed* of it: not only short words but short sentences, each carrying a new idea.' Introducing the poem in Nov. 1974, L called it 'my nearest thing to a lyric poem – or to a Georgian poem, if you're being uncomplimentary': Watt (1989), 174.

3 *distresses*: normally, 'afflicts'; but here, 'picks at the tresses of' (a sense not recorded in *OED*). 12 *classic Junes*: June is the height of the British horseracing season. There are ten top-level flat races alone, including the Coronation Cup, the Oaks, the Derby, the Queen Anne Stakes and the Ascot Gold Cup. 13 *against the sky*: Christopher Ricks notes the phrase, acknowledging the different setting, in Eliot's *The Love Song of J. Alfred Prufrock, 2: True Friendship. Geoffrey Hill, Anthony Hecht, and Robert Lowell Under the Sign of Eliot and Pound* (2010), 48. 25 *slipped their names*: Displacing the familiar phrase 'slipped their bridles': Booth (1992), 82. 30 *bridles*: Motion (1993), 188: 'strictly speaking it should be halters'. (Bridles would imply that the horses are to be ridden, whereas halters would not.)

Published on 28 Feb. 1964. L to CM, 17 Jan. 1962 (*SL*, 338): 'I should really rather wait until I can offer a solider collection than would be the case now [. . .] What I should like to do is write three or four stronger poems to give the whole thing some weight.' L to BP, 8 Apr. 1963 (*SL*, 351): 'Since writing last I have agreed to provide Fabers with another collection of poems.' To Norman Iles, 12 June 1963 (*SL*, 354): 'I have also just sent off a new collection of poems, very thin stuff. I believe they will not be published until the Spring. At present it is called THE WHITSUN WEDDINGS.' To MJ, 13 June 1963 (Bodl. MS Eng. c. 7426/97): 'I sent off my collection to Faber's on Tuesday. Provisionally called *The Whitsun Weddings* (TWW) it comprised 33 poems. Some are *very thin*, in fact I might knock out 2 even now. It's a poor harvest for 9 years, in fact I think it's definitely *worse* than the L.D. It has nothing like *If, My Darling* or *Maiden name*, poems that give the impression of *having plenty in hand*. The poetic quality is diluted. Too many depend on mere sentiment. It's all very depressing. But then, what isn't? I wonder if you think the title will do. I feel I'm getting a bit old for *The Way Things Go* or – well, what? I want to put that poem in the shop window, as it were.' To MJ, 4 Feb. 1964 (Bodl. MS Eng. c. 7427/80): 'Today I marked *The LD* & *The WW* to see wch I thought best – *The LD* won – more 1st & upper 2nd poems than *The W.W.* All I feel is *TWW* itself is a better poem than anythin [*sic*] in the *L.D.*'

L asked AT to comment on a t.s. of *TWW* before it went to Faber & Faber. Thwaite proposed alterations. To AT, 5 Oct. 1963 (*SL*, 358): 'I adopted only those I felt really sure of: the rest I can consider at my leisure, and if I find myself agreeing with you put them in at the proof stage.'

Here

DATE AND TEXT

Wkbk 6 (1/6/9) contains ten pages of drafts of the whole poem between '6. 9. 61' and the completion date '8 / 10 / 61'. Bemoaning his lack of progress with it, L describes it as 'a pointless shapeless thing about Hull' in a letter to MJ dated 11 Sept. 1961 (Bodl. MS

Eng. c. 7423/102). To MJ, in a letter begun on 8 Oct. 1961 (Bodl. MS Eng. c. 7423/117): '*Monday* Last night [. . .] I finished a dull poem called *Here* about ye Eastern Thridding' (Hull is in the former East Riding of Yorkshire). To MJ, 27 Oct. 1961 (Bodl. MS. Eng. c. 7424/10): 'I've sent my Hull poem to the *NS*, under the poor title of *Withdrawing Room*'. L must have changed the title at proof stage. Published in *New Statesman*, 62. 1602 (24 Nov. 1961), 788.

VARIANTS (from *New Statesman*, 1961)
15 suits] suites [This may be a misprint.]
19 terminate] terminal
29 And] Then,

L to RC, 9 Dec. 1961 (*SL*, 335): 'Thanks for the kind words about Here. No one much seems to have noticed it, though it is to my mind in direct linear succession to The North Ship – I mean just pushing on into a bloodier and bloodier area.' L in 1981, asked whether he intended the poem as a brief for retirement, the simpler life (*FR*, 59): 'Oh no, not at all . . . well, it all depends what you mean by retirement. If you mean not living in London, I suppose it might be interpreted along those lines. I meant it just as a celebration of here, Hull. It's a fascinating area, not quite like anywhere else. So busy, yet so lonely. The poem is frightful to read aloud: the first sentence goes on for twenty-four-and-a-half lines, which is three-quarters of the poem, and the rest is full of consonants.' L described it as being 'plain description' in a letter to RC, 21 Sept. 1962 (*SL*, 346). His prose account of Hull in 'A Place to Write' (1982), Hartley (1988), 74, contains several echoes of the poem: 'a city that is in the world, yet sufficiently on the edge of it to have a different resonance. Behind Hull is the plain of Holderness, lonelier and lonelier, and after that the birds and the lights of Spurn Head, and then the sea [. . .] giving Hull the air of having its face half-turned towards distance and silence, and what lies beyond them.' Note 'edges', 'Loneliness', 'silence', 'distance', 'beyond', 'Facing' (ll. 22, 25, 29, 30, 32). This account earlier formed the foreword to *A Rumoured City: New Poets from Hull*, ed. Douglas Dunn (1982).

Title Booth (1992), 164, notes the poem's trajectory through Hull and out into the Holderness peninsula towards the North Sea. 2 L to Professor Laurence Perrine, 11 Feb. 1980: 'I was thinking of a journey I took many times, catching the Yorkshire Pullman from King's Cross (London) at 5-20 p.m., changing at Doncaster, as you so rightly say at 8 p.m., and getting into a smaller train that arrived in Hull about 9 p.m. All these trains have been changed now, but on a summer evening it was a very pleasant journey. The "traffic all night north" one would catch sight of from the train on the M1 (motorway), mostly lorries that I imagined would carry on all night until they reached Edinburgh or Carlisle or somewhere like that': Hull DPL (2) 2/21/24. Cooper (2004), 158, compares MacNeice, *Letter to Graham and Anne Shepard*, 43–4: 'Traffic . . . | Always on the move' (from *Letters from Iceland*). **4** *halt*: L refers Prof. Perrine to the *Concise Oxford Dictionary*: 'railway stopping-place used for local services only and without regular station buildings'. **8** *piled gold clouds*: L to MJ, 28 Sept. 1961 (Bodl. MS Eng. c. 7423/111): 'I wonder if you've been out again up the 1 in 10 hill and watched the piled clouds moving. That was lovely, wasn't it?' *the shining gull-marked mud*: A photograph of this taken by L is reproduced in *AL*, 20 (Autumn 2005), 16. **10** Cf. Wordsworth, 'Earth has not anything to show more fair', 6: 'Ships, towers, domes, theatres and temples'. Noted by Raphaël Ingelbien in '"England and Nowhere": Contestations of Englishness in Philip Larkin and Graham Swift', *English*, 48 (Spring 1999), 37. There are other points of similarity: W's 'fields' (7; cf. L's 2, 23); W's 'sky' (7; cf. L's 'skies', 6); W's 'silent' (5; cf. L's 'silence', 25); W's 'the river' (12; cf. L's 7). **13** *trolleys*: trolley-buses, trackless vehicles powered from an overhead electric cable by means of a pole and trolley. They continued to operate in Hull until Oct. 1964: Regan (1992), 104. **19–20** The St Andrew's Fish Dock in Hull was opened in 1883 and closed in 1975. L to MJ, 3 May 1955 (Bodl. MS Eng. c. 7410/120): 'It's in the depth of fishy Hull. When the wind is in the south, the smell of fish reaches as far as the university.' To MJ, 11 Sept. 1961 (Bodl. MS Eng. c. 7423/104): 'Very fishy wind tonight!' **20** *the slave museum*: Wilberforce House in Hull. **25** *Loneliness*: reinforced by 'solitude', 'Isolate', 'removed', 'out of reach', ll. 5, 24, 32. L in Hull to Michael Hamburger, 10 Mar. 1966: 'It was delightful to see you here, at the end of this line into loneliness': Michael Hamburger, *Philip Larkin: A Retrospect* (2002), 27. L to MJ, 15 Oct. 1966 (Bodl. MS Eng. c. 7434/35–6): 'To live *beyond* Hull! Where removed lives loneliness clarifies. Yes, it does attract me.' L talking about Hull on *The South Bank Show*, 30 May 1982, London Weekend Television: 'The lonely place is always to me the exciting place.' **28** *Luminously-peopled air*: Cf. Gray, *Ode on the Spring*, 23: 'the peopled air'. Noted in Osborne (2008), 54–5, with an acknowledgement of Ted Carling.

Mr Bleaney

DATE AND TEXT
L stated in 'New Comment', broadcast on the BBC Third
Programme on 12 July 1961 (BBC T/29443), that he wrote the poem
'in one evening out of pure exasperation'. *Wkbk 4* (1/4/12) contains:
after '10 October 1954' (fourteen pages before), just over three
pages of drafts of the whole poem, dated '13 / 5 / 55' at the end;
and a second draft of stanza 5 dated '19 / 5 / 55' at the end. At the
outset, the title was 'Lodgers' and 'Mr Bleaney' was 'Mr Gridley',
but both were soon changed. Published in *The Listener*, 54. 1384
(8 Sept. 1955), 373, and in *New World Writing: A New Adventure
in Modern Writing*, 10th Mentor Selection (Nov. 1956), 148.

L to MJ, 17 Apr. 1956 (Bodl. MS Eng. c. 7413/69): 'You know, I've
come to think Mr *Bleaney* an extraordinarily good poem: it says
oceans, everything I feel on that topic. "Bed, upright chair, sixty-
watt bulb, no hook behind the door, no room for books or bags" –
every word a bullseye. And I love the dark recommencement "But if
he stood and watched the frigid wind –" coiling itself up for the final
clawing spring in *"one hired box"* – O a splendid poem.'
   The poem was prompted by L's bleak lodgings at 11 Outlands
Road in Cottingham, just outside Hull, which he took shortly after
taking up his post as University Librarian: Motion (1993), 247;
Brennan (2002), 25. In a letter to MJ dated 9 Oct. 1957 (Bodl. MS
Eng. c. 7417/4) L refers to 'that ghastly house in Outlands Road, the
Mr Bleaney house'. In Nov. 1974 he confirmed that the poem was
'about a real lodging-house, digs that weren't very satisfactory': Watt
(1989), 174. L to RC, 5 Oct. 1956: 'I am taking a new flat [. . .]
and look forward to banishing the shade of Mr Bleaney for good in
a few weeks': *SL*, 267. He refers to the time 'when I was living the
life of Bleaney' (as distinct from 'the life of Reilly', i.e. in luxury)
in a letter to MJ dated 23 Nov. 1956 (Bodl. MS Eng. c. 7415/6).
L in 1981: 'The first two-thirds of the poem, down to "But if", are
concerned with my uneasy feeling that I'm becoming Mr Bleaney,
yes. The last third is reassuring myself that I'm not, because he was
clearly quite content with his sauce instead of gravy, and digging the
garden and so on, and yet there's doubt lingering too, perhaps he
hated it as much as I did': *FR*, 589. Asked whether he wasn't being
presumptuous in judging Mr Bleaney by what he sensed himself, L in
1981 replied: 'I don't think so. Unless you think it's presumptuous
to judge anyone': *FR*, 58–9. Asked further whether the poem had

been given a false emphasis in his work, L commented: 'Well, no, not a false one. Excessive, perhaps. I've never understood why it's so popular: I thought the subject was peculiar to me, and yet everybody seems to understand it and like it. When you're an only lodger, your relation with your landlady is very delicate: she's constantly urging you to do what she wants – dig the garden, or sit with her in the evenings, instead of sloping off to your own room': *FR*, 59.

Title As Nicholas Jenkins notes in Leader (2009), 48, the unusual name may be traced to Brebis Bleaney (1915–2007), who was Scholar (1934–7), D.Phil. student, member of the College's first soccer eleven and of the Debating Society, and first Fellow and Tutor in Physics (1947–57) at L's Oxford college, St John's. He was in Oxford during the time L was there (1940–3). There is a minor character, a schoolboy, also called Bleaney in *Jill*, 73, as noted in Cooper (2004), 32, and John Goodby, 'Mr Larkin's Two Bleaneys', *N&Q*, NS 51. 2 (June 2004), 182–3.

2 *the Bodies*: L to Alan Bold, 16 Aug. 1972: 'I was brought up in Coventry, a great car-making town, and there used to be works there which we referred to rather by what they produced than by the name of the makers. "The Bodies" was a fictitious example of this, invented for its macabre overtones.' Quoted in Bold, ed., *Cambridge Book of English Verse 1939–1975* (1976), 210. 9 L to MJ, 3 May 1955 (Bodl. MS Eng. c. 7411/5), on his digs at 11 Outlands Road: 'No room for books of course.' 13–14 Overheard radios irritated L, who lived in rented accommodation till June 1974. To JBS, 12 Apr. 1943 (DP 174/2/62): 'The bastard wireless is bastard well on, relaying a bastard cinema organ.' To JBS, 29 Dec. 1943 (Hull DP 174/2/83): 'I'm changing digs soon [. . .] I am leaving because there's too much noise in the house with a radio *and* a kid.' To JBS, 8 Oct. 1944 (DP 174/2/103; *SL*, 93): 'Christ, the blasted wireless is loud', 'It's been on for hours. No wonder Dickens and Trollope and Co. could write such enormous books, if this bastard way of rotting the mind hadn't been thought up.' To JBS, 9 Feb. 1945: 'and (most of all) there is a radio in the next room blaring out all the childish inanity that the BBC see fit to afflict our ears with [. . .] I can write at a pinch if my fingers are dead and my bones aching with the cold, but not with a lot of rubbishy singing and music beating the air [. . .] But really writing is very difficult. The news (which I don't want to hear) has started, just too muffled for me to hear the words': *SL*, 97. To MJ, 3 July 1951 (Bodl. MS Eng. c. 7405/106): 'moving into this hell-house of blazing radio sets.

Don't know if I shall be able to stand it – it's strange to think that *silence* is a luxury to be purchased by 70 or so shillings a week.' To D. J. Enright, 26 Apr. 1955: 'At present I'm in lodgings, and while they're quite good as far as lodgings go I can't ignore the blasted RADIO which seems a feature of everyone's life these days, and it prevents me from sitting thinking and scribbling in the evening [. . .] It is on *now*, subjecting me to its pathological highpitched burble, damn it': *SL*, 240–1. Complaints about the overheard radio increase when he moves to Cottingham, first to Holtby Hall (to MJ, 28 Mar., 14 Apr. 1955: Bodl. MSS Eng. c. 7410/ 72, 73, 74, 76), and then (markedly) to Mrs Dowling's house at 11 Outlands Road (to MJ, 14 Apr., 27 Apr., 23 May 1955: Bodl. MSS Eng. c. 7410/97, 111, 7411/25, 26). Matters improved when he moved at the beginning of June 1955 to Mrs Squire's house at 200 Hallgate, Cottingham, though there was still the occasional complaint: to MJ, 17 June, 26 Sept. 1955 (Bodl. MSS Eng. c. 7411/77, 7412/39, 40); to JE, 26 Sept. 1955 (Bodl. MS Eng. c. 7449/23). **13** L to MJ, 27 Apr. 1955 (Bodl. MS Eng. c. 7410/111): 'Oh the wireless – gabble, gabble, gabble. I have the usual wool in my ears, but it doesn't help much.' To MJ, 23 May 1955 (Bodl. MS Eng. c. 7411/26): 'God, this radio [. . .] My earplugs give me a slight haddock, & are no good, as you can guess.' **14** *jabbering*: L to MJ, 23 Aug. 1954 (Bodl. MS Eng. c. 7409/14): 'I can hear Jordan's radio jabbering away downstairs – the little swine!' To MJ, 1 May 1955 (Bodl. MS Eng. c. 7410/118): 'I also hear the cuckoo in the morning in bed, before *Lift up your hearts* comes jabbering and booming through the house'; to MJ, 13 May 1955 (Bodl. MS Eng. c. 7411/20): 'Now the silly old *sod* has got the 8 o'clock news on, jabbering away'; to MJ, 4 May 1957 (Bodl. MS Eng. c. 7416/2): 'All this while the Cup Final was jabbering away.' *set*: radio or television. **16** *sauce*: In a bottle (probably 'HP' sauce), as distinct from freshly prepared gravy. Mr Bleaney has working-class tastes: Booth (2005), 213. **17** *the four aways*: colloq. for four games won away from home in Association Football; guessed correctly, they would pay a substantial dividend for a modest stake in the football pools. For a time, L himself tried the football pools (with Larkin's luck): L to MJ, 8 Nov. 1952; 16 Aug., 28 Sept., 2 Oct., 10, 22, 30 Oct., 5 Nov. 1954; 15 Feb., 9, 20, 29 Oct., 12 Nov. 1955 (Bodl. MSS Eng. c. 7407/124; 7409/8, 58, 61, 70, 80, 89, 93; 7410/52, 7412/54–5, 62, 76, 88.) To MJ, 11 Sept. 1961 (Bodl. MS Eng. c. 7423/104): 'Have filled up another pools coupon this week'. **18** *Frinton*: seaside resort in N.

Essex. L in 1959 expressed the view that holidays were 'based on an impotent dislike of everyday life and a romantic notion that it will all be better at Frinton or Venice': *FR*, 6. **20** *Stoke*: Stoke-on-Trent, Staffordshire. **21–8** L to MJ, 3 May 1955 (Bodl. MS Eng. c. 7411/5): 'I have no house no wife no child no car no motor mower no holidays planned for Sweden or Italy [. . .] I dread being one who *only* at 50 gains what everyone else has had since they were 25.' **24** *shaking off the dread*: Morrison (1980), 216, notes Sassoon, *Haunted*, 13–14: 'He thought: "Somewhere there's thunder," as he strove | To shake off dread; he dared not look behind him.' **25** L to Janet Gallup, 6 June 1984, Hull DPL (2) 2/24/85: 'No poet is ever entirely happy to say what poems "mean", but as far as "how we live measures our own nature" goes I simply meant that if we lead miserable lives then we are pretty miserable people, as indeed the next few lines make clear. I don't think this is quite the same as referring to the universal human condition.'

Nothing To Be Said

DATE AND TEXT
Wkbk 6 (1/6/11) contains three pages of drafts of the whole poem between '18 / 10 [1961]' and '25. x. 61'. Published in *London Magazine*, NS 1. 11 (Feb. 1962), 5–6. L to MJ, 8 Feb. 1962 (*SL*, 340): 'Dig the mugs in *Lond. Mag.* – they didn't correct my mispunctuation.' There was an extra comma after 'mornings' (l. 5).

L to MJ, 8 Feb. 1962 (*SL*, 340): 'I quite like the poem – "it doesn't rhyme, but it's true".'

11 Stan Smith notes the pig hunt in Golding's *Lord of the Flies* (1954), which L had read by 16 Jan. 1956 (*SL*, 255–6): 'Something for Nothing: Late Larkins and Early', *English*, 49 (Autumn 2000), 263.

Love Songs in Age

DATE AND TEXT
Wkbk 3 (1/3/6) contains fourteen pages of drafts of the whole poem (but with many versions not represented in the final poem) between '2-2-53' (five pages earlier) and '?3 Aug. 1953.' (The Hull cataloguer fails to identify the poem correctly.) *Wkbk* 4 (1/4/33) contains: after

'17 Oct [1956]', nine and a half pages of drafts of the whole poem, dated '26. xii. 56' at the end; a page of further drafts of stanzas 2 and 3 dated '1 Jan 57' at the end; immediately followed by a further draft of stanza 3 before '14 / 5 / 57' (seven pages later). Hull DPL 2/3/19, t.s. with holograph corrections = Hull t.s. 1. L writes '(unfinished)' below the text. Hull DPL 2/3/5, t.s. with holograph corrections = Hull t.s. 2. In l. 23 L has inserted a caret and suggested 'lamely?' in the margin as the word to be added. L to RC, 21 Sept. 1962 (*SL*, 345): 'If you are printing LOVE SONGS IN AGE, would you mind substituting "Love" for "It" in the last line?' In *TWW*, however, the reading was 'It'.

VARIANTS

Title [No title] *Hull t.s. 1.*

1 She] She'd *Hull t.s. 1*

7 they had] there they *Hull t.s. 2*

7–8 ~~To happen on them like this Picking~~ To pick them up one evening at the last | Drifted her senses round until they faced the past *Hull t.s. 1*

9–16

~~The~~ Their tunes, of course: each frank submissive chord,
    Ushering plainly
    Word after sprawling hyphenated word
    To that arpeggio fingering at the close,
    Flew to the warehouse of her memory
    (Darker the basement grows)
    And brought back heavy rooms, a broken set
    Of lustre-jugs, french windows dribbling in the wet. *Hull t.s. 1*

12 unfailing] familiar *Hull t.s. 2*

13 spring-woken] Spring-laden *Hull t.s. 2*

14 That] A *Hull t.s. 2*

15 That] A *Hull t.s. 2*

17–24

            But, after all, that cold much-mentioned fume
            The songs called love,
            Which innocence had forced her to assume
            Was love, and would come later; would be ~~wrung~~ lit
    With ~~From~~ news of casualty or sudden move,
            ~~From a subdued tongue; would Settling her to sit~~
            Persuading her to sit
    Long ~~From On~~ country evenings, hearing the wind rise,
            Sending to long-due letters immediate replies, *Hull t.s. 1*

19 sailing] ~~regrouped~~ reformed *Hull t.s. 2*

22 pile] put *Hull t.s. 2*

23 Was hard, ~~to do~~ without ^ admitting how   ^lamely? *Hull t.s. 2*

Additional lines

  Until, with footstep or undated note,

    Hat thrown aside,

  Love, bursting in, stoops to the naked throat,
  Then all her grief flares up and vanishes,
  Then from the glare of joy she cannot hide,
  Watching her farthest wishes

  In brilliant bitter semblance of a gown
    Woven for her sole shoulders coming stiffly down.

 [Commas after 'wishes' and 'shoulders' cancelled.] *Hull t.s. 1*

The poem was inspired by 'the pile of sheet music on his mother's piano': Brennan (2002), 52. 'The conclusion of the poem, like the opening, had been prompted by a Christmas visit to his mother': Motion (1993), 279. Cf. L himself, however, in 1964 (*FR*, 81–2): 'From time to time [. . .] one writes something that seems to have no bearing on one's character or environment at all. I can't for the life of me think why I should have wanted to write about Victorian drawing-room ballads: probably I must have heard one on the wireless, and thought how terrible it must be for an old lady to hear one of these songs she had learned as a girl and reflect how different life had turned out to be. Here is "Love Songs in Age".'

 21 *set unchangeably in order*: John Whitehead, *Hardy to Larkin: Seven English Poets* (1995), 228, notes an echo of the thirteenth-century Franciscan, Jacopone da Todi, 'Ordina questo amore, O tu che m'ami', translated in E. M. Forster's essay in *I Believe* (1939) as 'O Thou who lovest me set this love in order'. Forster remarks that the prayer was not granted and that he himself believes it never will be. Cf. Auden, *New Year Letter*, l. 52, 56, 60–1: 'For art had set in order sense', 'To set in order – that's the task', 'That order which must be the end I That all self-loving things attend'.

Naturally the Foundation will Bear Your Expenses

DATE AND TEXT

Wkbk 6 (1/6/1) contains two pages of drafts of ll. 1–12 on pages headed '14. 11. 60' and '15 / 11 / 60' (with '27. 11. 60' at the top of the next page), and a single page (1/6/5) with '22. 1. 61' at the top bearing a complete draft with the title '*From London Far*', dated '23 / 1 / 61' at the end. L to MJ, 11 Feb.1961: 'Here is *Naturally*. [. . .] It "came to me," I think, when washing up after listening to the Cenotaph service last November & thinking how much sooner I'd be there than going to India – in fact the two situations presented themselves so strongly in opposition that I was greatly <u>stricken</u>, and dyd Seek to Compose vpon Itt.': Bodl. MS Eng. c. 7422/89. Published in *Twentieth Century*, 170. 1010 (July 1961), 54, and in *Partisan Review*, 31. 3 (Summer 1964), [381].

See 'A *Lecturer* in drip-dry shirt arrayed', an earlier treatment of the same subject. L to RC, 11 July 1961 (*SL*, 330): 'I thought the poem worth printing if only for the title, but I hope it annoys all the continent-hopping craps.' L in 1964: 'rather a curious poem. It came from having been to London and having heard that A had gone to India and that B had just come back from India; then when I got back home, happening unexpectedly across the memorial service at the Cenotaph on the wireless, on what used to be called Armistice Day, and the two things seemed to get mixed up together. Almost immediately afterwards *Twentieth Century* wrote saying that they were having a Humour number and would I send them something funny, so I sent that. Actually, it's as serious as anything I have written [. . .] I've never written a poem that has been less understood; one editor refused it on the grounds, and I quote, that it was "rather hard on the Queen"; several people have asked what it was like in Bombay! There is nothing like writing poems for realizing how low the level of critical understanding is': *FR*, 25. The editor who refused it was C. B. Cox, as is made clear in L's letter of 11 Feb. 1961 to MJ. L in 1981: 'It's both funny and serious. The speaker's a shit. That's always serious': *FR*, 58.

    Title Osborne (2008), 79: 'a standard formulation from the realm of arts fellowships and academic foundations'. L in 1967 (*FR*, 28): 'You can earn your money talking about poetry in universities or hopping from one foundation to another or one conference to another [. . .] I'm a librarian [. . .] It depends on your temperament.' **1** *Comet*: jet aircraft pioneered by Sir Geoffrey de

Havilland. Its first commercial flight took off in May 1952. Several crashes gave it a reputation for disaster, and as Osborne (2008), 204, recalls, two with no survivors were at Karachi and Calcutta. Osborne: 'Bombay next?' 5 *Berkeley*: the University of California at Berkeley. L reading the poem gives the British pronunciation 'Barclay' (rhyming perfectly with 'darkly'). 7–8 L in 1964 (*FR*, 25): 'Certainly it was a dig at the middleman who gives a lot of talks to America and then brushes them up and does them on the Third and then brushes them up again and puts them out as a book with Chatto.' *Perceiving . . . darkly . . . mirror*: 'For now we see as through a glass, darkly; but then face to face': 1 Cor. 13: 12. Noted in Petch (1981), 7, 63. *Chatto*: Chatto & Windus, publishers. *the Third*: BBC radio network largely devoted to high culture; introduced in 1946 and renamed 'Radio 3' in 1967. 12 *the date*: 11 Nov., designated Armistice Day since 1918, and involving the laying of wreaths at the Cenotaph in Whitehall in commemoration of British citizens who died in war. Noting that Tom Driberg had written a letter to the *New Statesman* 'heartily agreeing with Larkin about his supposed attack on ceremonies for the war dead', RC comments that the poem 'is in fact a very hostile caricature of this smug anti-patriotism': Thwaite (1982), 36. R. L. Brett in Hartley (1988), 110, notes that the description of Armistice Day 'would have offended his [L's] own deeply held patriotism'. L to MJ, 13 Nov. 1960 (Bodl. MS Eng. c. 7422/45): 'Today I stumbled on the Cenotaph service at 10. 45 – I seem to do this every year, just as the Guards Massed Bands are playing *Nimrod* [from Elgar's *Enigma Variations*, and see the note on *Broadcast*, 5, below], & it harrows me to my foundations. These things seem to grow in power as one gets older.' In letters to MJ dated 5 Nov. 1970 and 14 Nov. 1971 (Bodl. MSS Eng. c. 7442/24, 7443/120), L tells her he has been watching the Remembrance Day service on television. To AT, 11 Nov. 1984 (*SL*, 723): 'Watched the Cenotaph ceremony as usual, that day when Queen and minister etc. Very moving.' 15–18 L, inconsistently, in 1964 (*FR*, 25): 'Why he should be blamed for not sympathizing with the crowds on Armistice Day, I don't quite know.' 21 *Auster*: the south wind; hence, the south. 22 L to CM after the publication of *TWW* in 1963: 'An awful thing – a Professor Lal has written to me from Calcutta highly delighted at my mentioning him [. . .] Am I fated to be *his* contact and *his* pal?': Thwaite (1982), 42. 23 *Morgan Forster*: the novelist E[dward] M[organ] Forster (1879–1970), known as 'Morgan' only to family and friends.

Broadcast

DATE AND TEXT
Wkbk 6 (1/6/3) contains three pages of drafts of the complete poem except for the title between '5 xi 61' and '6. xi. 61'. Published in *The Listener*, 67. 1713 (25 Jan. 1962), 157.

Brennan (2002), 57: 'I had been present at a live concert [by the BBC Symphony Orchestra in the City Hall in Hull] on 5 November 1961 which was simultaneously broadcast on the radio. Philip, who knew I was in the audience, listened at home. The inscription in my copy of the *Listener* [. . .] where the poem first appeared, reads: "To Maeve, who wd. sooner listen to music than listen to me", accompanied by a caricature of himself, enveloped in gloom beside his radio, while I sit nearby, lost in my own musical world, one of my gloves unnoticed on the floor.' L to MJ, 8 Feb. 1962: 'I don't know that it's worth saying anything except that my delight in you isn't pretended: you blot out anyone else. This was the first "love" poem I've written since *Maiden name* in about 1954, & I sh^d think both are pretty tenuous, pretty remote, as far as general approach goes. In fact I think this one just a shade ludicrous!': *SL*, 340. When MJ came to see that the poem was not about her, L commented: 'I didn't hesitate a moment about including it, because I didn't think it w^d bother you, and it seemed good enough': 10 Feb. 1964 (Bodl. MS Eng. c. 7427/89); 'I'm sorry about *Broadcast*, and I'm sure my distress was real. I suppose I don't really equate poems with real-life as most people do – I mean they are true in a way, but very much dolled up & censored': 18 Feb. 1964, *SL*, 366.

4 *'The Queen'*: (familiarly) the National Anthem ('God save our gracious Queen'). 5 'We also shared a love of Elgar, whom Philip found nostalgic and intensely moving [. . .] Perhaps it was not without significance that the first item on the programme which inspired "Broadcast" was this composer's *Introduction and Allegro for Strings*: "A snivel on the violins"': Brennan (2002), 53. L to MJ, 12 May 1957 (Bodl. MS Eng. c. 7416/11), on Elgar: 'he is a composer I feel drawn to, in my parochial way'; to MJ, 10 Aug. 1957 (Bodl. MS Eng. c. 7416/95): 'I do think Elgar a good composer at times.' 10 Brennan (2002), 57: 'a private joke, whose formulation, if not the specific adjective, was mine. They were an unusual colour of pearlised bronze, very smart, with stiletto heels and long, pointed toes [. . .] Philip raved about the shoes. He used to take them off my feet, hold them up, stroke them, put them down

on the sofa and continue to admire them; not just once, but every time I wore them. He thought they were the last word in fashion, until one day, slightly exasperated, I teased: "I don't know why you go on so about these shoes. They're almost out of fashion now [. . .] He laughed and said: "Well. I still adore them even if they are slightly outmoded!"'

Faith Healing

DATE AND TEXT

Wkbk 5 (1/5/31) contains ten pages of drafts of the whole poem except for the title after '19. 3 [1960]', dated '10 / 5 / 60' at the end. Published in *The Listener*, 64. 1634 (21 July 1960), 115, and in *Shenandoah*, 13. 2 (Winter [i.e. Jan.] 1962), 33.

L in 1964: 'I believe that art which takes its origin in other art is less likely to be successful than art founded in unsorted experience. I am ashamed, therefore, to have to admit that [. . .] "Faith Healing" [. . .] was written after seeing a film in which such a scene occurs. Still, it was a documentary film – the actors were real people who did not know that they were being photographed. This I hope mitigates the offence somewhat': *FR*, 86. L in 1981: 'Well, people want to be loved, don't they. The sort of unconditional love parents give if you're lucky, and that gets mixed up with the love of God – "dear child", and so on': *FR*, 58.

15 *idiot child*: Housman notoriously said of Robinson Ellis that he had the intellect of an 'idiot child': *A. E. Housman: Collected Poems and Selected Prose*, ed. Christopher Ricks (1988), 387. L applies the phrase to his colleague Arthur Wood in a letter to MJ dated 20 Oct. 1960 (Bodl. MS Eng. c. 7422/24). 19 *blort*: L to AT, 20 May 1960: '*blort* is intended: it is I think a variation of *blore* which is a dialect word meaning to bellow (like an animal). I am rather alarmed not to find *blort* in the dictionary, but D. H. Lawrence uses it somewhere, and I certainly don't mean *blurt*, which has a quite different meaning to my mind': *SL*, 313. (L is advising AT as producer of 'New Poems' on the BBC Third Programme on how the actor Hugh Dickson should read the poem in the broadcast on 24 July 1960.) To Judie Johnson, 16 Mar. 1965 (Hull DPL 5/6): 'It means a thick heifer-like bellowing. I don't know where I found it – one of Lawrence's dialect poems I believe.' Lawrence uses it in his poem *Tortoise Shout*, 62: 'I remember the heifer in her heat, blorting

and blorting through the hours, persistent and irrepressible'. L uses the word in *Round Another Point* (1951): 'If someone came to you blorting that he'd just seen a baby born' (*TAWG*, 494). 'Blort' is not in the *OED*, though 'blurt' and 'blirt' are. **19–20** Tim Trengove-Jones, 'Larkin's Stammer', *EIC*, 40. 4 (1990), 331, relates the specific form of the distress to the stammer L had till about the age of thirty (on which, see notes on *Next, Please*). **22** *all's wrong*: Cf. Housman, *More Poems* XXX 3: 'All's wrong that ever I've done and said'. **27–30** L to AT, 20 May 1960 (*SL*, 313): 'As regards the last line, what spreads slowly through them is (a) an immense slackening ache, (b) the voice above, (c) all the things (like love and happiness and success and kindness) that the passage of time has proved to them do not really exist and which they have therefore got into the habit of forgetting.' L told MB in a letter of 28 Mar. 1964 that he thought the ending 'one of the best things in the book': Brennan (2002), 169.

For Sidney Bechet

DATE AND TEXT
Wkbk 3 contains: two drafts of ll. 1–5 between '6. xii. 53' and '28 xii 53' (1/3/27); after '8 / 1 / 54', four pages of drafts of all but stanza 6, dated '15. 1. 54' at the end, immediately followed by a draft of the first four stanzas before '17 / 1 / 54' (1/3/34); a page of drafts of stanza 5 and additional lines between '23 Jan 1954' and '27. 1. 54' (1/3/38); just over a page of drafts of stanza 5 and additional lines between '27. 1. 54' and '9 iii 54' (1/3/40); and drafts of ll. 13–14 and 1–2 after '26 5 54' (1/3/51). Published in *Ark*, 18 (Nov. 1956), 58, and in *Listen*, 4. 1 (Autumn 1962), 8, with 'Sydney' for 'Sidney' and 'Storeyvilles' for 'Storyvilles' (l. 7) each time.

Title *Sidney Bechet*: Jazz musician (1897–1959), clarinet and soprano-saxophone player. L regarded him as 'one of the half-dozen leading figures in jazz': *AWJ*, 139, and thought that though there were not many perfect things in jazz 'Bechet playing the blues could be one of them': *RB*, 45. He invariably spoke of Bechet with admiration and approval (*AWJ*, 19–20, 60, 77, 149, 181, 216, for instance). **1** *narrowing and rising*: Bechet was famous for deviations in pitch ('note-bending') and for a wide, fast vibrato. John Lucas, 'Appropriate Falsehoods: English Poets and American Jazz', *The Yearbook of English Studies*, 17 (1987), 57–8, notes that

L expressed admiration for Bechet's 'Blue Horizon': 'six choruses of slow blues in which Bechet climbs without interruption or hurry from lower to upper register, his clarinet tone at first thick and throbbing, then soaring like Melba in an extraordinary blend of lyricism and power that constituted the unique Bechet voice, commanding attention the instant it sounded': *AWJ*, 41. *shakes*: V. Penelope Pelizzon, *AL*, 5 (Apr. 1998), 17: 'suggests the tremolo characteristic of Bechet's playing'. 1–2 John Whitehead, *AL*, 5 (Apr. 1998), 29, notes E. M. Forster's comparison of a Hindu raga performed by a singer and a drummer to 'Western music reflected in trembling water' in *The Hill of Devi* (1954), letter of 9 May 1921 (Abinger edn., xiv. 46). 2 Early in his career, Bechet played in New Orleans with jazz greats Clarence Williams (1893–1965) and Joe 'King' Oliver (1885–1938). 5 *quadrilles*: square dances for couples. 6 In 1962 L described the music of the great New Orleans players as 'a particularly buoyant kind of jazz that seems to grow from a spontaneous enjoyment of living': *AWJ*, 54. 7 *Oh, play that thing!*: The celebrated shout supplied on the first version of Oliver's *Dippermouth Blues* (1923) by double-bass player Bill Johnson (1872/4–1932), who played the banjo on the recording. John Osborne, 'Larkin, Modernism and Jazz', *Hungarian Journal of English and American Studies*, 9. 2 (2003), 15, 16, cites other, derivative sources: the opening ('Play that thing') of 'Jazz Band in a Parisian Cabaret' by African American jazz-poet Langston Hughes; the exhortation 'Play it, man, play it' in Bechet's 1932 recording of *Maple Leaf Rag*; the echoing in parodic falsetto of 'Oh, play that thing!' in the Fletcher Henderson Orchestra's reworking of Oliver's *Dippermouth Blues* as *Sugar Foot Stomp* (1925); and Louis Armstrong introducing a member of the Hot Five on the recording of *Gut Bucket Blues* (1925) by saying 'Oh, play that thing, Mr St Cyr'. *Mute glorious*: Cf. Gray's *Elegy written in a Country Churchyard*, 59: 'Some mute inglorious Milton'. Noted in Petch (1981), 7. Storyville was a thirty-eight-block red-light district in New Orleans famous for its jazz. *Mute*: Osborne, 'Larkin, Modernism and Jazz', 13, notes that Storyville was partially closed in 1917, and this contributed to the diaspora of New Orleans jazz players like Bechet. Leggett (1999), 72 and n.: 'Storyville is also the name of a record label that issued or reissued (licensed) traditional New Orleans jazz and the blues', including 'the "Sidney Bechet Sessions," reissued from sessions of 1946 and 1947 [. . .] it was most active in 1953–1955.' 9 *Sporting-house*: brothel. L uses the term in a 1964 review (*AWJ*, 106). *priced*:

because they are prostitutes. Cf. Proverbs 31: 10: 'Who can find a virtuous woman? For her price is far above rubies.' 11 *scholars*: Leggett (1999), 71: 'the sporting-house pianists, who were called "professors," perhaps because many of them gave piano lessons'. L mentions the 'professors' in reviews (*AWJ*, 106, 176). *manqués*: unfulfilled, unsuccessful. French, in acknowledgement of the French Quarter of New Orleans. 12 *personnels*: band members (*OED*, 1.b.). Leggett (1999), 71, quotes Jelly Roll Morton on 'using different personnels in the Red Hot Peppers band'. Osborne, 'Larkin, Modernism and Jazz', 13, notes that 'personnels *were* fluid in New Orleans bands of all sizes'. 14 *an enormous yes*: Cf. Carlyle's 'The Everlasting Yea' ('wherein all contradiction is solved'): *Sartor Resartus*, book 2, ch. 9. L to MJ, Easter Sunday 1964 (Bodl. MS Eng. c. 7427/121): 'I do feel defensive about that Bechet line: have they never heard the Beatles singing "She loves you – yeah, yeah, yeah – "? Or read the end of Molly Bloom's soliloquy? Why is it so bad? I thought when I wrote it that it just "got" love & Bechet & everything. Perhaps that's what's wrong with it!' *Crescent City*: New Orleans, located on a curve of the Mississippi River. 17 *long-haired*: OED, long-hair, *n.* 2. a.: 'a devotee of classical (as opposed to popular) music. (Freq. used contemptuously.)' Earliest example with this sense, 1936. Leggett (1999), 71, notes that Roy Bird, a New Orleans pianist, singer and songwriter, called himself 'Professor Longhair'. L to KA, 19 Sept. 1978: 'I switched on for your Kaleidoscope thing and got ten minutes of [. . .] longhair crap': *SL*, 589. *scored*: Bechet was a celebrated improviser.

Home is so Sad

DATE AND TEXT
Wkbk 5 (1/5/13) contains two complete drafts after '29. xii [1958]', dated respectively '30 xii 58' and '31 xii 58' at the end, followed by a further draft of the first two and a half lines. Hull DPL 2/3/2 is a t.s. with holograph corrections. Published in *Oxford Magazine*, 77. 24 (18 June 1959), 473, and in *The Listener*, 71. 1817 (23 Jan. 1964), 149.

VARIANTS (from Hull DPL 2/3/2)
Title [No title]
2 Shaped to] ~~Suiting~~ Shaped to
3 win] ~~bring~~ win

L to MJ, 30 Jan. 1964 (Bodl. MS Eng. c. 7427/74): 'It goes awfully slack in the middle.'

Title 'lightly contradicting a familiar cliché (that home is sweet)': James Booth, 'The Turf-Cutter and the Nine-to-Five Man: Heaney, Larkin, and "The Spiritual Intellect's Great Work"', *Twentieth Century Literature*, 43. 4 (Winter 1997), 379. 1 *Home*: 'I am actually writing this at my "home", which is what one always calls where one's surviving parent lives': L to BP, 7 Dec. 1963 (*SL*, 362). To MB, 13 Sept. 1972 (Brennan [2002], 55): 'I am going "home" (as I still call it) this weekend as of course I must & want to, but it is saddening to face the sad situation again.' To MJ, 9 Apr. 1957 (Bodl. MS Eng. c. 7415/123): 'Home was rather sad in its way.' To MJ, 12 Aug. 1962 (Bodl. MS Eng. c. 7425/41): 'Home is a sad place, anyway'. 10 *That vase*: Patrick Swinden, 'Larkin and the Exemplary Owen', *EIC*, 44. 4 (1994), 326, compares Wilfred Owen, *Conscious*, 7: 'What's inside that jug?' Cf. *Lines on a Young Lady's Photograph Album*, 27: 'Those flowers, that gate'. L pronounces 'vase' as /vɑːz/ in his recording.

Toads Revisited

DATE AND TEXT
Wkbk 6 (1/6/23) contains a draft of the last two lines between '21. ix. 62' and '27. 9. 62', and the latter date is followed by six and a half pages of drafts of the whole poem with the date '10. 10. 62' at the end. Published in *The Spectator*, 209. 7013 (23 Nov. 1962), 828.

L to MJ, 9 Nov. 1972 (Bodl. MS Eng. c. 7444/123): 'a nice poem, I think'. To MJ, 22 Nov. 1962 (Bodl. MS Eng. c. 7425/107): '"The toad work" is a nice personification. It's in a different metre from *Toads*, slightly – AA'BB' instead of ABA'B' – I use the "'" sign to indicate dissonance, or half-assonance as Peter de Vries calls it.' To JE, 22 Dec. 1962 (Bodl. MS Eng. c. 7453/118): 'it was sincere, I thought, but failed to grip'.

David Chandler, 'Larkin's Toad Revisited', *N&Q*, NS 50. 3 (Sept. 2003), 339, notes a comparable double attitude to the toad in *As You Like It*, 2. 1. 12–13: 'adversity, | Which like the toad, ugly and venomous, | Wears yet a precious jewel in his head.'

30 Betty Mackereth. On 12 Aug. 1962 L remarked to MJ on 'an astounding hair-do, like a half-loaf or a leg of mutton' that Betty had tried in Aug. 1961: Motion (1993), 327. L refers to her as 'Loaf hair'

in a letter to MJ dated 12 Feb. 1963 (Bodl. MS Eng. c. 7426/29), as 'my loaf-haired sec.' in a letter to RC, 9 Jan. 1975 (SL, 519), and as 'my loaf-haired secretary' and 'the l-h secretary' in letters to BP, 5 Aug. 1977 and 19 Mar. 1978 (Bodl. MS Pym 152/14, 26). A photograph is printed in Motion (1993), between pages 412 and 413. 35 Osborne (2008), 55, cites Kenneth Grahame's *The Wind in the Willows* (ch. 11): '"Here's old Toad!" cried the Mole . . . Mole drew his arm through Toad's'. 35–6 In Nov. 1974, L 'stressed that "Toads Revisited", in its coming to terms with work, represented his present views: he had now come to feel that "if he didn't work he'd just brood over the reviews and get pissed by lunchtime"': Watt (1989), 174. L to BP, 21 Aug. 1978 (Bodl. MS Pym 152/33): 'Found the perfect epigraph for "Toads Revisited" in Oscar Wilde's *Letters*: "Work never seems to me a reality, but a way of getting rid of reality." Oh yes!' L to JE, 9 June 1983: 'Life is depressing on all sorts of counts – *work*; well, that one-time refuge, I can see, is coming to a close [. . .] I positively dread retirement': SL, 696.

Water

DATE AND TEXT
Wkbk 3 (1/3/46) contains one and a half pages bearing a complete draft after '5 / 4 / 54', dated '6 / 4 / 54' at the end. Published in *Listen*, 2. 3 (Summer–Autumn 1957), [1], and in *Poetry and Drama Magazine*, 10. 2 (1958), 24. L to CM, 19 Mar. 1964 (SL, 367): 'A kind friend has pointed out to me that where I say "litany" [. . .] I mean "liturgy". I don't think this will sound as well, but sense must come first: is there any chance of getting it into the American edition, and could we make a note of it for any subsequent resetting here?' (The kind friend was MJ.) In *CP* (1988), 93: 'litany'; in *CP* (2003), 'liturgy'. In a letter to MJ dated 18 Apr. 1971 (Bodl. MS Eng. c. 7442/110), he favoured 'litany' again: 'Oh, in the paperb. *TWW* "litany" has been replaced by "liturgy". I rather wish I hadn't listened to you on this: it seems to wreck the whole verse, it's so heavy, as opposed to the dancingness of "litany" – "liturgy" anticipates *images* in the next line, too, the g sound. I don't think the meaning is sufficient gain, as no one knows what either word means anyway.' The present edition prints 'liturgy': it is the correct term, as L realised (a litany would not employ 'Images of sousing, | A furious devout drench'); and, despite his reservations, he did not ask his publisher for 'liturgy' to be changed back to 'litany'.

7 My] The *Listen (1957)*
liturgy] litany *TWW, 1964*

2 Cf. Eliot, 'Lancelot Andrewes' (1926): 'No religion can survive
the judgment of history unless the best minds of its time have
collaborated in its construction': *Selected Prose of T. S. Eliot*, ed.
Frank Kermode (1975), 180. 10 *the east*: Associated with Jerusalem
and Mecca, as John Osborne, Booth (2000), 162, notes.

The Whitsun Weddings

DATE AND TEXT

'I was looking at "The Whitsun Weddings" [the poem] just the other
day, and found that I began it sometime in the summer of 1957.
After three pages, I dropped it for another poem that in fact was
finished but never published. I picked it up again, in March 1958,
and worked on it till October, when it was finished. But when I
look at the diary I was keeping at the time, I see that the kind of
incident it describes happened in July 1955! So in all, it took over
three years': L in 1982 (*RW*, 75, where the square brackets round
'the poem' are L's). (The incident took place in Aug. 1955: see
below.) *Wkbk* 4 contains two and a half pages of drafts of stanza
1 between '14 / 5 / 57' and '16 / x / 57' (1/4/36), and twenty-three
pages of drafts of all but the last stanza between '16 / 3 / 58' and a
final page headed '6 / 9 / 58' (1/4/38). *Wkbk* 5 (1/5/8) contains seven
pages of drafts of the last two stanzas between the date '19. 9. 58'
and the completion date '18. 10. 58'. L's struggle with the poem
is documented in letters to MJ dated 12 May, 16 June, 29 July,
22 Sept. and 16 and 18 Oct. 1958: Bodl. MSS Eng. c. 7418/35,
38 (posted 16 May), 52, 70, 106, 120, 122. In the last of these,
he remarks: 'I've never known anything resist me so! Not even
Church G. wch I find I abandoned once [. . .] I have just hammered
it to *an* end, but really out of sheer desperation to see this fiendish
8th verse in some kind of order'. Hull DPL 2/3/4 = Hull t.s. 1. At
l. 49, at 'Just what', L has written 'All that?' in the margin; at l.
68, at 'would all', he writes 'reverse?' in the margin: Hull DPL
2/3/39 = Hull t.s. 2; signed in t.s. 'Philip Larkin'. In l. 16 'unique'
may be a typing error rather than a variant. Published in *Encounter*,
12. 6 (June 1959), 47–8, but read by Gary Watson on 3 Apr. 1959
on the BBC's Third Programme in AT's production 'New Poetry'.

16 uniquely] unique *Hull t.s.* 2
26 took for] thought were *Hull t.s.* 1
37 loud and] more than *Hull t.s.* 1; *Hull t.s.* 2
49 Just what] Just what All that? *Hull t.s.* 1
53 The] Some *Hull t.s.* 1
68 would all] would all all would? *Hull t.s.* 1
80 becoming] turning to *Hull t.s.* 1; *Hull t.s.* 2

L to AT, 17 Mar. 1959, before the BBC broadcast (*SL*, 301): 'I might just add a note about its reading: it is pitched if anything in an even lower key than usual, and the reader's task is to graduate from just talking – the first verse or two – to interested close description (at least, one hopes the listener will be interested). It is of course humorous, here and there, but any supercilious note should be rigorously excluded. Success or failure of the poem depends on whether it gets off the ground on the last two lines. It is asking a lot of a reader, I know, to achieve a climax in so small a compass, but unless this image succeeds with the listener I am afraid the poem will seem no more than pedestrian.' AT confirms that L said that the poem should be read on a 'level, even a plodding, descriptive note' and that the 'mysterious last lines should suddenly "lift off the ground"': *Phoenix*, 11/12 (Autumn and Winter 1973–4), 51.

L in 1964 (*FR*, 87): 'Every now and then you will see some happening or situation that prompts you to think that if only you could get that down, in a kind of verbal photography, you would have a poem ready-made. This was what I felt some years ago when I happened to see a series of wedding parties at a succession of stations on the way to London one hot Saturday afternoon. Their cumulative effect produced an emotion so strong that I despaired of ever getting it under control; in the end, however, it produced "The Whitsun Weddings".' L in 1981 (*FR*, 57): 'You can't say "The Whitsun Weddings", which is central to the book, is a sad poem. It was just the transcription of a very happy afternoon. I didn't change a thing, it was just there to be written down [. . .] You couldn't be on that train without feeling the young lives all starting off, and that just for a moment you were touching them. Doncaster, Retford, Grantham, Newark, Peterborough, and at every station more wedding parties. It was wonderful, a marvellous afternoon. It only needed writing down. Anybody could have done it [. . .] There's nothing to suggest that their lives won't be happy, surely? I defy you to find it.' L again in 1981: 'There's hardly anything of me in it at all. It's just life as it happened': Motion (1993), 287.

Motion, 287–8, provides the text of an interview L gave with Melvyn Bragg for the *South Bank Show*, 16 Apr. 1981: 'I hadn't realized that, of course, this was the train that all the wedding couples would get on and go to London for their honeymoon[;] it was an eye-opener to me. Every part was different but the same somehow. They all looked different but they were all doing the same things and sort of feeling the same things. I suppose the train stopped at about four, five, six stations between Hull and London and there was a sense of gathering emotional momentum. Every time you stopped fresh emotion climbed aboard. And finally between Peterborough and London when you hurtle on, you felt the whole thing was being aimed like a bullet – at the heart of things, you know. All this fresh, open life. Incredible experience. I've never forgotten it.'

In fact, L did not travel at Whitsun, and did not go all the way to London: the accounts in Motion (1993), 287, and Bradford (2005), 157, are inaccurate. L to MJ, 3 Aug. 1955 (Bodl. MS Eng. c. 7411/122): 'I went home on Saturday afternoon, 1.30 to Grantham – a lovely run, the scorched land misty with heat, like a kind of *bloom* of heat – and at every station, Goole, Doncaster, Retford, Newark, importunate wedding parties, gawky & vociferous, seeing off couples to London. My literary pleasure in this was damped by missing the 4.8 connection at Grantham.' (He tells MJ that he got a lift from a farmer to Melton Mowbray, and then caught a bus to Loughborough, arriving at 6.46.) To JE, 5 May 1959 (*SL*, 301): 'I hope it conveys something of the impressiveness of the occasion: it really was an unforgettable experience. In fact it took place on August Saturday 1955 [*sic*] – during that very fine weather, remember.' To Doreen Preston, 11 Apr. 1985 (Hull DPL (2) 2/25/188): 'when I came to look up the genesis of "The Whitsun Weddings" I found that not only did it not take place at Whitsun, but that I actually got out of the train at Grantham and took a motorbus to the Midlands to see my family, or what was left of them. Twenty years or so had made me believe the poem rather than what actually happened!'

The train journey at the beginning of *Jill* is similar in that it too 'conflates urban and pastoral in a momentary synthesis of random detail': Cooper (2004), 34.

Ian Milligan, 'Philip Larkin's "The Whitsun Weddings" and Virginia Woolf's "The Waves"', *N&Q*, NS 23. 1 (Jan. 1976), 23, notes parallels with a passage in Virginia Woolf's novel (the section begins '"How fair, how strange," said Bernard': Harcourt edn., 111–12): both contain 'the idea of a shared community of experience . . . In each the journey suggests the brevity of life, and its conclusion carries intimations of death, but in each there are reminders of continuity.' More specific parallels are noted below. Thomas Gibbons and David Ormerod, '"The Whitsun Weddings" and *The Waves*', *N&Q*, NS 40. 1 (Mar. 1993), 69–70, duplicate much of what Milligan notes whilst elaborating further: 'There is a train journey from the north of England to London. There is a shared preoccupation with marriage – other people's weddings, on Larkin's part, his own impending marriage on the part of Woolf's narrator. There is a joint preoccupation with the itemized enumeration of the landscape details [. . .] Both writers associate London with generation [. . .] The sense of participating in an important rite, where the hitherto unappreciated beauty of the lives of undistinguished strangers is grasped in an emotional epiphany, is common to both. This appreciation is common to the observers, but not to the participants.'

John Osborne, Booth (2000), 148–9, makes an extended comparison with Eliot, *The Waste Land*: 'both poems begin with a journey south [. . .] Both travel from heat and drought, with much play on the way shadows lengthen or contract in accord with the angle of the sun, to hints of regenerative rain. Both poems describe major rivers, Eliot's "Sweet Thames run softly till I end my song" [. . .] being a quotation from Edmund Spenser's "Prothalamium", a poem written, like "The Whitsun Weddings", to celebrate a multiple marriage. Both poems complicate these wholesome riverine images with descriptions of industrial waterways, Eliot's seedy urban pastoral ("I was fishing in the dull canal / On a winter evening round behind the gashouse") being closely paralleled in Larkin's description of "Canals with floatings of industrial froth". Both poems move towards a close with references to towers, London and polluted walls (*The Waste Land* describes "a blackened wall", "The Whitsun Weddings" has "walls of blackened moss" [. . .] Both end with the prospect of sexual regeneration – the restoration to potency of the Fisher King in *The Waste Land*, the consummation of the marriages in "The Whitsun Weddings" – alike symbolized by the yoking of the word "rain" to a present participle (Eliot's "bringing rain", Larkin's "becoming rain"). Add the parallelings of word and phrase (Larkin's "girls" marked off "unreally from the rest" invoking the [. . .] "unreal" of *The Waste Land*; or Eliot's "She . . . nearly died of young George" becoming "*I nearly died*" in "The Whitsun Weddings"'. This account may also be found in Osborne (2008), 60.

John Reibetanz notes that L has chosen 'the stanzaic form that Keats evolved for his great odes' (specifically, the rhyme scheme *ababcdecde*), but has 'revised the romantic outlook': '"The Whitsun Weddings": Larkin's Reinterpretation of Time and Form in Keats', *Contemporary Literature*, 17. 4 (Autumn 1976), 530, 537.

Title *Whitsun*: Christian festival beginning the seventh Sunday after Easter. Osborne (2008), 63, notes the fiscal reason for marriages occurring at this time: the British tax laws of the 1950s granted a married man's tax allowance for the previous year to couples who got married by the Whit deadline, and 'the rush to meet the tax deadline was most conspicuous in lower-income groups for whom every penny counts (and who go off on honeymoon by public transport)'. 1 *getting away*: From Hull, on the train to King's Cross, London. 8 *smelt the fish-dock*: See the note on *Here*, 19. 9–10 Osborne (2008), 61, compares Tennyson, *The Lady of Shalott*, 1–3: 'On either side the river lie | Long fields of barley and of rye, | That clothe the wold and meet the sky'. He notes the aptness of the train entering Tennyson's county of Lincolnshire. 11–12 See L's comments on the heat in his letter to MJ (above). John Osborne, Booth (2000), 149: 'distantly invokes the heat and lethargy of Tennyson's "The Lotos-Eaters"'. More particularly, cf. Tennyson, ll. 3–5, 15, 21: 'afternoon', 'afternoon', 'All round', 'the inner land', 'far inland'. 16 *flashed*: John Gross in Thwaite (1982), 83, notes 'an Odeon flashes fire' in Betjeman's *The Metropolitan Railway*, 32, and the 'melancholy kinship' ('Cancer has killed him. Heart is killing her') it establishes between the couples in the two poems. Cf. also Betjeman's *North Coast Recollections*, 53: 'The windows of Trenain are flashing fire'. 26 Peter Sheldon, who was Sub-librarian to L at Hull, recounts how L told him on at least two occasions that the line contained a punning reference to a student, Miss Porter, whom he professed to lust after: *AL*, 20 (Autumn 2005), 75. 28 *pomaded*: wearing scented hair-dressing. 40 Timms (1973), 95, notes 'the colour-names used by department stores to glamorize their products', as in *The Large Cool Store*, 11, and, in each case, an association with unreality. 54 Milligan, 23, notes a parallel in *The Waves* (Harcourt edn., III): 'Men clutch their newspapers a little tighter'. **55** *Free at last*: John Osborne, 'Larkin, Modernism and Jazz', *Hungarian Journal of English and American Studies*, 9. 2 (2003), 27 (2008), 66, catches the echo of the African-American spiritual 'I Thank God I'm Free At Last'. Also Osborne (2008), 66. **58–9** Stephen Derry, 'Tennyson's "Mariana" and Larkin's "The Whitsun Weddings"', *N&Q*, NS 42. 4 (December 1996), 448, notes *Mariana*, 55–6: 'The shadow of the poplar fell | Upon her bed, across her brow'. **62** Osborne (2008), 61, notes that in addition to *The Waste Land* (see above) L may be echoing '"Laugh! I thought I should 'ave died"' from Albert Chevalier's music-hall song *Wot' Cher!* or *Knock'd 'em in the Old Kent Road*, 8, 21. **65** *Odeon*: one of a chain of grand 1930s cinemas. See the note on l. 16. In a letter to MJ dated 22 Sept. 1951 (Bodl. MS Eng. c. 7406/29), L cited 'Odeons and Coca Cola' as examples of England's 'half borrowed vitality'. **70** L in 1982 (*RW*, 74): the line 'doesn't seem "diminutional" to me, rather the reverse, if anything. It's meant to make the postal districts seem rich and fruitful.' On London Weekend Television's *South Bank Show*, 30 May 1982, he stated that he was aiming at conveying 'overcrowdedness . . . but also fruitfulness'. John Whitehead, *Hardy to Larkin: Seven English Poets* (1995), 231, compares Auden, 'As I walked out one evening', 3–4: 'The crowds . . . | Were fields of harvest wheat'. **71** *aimed*: Milligan, 23, notes the description of a train bound for London in Virginia Woolf, *The Waves* (Harcourt edn., III): 'But we are aimed at her'. See also 'aimed' in L's interview with Melvyn Bragg (above). **73** *Pullmans*: luxurious railway carriages, usually with sleeping compartments (after US industrialist George M. Pullman, 1831–97). *blackened moss*: Stephen Derry (see 58–9 n., above), 448, notes *Mariana*, 1: 'blackest moss'. **77–9** Asked in 1981 'Did you intend to give an unqualified assent to hopefulness at the end of the poem, where you seem to be flirting with a romantic visionary quality?', L replied 'Yes' (*FR*, 57). **78–9** L told Jean Hartley that he got the idea from the arrows fired by the English bowmen in Laurence Olivier's film of *Henry V*: Jean Hartley (1989), 119. L to MJ, 3 Aug. 1955 (Bodl. MS Eng. c. 7411/125): 'did you see *Henry V* is to be shown at the Academy, Oxford St.? *I want to go*.' **79** *an arrow shower*: Spenser, *The Faerie Queene*, 5. 4. 38. 4: 'a sharpe showre of arrowes'; Milton, *Paradise Regained*, 3. 324: 'sharp sleet of arrowy showers'. Motion (1982), 78, invokes Blake's 'arrows of desire' and Cupid's arrows. **80** *Sent out of sight, somewhere*: John

Osborne, Booth (2000), 150, and Osborne (2008), 62, parallels Longfellow's *The Arrow and the Song*, 1–2: 'I shot an arrow in the air, | It fell to earth, I knew not where'.

Self's the Man

DATE AND TEXT
Wkbk 5 (1/5/10) contains two pages of drafts of the whole poem except for the title dated '5. xi. 58' at the beginning and '5 Nov 58' at the end. Hull DPL 2/3/3 (t.s.). Hull DPL 2/3/41 (t.s.), signed in t.s. 'Philip Larkin'. Not published till *TWW*.

VARIANTS (from *Hull DPL 2/3/3*)
Title [No title]
2 Arnold] Arthur
5 wasting] fouling
on] with
20 Arnold] Arthur

2 *Arnold*: Based on Arthur Wood (d. 1971), deputy librarian at the Brynmor Jones Library, Hull, 'a bookman, a plump, agreeable, ex-naval Glaswegian' who 'liked a proper lunch, soup, meat and two veg, and sticky pudding, eaten at a solid table with serious cutlery': Douglas Dunn in Thwaite (1982), 57. For photographs, see illustration 15 in *SL*; Motion (1993), opposite p. 412; *AL*, 1 (Apr. 1996), back cover. L invariably spoke of him with virulent loathing bordering on the absurd. For instance: to Ansell Egerton and JE, 26 July 1955: Wood 'has been successively taking the beginning of July, the end of July, & the beginning of August, as well as part of September that will cut across the part I want: I shd like to feed him into a hay chopper, popeyed little Scotch dad': *SL*, 246; to MJ, 11 Jan. 1956 (Bodl. MS Eng. c. 7412/124): 'I want to boot Wood round the university today, tomorrow, & all days to come till he comes apart'; to MJ, 14 Jan. 1956 (Bodl. MS Eng. c. 7412/133): 'God I'd like to see him sprayed with molten rubber or something'; to MJ, 29 Jan. 1957 (Bodl. MS Eng. c. 7415/69): 'I'd like to hire an eagle to come down & carry him off'; to MJ, 17 Mar. 1957 (Bodl. MS Eng. c. 7415/113): 'I'm sure I hate him much more than I hate anybody [. . .] Filthy little bread-buying swine [. . .] Why won't he die? He's never ill, you know. Much too selfish. *Horrible* little *grey creeping clot* of *self-interest*.' To MJ, 3 Nov. 1958 (*SL*, 294):

'Funnily enough, [tonight] I settled to write a short "comic" poem *à la Toads* – not very good, wanting a last line. It's based to some extent on Wood, horrible cadging little varmint.' **4** Cf. L's *Round Another Point* (1951): 'A wife can be with him twenty-three and a half hours a day': *TAWG*, 496. **7** *To pay for the kiddies' clobber*: Cf. *Round Another Point*: 'But what isn't a law of Nature is the idea that you should be happy [. . .] when you're having to cut down on fags because the kid wants a scooter': *TAWG*, 490. **9–16** L consistently represents Wood as henpecked. For instance, to MJ, 6 Feb. 1957: 'His wife won't let him go to Leeds on Saturday to a Library do because he won't be back in time to bath the baby – the elder': Bodl. MS Eng. c. 7415/77. **13** L to MJ, 19 Aug. 1955: 'Saw that stupid little sod Wood pushing the pram this afternoon – he makes me want to set dogs on him, the pop-eyed little ass. And buying a house is sort of binding me to Wood & all he represents. Oh hell! hell! hell!': Bodl. MS Eng. c. 7412/24. **15–16** Cf. *Round Another Point*: 'But what isn't a law of Nature is the idea that you should be happy [. . .] when you're writing a letter asking your mother-in-law to come and stay the summer': *TAWG*, 490.

Take One Home for the Kiddies

DATE AND TEXT
Wkbk 3 (1/3/47) contains two pages of drafts after '6 / 4 / 54', including a complete draft (entitled '<u>Pets</u>') dated '18. 4. 54'. *Wkbk 5* (1/5/34) contains another complete draft (entitled '<u>Take Home a Pet for the Kiddies</u>'), after '6. 8. 60', dated '13. 8. 60' at the end. Published in *The Listener*, 70. 1810 (5 Dec. 1963), 955.

Title Osborne (2008), 79: 'a shop-window slogan'.

Days

DATE AND TEXT
Wkbk 2 (1/2/38) contains a draft of two stanzas of six lines each, untitled, after '6 Feb [1951]' (stanza 2 was different at this stage) and a further draft of four lines just before '19. iii. 51'. In *Wkbk 3* (1/3/7) there is a complete draft on a single page dated '? 3 August 1953' at the foot. L to MJ, 5 Aug. 1953 (Bodl. MS Eng. c. 7408/53): 'I've written a tiny little poem since returning, hardly a poem at all.'

Published in *Listen*, 2. 3 (Summer–Autumn 1957), [1], and reprinted in *Poetry and Drama Magazine*, 10. 2 (1958), 24.

VARIANTS (from the 1953 letter)
Title [No title]
7 And to seek where they join

L to MJ, 5 Aug. 1953: 'Don't take it seriously, but it's a change from the old style [. . .] *Wednesday* I shouldn't think there's much danger of y^r taking it seriously, having just re-read it, but I can't rub it out.'
    7–10 From Ted Tarling's copy of *CP* (1988), Osborne (2008), 55–6, records a reversal of section 40 of Walt Whitman's *Song of Myself*: 'To any one dying, thither I speed . . . Let the physician and the priest go home' (ll. 22–4). L to MJ, 21 Nov. 1971 (Bodl. MS Eng. c. 7443/128): 'Did I tell you about my discovery in Larkin Studies? I was rereading *The Wind in the Willows*, & found within a few pages of each other "long coats" and "running" and "over the fields". Isn't that odd? It's where Toad crashes the car & is chased. I'm sure I got the words from there – hiding places thirty years deep, at least.' L is referring to ch. 10, where the last of the phrases he refers to is 'across fields'.

MCMXIV

DATE AND TEXT
Wkbk 4 (1/4/32) contains: just over a page of drafts of ll. 1–6 between '17 Oct [1956]' and '26. xii. 56' (ten pages later); a version of l. 1 between 1 Jan. and 14 May 1957. *Wkbk* 5 contains: five pages of drafts of stanzas 1 and 2, additional lines, and ll. 25–6 and 32 between '7 xi [1958]' and '21 xi 58'; a further two and a half pages of drafts of stanza 1 and additional lines (including 12–13) after '2 xii 58', with the last page headed '7. xii. 58' (1/5/11); a one-page draft of stanzas 3 and 4 after '2. 2 [1959]' dated '2 /3 / 59' at the end (1/5/15); a one-page draft of stanzas 3 and 4 after '15 / 2 [1960]' dated '16. 2. 60' (1/5/28) at the end; further drafts of stanza 3 between '17. 2. 60' and '22. 2 [1960]' (1/5/30); a further draft of ll. 17–20 on a page dated '16 3 [1960]' at the top (1/5/30); further drafts of stanzas 3 and 4 on a page dated '17. 5. 60' at the top, with the next page dated '11. 6 [1960]' (1/5/32). Published in *Saturday Book*, 20 ([10 Oct.] 1960), 153–4, and in *Poetry Review*, 52. 4 (Oct.–Dec. 1961), 201.

L to MJ, 6 Nov. 1954 (Bodl. MS Eng. c. 7409/97): '1914–1918: that drab patch on our century, grey-green, green-brown, the colour of churned mud, how really it is trembling with emotion if you look closely! A silly sentence, but you know what I mean. 1939–45 will never stir me as much: I don't think the reason's entirely in me, either.' L in 1964 stated that the poem 'is about the First World War, or the Great War as I still call it; or rather about the irreplaceable world that came to an end on 4 August 1914': *FR*, 85. Discussing Betjeman's poem *I.M. Walter Ramsden* in 1971, L refers to 'the "long-dead generations" going back beyond Ypres and the Somme to golden summers of Edward and Victoria': *RW*, 212. L in 1975: 'It takes an effort today to realize how completely unprepared, imaginatively, the men of 1914 and 1915 were for the horrors that awaited them': *RW*, 236.

L to BP, 20 Feb. 1964 (*SL*, 367): 'I'm rather fond of *MCMXIV* – it's a "trick" poem, all one sentence & no main verb!' He claimed, however, that this was 'entirely accidental, not a piece of daring experimentalism': *FR*, 85.

Title L in 1964: 'It is called "1914", but written in roman numerals, as you might see it on a monument. It would be beyond me to write a poem called "1914" in arabic numerals': *FR*, 85. Similarly, L on his recording of *TWW*: 'I should really announce the next poem, 1914, as m-c-m-x-one-v because that is the way the title is printed, in roman numerals.' He explained 'beyond me' more fully: 'the emotional impact of 1914 was too great for anything I could possibly write myself' ('Philip Larkin reads *The Whitsun Weddings*', Marvell Press LPV6). In Nov. 1974 L said he felt on writing the poem 'that "1914" was too harsh a title, and that he preferred the decent obscurity of the title he chose': Watt (1989), 174. ('Decent obscurity' is often taken as Edward Gibbon's phrase, but it comes from a parody of him in the *Anti-Jacobin*.) Christopher Ricks in Thwaite (1982), 125: ' When a poetry-speaker on the BBC ushers in a poem by saying "1914", you sympathize, since some title has to be given and he couldn't say "MCMXIV". Yet how much of the sense of loss is lost. How long the continuity was with ancient wars and with immemorial commemoration; how sharp is the passing of an era.' Charles Mundye notes that the date 'MCMXIV' is engraved on the northern face of the Cenotaph in Whitehall, London: *AL*, 19 (Spring 2005), 24.

1 *lines*: Of men volunteering for military service. 4 *the Oval*: Kennington Oval, London, where cricket matches have been played

since 1846. *Villa Park*: the home of Aston Villa football club in Birmingham. 8 *August Bank Holiday*: a public holiday, during 1871–1965 celebrated on the first Monday in August, when banks closed and other businesses were obliged to close also. **12–13** Virginia Woolf, *To The Lighthouse*, I. 4, III. 1: 'He called them privately after the Kings and Queens of England', 'the six children whom they used to call after the Kings and Queens of England'. **14–15** Barbara Everett, Salwak (1989), 135–6, notes 'tin advertisements of cocoa' in Vivian de Sola Pinto's poem *In The Train*, 6, published in *England*, an English Association anthology (1946). **15** *twist*: tobacco shaped into a thick cord. **15–16** Business hours of public houses were to be restricted by law in 1915. **20** *Domesday lines*: visible boundaries of landed properties in the record of the Great Inquisition or Survey of the lands of England (from the eleventh century onwards). **25, 26, 32** John Osborne, Booth (2000), 147–8, compares the refrain in Ezra Pound, *Hugh Selwyn Mauberley*, 4. 20, 23, 24: 'Daring as never before, wastage as never before', 'fortitude as never before', 'frankness as never before'.

Talking in Bed

DATE AND TEXT

Wkbk 5 contains: two pages of drafts of stanza 1 and single lines between '5 / 6' and '30 / 8' [1959] (1/5/20); stanza 1 in fair copy between '14. 9' and '4. 10 [1959]' (1/5/23); four and a half pages of drafts of the whole poem except for the title between '17. 2. 60' and '16 3 [1960]' (1/5/29); and a final complete draft after '9. 8. 60', dated '10 / 8 / 60' at the end (1/5/35). Published in *Texas Quarterly*, 3. 4 (Winter 1960), 193.

VARIANTS

6 disperses] disposes *Texas Quarterly, 1960*

MJ to L, 7 Feb. 1964 (quoted in *LTM*, 375 n. 4): 'I'm naturally not happy abt *Talking in Bed* because it will cause so much talking here, in & out of beds, & indeed elsewhere – what do you think yr Mother & relatives will make of it?'

   5 *incomplete unrest*: Christopher Ricks in Thwaite (1982), 129: 'alludes to the easy restfulness of the phrase "a complete rest" – a phrase newly completed unrestfully'. **11–12** Edna Longley, 'Larkin, Edward Thomas and the tradition', *Phoenix: A Poetry Magazine*, ed.

Harry Chambers, 11/12 (autumn and winter 1973/4), Philip Larkin issue, 81–2, notes a similar undercut climax (likewise the last lines of the poem) with the same rhyme in Edward Thomas, *And You Helen*, 21–2: 'And myself, too, if I could find | Where it lay hidden and it proved kind'.

The Large Cool Store

DATE AND TEXT
Wkbk 6 (1/6/7) contains five and a half pages of drafts of the whole poem after '16. 5. 61', dated '18. 6. 61' at the end. L to MJ, 18 June 1961 (Bodl. MS Eng. c. 7423/58): 'Busy Sunday as usual – have been crashing my M & S poem to a finish for the TLS. Dull stuff it is too.' Published in *TLS*, 3098 (14 July 1961), supplement i.

VARIANTS (from the *TLS*)
7 and] or

L to RC, 11 July 1961 (*SL*, 330): 'My shorties one is really pure Holbrook: it was finished in a terrific hurry, else I might have taken pains to iron out accidental resemblances to our David from it.' L seems to be joking: Holbrook's collection *Imaginings* (1960) sometimes describes everyday things and events, but there is no specific influence.

Hugh Underhill, 'Poetry of Departures: Larkin and the Power of Choosing', *Critical Survey*, 1. 2 (1989), 189, cites a precedent in MacNeice's *Belfast*, 9–12, for the 'democratic urban sensibility' listing items in shops: 'And in the marble stores rubber gloves like polyps | Cluster; celluloid, painted ware, glaring | Metal patents, parchment lampshades, harsh | Attempts at buyable beauty.'

Title Marks and Spencer's in Hull, where MB had bought some items that she showed to library staff, prompting L to visit the store for the frst time: Brennan (2002), 56–7. The store opened in Hull on 15 Aug. 1931, some thirty years before. 11–19 Cf. *The Whitsun Weddings*, 40–2. Timms (1973), 95, notes 'the colour-names used by department stores to glamorize their products'. 12 *Bri-Nylon*: brand name introduced by British Nylon Spinners in 1958. *Baby-Dolls*: women's pyjamas consisting of a loose-fitting top worn over shorts. Osborne (2008), 209, notes that the term was popularised by the 1956 film *Baby Doll*, scripted by Tennessee Williams. *Shorties*: Originally American slang, from 1942 (*OED*, shorty, 5).

A Study of Reading Habits

DATE AND TEXT

Wkbk 5 (1/5/37) contains a page and a half bearing a draft of the whole poem except for the title after '19. 8. 60', dated '20. 8. 60' at the end. Published in *Critical Quarterly*, ed. C. B. Cox, 2. 4 (Winter 1960), 351.

L to MJ, 22 Aug. 1960 (Bodl. MS Eng. c. 7421/125): 'On Friday I wrote a disrespectful little *jeu d'esprit* called *A Study of Reading Habits* [. . .] It needs a little polishing [. . .] the poem I have in mind remains obdurate.' To MJ, 10 Nov. 1960 (Bodl. MS Eng. c. 7422/43): 'I have given my "Books are a load of crap" poem to Cox for 5 gns. I hope it will upset people like John Wain ("I wish you wouldn't copy Kingsley").' L in 1964 (*FR*, 85): 'I have always tried to keep literature out of my poems as a subject, but I did once amuse myself by trying to describe the normal man's gradual abandonment of reading as a source of pleasure. When we are young, we identify ourselves with the hero; during adolescence, with the villain; but when we are grown up we see that our true likeness is to some minor and even contemptible figure, and this puts us off the whole business.' To Dr P. D. Pumfrey, 22 Feb. 1985: 'The poem describes how people who embrace reading as a form of escape through self-dramatisation ultimately are led to see themselves as they really are, and turn from reading to some quicker and more reliable form of escape (drink). So many people seem to think that the poem's last line is a serious expression of opinion by me. It is, in fact, highly ironic': Hull DPL (2) 2/25/167.

1–12 Philip Gardner notes 'shades of Biggles, Westerns, Jack the Ripper, and Count Dracula': *Dalhousie Review*, 48. 1 (Sept. 1968), 93. 1–2 L, 'Not the Place's Fault' (*FR*, 10): 'for quite long periods I suppose I must have read a book a day, even despite the tiresome interruptions of morning and afternoon school'. 7 Cf. 'When we broke up, I walked alone', 71–2: 'For I read eleven hours a day | And my specs are getting thicker'. 13 *Don't read much now*: Only late in life might this apply to L himself, and even then he seems to have read a fair amount. In 1972: 'Within reach of my working chair I have reference books on the right, and twelve poets on the left: Hardy, Wordsworth, Christina Rossetti, Hopkins, Sassoon, Edward Thomas, Barnes, Praed, Betjeman, Whitman, Frost and Owen [. . .] All in all, therefore, I should miss my books': *RW*, 86. In 1979: 'I virtually read only novels, or something pretty undemanding in the non-fiction line, which might be a biography. I read almost no poetry [. . .] I tend to go back to novelists, like Dick Francis, for instance; I've just been through his early novels again which I think are outstandingly good for what they are. And Barbara Pym, of course, whom I've written about. Dickens, Trollope – sometimes you go back to them for about three novels running. And detective stories: Michael Innes [. . .] Anthony Powell, Rex Stout, Kingsley Amis, Peter de Vries [. . .] I read Betjeman, Kingsley again, Gavin Ewart (who I think is extraordinarily funny). Among the illustrious dead, Hardy and Christina Rossetti. Shakespeare, of course': *RW*, 53. In 1982: 'I don't read much. Books I'm sent to review. Otherwise novels I've read before. Detective stories: Gladys Mitchell, Michael Innes, Dick Francis. I'm reading *Framley Parsonage* at the moment. Nothing difficult': *RW*, 70. **13–17** The language is coloured by usage that is American or originally American: *dude* (dandy), *yellow* (cowardly), *store* (shop), *stewed* (drunk).

As Bad as a Mile

DATE AND TEXT
There are two drafts one below the other, complete except for the title, in *Wkbk 5* (1/5/27), dated '4 / 2 / 60' and '9. 2. 60' respectively. Published in *Audit* (University of Buffalo), 1. 2 (28 Mar. 1960), 2, and in *The Listener*, 70. 1811 (12 Dec. 1963), 985.

VARIANTS
Title Bad] Good *Audit, 1960*

The poem is consistent with the view expressed in *A New World Symphony* (1948–54): 'The process of failure only needs starting, it will continue almost of its own accord': *TAWG*, 428.

    Title. Cf. the proverb 'A miss is as good as a mile'. **6** In Genesis ch. 3, the eating of the forbidden fruit, long supposed to have been an apple, brought death and the knowledge of good and evil. *unbitten*: Cf. Housman, *Additional Poems* III 1–4: 'When Adam walked in Eden young | Happy, 'tis writ, was he, | While high the fruit of knowledge hung | Unbitten on the tree.'

Ambulances

DATE AND TEXT
Wkbk 6 (1/6/2) contains eighteen pages of drafts of the whole poem between '29. 11. 60' and the date '14 / 1 / 61' at the end. The next page, dated '10. 1. 61' at the top, bears a version of l. 19: 'For in this deadened air takes place'. L to JE, 28 Nov. 1960 (*SL*, 322): 'Ought to have been doing my poem, such as it is [. . .] Now I must get back to my poem – I've decided I can half rhyme to *absorb*, so that's okay.' L to AT, 1 Feb. 1961 (*SL*, 323): 'The snag about the enclosed, apart from its being not much good, is that I have given it to Alan Ross for the April no. of the LM.' Read by Hugh Dickson on the BBC Third Programme on 24 July 1960, and published in *London Magazine*, NS 1. 1 (April 1961), [23], and in *Atlantic*, 208. 6 (Dec. 1961), 62.

1 Cf. 'Come then to prayers', 12. 2 *Loud noons of cities*: Cf. 'I should be glad to be in at the death', 2: 'loud cities'. 13–14 Cf. Auden, *New Year Letter*, 2. 476–8: 'the abyss I That always lies just underneath I Our jolly picnic'.

The Importance of Elsewhere

DATE AND TEXT
Wkbk 4 (1/4/15) contains three pages of drafts of the whole poem except for the title after '27 May '55', dated '13 / 6 / 55' at the end. Published in *The Listener*, 54. 1384 (8 Sept. 1955), 373. Repr. in *Humberside*, the magazine of the Hull Literary Club, 12. 2 (Autumn 1956), 31, and in *Listen*, 2. 4 (Spring 1958), 2.

L to JBS, 5 Nov. 1950 (*SL*, 167–8): 'As a matter of fact, the mad Irish aren't so mad: they can be very nice indeed. Their voices are incomprehensible most of the time – a Glaswegian, after a short stay in the USA, whining for mercy, but as my business is mainly connected with the educated ones I am not always quite at a loss. As a rule they are kind & even polite, but one gets a bit sick of feeling a foreigner all the time, & of the really-quite-excusable local patriotism that continually recurs, even in Queen's itself.' (L inadvertently wrote 'They voices', corrected by AT in *SL*.)
Raphaël Ingelbien, 'Seamus Heaney and the Importance of Larkin', *Journal of Modern Literature*, 24. 1 (Summer 2000), 474,

notes a similarity between the attitude expressed in the poem and Cyril Connolly's in 'England, not my England' in *The Condemned Playground: Essays 1927–1944*: 'Abroad, I was at least interesting to myself – in London I can't be even that'; 'It is better to be *depaysé* in someone else's country than in one's own' (1985 edn., with an introduction by L, pp. 205, 206). Connolly was a notable influence on L in his student days: Motion (1993), 202.

2–4 Contrast L to MJ, 5 Nov. 1951 (Bodl. MS Eng. c. 7406/70): 'My head buzzes with Irish voices [. . .] Ulster phrases pop off my lips like bubbles [. . .] I have almost given up the battle, and floating down the social tide feel my nationality & individuality & character submerging like empty cake-boxes.'

Sunny Prestatyn

DATE AND TEXT
Wkbk 6 (1/6/24) contains two and a half pages of drafts of the whole poem except for the title after '16. 10. 62', dated '20. 10. 62' at the end. Published in *London Magazine*, NS 2. 10 (Jan. 1963), 13.

VARIANTS
11 boss] black *London Magazine, 1963*

L in 1964 (*FR*, 89) stated that *Sunny Prestatyn* 'is rather difficult to describe [. . .] the scene is a railway station, only this time I am looking at one of those cheerful posters okayed by some seaside town's publicity manager, showing the most convenient shorthand for happiness, a beautiful girl. Unfortunately, some travellers have been at work and the result is funny or terrifying, whichever way you look at it. If you are like me, it is both [. . .] Some people think it was intended to be funny, some people think it was intended to be horrific. I think it was intended to be both': L on 'Philip Larkin reads *The Whitsun Weddings*', Marvell Press LPV6. See L's comments on pictorial billboards in the notes on *Essential Beauty*. When MB objected to the coarse language in the poem, L replied: 'That's exactly the reaction I want to provoke, shock, outrage at the defacement of the poster and what the girl stood for': Brennan (2002), 60.

Noting 'tits', 'crotch', 'cock', and 'balls' (ll. 12, 16), Osborne (2008), 162, points out that this vocabulary is being used only two years after the end of the ban on *Lady Chatterley's Lover* (and before the Beatles' first LP: see *Annus Mirabilis* and notes).

Title Prestatyn is a seaside resort in N. Wales. 2 *the poster*: Cooper (2004), 190, reproduces a discussion from *Today* magazine (17 Aug. 1963) of a series of British Railways' advertisements for holiday destinations, illustrated by posters of women in swimsuits. L refers to 'the poster we saw at Tweedmouth' when he mentions the poem in a letter to MJ dated 23 Oct. 1962 (Bodl. MS Eng. c. 7425/81). Don Lee, *AL*, 25 (Apr. 2008), 25, reproduces a rail poster for Prestatyn depicting in profile a smiling blonde woman in a swimsuit with the sea behind her. James Orwin reproduces another Prestatyn poster depicting in profile a blonde woman in a white swimsuit with breasts uplifted and arms spread, and with a coastline and what looks like an hotel behind her: *AL*, 27 (Apr. 2009), 13. As is duly noted, she is not kneeling on the sand. 10–20 Cf. 'great gouts of clay . . . flung against posters' (*Jill*, 215), and *A New World Symphony* (1948–54): 'On the pavement opposite a little boy began defacing a house-agent's advertisement': *TAWG*, 432. 17 *Titch Thomas*: the name of the proprietor of the pub 'The Lord Jersey' in Dylan Thomas's story 'Old Garbo', *Portrait of the Artist as a Young Dog* (1940). 'John Thomas' is slang for penis, and 'Titch' jokingly implies small size.

First Sight

DATE AND TEXT

Wkbk 4 (1/4/25) contains, after '20. 2. 56', two and a half pages of drafts of the whole poem except for the title, dated '26 / 2/ 56' at the end; a further draft on a single page, complete except for the title and less like the final version in the second verse, dated '3 March 1956' at the end. L to MJ, 26 Feb. 1956 (Bodl. MS Eng. c. 7413/19): 'Last night I wrote a few lines about lambs: wish I could finish them off as a companion-piece to the *Pigeons* I *still* haven't sent you [. . .] It was written dangerously quickly.' On fo. 20 of the letter he decides to 'reconsider the end', and on fo. 23 he provides a t.s., corrected in pencil and ink, of the whole poem, with *Pigeons*, under the heading 'Two Winter Pieces'. Published in the *Times Educational Supplement*, 2147 (13 July 1956), 933.

VARIANTS

Title Lambs *Bodl. MS*; At First *TES*.
2–4 When the lanes are blocked, and air | Clouds upon their bleating, know | Nothing but a whiteness where *Bodl. MS*

6–7 They can find ~~outside~~ beyond the fold, | Only wretchedness and cold. *Bodl. MS*

12–14 [They could not grasp it] [*alt.* Could they grasp it] if they knew, | ~~How their joy will~~ What will shortly wake and grow | Wider than the vanished [*alts.* forgotten? the absent?] snow. [?] *Bodl. MS* [The question marks, including the final one in brackets, are L's.]

L to MJ, 2 Mar. 1956 (Bodl. MS Eng. c. 7413/26): 'the point is that here they are, being interested & patient & accepting it all, *not knowing* how *temporary* all the misery is & how, in a week or so, *everything will suddenly "melt & change"* like a miracle'. To MJ, 12 June 1956 (Bodl. MS Eng. c. 7413/116–17): 'I've sent off the lambs poem: it will look a funny poem for this great glossy marrow-headed fellow to have written, in his big shell goggles and creaseless suit.' To MJ, 12 May 1958 (Bodl. MS Eng. c. 7418/37): '*Guinness* poetry book [*The Guinness Book of Poetry 1958*] came today, absolutely rotten *I* think, even including my *Lambs* wch looks v. 1910-ish and conventional.'

   Title 'In the end I called it *At first*. I didn't want to mention lambs in the title, since they aren't the *real* point, and if you call a thing *Lambs* people say *O yes! about lambs* – & off goes their attention, skating away, missing the whole point. Maybe *At first* isn't very good, though': to MJ, 12 May 1958. Osborne (2008), 79 notes the abbreviation of the cliché 'love at first sight'. 3 *unwelcome*: 'cold reception. *rare*': *OED*, citing only D. H. Lawrence, *Trespasses* (1912), 1. 2: 'A stranger was assured of his unwelcome'.

Dockery and Son

DATE AND TEXT

Wkbk 6 contains: a draft of ll. 1–2 on a page dated '13. 5. 62' at the top (1/6/30); nine pages of drafts of everything but the last stanza (6) between '4. 2. 63' and '3. 3. 63' (1/6/28); and four pages of drafts of stanzas 5 and 6 after '4. 3. 63', with the final page dated '28. 3. 63' at the top. Published in *The Listener*, 59. 1776 (11 Apr. 1963), 633.

L in July 1964 (FR, 90): *Dockery and Son* 'brings me back full circle to the character and environment business. A year or two ago I was visiting my college, and in conversation the don who had been Dean in my day remarked that a man who had been some years behind me now had a son at the place. This led me to reflect how very different our lives must have been, so different as to suggest different concepts of life behind them, and I wondered where these concepts came from. This is what "Dockery and Son" is about. It is the last poem [in *TWW*] I wrote, and so I have a particular affection for it. There is always the chance, after all, that one's last poem may turn out to be just that.' L to MJ, 7 Aug. 1966 (Bodl. MS Eng. c. 7433/103): 'I don't think I shall ever get past "Dockery & Son" – even after 3 years it seems the last word on life, my own tiny unimportant last word.' To MJ, 30 Oct. 1966: 'inside I've been the same, trying to hold everything off in order to "write". Anyone w^d think I was Tolstoy, the value I put on it. It hasn't amounted to much. I mean, I know I've been successful in that I've made a name & got a medal [The Queen's Gold Medal for Poetry, 1965], & so on, but it's a very small achievement to set against all the rest. This is *Dockery & Son* again – I shall spend the rest of my life trying to get away from that poem': *SL*, 387.

See L's statement in the notes on *Essential Beauty* on a poem being either 'true' or 'beautiful'.

Title As in business names, especially Dickens's *Dombey and Son*. In 'Dockery' Roger Day detects 'the hint of the nursery rhyme "Hickory, Dickory, Dock", with the suggestion of time recorded mechanically by a clock': Day (1987), 56. **1–2** 'Junior to you am I? But you've got a boy or a grandson at the place now. I haven't got anybody': Julian Hall's novel *The Senior Commoner* (1933), 119. In letters to JBS, L defends the novel, and admits to 'rereading it with great pleasure': 1 Apr. and 24 Sept. 1941 (Hull DP 174/2/ 20, 28). In another letter to JBS, 16 Aug. 1943 (DP 174/2/74), he reports: 'Incidentally, I still read Julian Hall ("The Senior Commoner") – some of it is masterly.' He acknowledges the specific debt to Hall in *Tracks*, 1 (Summer 1967), 5–10, and in a 1982 review states that he first read the novel 'over forty years ago', and quotes the passage (*RW*, 274, 277). **3** *Death-suited*: L had in fact attended a funeral. 'In March 1962 Philip went to the funeral, in Oxford, of Miss Agnes Cuming, Hull's former librarian, and when he returned I remember how he recalled the incidents described in "Dockery and Son" with vivid clarity as we met by chance at the foot of the main staircase in the Library': Brennan (2002), 58. **4–7** KA describes this as a 'tiny but exact glimpse' of L 'being fined by the Dean' during his undergraduate days: Thwaite (1982), 26. The Dean and Senior Tutor during L's time at St John's College, Oxford (1940–3) was W. G. Moore (1905–78), University Lecturer in French (1931–72), Fellow and Tutor in Modern Languages at St John's (1934–78). L to Norman Iles, 13 Dec. 1942 (*SL*, 49): 'Moore called me into his room for a little straight talk on the evils of drinking. Until now he's just regarded me as a drunk sot, but my persistently good reports are beginning to shake him.' For a different view of Moore, see the reminiscence by his grandson Nicholas Jenkins in *Leader* (2009), 47–9. **17** Cf. the description of an Oxford student in *Jill*, 53: 'Jackson, who wore a curious stiff collar'. *public*: (in Britain) private. **18** *killed*: In the Second World War (1939–45). **20–2** Sheffield was a regular changing point for L on train journeys. He mentions this in letters to MJ dated 29 Dec. 1957 and 20 Oct. 1959 (Bodl. MSS Eng. c. 7417/74, 7420/69). Paul Walker, *AL*, 28 (2009), 39, notes that L is literally accurate in that in 1963 he would have travelled from Oxford to Sheffield on the now closed Great Central Railway, which approached the city from the east (where the steelworks are), and would have changed for Hull at the now closed Sheffield Victoria Station. Walker also notes that the station had a buffet where L could have bought a pie. **25** *Unhindered moon*: L to JBS, between 9 Aug. and 14 Oct. 1951 (Hull DP 174/2/217, first page missing): 'under a full moon; it was fascinating, the full unhindered flood of unreal light – no one has really defined moonlight yet; essentially it's a mysterious light, a kind of parody of real light'. **35** *dilution*: A. T. Tolley notes that in Virginia Woolf's *To The Lighthouse* it is said of Lily Briscoe, the artist who did not marry, 'she need not marry . . . she need not undergo that degradation. She was saved from that dilution': Tolley (1997), 106, referring to p. 154 of the Harcourt, Brace edn. (1927). **43–4** Raphaël Ingelbien, 'From Hardy to Yeats? Larkin's Poetry of Ageing', *EIC*, 53. 3 (2003), 270, compares Yeats, 'Pardon, old fathers, if you still remain', 21–2: 'I have no child, I have nothing but a book, | Nothing . . .' **45–8** 'I'm very proud of those lines. They're true. I remember when I was writing it, I thought this is how it's got to end. There's a break in the metre; it's meant as a jolt': L in 1981 (*FR*, 50). **45** 'When I try to tune into my childhood, the dominant emotions I pick up are, overwhelmingly, fear and boredom. Although I have an elder sister, the ten years' difference in our ages made me for practical purposes an only child, and I suppose those feelings are characteristic': L in *Wkbk 5* (DPL 1/5/1). *first boredom*: 'There was a curious tense boredom about the house': L in *Wkbk 5* (DPL 1/5/1). In 1973: 'At that time I was not happy at school. Admittedly it was an affair of being more frightened than hurt, but it was being hurt sometimes, and being frightened was not very pleasant. And in any case it was an affair of being more bored than either. The very words physics, geography, algebra, chemistry still conjure up in my mind a pantheon of tedium': *FR*, 128. In 1981: 'My childhood wasn't unhappy, just boring': *FR*, 47. Cf. *Coming*, 12–13: 'And I, whose childhood | Is a forgotten boredom'. *then fear*: L's response to Jonathan Raban in 2003, when the line was quoted to him, was: 'Oh no no no, there's no boredom left for me I'm afraid, it's fear all the way': *AL*, 26 (Oct. 2008), 16. **48** 'How strange the advance towards age is, and how it frightens me': L to BP, 23 Sept. 1974 (Bodl. MS Pym 151/86).

Ignorance

DATE AND TEXT
Wkbk 4 (1/4/21) contains, after '21. 8. 55', three pages of drafts of the whole poem except for the title, dated '11/ 9 / 55' at the end. Published in *Listen*, 2. 1 (Summer 1956), 4.

In a letter to MJ dated 14 Jan. 1956 (Bodl. MS Eng. c. 7412/131), L lists the poem among 'dregs & throwouts' and describes it as 'v. poor & short'.

   12–13 *decisions . . . imprecisions*: The rhyme 'suggests a Prufrockian lineage for the persona': Steve Clark (1988, 1994) in Regan (1997), 104, thinking of T. S. Eliot, *The Love Song of J. Alfred Prufrock*, 32–3 ('indecisions . . . revisions'), 48 ('decisions and revisions'). Cf. *Aubade*, 31–3 ('vision . . . indecision').

Reference Back

DATE AND TEXT
Wkbk 4 contains: after '20 / 6 / 55', five pages of drafts of the whole poem except for the title, dated '5 / 8 / 55' at the end (1/4/18); one and a half pages of further drafts of stanza 3 dated '21. 8. 55' at the end (1/4/20). Published in *Listen*, 1. 4 (Autumn 1955), 8, and in *Paris Review*, 19 (Summer 1958), 37.

VARIANTS
Title Referred Back *Listen, 1955; Paris Review, 1958*

L to MJ, 12 Nov. 1955 (Bodl. MS Eng. c. 7412/91), on *Reference Back*: 'in my opinion my poem *was* wrong, but in this way: the subject of it was being brought into communication again with my mother by a record made when any such loss of communication w^d have been unthinkable: and the oddness thereof. But the poem w^d have come better from her! I shouldn't regard our relationship when I was one [i.e. one year old] as "a loss" but I suppose she might. In a sense it is written from her viewpoint, or my imagination of it [. . .] the poem is only papered over cracks too deep for me to think highly of it.' In a letter to MJ dated 14 Jan. 1956 (Bodl. MS Eng. c. 7412/131), he lists the poem among 'dregs & throwouts'.

    1 *pretty*: 'As applied to jazz, usually had pejorative connotations': Leggett (1999), 80, referring to Robert S. Gold, *Jazz Talk* (1975), 208. *you*: L's mother, Eva. '"Listen-with-mother", the title of the BBC radio programme, is a tag Larkin uses in jazz reviews (*AWJ*, 157, 231, 242) to categorise a kind of bland, unadventurous music that wouldn't offend one's mother': Leggett (1999), 80. 5 *home*: his mother's house. See *Home is So Sad*, and notes. 7 *Riverside Blues*: recorded in Chicago in 1923 by American jazz cornetist Joe 'King' Oliver (1885–1938) and his Creole Jazz Band. L had a postcard of Oliver and his band on his mantlepiece at work: letter to B. C. Bloomfield, 26 Sept. 1982 (*SL*, 679). However, as Leggett (1999), 81, notes, 'for Larkin, Oliver was dangerously close to the "listen-with-mother" category. Larkin admits that he is "something of a heretic about Oliver" (*AWJ*, 190), one of the giants of traditional jazz; wonders aloud if Oliver "was all he was cracked up to be" (*AWJ*, 145); and finally confesses, "I don't care for Oliver," whose trumpet solos he characterises as "full of that childish wa-wa stuff" (*AWJ*, 248)'. 9 *those antique negroes*: L in a 1957 review refers to 'ancient, unbelievable photographs of primal figures in band uniform or tuxedo': *RB* (1999), 27. Noted by Trevor Tolley in *AL*, 12 (Oct. 2001), 37. 11 Before 1925, when electric recording began, musicians made acoustic recordings by playing into a large horn, not a microphone. Noted by Trevor Tolley in *AL*, 29 (Apr. 2010), 32. 12 L was born in 1922. 13 *bridge*: A pun on bridge as 'a short section of four or eight bars that links the separate strains of composition': Leggett (1999), 81. 21 Cf. *Sad Steps*, 18. 21–2 Cf. L to MB, 7 Aug. 1962 (*SL*, 344), looking back over forty years: 'What little happens or is so isn't at all expected or agreeable. And I don't feel that everything could have been different if only I'd acted differently – to have acted differently I shd have needed to have *felt*

differently, to have *been* different, wch means going back years and years, out of my lifetime.'

Wild Oats

DATE AND TEXT
Wkbk 6 (1/6/18) contains two pages of drafts, the second of the whole poem, with the title '<u>Love Life</u>', between '10. 5. 62' and '12. 5. 62'. Published in *The Review*, 5 (Feb. 1963), 11.

VARIANTS (from *The Review*, 1963)
11 Gave] Bought
12 I got] That came
20 to] for

The poem relates to Ruth Bowman, whom L met in Shropshire in 1943 and to whom he was engaged from May 1948 to Sept. 1950, when she ended the relationship. There is a photograph of her opposite p. 268 in Motion (1993). L to MJ, 10 Feb. 1964 (Bodl. MS Eng. c. 7427/89) on the poem: 'I wouldn't have printed it if I hadn't believed she was all settled & happy.'
   Title To 'sow one's wild oats' is 'to commit youthful excesses or follies; to spend early life in dissipation or dissolute courses (usually implying subsequent reform)': *OED*. 3 KA told AT that this was a reference to Jane Exall, a friend of L's sometime fiancée Ruth Bowman who likewise lived in Wellington, Shropshire: *SL*, 126 n. KA described her as 'rather fine looking', and L told him that he would find her 'hard to resist if she gave me anything to resist', but admitted that when once he took her out 'all I got was a damp kiss on the ear': Motion (1993), 118. L's other references to her suggest that he found her sexually attractive: *SL*, 126, 135–6. He tells JBS in a letter of 2 Jan. 1951 (Hull DP 174/2/ 208): 'I took a friend of hers [Ruth's] out to lunch on my way back here – good-looking girl, but heavy going.' He describes her to MJ in a letter dated 23 Sept. 1954 (Bodl. MS Eng. c. 7409/50) as a girl he 'mutely admired at the time'. 4 Ruth Bowman: 'the only girl I have met who doesn't instantly frighten me away', 'we are sort of committed to each other by our characters, at least I think we are. I can't imagine, judging from the women I meet casually, that any other girl would come within a mile of my inner feelings. It's odd': L to JBS, 18 May and 18 June 1948 (*SL*, 147, 148). L to JBS, 10 July 1951: 'I find it

amazingly difficult to talk to girls – not through shyness, so much as ignorance & apathy. I don't *know* what to talk to them about & really don't make much of a job even of the old parlour tricks. Unless a girl is ½-way to meet me I am nowhere': *SL*, 172. **11–12** Ruth Bowman returned the engagement ring L had given her: Motion (1993), 194. **15** *I met beautiful twice*: Suzuyo Kamitani establishes from letters from Jane Exall to L, now in the Hull archive, that L had lunch dates with her in Leicester and Shrewsbury in Feb. and Dec. 1950, and that there is no evidence of further meetings: *AL*, 16 (Oct. 2003), 19. **22–3** L really did have the two photographs in his wallet: MB in *AL*, 10 (Oct. 2000), 31; Brennan (2002), 58.

Essential Beauty

DATE AND TEXT
Wkbk 6 (1/6/20) contains nine and a half pages of drafts of the whole poem between '28. 5. 62' and '26. vi. 62'. At this stage the poem had the titles '<u>Hoardings</u>' and '<u>Posters</u>'. L in a letter to MJ begun on 23 May 1962 (Bodl. MS Eng. c. 7425/9–11): 'Have added about 2 lines to my long no-good poem [. . .] it is just dull, like a mixture of John Holloway and bad Dylan Thomas [. . .] Thursday now, & a less agreeable evening – have crossed out all I wrote last night and more, cursing & bored and raging. I am no good, all washed up, can't even write a *bad* poem, let alone a good one [. . .] Oh, curse this poem, I think I shall chuck it – I am no booldy [*sic*] good.' Published in *The Spectator*, 209. 7006 (5 Oct. 1962), 530, when L asked RC in a letter dated 21 Sept. 1962 to make three corrections to the galley proof at ll. 21, 22 and 31, which bring these lines to the state of *TWW* printing (*SL*, 345). It was reprinted from *The Spectator* in *The Balkite*, Perry Jackson Grammar School Magazine, Doncaster, Special Issue (Nov. 1962), [25].

VARIANTS (from *The Spectator*, 1962)
12 the] two
26 A halfpenny] Three-halfpence
27 taste] drink

L to RC, 21 Sept. 1962 (*SL*, 345): 'Delighted to hear you can use Ess. Beaut. – it is pretty crappy, really. I should like to dedicate it to Richard Hoggart, but there.' (On Hoggart, see the note on *High*

Windows, 2.) To MJ, 7 Oct. 1962 (Bodl. MS Eng. c. 7425/71): 'On reflection I find it gets into a long skid towards the end, but the last line seems to me to "stand", as Vernon Watkins would say.' (L refers to Welsh poet Vernon Watkins, 1906–67, who was an early influence on him. See L's 1966 introduction to *TNS*, and a 1959 review of Watkins's *Cypress and Acacia* in *FR*, 226–7.) To Harry Chambers, 15 Jan. 1963 (Hull DPL (2) 2/4/58): 'it is not meant to be a <u>satire</u> on advertisements: to me they appear as something like the platonic forms, infinitely vulgarised, but none the less "essential" to our view of the world'. L in 1964 (*FR*, 80–1): 'Most people would agree that we don't, nowadays, believe in poetic diction or poetic subject-matter. All the same, I think there are certain received opinions still very much operative which the poet flouts at his peril. Take advertisements, for instance – like most people, I have always lived in towns, and am constantly seeing enormous pictorial billboards. When I was young, I condemned them as ugly and corrupting – that is the "poetic" attitude. Later I learned to ignore them. Recently I've grown quite fond of them: they seem to me beautiful and in an odd way sad, like infinitely-debased Platonic essences. Now this is quite the wrong attitude: unfortunately, it was the only one that produced a poem. I called it, obviously enough, "Essential Beauty".' L in 1981 (*FR*, 49): 'A more important thing I said was that every poem starts out as either true or beautiful. Then you try to make the true ones seem beautiful, and the beautiful ones true. I could go through my poems marking them as one or the other. "Send No Money" is true. "Essential Beauty" is beautiful. When I say beautiful, I mean the original idea seemed beautiful. When I say true, I mean something was grinding its knuckles in my neck and I thought: God, I've got to say this somehow, I have to find words and I'll make them as beautiful as possible. "Dockery and Son": that's a true one. It's never reprinted in anthologies, but it's as true as anything I've ever written – for me anyway.'

Title Keats, letter to Benjamin Bailey, 22 Nov. 1817: 'What the imagination seizes as Beauty must be truth – whether it existed before or not – for I have the same Idea of all our Passions as of Love they are all in their sublime, creative of essential Beauty.' Asked by Ms Diana Basham whether the phrase was an allusion to Keats, L replied on 26 July 1979: 'The short answer to your question is "Not consciously". However, I have read Keats's letter, many years ago, and it may well be that the phrase stuck in my mind', the poem 'sees advertisements as super-versions of parts of our lives, with all

the nasty bits left out': Hull DPL (2) 2/20/9. In Nov. 1974 L stated
that the title was 'meant to have philosophical implications': Watt
(1989), 1974. The Keats source is noted by Roger Craik, *AL*, 12
(Oct. 2001), 11. **18–19** Steve Clark and James Booth in Booth
(2000), 168, 201, note the parallel repetition of 'pure' in *March Past*,
14. **29** *As if on water*: Miraculously, like Jesus: Matt. 14: 25, Mark
6: 48, John 6: 19. **30** *drag*: inhalation of cigarette smoke (slang).

Send No Money

DATE AND TEXT
Wkbk 5 (1/5/39) contains twelve pages of drafts of the complete
poem with the title 'What Goes On' between '27-9. 60' and
'31. x. 60'; a page bearing a complete draft after '3. 11. 60' dated
'4. 11. 60' at the end, and a further draft of stanzas 2 and 3 after
'7. 11. 60' dated '7 Nov' at the end; and immediately after, another
version of l. 9. *Wkbk 6* (1/6/21) contains two drafts of the whole
poem on two pages between '10. 8. 62' and '21. 8. 62'. The first
draft is entitled 'Without Prejudice'; the second is untitled. Published
in *The Observer*, 8942 (18 Nov. 1962), 24.

See L's statement in the notes on *Essential Beauty* on a poem being
'true' or 'beautiful'.
    Title 'Refers obliquely to those discreet advertisements headed
"Send No Money", familiar in newspapers of the 1950s and 60s, in
which catalogues of embarrassing items such as hernia trusses would
be offered on credit': Booth (1992), 151. L quotes one such advert
in a letter to JE dated 5 May 1959 (*SL*, 302): 'SEND NO MONEY
except a P.O. for 6ᵈ and s.a.e. for first FREE lesson'. **1** *fobbed*:
cheated, 'taken in'. **3** Cf. *Débats, Round the Point* (1950): 'M. No,
trying to find out the truth about life, and express it. G. But that's
just what a writer does! M. Don't you believe it . . . remember the
great law of literature is: No one will enjoy reading what you did
not enjoy writing. Now when did "the truth about life" ever give
anyone a thrill?': *TAWG*, 478. Cf. the refrain in W. H. Auden's
'Some say that love's a little boy', 16, 32, 48, 56: 'O tell me the
truth about love'. **10** A green eye betokens jealousy or envy. In
Othello, 3. 3. 170, jealousy is 'the green-eyed monster'. L to MJ,
16 Aug. 1954 (Bodl. MS Eng. c. 7409/9): 'Ain't no green in my eye,
now, look you.' **21–4** 'Truth is so unattractive that I no longer wish
to establish it': L to MJ, 4 May 1957 (Bodl. MS Eng. c. 7416/5).

Raphaël Ingelbien, 'From Hardy to Yeats? Larkin's Poetry of Ageing', *EIC*, 53. 3 (2003), 272, compares Yeats, *The Coming of Wisdom with Time*, 3–5: 'Through all the lying days of my youth . . . Now I may wither into the truth.'

Afternoons

DATE AND TEXT

Wkbk 5 (1/5/21) contains three pages of drafts after '30 / 8 [1959]' dated '14. 9. 59' at the end. After 'unripe acorns' (l. 20), the draft ends: 'The sun is going down. | They are clothed in patience.' Hull DPL 2/3/42 is a t.s. with one holograph correction. Published in *Listen*, 3. 3–4 (Spring 1960), 5.

VARIANTS

Title [No title] *Hull DPL 2/3/42*; Before Tea *Listen, 1960*
22 has thickened] is thicker has thickened *Hull DPL 2/3/42*
24 the] one *Hull DPL 2/3/42*

1–8 See the notes on *Letter to a Friend About Girls*, 15–16. 1 Cf. *Winter Nocturne*, 11: 'faded summers'.

An Arundel Tomb

DATE AND TEXT

Wkbk 4 (1/4/24) contains, after '11 / 9 / 55', twenty pages of drafts of the whole poem, dated '15 / 2 / 56' at the end, and a further draft of the last stanza dated '20. 2. 56'. L tells MJ in a letter dated 7 Feb. 1956 (Bodl. MS Eng. c. 7413/1) that he has been 'hacking at the Tombs poem'. There follow three letters and a postcard dated 12 Feb. (fo. 7), 21 Feb. (fo. 10, p.c.), 22 Feb. (fo. 11), and 26 Feb. (fo. 19) in which he reflects on the problems of composition and quotes lines 37–42, 21–4, 34–6, and another version of 37–42. Finally, he includes the entire poem in t.s. with holograph corrections and additions in pencil (fo. 22).

Published in *London Magazine*, 3. 5 (May 1956), 33–4, in *Torch*, University of Hull, 7. 4 (Easter 1957), 25–6, and in *New Poems, 1957*, ed. Kathleen Nott, C. Day-Lewis, and Thomas Blackburn (1957), 84–5. L made handwritten corrections in his copy of *New Poems, 1957*, now at Hull.

9 left] right *Bodl. MS*

11 sharp] ~~faint~~ sharp *Bodl. MS*

21 would change] , changing *Bodl. MS (1st version)*; , turning *Bodl. MS (2nd version)*

22 Turn] Turns *Bodl. MS (1st version)*

Turn the old] Ushers their *Bodl. MS (2nd version)*

23–4 succeeding eyes begin | To look, not read] civilities begin | A new allegiance *Bodl. MS*

35 Above new wars, new subtlety *Bodl. MS*

scrap] ~~scrap~~ shell *L's copy of New Poems, 1957*

36 an] their *Bodl. MS (1st and 2nd versions), London Magazine, 1956;* ~~their~~ the *L's copy of New Poems, 1957*

39 come] grown [alt. come] *Bodl. MS (1st version)*

has come to be] ~~is all that we~~ has come to be *Bodl. MS (3rd version)*

40 and] fit *Bodl. MS (2nd version)*

Their single sign? as if to prove *Bodl. MS (3rd version)*

41 Our nearest instinct nearly true: *Bodl. MS (2nd version)*; Our early [   ] instinct true: *Bodl. MS (3rd version)*

42 What will survive] All that [*alt.* That what] survives *Bodl. MS (1st version)*; All that survives *Bodl. MS (2nd and 3rd versions)*

L to MJ, 12 Feb. 1956 (Bodl. MS Eng. c. 7413/7): 'It's complete except for the last verse, which I can't seem to finish [. . .] It starts nicely enough, but I think I've failed to put over my chief idea, of their lasting so long, & in the end being remarkable only for something they hadn't perhaps meant very seriously.' In the middle of the *Wkbk* drafts, L writes: 'Love isn't stronger than death just because two statues hold hands for six hundred years.' L in a letter to RC dated 21 Sept. 1962 (*SL*, 346): '*But I do think A. T. is a bit timey.*' L in 1981, discussing the view that he has tended to moderate hopefulness (*FR*, 57): *An Arundel Tomb* 'is rather a romantic poem; there's even less reservation in that. I don't like it much, partly because of this; technically it's a bit muddy in the middle – the fourth and fifth stanzas seem trudging somehow, with awful rhymes like voyage / damage.' Asked in 1981 whether he felt sceptical about the faithfulness preserved for us in stone, L replied: 'No. I was very moved by it. Of course it was years ago. I think what survives of us is love, whether in the simple biological sense or just in terms of responding to life, making it happier, even if it's only making a joke': *FR*, 58.

Title See the note on l. 18. L and MJ visited Chichester during a holiday on the south coast before returning to work in Jan. 1956: Motion (1993), 274. **1** *Side by side*: As they were originally: the two figures had been split up until the restoration of the tomb was begun in 1843 by sculptor Edward Richardson (1812–68). Until then 'the knight lacked both arms from below the shoulders [. . .] Her right hand was missing from the wrist [. . .] Richardson obviously did some historical research on other monuments of the period, and there are a number of couples who lie hand in hand which he could readily have studied.' However, Richardson's 'only invention was to place the knight's right-hand gauntlet in his left hand': *An Arundel Tomb*, Otter Memorial Paper no. 1, by Paul Foster, Trevor Brighton and Patrick Garland (1987; repr. 1988), 16–19, 32, with an illustration on p. 20. *their faces blurred*: 'Today the tomb is in a decayed state again': ibid., 21. **6** In reality, a reclining lion is under the earl's feet and a little dog is under the countess's: Foster, Brighton and Garland, 15, 17. **9–10** 'I wrote it *before* I learned about the restoration': L's reply to a question from Muriel Crane about this detail, quoted in *AL*, 3 (Apr. 1997). L to AT, 25 Mar. 1975: 'in fact I've got the hands the wrong way round, and it should be "right-hand gauntlet", not left-hand. A schoolmaster sent me a number of illustrations of other tombs having the same feature, so clearly it is in no way unique': *SL*, 522–3. L, again, in 1981: 'Everything went wrong with that poem: I got the hands wrong – it's right-hand gauntlet really – and anyway the hands were a nineteenth-century addition, not pre-Baroque at all': *FR*, 58. **10–12** Cf. Betjeman, *Sunday Morning, King's Cambridge*, 13–14: 'In far East Anglian churches, the clasped hands lying long | Recumbent on sepulchral slabs'. Noted by Bill Ruddick, '"Some ruin-bibber, randy for antique": Philip Larkin's Response to John Betjeman', *Critical Quarterly*, 28. 4 (Winter 1986), 68–9. **18** 'There does not survive, and there has never been recorded, a contemporary inscription to identify them; nor did Richardson invent one. The inscription to which Larkin refers was probably that on the piece of card placed beside the monument by the cathedral authorities. This identified the figures as Richard FitzAlan III, 14th Earl of Arundel and Surrey (1346–1397) and his countess': Foster, Brighton and Garland, 19–20. Foster, Brighton and Garland (21) suggest, on the evidence of the earl's biography and the type of armour he is shown wearing, that the effigy is of Richard FitzAlan II, 13th Earl of Arundel (*c*.1307–76). **20–1** L to MJ, 2 Mar. 1956 (Bodl. MS Eng.

c. 7413/26): 'Lehmann is taking *Tomb*: he doesn't like "voyage-damage", that's all. It occurs to me that I pronounce it "voij", not "voi. edj", wch makes it more acceptable, I think.' ('Lehmann' is English poet and man of letters John Lehmann, 1907–87, founder of *London Magazine*, 1954, and editor till 1961.) **31–6** L to MJ, 16 Mar. 1956 (Bodl. MS Eng. c. 7413/41): 'Proofs of the *Tomb* have come – the penult. verse (stanza) is really shocking: still, no time now.' **31** 'I think by "washing at their identity" I was trying to suggest that succeeding generations of visitors (or worshippers) in the cathedral (it is Chichester, you know) slowly detracted from the individual personalities of the earl and countess simply by being so different from them and knowing so little about them': L to P. E. G. Marshall, 11 Feb. 1980, Hull DPL (2) 1/21/15. **35** To MJ, 22 Feb. 1956 (Bodl. MS Eng. c. 7413/11): 'The other revisions we agreed are harder to do – I doubt if I *can* substitute the concept of the unaltered atmosphere around them for "new *wars*, new subtlety".' **37** Cf. Yeats, *The Lamentation of the Old Pensioner*, 6, 11–12 (repeated in 17–18): 'Ere Time transfigured me', 'Time | That has transfigured me'. **40** *blazon*: (from heraldry) description, record of virtues or excellencies. It was suggested by MJ when L asked her for a word of two syllables meaning a sign: Motion (1993), 275. To MJ, 22 Feb. 1956: 'I think myself "their final blazon" fairly satisfactory, carrying just the right overtones of heraldry & medievalism, so for the moment I'll keep your suggestion in reserve.' (She had obviously made a further suggestion.) **40, 42** *prove | love*: John Saunders compares the rhyme of 'proved' and 'loved' in the concluding couplet of Shakespeare, sonnet 116 (which deals with the power of love to transcend time): 'Beauty and Truth in Three Poems from *The Whitsun Weddings*', *Critical Essays on Philip Larkin: The Poems*, ed. Linda Cookson and Brian Loughrey (1989), 46. The rhyme occurs nine times in Shakespeare's sonnets, however, and cf. also Housman, *The Carpenter's Son*, 19–20: 'All the same's the luck we prove, | Though the midmost hangs for love', and Edward Thomas, *Words*, 40–1: 'As the earth which you prove | That we love.' **41–2** L to MJ, 26 Feb. 1956 (Bodl. MS Eng. c. 7413/19–20), when the last two lines were 'Our nearest instinct nearly true: | All that survives of us is love': 'The "almost" line wouldn't do if the last line was to start with *All*: I didn't think it pretty, but it was more accurate than this one, & I felt an ugly penultimate line would strengthen the last line. Or rather, a "subtle" penult. line w^d strengthen a "simple" last line. Sea-water mean?' To MJ, 2 Mar. 1956 (Bodl. MS Eng. c. 7413/26):

'Shall ponder the last two lines. I quite *like* the "almost" set up, but *don't* like that "That what" construction it entails.' **42** 'Larkin is consciously refuting *The Song of Solomon* 8: 6: "for love is strong as death"': Craig Raine, 'Counter-Intuitive Larkin' (2007), repr. in Leader (2009), 72. Osborne (2008), 80, notes 'the language of popular song', citing the Billy Wells album *Love Survives*, 'Our Love Will Survive' by Eddie Rabbitt, and the Donna Summer song 'True Love Survives' ('Only love will last forever, true love will survive').

HIGH WINDOWS

DATE AND TEXT

Published on 3 June 1974. L to JE, 3 Nov. 1974 (*SL*, 514): 'The new printing of *HW* came out, with 3 mistakes corrected but a new one introduced: there is talk of another – printing, not mistake.' The three mistakes were: 'parts retreat' for 'part retreats' (*Going, Going*, 10), 'out for kicks' for 'out of kicks' (*Posterity*, 17), and 'spent' for 'spend' (*Vers de Société*, 8). L pointed out all of them. **Title** L to Oliver Marshall, May 1974: 'The title I really wanted was *Living for Others*, only I could never write the title-poem. Perhaps one day I shall': *AL*, 15 (Apr. 2003), 18. L in 1981 (*FR*, 59): 'I called the book after it [the poem *High Windows*] because I liked the title.'

L to JE, 25 Sept. 1971 (Bodl. MS Eng. c. 7456/18): 'I have about 20 mediocre poems & need 10 good ones to make up a book, but there is no sign of my being able to write even mediocre ones.' To JE, 10 Dec. 1973 (Bodl. MS Eng. c. 7457/24): 'Proofs of *High Windows* have come, a slim desultory volume with a four-letter word on every page, or so it seems. 25 poems, and about 3 as good as, etc. Larkin goes downhill. I'll get the chop.' To WA, 12 May 1974 (Bodl. MS Res. c. 616): 'I have a new collection of poems coming out early next month. My advance copy seems full of four-letter words, not at all likely to please a JP! Perhaps you can ban it.' (WA had been appointed a Justice of the Peace.) The volume was published on 3 June 1974. L to BP, 5 June 1974, on *HW*: 'one day I hope I can write *happier* poems, but most of the things I think about aren't very cheerful': *SL*, 509. L in 1981, commenting on the view that there is a growing disenchantment in *HW*: 'Just me getting older, I suppose. What's disenchanted about describing a hospital, or a nursing home?': *FR*, 59. Interviewed by John Haffenden in 1981 (*FR*, 60): 'I'm glad if you find the poems in *High Windows* more compassionate: I don't know that they are. But one must be more aware of suffering as one grows older [. . .] I thought the poems were more of the same, you know. There are some quite nasty ones in it. "They fuck you up, your mum and dad" doesn't sound very compassionate.'

To the Sea

DATE AND TEXT
Wkbk 7 (1/7/32) contains eight pages of drafts after '14. 9. 69'. The last date written on the drafts is '6. 10. 69' at the top of a page, but another page of drafts follows that page and completes a draft of the whole poem. The next date in *Wkbk* 7 is '20. 10. 69', but the poem (except for the title) was completed by 8 Oct. 1969, when L told BP: 'I have just written a poem, wh^{ch} cheers me slightly, except when I read it, when it depresses me. It's about the seaside, & rather a self parody': *SL*, 420. Published in *London Magazine*, NS 9. 10 (Jan. 1970), 28–9, and in *Antaeus*, 12 (Winter 1973), 70–1.

L to MJ, 30 Oct. 1969 (Bodl. MS Eng. c. 7440/39): 'I'm afraid people will say it's the same stodgy old iambics. For my part I suspect it hasn't got over the Boudin atmosphere I wanted – it was aimed at being a Boudin, in its own way of course [. . .] The white steamer bit* pleases me. Still.   *dating from our Alnmouth holiday' (L is referring to French painter Eugène Boudin, 1824–98, famous for depictions of the sea and seashore.) To AT, 13 Jan. 1970: 'I am not too keen on it myself – it seems rather Wordsworthian, in the sense of being bloody dull': *SL*, 425.

L in 1981 (*FR*, 60): 'My father died when my mother was sixty-one, and she lived to be ninety-one. We used to take a week's holiday in the summer', *To the Sea* 'came when we were in Southwold, when I realized that I hadn't had a "seaside holiday" for years, and remembered all the ones when I was young.'

See the notes on *Holiday*, details of which are reworked in *To the Sea*.

9 *stuck in the afternoon*: Cf. Christopher Isherwood, *Lions and Shadows* (1938), 172: 'Far away a paddle-steamer is stuck in the afternoon sea'. L notes this in his diary and identifies Isherwood's 'Chalmers' (who writes this in a letter) as the novelist and short-story writer Edward Upward (1903–2009): Hull DPL (2) 1/1/10/ 47. **12** *transistors*: small portable radios. *OED*'s earliest example is from 1961. **20** *Famous Cricketers*: L in 1959: 'I sometimes think the slight scholarly stoop in my bearing today was acquired by looking for cigarette cards in Coventry gutters. There seemed to be a "Famous Cricketers" series every summer then': Motion (1993), 16; *FR*, 7. L acquired two sets of cricketers from Fred Holland in 1964: *AL*, 21 (Summer 2006), 33. L to Harold Pinter, 5 Jan. 1983 (*SL*, 686): 'I've been looking for my cigarette cards to see if I "had"

A. W. [Somerset cricketer Arthur Wellard] – I did once – but can't find them.' L's collection of Famous Cricketers cigarette cards was part of an exhibition at Wilberforce Hall, Hull, 9 Nov. 2002–31 Aug. 2003: *AL*, 15 (Apr. 2003), 21, 22. **21–2** L's parents, Sydney and Eva, met on a holiday in Rhyl on the N. coast of Wales on 6 Aug. 1906, and within three days Sydney had made up his mind that she would suit him: L in *Wkbk 5* (Hull DPL 1/5/1). L to MJ, 7 Aug. 1953 (Bodl. MS Eng. c. 7408/56), about his father: 'O frigid inarticulate man! He met my mother on the beach at Rhyl. He was there for 3 days only, on a cycling tour, but before leaving he had a picture of them taken together & exchanged addresses (I agree this doesn't sound especially fr. or inart.!), & despite a separation of several years his intentions didn't alter. I find all that very strange & romantic, partly because unlike the father I knew. He must have been as intensely idealistic as a young man as he was nihilistically disillusioned in middle age.'

Sympathy in White Major

DATE AND TEXT
Wkbk 7 contains a page of drafts of stanza 1 between '4. 8. 66' and '13. 1. 67', with the title 'The Toast' cancelled (1/7/15); and two and a half pages of drafts of the whole poem after '22. 8. 67', with the final page dated '31. 8. 67' at the top (1/7/22). The next date in the *Wkbk* is '5. 9. 67'. Hull DPL 1/7/78 is a t.s. with holograph corrections in pencil and ink loosely inserted at the back of *Wkbk* 7. Published in *London Magazine*, NS 7. 9 (Dec. 1967), 13. See the note on *Annus Mirabilis.*

VARIANTS (from DPL 1/7/78)
Title ~~SYMPHONY~~ SYMPATHY
  7 lift the lot] ~~raise it~~ lift the lot
private] ~~a~~ private
14 all concerned were] ~~all of us were everyone was~~ all concerned were
21 *How many*] For all their *1st version*
(– I ~~think of~~ watch the ~~lives~~ days becoming duller, *2nd version*
22 *here*] ~~here sent~~ *1st version*
~~I watch the~~ The finished leaves ~~spin~~ reared to and fro – , *2nd version*
23 *Here's to*] ~~He is~~ Here's to

John Whitehead, *Hardy to Larkin: Seven Poets* (1995), 234, mentions Kipling's *Gunga Din* as an influence. Specifically, both poems pay a tribute and both feature drinking; still more specifically, both poems mention 'gin' (Kipling, 1; L, 3), and L, 23, amalgamates 'Of all them blackfaced crew | The finest man I knew' and ''E was white, clear white, inside' (Kipling, 10–11, 45).

Title Barbara Everett in *EIC*, 30 (July 1980), repr. Regan (1997), 59, 60, compares Théophile Gautier's *Symphonie en Blanc Majeure* (c.1850), and James McNeill Whistler's *Symphony in White*, nos. 1 and 2 (1862, 1864). L to Dr Ernst Zillekens, 2 Aug. 1984: 'you don't mention that "Sympathy in White Major" is an echo of "Symphonie en Blanc Majeure" (Gautier). Nothing about white majors!': Hull DPL (2) 2/24/74. **4** *void*: 'the key Symbolist concept for the cosmic Nothingness to be confronted and embodied and so – in theory – overcome by Art': Everett in Regan (1997), 61.

17–23 Cf. L to MJ, 9 Aug. 1959 (his birthday): 'I drank my own health in a bottle of Guinness last night ("Well, Phil old man, the years go by, but I can only say once again that you're a damned decent sport it's a pleasure to know." "That's very good of you." "Straight as a die and always stands his round, plenty of grey matter too.")': Bodl. MS Eng. c. 7420/18. George Hartley, Hartley (1988), 305, notes the dated eulogistic platitudes, which Osborne (2008), 241, establishes as being mainly Victorian in origin. Alan Brownjohn once told AT that in Roget's *Thesaurus* under 937 Good man (editions vary) the consecutive entries run 'good sort, stout fellow, white man, brick, trump, sport'. **23** *whitest*: '*slang or colloq.* (by extension of <u>WHITE MAN</u> 2b; orig. *U. S.*) Honourable, square-dealing': *OED*, white, a. 4b. *The Whitest Man I Know* is the title of a popular poem by J. Milton Hayes (1884–1940), as Osborne (2008), 243, notes, and the phrase passed into general usage. (It is echoed, for instance, in Joyce's *Ulysses*, as Osborne, 244, notes, and in 1949 in ch. 12 of P. G. Wodehouse's novel *The Mating Season*.) L to MJ, 9 Oct. 1955 (Bodl. MS Eng. c. 7412/51): 'Kingsley inscribed a new one he'd sent to me <u>To Philip, the whitest man I know</u> – this was a jesting idea of mine, not realizing that the phrase actually occurs in the book, on p. 191.' L is referring to Amis's novel *That Uncertain Feeling* (1955).

The Trees

DATE AND TEXT

Wkbk 7 (1/7/20) contains nine pages of drafts, including the final version of stanzas 1 and 2, between '9. 4. 67' and '2 June 1967 | Birthday of T. Hardy 1840 | bloody awful tripe'. L to MJ, 23 Apr. 1967 (Bodl. MS Eng. c. 7434/126–7): 'I seem to have spent a rather fruitless week, spending the evenings sleeping or staring at an incomplete & v. modest poem [. . .]. The poem is four lines wch I thought all right, then four more lines wch are less good; now I really want four more about as good as the combined best of Wordsworth & Omar Khayyam to sort of lift the thing up to a finish.' On 3 June 1967 L sent a version of the poem based on these drafts in a letter to MJ (Bodl. MS Eng. c. 7435/40), with ll. 5–12 markedly different from the *HW* text. He includes a revised version with a letter to MJ dated 28 Apr. 1968 (Bodl. MS Eng. c. 7437/16): 'I enclose the other poem. Do you think it better than the first version? *Can* one write this sort of poem today? Should the first two lines of the last verse be improved? Should I use "thickened" to help the awkward "thresh" more directly, as "And yet the thickeninged castles thresh To fullgrown⁀⁀ every May"? Joo think it's any good?'

Published in *New Statesman*, 75. 1940 (17 May 1968), 659, in *Humberside*, Hull Literary Club, 17. 1 (Autumn 1971), 11, and in *Antaeus*, 12 (Winter 1973), 69.

VARIANTS (from the Bodl. MS)

5–12
The faint reclothing of midair
That thickens into restless towers
~~Suggests~~ Creates a different world from ours
Up to the edge of winter. There

A summer is a separate thing
That makes no reference to the past,
And may not even̶r be the last,
And mocks our lack of blossoming.

L in the letter of 3 June 1967: 'I celebrated TH's [Thomas Hardy's] birthday by *finishing* my sixteen year old's poem about spring etc. Well, completing a draft.' After the poem he writes: 'PAL (VI mod), eh? First verse all right, the rest crap, especially the last line.' L's reference to himself expands to 'Philip Arthur Larkin (form VI, modern)', i.e. the modern as distinct from the classical stream in the VIth of a grammar school.

1–2 Tim Trengove-Jones, 'Larkin's Stammer', *EIC*, 40. 4 (1990), 334, invokes Keats's maxim (in the letter to John Taylor, 27 Feb. 1818), about the necessity for poetry to come as naturally as leaves to a tree. **1, 12** Cf. *A New World Symphony* (1948–54): 'At each end trees were coming into fresh leaf': *TAWG*, 412. **4** Cf. Housman, *More Poems* VIIIA 3: 'Where trees are fallen, there is grief' (rhymed with 'leaf'); published in 1936. **9, 12** Cf. 'The poet has a straight face', 109: 'From the castle of leaves'; 'Long roots moor summer to our side of earth', 3: 'River-fresh castles of unresting leaf'. **9** *thresh*: M. W. Rowe, 'On Being Brunette: Larkin's schoolgirl fiction', *Critical Quarterly*, 43. 4 (2001), 53, quotes from L's 1943 prose piece *Ante Meridian* (*TAWG*, 235): 'hear the wind gently rustling their leaves, or thrashing them with stormy fierceness'. Unfortunately, the parallel is falsely strengthened by the misquotation of 'thrashing' as 'threshing'. **12** Osborne (2008), 56, notes '"Get that and start afresh; get that and start afresh"' in Virginia Woolf, *To The Lighthouse* [the section 'The Lighthouse', 11].

Livings

DATE AND TEXT
I *Wkbk* 7 contains: a draft of eleven lines of the opening of the poem between '19. 9. 71' and '7. 10 [1971]' (1/7/45); two pages of drafts of the whole poem (entitled 'Vocations') between '11 / 10 [1971]' and '16 / 10 / 71' (1/7/47); II *Wkbk* 7 (1/7/48) contains four and a half pages of drafts of the whole poem after '16. 10. 71', with the final page dated '23 / xi / 71' at the top; III *Wkbk* 7 (1/7/49) contains a draft on one page of ll. 1–12 between '23 / xi / 71' and '6. 12. 71', followed by one and a half pages of drafts of the whole poem between '6. 12. 71' and '10 Dec [1971]'. In a letter to MJ dated 9 Dec. 1971 (Bodl. MS Eng. c. 7444/9), L announced 'I'm trying to do one about Oxford' and quoted a version of ll. 1–8 of *Livings III*. All three were printed in *The Observer*, 20 (Feb. 1972), 28. In *Livings I*, 22, in *CP* (2003), 'worthwhile' replaced 'worth while', which in *CP* (1988) was correct.

VARIANTS (from the letter of 9 Dec. 1971)
III, 2 (~~Autumna~~ Nocturnal vapours make him wheeze):
3 so much the] a good deal

4 The arguers are more at ease –
8 Judas] Juggins

L to MJ, 13 Jan. 1972 (Bodl. MS Eng. c. 7444/22): 'I think they're
all good in different ways. Better than *Crow* anyway.' (L refers to
Crow, the 1970 vol. by British poet Ted Hughes.) To MJ, 16 Jan.
1972 (Bodl. MS Eng. c. 7444/25): '*The Gobserver* has accepted the
three poems and will print them together "when I have space" in
a pig's arse. I still like them. The 3rd verse of the King's Lynn one
isn't quite right: "big" and "great" clash, & the penultimate line
has six beats. Awgh. Perhaps I can maul it about in proof.' To C. B.
Cox, 23 Feb. 1972 (*SL*, 453): 'I found them rather fun to do myself
[. . .] they are miniature derivatives of Browning's dramatic lyrics, I
suppose. As for LIVINGS: well, I don't know – the way people live,
kinds of life, anything like that. I thought LIVINGS brought in the
Crockford element, too.' (*Crockford's Clerical Directory* provides
information on the clergy and the Church of England.) To Barbara
Everett, 30 July 1981 (*SL*, 653): 'I thought I was going to write a
sequence of lives, or livings, little vignettes, but it petered out after
three. They haven't any connection with each other, or meaning, but
are supposed to be exciting in their separate ways.'
  I '"Livings I" has an extraordinary sense of place (I once asked
Larkin if it were King's Lynn, and the guess was confirmed)':
Barbara Everett in Salwak (1989), 134. See L's comments above.
1 Everett, loc. cit., notes that in KA's *Take a Girl Like You* [ch.
18], Patrick Standish, the hero, pretends to be an expense-account
businessman who deals in dips. 4 *boots*: hotel servant who cleans
shoes. 10 L to KA, 12 Oct. 1943 (*SL*, 76–7) gives an account of
the regular customers at the Crown Hotel, Warwick, who include
a captain who makes awkward remarks and an auctioneer called
John Margetts. 18–19 Cf. Betjeman, *North Coast Recollections*, 22:
'When low tides drain the estuary gold'. 24 *nineteen twenty-nine*:
Everett notes that this is the first year of the great economic slump:
Salwak (1989), 133.
  II L to MB, 25 Dec. 1966: 'Oh for Christmas in a lighthouse!
Wouldn't it be lovely? The boom of the sea . . . the cry of the gulls
. . . the wireless . . . I wonder how one gets to be a lighthouse
keeper?': Motion (1993), 416. 3–6 In *My Home* (*TAWG*, 235)
L describes the sea breaking against rocks: 'Spray flies twenty
feet into the air, and the black rocks are submerged by a swelter
of white foam; will they ever emerge?' 5 Cf. Sassoon, *Storm and*

Sunlight, 11. 5: 'Small, chuckling rills, rejoice!' **12** *Grape-dark*: L to MJ, 5 Nov. 1951 (Bodl. MS Eng. c. 7406/68): 'At 4 30 today the sky here was murky & windy – grape coloured clouds, like great thumb-marks, rolling westward.' Cf. *Mother, Summer, I*, 4: 'grape-dark clouds'; *Light, Clouds, Dwelling-places*, 1: 'grape-dark sky'. **14** 'Peter Hoare thought the lighthouse keeper was Anglo-Saxon! *Anglo-Saxon?* Mad sod. They didn't have radio': L to MJ, 21 Feb. 1972 (Bodl. MS Eng. c. 7444/46). **20** L to MJ, 11 Mar. 1951 (Bodl. MS Eng. c. 7405/15): 'that kippered room of his'. **24** *the stare*: Of the moon. See *How to Sleep*, 5: 'The keen moon stares'; *Sad Steps*, 15: 'that wide stare' (of the moon). Cf. Auden, *Dover*, 41–3: 'a full moon . . . returns our stare'. Possibly – by association – the lighthouse beam, as in Virginia Woolf, *To the Lighthouse*, 11. 9: 'the lighthouse beam . . . sent its sudden stare over bed and wall in the darkness of winter'.

III Everett in Booth (2000), 26, notes a remark made in a letter to CM of 3 Aug. 1971 about a dinner at All Souls College, Oxford (*SL*, 445): 'I sat drunk in the smoking room at one in the morning and dreamed of a former existence.' **1** John Norton-Smith records in a note written opposite the opening of *Livings III* (1972 printing) that the first line was uttered by Saville Bradbury just before a dinner at Pembroke College, Oxford, in Feb. 1971, and that L, who was Norton-Smith's guest, remarked, 'That would make a good first line of a poem': Hull DP 176/56. Motion (1993), 415, misleads by adducing the first line of *Livings I*. **5** *advowson*: right of presentation to a church living. **6** *Snape*: Suffolk village. **7** *pudendum mulieris*: female genitals. **7–8** Cf. Robert Browning, *Soliloquy of the Spanish Cloister*, 15–16: 'What's the Latin name for "parsley"? | What's the Greek name for Swine's Snout?' **8** After betraying Jesus, Judas hanged himself (Matt. 27: 5); hence a connection with Jack Ketch, the common executioner (*c*.1663–86). In Punch and Judy shows, Mr Punch dupes him into putting his head in a noose (and thus hanging himself): *Oxford Dictionary of National Biography* entry on Ketch. **11** *jordan*: chamber-pot. 'Now *vulgar* or *dial*.' (*OED*). **12** *bogs*: toilets (slang). **19** *sizar*: undergraduate at Cambridge University or Trinity College, Dublin, who receives an allowance from his college. John Norton-Smith records that L and he discussed Dr Johnson's status when up at Pembroke College: '"servitor" or "sizar." I said': Hull DP 176/56. Oxford never had 'sizars', however. Barbara Everett points out that L has blended images from the ancient universities in the poem: 'Larkin's Edens', *English*, 31. 139 (Spring 1982), 44. **23** *Chaldean*: as determined by ancient astrology, magical.

Forget What Did

DATE AND TEXT

L to PS, 23 July 1952 (*SL*, 187): 'I am trying to write a little unrhyming poem about giving up a diary.' It took over nineteen years to be completed. *Wkbk* 7 contains three and a half pages of drafts of the whole poem except for the title between '30 1 67' and '12. 2. 67' (1/7/17); two pages of drafts of the whole poem between '6 / 8 / 71' and '19. 9. 71' (1/7/43), the latter being the date at the top of the next page. When the poem was reprinted in *CP* (2003), 'cicatrised' replaced the correct 'cicatrized' (l. 4) in *CP* (1988).

Commenting in 1981 that the poem was about 'getting away from the miseries of life', L continued: 'It's about a time when I stopped keeping a diary because I couldn't bear to record what was going on. I kept a diary for a long time, more as a type of great grumble-book than anything else. It's stopped now': *FR*, 60. L told MB in May 1974, during a break in their friendship that lasted from July 1973 to November 1974, that the poem directly concerned her: Brennan (2002), 63.

Title From ch. 2 of Susan Coolidge's novel *What Katy Did*, where Dorry keeps a journal written with subliterate grammar and spelling. Several entries record 'Forgit what did' until, on 1 April, he writes 'Have dissided not to kepe a jurnal enny more'. This source is identified by Marion Lomax in *Larkin with Poetry: English Association Conference Papers*, ed. Michael Baron (1997), 40. L to MJ, 7 Nov. 1950 (Bodl. MS Eng. c. 7403/115): 'Today has been quite devoid of incident: in fact, in the words of old holiday diaries, "forget what did".' To MJ, 4 Nov. 1958 (Bodl. MS Eng. c. 7419/5): 'Monday & Tuesday it's a case of "forget what did".'

High Windows

DATE AND TEXT

Wkbk 7 (1/7/7) contains six pages of drafts of the whole poem after '3. 3. 65', with the final page dated '23 / 3/ 65' at the top. At the end of the draft, apparently as a disillusioned alternative to the

(then) ending 'and is endlessness', L writes: 'and fucking piss'. *Wkbk*
7 (1/7/18) also contains a single page bearing a draft of the whole
poem dated '12. 2. 67'. Hull DPL 1/7/64 is a t.s. with holograph
corrections, loosely inserted at the back of *Wkbk* 7. Published in
Critical Quarterly, 10. 1 and 2 (Spring–Summer 1968), 55.

VARIANTS (from DPL 1/7/64)
18 ~~Their~~ The sun-~~sanctified~~ comprehending glass.
19 beyond it, the] ~~beyond,~~ beyond it, the ['it, the' inserted above a
caret]

L in 1981 (*FR*, 59): 'I think the end shows a desire to get away
from it all, not unlike "Dry-Point", in a way, or "Absences". I don't
think it very good: I called the book after it because I liked the title.
It's a true poem. One longs for infinity and absence, the beauty of
somewhere you're not. It shows humanity as a series of oppressions,
and one wants to be somewhere where there's neither oppressed nor
oppressor, just freedom. It may not be very articulate.'
   Title 'I have lived most of my working life in rooms at the top
of houses': L in 1974 (*RW*, 36). L to Gavin Ewart, 6 June 1980
(*SL*, 623): 'I hate living on the ground floor: all my poems were
written on top floors.' L in 1982 (*RW*, 57, 58): 'I took a University
flat [in Hull] and lived there for nearly eighteen years. It was the
top flat [. . .] I wrote most of *The Whitsun Weddings* and all of
High Windows there', 'The best writing conditions I ever had were
in Belfast, when I was working at the University there. Another
top-floor flat, by the way.' MB identifies the 'high windows' of
L's flat in Hull as the inspiration for the title of the poem and
the collection: Salwak (1989), 29. 'We admired in particular the
spacious attic sitting-room, with its arched high windows at tree-top
level, overlooking the park below': Brennan (2002), 26. However,
Raphaël Ingelbien rightly insists that '"high windows" are supposed
to be a purely mental image, rather than a verbal reality: "Rather
than words comes the thought of high windows"': *Philip Larkin
and the Poetics of Resistance*, ed. Andrew McKeown and Charles
Holdefer (2006), 23. 2 *fucking*: 'the 10th anniversary of CQ
[*Critical Quarterly*] is out containing "High Windows", another
Hoggart word, indeed the very Open Sesame of Hoggartism. Good
thing nobody reads anything. "Lackeen's usin' language"': L to MJ,
27 June 1968 (Bodl. MS Eng. c. 7437/77–8). 'Hoggart' is Richard
Hoggart (b. 1918), author of *The Uses of Literacy* (1957). Hoggart
was an expert witness at the *Lady Chatterley's Lover* trial in 1960,

and defended the book as a moral work containing words he had
heard on a building site on his way to court. L in 1981: 'these
words are part of the palette. You use them when you want to
shock. I don't think I've ever shocked for the sake of shocking': *FR*,
61. **3** *Taking pills*: Cf. L in the 1968 preface (28) to *AWJ*: 'cold-eyed
lascivious daughters on the pill'. **17–19** *Rather than words . . . the
deep blue air*: Cf. Virginia Woolf, *The Voyage Out*, ch. 11: 'Silence
fell upon one, and then upon another, they were all silent, their
minds spilling out into the deep blue air.' Stephen Medcalf in a letter
in the *TLS*, 5329 (20 May 2005), 15, compares a passage in Ursula
Le Guin's science-fiction novel *Planet of Exile* (1966): 'Outside the
high windows the air was the same translucent blue.' He comments
on the matching contexts: 'The poet, like Agat in the novel on his
planet, feels an alien in the world; others – perhaps the new liberated
generations – feel at home in it, like the native populations of Agat's
planet.' Cf. *Spring Warning*, 15–16: 'the sun that flashes from their
high | Attic windows'. **18** Andrew Motion, *Philip Larkin* (1982),
81, compares 'Shelley's "dome of many-coloured glass" between
life and death' (*Adonais*, 462). **19–20** Cf. 'Come then to prayers',
14. 'The radiant colour and the "nothingness" are too Mallarméan
to be only coincidentally similar. "*L'azur*" (the blue) is Mallarmé's
most consistent and philosophical symbol, delineating both the
necessity and the absence of the ideal [. . .] his poetry is full of "*De
l'éternel azur la sereine ironie*" (the calm irony of the endless blue)
[. . .] The poem [. . .] in which this image becomes most definitive
is "*Les Fenêtres*" (the Windows)': Barbara Everett, *EIC*, 30 (1980),
repr. Regan (1997), 64.

Friday Night in the Royal Station Hotel

DATE AND TEXT
Wkbk 7 (1/7/12) contains four pages of drafts of the whole poem
between '25/4 [1966]' and '20. 5. 66'. Published in the Sheffield
Morning Telegraph, 7 Jan. 1967, 12. L to BP, 13 Jan. 1967 (*SL*,
391): 'I had a sonnet in the Sheffield *Morning Telegraph* last
Saturday, which is how some people *start*, I suppose.' Hull DPL
1/7/56 is a cutting of this printing, dated '7 Jan 69' by L, with
'Facing' (l. 3) corrected to 'That face' in his hand. L to MJ, 12 Jan.
1967 (Bodl. MS Eng. c. 7447/55): 'I enclose my sonnet, published
on Saturday – there are bits I want to alter, but don't quite see how.
You know the R S Hotel at Hull? Of course, the best alteration

would be "Ears" for "Waves", transforming it, as always, into a happy poem, as you pointed out years ago. "Facing" should be "That face", I think, to get it into rhythm (syllable missing in both lines 1 and 2). Still, it's hardly an *Ode to Autumn*. Ode to your granny.' A revised version was published in *Humberside*, Hull Literary Club, 16. 1 (Autumn 1968), 33. L told Harry Chambers in a letter of 15 Nov. 1967 that it was 'no good' (*SL*, 398).

VARIANTS
3 That face] Facing *Morning Telegraph, 1967*

Title Motion (1993), 363: 'In March 1966 he paid a brief visit to Eva [his mother] in Loughborough, then hurried back to Hull to meet Monica, whom he had invited for Easter. Arriving at the railway station, he discovered her train was late, and turned into the Royal Station Hotel for a drink. In the gloomy, almost-empty bar he found the image of "a larger loneliness" than his own.' MB recalls that she and L often sat over a drink in the hotel's 'formal, lofty lounge. It was a more forbidding place then than it is now': Brennan (2002), 63. CM records that on a visit to Hull he stayed as L's guest in 'the gloomily splendid Station Hotel': Thwaite (1982), 41. Derek Spooner, 'Reflections on the place of Larkin', *Area* 32. 2 (2000), 211, records that the old Royal Station Hotel burned down in 1990. 6 Cf. L to MJ, 13 Jan. 1951 (Bodl. MS Eng. c. 7404/74): 'This afternoon I had afternoon tea in a sombre silent lounge of the Grand Central Hotel – 3/-. The silence could have been cut up & weighed on scales.' 10 *shoeless*: No shoes have been put outside room doors for cleaning. 13–14 Tim Trengove-Jones, 'Larkin's Stammer', *EIC*, 40. 4 (1990), 338, compares *Paradise Lost*, 4. 598: 'Now came still evening on'.

The Old Fools

DATE AND TEXT
Wkbk 8 contains: six pages of drafts of the first three stanzas (most of the third not corresponding to the final poem) after '12. 9. 72', with the last page dated '20. 10. 72' at the top (1/8/9); and six pages of drafts of the whole poem except for the title between '25. 11. 72' and the completion date '12. 1. 73' (1/8/11). Published in *The Listener*, 89. 2288 (1 Feb. 1973), 147.

L to JBS, 9 Mar. 1948 (*SL*, 146): 'Truly old age seems a terrible time, but I suppose one reaches it by easy stages.' To MJ, 3 June 1955 (Bodl. MS Eng. c. 7411/47): 'Old people fill me with fascinated terror.' To C. B. Cox, 10 Feb. 1973 (*SL*, 473): 'I don't know that TOF is so very good, but I felt I had to write it. It's rather an angry poem, but the anger is ambivalent – we are angry at the humiliation of age, but we are also angry at old people for reminding us of death, and I suppose for making us feel bad about doing nothing for them. The brutality of some of the phrasing (which aroused a nurse in Bath to condemn me as a young man too intent on scrambling up the ladder to care about people's feelings) no doubt evokes these feelings in us.' L in Nov. 1974: 'I've been thinking a lot about old age. Hence "The Old Fools"': Watt (1989), 174. L to R. Gore Graham, 16 Jan. 1976 (Hull DPL (2) 2/4/6): 'I think we are angry about old people – angry with them for making us feel guilty and responsible, and of course (in a materialistic age) for reminding us of our own mortality. This is the anger in the poem that others than you have found distasteful, and indeed it may be badly organized. But there is it.' When the poem was published in 1973 L told CM 'There's always so much *more* to say': Motion (1993), 425.

Title, 1 *Hamlet*, 2. 2. 220: 'These tedious old fools!' L to MJ, 23 Oct. 1952 (Bodl. MS Eng. c.7407/109), states that the French peasant comedy *Jofroi* is 'spoilt for me, like *King Lear*, by the fact that the hero is an old fool'. To MJ, 17 June 1955 (Bodl. MS Eng. c. 7411/81): 'It's this old fool I saw in the train when I was first coming here, gargling & gobbing like an old dredger.' 7 *sloped arms*: carried out army rifle drill, 'Slope arms!' being one of the relevant commands. 13 L to MJ, 28 Dec. 1950 (Bodl. MS Eng. c. 7404/50): 'people grow old & have to be looked after not because you like them but because they are *breaking up*'. 16–20 Robert Richman in *The New Criterion*, 4. 6 (Feb. 1986), 14, views the lines as a riposte to Hazlitt's famous remark in 'On the Fear of Death' (1822): 'There was a time when we were not: this gives us no concern – why then should it trouble us that a time will come when we shall cease to be?' 25 *lighted rooms*: Also in 'Evening, and I, young', 8. 27–34 Booth (1992), 158, notes 'the pondering, meditative mode of Eliot's *Four Quartets*'. 28–30 Cf. Auden, *Musée des Beaux Arts*, 3–4 (on suffering): 'how it takes place | While someone else is eating or opening a window or just walking dully along'. 34 *Rain-ceased*: Not in *OED*.

Going, Going

DATE AND TEXT
Wkbk 7 (1/7/51) contains two pages of drafts of the first four stanzas
with the date '10. 1. 72' at the top of each page. To MJ, 8 Jan. 1972
(Bodl. MS Eng. c. 7444/18): 'I've been pecking away at the poem
until I feel it's hopeless, like a crossword, so I've given it up.' To MJ,
13 Jan. 1972 (Bodl. MS Eng. c. 7444/22): 'I've stayed in labouring at
this craft of LIVING OFF THE BRITISH GOVT WHILE CRYING
UP THEIR ENEMIES verse. Finished the "commissioned" poem last
night, but it isn't any good. I'll never be laureate.' To CM, 13 Jan.
1972 (*SL*, 452): 'I have actually finished *a* poem, and thin ranting
conventional gruel it is.' *Wkbk 8* contains: three pages of drafts of the
whole poem apart from ll. 44–8 between '11. 1. 72' and '13. 1. 72'
(1/8/1); and two pages of drafts of stanzas 1, 2, 3, 8 and 9 between
'24 / 1 / 72' and '25 / 1 / 72' (1/8/3). Robert Jackson, a Fellow of
All Souls and a member of a government working party convened
under Raine, Countess of Dartmouth, to produce a report that would
eventually be entitled *How Do You Want To Live? A Report on the
Human Habitat*, asked L to write a poem about 'the environment'
which would be included with the report: Motion (1993), 418. The
poem, headed 'Prologue', was censored at the instigation of the
Countess when printed on p. xxi of the report, which was published
on 24 May 1972. L to RC, 31 May 1972 (*SL*, 459): 'Have you seen
this commissioned poem I did for the Countess of Dartmouth's report
on the human habitat? It makes my flesh creep. She made me cut
out a verse attacking big business – don't tell anyone. It was a pretty
crappy verse, anyway, not that she minded that.' Reprinted in *The
Observer*, 4 June 1972. L's revision of the text is in Hull DPL (2)
1/5/5 (t.s. with holograph corrections). The text before censorship
was restored in *HW*. L pointed out a misprint in *HW* to CM, 5 June
1974 (*SL*, 508): l. 10, 'parts retreat' for 'part retreats'.

VARIANTS
Title PROLOGUE *Hull DPL (2) 1/5/5*; Prologue *How Do You Want
To Live?*
4 the village louts] sports from the village ~~louts lot~~ *Hull DPL (2)
1/5/5*; sports from the village *How Do You Want To Live?*
24 ~~On the Business Page, a score~~ The pylons are walking; the
shore, *Hull DPL (2) 1/5/5*; The pylons are walking; the shore, *How
Do You Want To Live?* [Cf. 'Blind through the shouting sun', 4:
'walking pylons'.]

[Lines 25–30 cancelled in Hull DPL (2) 1/5/5; not represented in *How Do You Want To Live?*]
31 You] When ~~Y~~you *Hull DPL (2) 1/5/5*; When you *How Do You Want To Live?*
51 thick-strewn] thickly strewn *Hull DPL (2) 1/5/5*; *How Do You Want To Live?*

L to MJ, 22 Sept. 1951 (Bodl. MS Eng. c. 7406/29), on England: 'but really one wonders what will be the end of the place, one huge dismal wet imbecile Yanked-up slum, half-borrowed vitality (Odeons & Coca Cola), half exhausted mummery (the Lord Mayor's show)'.
Title Auctioneers' phraseology ('Going! Going!'), announcing something on the point of being sold ('Gone!'). **4** 'I didn't like the village tonight: it reeked of chips & louts': L to MJ, 26 May 1955 (Bodl. MS Eng. c. 7411/34). **20** *M1*: motorway, the first section of which was opened in Nov. 1959. **22–3** Osborne (2008), 200, invokes Blake, *There is no natural Religion*: 'More! More! is the cry of a mistaken soul; less than All cannot satisfy Man.' **28–30** Osborne, 201, recalls that though 'Grey area grants' were introduced on a small scale by Harold Wilson's Labour government in 1969, Edward Heath's Conservative government implemented them on a large scale in 1972, extending 'assisted area' status to the whole of North West England, Humberside and Yorkshire, including the Yorkshire Dales. **37–8** *the whole | Boiling*: all of it (slang). **40** *slum*: See L's comment above. *Europe*: Osborne, 201, notes the topical relevance of Edward Heath's signing in Brussels on 22 Jan. 1972 of the Treaty of Accession, which took the United Kingdom into the European Economic Community. **42** Osborne, 201, cites numerous examples of the criminal and sexual scandals that plagued the Macmillan and later the Heath years. **43** Osborne, 201, compares D. H. Lawrence, *Kangaroo*, ch. 12: 'It is the end of England. It is the end of the old England. It is finished. England will never be England any more.' **43–5** Hugo Williams, *TLS*, 29 Apr. 2005, 16, compares Betjeman, *Delectable Duchy*, 29–31: 'The slate-hung farms, the oil-lit chapels, | Thin elms and lemon-coloured apples – | Going and gone beyond recall'. Betjeman's poem was published in 1967.

The Card-Players

DATE AND TEXT
Wkbk 7 (1/7/37) contains a page and a half of two drafts of the whole poem except for the title between '6. 5. 70' and '8 / 5 / 70'. Published in *Encounter*, 35. 4 (Oct. 1970), [41].

Roger Day, '"That vast moth-eaten musical brocade": Larkin and Religion', in *Critical Essays on Philip Larkin: The Poems*, ed. Linda Cookson and Brian Loughrey (1989), 100–1, notes that the form of the poem, somewhat unexpectedly, is that of a sonnet rhyming *abbacddcefeggh* (though with the final line isolated).

Roger Craik, *AL*, 6 (Winter 1998/9), 18, notes striking parallel details in the description of a storm of rain and wind in the opening paragraph of Turgenev's short story *Biryuk*, in the only English translation available since 1950: 'the hard roots of hundred-year-old oaks and limes, which kept on intersecting the deep ruts left by cartwheels'. Craik comments astutely on the way in which L 'renders the details of the storm uniquely his own'.

Title A favourite topic of genre painters from the sixteenth century onwards, and especially popular among Dutch and Flemish painters of the seventeenth century. Though L adjudged Cézanne's painting *The Card Players* to be 'wonderful' (to JBS, 28 Oct. 1947: Hull DP 174/2/168), and may have felt some affinity with Cézanne's artistic ideals, as István D. Ráez maintains ('Space in Larkin and Cézanne', *Hungarian Journal of English and American Studies*, 9. 2, 2003, 119–25), it is details of paintings by Flemish artist Adriaen Brouwer (*c.*1605–38) such as *Scene at the Inn*, *Peasants Smoking and Drinking*, *Tobacco Inn* and *The Card Players*, that L draws upon, improvising some of his own. L had the idea of the poem in mind for some time. To MJ, 15 May 1965 (Bodl. MS Eng. c. 7430/55): 'Agitation on the part of the acquisition dept for the return of Adriaen Brouwer has led me to look at it again – fine stuff: a comforting world of its own – you are a great fat oaf, three-quarters drunk, sitting on a bench with a jug of beer in your hand, surrounded by cronies as ugly and disgusting as yourself. You are all smoking clay pipes: there's a good fire in the hearth. One man is flat out on the floor, having spewed (dogs are licking it up), another is pissing out of the back door. The candlelight shows patched clothes, broken cupboards: outside is wind, mud, winter. *But you are all right.*' To MJ, 3 June 1967 (Bodl. MS Eng. c. 7435/40): 'I'd like to do one on Dutch

tavern scenes now. "Jan Hockspew staggers to the door . . ."' To
MJ, 23 Nov. 1967 (Bodl. MS Eng. c. 7436/42): 'I think about Jan
Hogspewer (flor. 1600) sometimes these days – I would write a
poem about him if I believed poems about works of art were licit,
but I can't think of any way in which it would be.' To MJ, 10 Dec.
1967 (Bodl. MS Eng. c. 7436/57): 'I imagine I am like [. . .] some
character from Jan Hogspewer (fl. 1600) [. . .] We shall be two
Hogspewers together.' In a letter to MJ dated 7 Feb. 1968 (Bodl.
MS Eng. c. 7436/82) he describes the 'Winter' song at the end
of *Love's Labour's Lost* as 'direct, real Jan Hogspewer stuff'. To
MJ, 29 Feb. 1968 (Bodl. MS Eng. c. 7436/102): 'This is a night
for Jan Hogspewer & his friends to gather at the rush-strewn inn
with their long clay pipes. Glowing fire. Dogs lying about. Mugs
of beer. Eructations. Hands of greasy cards.' To MJ, 7 May 1968
(Bodl. MS Eng. c. 7437/30): 'Dark evening, nice to have fires &
lights on – Jan Hogspewer comes to mind again.' In a Christmas
card to MJ (n.d.) depicting 'The Card Players' by David Teniers
(1610–90), L remarks: 'It's the nearest I could get to anything I
like – cold outside, warmth & booze & smoke within': Bodl. MS
Eng. c. 7553/41. L to JE, 28 Nov. 1975 (*SL*, 533), on his receiving
the CBE at Buckingham Palace: 'I had to wait for about 1½ hours
(in a large "Dutch" room, to judge from the pictures – Rembrandt,
Rubens, but no Van Hogspeuw).' Bodl. MS Eng. c. 7459/23 is an
offprint dated 23 Aug.1980 sent by L to JE. It is taken from Gerald
Knuttel, *Adriaen Brouwer* (1962), 23, and describes Brouwer's
painting *Tobacco Inn*, which is in the Gallery of Dulwich College,
London: 'It is a tavern scene with two men in the foreground,
one smoking and the other filling his pipe [. . .] On the right a
man stands making water against the familiar post.' **5** Cf. *Jill*,
237: 'John left him lighting a long clay churchwarden pipe with
a glowing cinder held in a pair of tongs.' *clay*: (colloq.) clay-pipe
(*OED*, clay *n.* 6a). **12** *This lamplit cave*: Cf. MacNeice, *Autumn
Sequel*, vi. 8: 'In a firelit cave equipped with drinks and books'
(and note 'firelit', l. 5). **13** Roger Craik, *AL*, 12 (Oct. 2001),
11–12, notes Patrick Kavanagh, *The Great Hunger*, xi. 106–7:
'One of the card-players laughs and spits | Into the flame across a
shoulder'. Additionally, Kavanagh, xi. 125, has 'the ace of hearts'
in a rhyming position, and L's 'Outside, . . .' (l. 2) corresponds
to Kavanagh's (xi. 108). L included a three-page excerpt from
another part of Kavanagh's poem in *OBTCEV*. **14** John Osborne,
Booth (2000), 147, notes that the short double exclamation is a

favourite mannerism of Rimbaud. It is also favoured by Whitman. See *Absences*, 10; *Sad Steps*, 11–12; *Gathering Wood*, 11–12. *Rain, wind, and fire*: Cf. *King Lear*, 3. 2. 15: 'rain, wind, thunder, fire'. Also Burns, *Tam O' Shanter* (after a drinking bout): 'Despising wind, and rain, and fire'.

The Building

DATE AND TEXT

Wkbk 6 (1/6/16) contains sixteen pages of drafts after '17. 1. 62', with '24. 3. 62' at the top of the last page. The next date in the *Wkbk* is '10. 5. 62'. At this stage, the drafts relate only slightly to *The Building*, though some details are recognisable: see the notes on *Light, Clouds, Dwelling-places*, for which L drew on these drafts. *Wkbk 7* (1/7/50) contains seven pages of drafts of the first four stanzas and other lines (mostly not represented in the final poem) after '14. 12. 71', with the final page dated '9. 1. 72' at the top. *Wkbk 8* contains: four pages of drafts of the first seven stanzas and part of stanza 8, as well as the title 'The Meeting House' and lines mostly not represented in the final poem, after '13. 1. 72', with the final page dated '19. 1. 72' at the top (1/8/2); and four pages of drafts of the last three stanzas after '29 / 1 / 72' (1/8/4) . '9 Fdy 1972' is circled on the third page, and the next date in the *Wkbk* is '6 / 3 / 72' at the top of the page after the drafts. L to MJ, 16 Jan. 1972 (Bodl. MS Eng. c. 7444/25): 'The non commissioned one is now called "The Meeting House". It's the best thing about it.' Published in *New Statesman*, 84. 2139 (17 Mar. 1972), 356.

L to MJ, 22 July 1956 (Bodl. MS Eng. c. 7414/9): 'Hospitals are horrible places. My father said everyone could learn a lot from a spell in one.' To MJ, 11 Mar. 1961 (Bodl. MS Eng. c. 7422/109): 'I dread hospitals, & the very fact of being in one is enough to frighten me.' To MJ, 7 Oct. 1971 (Bodl. MS Eng. c. 7443/93): 'hospitals are always depressing'. To C. B. Cox, 3 Aug. 1972 (*SL*, 461): '"The Building" was (as you might expect) "inspired" by a visit to the hospital here about a crick in the neck which they couldn't do anything about and which passed off eventually of its own accord.' Once he had started the poem – see Motion (1993), 420 – L's mother had a fall, and, as he told Cox, this 'led to many dreary visits' to the hospital. Introducing the poem in Nov. 1974, L identified the hospital as Kingston General in Hull: Watt (1989), 173.

L to AT, 24 Jan. 1973 (*SL*, 472): 'the last real poem I wrote'.

41 *terraced streets*: Cf. *The Large Cool Store*, 6, and *Light, Clouds, Dwelling-places*, 15: 'terraced houses'. **43** *separates*: items of clothing that may be worn in various combinations. *OED*'s earliest example is from 1945. *O world*: Booth (2005), 189, catches a 'faint echo' of Shelley's 'O world! O life! O time! | On whose last steps I climb'. **45–7** 'Once removed from the outside world we see it as a touching dream to wch everyone is lulled, but from wch we awake when we get into hospital. In there is the only reality. There you see how transient and pointless everything in the world is. Out there conceits and wishful thinking': L's MS note, Hull DPL 11.

Posterity

DATE AND TEXT

Wkbk 7 (1/7/28) contains drafts of ll. 1, 18 and 17 on a page dated '24. 4. 68' at the top, immediately followed by one and a half pages of drafts of the whole poem between '2. 6. 68' and '17. 6. 68'. Published in *New Statesman*, 75. 1946 (28 June 1968), 876. L to CM, 16 Apr. 1974 (*SL*, 503), on l. 17: 'I don't think it is a misprint – "out of kicks" is what I wrote.' In a letter of 16 Oct. 1974 (*SL*, 513), L directed CM to correct 'out for kicks' in a reprint of *HW*, which was done.

L to MJ, 16 June 1968 (Bodl. MS Eng. c. 7437/71): 'I have been pegging on with *Posterity* – perhaps I'll enclose a draft – in case you think I've spoilt it let me say that, as usual, I thought of the last line first. Jake B came second – I didn't "think of Mʳ Balokowsky" [. . .] Of course, it's about my favourite theme that people will never be unhappy again as we are unhappy – we were born in the very tip of the shadow – Everything I write now seems to come back to this.' To MJ, 30 June 1968, on *Sad Steps* and *Posterity* (Bodl. MS Eng. c. 7437/81): 'How did you think the poems looked? I like them drunk, prefer *Posterity* sober. It must be the title. It gets in Yanks, Yids, wives, kids, Coca Cola, Protest, & the Theatre – pretty good list of hates, eh?' To CM, 16 Apr. 1974 (*SL*, 503): 'I suppose what Jake is trying to say is that I am one of those old-type natural fouled-up guys you read about in Freshman's Psych., someone who has always been fouled-up and wasn't made like it accidentally and isn't doing it for kicks. I agree the construction is a bit shaky, but I hope the meaning comes over.'

L to Richard Murphy, quoted in Osborne (2008), 211: 'I'm sorry if Jake Balokowsky seemed an unfair portrait. As you see, the idea of the poem was imagining the ironical situation in which one's posthumous reputation was entrusted to somebody as utterly unlike oneself as could be. It was only after the poem had been published that I saw that Jake, wanting to do one thing but having to do something else, was really not so unlike me, and indeed had probably unconsciously been drawn to my work for this reason, which explains his bitter resentment of it.' See L's other poem *Dear Jake*.

3 *Kennedy*: John F. Kennedy University in California, founded in 1964? Perhaps L imagines the name as a likely one. **10** The metre duly requires the American stress on the first syllable of 'research'. **11** *on the skids*: (colloq.) on the way to defeat or ruin. OED: 'orig. *U.S.*' **13** *Protest Theater*: The 1960s were notable for social protest in the U.S.A., especially against the Vietnam War, and this was reflected in many theatrical productions. **16** *Freshman*: first-year university student.

Dublinesque

DATE AND TEXT
Wkbk 7 (1/7/39) has just over a page of drafts of the whole poem except for the title between '1. 6. 70' and '6 / 6 / 70'. Published in *Encounter*, 35. 4 (Oct. 1970), [41].

L to MJ, 7 June 1970 (Bodl. MS Eng. c. 7441/ 66): 'I had an odd dream on Friday, wch I transcribed into verse last night, or into *lines*, anyway.' In a letter to MJ dated 11 June 1970 he refers to 'the dream poem wch I've called *Dublinesque*. It's pretty thin, in fact pretty bad.' (Nevertheless, he sent it with *The Card-Players* to *Encounter*.) On 16 Oct. 1970 L told MB that the origin of the poem was 'a dream – I just woke up and described it': Motion (1993), 395; *AL*, 3 (Apr. 1997), 14.

L paid a visit to Dublin with MJ in the summer of 1969: Maeve Brennan, 'Letters from Ireland', *AL*, 3 (Apr. 1997), 13.

2 *AGIW*, 172: 'The water was the colour of pewter, for the afterglow had faded rapidly and left a quality of light that resembled early dawn.' L to MJ, 28 Dec. 1950 (Bodl. MS Eng. c. 7404/49): 'I shall always remember your plaid coat & golden hair moving fearfully through the heavy pewter-coloured light of St Lucy's Day in

Ludlow Castle.' To MJ, 20 Nov. 1965 (Bodl. MS Eng. c. 7431/94):
'I do remember Ludlow very faintly. A bridge, some flare-lit market
stalls, some pewter afternoon winter light.' 22 Names and the Irish
setting recall for Hugo Williams (*TLS*, 29 Apr. 2005, 16) Betjeman's
Ireland with Emily, 3–4: 'Now the Julias, Maeves and Maureens |
Move between the fields to Mass'.

Homage to a Government

DATE AND TEXT

Wkbk 7 (1/7/26) contains six and a half pages of drafts after
'30. 1. 68', with the final page dated '7. 3. 68' at the top. At this
stage only the first stanza is recognisable as part of the final poem.
Wkbk 7 (1/7/30) also contains eight pages of drafts of the whole
poem (with the title 'Homage To a Prime Minister') between
'18. 11. 68' and '10 Jan 69'. L to MJ, 12 Jan. 1969 (Bodl. MS Eng.
c. 7438/91): 'spent the evening [. . .] brooding over my political
poem. I thought I had it finished, and indeed wrote a letter to the
Sunday Times to accompany it, but this morning it seems bad again,
& I don't think I shall send it.' To MJ, 15 Jan. 1969 (Bodl. MS
Eng. c. 7438/94): 'In the end I sent the political poem to the *Sunday
Times*, but have had no response. It's quite undistinguished & indeed
the end fails – if they print it I'll say why it fails. But they may send
it back. Probably the kindest thing.' Published in the *Sunday Times*,
19 Jan. 1969, 60. Uniquely, L appends the date '1969' to the poem
in *HW*: omitted in *CP* (1988), 171; reinstated in *CP* (2003), 141.

L to MJ, 30 June 1968 (Bodl. MS Eng. c. 7437/81): 'I long to write
a political poem – the withdrawal of troops east of Suez started
me, now I see someone boasting that in a few years' time we shall
be spending 'more on Education than "Defence"' – this shocks
me *to the core*, & I seriously feel that *within our lifetime* we shall
see England under the heel of the conqueror – or what *used* to be
England.' In Nov. 1974: 'I'm not normally known as a political
poet; my one political poem is "Homage to a Government" which
was written about the government in power in 1969': Watt (1989),
174. In 1979, noting that the poem 'has been quoted in several
books as a kind of symbol of the British withdrawal from a world
role', L commented: 'I don't mind troops being brought home if
we'd decided this was the best thing all round, but to bring them
home simply because we couldn't afford to keep them there seemed

a dreadful humiliation': *RW*, 52. When a letter from Sir Arthur de la Mare, High Commissioner in Singapore from 1967 to 1970, complaining about what he called 'the second British surrender in Singapore', was printed in the *Daily Telegraph* on 19 Feb. 1982, three days later L sent him a copy of the poem 'on this subject that I wrote at the time': Hull DPL (2) 2/18/60. (L seems to be referring to the subject of troop withdrawal, and not only from Singapore.) L remarks in the letter that 'the title of course is ironical'.

The poem is concerned with the decisions of Harold Wilson's Labour government to bring home British troops from Aden, following a civil war there in 1965–7, and to disband the Far Eastern command and withdraw British forces from Singapore just before 1967. Aden had been made a crown colony in 1937, had been given partial self-government in 1962, and had joined the South Arabian Federation of Arab Emirates in 1963. Historian Trevor Lloyd notes: 'Aden in 1967 was the most clear-cut case of a local independence movement dictating the timetable of departure to the British by force of arms': *Empire: The History of the British Empire* (2001), 195; quoted by Rory Waterman in *AL*, 27 (Apr. 2009), 28, to show that in reality 'the Imperial forces were militarily ousted. Larkin portrays the British Empire in the late 1960s as more potent than it actually was. In his poem the British Government *chooses* (albeit incorrectly) to leave.'

Palmer (2008), 126, likens the scathing rhetorical repetition of 'and it is all right', 'And this is all right', and 'Which is all right' to a similar strategy of repetition ('Brutus says . . . And Brutus is an honourable man') in Mark Antony's funeral oration in *Julius Caesar*, 3. 2. 83–95.

9 Cf. Bernard Spencer, *A Thousand Killed*, 7: '(That fighting was a long way off)'.

This Be The Verse

DATE AND TEXT
A version with variant wording in stanza 1 was included in a letter to AT of 14 Apr. 1971 (*SL*, 437): 'I've dashed off a little piece suitable for Ann's next Garden of Verses.' (L refers to Robert Louis Stevenson, *A Child's Garden of Verses*, 1885. Ann Thwaite edited an annual of new writing for children, *Allsorts*, 1968–75.) The same variants are in the version sent to MJ in t.s. with a letter postmarked 15 Apr. 1971 (Bodl. MS Eng. c.7442/106): 'Little Easter

poem – ought to be dedicated to D. Holbrook.' (David Holbrook, 1923–2011, published *Children's Games*, 1957, and *Children's Writing*, 1967.) The t.s. is reproduced in facsimile in *LTM*, [417]. In a letter to MJ dated 18 Apr. 1971 (Bodl. MS Eng. c. 7442/109), L had further thoughts: 'Talking of pwetry, as Kingsley used to call it. I suggest

> They fill you with the faults they had
>   And add some extra, just for you.

I think this is better. Or do you think

> They foist on you the faults etc?

That might be better. *Causons, causons, mon bon.* "Foist" is faintly farcical, wch is good – better than "fill". Shall it be foist? (The last shall be foist.) No: there is then too much emphasis on the two *you*s.' (L quotes Henry James's invocation in the detached notes to *The Ivory Tower*, 4 Jan. 1910. It means 'Let's chat, let's chat, my Muse'.) Hull DPL 1/7/68 is a t.s. loosely inserted at the back of *Wkbk* 7. It contains only one variant, an error: 'anothers" for 'another's' (l. 8). Published in *New Humanist*, 86. 8 (Aug. 1971), 253.

VARIANTS (from letters of 14 and 15 Apr. 1971)
3 fill you with] hand on all
4 extra] fresh ones

L to JE, 6 June 1982 (*SL*, 674): '"They fuck you up" will clearly be my Lake Isle of Innisfree. I fully expect to hear it recited by a thousand Girl Guides before I die.'
Title Robert Louis Stevenson, *Requiem*, 5: 'This be the verse you grave for me'. Noted in Petch (1981), 8. **1** L in *Wkbk* 5 (Hull DPL 1/5/1), on his parents' marriage: 'Certainly the marriage left me with two convictions: that human beings should not live together, and that children should be taken from their parents at an early age [. . .]. I think the worst thing about families is the way your parents impose their own neurotic deficiencies & patterns on you': L to MJ, 10 Nov. 1968 (Bodl. MS Eng. c. 7438/45). In 1979 (*RW*, 48): 'I wouldn't want it thought that I didn't like my parents. I did like them. But at the same time they were rather awkward people and not very good at being happy. And these things rub off.' Interviewed by John Haffenden in 1981 (*FR*, 60): '"They fuck you up, your mum and dad" doesn't sound very compassionate. [Haffenden: *It's very funny, though*.] It's perfectly serious as well.' L in 1981 on

using bad language in his poems (*FR*, 61): 'these words are part of the palette. You use them when you want to shock. I don't think I've ever shocked for the sake of shocking. "They fuck you up" is funny because it's ambiguous. Parents bring about your conception and also bugger you up once you are born. Professional parents in particular don't like that poem.'

How Distant

DATE AND TEXT
Wkbk 7 (1/7/10) contains three pages of drafts of the whole poem after '20. 11. 65', finishing on a page dated '24/ 11/ 65' at the top. The next date, at the top of the next page, is '2. 12. 65'. Published in *The Listener*, 78. 2013 (26 Oct. 1967), 521.

Sad Steps

DATE AND TEXT
Wkbk 7 (1/7/27) contains a draft of ll. 13–14 on a page dated '7. 3. 68', immediately followed by eight pages of drafts of the whole poem except for the title after '22. 3. 68', with the final page dated '24. 4. 68' at the top. L on 24 Apr. to MJ (Bodl. MS Eng. c. 7437/12): 'I think I've just *finished* the moon poem – if so, I'll send it. It's pretty unoriginal, just another moon poem. And now I look up *Shut Out That Moon*, as Scannell says he is going to have it in his programme – it isn't at all the same sentiment, but I suppose all moon poems are the same.' (L refers to Hardy, *Shut Out That Moon*, on which see the note on l. 12. 'Scannell' is Vernon Scannell, 1922–2007, English writer and broadcaster, who broadcast the poem on 7 June 1968: see *LTM*, 386 n.) L included a t.s. of the poem with a letter to MJ dated 28 Apr. 1968 (Bodl. MS Eng. c. 7437/17). Published in *New Statesman*, 75. 1946 (28 June 1968), 876.

VARIANTS (from the Bodl. MS)
Title [No title]
16 a reminder] like a statement
17 it can't] will not

Title Sidney, *Astrophil and Stella*, 31. 1: 'With how sad steps, ô Moone, thou climb'st the skies'. Noted by Bernard Bergonzi, 'Davie, Larkin and the State of England', *Contemporary Literature*, 18. 3

(Summer, 1977), 357. L to Katherine Duncan-Jones, 28 Oct. 1985 (Bodl. MS Eng. c. 5734/58): 'The connection between "Sad Steps" and Sidney is tenuous in the extreme – I suppose I just thought it a good idea at the time. It wasn't. My poem has nothing to do with love, or disdainful beauties, or anything like that.' Also *King Lear*, 5. 3. 263–4: 'from your first of difference and decay | Have followed your sad steps'. **4** *Four o'clock*: Bergonzi, 357, catches an echo of Eliot's *Rhapsody on a Windy Night*, which marks time in such a manner (e.g. 'Twelve o'clock', l. 1) and includes 'Four o'clock' specifically (l. 70). Also Eliot, *Preludes*, 1. 3: 'Six o' clock.' See TNS XVI, and notes. *wedge-shadowed gardens*: MB recalls that this was the view from the rear of L's flat in Hull: Salwak (1989), 29. **7–8** Cf. James Thomson, *Sonnet* ('Through foulest fogs of my own sluggish soul'), 3: 'Through sulphurous cannon-clouds that surge and roll'. **11** *Lozenge*: 'A plane rectilinear figure, having two acute and two obtuse angles; a rhomb, "diamond"' (*OED*, 1); a shield of such a shape with arms emblazoned on it (1a.) *Medallion*: large medal. Raphaël Ingelbien notes that Laforgue calls the moon 'Blanc médaillon' in *Litanie des premiers quartiers de la lune*, 3: *Philip Larkin and the Poetics of Resistance*, ed. Andrew McKeown and Charles Holdefer (2006), 24. Petch (1981), 100: 'The traditional symbolic associations of the moon . . . are deflated.' **11–12** Bergonzi, 358: L is 'imitating a characteristic construction of French symbolist poetry', and 'the appositional phrases in the vocative, the exclamations, are a noticeable feature of, for instance, Laforgue's *Dernier Vers*'. John Osborne, Booth (2000), 147, notes that the short double exclamation is a favourite mannerism of Rimbaud. See *Absences*, 10; *The Card-Players*, 14; *Gathering Wood*, 11–12. **12** *Immensements*: Bergonzi, 358, notes that the word does not exist in English or French but that it 'impressionistically parodies Laforgue or Rimbaud'. John Wiltshire in *Cambridge Quarterly*, 19. 3 (1990), 264, recalls 'Immense Orion's glittering form' from Hardy's *Shut Out That Moon*, 9. **16–17** Blake Morrison notes L's reference to the 'peculiar heartless, savage strength' of childhood in a 1959 review (*RW*, 111): *PN Review*, 14. 4 (Nov. 1976), 46. **17** *that it can't come again*: Cf. Housman, *A Shropshire Lad* XL ('Into my heart an air that kills'), 8: 'And cannot come again', and *ASL* II ('Loveliest of trees'), 6: 'Twenty will not come again'. Noted in Morrison (1980), 201. L included both poems in *OBTCEV*. Cf. 'An April Sunday brings the snow', 12: 'and not to come again'. **18** Cf. *Reference Back*, 21: 'Blindingly undiminished'.

Solar

DATE AND TEXT
Wkbk 7 (1/7/2) contains seven pages of drafts of the whole poem
except for the title between '6. 10. 64' and '4 Nov. 1964.' L to MJ,
13 Oct. 1964 (Bodl. MS Eng. c. 7429/10): 'I've finished my little
poem about the sun.' Hull DPL 1/7/69 is a t.s. with holograph
corrections, loosely inserted at the back of *Wkbk* 7: revising l. 18,
L did not convert the initial capital in 'Our' to lower case, though
the capitals in 'Daily' and 'Hourly' indicate that he wished these
words to come before 'our'. Published in *Queen*, 426. 5594 (25 May
1966), 47. Sending a typed copy to Vernon Watkins with a letter of
4 Feb. 1967, L described it as 'not recent, not unpublished': *SL*, 392.

VARIANTS
18 ~~Daily~~ Hourly Our needs ~~humbly~~ DPL 1/7/69; Hourly our needs
Queen, 1966

L to MJ, 13 Oct. 1964 (Bodl. MS Eng. c. 7429/10): 'it's the sort of
thing anyone could write, and indeed it ought to be much longer &
deeper & altogether better, but one can't be on one's high horse all
the time.' L in 1981 (*FR*, 61): '"Solar" was the first poem I wrote
after *The Whitsun Weddings*. Nobody's ever liked it, or mentioned
it. It was unlike anything I'd written for about twenty years, more
like *The North Ship*.' To the suggestion that critics may have found
that it didn't comport with the general run of what L's poems say, L
replied: 'So much the worse for them. It's a feeling, not a thought.
Beautiful': *FR*, 61.

   Terry Whalen, *Philip Larkin and English Poetry* (1986), 71, finds
the poem 'Lawrentian in its valuing of the mysterious presence
of the sun', and quotes the end of Lawrence's *Apocalypse* (1931):
'What we want to destroy is our false, inorganic connections,
especially those related to money, and re-establish the living organic
connections, with the cosmos, the sun and earth, with mankind and
nation and family. Start with the sun, and the rest will slowly, slowly
happen.' Dr S. N. Prasad, *AL*, 28 (Oct. 2009), 34–5, relates the
poem to ancient traditions of sun-worship.

   Merle Brown, 'Larkin and his Audience', *Iowa Review*, 8. 4 (Fall
1977), 120, compares the poem in general terms to another direct
address to the sun, Thom Gunn's *Sunlight*. More particularly: Gunn,
21–2 ('yellow center of the flower, | Flower on its own, without
a root or stem'), L, 6 (Single stalkless flower'); Gunn, 23 ('Giving

all color and all shape their power'), L, 21 ('You give for ever'); Gunn, 28 ('Petals of light'), L, 11 (Your petalled head of flames'). Christopher Fletcher, 'Echoes of David Gascoyne's "September Sun: 1947" in Philip Larkin's "Solar"', *N&Q*, NS 49. 4 (Dec. 2002), 500–1, cites evidence of the strong influence of Gascoyne's poem: the three-verse structure, the direct address to the sun, the ideas of overflowing abundance and self-sufficiency, the floral imagery associated with both life and fiery destruction, and the monetary metaphor.

1 Cf. D. H. Lawrence, *Prayer* ('Give me the moon at my feet'), 6–7: 'For the sun is hostile, now | his face is like the red lion'. Cf. 'Long lion days'. 18–21 Cf. the ladder in Jacob's dream when 'the sun was set', with 'the angels of God ascending and descending on it' (Genesis 28: 11, 12). Noted in Palmer (2008), 103. 20 *Unclosing*: Cf. *Thaw*, 2: 'The sun its hand uncloses like a statue'. 20–21 Day (1987), 77, compares Ps. 104: 28: 'That thou givest them they gather: thou openest thine hand, they are filled with good'.

Annus Mirabilis

DATE AND TEXT
Wkbk 7 (1/7/21) contains two pages of drafts, the first of stanza 1 and 2 after '16. 6. 67', the second of the whole poem except for the title between '2. 7. 67' and '12 July 67'. There are two t.s. versions inserted loosely at the back of *Wkbk* 7: DPL 1/7/60, which is identical to the published text; and 1/7/81, with the title and a holograph correction in pencil. Published in *Cover* [Oxford], 1 (Feb. 1968), 12, with indentation of lines 2, 3 and 5 of each stanza, and with l. 13 omitted in error and l. 14 indented. L to Harry Chambers, 15 Nov. 1967 (*SL*, 398): 'I sent a short poem called *History* to an Oxford magazine called *Cover* & another [*Sympathy in White Major*] to the *London Mag.* for, I *think*, their December number. Neither is good.' Repr. in *London Magazine*, NS 9. 10 (Jan. 1970), 29, and in *Michigan Quarterly Review*, 9. 3 (Summer 1970), 146. L parodies the opening in a letter to AT of 3 Sept. 1984 (*SL*, 718): 'Sexual intercourse began In 1895, Before I was alive – '.

VARIANTS
Title HISTORY *Cover, 1968*
7 sort] kind *Cover, 1968*
12 Everyone] ~~Both sexes~~ Everyone *DPL 1/7/81*

Title 'The Wonderful Year', as in Dryden's (nationalistic and celebratory) poem with the same title. **1–3, 16–18** Cf. A. P. Herbert, *Lines for a Worthy Person who has drifted by accident into a Chelsea revel*, 21–4: '*As my poor father used to say | In 1863, | Once people start on all this Art | Goodbye, moralitee!*' The refrain is repeated with the variations '*Farewell, monogamee!*' and '*Farewell, moralitee!*' (ll. 50, 77). The poem is included by KA in *The New Oxford Book of Light Verse* (1978), 224–6, and Christopher Ricks drew my attention to it. L included a poem by Herbert in *OBTCEV*. **4–5, 19–20** Lawrence's novel *Lady Chatterley's Lover* (expurgated edn., 1928; unabridged, Paris, 1929) was released for sale in Britain in unabridged form following the case of *Regina* v. *Penguin Books* at the Old Bailey, London, 20 Oct.–2 Nov. 1960. L to JBS, 28 Jan. 1948 (*SL*, 144): 'I reread *Lady C* recently & thought it grand – the English one, I'm afraid. The French one never came. I think it will live, like anything – parts of it made me laugh deeply.' In a letter dated 10 Nov. 1960 to MJ (Bodl. MS Eng. c. 7422/42), L expressed reservations about it as a novel, but felt obliged to 'acquit it of indecent – or at any rate pornographic – intention'. He had organised an exhibition concerned with the novel at the Brynmor Jones Library. **5, 20** *Please Please Me*, the first long-playing record ('LP') by the Beatles (1960–70), was released in the UK on 22 Mar. 1963. 'Philip fell under the sway of the Beatles in the 1960s [. . .] long after the group disbanded, their tunes held a special place in his affections, for they stood for a happy and successful period of his life': Brennan (2002), 54.

Vers de Société

DATE AND TEXT

Wkbk 7 contains: the first two and a half lines between '4 Nov. 1964' and '13. xi. 64' (1/7/3); and six pages of drafts of the whole poem except for the title between '25 / 4 / 71' and '20 / 5 / 71'. At this stage L cancelled the title '<u>The Big Wish</u>' and tried the alternatives '<u>Society</u>', '<u>Social Life</u>', and '<u>Verses of Society</u>'. To MJ, 15 May 1971 (Bodl. MS Eng. c. 7443/5): 'I've just spent a not very profitable evening trying to finish off a poem, and making it bad Aldous Huxley, i.e. Aldous Huxley.' To MJ, 23 May 1971 (Bodl. MS Eng. c. 7443/15): 'I've almost finished my crowd-of-craps poem – shall I call it <u>Vers de Societée</u>? How d'you pronounce it? Vair duh soce-yatay? Don't want to have a poem I can't pronounce.'

Hull DPL 1/7/71 is a t.s. loosely inserted at the back of *Wkbk 7*.
Published in *New Statesman*, 81. 2100 (18 June 1971), 854. L
pointed out the misprint 'spent' for 'spend' in l. 8 of the *HW* text to
AT, in a letter of 21 May 1974 (*SL*, 506).

L to JBS, 22 Jan. 1942 (Hull DP 174/2/38): 'I like being alone and
just seeing other people when I want to and not until. Lawrence's
stresses on being alone seem almost pointless to me: the whole thing
is so childishly simple: Company: Lot of shags talking shag. Solitude:
Enjoying oneself. The choice doesn't give me much of a headache.'
R. J. C. Watt reports that when L introduced the poem at a reading
in Nov. 1974 he said it is '"meant to be a funny poem, but in fact it's
very serious" (this of course with a twinkle in the eye': Watt (1989),
174. L on *Desert Island Discs* in 1976 (*FR*, 103): 'I never think of
myself as a gregarious man but having thought about your island
for a few weeks I've come to the conclusion that I probably am.
I should be very happy there for about twenty-four hours, and fairly
happy for another forty-eight hours, but after that I suspect that I
should miss people and society in general.' In 1979: 'I find the idea
of always being in company rather oppressive; I see life more as an
affair of solitude diversified by company than an affair of company
diversified by solitude. I don't want to sound falsely naïve, but I
often wonder why people get married. I think perhaps they dislike
being alone more than I do. Anyone who knows me will tell you that
I'm not fond of company. I'm very fond of people, but it's difficult to
get people without company': *RW*, 54. L in 1985, after noticing that
'there are no people' in Andrew Young's poetry and finding that 'the
silence, the absence are in the end intimidating' (*FR*, 376): 'To walk
all day without meeting a soul can be refreshing and restoring. But
at last one is glad to get back to humankind again' (377).
   Title A genre of social or familiar poetry, popular in Victorian
and Edwardian England. See Carolyn Wells, *A Vers de Société
Anthology* (1907). **1** *My wife and I*: L to MJ, 20 Mar. 1963
(Bodl. MS Eng. c. 7426/61): 'Am *maddened* by *inescapable sudden
My-wife-and-Is* tonight *& tomorrow night – how do people
think poetry gets written*?' To MJ, 28 Oct. 1963 (Bodl. MS Eng.
c. 7427/36): 'This has been a relatively quiet week, no reviews,
no jazz, no my-wife-and-Is.' *craps*: L to JBS, 15 Aug. 1944 (*SL*,
89): 'some crap I dimly knew at Oxford'; to KA, 20 Dec. 1945
(*SL*, 111): 'sum crap like that'; *No for an Answer* (1948–54):
'Becomes engaged to a minor crap?': *TAWG*, 356; to MJ, 6 Feb.

1957 (Bodl. MS Eng. c. 7415/76): 'a frightful shower of craps'. The expression occurs in several of L's letters (*SL*, 227, 304, 330; Bodl. MSS Eng. c. 7428/108, 7431/98, 7436/76, 7437/21), and in KA's more frequently (Amis, *Letters*, 220, 269, 270, 293, 294, 336, 352, 357, etc.). **2** KA to L, 19 Feb. 1954 (Amis, *Letters*, 372): 'Some sods coming tonight to drink my drink and waste my time.' **3** *In a pig's arse*: KA to L, 8 Sept. 1952 (Amis, *Letters*, 291): 'Nasty little toady in a pig's arse'; to L, 14 Aug. 1961 (Amis, *Letters*, 594): 'Yes, in a bull's arse it has'; Amis's novel *I Want It Now* (1968; repr. 1988), 197: 'In a pig's arse I'll come see him again.' L to MJ, 17 Sept. 1970 (Bodl. MS Eng. c. 7441/121): 'In a pig's arse he can rent my flat.' Echoed, after the poem, by L to MJ, 16 Jan. 1972 (Bodl. MS Eng. c. 7444/25): 'Only Connect in a pig's arse'; to KA, 11 Aug. 1972 (*SL*, 462): 'in a pig's arse I did'. The *OED* (pig *sb.*, III, phrases 12) regards the phrase as chiefly N. American or Australian slang expressing emphatic disbelief, rejection or denial. **5** *The gas fire breathes*: As in *Best Society*, 26. Cf. MacNeice, *Schizophrene*, 9: 'Hearing the gasfire breathe monotonously'. **9–10** *washing sherry*: 'What Dylan Thomas calls "washing sherry"': L to MJ, 12 Oct. 1957 (Bodl. MS Eng. c. 7417/7). See 'A Visit to America' (1953), printed in *The Listener*, 22 Apr. 1954, and repr. in *On the Air with Dylan Thomas: The Broadcasts*, ed. Ralph Maud (1991), 276. *canted | Over*: 'Almost everyone was shorter than he and this explains that awkward characteristic stoop as his increasing deafness made intricate conversation difficult': B. C. Bloomfield, *Brought to Book: Philip Larkin and his Bibliographer* (1995), 16. **11** *Which*: UK magazine of Which? Ltd, formerly known as the Consumers' Association (founded in 1957). Also mentioned in *The Dance*, 123. **16–17** Tom Paulin (1990), repr. in Regan (1997), 172–3, notes a parallel comparison of the moon to a sword blade in Yeats, *Meditations in Time of Civil War*, III *My Table*, 2, 10: 'a changeless sword . . . Curved like new moon, moon-luminous'. Cf. L's earlier poem 'Numberless blades of grass', 2–3: 'And only one thin blade | That is the moon'. **19, 34** L to MJ, 17 Oct. 1950 (Bodl. MS Eng. c. 7403/78): 'And I am not really at peace even alone, since I think it is weak & selfish to like being alone.' **22–3** Cf. 'Do unto others as you would have done unto you': Luke 6: 31. **24** *Virtue is social*: Cf. *Best Society*, 22: 'Our virtues are all social'.

Show Saturday

DATE AND TEXT
Wkbk 8 (1/8/15) contains ten and a half pages of drafts of the whole poem except for the title between '13. 10. 73' and '19. 1. 74', with '3. 12. 73' and '4 / 12 / 73' on the tenth page. Further drafts of the final stanza and all but the last line and a half of the penultimate stanza appear between '4/ 12/ 73'and '19. 1. 74'. L to AT, 10 Dec. 1973 (*SL*, 494–5): 'I've spent a good deal of time recently writing the enclosed poem (C. Day-Lewis rides again), and now can't decide if it's worth publishing [. . .] I don't know whether to shove it into HIGH WINDOWS, of which I have now had the proofs and which they want back by January 4th. It would add bulk and roughage, I suppose – both much needed qualities.' When *HW* was in proof, L sent it to CM for inclusion between *Vers de Société* and *Money*. Then he told CM on 28 Dec. 1973 that 'stanza three has its rhymes all wrong, and I shall have to re-write it', and, on 7 Jan. 1974, that 'One line has six beats': Motion (1993), 436. Published in *Encounter*, 42. 2 (Feb. 1974), [20–1]. In l. 41 L had mistyped 'From' for 'For', and AT corrected it to 'For'.

VARIANTS (from *Encounter*, 1974)
13 Folks] Folk
22 immobile] convulsive
that end in] to sudden
23 With] And

Title The 'show' is identified in Motion (1993), 437, as Bellingham Show in Northumberland, which L and MJ visited most years after she had moved to Haydon Bridge. In 1973 they visited the show after a fortnight's holiday in Scotland. The poem is reminiscent of the detailed account of 'a local gymkhana in a large field on the outskirts of the next village' in *A Girl in Winter* (1947; repr. 1975), 109–12, as John Bayley, Hartley (1988), 210, notes. *5–6 squealing logs | (Chain Saw Competition)*: Cf. Betjeman, *Summoned by Bells*, 2.61–2: 'whining saws, would thrill me with the scream | Of tortured wood'. 18 *Two young men in acrobats' tights*: 'the Harrington Brothers, who appeared at Bellingham every year': Motion (1993), 437. Bodl. MSS Eng. c. 7436/35c, 35d, are L's photographs of the wrestling match, which date from 1967. The wrestlers are wearing light-coloured tights and dark trunks. **22** *immobile*: In his recording of *HW*, L stressed the first, rather than the second, syllable of the word. Admitting his error, he told AT, 23 Aug. 1975 (*SL*, 529): 'I don't think I've ever heard anyone use the word. Hum. My pronunciation *is* rather built into the run of the lines, wch means I can't do much about it, except in future.' **45** *sports finals*: newspapers containing final sports results. **49–50, 52** The alliteration and compounding evoke Old English. Barbara Everett notes the 'dense semi-monosyllabic style distantly related to Old English alliterative verse': 'Larkin's Edens', *English*, 31. 139 (Spring 1982), 50.

Money

DATE AND TEXT
Wkbk 8 (1/8/12) contains three pages of drafts of the whole poem (with three titles: 'Bank Statement', 'Financial Statement', and 'Prices & Incomes') after '11. 2. 73', with the final page dated '19. 2 [1973]' at the top. Published in *Phoenix: A Poetry Magazine*, ed. Harry Chambers, 11/12 (autumn and winter 1973/4), 5, without indentation of alternate lines.

1 *Quarterly*: Barbara Everett, Booth (2000), 13, notes that this 'involves those statements of savings or investment accounts which all banks send out at three-monthly intervals'. She quotes (14) from a letter to JE of 18 Jan. 1973 (*SL*, 472), a month before the poem was written: 'The account book seems a cheerless symbol: is it *really* necessary? I keep an eye on my bank balance, but I suppose that's locking the stable door, etc.' **11** *screw*: earnings (slang). As also in 'What have I done to be thirty-two?', 3. **12** *in the end . . . a shave*: In a letter to AT dated 24 Mar. 1991, KA recalls L telling him of his father, a couple of days before his death, remarking, 'My last shave': Amis, *Letters*, 1105. Palmer (2008), 121, detects a still more eerie precision: 'Larkin could have chosen . . . anything everyday and inexpensive . . . the reference is to the rites that attend the preparation of a corpse for burial. Just as the finger- and toenails grow after death, so does the beard, and it is still common practice to clean-shave the cadaver's face.' **13** *money singing*: Cf. Auden, *They*, 21: 'Our money sang'. Noted by James Fenton, 'Wounded by Un-Shrapnel', *The New York Review of Books*, 48. 6 (12 Apr. 2001). **15–16** Cf. 'The poet has a straight face', 33–4: 'under the spread of the moon | The cities lie ruined and mad'. Roger Craik, *AL*, 12 (Oct. 2001), 11, catches an echo of Joan Barton, *The*

Mistress, 4–5: 'A sort of cottage orné at the gates, | Ridiculous and sad'. L included the poem in *OBTCEV*. 16 *intensely sad*: 'his own characteristic intensely sad, intensely penetrating note': L in 1962 on Hardy (*RW*, 145).

Cut Grass

DATE AND TEXT
Wkbk 7 (1/7/42) contains a draft of the whole poem except for the title on a single page between '2 / 6 / 71' and '3 / 6 / 71'. L to MJ, 3 June 1971: 'Am trying to write an ethereal little song, nothing like *This be the verse* or *Vers de Soc.*, about the time of year': Bodl. MS Eng. c. 7443/30. Hull DPL 1/7/66 is a t.s. inserted loosely at the back of *Wkbk 7*. Published in *The Listener*, 86. 2209 (29 July 1971), 144.

L to MJ, 20 July 1971 (Bodl. MS Eng. c. 7443/62): 'I wish someone good would set it to music – that shows it's no good, of course.*
*I sing it to a sort of whine made up by myself, minor changing to major at "Of young-leafed June", v. voluptuous.' To MJ, 29 July 1971 (Bodl. MS Eng. c. 7443/68): '*The Listener* printed *Cut Grass*. Looks rather crazy, though a good antidote to all the vulgar stuff. "Real pwetry".' To MJ, 1 Aug. 1971 (Bodl. MS Eng. c. 7443/71): 'Enclosed is *Cut Grass* – I expect it still "lacks impact". Its trouble is that it's "music", i.e. pointless crap. About line 6 I hear a kind of wonderful Elgar river-music take over, for wch the words are just an excuse [. . .] There's a point at wch the logical sense of the poem ceases to be added to, and it continues only as a succession of images. I like it all right, but for once I'm not a good judge.'

Title Cf. Ps. 37: 2: 'they shall soon be cut down like the grass'; Ps. 103: 15: 'As for man, his days are as grass: as a flower of the field, so he flourisheth'; Isa. 40: 6: 'All flesh is grass'. 4 Cf. Keats, *The Fall of Hyperion*, 1. 382: 'Long, long, these two were postured motionless' (with 'builded' in the next line). 8 Cf. Housman, *A Shropshire Lad* XXXIX 8, 11: 'The hedgerows heaped with may', 'high snowdrifts in the hedge'. 10 *Queen Anne's lace: Anthriscus sylvestris*, cow parsley, which bears clusters of small white flowers. 11–12 Cf. Louise Bogan, *Summer Wish* (1929), 118: 'hills that are builded like great clouds'. Christopher Ricks drew my attention to this.

The Explosion

DATE AND TEXT
Wkbk 7 (1/7/34) contains four and a half pages of drafts of the whole poem except for the title after '7. 12. 69', with the final page dated '5. 1. 70' at the top. The next page is dated '10 3 70' at the top. Hull DPL 1/7/75 is a t.s. loosely inserted at the back of *Wkbk* 7. It differs from the *HW* text in one variant wording, and ll. 16–18 are not underlined to be rendered in italic. L included a copy with a letter to MJ dated 6 Jan. 1970 (Bodl. MS Eng. c. 7440/78, 79, with ll. 16–18 marked 'Italics' in ballpoint pen). L to JE, 18 Mar. 1970 (*SL*, 428): 'I last wrote "a poem" on Christmas morning, & today learnt it will be "Poem of the Month" for June or July.' Published by Poem of the Month Club Ltd in June 1970, and reprinted in *The Listener*, 88. 2264 (17 Aug. 1972), 208. L to MJ, 28 June 1970 (Bodl. MS Eng. c. 7441/81): 'I've altered it slightly, not really for the better: "*Plain* as lettering . . . *Larger* than in life" . . . – I don't think larger will do: I'll have to think of another word.' In his account of the Hull t.s., A. T. Tolley misses out 'in' in 'Plainer than in life' and 'Larger than in life': Tolley (1997), 111.

VARIANTS
22 Larger] Plainer *Hull t.s., Bodl. t.s.*

L introducing the poem on BBC Radio Three, 9 Aug. 1972 (*FR*, 92): 'What I should like to do is to write different kinds of poems that might be by different people. Someone once said that the great thing is not to be different from other people but to be different from yourself. That's why I've chosen to read now a poem that isn't especially like me, or like what I fancy I'm supposed to be like.' L in 1981 (*FR*, 61): 'I heard a song about a mine disaster; a ballad, a sort of folk song. I thought it very moving, and it produced the poem. It made me want to write the same thing, a mine disaster with a vision of immortality at the end – that's the point of the eggs. It may be all rather silly. I like it.' L to MJ, 6 Jan. 1970: 'Enclosed (I hope) is my version of the Trimdon Grange Explosion. *Don't tell a soul* where I got the idea from.' To MJ, 11 Jan. 1970 (Bodl. MS Eng. c. 7440/83): 'The emotions the song roused in me were very strong. The song is better, though – more coaly & local & shining – "Where explosions are no more"! Couldn't beat that.' The ballad *The Trimdon Grange Explosion,* by Thomas Armstrong, is about the mining disaster at Trimdon near Durham on 15 Feb. 1882, in which seventy-four men and boys died. L quotes the end of the last line. He heard the ballad on *The Collier's Rant: Mining Songs of the Northumberland–Durham Coalfield* (1962). To MJ, 5 Mar. 1970 (Bodl. MS Eng. c. 7440/120): 'It led me to play the record & enjoy again "Runnin' for the Odd 'Un".' Peter Hollindale, *Critical Survey*, 1. 2 (1989), 142–3, deserves credit for relating L's poem to nineteenth-century disaster ballads (including *The Trimdon Grange Explosion*) without knowing what L said about the source of his inspiration. Motion (1993), 394–5, relates L's poem to a television documentary about the mining industry that L watched with his mother at Christmas in 1969.

L to MJ, 11 Jan. 1970 (Bodl. MS Eng. c. 7440/83): 'I have reservations: what time of year do larks lay eggs? Would it be as sunny as that? I think I might put the verse "The dead . . . " in italics, to bring the reader up short a bit & show someone is speaking (the minister). On the whole I think it does, though.'

Edna Longley, Hartley (1988), 228, views the poem as 'Larkin's only approximation to the visionary spirit of Baudelaire's *La Mort*'. Alan Brownjohn, *Philip Larkin* (1975), 25, notes L's adroit adaptation of the metre of Longfellow's *The Song of Hiawatha*, and Peter Hollindale, op. cit., 141, notes additionally that Longfellow and L both balance verbs of impetus in the past tense with verbs of stasis (participles) in the present. William Wootten, 'In the Graveyard of Verse', *London Review of Books*, 9 Aug. 2001, 23–4, relates the poem to *The Collier*, an early poem by Vernon Watkins (whom L met and was influenced by during his college years): in it a young miner brings 'spotted eggs from the trees' (l. 20), mining is represented as burial, and a mining disaster is transformed into a golden vision ('gold' occurs in ll. 36, 44).

4, 8, 13 *came men in pitboots . . . Came back . . . came a tremor*: Osborne (2008), 71, notes Longfellow's fondness for such parallelism ('Down the rivers, o'er the prairies, | Came the warriors of the nations, | Came the Delawares and Mohawks, | Came . . .': *The Peace-Pipe*, 58–61). **10** *moleskins*: work trousers made of hard-wearing heavy cotton fabric. **11** Osborne (2008), 71, notes that Longfellow often has series of disyllabic words (as might be expected with his metre). **13–15** The momentousness of an earthquake and a solar eclipse recalls such events reported at Christ's crucifixion: Matt. 27: 45, 51. Noted by A. T. Tolley, *My Proper Ground: A Study of the Work of Philip Larkin and its Development* (1991), 120. **16** Cf. *The Trimdon Grange Explosion*, 15: 'Death will pay us all a visit, they have only gone before'.

18 Cf. 1 Cor. 13: 12 'For now we see through a glass, darkly; but then face to face'; 3 John 5: 14: 'But I trust I shall shortly see thee, and we shall speak face to face'. Noted in 'Counter-Intuitive Larkin' (2007), repr. in Leader (2009), 76, by Craig Raine, who also comments (77) that though the closest match for Larkin's phrasing is in R. F. Weymouth's 1903 translation of the New Testament ('but then we shall see them face to face'), 'Larkin is covered. He's quoting from the chapel walls.' 19 The combination of coal-mining and chapel-going suggests a location in South Wales to John Osborne, who notes that L's use of 'valley' in the drafts would confirm this: *AL*, 6 (Winter 1998/9), 33. 23–4 *walking . . . towards them*: Cf. *The Trimdon Grange Explosion*, 39: 'We may meet the Trimdon victims'. 25 While conceding that the eggs may be 'a moving image of the fragility of life', James Booth, *AL*, 22 (Oct. 2006), 6, expresses unease at L's apparent naivety in thinking that the miner's lodging the nest in the grass (l. 9) restores it to the parent birds: 'the miner himself has already destroyed the potential life of these eggs by pulling the nest out of the grass . . .There is something very problematic about the unbrokenness of the shells as an image of life, since unbroken or not, the miner has ensured that these eggs can never hatch.'

OTHER POEMS PUBLISHED
IN THE POET'S LIFETIME

BEFORE *THE NORTH SHIP*

Winter Nocturne

DATE AND TEXT

Published in *The Coventrian* (magazine of Larkin's school), 158
(Dec. 1938), 559. Possibly written earlier that year: in Hull DPL
(2) 1/1/10/19 L gives the date 'Summer, 1938' as the time when he
'began to write poetry of a descriptive kind, about trees and the
sky and the seasons', and he gives *Winter Nocturne* as an example.
Reprinted in *CP* (1988), 225, and in Tolley (2005), 4. Both print
from L's t.s. (Hull DPL 3/1), though, misleadingly, they mention only
the first printing.

VARIANTS (from *The Coventrian*)
2 footsteps] footstep
3 drips] drops

Against a cutting of the printing in *The Coventrian*, L writes
'efficient halma': Hull DPL (2) 1/1/10/19. ('Halma' is a chequer-
board game.)
   1 L to JE, 20 May 1979 (*SL*, 601): '"Mantled in grey, the dusk
steals/creeps? slowly in" . . . still true!' Perhaps a reminiscence of
Milton, *Paradise Lost*, 4. 598–9: 'Now came still evening on, and
twilight grey | Had in her sober livery all things clad'. 11 *faded
summers*: Cf. *Afternoons*, 1: 'Summer is fading'. 11–14 *faded . . .
still: bowing, the woods . . . Dark . . . and leaves the world alone*:
Cf. Gray, *Elegy written in a Country Churchyard*, 5, 6, 28, 4: 'fades
. . . stillness . . . How bowed the woods . . . And leaves the world to
darkness and to me'.

Fragment from May

DATE AND TEXT
Published in *The Coventrian*, 158 (Dec. 1938), 560. Reprinted in *CP*
(1988), 226, and in Tolley (2005), 5.

477

5–6 Cf. Wordsworth, 'I wandered lonely as a cloud', 4–6: 'A host, of golden daffodils . . . Fluttering and dancing in the breeze'.

Summer Nocturne

DATE AND TEXT
Published in *The Coventrian*, 159 (Apr. 1939), 593. Reprinted in *CP* (1988), 227, and in Tolley (2005), 11, in each case with a full stop for the comma at the end of l. 5 and a colon for the semicolon at the end of l. 6.

Street Lamps

DATE AND TEXT
Published in *The Coventrian*, 160 (Sept. 1939), 644. Reprinted in *CP* (1988), 230, and in Tolley (2005) with the comma missing at the end of l. 10.

1–4 Reminiscent, in setting and in metaphor, of Eliot, *The Love Song of J. Alfred Prufrock*, 4 ('half-deserted streets'), 15–16ff. ('The yellow fog that rubs its back upon the window-panes, I The yellow smoke that rubs its muzzle on the window-panes'), and *Preludes*, I. 11, 13 ('at the corner of the street', 'the lighting of the lamps'). 3–4 Marcus Italiani notes a similar personification in Eliot's *Rhapsody on a Windy Night*, 8–9, 14–16, etc. ('Every street lamp that I pass I Beats like a fatalistic drum'; 'The street-lamp sputtered, I The street-lamp muttered, I The street-lamp said'): 'Philip Larkin – "A Youth in Winter"', *Philip Larkin's 'Best Society', Politische Einstellung und Gesellschaftskritik*, ed. Sascha Arnautovic and Marcus Italiani (2006), 12–13.

Spring Warning

DATE AND TEXT
Published in *The Coventrian*, 161 (Apr. 1940), 689. Reprinted in *CP* (1988), 237, and in Tolley (2005), 64. In each case, only *The Coventrian* is cited, but the source followed is L's t.s. (Hull DPL 3/1), and in each case also a colon is printed for the semicolon at the end of l. 2.

VARIANTS (from *The Coventrian*)
3–5 [Not indented]
 6 turf] grass
10 mutter] mutter softly
12–14 [Not indented]

15–16 Cf. *High Windows*, 17–18: 'Rather than words comes the thought of high windows: | The sun-comprehending glass'. 18 Cf. *Light, Clouds, Dwelling-places*, 29: 'Riding down into the blinding gulch.'

Last Will and Testament

DATE AND TEXT
Published in *The Coventrian*, 162 (Sept. 1940), 734–5, where the authors were identified as 'B. N. Hughes and P. A. Larkin'. Hughes told Jeff Vent that they composed the first verse together and after that each wrote alternate verses. Reprinted in *CP* (1988), 250–2, and in Tolley (2005), 129–31, with the titles 'Wizards' and 'Magnets' in l. 31 in italics (as in the present edition).

Annotation of this poem has benefited considerably from information supplied by Jeff Vent and, through him, by A. P. Montgomery.
   The poem imitates *Auden and MacNeice: Their Last Will and Testament* in *Letters from Iceland* (1937), as Motion (1993), 33, notes.
   2 *Bernard Noel Hughes*: 1921–2010; he was at school with L and went up to St John's College, Oxford, with him in 1940. For further information, see *SL*, xxviii. **3** *Philip Arthur Larkin*: L's full name. **12** *viscera*: entrails. **15** *panatrope*: brand-name of an (electric) record-player. *OED*'s earliest example is from 1926. **27** *Kipling's 'If'*: a poem about the virtues of manliness ('If you can keep you head when all about you | Are losing theirs and blaming it on you'). **30** *swimming master*: Mattocks. **31** *Magnets* . . . *Wizards*: boys' magazines. **36** *French master*: Head of Modern Languages G. H. ('Freddie') Horne. *Maginot Line*: the line of fortifications built before the 1939–45 war along France's eastern border, and in which the French placed excessive confidence. Named after André Maginot (1877–1932), French Minister of War. **38** *English Master*: L. W. Kingsland, who succeeded M. T.

Mason on his retirement. On Mason, see the note on *Coventria*,
21. 40 *German master*: Frank Liddiard. 42 *Iron Cross*: German
and Austrian military decoration for distinguished services in
war. 43 *Art Master*: the unpopular C. B. Shore. 44 *Philistines*:
uncultured persons, as in Arnold's *Culture and Anarchy* (1869).
51 *the Carpenter*: He in fact combined the roles of carpenter,
groundsman and Head's gardener. 52 *Paul Montgomery*: [Arthur]
Paul Montgomery attended the school, 1933–40. 54 *H. B. Gould*:
Herbert Barrington Gould, who attended the school, 1930–40. He
was killed in an air raid *c*.1941. 55 *William Rider*: William [Henry]
Rider (d. 2005), who attended the school, 1933–40. After war
service, he read law at Birmingham University, and for many years
worked locally at the law firm of Ward & Rider. Colin Gunner to
L, 2 Nov. 1971 (Hull DP 179/2/6): '*BILL RYDER* is an oak tree of
local responsibility – solicitor, Golf Club, Round Table – the lot.' 61
Percy Slater: Philip Slater, who attended the school, 1933–40. 65
F. G. Smith: Frank George Smith, who attended the school, 1933–
40. He went up to Oriel College, Oxford, but, owing to the college
being taken over by the Ministry of Information, spent much of his
time at Hertford College. He had a career in schoolteaching, ending
at Trinity School, New York, where he taught classics for over
twenty years. Colin Gunner to L, 2 Nov. 1971 (Hull DP 179/2/6):
'*F. G. Smith* I met years ago in a pub and was in New York as a
teacher. Also a homo!' 66 *Cutex*: brand of nail varnish remover. Jeff
Vent recounts that L did in fact leave Smith a compact and some
Cutex. 68 *Coventrian*: the school magazine. *Ian Fraser*: Ian [Weir]
Fraser, who attended the school, 1935–41.

Ultimatum

DATE AND TEXT
Before July 1940. Included in *FP*, and in *ChP* as (ii) of 'Two
Preliminary Sonnets', (i) being 'The world in its flowing is various;
as tides'. Published in *The Listener*, 24. 620 (28 Nov. 1940), 776
(not Oct. 1940, as L told RC in a letter of 27 July 1955: *SL*, 247).
L, 'Not the Place's Fault' (*FR*, 11): 'during the cloudless summer
of 1940 I sent four poems to *The Listener*. I was astonished when
someone calling himself J.R.A. wrote back, saying he would like to
take one (it was the one I had put in to make the others seem better,
but never mind)'. J. R. Ackerley (1896–1967) was literary editor
of *The Listener*, 1935–59. The poem is reprinted by AT in *The*

Survival of Poetry: a Contemporary Survey, ed. Martin Dodsworth
(1970), 38, in *CP* (1988), 243, and in Tolley (2005), 97, where
Tolley does not record that the poem is in *ChP*.

VARIANTS
Title Sonnet *FP*; [No title in *ChP*]
7 saying] maxim *FP*
11 Remember] Think of *FP*
when] as *FP*, *ChP*
12 safety] freedom *FP*, *ChP*

'Nicely obscure': L's comment written to the right of the title in *FP*.
Motion (1993), 34: 'Audenesque . . . Half-buried under its
literary borrowings.' Bradford (2005), 40: 'reads like a thesaurus of
Auden's phrasings and metrical orchestrations'. Nicholas Jenkins in
Leader (2009), 49: 'paralysingly Audenesque, not least in its almost
voluptuous sense of menace and doom'.
9 Cf. MacNeice, *The Hebrides*, 100–10: 'death is still | No lottery
ticket', 'On those islands | Where no train runs on rails', 'There
is still peace though not for me and not | perhaps for long – still
peace'. 13 *lianas*: tropical climbing plants.

Story

DATE AND TEXT
Begun Oct. 1940. Referring to the poem, L tells JBS in a letter of
Mar. 1942 (Hull DP 174/2/39) that 'It seems amazing that I wrote
that about 18 months ago, in my first term.' Poem XXXII in *ChP*.
Published in *Cherwell*, 61. 4 (13 Feb. 1941), 50, in a continuous
text. However, on a cutting (DPL 3/1) L indicates that there should
be gaps after ll. 8 and 13, and these were inserted in *CP* (1988), 257,
and in Tolley (2005), 141.

VARIANTS (from *ChP*)
Title [No title]
11 Yet he at times] And yet sometimes
13 the children and the rocks] all the rocks and children

A Writer

DATE AND TEXT
Poem XXXIII in *ChP*. Published in *Cherwell*, 62. 2 (8 May 1941),
20. On a photocopy of the printed text (Hull DPL 3/1) L writes
in 'away' after 'Explained' in l. 11, and this corrected version was
reprinted in *CP* (1988), 263, and in Tolley (2005), 151.

VARIANTS (from *ChP*)
Title [No title]
10 his] a
lying] frightened
11 Explained away] Could tolerate
14 did not see] never saw

Stan Smith notes that the poem is modelled most directly on Auden's
'A shilling life will give you all the facts', but mixes in a pastiche
of Auden's *In Time of War* sequence: 'Something for Nothing: Late
Larkins and Early', *English*, 49 (Autumn 2000), 264.

3 Smith, 265, notes the repetition of 'Nothing' in Auden's
Matthew Arnold, and, more generally, that the poems 'share key
rhymes on "face"' and 'focus on the idea of a thwarted, solitary
gift'. 10 Smith, 265, views L's 'foolish, lying race' as the equivalent
of Auden's 'gregarious optimistic generation' in *Matthew Arnold*,
15. 13–14 Smith, 265, notes the motif in Auden's *September 1,
1939*, 42–4, of not recognising the face in the mirror to be one's
own.

May Weather

DATE AND TEXT
Published in *Cherwell*, 62. 6 (5 June 1941), 92: copy-text. Hull
DPL 2/2/48 (t.s.). Reprinted from *Cherwell* in *CP* (1988), 261,
and in Tolley (2005), 153. On pp. 153–4 Tolley also reprinted L's
revised version from *7P*, which dates from Jan. 1942, later than the
Cherwell printing.

VARIANTS (from *7P*)
1 A week ago today
13 was] is
14 Then] Now
15 impressive] enormous

1–2 On a cutting of the *Cherwell* printing (Hull DPL 3/1) L quotes *After-Dinner Remarks*, iv. 13–14: 'so, while summer on this day | Enacts her dress rehearsals'.

Observation

DATE AND TEXT
'18 / xi / 41' is written by L on Hull DPL 2/2/49 (t.s. with holograph corrections). A version of the first two lines is written below a draft of 'Sailors brought back strange stories of those lands' (Hull DPL 2/2/45), written between Apr. and 18 Nov. 1941. On 20 Nov. 1941 L included the whole poem except for the title in a letter to JBS (*SL*, 28). Poem VII in *7P*. It was published with the title *Observation* in the O[xford] U[niversity] L[abour] C[lub] B[ulletin], 3. 7 (22 Nov. 1941), 10.

On cuttings (Hull DPL 3/1; Bodl. MS Facs. c. 1670) L corrects 'is the air' to 'it is air' in l. 6 and 'the' to 'our' in l. 7, and these revisions were incorporated in the text printed in *CP* (1988), 264, and in Tolley (2005), 158.

VARIANTS
Title [No title] *letter to JBS* or *7P*; ~~Sonnet at the Junction~~ [No alternative title] *Hull DPL 2/2/49*
1–8 [Continuous in letter to JBS and *7P*]
  2 dreams] books
  meet] touch *DPL 2/2/45*
  4 proofed against] free from all
  suspense] expense *7P*
  6 walk] ~~stand~~ walk *Hull DPL 2/2/49*
  8 When] Where *letter to JBS*
9–14 [Continuous in *letter to JBS*]
  10 Machine-gun] Rifle *7P*
  13 picturesque] ~~picturesque~~ beautiful picturesque *Hull DPL 2/2/49*

Disintegration

DATE AND TEXT
Published in O[xford] U[niversity] L[abour] C[lub] B[ulletin] (Feb. 1942). Reprinted in *CP* (1988), 266, and in Tolley (2005), 167.

8 *shaven lawn*. As in MacNeice, *Autumn Journal*, 2; from Milton,

Il Penseroso, 66: 'smooth-shaven green'. See *Hard Lines, or Mean Old W. H. Thomas Blues*, 19. **17** *simian*: ape-like.

Mythological Introduction

DATE AND TEXT
Published in *Arabesque*, [2] (Hilary Term [Jan.–Mar.], 1943), 5, and then in *Oxford Poetry 1942–3*, ed. Ian Davie (12 June 1943), 42 (copy-text). Reprinted from the latter source in *CP* (1988), 268, and in Tolley (2005), 199, though in both cases the first printing is the only early source mentioned.

VARIANTS (from *Arabesque*)
5–8 [Not indented]
  7 crossroads] crossways
  9 She rose up] Rising
  10 And] She

L to JBS, 14 May 1943 (Hull DP 174/2/64) judges it to be 'fairly good', but in another letter to JBS, 15 June 1943 (Hull DP 174/2/67) he pronounces both it and *Poem* ('I dreamed of an outstretched arm of land', later *TNS* XXI) 'rather gutless'.

A Stone Church Damaged by a Bomb

DATE AND TEXT
Possibly by 16 Mar. 1943, when L told JBS, 'I am trying to gatecrash another anthology, or have I told you? Nothing exciting, "Oxford Poetry" 1942–3': *SL*, 55. The poem appeared in *Oxford Poetry 1942–3*, ed. Ian Davie (12 June 1943), 41: copy-text. Davie states in his prefatory note that the anthology '*has been made, as far as possible, representative of the poetry written by members of the university within the last year; that is, from the Spring of 1942 to the Spring of 1943*'. Reprinted in *CP* (1988), 269, and in Tolley (2005), 200.

L to JBS, 14 May 1943 (Hull DP 174/2/64), mentioning the three poems published in *Oxford Poetry*: '1 is very good, 1 is fairly good, and 1 is rather stupid and bad.' To JBS, 15 June 1943 (Hull DP 174/2/67), referring to this poem: 'The first one is all right except for the last line.' To KA, 19 Oct. 1943 (*SL*, 80): Ian Davie 'says that out of the 14 reviews of "Oxford Poetry" he has seen, 5 mention

"A Stone Church Damaged by a Bum" and one quotes it in full, so you can take me, young Amis, as the organ-voice of Old England. The genital-organ voice.' (L refers to Tennyson, *Milton*, 3: 'God-gifted organ-voice of England'.)

Motion (1993), 49, relates the poem to L's memories of German air raids on Coventry in 1940. The cathedral was famously destroyed and its ruins much photographed thereafter.

BEFORE *THE LESS DECEIVED*

Plymouth

DATE AND TEXT
Wkbk 1 contains: a draft of nine lines, including ll. 1–4 (1/1/27), after '11. 4. 45', dated '10 / 6 / 45' at the end; a complete draft (1/1/29) dated '15 / 6 / 45' at the end; and a further draft of ll. 13–18 (1/1/29) dated '25 / 6 [1945]' at the end. Hull DPL 2/2/8 is a t.s. with one holograph correction in pencil. Included in *ITGOL*. Published in *Mandrake*, 3 (May 1946), 19 (copy-text), where it and *Portrait* (see next poem) were attributed to 'Phillip Larkin'. On a photocopy now in Hull DPL 3/1 L corrected this and remarked 'Good old JBW', referring to John Wain, who edited the magazine. Reprinted in *CP* (1988), 307, and in Tolley (2005), 279. L did not correct 'rust' in l. 13 on the photocopy, but the texts in *Wkbk 1* and Hull DPL 2/2/8, and the revised text in *ITGOL*, all have 'rest', which strongly suggests that 'rust' is a misprint. In the present edition, therefore, 'rest' (despite 'the rusted hands rest on a stick' in 'Evening, and I, young', 32).

VARIANTS
14 be] ~~lie~~ be *Hull DPL 2/2/8*; lie *ITGOL*
15 casual] common *Hull DPL 2/2/8, ITGOL*
16 Lying in] Symbols that *ITGOL*
for] through *ITGOL*
17 chance lives] a chance life *Hull DPL 2/2/8*; my life *ITGOL*
had not] never *ITGOL*

11 *rivers of Eden*: Gen. 2: 10, 13, 14. *rivers of blood*: Ps. 78: 44: 'turned their rivers into blood'; Rev. 16: 4: 'the rivers . . . became blood'.

Portrait

DATE AND TEXT

The unique draft in *Wkbk 1* (1/1/39) of the whole poem except for the title comes after '23 / 9 / 45', and is dated '7. 10. 45' at the end. *CP* (1988), 309, *CP* (2003), 208, and Tolley (2005), 287, all give this wrongly as 7 Nov. 1945. Published in *Mandrake*, 3 (May 1946), 19: see the note on the previous poem. L corrected the misprint 'grown' to 'grow' (l. 7) on a photocopy of this printing now in Hull DPL 3/1. The copy-text is the 1946 printing, with this correction. Included in *ITGOL*.

VARIANTS
Title The quiet one *ITGOL*

Fiction and the Reading Public

DATE AND TEXT

Wkbk 1 contains: a draft of ll. 1–3 after '13 May [1949]' (1/1/78); a draft of ll. 1–8 and an additional eight lines (possibly an alternative version of 9–16), and a page of drafts incorporating the title, verse 1 and parts of verses 2 and 3 between '18. 5. 49' and '31. 12. 49' (1/1/80); a draft of twelve lines, some of them related to verse 2, in Hull DPL 1/2/56, part of page 79 torn from *Wkbk 1*, with the date '19. v. 49' on the other side; and a complete draft dated '25. 2. 50' (1/1/96). Included in Hull DPL 4/10 (t.s.), *Round the Point*, 'débat inédit', 1950: see *TAWG*, 471–2. Published in *EIC*, 4. 1 (Jan. 1954), 86 (copy-text), and in *CP* (1988), 34.

VARIANTS (from Hull DPL 4/10)
13 plaits up the threads] 'plaits up the threads'
14 ~~And m~~Makes 'all for the best' ['the' inserted above caret]
15 That we may] So that we can
19 bull] balls
21 And let me suck up your sensations
22 Laugh, weep, masturbate
23 ~~If you~~ Just

L to MJ, 26 Aug. 1951 (Bodl. MS Eng. c. 7405/133): 'I sent a bit of doggerel to Bateson – a sort of splenetive A. P. H. [A. P. Herbert, 1890–1971] poem about novel-writing.' (F. W. Bateson, 1901–78, founded *Essays in Criticism* in 1951, and edited the journal till

1972.) When it was to be published in *EIC*, L referred to the poem as 'a short jeering poem of mine' that was 'written in 1950': to MJ, 7 July 1953 (Bodl. MS Eng. c. 7408/33). In a letter of 13 Apr. 1976 (*SL*, 537–8), L suggested it to KA for his *New Oxford Book of Light Verse*. (It was included.) L to KA, 18 June 1976 (*SL*, 543): 'hope it looks as good as you remember'.

Title Q. D. Leavis, *Fiction and the Reading Public* (1932). 1, 2 *Give me . . . Give me*: Giving the reader what he or she wants is a cliché. 8 L in 1982 (*RW*, 71): 'I can't understand these chaps who go round American universities explaining how they write poems: it's like going round explaining how you sleep with your wife.' 19 *bull*: rubbish, nonsense, 'bullshit'; *OED*, *n*.⁴ 3: 'slang (orig. U.S.)'. 24 Perhaps, as Osborne (2008), 24, suggests, a particular irony: F. R. Leavis's *The Great Tradition*, with its opening 'The great English novelists are . . .', was published in 1948.

BEFORE *THE WHITSUN WEDDINGS*

Pigeons

DATE AND TEXT
There are four holograph drafts, two of which are complete (Hull DPL 1/2/54). The second complete draft, with the title 'Pigeons in Winter', is dated '27 xii 55'. L sent a corrected t.s. of this poem and *Lambs* (later *First Sight*) under the heading 'Two Winter Pieces' with a letter to MJ dated 26 Feb. 1956 (Bodl. MS Eng. c. 7413/23). He originally regarded the two poems as companion-pieces: to MJ, 26 Feb. 1956 (Bodl. MS Eng. c. 7413/19). Published in *Departure*, 4. 11 (Jan. 1957), 2 (copy-text), and in *CP* (1988), 109.

VARIANTS
2 against] ~~against~~ to Bodl. MS

Tops

DATE AND TEXT
Wkbk 3 (1/3/20) contains, after '13 x. 53' (seven pages earlier), two pages bearing two complete drafts, each with the title 'You're the tops', dated '22. x. 53' and '24. x. 53' respectively. Published in *Listen*, 2. 2 (Spring 1957), 6, (not 3. 2, as Bloomfield, 102, states). L notes on a cutting of the *Listen* printing (Hull DPL 3/1), 'Orig.

called "You're the tops"'. Reprinted in *CP* (1988), 76, and *CP* (2003), 175, with 'tiny first' for 'first tiny' (l. 20).

L refers to it as 'an old no-good one you haven't seen called *Tops*' in a letter to MJ dated 8 May 1956 (Bodl. MS Eng. c. 7413/87). He owned a spinning top: *AL*, 15 (Apr. 2003), 21.

Success Story

DATE AND TEXT
Wkbk 3 (1/3/41) contains four pages of drafts after '27. 1. 54', including two complete drafts dated '9. iii. 54' and '11-3-54' respectively. Published in *The Grapevine*, University of Durham Institute of Education, 4 (Feb. 1957), 8, and in *Beloit Poetry Journal*, 8. 2 (Winter 1957–8), 36. Reprinted in *CP* (1988), 88.

VARIANTS (from *The Grapevine*, 1957)
4 *I*] *you*
5 They] we
6 that I] I that

In a letter to MJ dated 22 Oct. 1954 (Bodl. MS Eng. c. 7409/82), L expressed the view that 'Waiting for breakfast, while she brushed her hair' (*TNS* XXXII, to which see notes) said more about him than anything else '(except *To fail*)'. **12** *forbidding fruit*: Cf. 'forbidden fruit': the fruit forbidden to Adam and Eve (Gen. 2: 17), as in Milton, *Paradise Lost*, 1. 1–2: 'the fruit | Of that forbidden tree'; often referring to illicit love.

Modesties

DATE AND TEXT
In *Wkbk 1* (1/1/76) five pages of drafts after '18. 3. 49' are followed by a fair copy dated '13 May 1949' at the end. Poem II in *XX Poems*: copy-text. Reprinted in *Humberside* (Hull Literary Club), 13. 1 (Autumn 1958), 29, in *Poetry Book Society Bulletin*, 40 (Feb. 1964), 1–2, in *Encounter*, 22. 3 (Mar. 1964), 28, and in *CP* (1988), 26.

In a letter to MJ dated 26 Nov. 1950 (Bodl. MS Eng. c. 7404/1), L confessed to liking the poem.

5, 7 *pence* | *sense*: Rhyme in W. B. Yeats, *September 1913*, 1, 3.

Breadfruit

DATE AND TEXT
Wkbk 6 contains a draft of the whole poem on a single page dated
'19. 11. 61' at the top and '19. xi. 61' at the end. Published in a
revised text in *Critical Quarterly*, ed. C. B. Cox, 3. 4 (Winter 1961),
309. CP (1988), 141, printed 'brides' for 'bribes' (l. 3); corrected in
1988 reprint.

L told MB the poem was written 'out of frustration when you
refused to come round last night!': Brennan (2002), 59. L to RC, 9
Dec. 1961 (*SL*, 335): 'Dig a little squib of mine called Breadfruit in
Cox's mag – bitterly regret letting him have it, as it is just about the
worst poem I have ever let get set up. Don't get any breadfruit up
here, I can tell you.'
    Title Melon-sized fruit from the South Sea islands, etc. HMS
Bounty set sail in 1787 in search of breadfruit plants, and the crew
formed intimate relationships with the native women on Tahiti,
where the fruit was cultivated. On 'Whatever they are' (ll. 2, 16),
Douglas Porteous, *AL*, 24 (Oct. 2007), 23, comments: 'This . . . is
not ignorance. Larkin the librarian knew all about Captain Bligh.'
The 1935 film of *The Mutiny on the Bounty*, starring Charles
Laughton and Clark Gable, raised consciousness of the expedition.
A remake, starring Marlon Brando, was scheduled for 1962. There
may, too, be a reminiscence of Eliot, *Fragment of an Agon*, 55, 61–3:
'*Where the breadfruit fall*', '*Where the Gauguin maids . . . Wear
palmleaf drapery.*' 6 *Mecca*: dance-hall.

BEFORE *HIGH WINDOWS*

Love

DATE AND TEXT
Wkbk 6 (1/6/25) contains six and a half pages of drafts of the whole
poem between '7. xi. 62' and '7. 12. 62'. Published in *Critical
Quarterly*, 8. 2 (Summer 1966), 173. Reprinted in CP (1988), 150.
Hull DPL 1/8/40 is a t.s. with a holograph correction, inserted
loosely at the beginning of *Wkbk 8*. The copy-text is the latest

version, Hull DPL 1/6/43, a t.s. loosely inserted at the front of *Wkbk* 6 which contains revisions of the *CQ* version.

VARIANTS
4 an] someone's *DPL 1/8/40, CQ, 1966*
8 How can you] Who can *DPL 1/8/40, CQ, 1966*
9 Putting] With putting *DPL 1/8/40*
12 ignore] deny *DPL 1/8/40, CQ, 1966*
13 Still] ~~Still~~ Yet ?Well *DPL 1/8/40*; Yet *CQ, 1966*
or] and *DPL 1/8/40*
14 suits] still suits *DPL 1/8/40, CQ, 1966*
15 Something the bleeder who *DPL 1/8/40*
found] who *CQ, 1966*
16 Can't manage either view *DPL 1/8/40 CQ, 1966*
17–18 Alone feels the lack of – | And he can jack off. *DPL 1/8/40*

L to MJ, 21 May 1966, referring to C. B. Cox: 'He is going to print a poem of mine (called *Love*) I cut out of *TWW* as too shallow & offensive. Looks jolly good now': Bodl. MS Eng. c. 7433/39. To Cox, 3 Oct. 1969 (*SL*, 419): 'I thought it rather good'. To Campbell Burnap, 26 Apr. 1976 (Hull DPL (2) 2/16/57): '"Love" would normally have been collected in *High Windows*, but I thought there were enough poems striking that particular note without it, and so I left it out.' L in 1979 (*RW*, 54): 'I think living with someone and being in love is a very difficult business anyway because almost by definition it means putting yourself at the disposal of someone else, ranking them higher than yourself. I wrote a little poem about this [quotes two verses of *Love* and refers to third verse]. I think love collides very sharply with selfishness, and they're both pretty powerful things.'
15 *bleeder*: contemptible person; '*low slang*' (*OED*).

'When the Russian tanks roll westward'

DATE AND TEXT
L includes it in a letter to BP dated 18 Mar. 1969 (Bodl. MS Pym 151/56). Published in *Black Paper Two: The Crisis in Education*, ed. C. B. Cox and A. E. Dyson (London, Critical Quarterly Society, 1969), 133, and reprinted in *CP* (1988), 172.

L to C. B. Cox, 22 Aug. 1969 (*SL*, 418): 'Yes, do use my couplet: fake up a quotation to precede it, e.g. "For the first time in history

Her Majesty's Government is spending more on education than on the armed services" – Rt Hon Edward Short, Minister of Education.' There was no need for faking: when the couplet was quoted in *The Times* on 8 Oct. 1969, the columnist 'PHS' cited Short's speech containing the statement exactly as given by L as having prompted it. L to MJ, 20 May 1968 (Bodl. MS Eng. c. 7437/41): 'I do sympathise with you over these poxy students. Don't they look a fearful crew at Essex. And the staff sound just as bad.' L to MJ, 10 Aug. 1968 (Bodl. MS Eng. c. 7437/117–18): 'I'd like to write a poem about the next war, & how the LSE Fusiliers will go into action, flanked by the Essex University Dragoons, not to mention the Pakistani Artillery & West Indian Marines. They'd hold the enemy up for as long as it took them to be able to stand up and laugh at the same time.'

L to BP, 18 Mar. 1969: 'I feel deeply humiliated at living in a country that spends more on education than on defence': Bodl. MS Pym 151/56. In a letter of 13 Apr. 1976 (*SL*, 537), L suggested the poem to KA for inclusion in his *New Oxford Book of Light Verse*. (It was not chosen.)

2 *Colonel Sloman's Essex Rifles*: Dr Albert E. Sloman was Vice-Chancellor of the University of Essex. *L.S.E.*: the London School of Economics, well known at the time for student protests. In his letter to BP, L adds the comment 'Or possibly that mythological company known in the War as "The King's Own Enemy Aliens": Pioneers, were they?'

How

DATE AND TEXT
Wkbk 7 (1/7/36) contains a draft of the whole poem except for the title on a page dated '10. 4. 70' at the top. '6. 5. 70' is at the top of the next page. Hull DPL 1/7/62 is a t.s. with holograph corrections, inserted loosely at the back of *Wkbk* 7. Published in *Wave*, 1 (Autumn 1970), 32 (copy-text), and reprinted in *CP* (1988), 176.

VARIANTS (from DPL 1/7/62)
Title [No title]
7 now for kindness] ~~to be quiet now~~ of kind climates
8 Spring is held back, somewhere.
10 ~~And widely separated~~ h~~H~~eld apart ~~by~~ ~~Parted~~ Separated by
11 ~~By~~ Of housing estates, ~~of~~ and children

4 Motion (1993), 420, notes that L could see Hull Royal Infirmary from the university library where he worked. 7 *kindness*: 'I wish the second verse were better. I think "mildness" instead of "kindness", don't you?': L to MJ, 5 Nov. 1970 (Bodl. MS Eng. c. 7442/24).

Heads in the Women's Ward

DATE AND TEXT
Wkbk 8 (1/8/5) contains a unique draft on a page dated '6 / 3 / 72' at the top. Hull DPL 1/8/37 is a t.s. with holograph corrections in pencil, loosely inserted at the front of *Wkbk 8*. The copy-text is Hull DPL (2) 1/5/4 (t.s.). Published in *New Humanist*, 1. 1 (May 1972), 17, and reprinted in *CP* (1988), 194.

VARIANTS (from Hull DPL 1/8/37)
3 stand] ~~stick~~ stand
9 Smiles are for youth] ~~In youth is joy Joy is~~ Smiles are for youth
For] ~~In~~ For

L to KA, 18 May 1972 (Huntington MS AMS 353-393): 'My Mother is in a Nursing Home, not very well, wch is a worry & v. time-consuming: also starts up a chain-reaction of <u>gloomy reflections</u> on one's own account.'

Continuing to Live

DATE AND TEXT
Wkbk 3 (1/3/48) contains two pages of drafts after '18. 4. 54', including a complete draft dated '24. 4. 54' at the end. Hull DPL 2/3/8, is a t.s. with holograph corrections. In l. 10 L inserts a caret and writes 'can' in the margin as the word to be added. Published in *A Keepsake for the New Library*, School of African and Oriental Studies, University of London, 5 Oct. 1973, p. [9], with the misprint 'is' for 'it' (l. 18): this, with the misprint corrected, is the copy-text. Reprinted in *CP* (1988), 94.

VARIANTS (from Hull DPL 2/3/8)
7 Discarding them, ~~might~~ we might draw a full house!
10 command] can command
18 what it] ~~where that~~ what it
19 Since it ~~only~~ applied only ~~to one person man~~ once, ~~to~~ but ~~to~~ to one person once,

20 ~~And that one Who now is Who's now~~ dying. And that one dying.

L described it to B. C. Bloomfield, 27 June 1973 (SL, 484), as 'a completely unpublished mediocre poem'.

10 *lading-list*: official inventory of a ship's cargo. 17 *that green evening*: Cf. Keats, *Endymion*, ii. 71: 'the green evening'.

AFTER *HIGH WINDOWS*

The Life with a Hole in it

DATE AND TEXT
Wkbk 8 (1/8/19) contains a draft of the whole poem on a single page dated '7. 8. 74' at the top and '8 / 8/ 74' at the bottom. Printed on p. [25] of the *Poetry Supplement* which L compiled for The Poetry Book Society (Christmas, 1974), and reprinted in *CP* (1988), 202.

L to B. C. Bloomfield, 4 Dec. 1974 (SL, 515), on the poem: 'what my old friend Edmund Crispin calls "demotic", I believe'. L sending the poem to KA, 13 Apr. 1976 (SL, 537), when KA was collecting material for his *New Oxford Book of Light Verse*: 'it's hardly "light verse"'.

Title Booth (1992), 100, notes the advertising slogan for Polomints: 'the mint with the hole'. **9–16** 'I've never written anything it wasn't a pleasure to work at. All this 500 words a day stuff is so much bilge': L to MJ, 1 Nov. 1951 (Bodl. MS Eng. c. 7406/65). 'I was about 23, & hoped I was going to lead that wonderful 500-words-a-day on-the-Riviera life that beckons us all like an *ignis fatuus* from the age of 16 onwards, but alas I wasn't good enough': L to BP, 18 Nov. 1961, looking back at the time he wrote *AGIW* (SL, 334). 'I felt a bit cheated. I'd had visions of myself writing 500 words a day for six months, shoving the result off to the printer and going to live on the Côte d'Azur, uninterrupted except for the correction of proofs. It didn't happen like that – very frustrating': L in 1979 on his attempts to write a third novel after the publication of *AGIW* in Feb. 1947 (RW, 49). L to Jonathan Price, 22 Dec. 1984 (SL, 725): 'Please don't think (if you did) that I was knocking the sh. in the sh. ch. – he was the man my hero most wanted to be, while the sp. sch. sod was the man he least wanted to be. What happens [. . .] is something in between.' **14** John Osborne, Booth (2008), 148, notes the echo of W. H. Auden's earliest *Shorts*: 'many a spectacled sod'. **17–24** L to MB, 7 Aug. 1962 (*SL*, 344): 'Looking back on my first 40 years, I think what strikes me most is that hardly any of the things that are supposed to happen or be so do in fact happen or are so. What little happens or is so isn't at all expected or agreeable. And I don't feel that everything could have been different if only I'd acted differently – to have acted differently I shd have needed to have *felt* differently, to have *been* different, wch means going back years and years, out of my lifetime.' To MJ, 18 Sept. 1966 (Bodl. MS Eng. c. 7434/6): 'I have never in my life felt I had free will, have you?'

'I hope games like tossing the caber'

DATE AND TEXT
1977, when it was published in the in-house magazine of Faber and Faber, *Newslink*, 20 ([Nov.] 1977), [3]. The limerick was sent by L on the back of a card depicting a Scotsman trying to pull a telegraph pole out of the ground. Reprinted in Thwaite (1982), 46, where CM describes it as the 'Second Faber Limerick' (the first being 'There was an old fellow of Kaber').

Aubade

DATE AND TEXT
Wkbk 8 contains: seven and a half pages of drafts (with the title '<u>Aubade</u>') of the first two stanzas and the first four lines of the third, as well as other lines not represented in the final poem, after '11. 4. 74', with the last page dated '7. 6. 74' at the top (1/8/18); and a draft of ll. 1–7 on a page dated '18. 5. 77' at the top, followed by ten pages of drafts of the whole poem after '28. 5. [1977]', dated '29. 11. 77' at the end.

L to BP, 27 June 1977: 'I get up at 6 when I can and try to add to a poem about DEATH. Not making much progress, but one can only hope – to finish the poem, I mean. It was begun in 1974': Bodl. MS Pym 152/13. To WA, 13 Dec. 1977 (*SL*, 573): 'I did round off an old one recently and it will appear in the TLS called *Aubade*.' To JB, 14 Jan. 1978 (*SL*, 576): 'The first three stanzas had been hanging about since 1974, and I finished them off this Autumn.' Similarly, L to George Hartley, 6 Mar. 1978: Hartley (1988), 4. L completed the poem after his mother's death on 17 Nov. 1977 at the age of

91. L to Simon Petch, 26 July 1981 (*SL*, 652): 'the only substantial poem I have done since *High Windows*'. To B. C. Bloomfield, 6 Dec. 1977: 'See the *TLS* on 23 December for a real infusion of Christmas cheer by yours truly! Don't miss this! Green stamps given': *AL*, 4 (Oct. 1977), 22. Published in *TLS*, 3952 (23 Dec. 1977), 1491. Amis, *Memoirs* (1991), 62, notes that L 'published it separately as a little pamphlet': for details see Bloomfield (2002), 47. I have seen a copy in which L supplied the missing 'this' in l. 27. Reprinted in *CP* (1988), 208–9.

L to WA, 13 Dec. 1977 (*SL*, 573): 'Many thanks for writing so kindly about my mother. It has been a depressing year since about March, when she began to deteriorate (she had been in a nursing home for nearly six years), and the last few months of her life were scarcely livable. She would have been 92 in January!' L to Hartley, 6 Mar. 1978: 'My mother's death was a sad business, but the preceding year or so had been increasingly difficult for her; she could not move, or read, or make herself understood, and she was going blind. It was all a strange background against which to finish off the poem': Hartley (1988), 4. To Hartley, 30 Nov. 1977: 'it feels like the end of an era': Hartley (1988), 4.

L to MJ, 8 Nov. 1952 (Bodl. MS Eng. c. 7407/125–6): 'To me, since death is the most important thing about life (because it puts an end to life and extinguishes further hope of restitution or recompense, as well as any more experience), so the expression of death & the effects of death are the highest planes of literature [. . .] and should not be lightly loosed upon the populace [. . .] after death there's nothing.' To MJ, 19 Feb. 1955 (Bodl. MS Eng. c. 7410/62–3): 'I can't imagine how people can say "no use worrying about it, it's inevitable." That's *exactly why* I worry.' To MJ, 21 Mar. 1960 (Bodl. MS Eng. c. 7421/56): 'the terrors of life, that mostly I try to forget – death of loved ones, death of me'. To WA, 9 June 1977 (Bodl. MS Res. c. 616): 'I get less used to the fact of death as I grow older, & I was never very used to it.' To Kenneth Hibbert, 23 June 1977, Hull DPL (2) 2/15/143: 'I think death is the hardest thing in the world to come to terms with.' To KA, 12 Aug. 1977 (Huntington MS AMS 323-393): 'Poetry, that rare bird, has flown out of the window and now sings on some alien shore. In other words I just drink these days . . . I wake at four and lie worrying till seven. Loneliness. Death. Law suits. Talent gone. Law suits. Loneliness. Talent gone. Death. I really am not happy these days.' To BP, 14 Dec. 1977 (*SL*, 574):

'The TLS is going to print my in-a-funk-about-death poem [. . .] The death-throes of a talent.' To JB, 14 Jan. 1978 (*SL*, 576): 'I have had several other letters, including one from a lady of 72 who says she felt as I did once but now doesn't mind – the body "gets ready". Hum.' To BP, 14 Feb. 1978: '"Aubade", the death thing, or rather fear-of-death thing': Bodl. MS Pym 152/24. To W. G. Runciman, 26 Nov. 1978 (*SL*, 591): 'nothing really expunges the terror [of death]: it remains a sort of Bluebeard's chamber in the mind, something one is *always* afraid of – and this is bad for one'. To KA, 28 Oct. 1979 (*SL*, 608): 'I don't know that I ever expected much of life, but it terrifies me to think it's nearly over.'

Seamus Heaney, *The Redress of Poetry* (1995), 155–6, notes the transforming relocation of 'unresting' (l. 5), 'afresh' (l. 10), and 'dead' (l. 9) from *The Trees*, 9, 11, 12.

Christopher Fletcher in *N&Q*, NS 54. 2 (June 2007), 179–81, relates the poem to Betjeman's *Before the Anaesthetic, or A Real Fright*: L's 'The sure extinction that we travel to' is a response to Betjeman's 'Is it extinction when I die?'; L 'more succinctly identifies and rejects . . . liturgical sophistry'; L's 'The anaesthetic from which none come round' relates to Betjeman's title; and 'Betjeman's image of the last letter – to be posthumously received – is picked up and redelivered in Larkin's ominous concluding line "Postmen like doctors go from house to house".'

Title Traditionally, a joyful greeting of the dawn or a lament that lovers must part at dawn. L had precedents for an anti-aubade or for a bleaker modern aubade in poems with the same title by Empson and MacNeice, as Grevel Lindop notes: *British Poetry since 1970: A Critical Survey*, ed. Peter Jones and Michael Schmidt (1980), 53. 1 *I work all day*: L to BP, 17 Oct. 1968 (*SL*, 406): 'I wish I didn't have to work so hard: every day, all day.' To JE, 11 Jan. 1974 (*SL*, 498): 'my life at present resembles that of the French *plongeurs* in *Down & Out in Paris & London* – work all day, drink at night to forget it'. L in 1982 (*RW*, 57): 'My life is as simple as I can make it. Work all day, then cook, eat, wash up, telephone, hack writing, drink and television in the evenings.' L was always hard-working. To Michael Hamburger, 23 Oct. 1942: 'The reason for my lack of time for civilised occupations is, quite simply, work. I work all day': *PN Review*, 14. 4 (Dec. 1987), 73. *get half-drunk at night*: 'I am getting more of an alcoholic: I sit half-stewed each night': L to Richard and Patsy Murphy, 8 July 1957 (*SL*, 278). To C. B. Cox, 7 May 1981 (Hull DPL (2) 2/22/28): 'Despite a life-long opposition to work, I can't think what on earth I should do without it, bar drink myself to death.' Leggett (1999), 94, 97, notes that the first line is 'a blues line', and that 'working and drinking are the common properties of the blues, drinking most often as a way of coping with despair'. RC records that 'there was also talk . . . of a Blues version [of *Aubade*] – the first line coming in perfectly, perhaps the sign of a real "influence"': Thwaite (1982), 35. **2** *Waking at four*: See the letter to KA quoted above. Leggett (1999), 98, notes that this continues the blues convention of line 1 by alluding to 'one of the most common of all blues openings – "I woke up this morning" – but rephrasing it in nonblues language'. He also notes that the early morning is the time of the blues, and that 'it is also customary for the blues to specify the hour, and four o'clock turns out to be the most popular blues time for waking'. See the note below on l. 41. **3** Cf. *Jill*, 41, where John Kemp lies in bed in a state of fear 'watching the light grow round the edges of the shutters'. **4–10** L to PS, 3 Feb. 1954 (*SL*, 223): 'The passage of time, and the approach and arrival of death, still seems to me the most unforgettable thing about our existence.' L in 1959, reviewing John Betjeman (*FR*, 212): 'Fear of death is too much of a screaming close-up to allow the poetic faculty to function properly, but demands expression by reason of its very frightfulness.' Jean Hartley (1989), 72, records that 'fear of death was a subject which featured frequently in his conversation'. **6** Cf. Hugh MacDiarmid, *At My Father's Grave*, 7–8: 'A livin' man upon a deid man thinks, | And ony sma'er thocht's impossible.' **8–10** L reviewing *The Oxford Book of Death* in 1983 (*FR*, 347): 'What might with some justice be called the majority view, however – death is the end of everything, and thinking about it gives us a pain in the bowels – is poorly represented.' **9** *and being dead*: 'On first reading these words, I at once remembered a conversation that ended with Philip saying, "I'm not only [or perhaps "not so much"] frightened of dying," then shouting, "I'm afraid of being dead!"': Amis, *Memoirs* (1991), 62. Bruce Montgomery wrote a poem called 'Song After An Operation', which ended 'Death will soon be driving back, for the last time | But checked by decent rhymester's soothing rhyme, | Less in his terror'. On the t.s. L pencilled the comment: 'Well, I hope so. Personally I find it gets worse': Bodl. MS Eng. c. 3917/116. **16–18** L to Ray Brett, 25 Nov. 1977: 'It's just the thought of someone being wiped out of existence for ever that is so hard to comprehend': Motion (1993), 467. L in 1979 (*RW*, 55): 'If you ask why does it bother me, I can only say I dread endless

extinction.' L reviewing Richard Perceval Graves's *The Brothers Powys* in 1983 (*FR*, 340): 'But for Llewelyn the thought of extinction was unforgettable ("cold nights, cold years, cold centuries, alone in a cold elm-wood coffin"), while also heightening his awareness of physical existence and making the duty of self-fulfilment more compelling.' L in 1983 (*FR*, 345): 'Man's most remarkable talent is for ignoring death. For once the certainty of permanent extinction is realized, only a more immediate calamity can dislodge it from the mind, and then only temporarily.' **17** Cf. Edward Thomas, *The Glory*, 27–8: 'How dreary-swift, with naught to travel to, | Is Time?' **18–19** Andrew Swarbrick, *Out of Reach: The Poetry of Philip Larkin* (1995), 94, notes the reminiscence of *Wires*, 4: 'Not here but anywhere'. **21–2** Cf. *Midsummer Night, 1940*, 17–18: 'a pervading fear | No jolly laugh disperses'. **22–3** L to JBS, 17 Aug. 1943 (Hull DP 174/2/75): 'religion – well, nobody gives a darn for that any longer, not in England, anyway. Methodism caught on fine in the 18th century, but it's worn thin now.'
23 *musical*: L, choosing Thomas Tallis's *Spem in alium* on *Desert Island Discs* in 1976 (*FR*, 105–6): 'Well, I should want something for Sundays which suggests Church music. There's an enormous amount to choose from, and I think oddly enough Church music is a kind of music I like very much in the same way as jazz. I don't know why this should be so, unless agnostics are naturally romantic about religion, but I could pick any one of ten or twenty records.' **25–6** L to Thomas R. Arp, 23 Sept. 1980 (Hull DPL (2) 2/21/39): 'the sentence in inverted commas in "Aubade" is not a quotation, although it was meant to sound like one'. The sentence was not in fact printed in inverted commas. In the *TLS*, it was in roman, and the rest of the poem was in italic; in the pamphlet printing, it was in italic. **27–9** Cf. Eliot, *Gerontion*, 59–60: 'I have lost my sight, smell, hearing, taste and touch: | How should I use them for your closer contact?' Noted by Roger Craik in *Notes on Contemporary Literature*, 33. 2 (Mar. 2003), 8–9. **27–30** 'This fear had arisen in conversation too': Amis, *Memoirs*, 62. **30** 'Tell me, as a Professor of English, are you offended by "None come round"? Would you be happier with "None comes round"? As a natural illiterate, I never think of these things until it is too late. But it could be changed if the poem is ever collected': L to C. B. Cox, 12 May 1982 (*SL*, 669). **31–3** *vision . . . indecision*: Cf. Eliot, *The Love Song of J. Alfred Prufrock*, 32–3, 48: 'And time yet for a hundred indecisions, | And for a hundred visions and revisions', 'decisions

and revisions'. Also Hardy, *I Say, 'I'll Seek Her'* (publ. 1909), 6, 7: 'vision . . . indecision'. See *Ignorance*, 12–13. 36–7 Hugo Williams, *TLS*, 29 Apr. 2005, 16, notes Betjeman's *Loneliness*, 17–18: 'The tasteful crematorium door | Shuts out for some the furnace roar'. Betjeman's poem was published in 1971. 37–9 Cf. Eliot's *Gerontion*, 43–4: 'Think | Neither fear nor courage saves us'. Noted by Roger Craik, op. cit., 9. 41 *Slowly light strengthens*: Cf. Hardy, *Four in the Morning*, 1–2 (and note the time): 'At four this day of June I rise: | The dawn-light strengthens steadily'. 42–4 Roger Craik, *AL*, 12 (Oct. 2001), 12, compares the 'lurching rhythms which eliminate hope' in two choruses from Eliot's *Murder in the Cathedral*: 'a fear which we cannot know, which we cannot face, which none understands', 'a new terror has soiled us, which none can avert, none can avoid'. L included both choruses in *OBTCEV*. 45 *telephones crouch*: Edward Wilson, 'Philip Larkin's "Aubade" and Barbara Pym's *A Glass of Blessings*', *N&Q*, NS 40. 4 (Dec. 1993), 505–6, notes the unusual image in ch. 13 of Barbara Pym's novel, *A Glass of Blessings* (1958), a favourite of his (*SL*, 426): 'the telephone crouching on the floor alone, ringing unheeded'. Stephen Derry in *N&Q*, NS 44. 3 (Sept. 1997), 365, suggests that L is responding reciprocally and deliberately to Pym's borrowing of a quotation from his *Ambulances* in her *Quartet in Autumn*. The case is strengthened by the fact that that novel was published on 1 Sept. 1977, and the image of the crouching telephones first occurs in *Wkbk 8* on a page dated '18. 8. 77' at the top. It looks as though L had seen an advance copy. 45–50 'Somewhere within its rising rhythm at the end there stirs a memory of a famous poem that Larkin probably read when young, "Le Cimetière Marin" by Valéry – with the unforgettable last stanza that begins: *Le vent se lève . . . il faut tenter de vivre*. Some ironical ghost of that phrase moves within Larkin's "Aubade", as is hinted perhaps by its French title': Barbara Everett in Salwak (1989), 138. 49 A long-held resigned attitude of L's. To JBS, 16 Aug. 1943 (Hull DP 174/2/74): 'Still, work must be done'. See notes on *Toads* and *Toads Revisited*. 50 L in 1984: 'Some doctor read that last line "Postmen like doctors go from house to house" and said, "It's years you know since doctors did house to house visiting." But I said "No. It isn't postmen, comma, like doctors, comma, but just postmen like doctors." I meant the arrival of the postman in the morning is consoling, healing': A. N. Wilson, 'Honouring the Hermit of Hull', *The Times*, 16 Feb. 1984, 10.

DATE AND TEXT

Wkbk 8 (1/8/29) contains a page of drafts dated '27. 2. 78' at
the top and the completion date '2 / 3 / 78' below a draft of the
whole poem. L to CM, 2 Mar. 1978 (*SL*, 580): 'I'm no good at this
lapidary lark. All three nights' thought can produce is [the poem
follows, entitled '1952–1977']. Published in *TLS*, 3977 (23 June
1978), 704. L had been asked by CM on behalf of the Trustees of
the Queen Square Garden to write a short poem to commemorate
the Queen's Silver Jubilee. It and a poem by Ted Hughes were
inscribed on paving stones around a bowl of Portland stone, four
feet in diameter, in Queen Square, London. L to BP, 17 June 1978:
'two slabs of stone bearing quatrains by Ted Hughes & I': Bodl. MS
Pym 152/29. AT in *CP* (1988), 210, and *CP* (2003) prints lower-case
letters at the beginnings of lines 2–4. However, the texts in *Wkbk 8*,
the letter to CM and the *TLS* all have capitals. The title, omitted in
1988, was reinstated in 2003.

VARIANTS

3 there was] ~~We had~~ There was *letter to CM*

Christopher Ricks has pointed out to me a parallel in lines 1–4 of a
song by John Dowland on Elizabeth I: 'Time stands still with gazing
on her face. | . . . | All other things shall change but she remains the
same, | Till heavens changed have their course and Time hath lost his
name.'
    1 *nothing stood*: Cf. Housman, *A Shropshire Lad* XII 10:
'Nothing stands that stood before'. 4 *She*: Queen Elizabeth II. L in
1979 (*RW*, 50): 'one's always suspicious of change'.

Femmes Damnées

DATE AND TEXT

Aug.–Sept. 1943, and before 13 Sept., when L tells KA in a letter
that Bruce Montgomery likes best the last poem [this one] in the
copy of *Sugar and Spice* sent to him: *SL*, 69. The copy-text is
Hull DPL 1/8/43, a t.s. dated '1943' in t.s., loosely inserted at the
beginning of *Wkbk 8*. The text is identical to that in the Hull copy
of *Sugar and Spice*, DPL (2) 1/11. The Bodleian copy of *Sugar and
Spice* (MS Eng. c. 2356), the one sent to Montgomery, differs slightly
in punctuation and other minor details. Published in *Sycamore*

Broadsheet, 27 (1978), and in *CP* (1988), 270, *TAWG*, 246, and Tolley (2005), 205.

L to KA, 16 Sept. 1943 (*SL*, 70): 'I am glad you liked Brunette's poems: I think all wrong-thinking people ought to like them. I used to write them whenever I'd seen some particularly ripe schoolgirl, or when I felt sentimental: "Fam Damnay" was written for fun, but I'm glad you liked it; I wanted to put in something about "bare shoulders" but couldn't find room. A pity.' L described it to BP, 17 June 1978, as 'an odd little triptych' (*SL*, 582). L's note printed on *Sycamore Broadsheet*: 'The piece is evidence that I once read at least one "foreign poem", though I can't remember how far, if at all, my verses are based on the original.'

L's poem derives from Baudelaire's *Femmes Damnées*. Andrew Motion, *Philip Larkin* (1982), 73–4: 'Both poems describe two sensuously tragic lesbians . . . and contain marked similarities of phrasing.' Graham Chesters, 'Larkin and Baudelaire's Damned Women', *Making Connections: Essays in French Culture and Society in Honour of Philip Thody*, ed. James Dolamore (1999), 81–92, comments on the changes L makes to the original to produce 'a stereotypical English reserve': Baudelaire's poem is reduced by eighty lines; details of suburbia (milk and newspaper delivery, the Green Line bus) and of the domestic interior (cushions from Harrods, book titles, degree photograph) are introduced; Second-Empire Hellenic names adopted by courtesans, Hippolyte and Delphine, are changed to Rosemary and Rachel; 'Rosemary's hands are clasped in a gesture of puritanical repentance whereas Baudelaire's victim has "ses bras vaincus, jetés comme de vaines armes" ['her defeated arms thrown wide like futile weapons'], indices of a voluptuous surrender'; 'Rosemary's remorseful weeping, expressed in the minimal syntax, contrasts with the much more ambiguous tears shed by Hippolyte: "De ses yeux amortis les paresseuses larmes" ['listless tears from her lacklustrous eyes']'; 'Baudelaire seeks to give his women some kind of epic status; he captures Hippolyte's bewildered search for her lost innocence in a layered simile [. . .] Larkin/Brunette chooses the understated "She stares about her", and, by transferring the lost decency to the walls and their healthy books and uplifting photograph, refuses the symbolist images of transcendent purity (voyages, horizons, blue skies). In the midst of this "point-of-view" sequence, the parenthesis uses its dislocative power to spin the reader's attention to the true symbols of Rosemary's despoliation,

the lost ribbon and the falling hair'; L cuts the dialogues between
the women and the final moralising tirade ('Descendez, descendez,
lamentables victimes . . .' ['Go down, go down, lamentable victims'])
by the poet. Timothy Chesters, *AL*, 22 (Oct. 2006), 23 additionally
notes that Delphine's drinking 'voluptueusement I Le vin de son
triomphe' ['voluptuously I The wine of her triumph'] survives merely
as the smell of wine in the room (l. 11).

Title See L's comments in his preface to *Sugar and Spice*
(Appendix 1) on the two poems with French titles. 4 *Guardian*:
British national daily newspaper. 10 *Harrods*: London department
store. 10–11 Graham Chesters, op. cit., 89–90, compares
Baudelaire's 'profonds coussins tout imprégnés d'odeur' ['deep
cushions redolent of perfume'], 'although even here the Baudelairean
cushions are more likely to have been scented with incense, amber
and musk'. 15–16 Reminiscent, as Osborne (2008), 167, notes,
of the account of the photos and books in the room in Eliot,
A Cooking Egg, 3–8: '*Views of Oxford Colleges* I Lay on the
table, with the knitting. I Daguerrotypes and silhouettes, I Her
grandfather and great great aunts, I Supported on the mantelpiece
I An *Invitation to the Dance*.' 17–20 Motion (74) notes the close
parallel to ll. 13–16 of Baudelaire's poem: 'Étendue à ses pieds,
calme et pleine de joie, I Delphine la couvait avec des yeux ardents,
I Comme un animal fort qui surveille une proie, I Après l'avoir
d'abord marquée avec les dents.' ['Lying at her feet, calm and filled
with joy, I Delphine gazed at her hungrily, with burning eyes, I Like
a strong animal watching a prey I Which it has already marked with
its teeth.'] For Claude Rawson, 'Larkin's Desolate Attics', *Raritan*,
11. 2 (1991), 42, 'Larkin's lines have much more in common (down
to the woman's name) with the flat social notation of Eliot's Sweeney
poems than with the Baudelairean grandiloquence of doomed
sensuality'. Osborne (2008), 167, suggests that 'Rachel's name and
feline ferocity invoke the "Rachel *née* Rabinovitch" who "Tears at
the grapes with murderous paws" in [Eliot,] *Sweeney Among the
Nightingales*, [23–4]'.

'New eyes each year'

DATE AND TEXT
Brenda Moon, *AL*, 8 (Oct. 1999), 11: 'On 8th March 1979, to
celebrate the Library's fiftieth anniversary, one or two of us printed a
keepsake to mark the occasion, on the Library's Albion hand press.

I asked Philip whether we might distribute it at the celebration lunch for the Library Committee. "What are you going to put in it?" he asked. I was about to explain that keepsakes don't have insides, when I thought better of it. "A poem, perhaps?" The next day I found the poem "New eyes each year" on my desk.' Bloomfield (2002), 46, provides further bibliographical information, but does not make it clear that the version of the keepsake containing the verse was the second issue. L to BP, 18 Mar. 1979: 'I haven't written anything but an 8-line verse for a commemorative "keepsake" on the library's 50th birthday, printed on an old press in the basement': Bodl. MS Pym 152/38. Item 51 in the catalogue to *Philip Larkin: his life and work*, an exhibition held in the Brynmor Jones Library, Hull, 2 June–12 July 1986. Reprinted in *CP* (1988), 212.

The Mower

DATE AND TEXT

Wkbk 8 (1/8/32) contains a draft of the whole poem (entitled 'The Hedgehog') on a single page dated '12. 6. 79' at the top and bottom, which is two days after L told JE, 'This has been a rather depressing day: killed a hedgehog when mowing the lawn, by accident of course. It's upset me rather': *SL*, 601. Three identical t.s. versions are inserted loosely in *Wkbk 8*, two at the beginning, one at the end: Hull DPL 1/8/35, 38, 47 (copy-text). Published in *Humberside*, Hull Literary Club Magazine, 20. 1 (Autumn 1979), 16–17, and in *J S R Farms Autumn Newsletter*, [14] (9 Nov. 1979), 12. Reprinted in *CP* (1988), 214.

L to BP, 22 Apr. 1979: 'At Easter a hedgehog woke up in my garden, & accepted milk, but I think it has gone back to sleep as subsequent saucers have remained untouched': Bodl. MS Pym 152/39. To JE, 20 May 1979: 'At Easter I found a hedgehog cruising about my garden, clearly just woken up: it accepted milk, but went back to sleep I fancy, for I haven't seen it since': *SL*, 601. L's photograph of the hedgehog sipping milk (Mar. 1979) is on the front cover of *AL*, 22 (Oct. 2006), and the detail of the hedgehog is enlarged on p. 6 of the same issue. MJ recalled: 'When it happened, he came in from the garden howling. He was very upset. He'd been feeding the hedgehog, you see – he looked out for it in the mornings. He started writing about it soon afterwards': Motion (1993), 475. L's secretary, Betty Mackereth, recalls L telling her of the incident in the office the next morning 'with tears streaming down his face': *AL*, 20 (Autumn 2005), 48. L's tender feelings for hedgehogs are registered in letters to MJ: 'Commotion downstairs – hedgehog on the path! Rolled up, but breathing!', 'But what a pleasant visitor! Dear little thing!', 'Is it just passing through, I wonder, or does it live in the garden?': 6 Aug. 1955; Bodl. MS Eng. c. 7412/4; seeking out a hedgehog in a colleague's garden, 'Rather nice!': 12 May 1957; Bodl. MS Eng. c. 7416/13; 'They're charming creatures': 17 May 1962; Bodl. MS Eng. c. 7425/7. Cards sent to MJ on 5 Aug. 1964 and 22 Feb. 1983 bear a photograph of a hedgehog on the front: Bodl. MSS Eng. c. 7428/103, 7445/72.

Christopher Fletcher, *N&Q*, NS 52. 1 (Mar. 2005), 102–3, notes similarities with Edmund Blunden's poem *Young Fieldmouse*, published in *Poems of Many Years* (1957): 'In each case technology deals the damaging blows; but uncut grass also contributes to the unfortunate fate of both animals, offering misleading protection from the modern reaper.'

Title Cf. the pastoralism of Marvell's 'Mower' poems. 7 James Booth observes that hedgehogs 'are nocturnal animals and do not "get up" in the morning', and therefore that the one L inadvertently killed 'was almost certainly . . . diseased [or] already dead when Larkin's mower hit it': *AL*, 22 (Oct. 2006), 5.

Bridge for the Living

DATE AND TEXT
First mentioned by L to CM, 24 Oct. 1973 (*SL*, 490): 'I have been asked to write something about the Humber Bridge (due 1976) that could be set to music and sung by the Hull Choral Union.' *Wkbk 8* (1/8/21) contains: two pages of drafts of the last four stanzas after '28. 1. 75', with the last draft on a page dated '11. 2. [1975]' at the top; and a draft of stanza 3 and the first two lines of stanza 4 dated '3. 4. [1975]'. Booth (2005), 202, records that eleven sides of pencil drafts appear between the dates 30 May and 27 July 1975 in a manuscript notebook that went to Maggs Bros. Ltd. Commissioned by Sidney Hainsworth of the Hull business Fenner's, the cantata, with music composed by Anthony Hedges, was first performed at the City Hall, Hull, on 11 Apr. 1981 to celebrate the opening of the bridge. Printed in *A Garland for the Laureate: Poems presented to Sir John Betjeman on his 75th birthday* (1981), and in *Poetry Book Society Supplement*, Christmas 1981. L to Andrew Motion, 16 Sept.

1981 (*SL*, 657): 'there is a little epigraph explaining that it is simply "words for music" that I hope you have included. If not, I'll add it to the proof.' Reprinted in *CP* (1988), 203–4.

L to BP, 22 Jan. 1975 (*SL*, 521): 'One of my waking nightmares is a local business man who is trying to commission a "choral work" – *possibly about the Humber Bridge* – words by me, music by some thrusting young fellow from the Music Department. He is having us both to lunch on Monday. Sometimes I think my brain is going.' L to KA, 25 June 1975 (Huntington MS AMS 353-393): 'I am trying to write words for a choral work on the Humber Bridge. I get up at 6 a.m. to do this. It's the only time I'm not drunk.' L to BP, 22 July 1975 (*SL*, 528): 'A local industrialist has bullied me into writing words for *a choral work to celebrate the Humber Bridge*, and this haunts the troubled midnight and the noon's repose. I wish a thousand times over I'd said no. What can one *say* about such a thing? And say *in advance*? That seems to me the worst of "public" poetry: it's not the public element, it's having to write *in advance* of Princess Anne's wedding or whatever it is. I take comfort in Beaumarchais' assurance that what is too silly to be said can be sung.' ('The troubled midnight and the noon's repose': Eliot, *La Figlia Che Piange*, 24.) To Anthony Hedges, 15 Dec. 1975 (*SL*, 534): 'I enclose a copy of (to use W. B. Yeats's title) words for music perhaps. The shape and theme is I suppose sufficiently obvious: the first part describes Hull's essential loneliness, and is descriptive and slow-moving, the second tries to feel cheerful about the ending of this loneliness through the agency of the bridge, and I suppose could be called celebratory. I am concerned to hear that forty lines will produce only eight minutes music [. . .] Looking at my four collections, I find that I have never written even 100 lines on any subject, even when I have grouped poems together; in fact I have exceeded 40 lines on eleven occasions only.' Hedges reports: 'I told Philip it was half-length, and he said there was nothing more he could do, so I produced a long slow introduction and lots of repetition': Motion (1993), 487. L to BP, 29 Dec. 1975, (*SL*, 535): 'I actually strung together 40 lines of rubbish about (well, more or less) the Humber Bridge & this region in general, and passed them on to the composer. No word yet! When I said I'd done 40 lines, he said they w^d last about 8 minutes: these chaps like something like Spenser's *Epithalamion* that just goes on & on. In fact 40 lines is *very long* for me.' L to JB, 14 May 1980 (*SL*, 621): 'The Humber Bridge is still unfinished, which suits me all right as when it *is* finished the Hull Philharmonic Society will perform a choral work specially written for the occasion for which I was mad enough to provide the words.' To Anthony Hedges, 16 Apr. 1981 (*SL*, 647–8): 'For my part, I owe you deep gratitude for the way you handled my "words" – I was afraid they were too much of a formal "poem", but that is the only thing I have had any experience of writing. It was splendid the way you transmuted the formality into an emotional statement.'

Title Hedges reports: 'Eventually I got something forty lines long with no title . . . When I finished I wrote "A Humberside Cantata" on the score but the title . . . was pressed on us by our commissioners. Philip told me he thought it made it sound like a card game Instruction Manual for adults': Motion (1993), 487. **1, 3** Motion (1993), 488, notes the 'water | daughter' rhyme used earlier in *Spring*, 10–11. **20** Cf. Housman, prefatory verse to *A Shropshire Lad* L: '*Clunton and Clunbury,* | *Clungunford and Clun*'; Eliot, *Four Quartets, Burnt Norton*, 3. **22**: 'Hampstead and Clerkenwell, Campden and Putney'. **38, 40** Cf. Kingsley Amis, *Masters* (from *A Case of Samples* [1956], 22–3): 'For it is by surrender that we live, | And we are taken if we wish to give'.

'When Coote roared: "Mitchell, what about this jazz?"'

DATE AND TEXT
Feb. 1970, when it was inscribed by L on a complimentary copy of *AWJ* given to Donald Mitchell. Published in Thwaite (1982), 75.

1 *Coote*: Sir Colin Coote DSO (1893–1979), Editor of the *Daily Telegraph*, 1950–64. *Mitchell*: Donald Mitchell (b. 1925), member of the music staff of the *Daily Telegraph*, 1959–64; founder in 1965 of Faber Music Ltd; Professor of Music, Sussex University, 1971–6; publications on Britten and Mahler. **2** L reviewed jazz records for the *Daily Telegraph*, 1961–71.

'Dear CHARLES, My Muse, asleep or dead'

DATE AND TEXT
Published in *Poems for Charles Causley* (1982), which marked Causley's sixty-fifth birthday. Reprinted in *CP* (1988), 217–18.

The poem was commissioned by 'friends of friends' of L, and he thought it 'doggerel': Motion (1993), 491.

Title *CHARLES*: the poet Charles Causley (1917–2003). He was born and educated in Launceston, Cornwall, and spent most of his working life as a teacher there. **3** *the frozen North*: Of England (i.e., Hull). **6** *that Roman*: the Emperor Augustus. **7** *a Leo*: born under the sign of the zodiac, the Lion, 24 July–23 Aug. *same as me*: L was born on 9 Aug. 1922.

'By day, a lifted study-storehouse'

DATE AND TEXT
Before 26 Oct. 1983. It was written as an eightieth birthday tribute to Sir Brynmor Jones, Vice-Chancellor of the University of Hull, 1956–72.

For the occasion, fourteen fair copies were printed on the Albion Press housed in the Brynmor Jones Library. Bloomfield (2002), 48, provides further bibliographical information. Item 56 in the catalogue to *Philip Larkin: his life and work*, an exhibition in the Brynmor Jones Library, 2 June–12 July 1986. Reprinted in *CP* (1988), 220.

Party Politics

DATE AND TEXT
Published in *Poetry Review*, 73. 4 ([Jan.] 1984), 4. Bloomfield (2002), 125, gives the volume number wrongly as 77. Commissioned by the magazine's editors Tracey Warr and Mick Imlah to appear in a special issue on 'Poetry and Drink': Motion (1993), 505. Reprinted in *CP* (1988), 221.

Title Pun on 'political party'.

POEMS NOT PUBLISHED
IN THE POET'S LIFETIME

'Who's that guy hanging on a rail?'

DATE AND TEXT
In a postscript to a letter to L postmarked 2 Nov. 1971 (Hull DP
179/2/7), Colin Gunner gives the lines, and adds: 'Mint, vintage
Larkin. Composed beside Walls Ice Cream Cart Warwick Rd. 1936'.
I have corrected Gunner's typographical errors and converted a
comma at the end of line 1 (a full stop when he gives it again on 26
Mar. 1981) to a question mark. In a letter to L dated 3 May 1985
(Hull DP 179/2/36) Gunner gives the text (barring typographical
errors) as 'Who dat guy hanging on a rail. You know, I know A.
B. Sale'. I choose his earliest version, which is accompanied by the
most detailed information he supplies, and which is confirmed by his
second version.

2 *A. B. Sale*: 1884–1959. A genial figure, he taught various
subjects at King Henry VIII School, Coventry, including English,
Mathematics, Latin, Geography, History, Drawing and Scripture; he
had charge of games at the school for more than twenty years; he
introduced the house system; and with the wife of headmaster John
Lupton he managed the Tuck Shop. L in DPL (2) 1/1/10, a collection
of schoolboy writings, 'Tour of K. H. S.': 'Now this is the tuckshop.
Here Major Sale dispenses light refreshment to the boys – such
a favourite': *AL*, 13 (Apr. 2002), 24. Gunner to L, 3 May 1985,
discussing a photograph of an old boys' cricket team of the early
1930s (Hull DP 179/2/36): 'Figure on left in white coat MUST be
A. B. Sale fresh from his libations in the Railway Tavern.'

Coventria

DATE AND TEXT
Early 1938. T.s. in a letter to Colin Gunner: DPL (2)1/4/9.
Published in Tolley (2005), 3. Tolley prints 'Heads [*sic*]' in l. 5 and
'Vergils [sic]' in l. 14 instead of correcting L's errors, but leaves
the possessives 'Saints' and 'Phips' in l. 13 as they are. In l. 15, he
misrepresents 'Fahve Ell' (i.e. class 5L) as an unmetrical 'Fahve

E 1'. Cf. L to Gunner, 9 Feb. 1980 (Hull DP 179/18), mentioning a schoolmate he has heard from: 'I used to do chemistry with him in 4L'.

As S. S. Prawer notes in *TLS*, 5329 (20 May 2005), 15, the poem is a parody of the school song, current when L was there. The words are by F. H. Metcalf:

> We are the School at the top of the hill
> That Henry the King did will,
>   John Hales so to found when he got him his lands
> And his coffers with treasure did fill.
>   Henry the King, John Hales the Clerk,
>   To us did richly give!
>   Religioni et Reipublicae
>   With us shall ever live!
>
>   On field and in room, wherever we may be,
> Though the task be drear and grim,
>   Though pressed to the full and the way be hard,
> May our courage never dim!
>   Henry the King, John Hales the Clerk,
>   To us did richly give!
>   Religioni et Reipublicae
>   With us shall ever live!
>   When we look back, in the years yet to be,
> And our days live again in thought –
>   Our work that was hard, our friends and our foes,
> The games that were fiercely fought –
>   God give us grace that memory be sweet,
>   When we dream of our boyhood strife!
>   Religioni et Reipublicae
>   With us to the end of life.

1–2 The boys-only grammar school, King Henry VIII School, Coventry, was founded in 1545. L attended it from 1932 to 1940. It moved from its original position in the city to its hilltop site in 1885. 5 *The Head's a lout*: The headmaster from 1931 to 1949 was Albert Alfred Charles Burton (1889–1967), Oxford BA (1912), MA (1915), known as 'Monty' (after the outfitters Montague Burton and Sons). He was a charismatic and unpredictable man, slovenly in appearance and violent in discipline. L called him 'the resident thug': Motion (1993), 18. Roy Burgess, *AL*, 13 (Apr.

2002), 29–31 attempts some rehabilitation of Burton's image, but only succeeds in portraying him as an irascible dictator. 'Burton was indeed a thug': L's contemporary Noel Hughes, *AL*, 14 (Oct. 2002), 14. *Hardy's*: In a letter to Gunner, 9 Feb. 1980 (Hull DP 179/18), L mentions 'our old friend Squiff ("Shepherd! Bring me a spatula-full of graphite!") Hardy'. Leslie Thomas Newell Hardy (b. 1909) took a first in Natural Sciences at Cambridge in 1931, and was senior science master at the school from 1935 to 1942. He features in L's schoolboy piece 'Tour of K. H. S.': *AL*, 13 (Apr. 2002), 25. **13** *Saint's*: Henry Lancelot Basil Saint (b. 1911) took a first in mathematics at Liverpool, and joined the school staff in 1936. *Phip's*. Hugh Myrddin ('Phippy') Phillipson (b. 1907), took a first in classics at Manchester, and was senior classics master at the school from 1934 to 1940. He is identified in a letter from L to Gunner, 6 Sept. 1971 (*SL*, 445). The two masters also feature in L's 'Tour of K. H. S.': *AL*, 13 (Apr. 2002), 24–5. **15** *shoot*: shut (in a Midlands accent). **21** *The Grand Old Man*: Mark Theakston Mason (b. 1879), L's English teacher. He graduated in the second class in classics at Cambridge, and taught at the school from 1906 until he retired in 1938 (the year of L's poem). L to Gunner, early 1938, on his (L's) school report, Hull DPL (2) 1/4/9: 'and one "VERY GOOD" from no other than the Grand Old Man [. . .] He knows a fellow's worth [. . .] came top in term and exam in English Lang. and Art'. L to Gunner, 21 Aug. 1971 (Hull DP 179/2/5): 'Almost heard the ghostly voice of M. T. Mason booming "ER – LURKIN!!" from that far away era.' *Bunyan*: John Bunyan (1628–88), author of *The Pilgrim's Progress*.

Thought Somewhere in France 1917

DATE AND TEXT
?Winter 1938/9. The date is suggested by a comment L makes just after the poem in Hull DPL (2) 1/1/10/19: 'Through the winter of 1938–9 I continued to write poems, all of much the same kind.' The poem, and other early poems, were collected by L in 'The Happiest Days': see the note on 'The sun was battling to close our eyes'. Hull DPL (2) 1/1/10/19 (t.s.). In l. 7 the final 'g' in 'bringing' is added in pencil. Published in Tolley (2005), 6.

VARIANTS (from Hull DPL (2) 1/1/10/19)
4 with] ~~against~~ with

Introducing the poem, L writes: 'and also (for I had turned Pacifist)'. In the t.s., he comments: 'It is not an imitation of anyone: in fact, I did not read poetry at all.' Against the poem in the t.s., he writes: 'balls. possibly historically incorrect, too. certainly illogical.'

2 The First Opium War between Britain and China, 1840–2.

What the half-open door said to the empty room when a chance draft ruffled the pages of an old scorebook which happened to be lying on the top of a cupboard when the last blazer had gone home

DATE AND TEXT
1938/9. Hull DPL (2) 1/1/10/21 (t.s. with holograph corrections in ink). Published in Tolley (2005), 9 with 'top' for 'the top' in the opening section. This section has the force of a long title, and the fact that L writes disparagingly 'little better than the verse' against it in the t.s. strongly suggests that it is indeed a title. I retain the lineation and letter-case of the title, but print it in larger type.

VARIANTS (from Hull DPL (2) 1/1/10/21)
4 blow'st] ~~blowst~~ blow'st
day] days
week] weeks

1–2 Cf. *As You Like It*, 2. 7. 175–6: 'Blow, blow, thou winter wind | Thou art not so unkind'.

Butterflies

DATE AND TEXT
Spring/summer 1939. For date and context see the note on 'The sun was battling to close our eyes' (below). 'Darling' (l. 14) would suggest one of the love-affairs L mentions in that poem. Hull DPL (2) 1/1/10/20 (t.s.). Published in Tolley (2005), 8, with 'white robed' for 'white-robed' (l. 8).

L writes on the t.s.: 'written variously on a cycle tour. not very good. pretty bloody, actually. ANUS'.

A Meeting – Et Seq. (2)

DATE AND TEXT
Spring/summer 1939. See the note on 'The sun was battling to close our eyes' (below). The declaration in l. 6 would suggest one of the love-affairs L mentions in that poem. Hull DPL (2) 1/1/10/21 (t.s.). Published in Tolley (2005), 10.

The t.s. is accompanied by holograph additions and comments, all of them vilificatory. To ll. 1, 5 and 15 L adds 'outside the shithouse'; in l. 3 he brackets off 'scimitar' and replaces it with 'dose of salts'; to l. 10 he adds 'into the bogs', to l. 11 'and had a good shit', and to l. 13 'there was no paper'. To the right of the poem he writes: 'bloody awful. sincerity no excuse for bad verse & banality – or is it? There is not a line of this shitty thing that is free from the most execrable vulgarity or BAD TASTE!!!! balls shit all cunt ass-hole.' Below the poem he writes: 'a case of the fart being greater than the hole.'

14, 16 *furled | world*: Rhyme in Housman, *R. L. S.* (*Additional Poems* XXII), 2, 4.

The Ships at Mylae

DATE AND TEXT
8 July 1939: 'July 8th. – At night write poetry. "Ships at Mylae": I think fair. Good idea badly worked out' (L's note). The copy-text is that in *1st Coll*. Published in Tolley (2005), 18–19, with 'Snow' for 'snow' (l. 6).

Title, 25–6 '"Stetson! | You who were with me in the ships at Mylae!"': Eliot, *The Waste Land, I, The Burial of the Dead*, 69–70. Noted by Stephen Regan, 'Philip Larkin: a late modern poet', *The Cambridge Companion to Twentieth-Century English Poetry*, ed. Neil Corcoran (2007), 147. The Battle of Mylae (260 BC) was between the Romans and the Carthaginians. **3** Cf. Eliot, *Preludes*, 9: 'The showers beat' (rhymed with 'street'). **12** Cf. Milton, Sonnet XVII ('Lawrence of virtuous father virtuous son'), 2, 4: 'Now that the fields are dank, the ways are mire', 'a sullen day'. **25** L's schoolfriend Earnest Stanley Sanders. **26** *argosies*: A Keatsian word, as in *The Eve of St Agnes*, xxx. 7: 'in argosy transferred'. **27** *mounting foam*: Cf. Tennyson, *The Lotos-Eaters*,

2: 'This mounting wave'. **37** Cf. Hopkins, *Binsey Poplars*, 2: 'the leaping sun'.

Alvis Victrix

DATE AND TEXT

12 July 1939: 'The poem was conceived July 11th, and written July 12th. The version here is inferior to one sent to F. G. Smith, but is the original in all but one word' (L's note). The copy-text is that in *1st Coll*. Published in *AL*, 8 (Oct. 1999), 18, with 'nose' for 'rose' (l. 9) and 'bold' for 'bolt' (l. 14), the latter error acknowledged in *AL*, 9 (Apr. 2000), 20. The text in Tolley (2005), 20, is correct.

Title 'Alvis Victorious', by analogy with the heading to ch. 6 in D. H. Lawrence's *The Rainbow*: 'Anna Victrix'. *Alvis*: Coventry-based manufacturer of luxury and sports cars, 1919–67. **2** *the Albany Road*: In Coventry. **12** Cf. Tennyson, *In Memoriam*, xi. 17: 'Calm on the seas, and silver sleep'.

Stanley en Musique

DATE AND TEXT

15 July 1939: 'July 15th. – at night type out "Alvis Victrix" and write "Stanley en Musique": Eliotian but amusing. Somehow one can't be serious about Sanders. He is too – how shall I put it? Oh, I don't know' (L's note). L also notes on the t.s.: 'l. 16: This line. Although complete in the original, still awaits satisfactory completion.' The copy-text is that in *1st Coll*. Published in Tolley (2005), 21, with 'grow' for 'Grow' (l. 16).

Note by L on the page following: '(The next of the Stanley poems was "Stanley à tatons". It was the first effort at serious writing on this subject, and is not included here partly because it is a bad poem, and partly because it is untrue. But the diary comment ran: "He has now become Adolescence to me-pre-natal, I mean." This is a decided link between the earlier poems and the later ones.)'.

Title *Stanley*: Earnest Stanley Sanders, not 'Saunders', as Tolley (2005), 21n., states, who attended King Henry VIII School, Coventry, 1933–9. He was a year younger than L: Fred Holland, *AL*, 20 (Autumn 2005), 84. **3** *Dresden shepherdesses*: Cf. Eliot,

Aunt Helen, 10: 'The Dresden clock'. **9–12** L's handwritten note opposite these lines on the t.s. in *1st Coll*: 'Oh – no! Who's been reading T. S. Eliot?' Stephen Regan, 'Philip Larkin: a late modern poet', *The Cambridge Companion to Twentieth-Century English Literature*, ed. Neil Corcoran (2007), 147: 'The Stanley Poems take their inspiration from Eliot's Sweeney poems, skilfully adopting their ironic tone and supercilious detachment. "Stanley en Musique" and "Stanley et la Glace" are written in the lean quatrains of "Sweeney Among the Nightingales" and their comically pretentious French titles recall poems written by Eliot under the influence of Baudelaire and Laforgue.' **16** From the film *The Night is Young* (1935). L's handwritten note at this line on the t.s. in *1st Coll*: 'NB this is *not* a coarse jest. At least not very.'

Founder's Day, 1939

DATE AND TEXT
Summer 1939. Founder's Day is 23 July. Hull DPL (2) 1/1/10/23 (t.s. with holograph correction). Published in Tolley (2005), 12–13.

VARIANTS (from the Hull t.s.)
26 tall] ~~dark~~ tall

27 *John Hales*: a Coventry man of great wealth, Clerk of the Hanaper under Henry VIII, and founder in 1545 of the Free Grammar School under letters patent from the king.

Collected Fragments

DATE AND TEXT
Summer 1939. 'July Rain' and, in '4', 'now the slow movement of summer has been played to its close', would suggest such a date, and perhaps too there is a trace of the summer love-affair in '2' and '3' (on which, see the note on 'The sun was battling close to our eyes', below). DPL (2) 1/1/10/22 (t.s.). The four pieces are numbered by L. I follow the format of his text. It is not clear whether the headings he gives are intended as titles. Not previously published.

Against '1' and '2' L writes 'fair'; against '3', 'bad'; against '4', 'good'.
    (2) 4 *this falling sky*: Cf. Housman, *A Shropshire Lad* XLIX ('Think no more, lad; laugh, be jolly'), 6: 'the falling sky'; *Additional*

Poems XIV ('"Oh is it the jar of nations'), 7: 'To shore up the sky from falling': *Last Poems* XXXVIII (*Epitaph on an Army of Mercenaries*), 1: 'the day when heaven was falling'. (4) *Der tag*: the day.

'The sun was battling to close our eyes'

DATE AND TEXT

1938/9, possibly spring/summer 1939, and certainly before 9 Aug. 1939 (L's 17th birthday). L to JBS, 16 Apr. 1941 (*SL*, 12), quoting the poem: 'written when I was *sixteen*!!' Hull DPL (2) 1/1/10/20 (t.s.); included in *ChP* (copy-text). Published in Tolley (2005), 7, without a mention of the earlier t.s. text.

Between *Thought Somewhere in France 1917* and this poem, L's t.s. reads: 'Through the winter of 1938–9 I continued to write poems, all much of the same kind, faintly influenced by Keats and Aldous Huxley, until in the spring I broke into freer verse when I re-fell in love with someone. Then poems became much more personal and more frequent, for I remained in love during the whole summer though not with the same person. Here are those I want to keep from the first book of poems ("The Happiest Days").'

On the earlier t.s. L writes: 'This is probably as good a poem as I have ever written. It is that rare thing: a completely original poem by P A Larkin.' L to JBS, 16 Apr. 1941 (*SL*, 12): 'Much nearer Lawrence than Auden, anyway.'

5 *dusty trees*: As in Eliot, *The Waste Land, III, The Fire Sermon*, 292.

Chorus from a Masque

DATE AND TEXT

Aug. 1939: to the right of the opening in *PAug40* L writes: 'this is a year earlier than all the other shit & isn't it better?' Poem XVI in *PAug40*; VII in *ChP* (copy-text). Published in Tolley (2005), 55, with 'or' for 'and' in l. 7. The chorus is from *Behind the Façade*: see Tolley (2005), 335.

Stanley et la Glace

DATE AND TEXT
14 Sept. 1939. 'Sept. 14th. – Write "Stanley et la Glace". Not very good.' (L's note). 'July' is cancelled and 'Sept.' written above it. In *1st Coll.* Published in Tolley (2005), 50.

See the notes on *Stanley en Musique*.
   19 *coiled ice-cream*: L's handwritten note opposite the phrase on the t.s. in *1st Coll*: 'coiled dogshit 1946'.

Erotic Play

DATE AND TEXT
19 Sept. 1939. L's note in his diary: 'Sept. 19th. – Morning, another episode of "Erotic Play" (I write a poem called this).' T.s. in *1st Coll.* Published in Tolley (2005), 51, with 'side' for 'wide' (l. 7).

3 L's note: 'l. 3 cf. Ronsard.' He refers to the opening of no. XXIV of *Sonnets pour Hélène* (1575): 'When you are really old'.

The Days of thy Youth

DATE AND TEXT
Begun 25 June 1939. L's note on the t.s.: 'June 25th. – In morning read "Ecclesiastes" – *very* good – and write a quite good poem.' Hull DPL (2) 1/1/10/24 = Hull t.s. 1; t.s. 2, a revised text, is in *1st Coll* (copy-text). The earlier t.s. version was published by James Booth in *AL*, 13 (Apr. 2002), 27, with the second line missing. Published in Tolley (2005), 17, with a comma between 'wind' and 'is' (l. 5).

VARIANTS (from Hull t.s. 1)
   8 But we are here, to enjoy the endless second
  11 flourish, and, then] flourish: then
  14 Far away] Many leagues off

On DPL (2) 1/1/10/24 L writes: 'Is this good? I rather like it. It's probably bad but by God I do like it. It hits me bash in the bowels!' Booth in *AL*, 13, mistranscribes: 'oh God', and no exclamation mark after 'bowels'.

Title Ecclesiastes 11: 9: 'Rejoice, O young man, in thy youth; and let thy heart cheer thee in the days of thy youth'; 12: 1: 'Remember now thy Creator in the days of thy youth, while the evil days come not, nor the years draw nigh, when thou shalt say, I have no pleasure in them'. **9** *under the sun*: Repeated phrase in Ecclesiastes: 1: 3, 9, 13, etc. **13** Cf. Rupert Brooke, *The Soldier*, 8: 'Washed by the rivers'. **16** Ecclesiastes 4: 12: 'And if one prevail against him, two shall withstand him; and a threefold cord is not quickly broken'; 12: 6 (in the context of death): 'Or ever the silver cord be loosed'. L's note on the MS reads 'l. 16. "this cord": window cord in pavilion'.

(À un ami qui aime.)

DATE AND TEXT
Sept.–Oct. 1939. L in Hull DPL (2) 1/1/10/25: 'Before 1939 was out, the war started and I wrote two more books of poems. One was "Poems in War" (Sept. 3rd–Oct. 7th). These poems are influenced by the modern Left-wing school, generally, whom I read avidly, especially Auden. It included a masque: "Behind the Facade", which I'll keep. "One O'Clock Jump" the other was called, not that the titles had anything to do with the contents. Towards the end they became gritty. Here are the best:' There follow the next 22 poems, (À *un ami qui aime.*) being the first, numbered by L.

Hull DPL (2) 1/1/10/25 (t.s.). Published by James Booth in *AL*, 13 (Apr. 2002), 28, with an acute rather than a grave accent on the last syllable of 'Relaxed' (l. 2), and in Tolley (2005), 24, without parentheses round the title or an accent on the last syllable of 'Relaxed' (l. 2). In the present edition, as in Tolley (2005), a grave accent has been added to the 'A' in the title.

On the t.s., to the right of verses one and two respectively, L writes: 'efficient halma-playing' and 'philosophy banal, true, & impossible'. ('Halma' is a chequerboard game.)

'The grinding halt of plant, and clicking stiles'

DATE AND TEXT
Sept.–Oct. 1939. Hull DPL (2) 1/1/10/25 (t.s., with line numbering). Tolley (2005), 25–8, reproduces L's errors 'news-sellers' (l. 58, for 'news-seller's') and 'dew-flicked' (l.91, for 'dew-flecked') appending

'[sic]' and '[sic]' respectively, but misses 'crakt' (for 'crackt', l. 41)
and prints 'motor bike' for 'motorbike' (l. 88). In the present edition
a comma has been inserted after trousers in l. 22; 'One' (l. 52) has
been corrected to 'one' (as in Tolley silently); 'clash the cogs' (l. 74)
has been emended to the idiomatic 'crash the cogs'; a full stop has
been inserted after 'over)' (l. 86); and the number of dots L inserts at
various points has been regularised each time to three.

On the t.s., to the right of ll. 1–10, L writes: 'amazingly advanced,
but shit. Also inexact. Also balls also cock & two edged prick.' To
the left of ll. 33–40, he writes: 'and shit in the shithouse'. To the left
and right of ll. 93–6: 'canting cunt' and 'ballocks'; and at the end of
the poem: 'anus . . . anus . . . balls and ballocks and anus . . .'
  16 *Hearsall Common*: large grassy area in Earlsdon, Coventry.
18 *Ratisbon*: Regensburg, site of a battle between France and
Austria in Apr. 1809. 41 *'Land of Hope and Glory'*: Song with
words by A. C. Benson (1862–1925), written as a coronation ode
for King Edward VII in 1902. It was set to the tune from the trio
section of Pomp and Circumstance March no. 1 by Elgar (1857–
1934) and became a second national anthem. 89–90 Matt. 26: 40:
'And he cometh unto the disciples, and findeth them asleep, and
saith unto Peter, What, could ye not watch with me one hour?' Also
Mark 14: 37.

'Smash all the mirrors in your home'

DATE AND TEXT
Sept.–Oct. 1939. Hull DPL (2) 1/1/10/28 (t.s.). ll. 1–8 and 25–32 are
run through with diagonal wavy lines. Published in Tolley (2005),
29–30. The syntax of 'Feed love fires intellect' (l. 29) is problematic.
Possibilities are that 'Feed' should be 'Freed' (so that 'fires' is a
transitive verb with 'Freed love' as its subject); or, that 'fires' should
be 'fire's' (so that 'love' is 'fire's intellect', the object of 'Feed'). I opt
for the latter: 'Feed . . . till' is a credible sequence, and, clinchingly,
the parallel between the imperatives 'Feed' and 'lose' (l. 31) is more
convincing than the sequence 'Freed . . . lose' would be.

To the right of the first verse, L writes: 'bloody awful, I loath this.
But revealing like Hell.' He pronounces verse 2 'all right!' and verse
3 'also not too bad'; to the right of the fourth verse he writes 'SHIT'.
  1–8 The commands recall those in Auden's 'Stop all the clocks,

cut off the telephone'. **6** *scullery*: back kitchen. **12** *Cornish pasties*: seasoned meat and vegetables cooked in cases of pastry. **13** *the Jew blinks in a doorway*: Cf. Eliot, *Gerontion*, 8: 'the Jew squats on the window sill'. **21** *blimpish*: rotund, pompous, disliking new ideas.

'Watch, my dear, the darkness now'

DATE AND TEXT
Sept.–Oct. 1939. Hull DPL (2) 1/1/10/28 (t.s.) Published in Tolley (2005), 31.

On the t.s. L draws a line from the previous poem to this one, and writes 'remarkable contrast', 'remarkable shit'. To the right of the first verse, he writes: 'also shit. philosophy banal, true & impossible'.

'Has all History rolled to bring us here?'

DATE AND TEXT
Sept.–Oct. 1939. Hull DPL (2) 1/1/10/30 (t.s.). Published in Tolley (2005), 34, with 'history' for 'History' (l. 1), and with L's ungrammatical 'he' for 'him' (l. 23).

To the right of l. 1 on the t.s., L writes 'rot', and, at the end of the poem, 'BALLS. BALLOCKS. I don't know! might be possible.'

'In a second I knew it was your voice speaking'

DATE AND TEXT
Sept.–Oct. 1939. Hull DPL (2) 1/1/10/30 (t.s.). Published in Tolley (2005), 35.

To the right of the poem on the t.s., L writes 'bosh'.

(A Study in Light and Dark)

DATE AND TEXT
Sept.–Oct. 1939. Hull DPL (2) 1/1/10/31 (t.s.). Published in Tolley (2005), 36, without brackets round the title, and with 'capitalists'

(l. 8) corrected silently to 'capitalist's'. I supply a full stop at the end of l. 13.

To the right of the poem, L writes 'trash', 'this ought never to have been written', and 'this is a lot of cunt'.

'Within, a voice said: Cry!'

DATE AND TEXT

Sept.–Oct. 1939. Hull DPL (2) 1/1/10/ 32 (t.s.). Published in Tolley (2005), 38, with 'you;' missing from the end of l. 9.

To the right of the first verse on the t.s., L writes 'queerly attractive' and 'also rather original'.

'What is the difference between December and January?'

DATE AND TEXT

Sept.–Oct. 1939. Hull DPL (2) 1/1/10/33 (t.s.). Published in Tolley (2005), 39.

On the t.s. L writes: 'more shit'.

To a Friend's Acquaintance

DATE AND TEXT

Sept.–Oct. 1939. Hull DPL (2) 1/1/10/33 (t.s.). Published in Tolley (2005), 41, with a full stop instead of the comma after 'honey' (l. 9).

On the t.s. L writes 'funny, but personal. no it is: it's quite amusing'.

To a Friend

DATE AND TEXT

Sept.–Oct. 1939. Hull DPL (2) 1/1/10/34: t.s. with holograph corrections. Published by James Booth in *AL*, 13 (Apr. 2002), 28. Tolley (2005), 42, prints the ungrammatical 'years' for 'year' in l. 16, and yet remarks (as he could have done often elsewhere) that it is 'probably a typing error'. He prints 'trace' for 'form' (l. 6) and 'a' for 'the' (l. 19). He also states that L's holograph corrections to the t.s. 'do not permit the construction of a corrected version'. In fact, as Booth demonstrated three years before, they do.

VARIANTS (from the Hull t.s.)
 6 form] ~~trace~~ form
14 trace] ~~trace breath~~ trace

On the t.s. L writes 'pretty bad', 'I don't know! this has its points', and 'So has a porcupine'. At the end of l. 7 he writes 'senseless!'. In l. 20 he rings 'rests' and 'summer' drawing lines back to 'summer' and 'rest' (each word ringed) in l. 13, and writes 'is this cross reference justifiable?'

The poem is an imitation of Auden's *Lullaby* ('Lay your sleeping head, my love'), as Adam Kirsch, *TLS*, 5328 (13 May 2005), 9, notes.

A Farewell

DATE AND TEXT
Sept.–Oct. 1939. Hull DPL (2) 1/1/10/34 (t.s.). Published in Tolley (2005), 43.

On the t.s L writes 'awful' and 'fucked'.

Young Woman's Blues

DATE AND TEXT
Sept.–Oct. 1939. Hull DPL (2) 1/1/10/35 (t.s.). Published in Tolley (2005), 44, with 'Woman' in the title, despite the fact that L has corrected it by hand on the t.s. to 'Woman's'.

On the t.s. L writes 'worse than awful'.

'Lie there, my tumbled thoughts'

DATE AND TEXT
Sept.–Oct. 1939. Hull DPL (2) 1/1/10/35 (t.s. with one holograph correction). Published in Tolley (2005), 45.

4 Queer] ~~a queer~~ Queer
9 we are] ~~I am~~ we are

On the t.s. L writes 'compact but largely pointless', 'But quite good'.

'Now the shadows that fall from the hills'

DATE AND TEXT

Sept.–Oct. 1939. Hull DPL (2) 1/1/10/35 (t.s.). Published in Tolley (2005), 46, with L's error 'that' (for 'than') reproduced in l. 8, and '[sic]' appended.

On the t.s. L writes 'this has its intellectual points'.

'The pistol now again is raised'

DATE AND TEXT

Sept.–Oct. 1939. Hull DPL (2) 1/1/10/36 (t.s.). Published in Tolley (2005), 47.

On the t.s. L marks verse 3 and writes 'This verse quite good'.
    18–19 Cf. Eliot, *The Love Song of J. Alfred Prufrock*, 120, 131: 'I grow old . . . I grow old', 'Till human voices wake us, and we drown'.

'Autumn has caught us in our summer wear'

DATE AND TEXT

Late 1939. Poem V in *ChP*. Published in *CP* (1988), 233, and in Tolley (2005), 52, without a comma after 'berries' (l. 9), and with L's erratic typing in the indentation of lines 4, 7, 10 13, and 16 regularised. I regularise slightly differently. In the t.s. l. 4 is clearly aligned with l. 1; and though the first lines of the next two verses are slightly indented, ll. 10 and 16 are aligned with the opening line in each case. Accordingly, I do not indent ll. 4, 10, and 16.

9 *Harvest Festival*: thanksgiving service for the completion of harvest in which the church is usually decorated with grain, fruit, etc. 11–12 Wordsworth rhymes 'shall be' with "piety' in 'My heart

leaps up when I behold', 8–9. **15** *achingcold*: Not in *OED*. Cf. John Wilmot, Earl of Rochester, *Song of A Young Lady to her Antient Lover*, 4: 'Aking, shaking, Crazy, Cold'.

Evensong

DATE AND TEXT
?Late 1939. Dated 'Thursday'. Letter (t.s. with holograph additions) to JBS (Hull DP 174/2/10). Published in Tolley (2005), 53.

In the letter L describes the poem as 'Huxleyan and bad. (paradox)'. After the poem, he writes: 'My God! If these are my contemporaries – and they are, easily – then I am a king amongst men. (This thought inspired the first verses.) But then one comes to the last verse . . . and one wonders. Am I wrong? And thousands of thousands of inarticulate voices reply, "We are right." Pigs. Dogs. Goats. Monkeys. (all quite calmly.)'.
    4 As, famously, in Petrarch, *Canzoniere*, no. 199. **15** *every wise man's son doth know*: *Twelfth Night*, 2. 3. 43. **16** Ancient proverb '*vox populi, vox Deï*', quoted by Alcuin in a letter to Charlemagne before 804.

'This is one of those whiteghosted mornings'

DATE AND TEXT
1939. Poem II in *ChP*. Published in Tolley (2005), 14.

'We see the spring breaking across rough stone'

DATE AND TEXT
1939. Poem III in *ChP*. Published in *CP* (1988), 228; and in Tolley (2005), 15, without stanza division after l. 8 or l. 12.

'Why did I dream of you last night?'

DATE AND TEXT
1939. Poem VI in *ChP*. Published in *CP* (1988), 231, and in Tolley (2005), 54.

'The cycles hiss on the road away from the factory'

DATE AND TEXT

8 Feb. 1940: L wrote the date 'Feb. 8th' in pencil at the foot of the
page of the t.s. of *VOTH*, in which it was poem XII (copy-text).
Published in Tolley (2005), 59.

At the foot of the page of the t.s., L writes in pencil 'trash'.

'So you have been, despite paternal ban'

DATE AND TEXT

16 Mar. 1940. 'March 16th' is written on the t.s. of *VOTH* by L.
Poem IV in *VOTH*; poem X in *ChP* (copy-text). Published in *CP*
(1988), 236, and in Tolley (2005), 60.

At the foot of the page in *VOTH*, L writes 'why?' in ink. L in his
diary, 16 Mar. 1940 (Hull DPL (2), 1/1/10/ 53): 'Thought out an
interesting theory about art today. An interesting branch of poetry &
painting would be solely to stimulate the emotions, and to obscure
the meaning of the artist as much as possible. Thus every reader
could place his own construction on the poem & everyone would be
happy. Write a poem today on these lines: "So you have been."'

'Through darkness of sowing'

DATE AND TEXT

18 Mar. 1940: see the note on 'Nothing significant was really said'.
Poem V in *VOTH*; poem IX in *ChP* (copy-text). Published in Tolley
(2005), 61, but, unaccountably, from the earlier text in *VOTH*. The
ChP text has a comma at the end of l. 5 and no commas after 'you'
and 'leaf' in l. 17.

At the foot of the page in the *VOTH* t.s., L writes 'all right'.

'Falling of these early flowers'

DATE AND TEXT

Begun Sept.–Oct. 1939. Hull DPL (2) 1/1/10/33 = Hull t.s. 1; poem
III in *VOTH* (copy-text). Published in Tolley (2005), 40.

VARIANTS (from Hull t.s. 1)
4 Yet the north-blown chimney-sign,
5 stairs] pears,
6 deeper] keener

Above the poem on the earlier t.s., L writes 'Piss'. Marking ll. 3–5, he writes 'these lines have been altered. Anyway they're all but nonsensical.' At the foot of the page of the *VOTH* t.s., he writes 'trash'.

'Praise to the higher organisms!'

DATE AND TEXT
Begun Sept.–Oct. 1939. Hull DPL (2) 1/1/10/36 = Hull t.s. 1; poem VI in *VOTH* (copy-text). Published in Tolley (2005), 48.

VARIANTS
Title A song of praise *Hull t.s. 1*

L writes 'Yoomour' on the earlier t.s. and again on the VOTH t.s.
   10 *D. H. Lawrence*: eminent novelist and poet (1885–1930), whom L when young greatly admired: see, e.g., *SL*, 49–56.

'(from James Hogg) | Lock the door, Lariston, lock it, I say to you'

DATE AND TEXT
Begun Sept.–Oct. 1939. Hull DPL (2) 1/1/10/29 (t.s. with holograph corrections); poem VIII in *VOTH* (copy-text). Published in Tolley (2005), 33, with '(from James Hogg)' in italics.

VARIANTS (from Hull DPL (2) 1/1/10/29)
Heading (To James Hogg, 1770–1835)
12 Leap from your ~~armchair, and charge up the syringe~~; inglenook ~~it's now~~ no time to cringe
13 Lock] O, lock

At the foot of the page of the *VOTH* t.s., L writes in ink 'why?'
   Title James Hogg: Scots poet and novelist (1770–1835). 1 James Hogg, 'Lock the door, Lariston, lion of Liddesdale, | Lock the door, Lariston, Lowther comes on'.

'Turning from obscene verses to the stars'

DATE AND TEXT
Begun Sept.–Oct. 1939. L to JBS, 31 Oct. 1945 (*SL*, 111): 'Do you remember that poem I wrote at school, ending [quotes last verse]'. Hull DPL (2) 1/1/10/29 = Hull t.s. 1; poem X in *VOTH* (copy-text). Published in Tolley (2005), 32.

VARIANTS
19–20 But time likes me, and draws | Me near her shining teeth *Hull t.s. 1*

In the earlier t.s., to the right of the first verse, L writes 'amusing meditation'. To the right of the second verse, he writes 'well? I think this is good.' At the foot of the page in the *VOTH* t.s., he writes 'a bit pointless'.

  5 *Hamlet*, 3. 2. 221 (Folio reading): 'The lady protests too much, methinks'. 17–20 L to JBS (*SL*, 111): 'I don't feel as strongly as that nowadays! But it is true for me, I believe. Norman [Iles?] gave me a long harangue on the necessity for "living" – it doesn't convince me. We've had enough living.'

'Autumn sees the sun low in the sky'

DATE AND TEXT
Begun Sept.–Oct. 1939. Hull DPL (2) 1/1/10/31 = Hull t.s. 1; poem XI in *VOTH* (copy-text). Published in Tolley (2005), 37.

VARIANTS (from Hull t.s. 1)
Title Autumn refrain
10 the] those

To the right of the title in the earlier t.s., L writes 'halma'. (Halma is a chequerboard game.) At the foot of the page of the t.s., he writes 'grrr!'
  5 L to JBS, 15 June 1941 (Hull DP 174/2/24): 'I am in freckled shade. (Does this look like fuckled?) "The trees stand in the setting sun | I in their freckled shade . . ."'

Prologue

DATE AND TEXT
Before 28 Mar. 1940. L added 'March 28th' by hand to '1940' on
the title page of *VOTH* (copy-text). Published in Tolley (2005), 56.

Separated from its original context, the poem is no longer a
prologue, but see the note on the title of *Epilogue* below.

'Standing on love's farther shores'

DATE AND TEXT
Before 28 Mar. 1940. Poem I in *VOTH* (copy-text). Published in
Tolley (2005), 58, with 'traces' for 'trace' (l. 14).

At the foot of the page of the t.s. L writes 'ugly' in ink, and in pencil,
'But how *true!*'

Epilogue

DATE AND TEXT
Before 28 Mar. 1940. *VOTH*; poem XIV in *ChP* (copy-text). The
poem was an epilogue to *VOTH*, but not to *ChP*, but L preserved
the title in *ChP*. L's typing is somewhat erratic in the version in *ChP*,
and I revert to the format of the poem in *VOTH*. Published in Tolley
(2005), 63, with a colon for the semicolon after 'Kill' (l. 5).

L's note at the foot of the page in the *VOTH* t.s.: 'well? July 1940'.

Remark

DATE AND TEXT
L's diary, 10 Apr. 1940, Hull DPL (2) 1/1/10/55: 'Type out
"Remark", a little epigram in the "eyes in which" metre. Says what I
want to say.' In *FP*. Published in Tolley (2005), 67.

L's note pencilled to the right of the title on the t.s.: 'Overly cynical'.

Long Jump

DATE AND TEXT
21 Apr. 1940. L records 'write "Long Jump"' on this day in his diary: DPL (2) 1/1/10/49. Hull DPL (2) 1/3/9d (t.s.). Published in Tolley (2005), 65–6, with the comma missing after 'strange' (l. 18). L's indentation of lines in the t.s. is somewhat erratic at ll. 21 and 28–9. In the present edition, as in Tolley, the lines are printed ranged left.

'Quests are numerous; for the far acid strand'

DATE AND TEXT
4 May 1940, the day on which L records 'Write "Quests are numerous."' in his diary: Hull DPL (2) 1/1/10/49. Poem XXII in *ChP*. Published in Tolley (2005), 75, with 'acrid' for 'acid'.

'For the mind to betray'

DATE AND TEXT
10 June 1940. 'June 10th' is pencilled by L to the left of the first verse on Hull DPL 2/2/3 (t.s. with holograph corrections). See the notes on 'For who will deny' (below). Published in Tolley (2005), 76.

VARIANTS (from Hull DPL 2/2/3)
12 ~~Myself~~ Not me ~~And~~ Yet

'For who will deny'

DATE AND TEXT
10 June 1940. In *FP*, as epigraph. Cf. the closing lines of 'For the mind to betray'. Published in Tolley (2005), 87.

At the foot of the page of the t.s., L writes in pencil 'Not bad, that'.

3 *Not me*: Cf. Housman, *More Poems* XXIII ('Crossing alone the nighted ferry'), 4: 'Count you to find? not me'.

Poem ('Still beauty')

DATE AND TEXT
12 June 1940. 'June 12ᵗʰ' pencilled by L below the text on Hull DPL
2/2/3 (t.s. with one holograph correction). Included in FP with the
heading 'Poem': copy-text. Published in Tolley (2005), 77.

VARIANTS (from Hull DPL 2/2/3)
20 quick] ~~quick~~ my slim

'Now we get to the real rubbish': note pencilled by L to the right of
the title and first two lines on the t.s.

Midsummer Night, 1940

DATE AND TEXT
'June, 1940' written by L on the title-page of FP. Midsummer Night
was on 24 June. In FP; poem XVI in ChP (copy-text). Published in
CP (1988), 244–5 and in Tolley (2005), 99–100, in each case with
the error 'shows' for 'showers' (l. 29). Tolley cites FP but not ChP,
though it is from ChP that he (mis)prints. In the present edition
'unison' (FP) is preferred to 'union' (ChP) in l. 20: there is ample
evidence of mistyping in ChP, and 'sneer in unison' makes better
sense and metre.

'Lay off Auden, my son!': L's note to the right of the title in FP.
   Title Perhaps suggested by *A Midsummer Night's Dream*, as
Osborne (2008), 54, suggests, though 'midsummer night' is common
enough (*OED*). **1–2** Cf. Housman, *More Poems* XXXIII ('On
forelands high in heaven'), 27–8: 'And lamps in England lighted, |
And evening wrecked on Wales'. A. T. Tolley, *My Proper Ground:
A Study of the Work of Philip Larkin and its Development* (1991),
5, cites 'Night moves over China' from Auden. The earlier version
of Auden's poem *Commentary*, at the end of the sonnet sequence
In Time of War, provides a better verbal parallel: 'Night falls
on China' (l. 250); see *The English Auden: Poems, Essays, and
Dramatic Writings, 1927–1939*, ed. Edward Mendelson (1977),
269. **11** Cf. *The Merchant of Venice*, 5. 1. 1: 'In such a night as
this', echoed seven times as 'In such a night'. Noted in Osborne
(2008), 54. **17–18** Cf. *Aubade*, 21–2: 'a special way of being afraid |
No trick dispels'.

Two Sonnets

DATE AND TEXT
Before July 1940. In *FP*. In *The Conscript*, 10, L has typed 'was' through 'were'. Published in Tolley (2005), 93–4, with 'killing' for 'the killing' in *The Conscript*, 9.

Above the first title L pencilled 'Tripey'.

   1 The Conscript Stan Smith notes that Auden opens *In Time of War* abruptly like this ('So from the years the gifts were showered'): 'Something for Nothing: Late Larkins and Early', *English*, 49 (2000), 262.

Further Afterdinner Remarks

DATE AND TEXT
Before July 1940. In *FP*. Published in Tolley (2005), 95–6, with '(extempore)' in the same line as the title and with 'square:' (l. 26) transposed to the end of l. 27.

Above the title in the t.s., L writes in pencil 'Likewise tripish'.

Historical Fact:

DATE AND TEXT
Before July 1940. In *FP*. Published in Tolley (2005), 98.

'But as to the real truth, who knows? The earth'

DATE AND TEXT
Before July 1940. The lines were originally ll. 49–54 of *Long Jump*, written on 21 Apr. 1940. This later text has different punctuation at two points, and L clearly was now regarding it as a self-sufficient poem. In *FP*. Published in Tolley (2005), 101.

L pencilled 'Not bad either' below the text.

'It is late: the moon regards the city'

DATE AND TEXT
By 23 Aug. 1940, when L sent it to JBS with 'A birthday, yes, a day without rain' for his birthday. Hull DP 174/2/17 (t.s. with holograph correction in ink). Published in Tolley (2005), 102, with a comma for the full stop at the end of l. 7, 'portraits' for 'portrait' (l. 16), and 'Offer' for 'Offers' (l. 20).

VARIANTS (from Hull DP 174/2/17)
28 by] ~~and~~ by

28 *by losing, save*: Cf. 'For whosoever will save his life shall lose it; but whosoever shall lose his life . . . shall save it': Mark 8: 35, etc.

'A birthday, yes, a day without rain'

DATE AND TEXT
For the date, see the note on the previous poem. 'Jim' in l. 7 is JBS. Hull DP 174/2/17 (t.s.). Published in Tolley (2005), 103.

'Art is not clever'

DATE AND TEXT
Before Sept. 1940. Poem I in *PAug40*; XVIII in *ChP* (copy-text). Published in Tolley (2005), 104, with 'has meant' for 'meant' in l. 6.

'O today is everywhere'

DATE AND TEXT
Before Sept. 1940. Poem IV in *PAug40*. Published in Tolley (2005), 110.

L's MS note to the right of the title on the t.s.: 'Now we reach the real cess . . .'
14 *endless roads*: Cf. Housman, *A Shropshire Lad* LX ('Now hollow fires burn out to black'), 7: 'the endless road'.

Creative Joy

DATE AND TEXT
Before Sept. 1940. Poem VI in *PAug40*. Published in Tolley (2005), 112.

Opposite the title and opening lines in the t.s., L wrote: 'a little bit of pseudo autobiography'.

'The spaniel on the tennis court'
Before Sept. 1940. Poem X in *PAug40*. Published in Tolley (2005), 116.

Schoolmaster

DATE AND TEXT
Before Sept. 1940. Poem XI in *PAug40*, XXVII in *ChP* (copy-text). In l. 14 of the *PAug40* text the parentheses are added in pencil to the t.s. Published in *CP* (1988), 248, and in Tolley (2005), 117.

L to MJ, 6 Feb. 1951 (Bodl. MS Eng. c. 7404/102): 'I'm always sorry for schoolmasters anyway, on principle.'

'When we broke up, I walked alone'

DATE AND TEXT
Before Sept. 1940. Poem XII in *PAug40*. L mistypes 'talkabout' and 'thinkthat' (ll. 55, 81), and in l. 96 corrects 'acheive'. Published in Tolley (2005), 118–21.

VARIANTS
78 is] ~~am~~ is *PAug40*

43–4 The poem seems to be imaginary. **49** *Molière*: French comic playwright (1622–73). **50** *Hugo*: Victor Hugo (1802–85), poet, dramatist and novelist; the leading figure in French Romanticism. **51** *Garibaldi*: Giuseppe Garibaldi (1807–82), Italian patriot and national hero. **52** *in 1862*: Garibaldi wished to liberate Italy, and to that end decided to take on the Papal States, vowing that he would enter Rome as a victor or perish beneath its walls. **59** *Langland*:

c.1330–86. *Shelley*: 1792–1822. 60 *Auden*: 1907–73. *Donne*: 1572–1631. 72 Cf. *A Study of Reading Habits*, 7: 'inch-thick specs'.

'From the window at sundown'

DATE AND TEXT
Before Sept. 1940. Poem XIII in *PAug40*; XXI in *ChP* (copy-text). Published in Tolley (2005), 122.

'You've only one life and you'd better not lose it'

DATE AND TEXT
Before Sept. 1940. Poem XIV in *PAug40*. Published in Tolley (2005), 123–4, with L's error 'preceeding' in l. 1 of 'Envoi' uncorrected (and no ['*sic*']).

L's note written on the *PAug40* t.s.: 'O a lovely slop of dung, this –'.
   Title Matt. 10: 39: 'He that findeth his life shall lose it: and he that loseth his life for my sake shall find it'; John 12: 25: 'He that loveth his life shall lose it'; etc.

'The question of poetry, of course'

DATE AND TEXT
Before Sept. 1940. Poem XV in *PAug40*. Published in Tolley (2005), 125.

L's note written on the *PAug40* t.s.: 'Likewise 2'. After 'kissed' (l. 7) he writes '(pissed?)'.

Rupert Brooke

DATE AND TEXT
Before Sept. 1940. Poem XVII in *PAug40*. Published in Tolley (2005), 126, with L's error 'opthalmic' (l. 10) faithfully reproduced (and no '[*sic*]').

VARIANTS (from *PAug40*)
   4 life passed] life passed lived?
   12 water] ~~by~~ water

Title English poet (1887–1915). **5** Brooke's family home was at Rugby, Warwickshire. In a letter to Lady Eileen Wellesley dated July 1914, Brooke rhapsodises over Warwickshire: 'It's the sort of county I adore. I'm a Warwickshire man . . . I know the *heart* of England.' **6** *Munich*: He visited Munich, Jan.–Apr. 1911. *Tahiti*: He was there in Feb.–Mar. 1914. See his poem *Tiare Tahiti*. **8** His five idealistic sonnets (1914), entitled *Peace, Safety, The Dead, The Dead* and *The Soldier*. **10–11** Among the various maladies he suffered from during his years at Rugby School (1901–6) was ophthalmia, or pink-eye. At King's College, Cambridge (1906–9) he suffered at one point from nervous exhaustion. **11** He won a scholarship at King's College, Cambridge. **12** *poisoned by coral and water*: While swimming in Tahiti at the end of Feb. 1914, Brooke scraped his leg on coral. The poisoning that ensued, which was aggravated by his subsequent swimming, contributed to his death, on 23 Apr. 1915, from septicaemia following a mosquito bite on the lip. *sun's enemy*: Brooke was very fair-complexioned. To Lascelles Abercrombie from Egypt, 6 Apr. 1915: The Sun God 'distinguished one of his most dangerous rivals since Marsyas among the X thousand tanned and dirty men blown suddenly on these his special coasts a few days or weeks ago. He unslung his bow. I lie in an hotel, cool at length, with wet clothes on my head and less than nothing in my belly': *The Letters of Rupert Brooke*, ed. Geoffrey Keynes (1968), 677. To Violet Asquith, 9 Apr. 1915: 'I've been a victim to the sun. He struck me down': *Letters*, 678. Brooke's fatal infection responded at one point to the dieting prescribed for mild sunstroke: Christopher Hassall, *Rupert Brooke: A Biography* (1964), 507. **13** In addition to the deaths of many friends in the war, Brooke's brother Richard died of pneumonia in 1907, and his brother Alfred was killed in battle in France on 14 June 1915. **14** *foretold his death*: Brooke countenanced the possibility of his death in the opening of *The Soldier*: 'If I should die, think only this of me'.

Postscript | On Imitating Auden

DATE AND TEXT
Before Sept. 1940. In *PAug40*, with the heading 'POSTSCRIPT. | On Imitating Auden'. Published in Tolley (2005), 127, with the subtitle italicised.

'The earliest machine was simple'

DATE AND TEXT
Autumn 1940: L writes the date on the t.s., Hull DPL 2/2/4. The comma after 'logic' (l. 15) is added by hand. Published in Tolley (2005), 132–3.

'Mr. A. J. Wilton'

DATE AND TEXT
Late Nov. 1940. The lines were written in the 'Suggestions Book' of the Junior Common Room (JCR B. 7), of St John's College, Oxford, and were signed 'Yours thoughtfully | Philip A. Larkin'. They appear a few pages before an entry written on the last day of term (*c*.6 Dec.). Published by John Kelly in the college's *TW Magazine* (Summer 2005), 18.

Peter Deyong, a fellow undergraduate, had written a verse squib accusing Arthur Wilton of removing a card from the JCR against standing orders. Wilton's reply, in verse, began: 'To remove a card from the JCR | Is the action of a dastard'. Another undergraduate, C. W. H. Young, altered 'dastard' to 'Bastard'. Deyong replied: 'He sure is no Milton | Our Wilton'.

4 *Bastard*: L supplies the dates of epigrammatist Thomas Bastard.

'There's a high percentage of bastards'

DATE AND TEXT
Included in a letter to JBS dated 19 Dec. 1940: Hull DP 174/2/14. Previously unpublished.

VARIANTS (from the letter)
9 pee] ~~piss~~ pee
10 large] ~~high~~ large
14 arsing] ~~snooping~~ arsing

L in the letter: 'On my second day here I went about chanting bawdy songs in childish defiance. (Parlour tricks) including one I made up myself & which never amounted to more than [verse] Sung very slowly & deliberately. Would be funny if you were all pissed. I'll sing it sometime.'

The language of the letter and the poem is that typically found in the correspondence between L and JBS. Often a letter from one could readily be taken to be from the other – which shows a capacity in L for sympathetic mimicry, also notably seen in his correspondence with KA.

Christmas 1940

DATE AND TEXT

19 Dec. 1940. L included it in a letter to JBS dated 20 Dec. 1940 (Hull DP 174/2/15), in which he comments: 'I scribbled this in a coma at about 11.45 pm. last night. The only thing is that its impulse is not purely negative – except for the last 2 lines, where I break off into mumblings of dotage.' Published in *SL*, 8, and in Tolley (2005) 135, with capitals at the beginnings of ll. 9 and 11, a practice I also follow. There are early poems that have lower-case letters at the beginnings of lines, but the earlier short line in this poem begins with a capital. Tolley has 'fields' for 'field' (l. 1), 'on all' for ' to all on' (l. 5), and 'them as' for 'as them' (l. 7) .

VARIANTS

3 tree and farm] ~~field and~~ tree and farm *Letter to JBS*

Ghosts

DATE AND TEXT

Included in a letter to JBS dated 20 Dec. 1940 (Hull DP 174/2/16). In l. 13 'happy' is inserted above a caret. Published in *SL*, 10, and in Tolley (2005), 136, the latter with 'moths' for 'moth' (l. 14).

L in the letter: 'Have just written the above in about ½ hour – actually a great speed. Lousily technically done, but I wanted to send it to you to show you my *real* talent – not the truly strong man but the fin de siècle romantic, not the clinically austere but the Peg's Paper sonneteer, not Auden but Rupert Brooke.'

Poem ('Walking on the summer grass beneath the trees')

DATE AND TEXT

?Late 1940. Hull DPL 2/2/5. The poem on Hull DPL 2/2/4, 'The earliest machine was simple', is dated 'autumn 1940' in L's hand on the t.s. Published in Tolley (2005), 79.

Prayer of a Plum

DATE AND TEXT

?1940. Hull DPL 2/2/43 (t.s.). Published in Tolley (2005), 80.

'A bird sings at the garden's end'

DATE AND TEXT

?1940. Hull DPL 2/2/44 (t.s.). Published in Tolley (2005), 81–2, with 'hotels [sic]' in l. 44.

At the end of the t.s. L has typed '(This MS has been badly gnawed by Flemish rabbits.)'

7, 19, 23–4, 42 The questions recall Prufrock's, especially those beginning 'Shall I': Eliot, *The Love Song of J. Alfred Prufrock*, 70, 122. 8 Cf. Eliot, *The Waste Land, I The Burial of the Dead*, 28–9: 'Your shadow at morning striding behind you | Or your shadow at evening rising to meet you'. 37 *on the bank*: With 'canal' (ll. 20, 59), may recall *The Waste Land, III The Fire Sermon*, 16–17: 'on the bank . . . the dull canal'. 53–4 *run away | another day*: Cf. the proverb 'He who fights and runs away, may live to fight another day'. 57 *Woolpack*: Common name for a pub or hotel. In a letter to MJ dated 21 Dec. 1952 (Bodl. MS Eng. c. 7408/178), for instance, L mentions the Woolpack Hotel, Warwick.

'I should be glad to be in at the death'

DATE AND TEXT

?1940. Hull DPL 2/2/19 (t.s.). Published in Tolley (2005), 85.

On the t.s. L has typed 'from "Poems for a National Day of Prayers", Faeber and Fwaeber'.

Title Cf. Eliot, *Journey of the Magi*, 43: 'I should be glad of another death'. **2** *loud cities*: Cf. *Ambulances*, 2: 'Loud noons of cities'.

Chant

DATE AND TEXT
?1940. Hull DPL 2/2/17 (t.s.). Published in Tolley (2005), 86, with 'aeropanes [*sic*]' (l. 3).

Hard Lines, or Mean Old W. H. Thomas Blues

DATE AND TEXT
?1940. Hull DPL (2) 1/3/9a (t.s.). Published in Tolley (2005), 73–4, with 'whiskey [sic]' (l. 13). However, L favoured this spelling at the time and for quite some time afterwards, and did so whether he was referring to the Scotch, Irish or Bourbon varieties: in letters to JBS at Hull (1941–51), and letters and cards to MJ (1946–84) and JE (1954–85) at the Bodleian, he writes 'whiskey' thirty-five times and 'whisky' fourteen times, the latter being confined to the 1960s and 1980s. Inconsistently, Tolley leaves 'whiskey' in *Leave*, 10 (p. 177).

On the t.s. at the end of the poem L writes: 'This reminds me of work by some very bad, impudent poet – George Barker, say, or far worse.' He also marks verses 1, 4, 5, 7, 10, and 11 with crosses, and the others with ticks.

Title 'W. H. Thomas' is a mixture of W. H. Auden (1907–73) and Dylan Thomas (1914–53). **12** Cf. Thomas, 'The force that through the green fuse drives the flower' (opening line). **13** Thomas was a notable drinker. **15** Ogres turn up intermittently in Auden's poems. **19** *lawns . . . shaven*: Cf. Milton, *Il Penseroso*, 66: 'the dry, smooth-shaven green'; MacNeice, *Autumn Journal*, 2: 'shaven lawn'. See *Disintegration*, 8. **37** *prom*: promenade, where people walk along the seafront.

'O won't it be just posh'

DATE AND TEXT
5 Feb. 1941, in a letter to his sister Catherine: Hull DLN Correspondence 3/2. Previously unpublished.

L introduces the verse: 'I will sign off now with my signature tune "Forward lads" (tune – "Rock of Ages")'. After them, he writes: 'Sung in tones of beautiful youthful hope.' 2 *Boche*: Slang for German. 4 *'un*: Hun (slang for German).

VARIANTS
5 earth's treasure will be mine] ~~the hour will pass like war~~ earth's treasure will be mine *Hull MS*

'Having grown up in shade of Church and State'

DATE AND TEXT
Begun 8 June 1939. Note by L in *1st Coll*: 'June 8th. – Pleasant enough day. Cricket – 11 runs. Write two good sonnets at night.' In *1st Coll*; poem IV in *ChP* (copy-text). Published in *CP* (1988), 229, and in Tolley (2005), 16, with the title of the magazine *Modern Boy* in l. 8 in italics (as in the present edition).

VARIANTS (from *1st Coll*)
Title Untitled Sonnet
5 With] A

1 The motto of L's school, King Henry VIII School, Coventry, is 'Religioni reipublicae' ('For Religion and the State'). Noted by Fred Holland, *AL*, 20 (Autumn 2005), 85 (but with the motto incorrect). See the notes on *Coventria*. 3 *the Test Match*: cricket match, here between England and a visiting national team, as one of a series. *Lent*: the period from Ash Wednesday to Easter Eve during which it is customary to fast in some way. 8 *Modern Boy*: boys' magazine. 14 'I don't mind diagnosing a simple case of good old sex' is Grimes's comment on the relationship between Margot Beste-Chetwynde and her black lover Chokey in Waugh's *Decline and Fall*, ch. 10. L's note in *1st Coll*: 'Acknowledgements to Evelyn Waugh.'

'When the night puts twenty veils'

DATE AND TEXT
Begun before Sept. 1939. Poem VIII in *ChP*, t.s. with one holograph correction in ink. Published in *CP* (1988), 232, and in Tolley (2005), 23.

VARIANTS (from *ChP*)
14 no] not

'Nothing significant was really said'

DATE AND TEXT
Begun 18 Mar. 1940: see below. Included with a letter to JBS dating from before 14 Dec. 1940 (Hull DP 174/2/12); poem IX in *VOTH*; poem XI in *ChP* (copy-text, in which 'me' in l. 12 is inserted by hand). Published in *CP* (1988), 235, and in Tolley (2005), 62.

VARIANTS
12 break] leave *VOTH*

L's diary, 18 Mar. 1940 (Hull DPL (2) 1/1/10/53–4): 'Today write two poems: "Nothing significant was really said" and "Through darkness of sowing". Former vaguely about le vert paradis. Latter inspired by a meeting & short talk with Whitelaw during which I am convinced that beauty, as such, cannot be explained in any other terms. This unoriginal thought forms the poem. [Quotes 'You are the reason | From reason unwrapped.'] The two poems (future generations note) show my two poetic techniques – mature and spontaneous. I thought day [*sic*] about "Sonnet" but "Poem" was done in a minute. Which is superior?' L's handwritten note on the t.s. sent with the letter to JBS: 'Jim – this is the poem I was vaguely talking about. All characters entirely fictitious. Philip.' At the foot of the page in the *VOTH* t.s., L writes 'all right'.

  1 *Nothing*: Stan Smith notes that this is the opening word of sonnet XXV in Auden's sequence *In Time of War* ('Nothing is given: we must find our law'), a poem which also 'sharply distinguished conventional assumptions of self and role from the existential loneliness of the exceptional individual': 'Something for Nothing: Late Larkins and Early', *English*, 49 (Autumn 2000), 262. 11 Smith, 261: 'Even the exclamatory "O" with which the direct reported speech breaks into the narrative is classic early Auden. Twelve poems in *The English Auden* actually begin with "O", of which four issue directly in semi-rhetorical questions.'

'Prince, fortune is accepted among these rooms'

DATE AND TEXT
Begun before 28 Mar. 1940, when it was included as poem VII in
VOTH. Poem XII in *ChP* (copy-text). Published in Tolley (2005),
57, with the misprint 'vith' for 'with' (l. 2).

VARIANTS
3 Of] From *VOTH*

At the foot of the page in the *VOTH* t.s., L writes 'pretty bad'.

'The hills in their recumbent postures'

DATE AND TEXT
Begun before 28 Mar. 1940, when it was included in *VOTH*. Hull
DPL (2) 1/1/10/37 = Hull t.s. 1; poem II in *VOTH*; poem XIII in *ChP*
(copy-text). Published in *CP* (1988), 234, and in Tolley (2005), 49.

VARIANTS
Title ~~Homage to Daddy Lamartine~~ Ein alte Geshiete *Hull t.s. 1*
6 mortal] closing *Hull t.s. 1*; <u>closing</u> mortal? *VOTH*
7 fall] ~~die~~ fall *Hull t.s. 1*
among] amongst *VOTH*
8 the] ~~the~~ this *Hull t.s. 1*

On the earliest t.s. L writes 'efficient'.

'At once he realised that the thrilling night'

DATE AND TEXT
?Begun before 10 June 1940. Hull DPL 2/2/3 (t.s.). The next two
poems in DPL 2/2/3 are dated by L 'June 10th' and 'June 12th'
respectively, and DPL 2/2/4 is dated 'autumn 1940'. The title
on DPL 2/2/3 is written in ink and enclosed in square brackets
by L. Included in *ChP* (XVII, as 'Two Versions (ii)'; (i) being
'Unexpectedly the scene attained'). The *ChP* text is the copy-text.
Published in Tolley (2005), 78.

VARIANTS (from Hull DPL 2/2/3)
Title [Mary had a little lamb in Arabic.]

After-Dinner Remarks

DATE AND TEXT

Begun before July 1940. In *FP*; poem XV in *ChP* (copy-text). In *ChP* Section II of the poem is irregularly designated 'ii' (rather than 'II'), and 'have' (122) is inserted by hand. Published in *CP* (1988), 238–42, and in Tolley (2005), 88–92, with, in the latter case, a full stop for the comma at the end of 29, 'delay' for 'decay' in 85, and a missing comma at the end of 87.

VARIANTS (from FP)
15 the] its
17 I think of] ~~Forming~~ I think of
19 the] those
27 living flesh beneath] flesh as living as this
34 clean] cleanse
38 these] ~~these~~ this
65 serves] saves
70 leaves] leave
71 starts] sets
77 and tall] or slim
110 her] its
126 Or] And

L's note pencilled above the title in *FP*: 'This is good'.
   6 Cf. Milton, *On the Morning of Christ's Nativity*, 46–8: '. . . Peace, | She crowned with olive green, came softly sliding | Down through the turning sphere'. 7–8 L quotes the lines in a letter dated 15 June 1941 to JBS (Hull DP 174/2/24). 61 *living is a dreadful thing*: Cf. *Measure for Measure*, 3. 1. 115: 'Death is a fearful thing'. 94 *Aaron*: The first high priest of Israel, who did his duty and prevailed despite being spoken against (Num. 16, 17). *a Tess*: In Hardy's *Tess of the D'Urbervilles*, 'A Pure Woman', who adapts her personal life to difficult circumstances, which eventually prove tragic. 101 *reechy*: filthy (as, most familiarly, in *Hamlet*, 3. 4. 168); a variant of 'reeky' (lit. 'smoky'). 109–10 Cf. the revised version of *May Weather*, 1–2: 'A week ago today | Rehearsals were begun'. 123 *our tub of thought*: Diogenes, leader of the Cynics, who scorned riches and the ordinary pleasures of life, made a tub his dwelling. Milton, *Comus*, 708: 'the Cynic tub'.

'Unexpectedly the scene attained'

DATE AND TEXT
Begun before Sept. 1940. Poem II in *PAug40*; poem XVII in *ChP* (as 'Two Versions (i)', (ii) being 'At once he realised that the thrilling night'): copy-text. Published in Tolley (2005), 105, with semicolons instead of commas after 'stars' and 'darling' (l. 3) and 'waters' instead of 'water's' (l. 5).

VARIANTS (from *PAug40*)
4 trees] leaves
5 water's] waters'

13 *lianas*: climbing and twining plants in tropical forests.

'There are moments like music, minutes'

DATE AND TEXT
Begun before Sept. 1940. Poem V in *PAug40*; poem XIX in *ChP* (copy-text). Tolley (2005), 111, acknowledges that the poem is included in *ChP*, but, unaccountably, he largely reproduces the earlier text of *PAug40*. However, from the *ChP* text, he prints a comma after 'harangue' (l. 6) and 'chords of' (l. 13), and he leaves out a comma after 'organ' (l. 13).

VARIANTS (from *PAug40*)
7 simple] the simple
like] of
8 plain] as plain
10 the moving] moving
13 chords of] to

In *PAug40* L underlined 'of art' in l. 7 and wrote 'of *what*' below it.

'Could wish to lose hands'

DATE AND TEXT
Begun before Sept. 1940. Poem IX in *PAug40*; poem XX in *ChP* (copy-text). In *PAug40* the changes in ll. 8 and 9 are made in ink. Published in Tolley (2005), 115, with 'nails' for 'nails" (l. 3).

VARIANTS (from *PAug40*)
7 Inwards] Downwards
8 lose] loses
9 or] or be

On the t.s. in *PAug40* L wrote: 'Sod. Pinched from George Barker.'

'There is no language of destruction for'

DATE AND TEXT
?Begun late 1940. L quoted it in full in a letter to JBS dated 16
Apr. 1941 (*SL*, 12 n.). Poem XXVIII in *ChP* (t.s. with holograph
correction). Published in *CP* (1988), 249, and in Tolley (2005), 128.

VARIANTS (from *ChP*)
4 upright] the upright

L in the letter: 'Here's another Sonnet I found, obscurely scrawled
in pencil on the back of another one: [quotes poem] Elementary but
quite nice.'

'Out in the lane I pause: the night'

DATE AND TEXT
Begun 18–19 Dec. 1940. L to JBS, 20 Dec. 1940 (*SL*, 5): 'I wrote
a poem the last 2 nights which I will copy out for you if I can find
it. Ah yes. It's highly moral, of course. ['Out in the lane I pause:
the night', complete].' Poem XXX in *ChP*. Published in *CP* (1988),
253–4, and in Tolley (2005), 137–8.

VARIANTS (from the letter to JBS)
17 endless love and hope] fear and endless hope
31 what] as
33 gasping] cubic
43 those] the

1 Cf. Auden, 'Out on the lawn I lie in bed'. Noted in A. T. Tolley,
*My Proper Ground: A Study of the Work of Philip Larkin and its
Development* (1991), 5. Note in particular Auden, l. 3, and L, l. 3:
'overhead'; Auden, l. 29, 'silent walkers', L, l. 10, 'lonely walkers'.
Tolley also notes that the stanza form seems to have been inspired

by – it is very similar though not identical – Auden's 'Brothers, who when the sirens roar'.

New Year Poem

DATE AND TEXT

'December 31st | 1940' is typed below the t.s. text in *ChP*. On 16 Apr. 1941 L included it in a letter to JBS (Hull DPL 174/2/227, a t.s. with holograph corrections). Poem XXXI in *ChP* (copy-text). On the *ChP* t.s. 'T' looks to have been typed through 'W' in 'Where' (l. 8); and 'that' in 'through that' (l. 33) is inserted by hand. Published in *CP* (1988), 255–6, and in Tolley (2005), 139–40, in each case with a semicolon for the colon at the end of l. 41.

VARIANTS (from the letter to JBS)

6 The ~~lorries~~ buses bearing their ~~gangs~~ hands back from the ~~bricks~~ works

7 home from bricks –] ~~from the works~~ back from bricks,

8 lorry] ~~truck~~ lorry

21 a laugh] laugh

35 all must take] give to all

36 these] their

38 glove] ~~hand~~ glove

39 results] result

42 Tomorrow] For tomorrow

L in the letter (*SL*, 12): 'the "New Year Poem" which I enclose too is buggering fine'.

42–3 Cf. the repetitions of 'Tomorrow . . .' in Auden's *Spain* (1937), 81, 84, 85, 88, 90, 93, 95. Noted in A. T. Tolley, *My Proper Ground: A Study of the Work of Philip Larkin and its Development* (1991), 5.

'Evening, and I, young'

DATE AND TEXT

By 30 Apr. 1941. Poem XXIII in *ChP*. Published in Tolley (2005), 145–6, with the comma missing at the end of l. 28.

At ll. 30–2 on the t.s., L writes 'my best lines, easily. (April 1942) | endorsed Nov 1944'. He also marks ll. 24–5 and asks 'Eh? Nothing can save the rocks that fall on your mind from your mind falling on them?'

8 *lighted rooms*: Also in *The Old Fools*, 25.

'Stranger, do not linger'

DATE AND TEXT
By 30 Apr. 1941. Poem XXIV in *ChP*. Published in Tolley (2005), 147.

The Poet's Last Poem

DATE AND TEXT
By 30 Apr. 1941. Hull DPL 2/2/50 is a t.s. with holograph corrections; poem XXV in *ChP* (copy-text). Published in Tolley (2005), 149, with 'la-bas' corrected to 'là-bas' (l. 20), as in the present edition.

VARIANTS (from Hull DPL 2/2/50)
Title [No title]
  5 the air] air
12 Dreamed-of] ~~Musical~~ And dreamed-of
12–13 [No break]

'The world in its flowing is various; as tides'

DATE AND TEXT
By 30 Apr. 1941. Included in item XXIX in *ChP* as (i) of 'Two Preliminary Sonnets'. (ii) is 'But we must build our walls, for what we are', published as *Ultimatum*. Published in Tolley (2005), 150.

'Time and Space were only their disguises'

DATE AND TEXT
By 30 Apr. 1941. Poem XXXIV in *ChP*. Published in *CP* (1988), 260, and in Tolley (2005), 144, with 'premiere' corrected to 'première' (l. 13), as in the present edition.

'The house on the edge of the serious wood'

DATE AND TEXT
By 30 Apr. 1941. Poem XXXV in *ChP* (copy-text). Hull DP
174/2/223 (t.s.). Published in *CP* (1988), 258–9, and in Tolley
(2005), 142–3, in each case with 'These' for 'Those' (l. 41) and with
L's error 'hearts' corrected silently to 'heart's' (l. 41). In l. 12 of the
t.s., 'they' is very faint. It is cancelled, and 'they' is confirmed by
hand in the left margin.

VARIANTS
36 told] aware *Hull DP 174/2/223*

'Out of this came danger'

DATE AND TEXT
By 30 Apr. 1941. Hull DPL 2/2/50 (t.s.). From a six-part poem of
which two parts and a fragment survive. This is part (v), part (vi)
being *The Poet's Last Poem*. Published in Tolley (2005), 148.

1–4 Adam Kirsch, *TLS*, 5328 (13 May 2005), 9, notes L practising
Auden's half-rhymed lines.

The Dead City: A Vision

DATE AND TEXT
?By 30 Apr. 1941. The poem is numbered 'XIX' and may have been
prepared for possible inclusion in *ChP*. Hull DP 174/2/224 (t.s.). In
the present edition 'a vision' has been regularised to "A Vision', and
'beseigers' in l. 2 has been corrected. Previously unpublished.

'At school, the acquaintance'

DATE AND TEXT
Included in a letter to JBS dated 21 May 1941 (Hull DP 174/2/23).
Published in Tolley (2005), 152, with 'And wish' for 'And a wish'
(l. 6) and 'deflating' for 'defeating' (l. 8).

VARIANTS (from the letter)
18 But weakness] But of weakness

L in the letter: 'You've read it before, I know, but it restruck me as having a standard of competence in imitation that I hadn't expected. However, it is *nowhere near Auden* – as you know.'

'The wind at creep of dawn'

DATE AND TEXT
Included in a letter to JBS dated 15 June 1941 (Hull DP 174/2/24). Poem IV in *7th Coll* (copy-text), in the preface to which L gives the year. Published in Tolley (2005), 155.

'Those who are born to rot, decay –'

DATE AND TEXT
It is in L's fragmentary short story *Peter* (Hull DPL 4/6); published by James Booth in *AL*, 11 (Apr. 2001), 13–23, with the poem on p. 19. Booth plausibly places the story in Oct. 1941 (ibid., 13). See *After-Dinner Remarks*, 85–90.

In the story, Peter repeats 'a verse to himself written during an attack of adolescent melancholia [. . .] The polish of the verse surprised him.'

'O what ails thee, bloody sod'

DATE AND TEXT
4 Dec. 1941, in a letter to JBS written in ink (Hull DP 174/2/35). Published in Tolley (2005), 159, as a continuous text, whereas the poem is written by L in quatrains. There are other errors: a semicolon for the colon at the end of l. 4; 'garden's' for 'gardens'' (l. 10); 'and' for 'on' (l. 15); a comma for the semicolon at the end of l. 17; and 'In' for 'Ere' (l. 22).

VARIANTS (from the letter)
  6 cosy fun] ~~home~~ cosy fun
  26 brown] ~~brought~~ brown

L in the letter: 'This is the latest work of the brilliant new Post-Masturbationist poet, Shaggerybox McPhallus. His new book of verse, "The Escaped Cock", deals almost exclusively with problems of intense spiritual value . . .'

1–4 Cf. Keats, *La Belle Dame sans Merci*, 1–4: 'O what can ail thee, knight at arms, | Alone and palely loitering? | The sedge has wither'd from the lake, | And no birds sing.' **8** Keats, 8: 'And the harvest's done'. **21** Keats, 45: 'And this is why I sojourn here'. **22** Cf. Milton, sonnet XVI ('When I consider how my light is spent'), 2: 'Ere half my days'.

'After the casual growing-up'

DATE AND TEXT
Included with a letter of 21 May 1941 to JBS (Hull DP 174/2/23): Hull DP 174/2/225 (t.s.), with L's note on it to JBS ('my latest – legible, I hope | Philip'); Hull DPL 2/2/46 (t.s.); poem IV in 7P (copy-text). Published in Tolley (2005), 160.

VARIANTS
Title Fable *Hull DP 174/2/225* <u>FABLE.</u> *Hull DPL 2/2/46*
  9 up] ~~on~~ up *Hull DP 2/2/46*
  11 Flames] Flame *Hull DP 174/2/225; Hull DPL 2/2/46*
  15 [Not split in *Hull DP 174/2/225* or *Hull DPL 2/2/46*]
  16 horse he stood] sack he slumped *Hull DP 174/2/225; Hull DPL 2/2/46*
  17 not] was not *Hull DP 174/2/225; Hull DPL 2/2/46*
  24 clouds] chains *Hull DP 174/2/225;* ~~skeins~~ clouds *Hull DP 2/2/46*

L in the letter: '"Fable" is possibly bad technically, but as regards content it is one of my most important poems. For better readings divide by paragraphing line 15 (". . . falling [|] They . . .") Even so, it has three really good Auden lines in it (consecutive). I leave you to find them.'

'There behind the intricate carving'

DATE AND TEXT
Quoted in a letter to JBS dated 15 June 1941 (Hull DP 174/2/24). Poem II in 7P (copy-text), where L has marked the last three lines and written 'true' in the margin. Published in Tolley (2005), 156.

VARIANTS (from the letter to JBS)
3 book] ~~book~~ word

7–8 By inflexion in a sentence show | That only those who pardon know.

'Sailors brought back strange stories of those lands'

DATE AND TEXT

Begun between Apr. and 18 Nov. 1941. Hull DPL 2/2/45 is a t.s.
with holograph corrections and a version of the first two lines
of *Observation*. The copy-text is the revised text, poem V in 7*P*.
Published in Tolley (2005), 161, with L's error 'travellers' in l. 6
reproduced with '[sic]'.

VARIANTS (from DPL 2/2/45)
  6 point] ~~guide~~ point
  way] ~~home~~ way
  7 ecstasy] ~~liberty~~ ecstasy
  9 maps deceived them] ~~ruinous falsehood~~ maps deceived them
  12 vessels under] ~~coracles on~~ vessels against

Dances in Doggerel

DATE AND TEXT

Begun between Apr. and Dec. 1941. Poem VI in 7*P*. Published in
Tolley (2005), 162–4.

VARIANTS (from 7*P*)
74 ~~one~~ I

63, 64 *river* | *quiver*: Rhyme in Tennyson, *The Lady of Shalott*, 10,
13 (also with the same metre).

Lines after Blake

DATE AND TEXT

Begun between Apr. and Dec. 1941. Included as a supplementary
(unnumbered) poem in 7*P*: copy-text. Published in Tolley (2005),
165, with 'time' for 'Time' (l. 1).

The Blakean elements comprise metre and couplets, pithy wisdom,
abstractions, personifications and metaphors, and successive
rhetorical questions.

'I don't like March!'

DATE AND TEXT

By 7 Mar. 1942, when it is included in a letter to JBS (Hull DP 174/2/ 41). Published in Tolley (2005), 168, with a semicolon for the exclamation mark at the end of l. 1, and with L's error 'Its' silently corrected to 'It's' (l. 2).

L introducing the poem in the letter: 'To quote T. E. Hulme: "Warmth's the only stuff of poetry" – Yes sir! I long for the relaxed muscles of summer – tired of winter. But it's March – we're nearly through it. Permit me to extemporize.' To the right of the first verse he writes: '(Acknowledgements to Auden, MacNeice and Bugger E. Box-McPhallus)'. To the right of the second: '(Acknowledgements to Dylan Thomas, Henry Treece, Terence Tiller, and P. A. Larkin-in-the-shithouse)'.

3–4 Cf. the nursery rhyme 'The North Wind doth blow | And we shall have snow'. 13–14 Cf. Matt. 17: 5: 'a voice out of the cloud'. Also Mark 9: 7, Luke 9: 35.

'The doublehanded kiss and the brainwet hatred'

DATE AND TEXT

Mar. [1942]: MS letter to JBS (Hull DP 174/2/39). The year can be established from the fact that L refers in the letter to Story ('Tired of a landscape'), published on 13 Feb. 1941, as having been written about 18 months previously. Published in Tolley (2005), 169, with 'of' for 'at' (l. 4) and 'done' for 'alone' (l. 7).

VARIANTS (from the letter)
7 alone I] ‡ alone I

L introducing the poem in the letter: 'I have quite changed my style of writing, probably for the worse, having become soaked in Dylan Thomas. Here is the latest:'.

'A day has fallen past'

DATE AND TEXT
Apr. 1942. The sheet bearing this and the next poem also bears the heading 'poems. April | 1942'. Hull DPL 2/2/41 (t.s.). The poem is numbered '(1)'. Published in Tolley (2005), 170.

'If days were matches I would strike the lot'

DATE AND TEXT
Apr. 1942. Hull DPL 2/2/41 (t.s.); poem X in *7th Coll* (copy-text). Published in Tolley (2005), 171.

'I walk at random through the evening park'

DATE AND TEXT
Apr. 1942. The t.s. is stapled to the sheet bearing the previous poem. Hull DPL 2/2/41 (t.s.). Published in Tolley (2005), 172, with 'tickets' for 'ticket' in l. 24.

'At the flicker of a letter'

DATE AND TEXT
?Begun late Nov. 1940. Line 3 of the poem specifies 'late November'. A slightly different version of the first stanza is quoted in a letter to JBS, 20 Dec. 1940 (*SL*, 6), and the text was revised as poem II in *7th Coll* (copy-text), in the preface to which collection L states that the poem was written in 1940. Published in Tolley (2005), 134, with L's error 'november' in l. 3 silently corrected.

VARIANTS (from the letter to JBS)
2 frozen] leaden
3 at] ~~in~~ at

L in the letter: 'A poem is written because the poet gets a sudden vision – lasting one second or less – and he attempts to express the whole of which the vision is a part. Or he attempts to express the vision [. . .] I am not trying to imitate Auden: I am juggling with sounds and associations which will best express the original vision. It is done quite intuitively and esoterically.'

'Where should we lie, green heart'

DATE AND TEXT

Between Apr. and 10 July 1942. Poem I in *7th Coll.* Published in Tolley (2005), 173, with L's erratic indentation in l. 1 corrected.

'I am the latest son'

DATE AND TEXT

Between Apr. and 10 July 1942. Poem III in *7th Coll.* Published in Tolley (2005), 174.

1 Perhaps influenced by Vernon Watkins, *The Collier*, 4: 'I was the youngest son'. L may have been further influenced by the poem: see the notes on *The Explosion*.

'This triumph ended in the curtained head'

DATE AND TEXT

Between Apr. and 10 July 1942. Poem V in *7th Coll.* Published in Tolley (2005), 175.

'The sun swings near the earth'

DATE AND TEXT

Between Apr. and 10 July 1942. Poem VI in *7th Coll.* Published in Tolley (2005), 176.

Leave

DATE AND TEXT

Between Apr. and 10 July 1942. Poem VII in *7th Coll.* Published in Tolley (2005), 177–80, with the misprint 'kind's of' (l. 3) and with 'Homer' for 'Horner' (l. 78).

2 *cretonned*: decorated with patterned cotton cloth. 44 *Corona*: a size of cigar. 51 *Huns*: (derogatory for) Germans. 65 *Rover*: Make of car. 70-1 *make | belly-ache*: The rhyme is in Housman, *A Shropshire Lad* LXII 5, 6. 78–9 The rhyme is from the opening of the nursery rhyme 'Little Jack Horner | Sat in a corner'.

'As the pool hits the diver, or the white cloud'

DATE AND TEXT
Between Apr. and 10 July 1942. Hull DPL (2) 1/4/2 (t.s. with
holograph corrections; headed '<u>Poem</u>'); poem VIII in *7th Coll* (copy-
text). Published in Tolley (2005), 181, with L's typing error 'secred'
in l. 10 silently corrected.

VARIANTS (from Hull DPL (2) 1/4/2)
  8 warning] ~~logic~~ warning
10 sacred] ~~sacred~~ secret

'Flesh to flesh was loving from the start'

DATE AND TEXT
Between Apr. and 10 July 1942. Hull DPL (2) 1/4/1 (t.s., headed
'Sonnet'); poem IX in *7th Coll* (copy-text). Published in Tolley
(2005), 182 with extra space before and after the three dots.

VARIANTS (from Hull DPL (2) 1/4/1)
  6 crying] weeping
11 will call you blood] must call you Time
14 hanging] ~~hiding~~ hanging

July Miniatures

DATE AND TEXT
Between Apr. and 10 July 1942. Item XI in *7th Coll*. Published in
Tolley (2005), 183, with 'miniatures' (unregularised) in the title.

'Blind through the shouting sun'

DATE AND TEXT
Between Apr. and 10 July 1942. Poem XII in *7th Coll*. Published in
Tolley (2005), 184.

4 *walking pylons*: Cf. the version of l. 24 (recorded in Variants) of
Going, Going: 'The pylons are walking'.

The Returning

DATE AND TEXT

Between Apr. and 10 July 1942. Poem XIII in *7th Coll*. Published in
Tolley (2005), 185.

VARIANTS

7 By] In By *7th Coll*

6 *Drives their dry blood*: Cf. Dylan Thomas, 'The force that through
the green fuse drives the flower', 7: 'Drives my red blood'.

Now

DATE AND TEXT

?Mid-1942. Hull PL (2) 1/4/3 (t.s.). Published in Tolley (2005), 186,
with 'victim' for 'victims' (l. 2).

'The poet has a straight face'

DATE AND TEXT

In his diary, L records on 23 Apr. 1940 'Type out "Poem" "Study in
4 parts"': Hull DPL (2) 1/1/10/49. When he notes on 9 May which
verses he likes (I–2, 4, 5, 6; II–2, 3, 4; III–4; IV–2, 3, 5, 6), it is clear
that the poem was a longer one at this stage.

Hull DPL 2/2/38: t.s. with holograph corrections and additions
in ink. This is a later version than the one previously typed out. In
DPL 2/2/38 it comes after *A Member of the 1922 Class Reads the
1942 Newspapers* and precedes *Sonnet: Penelope, August, 1942*,
and the line 'A single body's achievement of nineteen years?' would
also point to a date before L's twentieth birthday on 9 Aug. 1942. It
has no title. It is possible in all cases but two to discern a single final
version: there are uncancelled alternative versions in ll. 33 and 93. In
these cases I print the latest version in the text, and record the other
uncancelled version below. At ll. 19, 24, 37 and 50, L has inserted
words by hand.

Published in Tolley (2005), 68–72, with no mention of the
source of the text, and with the title 'Poem: Study in Four Parts',
a comma for the full stop at the end of l. 2, a comma after 'face'
(l. 19), 'complete' for 'caught' (l. 21), 'Now' (cancelled in the MS)
for 'And' and 'to' for 'can' (l. 38), a semicolon for the colon at the

end of l. 44, 'a' for 'the' (l. 89), and 'the sun' for 'sun' (l. 101). At ll. 87–8, Tolley misses or misunderstands L's reordering of the lines (the effect of which is to cancel the first version): L encircles 'soft as a licking candle say my wish' and indicates by an arrow that it is to follow 'Over the wine of memory and hoping'. Tolley's question mark in square brackets after 'mad' at the end of l. 34 is not in the t.s. or in the handwritten revisions to it, but is his signal that he cannot read L's handwriting.

VARIANTS (from Hull DPL 2/2/38)
18 with a] ~~from the~~ with a
19 interesting] ~~own beautiful~~ interesting
of all the] of
20 evening] ~~country~~ evening
22 catalogued] ~~classified~~ catalogued
24 simple images] image *1st version*
25 But] ~~Then~~ But
28 eaten] ~~bitten spotted~~ eaten
29 Strayed] ~~Wandered~~ Strayed
30 And] ~~And Now~~ And
hill] hill~~side~~
32 Are] ~~Were~~ Are
wheat] ~~fish fire flames~~ wheat
33 ~~And more than houses are breaking~~ *1st version*
While] And While *2nd version*
34 ~~Now death is soaring down from every moon~~ *1st version*
Under the echoing moon *2nd version*
lie] ~~are~~ lie *3rd version*
37 the paths] paths
50 prayerless dead] dead
54 no] ~~the~~ no
59 a house] ~~an inn~~ a house
66 in] ~~at~~ in
70 childhoods] child~~ishness~~hoods
71 Those] ~~The~~ Those
82 ~~Your mind passing the kindnesses like cakes,~~ Flushed and timid are the kindnesses
83 ~~Eager to return to the familiar life~~ And wanting the old unnoticed life again,
87–8 ~~And soft as a licking candle say my wish | Over the wine of memory and hoping,~~ And over the wine of memory and hoping | Soft as a licking candle say my wish,

91 prayer] ~~praising~~ prayer
92 in] ~~of~~ in
93 May out] Out *1st version*
97 striking arrow] arrows thrust ~~striking~~ striking arrow

Entries in L's diary, Hull DPL (2), 1/1/10/ 49: 23 Apr. 1940, 'The first time I have fully stated my dilemma'; 1 May 1940, 'I still rather like it'; 9 May (referring to the verses he likes), 'They have a skilful ease of expression I didn't think I could achieve. There is some badly-expressed tripe, but on the whole it is a successful and significant poem.'

   34 Cf. *Money*, 15–16: 'the churches ornate and mad | In the evening sun'. **70** *forgotten childhoods*: Cf. *Coming* 12–13: 'whose childhood | Is a forgotten boredom'. **72** *Lawrence*: D. H. Lawrence (1885–1930). **102–3** Cf. *TNS*, VII 1–2: 'The horns of the morning | Are blowing, are shining'. **104, 106** Cf. *TNS*, XX 1–2: 'a girl . . . a dazzling field of snow'. **108–9** Cf. 'Long roots moor summer to our side of earth', 3: 'River-fresh castles of unresting leaf'; *The Trees*, 9: 'Yet still the unresting castles thresh'.

To James Sutton | Poem

DATE AND TEXT
By 17 Aug. [1942], when it was included as a separate t.s. with a letter to JBS (Hull DP 174/2/51). On another version of the poem, Hull DPL (2) 1/3/9b (t.s.) [copy-text], L has written 'August 1942?'. On this text, L has written 'To James Sutton', and made a correction in l. 13 by hand. The correction, and the querying of the date, suggest that this is a later text than the one sent in the letter to JBS. Published from the t.s. accompanying the letter to JBS in *AL*, 14 (Oct. 2002), 8, by Don Lee and James Booth; and in Tolley (2005), 187, with 'lubber's' for 'lubbers'' (l. 21). In neither case is the existence of the later t.s. version acknowledged.

VARIANTS
13 Yet] For *Letter to JBS*; ~~For~~ Yet *Hull DPL (2) 1/3/9b*

6 *birdless*: Also in *TNS*, *Songs*, 65°N, 12 ('The birdless sea'), and *Next, Please*, 23 ('birdless silence').

'Llandovery'

DATE AND TEXT

The first two lines also appear in a letter of 14 July 1942 to KA
(Hull DPL 5/1; *SL*, 37): 'This discovery does not please me. Nice
word, discovery. | Llandovery | Is responsible for the discovery . . .
| Completion, please.' The poem is included in a letter of 20 Aug.
1942 to KA (Hull DPL 5/1 [t.s.]). Published in *AL*, 14 (Oct. 2002),
10, and in Tolley (2005), 189. Tolley prints 'women' for 'wemen'
(l. 4), and a question mark at the end of the text which belongs not
with the text of the poem but with L's question prefacing it: 'Did I
send you [poem]?'

Title The name is of an upper Towy valley market town in Wales.

Fuel Form Blues

DATE AND TEXT

It was included with a letter to KA dated 20 Aug. 1942 (Hull DPL
5/1); *AL*, 14 (Oct. 2002), 9–10; *SL*, 42–3: 'I enclose Fuel Form
Blues, composed & illuminated at the office.' The copy-text is Hull
DPL 5/1. The poem is typed, the title handwritten, and the text is
accompanied by L's drawing of a jazz band. Published in Tolley
(2005), 188, with L's 'wont' (l. 13) corrected silently to 'won't', but
without italicisation of 'see' (l. 2), signalled in the t.s. by underlining.

L had a temporary summer job as a clerk in the Borough Treasurer's
Office, Jury Street, Warwick: 'Work consists of reducing a fucking
great pile of Fuel Rationing forms (numbering several thousand –
about five, I should think) into a fucking great pile of Fuel Rationing
forms in alphabetical order of streets and numbers according to
the Rate Book, whose numbering goes NOT 1-2-3-4-5-6 but 2-4-
6-5-3-1. WHY? Because, once upon a time, a rate collector used to
walk up the street and down the other side. Consequently, you have
to sort 60 forms out of 5,000 of one street, say, divide them into
odds and even numbers, and then fit them together in the manner
described, pausing to look up in the rate book to find where a house
occurs when some son of a shit-bespattered cock chooses to call
his hovel "Oakdene" instead of "27". There are quite a number of
streets in Warwick': to KA, 4 Aug. 1942 (*SL*, 40). L in an untitled
prose fragment written at the time: 'Mr. Wilson, the Treasurer and

also the Local Fuel Overseer, came in with his pipe and an armful of forms. We had to sort them into streets. In all there were about five thousand of them, and I knew very few of the streets, having spent only three vacations in the town. However, we settled down. It was like sorting an enormous pack of playing cards into suits': Hull DPL (2) 1/3/11; *AL*, 14 (Oct. 2002), 5.

'When you sing the blues, you sing a rhymed couplet (with the first line repeated) against a twelve-bar progression of the common chord on the keynote, the chord of the sub-dominant, the chord of the dominant, and the chord of the dominant seventh. It is a loose, monotonous form, easily fitted to physical movement like lifting or scrubbing, and it is the American Negro's most characteristic expression': L in a 1960 review (*RB*, 43).

Poem ('I met an idiot at a bend in the lane')

DATE AND TEXT
20 Aug. 1942: dated by L on the t.s. Hull DPL 2/2/18 (t.s.).
Published in Tolley (2005), 190.

10 Cf. 1 Cor. 13: 11: 'when I became a man, I put away childish things'.

'The canal stands through the fields; another'

DATE AND TEXT
23–8 Aug. 1942: dated by L on the t.s. Hull DPL (2) 1/3/9c (t.s.).
Published in Tolley (2005), 191–2, with L's mis-spelling 'bombsight' for 'bombsite' (l. 35) uncorrected.

Planes Passing

DATE AND TEXT
?Begun 1940. L quotes a version of the first seven lines in a letter to JBS dated 5 Aug. 1942 (Hull DP 174/2/50), remarking 'I have also changed my poetic style, writing pompous, windy effusions of the war in the style of Stephen Spender.' Hull DPL 2/2/47 (t.s.).
Published in Tolley (2005), 84.

  2 drumhead] drumskin
3–4 Where, leaving soft trails of sound, | The separate bombers
crawl:

Aeroplanes appear regularly in Spender's poems. L is thinking
of war poems such as *Thoughts During an Air Raid* (1939). The
only specific influence, a similar opening in Spender's *Ultima Ratio
Regum* (1939), is noted in Andrew Swarbrick, *Out of Reach: The
Poetry of Philip Larkin* (1995), 10: 'The guns spell money's ultimate
reason | In letters of lead on the spring hillside'.

'As a war in years of peace'

DATE AND TEXT
'Written August 1940: revised September 15th 1942. Coventry–
Warwick. This is the first instance of a poem being revised': L's note
below the revised version inserted after the first version in *PAug40*.
L also pencils 'aaoh' next to ll. 16–17 of the revised version and
'ooo-er' beneath his note about the revision. Poem VII in *PAug40*;
XXVI (but misnumbered XVI) in *ChP*; revised version inserted
in *PAug40* (copy-text). In his note on the textual sources, Tolley
(2005), 114, mentions *PAug40* and *ChP*, and reproduces L's note
about the revision of the text. The version he prints on p. 113 is not
that in *PAug40*: it is the *ChP* text (Apr. 1941), which AT printed in
CP (1988), 246 (when he should have chosen the revised text of 15
Sept. 1942 inserted with L's note in *PAug40*). The revised version is
in Tolley (2005), 114.

The first *PAug40* text:

> As a war in years of peace
> Or in war an armistice
> Or a father's death, just so
> Our parting was not visualized
> When from the further side I gazed   5
> Occasionally, as likely sorrow,
>
> For parting is no simple act
> Scenery-shifting for the next,
> Parting is a trailing streamer,
> Lingering like leaves in Autumn   10

Thinning at the winter's comb –
No more impressive nor supremer;

If so, then still is less than death,
The only parting; on a hearth
Or passing street, always the meeting   15
And the wondering brain and eye
Quickly consulting memory
That follow or precede that greeting.

Only another case, perhaps,
Arranges our predestined shapes: 20
That of brilliant passing liner
Or the miraculous interpretation
Of the simple composition –
Jewels life throws up as a miner.

And so, being caught quite unawares   25
By petition for some gracious tears,
I ponder on the consequence
Of never seeing this, nor saying
What, remembered, still seems glowing
As all of you. Indifference?   30

VARIANTS (to first *PAug40* text from *ChP*)
 7 simple] single
18 That] ~~That~~ That
24 as] like

A Member of the 1922 Class Looks to the Future

DATE AND TEXT
?Late 1942. Hull DPL 2/2/21 (t.s.). Published in Tolley (2005), 193,
with L's 'shant' uncorrected (l. 2).

8 *Cologne*: Bombed in 262 raids during World War II, including the
first 1,000-bomber raid on the night of 30–31 May 1942. *Coventry*:
Suffered severe damage from air raids during World War II, most
notoriously on 14 Nov. 1940. 13 The Nazis under Hitler ruled
Germany from 1933 to 1945.

A Member of the 1922 Class Reads the 1942 Newspapers

DATE AND TEXT

?Late 1942. Hull DL 2/2/37 (t.s. with holograph corrections of errors, mostly of typing). Published in Tolley (2005) 193–4, with L's 'wont' (l. 2) uncorrected.

Below the poem in the t.s. is L's drawing of a goofy bespectacled figure wearing a bow-tie saying 'By Jove, yes, I thoroughly agree, eh?'

18 *Eton*: Eton College, Windsor, a school associated with wealth and privilege. 20 A sign of regional or vulgar speech.

A Democrat to Others

DATE AND TEXT

?Late 1942. Hull DPL 2/2/21 (t.s.). Published in Tolley (2005), 195.

'After a particularly good game of rugger'

DATE AND TEXT

By 8 Nov. 1942, when it is quoted in a letter to Norman Iles. Published in *SL*, 47, and in Tolley (2005), 196.

1 *rugger*: rugby football (slang). 3 *scrum*: scrummage, in which two sets of forwards pack themselves close together with their heads down and try to push their opponents off the ball while heeling it out into open play.

Poem ('The camera of the eye')

DATE AND TEXT

'Unfinished, circa December, 1942': L's note on the t.s., Hull DPL 2/2/42. Published in Tolley (2005), 197, with 'around' for 'round' (l. 11) and 'thickened' for 'quickened' (l. 20).

9 *Aleaf*. Not in OED.

'(from the back) | We're Middleton Murry & Somerset Maugham'

DATE AND TEXT
Included in a letter to JBS dated 2 Jan. 1943 (Hull DP 174/2/55).
Previously unpublished.

The lines are written in imitation of the traditional song with refrain
'*Vive l'Amour*', which opens variously with 'Let every good fellow
now join in our song' or 'Let every good fellow now fill up his glass'.

2 *Middleton Murry*: [John] Middleton Murry (1889–1957),
prolific English man of letters and advocate of commitment to
the spiritual inner self. *Somerset Maugham*: [William] Somerset
Maugham (1874–1965), novelist, short story writer, and
playwright. 5 *Lawrence*: D. H. Lawrence (1885–1930).

Songs of Innocence and Inexperience

DATE AND TEXT
The Hull catalogue assigns it to 1943–6, but the joint authorship
of P. S. Brown, Edward duCann and L makes L's time at St John's
College, Oxford (Oct. 1940–June 1943) much more likely. It is not
known who composed individual poems in the sequence, which runs
Soul, *Birth*, *The Death of Life*, 'A broken down chair sprawls in the
corner', *To Ursula* and *Spoonerism*. The copy-text is Hull DPL (2)
1/3/7. Published in Tolley (2005), 364–8, prefaced by a prose piece
called 'Marie' that seems not to relate to the poems. Tolley gives Philip
Brown as 'B. S. Brown', and in the first paragraph of the prose 'on to'
for 'onto' and 'was' for 'was ever'. In the poems, he gives 'woods and
animals' for 'woods of animals' in *The Death of Life*, 9; 'useless' for
'useful' in 'A broken down chair sprawls in the corner', 4; a semicolon
for the colon at the end of *To Ursula*, 5; a semicolon for the colon at
the end of *Spoonerism*, 2; and a comma for the full stop at the end
of *Spoonerism*, 6. He corrects several typographical or spelling errors
('Theother', 'fashoned', 'symbal', 'cacophany') silently.

Title After William Blake's *Songs of Innocence* and *Songs of
Experience*. **Soul 1–2** Possibly a reminiscence of Housman,
'Crossing alone the nighted ferry | with the one coin for fee'
(in which case the oarsman is Charon, who ferries the souls of
the dead across the River Styx in the underworld). **To Ursula**

Ursula Brangwen is a character in Lawrence's *Women in Love* who seeks, and finds, sexual and personal fulfilment. Lawrence regarded Mexico as a place of mysterious liberation (as in *The Plumed Serpent*). He visited it in 1923 and 1924. **Spoonerism** An unfortunate utterance in which sounds are switched (as in 'half-warmed fish' for 'half-formed wish', 'shoving leopard' for 'loving shepherd'), characteristic of the Revd William Spooner (1844–1930) of New College, Oxford.

If approached by Sir Cyril Norwood

DATE AND TEXT
Oct. 1940–June 1943. Published by Nick Russel in Hartley (1988), 87.

1 Sir Cyril Norwood: 1875–1956. President of St John's College, Oxford, 1934–46.

Letters

DATE AND TEXT
It appears in *Wkbk 1* (1/1/6) with the date '(*Summer 1943 – June* [?])'. It is a draft without uncancelled alternative readings. Previously unpublished.

Blues

DATE AND TEXT
12 July 1943: MS letter to JBS (Hull DP 174/2/70). Published in Tolley (2005), 201, as continuous text instead of the three-line stanzas of the MS. In the present edition the ampersand in l. 3 is retained (Tolley substitutes 'and' and sacrifices informality), and, as in Tolley, a needed comma is inserted at the end of line 2.

Immediately after the poem L writes '(enter Pee Wee Russell)': this should, I think, be part of the text, on the grounds that L writes a horizontal line *after* this to section off the text from the rest of the letter.

Below this, he comments 'The above blues has been in my head some time, I think it's awfully good. (Swells up & bursts).' See the discussion of blues in the note on *Fuel Form Blues*. 10 *Pee Wee*

Russell: 1906–69, jazz musician (saxophone and clarinet player). See the note on 'And did you once see Russell plain?', 1.

'The – er – university of Stockholm – er – '

DATE AND TEXT
28 July 1943: MS letter to JBS (Hull DP 174/2/72). Published in Tolley (2005), 202.

2 *Jung*: Swiss psychologist Carl [Gustav] Jung (1875–1961).

The False Friend

DATE AND TEXT
Aug.–Sept. 1943, and before 13 Sept., when L tells KA in a letter that Bruce Montgomery likes the last poem in the collection *Sugar and Spice* best (*SL*, 69). (The last poem was *The School in August*.) In *Sugar and Spice*: Hull DPL (2) 1/11; Bodl. MS Eng. c. 2356. Published in *TAWG*, 244; and in Tolley (2005), 203, with the last line detached from the stanza.

Bliss

DATE AND TEXT
The poem is in *Sugar and Spice*; see the notes on the previous poem for details of date and text. A slightly different version appears in a letter of 20 Aug. 1943 to KA (*SL*, 64). Published in *TAWG*, 245, and in Tolley (2005), 204.

VARIANTS (from the letter to KA)
[No indentation of lines]
 5 stable] stables
13 up] in up
16 It's twelve] Twelve

6 *junior B.S.A.*: bicycle made by the Birmingham Small Arms company. 10 *W. H. Smith & Son*: newsagents and booksellers. 14–15 *Handling Horses: Hints and Principles for the Training and Education of Horses and their Riders* by Lieutenant-Colonel P. D. Stewart was first published in 1943.

Ballade des Dames du Temps Jadis

DATE AND TEXT
The poem is in *Sugar and Spice*; see the notes above on *The False Friend* for details of date and text. Published in *TAWG*, 247–8. In l. 54 L typed 'Elspeth, Elizabeth, and Esme', and then cancelled 'and' in pencil. The cancellation is not present in Bruce Montgomery's copy (Bodl. MS Eng. c. 2356). L added an erratum slip: 'Line 27 of this poem should of course read: "Brenda and Wenda and brown-legged Jill . . ."' The line previously read 'Wenda and Brenda and brown-legged Jill – '. Published in Tolley (2005), 206–7, with 'Esmé' for 'Esme' in l. 54, and with L's original line in the body of the poem and the erratum note appended.

Title 'Ballad of the ladies of old'. **1–3 marginal comment** *'old, unhappy, far-off things'*: Wordsworth, *The Solitary Reaper*, 19. **4** *dabbled with the dew*: Cf. Keats, *Endymion*, i. 683: 'Dew-dabbled'; Yeats, *The White Birds*, 5: 'dew-dabbled'. **20** *'The Londonderry Air'*: anthem of Northern Ireland, usually set to the words of *Danny Boy*. **21** *take the veil*: become a nun. **33–6 marginal comment** Yeats, *To a Child Dancing in the Wind*, 12. **34** *Aertex*: cellular cloth, since 1888. **35** *Rosalind*: In *As You Like It*. **51** *lemon-caley*: effervescent flavoured powder; sherbet.

Holidays

DATE AND TEXT
The poem is in *Sugar and Spice*; see the notes above on *The False Friend* for details of date and text. In the present edition 'Stratford on Avon' in the headnote is regularised to 'Stratford-on-Avon' (as in line 1). Published in *TAWG*, 249; and in Tolley (2005), 208, with 'saddle bags' for 'saddlebags' (l. 4), and a semicolon for the colon at the end of l. 12.

Dedication *Shakespeare Memorial Theatre*. Opened on 23 Apr. 1932 following the destruction of the original 1879 theatre by fire. **10–14** Female characters respectively from *As You Like It*, *Twelfth Night*, *The Merchant of Venice*, *Much Ado About Nothing*, *The Merchant of Venice*, *Cymbeline*, *The Tempest*, *Antony and Cleopatra*, *Romeo and Juliet* and *Othello*. **12** *The Tempest*, 5. 1. 186 (Miranda): 'O brave new world'. **14** *Othello*, 5. 2. 47

(Desdemona to Othello before he smothers her): 'Some bloody passion shakes your very frame'.

The School in August

DATE AND TEXT
The poem is in *Sugar and Spice*; see the notes above on *The False Friend* for details of date and text. Published in Hartley (1988), 43, *CP* (1988), 271, and Tolley (2005), 209, all with 'dimmed' for 'dim' in l. 3. In *TAWG*, 250, 'dim' is correctly printed, and James Booth notes that, also in l. 3, 'hollow' is underlined in pencil and 'empty?' suggested in the margin, but not in Bruce Montgomery's copy (Bodl. MS Eng. c. 2356). A version with variants is printed in *TAWG*, 5.

VARIANTS
Dedication TO | Jacinth
5 creeps between the chairs] creeps, until
6 The sun is seen no more

L told George Hartley that it was 'the best poem of my suppressed Betjeman period': Hartley (1988), 6. **18** *turn grey*: Terry Castle, 'The Lesbianism of Philip Larkin', *Daedalus* (Spring 2007), repr. in Leader (2009), 97, suggests an echo of Pope, *The Rape of the Lock*, 5. 25–6: 'But since, alas! frail Beauty must decay, | Curl'd or uncurl'd, since Locks will turn to grey'.

Fourth Former Loquitur

DATE AND TEXT
?Aug.–Sept. 1943. MS appended to the previous five poems in the collection *Sugar and Spice*: Hull DPL (2) 1/11. Not represented in the Bodleian MS of *Sugar and Spice* (Eng. c. 2356). Published in *TAWG*, 251–2, with 'shock headed' for 'shock-headed' (l. 9), and in Tolley (2005), 210–11, with 'Shelly' (l. 14), 'shadow' for 'shadows' (l. 23), 'tack' for 'talk' (l. 38), and commas missing after 'Jill' (l. 9) and 'sprawled' (l. 12). The variants 'brown-legged' (l. 31) and 'brownlegged' (l. 37) are in the MS. The second part of l. 32, 'in just a week', does not begin with a capital (whereas the second parts of ll. 7 and 29 do): it should, I think, be continuous with 'And at your feet, three more:'. James Booth has told me independently that he thinks so too. I have added a full stop at the end of l. 34.

VARIANTS (from Hull DPL (2) 1/11)

7 When] ~~Now~~ When
9-10 ~~her blazer full~~ | ~~Of apple cores~~ the pockets of | Her blazer
10 crumbs] ~~coconut~~ crumbs
11 matured] ~~that~~ matured
12 By] ~~With~~ By every minute.~~When will there be again another such~~
Additional lines ~~Another July evening run its course,~~ | ~~And we be~~
~~suffered to sprawl here~~ Here we sprawled, barelegged,
13 talked] ~~chat~~ talked
14 heard] ~~hear~~ heard
21 filmy] ~~films of~~ filmy
32 ~~A group of us to~~ in just a week
34 houses] ~~homes~~ houses

Title *Loquitur*: speaks. 3 *pav.*: pavilion (colloq.). 11 Cf. Hardy,
The Sun on the Bookcase, 1-2: 'the sun | Smears the bookcase with
winy red'. 18 *Todhunter's Algebra*: *Treatise on Algebra* by Isaac
Todhunter (1888, etc.).

'I would give all I possess'

DATE AND TEXT
Early Oct. 1943, when it is included in a letter to KA, possibly
before another letter dated 12 Oct. Copy in Hull DPL 5/1.
Previously unpublished.

L in the letter: 'This is what is known as a "cri du cock."'

'Sent you a letter, but it had to go by boat'

DATE AND TEXT
Included in a letter to JBS dated 25 Oct. 1943. Published in *SL*, 81,
with the comma missing from the end of l. 1.

L prefaces the lines with comments on a letter he sent earlier to JBS:
'The letter was a fraction heavier than Air Mail weight so has gone
off the long way.' After the lines, he writes: '(singer exits hurriedly,
Allen, Russell, and Freeman covering his retreat by a cataclysmic
discord produced by three long wails, each on a different and
antagonistic note)'. See the note on *Fuel Form Blues*.

'The wind that blows from Morpeth'

DATE AND TEXT
Included in a letter to KA dated 8 Nov. 1943. Published in *SL*, 83.

L writes against the lines: 'with its flabbiness and utter lack of merit it might be from Aviator Loq', a reference to Ian Davie's book of poems *Aviator Loquitur* (1943), as AT notes (*SL*, 83).
  1 *Morpeth*: town in Northumberland, NE England. 7–8 *Macbeth*, 2. 2. 35, 40–1: 'Macbeth doth murder sleep . . . Glamis hath murdered sleep, and therefore Cawdor | Shall sleep no more, Macbeth shall sleep no more.'

Address to Life, by a Young Man Seeking a Career

DATE AND TEXT
The main poem dates from before Sept. 1940. The postscript, 'I'm sorry to say that, as life looks today', dates from 29 Nov. 1943. Below this, on 10 Aug. 1944, L wrote the comment 'How true, how true, how true'. Poem III in *PAug40* (t.s.), with the postscript added by hand. Published in Tolley (2005), 106–9, with a comma after 'that' in the postscript, whereas L inserts 'that' after 'say,'. In the present edition a full stop has been added after 'enjoyment' at the end of the postscript, as in Tolley.

VARIANTS (from the postscript)
95 only pulling] ~~rubbing~~ only pulling
96 the slightest] ~~my only~~ the slightest

18 *the spires*: Of Oxford, 'that sweet city with her dreaming spires', as Matthew Arnold called it (*Thyrsis*, 19). 40 *the Pan*: final stage of deterioration, as in 'going down the pan'. 73 *M.P.*: Member of Parliament. 90 *Wellington*: small Shropshire town where L was appointed as a librarian in Dec. 1943. 92 *Duke Ellington*: celebrated jazz composer and bandleader (1899–1974).

'What ant crawls behind the picture?'

DATE AND TEXT
?1943. Hull DPL (2) 1/2/5 (t.s.). Published in Tolley (2005), 224, with 'calalier [*sic*]' in l. 2 and 'sheperd [*sic*]' in l. 8. Tolley corrects

two other typing slips silently: 'Black' for 'Blacks' (l. 13) and the slight indentation of l. 18. He also prints a semicolon for the colon after 'horse' (l. 4).

10 *Grand Guignol*: Le Théâtre du Grand Guignol, a small Parisian theatre (1897–1962) specialising in naturalistic horror shows. 15 *spurning the albatross*: As in Coleridge's *The Rime of the Ancient Mariner*. 17 *landgirl*: member of the Women's Land Army, established in 1917 for work on the land in wartime.

'Someone stole a march on the composer'

DATE AND TEXT
?1943. Hull DPL (2) 1/2/5 (t.s.). Published in Tolley (2005), 225, with 'theif [sic]' and 'laughted [sic]' in l. 7.

1 *stole a march on*: gained an advantage over. 4 *Non compos*: *non compos mentis*, not in his right mind.

'Did you hear his prayer, God?'

DATE AND TEXT
?1943. Hull DPL (2) 1/2/5 (t.s.). Published in Tolley (2005), 226.

Leap Year

DATE AND TEXT
?1943. Hull DPL (2) 1/3/10 (t.s.). Published in Tolley (2005), 227, with 'pillar box' for 'pillarbox' in l. 15. In the present edition 'brassiere' in l. 5 is converted to 'brassière'.

'Some large man had a pendulous eyeball'

DATE AND TEXT
?1943. Hull DPL (2) 1/3/10 (t.s.). Published in Tolley (2005), 228, with L's typing error 'wuth' in l. 9 corrected silently to 'with'.

End

DATE AND TEXT
?1943–4. Hull DPL 2/2/15 (t.s.). The poem is numbered with an encircled '7', and there is a tick against it in the left margin. Below the poem in the t.s. is a drawing by L of a king looking in alarm at a large bone on a plate. Published in Tolley (2005), 230.

On Poetry

DATE AND TEXT
?1943–4. Hull DPL 2/2/15 (t.s.): copy-text. Published in Tolley (2005), 231.

Inscription on a Clockface

DATE AND TEXT
?1943–4. Hull DPL 2/2/12 (t.s.): copy-text. Published in Tolley (2005), 232, with 'is' inserted after 'this' in l. 1.

'Wall up the day in words'

DATE AND TEXT
?1943–4. Hull DPL (2) 1/2/5 (t.s.). Published in Tolley (2005), 233.

1 Cf. 'Where was this silence learned', 3.

'There is snow in the sky'

DATE AND TEXT
1943–4. Bodl. MS Eng. c. 2357/12, where it is numbered 'iv.', and Hull DPL 2/2/10 (t.s.). The two texts date from the same period and are identical. Published in Tolley (2005), 234.

7–8 Cf. Yeats, *Sailing to Byzantium*, 10: 'A tattered coat upon a stick'. 8 Crossed bones (with a skull) constitute the emblem on the flag (the 'Jolly Roger') flown by a pirate ship.

'If I saw the sky in flames'

DATE AND TEXT
1943–4. Bodl. MS Eng. c. 2357/12, where it is numbered 'v.'; Hull
t.s. (DPL 2/2/11): copy-text. It is not possible to determine which
of the two versions is later. In the present edition the Hull version,
with its striking image of the sunk ship in ll. 7–8 and slightly more
economical wording, has been chosen. Published in Tolley (2005),
235.

VARIANTS (from the Bodl. MS)
3 Each constellation] The constellations
4 to have] I had
5 Ridden] And ridden
6 fills] is filled
7–8 Like a jar brimful of smoke, or a room | Filling at last with
shadows –
9 to have] I had
10 Ridden] And ridden

'When this face was younger'

DATE AND TEXT
1943–4. Hull DPL 2/2/27 (t.s.). Bodl. MS Eng. c. 2357/12, where
it is numbered 'iv.', dates from the same period. It is not possible to
determine which of the two is the later version. In the present edition
the Hull version has been chosen, on aesthetic grounds: the shift
to the present tense in ll. 6–7 is more dramatic. Published in Tolley
(2005), 236.

VARIANTS (from the Bodl. MS)
Title Maid's Song.
6 is] was
7 loves] loved

1, 4 Cf. 'Why should I be out walking', 5–7.

'Honour William Yeats for this success'

DATE AND TEXT
1943–4. It appears on p. 14 of Bodl. MS Eng. c. 2357, where it is
numbered 'ix'. Previously unpublished.

1 *William Yeats*: Yeats as named in Auden's *In Memory of W. B. Yeats*, 43.

Poem ('Summer extravagances shrink')

DATE AND TEXT
1943–4. Hull DPL 2/2/20 (t.s. with holograph addition and correction). Published in Tolley (2005), 237. Tolley inserts 'a' before 'shapely' (l. 4), and misses both 'Poem' in pencil on the t.s. and the correction in pencil in l. 21 (see below). He catches 'the' in pencil before 'aristocratic' (l. 21).

VARIANTS (from Hull DPL 2/2/20)
21 Where] ~~Although~~ Where

'If I wrote like D. H. Lawrence, I wouldn't need to drink no beer'

DATE AND TEXT
Included in a letter to JBS dated 12 Mar. 1944 (Hull DPL 174/2/88). I have added stops after Lawrence's initials. Previously unpublished.

The lines are in the style of a blues lyric (see the note on *Fuel Form Blues*). After them, L remarks 'Alas, I [for 'it'] cannot be.'.
1–2 *D. H. Lawrence*: novelist and poet, whom L greatly admired.

Poem ('Last night, by a restless bed')

DATE AND TEXT
Dated '15. iv. 44' by L on p. 20 of Bodl. MS Eng. c. 2357, where the poem occupies pp. 19–20. Previously unpublished.

VARIANTS
33 hope] ~~grief~~ hope *Bodl. MS*

9 *trick*: cards played and won ('taken') in one round, collectively.

Girl Saying Goodbye

DATE AND TEXT

Included in a letter of 21 Apr. 1944 to JBS (Hull DP 174/2/91). It appears, in an identical text, on p. 15 of Bodl. MS Eng. c. 2357, where it is numbered 'xv'. Published in Tolley (2005), 250, with 'on earth' for 'earth' (l. 7).

'Mary Cox in tennis socks'

DATE AND TEXT
Dated '1 July | 1944' by L on the holograph MS written on the front cover of the programme for *Dear Brutus* by the King Henry VIII School Dramatic Society, 1944, Hull DPL (2) 1/3/14. The verso bears L's sketch of Mary Cox holding a tennis racket. Published in Tolley (2005), 251, with 'Summer' twice in l. 13. However, L's lower-case 's' at the beginning of words is quite tall compared to his other lower-case letters, and the 's' in the second 'summer', for instance, is the same size as that in 'still' two lines later. I therefore print 'summer'.

VARIANTS
15 Yet] Yet ~~But~~ MS

'Small paths lead away'

DATE AND TEXT
Bodl. MS Eng. c. 2357/5, where it is numbered 'ii.', dates from 1943–4. Dated '29. 8. 44' in L's hand on the Hull t.s. (DPL 2/2/14), where it is also numbered 'ii.'. Published in Tolley (2005), 253.

'Sheaves under the moon in ghostly fruitfulness'

DATE AND TEXT
Dated '6. 10. 44' in *Wkbk 1* (1/1/4). Published in Tolley (2005), 255, with 'in' for 'with' (l. 2). It is a draft, but there are no uncancelled alternative readings and a latest version can be discerned. Tolley ought, however, to have recorded that L cancelled ll. 7–12 with a diagonal line.

[Crewe]

DATE AND TEXT
L's is a reworking, in pencil, of Bruce Montgomery's poem 'CREWE' (Bodl. MS Eng. c. 2762/10). The envelope containing the MS is addressed to L in BM's handwriting and is postmarked 3 Nov. 1944. In l. 3 'That' is written through 'Cro'[?wd], and in l. 4 'they part upon' is cancelled in favour of 'wheels part them on'. Previously unpublished.

Bruce Montgomery's poem:

Crewe
Corruption stands in his eye:
And in hers the images of death
Crowd like bare branches in an autumn sky.
With a kiss, on a breath they part, in a sigh:
Dividing love the wheels move
And on the windy platform only I
Am left, remembering
That where the rose blooms
The roots crawl;
Where the bright gold dyes them
The leaves fall.

Title *Crewe*: major railway junction in Cheshire, England.

'Why should I be out walking'

DATE AND TEXT
In *Wkbk 1* (1/1/14), there are two drafts after '2. xi. 44', the first cancelled by a diagonal line, the second, with no uncancelled alternative readings, dated '9 xi 44' at the end. Published in Tolley (2005), 264, with 'the' for 'a' (l. 2).

5–7 Cf. 'When this face was younger', 4.

'We are the night-shite shifters shifting the shite by night and shouting'

DATE AND TEXT
Included in a letter to JBS dated 10 Dec. 1944 (Hull DP 174/2/108). Previously unpublished.

L in the letter: 'Pardon this inconsequentiality, but I like that song, to the tune of Colonel Bogey, I think – or some well known Sousa march.'

'Snow has brought the winter to my door'

DATE AND TEXT
Hull DPL (2) 1/1/14/27, a torn-out page from *Wkbk 1*, identified by A. T. Tolley as p. 40: *AL*, 11 (Apr. 2001), 24. The lines are dated '8. 1. 45'. They are a draft, but they contain no uncancelled alternative versions. Published by Tolley in *AL*, 11 (Apr. 2001), 24, and in Tolley (2005), 265, the latter with 'on to' for 'onto' (l. 8).

To S. L.

DATE AND TEXT
A draft written after '8. 1. 45' is dated '13. 1. 45' at the end on the page torn out from *Wkbk 1* (Hull DPL (2) 1/1/14/27). Tolley in *AL*, 11 (Apr. 2001), 25, printed from this draft (though with 'For' instead of 'To', written through 'For', in the title '*To My Father*'). In the present edition the text is from the later t.s. version, from Bodl. MS Eng. c. 2357/23, where it is the first of three items under the heading 'Scraps, January 1945'.

Title *S. L.*: L's father Sydney Larkin (1884–1948).

'Because the images would not fit'

DATE AND TEXT
Wkbk 1 (1/1/15) contains two versions on a single page after '3. xi. 44', dated '13. 1. 45' and '14. 1. 45' respectively. The first is cancelled by a diagonal line. Tolley wrongly records 'two versions deleted'. The poem appears on p. 23 of Bodl. MS Eng. c. 2357 as

the second of three items under the heading 'Scraps, January 1945'. Published in Tolley (2005), 267, from the second draft, with a full stop for the colon at the end of l. 5. In the present edition the text is from the later t.s.: Bodl. MS Eng. c. 2357/23.

'Days like a handful of grey pearls'

DATE AND TEXT
Wkbk 1 (1/1/16) contains two pages of drafts after '14. 1. 45', and the final draft is dated '16. 1. 45' at the end. Hull DPL 2/2/34 (t.s.): copy-text. It appears on p. 23 of Bodl. MS Eng. c. 2357, where it is numbered '(iii)' under the heading 'Scraps, January 1945'. Published in Tolley (2005), 268.

VARIANTS
3 hours and miles] miles and hours *Bodl. MS*

'Numberless blades of grass'

DATE AND TEXT
The drafts are in *Wkbk 1* (1/1/17) and come after '16. 1. 45'. The second (final) draft, which has no uncancelled alternative readings, is dated '19. 1. 45' at the end. Published in Tolley (2005), 269, with 'further' for 'farther' (l. 7) and 'full' for 'fall' (l. 12), and without a comma after 'moon' (l. 11).

2–3 Cf. *Vers de Société*, 16–17: 'the moon thinned | To an air-sharpened blade'.

'Draw close around you'

DATE AND TEXT
The two pages of drafts in *Wkbk 1* (1/1/20) come after '5-2-45', and the final draft is dated '14. 2. 45' at the end. The copy-text is the fair copy in Bodl. MS Eng. c. 2357/2. Published in Tolley (2005), 271, from *Wkbk 1*, with 'your love' (l. 2), but *Wkbk 1* and the Bodl. MS both have only 'love'.

'I have despatched so many words'

DATE AND TEXT
There are a draft and two fair copies after '14. 2. 45' in *Wkbk 1*
(1/1/22), dated respectively '25. ii. 45', '25. ii. 45' and '26 ii. 45'.
The first draft is headed '<u>Quatrain</u>', and both it and the first fair
copy are cancelled by a diagonal line. Both fair copies differ in l. 2
from Hull DPL 2/2/16 (t.s.), which is the copy-text. Published in
Tolley (2005), 272, with the title 'Quatrain', but the t.s. version does
not have a title. Tolley also records '2 TS', but there is only one.

'Where was this silence learned'

DATE AND TEXT
The single draft in *Wkbk 1* (1/1/23) is dated '27. ii. 45'. Bodl. MS
Eng. c. 2357/1; Hull DPL 2/2/16 = Hull t.s. 1; Hull DPL 2/2/28 = Hull
t.s. 2 (copy-text). Published in Tolley (2005), 273, unaccountably
from Hull t.s. 1 (and with a comma after 'that', l. 10, that is not in
t.s. 1, though it is in t.s. 2).

VARIANTS
5 Over] Along *Hull t.s. 1, Bodl. MS*
7 Less delicate of feather *Hull t.s. 1, Bodl. MS*
8 their least] such sights *Hull t.s. 1, Bodl. MS*
9 Proud music on your part *Hull t.s. 1, Bodl. MS*

1 Cf. 'Wall up the day in words', 1.

'Ride with me down into the spring'

DATE AND TEXT
The page bearing two drafts in *Wkbk 1* (1/1/25) comes after 1 Mar.
1945, and the second draft, which has no uncancelled alternative
readings, is dated '16. 3. 45' at the end. Published in Tolley (2005),
275, with 'now' as the last word in l. 10, though it is cancelled in
the MS.

'Safely evening behind the window'

DATE AND TEXT

In *Wkbk 1* (1/1/26) a single draft, without uncancelled alternative readings, comes after '16. 3. 45', and is dated '11. 4. 45' at the end. Published in Tolley (2005), 276, with 'drowsed' for 'aroused' (l. 2), 'the' for 'its' (l. 5), a comma after 'Trees' (l. 3), and a comma for the semicolon after 'cradled' (l. 6).

Song with a Spoken Refrain

DATE AND TEXT

The complete draft, entitled 'Song with a spoken chorus', in *Wkbk 1* (1/1/28) is dated '10 / 6 / 45'. Hull DPL 2/2/8 (t.s., with a correction in pencil) is the copy-text. Published in Tolley (2005), 278.

VARIANTS

Title ~~Chorus~~ Refrain *Hull DPL 2/2/8*

'Happiness is a flame'

DATE AND TEXT

The two pages of drafts in *Wkbk 1* fall between '25 / 6 [1945]' and '2 / 7 / 45'. Hull DPL 2/2/9 (t.s.) is the copy-text. Published in Tolley (2005), 280–1, with an unnecessary '[*sic*]' after 'has' (l. 20). The drafts have 'When all else has been taken' and 'When all else has felt and spoken'.

'Lie with me, though the night return outside'

DATE AND TEXT

The draft in *Wkbk 1* (1/1/31) is dated '2 / 7 / 45'. There are two t.s. versions: Hull DPL 2/2/6 = Hull t.s. 1, where the poem is numbered '1' (encircled), with 'When trees are quiet' numbered '2', and 'The dead are lost, unravelled', '3'; and Hull DPL 2/2/29 = Hull t.s. 2, which is the copy-text. Published in Tolley (2005), 282.

VARIANTS

1 return] returns *Hull t.s. 1*

'When trees are quiet, there will be no more weeping'

DATE AND TEXT
Hull DPL (2) 1/1/14/37, a torn-out page from *Wkbk 1*, bears two drafts, the first cancelled by a diagonal line, dated '22 / 7 / 45' and '24 / 7 / 45' respectively. Hull DPL 2/2/6 = Hull t.s. 1, numbered with an encircled '2'; Hull DPL 2/2/32 = Hull t.s. 2 (copy-text). Tolley published the version from the second *Wkbk* draft in *AL*, 11 (Apr. 2001), 25–6. In Tolley (2005), 277, he follows Hull t.s. 2.

VARIANTS
5 speculating] ~~lacerating~~ speculating *Hull t.s. 1*
7 all] these
an] find *Hull t.s. 1*

'The dead are lost, unravelled; but if a voice'

DATE AND TEXT
Wkbk 1 (1/1/33) contains: a draft of the first four and a half lines dated '20. 8. 45'; a draft of ll. 1–8 dated '21. 8. 45'; a draft of the whole poem dated '23 / 8 [1945]', followed by a second version of ll. 9–14, and a second complete draft dated '23 / 8 / 45' at the end. The first five and a half lines are quoted in a letter to KA dated 22 Aug. 1945 (*SL*, 108). Hull DPL 2/2/6 (t.s.) is the copy-text. Published in Tolley (2005), 283.

L on the excerpt in the letter to KA: 'I think it is true, but it never does to write things you think are true. Only things you think are beautiful.'

'Lift through the breaking day'

DATE AND TEXT
The two pages of drafts in *Wkbk 1* (1/1/35) come after '23 / 8 / 45', and the final draft is dated '27 / 8 / 45' at the end. Hull DPL 2/2/35 (t.s.); *ITGOL* (copy-text). Published in *CP* (1988), 308, and in Tolley (2005), 284.

15 Pope, *Pastorals*, 'Summer', 76: 'And all things flourish where you turn your Eyes'.

'Past days of gales'

DATE AND TEXT
The one and a half pages of drafts in *Wkbk 1* (1/1/40) come after 7 Oct. 1945, and a final complete draft is dated '17-x.-45'. Hull DPL 2/2/23 (t.s.); *ITGOL* (copy-text). Published in *CP* (1988), 310, and in Tolley (2005), 288, with the date given wrongly as 17 Nov. 1945, probably owing to a misreading of L's 'x.' as 'xi'; but the full stop after 'x' is too small to be 'i', and the drafts are followed by drafts of 'The cry I would hear' from October.

'The cry I would hear'

DATE AND TEXT
There are three drafts in *Wkbk 1* (1/1/41) after '17-x-45', of which 2 and 3 are dated '18 / x / 45' and '24 / x / 45' respectively. These drafts are cancelled by a diagonal line. Published in Tolley (2005), 286.

'Who whistled for the wind, that it should break'

DATE AND TEXT
The two complete drafts in *Wkbk 1* (1/1/43) come after '24 / x / 45' and are dated '14. 12. 45' and '15. 12. 45' respectively. The copy-text is that in *ITGOL*. Published in *CP* (1988), 311, and in Tolley (2005), 289.

1 *whistled for the wind*: the common practice of sailors, who superstitiously whistled for a wind during a calm and refrained from whistling during a gale (*OED*, whistle *v*. 1 n).

'Sky tumbles, the sea'

DATE AND TEXT
There are two complete drafts in *Wkbk 1* (1/1/47), dated '23. 2. 46' and '26. 4. 46' respectively. Hull DPL 2/2/36 (t.s. with holograph corrections to l. 12) is the copy-text. Published in Tolley (2005), 292, with no mention of the corrections.

VARIANTS (from DPL 2/2/36)
12 ~~And be contented to wait~~ *1st version* [with 'ed' added to 'content' in holograph]; ~~And do n~~Nothing but wait? *2nd version*

'Sting in the shell'

DATE AND TEXT
In *Wkbk 1* (1/1/51) there is a complete draft dated '15 May 1946'. Published in Tolley (2005), 294, with 'Out races' for 'Outraces' (l. 9) and without acknowledgement that 'All' is written to the left of 'Ten' (l. 11).

VARIANTS (from *Wkbk 1*)
11 All] Ten [*alt.* All]

'A stick's-point, drawn'

DATE AND TEXT
Hull DPL 1/2/57 is a page torn from *Wkbk 1* just after p. 43. It bears three drafts of the poem, the first with the title 'For I. C. L.' dated '30. 5. 46', the third dated '3 - 6. 46'. (The other side bears 'There is no clearer speaking'.) Hull DPL 2/2/31 (t.s.) is the copy-text. Published in Tolley (2005), 295, with the title 'The point of a stick'; but there is no title in the t.s.

'There is no clearer speaking'

DATE AND TEXT
Hull DPL 1/2/57 is a page torn from *Wkbk 1* just after p. 43. On one side is this poem, dated '12 - 6 - 46'. Hull DPL 2/2/30 (t.s.): copy-text. Published in Tolley (2005), 296, with no record of the *Wkbk* version (but dated from it).

'THE MAYOR OF BRISTOL WAS DRINKING GIN'

DATE AND TEXT
Hull DPL 5/1, copy of a letter to KA dated 17 July 1946, in a passage omitted in *SL*, 119. Previously unpublished.

Beggars

DATE AND TEXT
Drafts of lines begin in *Wkbk 1* after 19 Jan. 1945, and the main
draft (1/1/18) is dated '5. 2. 45 / 6. 10. 46'. Bodl. MS Eng. c.
2357/24. Hull DPL 2/2/33 (t.s., with 'on' inserted by hand in l. 22)
is the copy-text. Published in Tolley (2005), 270.

VARIANTS (from the Bodl. MS)
Title [No title]
3 Frightening] Scaring the
5–6, 11–12, 17–18, 23–4 Lean days, lean days, | Who will shelter us?
19–22 Rich men kneel to pray | And their beds are warm, | When
the nights come | We find no charity;

'When the tide draws out'

DATE AND TEXT
In *Wkbk 1* (1/1/35) the drafts come after 27 Aug. 1945. A complete
draft is dated '9. 9. 45', and a second draft of ll. 17–24, '23 / 9 / 45'.
Below that, L writes 'corrected 6 / 10 / 46'. Hull DPL 2/2/22 (t.s.
with holograph corrections) is the copy-text. Published in Tolley
(2005), 285, with 'at shore' for 'at the shore' (l. 10).

VARIANTS (from DPL 2/2/22)
23 but no minute stirs] ~~but who now has~~ prayers *1st version*; but
~~still nothing~~ no minute stirs *2nd version*
24 ~~That do not seem to mimic the grey gull?~~ *1st version*; ~~Nor
mounts the air~~ No day ~~Nothing~~ mounts up to follow the grey gull.
2nd version

Blues Shouter

DATE AND TEXT
In *Wkbk 1* (1/1/65) the two pages of drafts come after 'Oct 5, 1946'
and are dated '8 / xi / 46' at the end. L indicates the position of
verse 1 by encircling it and redirecting it with an arrow from below
verses 2 and 3. There are drafts of ll. 1–4 and 17–20 cancelled by
diagonal lines, leaving a clear complete version without uncancelled
alternative readings. Published in Tolley (2005), 310, with verse 1 in
roman (though in both drafts it is underlined to signal italics), and
with a full stop for the comma after 'diamond' (l. 16).

In a 1964 review to which he gave the title 'Shout It, Moan It', L traced modern pop music to 'the blues of the shouters, not the moaners': *AWJ*, 124.

'That girl is lame: look at my rough'

DATE AND TEXT

In *Wkbk 1* (1/1/66) there are two drafts on a single page after '8 / xi / 46', the second complete and dated '13. xi. 1946'. The copy-text is Hull DPL 2/2/26, a t.s. with a holograph correction in l. 11 and, below the text, holograph drafts of l. 9 and part of 10. Published in Tolley (2005), 311, with no mention of the holograph corrections and with the comma missing at the end of l. 7.

VARIANTS (from DPL 2/2/26)

10 By such a turning of the world from pain *1st version* [t.s.] so free from] ~~untouched by~~ so free from *2nd version*
11 All would have been made new] That all would be renewed *1st version* [t.s.]; ~~That all would be received have been changed be as new~~ All w^d have been ~~be~~ made new *2nd version*
But] ~~And~~ But

11 *All would have been made new*: Cf. Revelation 21: 5: 'Behold, I make all things new'.

'Voices round a light'

DATE AND TEXT

In *Wkbk 1* (1/1/67), after '15. xi. 1946', '17 / xii / 46' is written below a final (complete) draft and again below a fair copy. Hull DPL 2/2/25 (t.s. with holograph corrections) is the copy-text. Published in Tolley (2005), 312. Tolley does not record that the last stanza is cancelled by a diagonal line that goes through 'Unfearing' at the beginning of l. 18; that ll. 13–17 (i.e. not the whole stanza) are redrafted in holograph; and that L has written 'alter?' in the top left corner of the sheet. The text is therefore of questionable completeness, though it is a borderline case. Tolley prints 'Now' for 'New' in l. 13.

VARIANTS (from DPL 2/2/25)
15 That] ~~That It~~ That

Laforgue

DATE AND TEXT
Included in a letter of 11 Jan. 1947 to KA: copy in Hull DPL 5/1.
Published in *SL*, 133. I have restored the punctuation of the MS,
but have regularised the title to accord with those in L's published
poems.

L to KA: 'I think there is no man in Ennglad now who can "stick
words into us like pins" [Ooh! doesn't that sound like a line from
an *Auden sonnet* about a dead wordwriter? You know the kind
of thing: [poem] like he can but he doesn't use his words to any
advantage.'
   AT notes in *SL*, 133, that L's choice of the French poet Jules
Laforgue (1860–87) 'seems gratuitous', though Auden did write a
sonnet about Rimbaud.

'And did you once see Russell plain?'

DATE AND TEXT
Included in a letter of 11 Jan. 1947 to KA (copy in Hull DPL
5/1), in a passage omitted in SL, 134. Previously unpublished.

L comments: '*Down Beat* reports that, after ten years, Russell is
leaving Nick's and taking up residence at the Club Condon. *Plus
ça change, plus c'est la même chose*. Apparently Russell & Condon
don't get on very well, but as Russell says "I can always talk to
Dave Tough."' *Down Beat* is an American magazine, founded in
1934, that covers jazz, the blues, etc. Nick's and Club Condon were
famous jazz clubs in New York City, and Dave Tough (1907–48)
was a celebrated jazz drummer.
   The lines imitate Robert Browning's *Memorabilia*, 1–4: 'Ah, did
you once see Shelley plain? | And did he stop and speak to you? |
And did you speak to him again? | How strange it seems, and new!'
   1 *Russell*: American jazz clarinetist 'Pee Wee' Russell (1906–69).
L wrote about him with often strong approval (*AWJ*, 34, 81, 156,
225), stating that in the 1930–45 period he 'had no peers' (226).
Latterly he was less enthusiastic (213). 2 *Condon's*: American jazz
banjoist, guitarist and bandleader 'Eddie' Condon (1905–73). L
admired his music-making in the 1930s, but in the 1960s accused
him of 'musical somnambulism': *AWJ*, 144. 3 *Da-da*: Dadaism

was an international avant-garde art (or anti-art) movement
(*fl.* 1916–22) that advocated (often scandalously) abstraction and
experimentalism.

'From this day forward, may you find'

DATE AND TEXT
1947: written in Sydney Larkin's 1947 diary from Philip. Hull MS
DPL (4) 9/6. Previously unpublished.

1 *you*: L's father Sydney.

'Coming at last to night's most thankful springs'

DATE AND TEXT
The two drafts in *Wkbk* 1 (1/1/24) come after '27. ii. 45', and the
second draft is dated '1.3. 45' at the end. Bodl. MS Eng. c. 2357/1;
Hull DPL 2/2/16 (t.s.); *ITGOL* (copy-text). Published in *CP* (1988),
306, and in Tolley (2005), 274.

VARIANTS
2 sharply] long since *Bodl. MS, Hull t.s.*
3 Ambered in memory] In memory's amber *Bodl. MS, Hull t.s.*
4 A] Some *Bodl. MS, Hull t.s.*
8 not my] no such *Bodl. MS, Hull t.s.*
9 The] His *Bodl. MS, Hull t.s.*
11 full] white *Bodl. MS*

Deep Analysis

DATE AND TEXT
The drafts in *Wkbk* 1 (1/1/45), including a draft of the whole poem,
come between '15. 12. 45' and '23. 2. 46'. Included as a revised
text in *ITGOL* (copy-text). Published in *CP* (1988), 4, and in Tolley
(2005), 291, with the date Apr. 1946.

John Carey in Booth (2000), 54–5, relates the poem to L's
attendance at a series of seminars given in Oxford by the Jungian
psychologist John Layard, who taught that 'women should be
the priestesses of the unconscious and help men to regain all the

vision they have lost [. . .] What women must do is – as they are in the unconscious, rubbing shoulders with all these archetypes and symbols that man so needs – is bring them up and give them to man': quoted in Motion (1993), 61. In a letter dated 15 May 1941, L told his sister Catherine that attending Layard's class 'was like an evening spent with truth': Hull DLN Correspondence.

'Come then to prayers'

DATE AND TEXT
In *Wkbk* 1 (1/1/50) there are two pages of drafts dated '13 May 1946' at the end, followed immediately by another, nearly complete draft dating from 13–14 May 1946. A t.s. is also pasted into the *Wkbk*. Revised text in *ITGOL* (copy-text). Published in *CP* (1988), 5, and in Tolley (2005), 293.

VARIANTS (from *Wkbk* t.s.)
23 shadows] shallows

12 Cf. *Ambulances*, 1: 'Closed like confessionals' 14 Cf. *High Windows*, 20: 'Nothing, and is nowhere, and is endless'.

'And the wave sings because it is moving'

DATE AND TEXT
In *Wkbk* 1 (1/1/53) is just over a page of drafts after '14 May 1946', below which L has written '(finished) 14 Sept. 1946'. There is also a t.s. version in the *Wkbk* that Tolley (2005), 298, does not record. He does record 'WKBK (torn-out page)': this is Hull DP (2) 1/4/21. Revised text in *ITGOL* (copy-text). Published in *CP* (1988), 6–7, and in Tolley (2005), 297–8.

VARIANTS
19–20 From unreflection or hours salted with thought, [*Additional line between 19 and 20 in Wkbk t.s.*]

24 Cf. Milton, *Paradise Lost*, vii. 402 (on fish): 'Glide under the green wave'.

Two Guitar Pieces

DATE AND TEXT
In *Wkbk 1* (1/1/51), after '14 May 1946', there is a complete draft of piece I dated '15 Sept 1946' at the end. Further drafts of both pieces follow (1/1/57), the first with '(finished) 15 Sep 1946' at the end, the second '(finished) 18 Sept 1946'. There is also a t.s. of ll. 1–4 and the first word of 5. Revised text in *ITGOL* (copy-text). Published in *CP* (1988), 8–9, and in Tolley (2005), 299–300.

VARIANTS
I 5 Dark] Bare *Wkbk t.s.*

I 2 *Wheatstraws*: not in *OED*. II 5 *platz*: not in *OED*.

Träumerei

DATE AND TEXT
In *Wkbk 1* (1/1/60) there are two drafts on consecutive pages, complete except for a title, dated '26 Sep' and '27th Sept' [1946] respectively. Revised text in *ITGOL* (copy-text). Published in *CP* (1988), 12, and in Tolley (2005), 303.

Title After the piano piece from Schumann's *Kinderszenen*, 'Dreaming'.

To a Very Slow Air

DATE AND TEXT
In *Wkbk 1* (1/1/61) there are two complete drafts, dated '28 Sep 46' and '29th Sep' respectively. (The title at this stage was 'Slow song'.) Hull DPL 2/2/24 is a t.s., and the copy-text is from *ITGOL*. Published in *CP* (1988), 13, and in Tolley (2005), 304.

VARIANTS (from Hull DPL 2/2/24)
Title Slow song
10 Our] The
clothing, our elapsing] clothing of our human

'At the chiming of light upon sleep'

DATE AND TEXT
In *Wkbk 1* (1/1/62) there are two pages of drafts after '29th Sep
[1946]' and the final (complete) draft is dated '4 Oct 1946'. Revised
text in *ITGOL* (copy-text). Published in *CP* (1988), 14, and in
Tolley (2005), 305.

6 *Michaelmas*: the feast of St Michael, 29 Sept.; the Oxford term
beginning soon afterwards. 7 *a green world*: Cf. Keats, *Endymion*,
i. 16: ' the green world'. 27–8 *Paradise Lost*, 11. 104–5: 'from the
Paradise of God | Without remorse drive out the sinful pair'; 7.
537 (Eden): 'this delicious grove'; *undeciduous*: imitates Miltonic
Latinate polysyllables, though the word does not occur in Milton's
poetry. *OED*'s earliest example is Elizabeth Barrett Browning, *Casa
Guidi Windows* (1851), 2. 380: 'immemorial, undeciduous trees'.

'Many famous feet have trod'

DATE AND TEXT
In *Wkbk 1* (1/1/63) there are four pages after '4 Oct. 1946'
bearing a complete draft, below which L has written 'Finished
Oct. 15 1946'. L to JBS, 16 Oct. 1946 (*SL*, 127): 'I am in a queer
state at present: I have just finished a poem – a long one for me,
a hundred-odd (very odd) lines – and am feeling the backwash of
unachievement.' Revised text in *ITGOL* (copy-text). Published
in *CP* (1988), 15–18, and in Tolley (2005), 306–9, in each case
with the comma missing after 'sleep' at the end of l. 35. Tolley has
'observe' for 'obverse' in l. 30.

L to JBS, 16 Oct. 1946 (*SL*, 127): 'In the poem I tried to express
something of an attitude and I don't even think I have expressed
it, let alone getting the accents right & into proportion or writing
patches of sheer beauty. The attitude is that sorrow is personal
& temporal, joy impersonal & eternal; but I have mainly wasted
my time in arguing in verse that the whole of knowledge can
be divided so: [diagram of death and life, with life divided into
sleeping and waking, and waking divided into sorrow and joy].
This took a lot of time & while it provided a frame probably
obscured my meaning. What I feel is that death can ballock life.
It does. But life can ballock death by means of sex (creating new

life) or (less certainly) art. <u>BUT</u> as it is no consolation (I imagine) when the Reaper is knocking on your door to reflect that you have fine sons & daughters, I postulate that life can only ballock death impersonally, while death ballocks you personally. <u>FURTHER</u>, that the emotion of being ballocked by death personally is sorrow, and the emotion of ballocking death impersonally is joy. And much more on the same theme.'

20 Cf. Yeats, *Easter 1916*, 57–8: 'Too long a sacrifice | Can make a stone of the heart'.

Thaw

DATE AND TEXT

In *Wkbk 1* (1/1/69), the two drafts, including a complete one, come between '17. xii. 46' and '15. xii. 47'. Hull DPL 2/3/26 is a t.s. with a correction and uncancelled alternative in holograph in the title, and further corrections in l. 9, and (in punctuation) in ll. 10, 12 and 13. The poem is numbered 'V' in t.s. Revised text in *ITGOL* (copy-text). In l. 9 L has typed 'among' twice. Published in *CP* (1988), 19, and in Tolley (2005), 313. Neither mentions the DPL 2/3/26 text, and though both mention *ITGOL*, the text printed is not from that source.

VARIANTS (from DPL 2/3/26)
Title The [*alt.* A] T̶thaw ['Thaw' in t.s.]
  2 its] his
  3 Distantly] Deliberately
  6 run] course
  9 causing to fall] Before them falls
10 Stiffened from memory, forestloads of grief.
13 forget] discount

2 Cf. *Solar*, 20: 'Unclosing like a hand'.

'An April Sunday brings the snow'

DATE AND TEXT

In *Wkbk 1* (1/1/72) there is a fair copy dated '4 April [1948]'. Published in *CP* (1988), 21, with the comma missing at the end of l. 1.

1–3 There were plum trees in the back garden of the Larkin home at 73 Coten End: *AL*, 14 (Oct. 2002), 32; 15 (Apr. 2003), 31; 16 (Oct. 2003), 6. Osborne (2008), 181, notes Vernon Watkins, *Music of Colours: White Blossom*, 7, 9, 36: 'The spray looked white until this snowfall . . . White is not white again . . . Spirals of blossom, their green conspiracy'. But remember Housman's botanical precision in *Last Poems XXXIV* (*The First of May*), 9: 'The plum broke forth in green' (contrasted with 'The pear stood high and snowed' in the next line). **5–8** L to MJ, 4 Apr. 1948 (Bodl. MS Eng. c. 7403/11): 'My holiday was rather as I expected – my poor father grew steadily worse & died on Good Friday. Since then mother & I have been rather hopelessly looking at the stock in the house – this morning I shifted 100 lbs of jam – 1945, 1946, & 1947 years – and about 25 Kilner jars of bottled fruit [. . .] I don't know what will happen to it all – I don't like sweet things, you remember.' **6** *you*: L's father Sydney, who died of liver cancer on 26 Mar. 1948. **9** John Carey, Booth (2000), 62, compares George Herbert, *Love III*, 18: 'So I did sit and eat'. He also notes L's 'sweet' (l. 11) and Herbert's 'sweetly' (l. 5). **12** See the note on *Sad Steps*, 16–17.

'And yet – but after death there's no "and yet"'

DATE AND TEXT
After 'April Sunday [1948]'. The copy-text is Hull DPL (2)1/1/14/14, a draft on a torn-out page from *Wkbk 1*. Published by A. T. Tolley in *AL*, 11 (Apr. 2001), 26, by David Rees in *AL*, 18 (Autumn 2004), 23–4, and in Tolley (2005), xx–xxi.
It is not clear whether the lines represent a complete poem. Tolley (p. 24) calls it 'Fragment(?) of a poem', yet judges, with some plausibility, that it 'seems complete as it stands' (26). He acknowledges that 'there are illegible remnants of erased lines' below the lines, and that the rhyme scheme (whether by design or not) is not consistent towards the end. There can be no editorial certainty in such cases: the lines are included in the present edition on the chance that they may constitute a complete poem.

2 *you*: L's father Sydney. *burned*: His body was cremated on 31 Mar. 1948.

'I am washed upon a rock'

DATE AND TEXT
In *Wkbk 1* (1/1/73) a draft of ll. 13–20 and a complete draft are
each dated '18. 3. 49'. Hull DPL 2/3/35 (t.s.) is the copy-text.
Published in *CP* (1988), 23, with 'blocks' for the subjunctive 'block'
in l. 8. (*Wkbk 1* also has 'block'.)

L to JBS, 7 Apr. 1946 (*SL*, 116): 'It's very easy to float along in a
semi-submerged way, dissipating one's talent for pleasing by amusing
and being affectionate to the other [. . .] but I find, myself, that this
letting-in of a second person spells death to perception and the desire
to express, as well as the ability. Time & time again I feel that before
I write anything else at all I must drag myself out of the water, shake
myself dry and sit down on a lonely rock to contemplate glittering
loneliness. Marriage . . . is impossible if one wants to do this.'

   1 L to MJ, 30 Oct. 1966 (*SL*, 387): 'I feel I am landed on my
45th year as if washed up on a rock, not knowing how I got here or
ever having had a chance of being anywhere else.' 4 Cf. Housman,
A Shropshire Lad XXII ('The street sounds to the soldiers' tread')
3–4: 'A single redcoat turns his head, | He turns and looks at
me.' 6 *lonely cloud*: Cf. Wordsworth, 'I wandered lonely as a cloud'.

Neurotics

DATE AND TEXT
The two pages of drafts in *Wkbk 1* (1/1/74), which include a
complete draft, fall between '18. 3. 49' and '13 May 1949'. Hull
DPL 2/3/32 (t.s.) is the copy-text. Published in *CP* (1988), 22.

VARIANTS
9 unfinished] ~~unpitied~~ unfinished *Hull DPL 2/3/32*

On Being Twenty-six

DATE AND TEXT
In *Wkbk 1* (1/1/75), the page of drafts of ll. 19–42 and some
additional lines fall between '18. 3. 49' and '13 May 1949'. Hull
DPL 2/3/33 (t.s.) is the copy-text. Published in *CP* (1988), 24–5.

VARIANTS
45 That if chance dissipates ~~the last~~ *Hull DPL 2/3/33*

'Sinking like sediment through the day'

DATE AND TEXT

In *Wkbk 1* (1/1/77) a draft is followed by a fair copy dated '13 May [1949]'. With *Wkbk 2* (1/2/50) is a part of page 76 torn from *Wkbk 1* bearing a draft of stanzas 2 and 3 dated '13 May '49'. In the copy-text, Hull DPL 2/3/27 (t.s.), the poem is numbered 'III', possibly because L was considering it for *XX Poems*. Published in *CP* (1988), 27.

1 Cf. Virginia Woolf, *The Waves* (1931), Harvest edn., 184: 'As a drop falls from a glass heavy with some sediment, time falls.'

'In our family'

DATE AND TEXT

With *Wkbk 2* is part of p. 76 torn out from *Wkbk 1*. These lines are on the other side of the sheet bearing stanzas 2 and 3 of 'Sinking like sediment through the day', and they are dated '13. 5. 49' at the end. Published by Olivia Cole in the *Sunday Times*, 8 Oct. 2006.

To Failure

DATE AND TEXT

In *Wkbk 1* (1/1/79), after '13 May [1949]' there are two complete drafts on three consecutive pages, the second draft dated '17 May 1949', and a fair copy dated '18. 5. 49'. Hull DPL 2/3/37 (t.s. with holograph corrections) is the copy-text. Published in *CP* (1988), 28, without the parentheses in the last line.

VARIANTS (from Hull DPL 2/3/37)
3 butchered] butchered ~~bleeding?~~
6 charges] ~~debit payments~~ charges

Epigram on an Academic Marriage

DATE AND TEXT

Hull DPL 1/2/56 is part of page 79 torn from *Wkbk 1*. This poem is on one side, dated '19. v. 49'. (The other side bears part of a draft of *Fiction and the Reading Public*.) In the present edition capitals have been added to 'academic marriage' in the title. Published by Olivia Cole in the *Sunday Times*, 8 Oct. 2006.

My Home

DATE AND TEXT
?May 1949. Above the text, in t.s., L cancels 'On being twenty-six', which dates from May 1949. Note 'post-war cars' (l. 10). Hull DPL 2/3/31 (t.s.) is the copy-text. In the present edition the title 'My home' has been regularised to 'My Home'. Previously unpublished.

Compline

DATE AND TEXT
There are three pages of drafts in *Wkbk 1* (1/1/91), including a complete draft dated '12. 2. 50'. The copy-text is Hull DPL 2/3/29 (t.s. with holograph title and corrections). Published in *CP* (1988), 31, with *'will'* for *'Will'* in l. 3, 'notes' for 'rites' in l. 13, and 'the' in l. 15 without a record of the uncancelled alternative 'a'. The word written above 'a' is not 'the' but 'one': the first letter is too short for 't', and matches L's formation elsewhere of initial 'o' (for instance, in Hull DPL 2/3/8, in 'one' in each of the last two lines); and the version in *Wkbk 1* has 'one'. In addition to specific cancellations in l. 13, ll. 13–15 are cancelled, and a corrected version is written below.

VARIANTS (from Hull DPL 2/3/29)
13 ~~Let a million prayers As many prayers may well beseech~~ Better ~~an~~ that endless rites beseech
14 ~~As many nights, as many dawns:~~ As many nights, as many dawns,
15 ~~God casually may grant a wish~~ If finally God grants a [*alt.* one] wish

Title In Catholic ritual, the last service of the day. 3 From the Lord's Prayer (Matt. 6: 10; Luke 11: 2). 4 *Produce*: extend. *OED* cites Sir Thomas Browne, *Religio Medici* (1634): 'produce a mans life unto threescore'. 5 Eccles. 11: 7: 'a pleasant thing it is for the eyes to behold the sun' (the closest biblical parallel).

How to Sleep

DATE AND TEXT
In *Wkbk* I (1/1/97) there is a complete draft dated '8 / 3 / 50' and
two further drafts of verse 3 dated '10 / 3 / 50' at the end. The copy-
text is Hull DPL 2/3/25 (t.s.). Published in *CP* (1988), 35, with
'sleep' in the title regularised to 'Sleep', as in the present edition.

5 *stares*: Cf. *Livings*, II 24: 'Through the stare travelling'.

The Literary World

DATE AND TEXT
Wkbk 2 (1/2/5) contains a page bearing a draft of the whole poem
except for the title after '17. 3. 50', dated '20 / 3 / 50' at the end.
The copy-text is Hull DPL 2/3/30 (t.s.). To the right of the last line
of section I on the t.s., L has written '<u>Five</u>, Christ.' Published in *CP*
(1988), 38. The title 'The literary world' has been regularised to
'The Literary World', as it was in *CP*.

I Quotation From *The Diaries of Franz Kafka 1910–1923*, ed. Max
Brod and trans. Joseph Kresh (1948), 11: entry for 1910, probably
May. 3–4 *an irresistible force meeting an | immoveable object*:
The classic logical paradox: if a force is irresistible, no object is
immoveable, and vice versa. II L in 1980, reviewing Robert Bernard
Martin's *Tennyson: The Unquiet Heart* (FR, 314–15): 'In fact the
character he draws is of someone demanding much from others,
and not giving a great deal in return: Edward Lear, for instance, was
amazed at the invalid Emily Tennyson's constant attention to her
husband: "What labour for him! – and how little he seems to regard
it!"' 19 *Doing his . . . business*: (euphemism) defecating (*OED*,
business, 15. c., to do one's business: 'to ease oneself').

Strangers

DATE AND TEXT
Wkbk 2 (1/2/8) contains two and a half pages of drafts of the whole
poem between '19. 5. 50' and '20. 5. 50', and a further draft of
ll. 9–13 before '23. 5. 50'. Hull DPL 2/3/24 (t.s.) is the copy-text.
Published by AT in Hartley (1988), 45, and in *CP* (1988), 40. AT
notes that in the t.s. the poem is headed by a Roman 'VII', 'as if at

one time Larkin considered it a candidate for his privately printed booklet *XX Poems* (1951)': Hartley (1988), 44.

'Under a splendid chestnut tree'

DATE AND TEXT

Wkbk 2 contains: three pages of drafts of the opening lines and additional lines between '28. 5. 50' and '1. 6. 50' (1/2/14); a half-page draft of the opening lines between '1. 6. 50' and '2-6-50'; and five and a half pages of drafts of the whole poem after '2-6-50' (1/2/16). The next date in the *Wkbk* is '17 July [1950]'. Hull DPL 1/2/55 (t.s. corrected in pencil) bears the date 'June 1950' and is the copy-text. Line 8 is preceded by an arrow in pencil signalling indentation. Published in *CP* (1988), 43–4, without indentation of l. 8, with a hyphen inserted in 'gas lights' (l. 36) and a comma, cancelled in the t.s., after 'cup' (l. 38). For consistency ll. 21 and 34 are indented in the present edition.

VARIANTS (from DPL 1/2/55)
4 Clamping] ~~Making~~ Clamping
9 a] ~~this~~ a
scum] ~~smear~~ scum
24 But] ~~And~~ But
27 Thus] ~~So And~~ Thus
36 gas] ~~street~~ gas
39 the] ~~their~~ the

1 Longfellow, *The Village Blacksmith*, 1: 'Under the spreading chestnut tree'. 20 *hortus siccus*: arranged collection of dried plants. L to MJ, 25 Aug. 1959 (on her garden): 'it's probably a *hortus siccus* by now, only the weeds thriving with their long roots': Bodl. MS Eng. c. 7420/28. 22 *tsetse flies*: insects, abundant in tropical and southern Africa, whose bite can be fatal to animals. 28, 29 *fir | her*: Rhyme in Housman, *Last Poems* XXII ('The sloe was lost in flower'), 6, 8. 33–4 *stained unsightly breath | Of carious death*: John Osborne, Booth (2000), 148, compares Eliot, *The Waste Land*, V. *What the Thunder Said*, 18: 'Dead mountain mouth of carious teeth'. 35–6 *listen | glisten*: The rhyme is in Keats: *Endymion*, iii. 241–2; ''Tis the witching time of night', 3–4, 15–16, 24–5; but also (note 'children', l. 36) in Irving Berlin's *I'm dreaming of a white Christmas* (1942), 3: 'Where treetops glisten, and children listen'.

In a 1974 review L listed the song among 'pieces that are not so much songs as bits of the twentieth century': *RB*, 97.

'Westminster's crown has gained a special jewel'

DATE AND TEXT
Included in a letter dated 28 Nov. 1950 to MJ (Bodl. MS Eng. c. 7404/11). Published in *LTM*, 24, with the letter misdated 25 Nov. 1950. For a simplified version of the epigram, see 'Teevan touched pitch: the pitch was very wild', sent to MJ in a letter dated 18 Dec. 1950.

The epigram accompanied a press cutting of a photograph of Thomas Teevan (see below), who had just been elected a Member of Parliament. L comments: 'The above not very coherent epigram sprang unwatched from the contemplation of this inset. No particular news: the voting was very close as you'll have seen. He's only 23, by the way. I hadn't realised that.' L to MJ, 8 June 1951 (Bodl. MS Eng. c. 7405/84): 'Next week is "Twalfth" week [. . .] Needless to say Teevan is waddling about: fat deceitful vulgar Irish fool.' In a letter to MJ dated 24 Oct. 1951 (Bodl. MS Eng. c. 7405/53), L reports on hearing a speech by Teevan: 'His sentiments on the whole were no more gross & stupid than most political speeches, he was not *disgustingly* anti-Catholic (though strongly), & he was not an awfully good speaker. I suppose he will get in again.' In a letter to MJ dated 28 Oct. 1951 (Bodl. MS Eng. c. 7405/59), he notes that 'Belfast has vindicated itself & got Teevan out.' L to MJ, 10 Oct. 1954 (Bodl. MS Eng. c. 7409/70): 'Tom Teevan is dead, of pneumonia, at 27. A curious shoddy Irish version of the Younger Pitt. Do you know, he was Chairman of his Town Council at 21? And Westminster at 23 or 24.'

3 *Churchill*: Sir Winston Churchill (1874–1965), British Prime Minister, 1940–5, 1951–5. *Wilde*: Oscar Wilde (1854–1900), Irish playwright and poet. 4 *Teevan*: Thomas Teevan (1927–54), MP for Belfast West, 29 Nov. 1950–5 Oct. 1951. L refers to the proverbial saying originating in Ecclesiasticus 13: 1: 'He that toucheth pitch shall be defiled therewith'.

'Teevan touched pitch: the pitch was very wild'

DATE AND TEXT
Included in a letter to MJ dated 18 Dec. 1950 (Bodl. MS Eng. c. 7404/39). L: 'By the way, I've simplied my Teevan crack.' In the present edition L's 'T.' in the letter has been expanded to 'Teevan', as the scansion requires. Previously unpublished.

See the notes on 'Westminster's crown has gained a special jewel'.

The Spirit Wooed

DATE AND TEXT
?1950. Hull DPL 2/3/34 (t.s. with one holograph correction of punctuation). Published in CP (1988), 46.

To My Wife

DATE AND TEXT
Wkbk 2 (1/2/37) contains four and a half pages of drafts of the whole poem except for the title after '6 Feb [1951]', dated '19. iii. 51' at the end. With Wkbk 2 (1/2/53) is a t.s. dated '19. 3. 51' in L's hand: copy-text. Published in CP (1988), 54, with 'my' in the title regularised to 'My', a change also made in the present edition.

Bradford (2005), 30, regards the poem as 'a savagely economical account of his parents' marriage and could indeed have been uttered by his father'.
   Deborah Bowman in Leader (2009), 166, notes that the sonnet has the same rhyme-scheme as Auden's Who's Who, and that the syntax and rhythm of l. 13 echo Auden's In Memory of W. B. Yeats, 41: 'A way of happening, a mouth'.
   14 hypostasis: essence.

The Dedicated

DATE AND TEXT
A complete draft in Wkbk 1 (1/1/58) is dated '18. Sep. 1946'.
Included in ITGOL; poem XVII in XX Poems (copy-text). Reprinted in CP (1988), 10, and in Tolley (2005), 301.

VARIANTS (from *ITGOL*)
Title [No title]
12 using] uses

19 *the dove*: Representing peace, as in Hopkins's sonnet *Peace*: noted in Palmer (2008), 92. **21** *depart*: leave, quit. *OED*, *v.* 8 (*trans.*): 'Now *rare*, exc. in phr. *to depart this life*.'

Oils

DATE AND TEXT
Wkbk 2 (1/2/2) contains four and a half pages of drafts of the whole poem except for the title between '12. 3. 50' and '14. 3. 50'. Revised as poem X in *XX Poems*, where it was the first of two poems under the title *Two portraits of sex*: copy-text. (The second was *Etching*, reprinted as *Dry-Point* in *TLD*.) Reprinted in *CP* (1988), 36, and in *CP* (2003), 171, from *XX Poems*, with 'abdicated' for 'abdicating' (l. 2).

L to MJ, 18 Oct. 1954 (Bodl. MS Eng. c. 7409/75): 'Have been fiddling around since eight with a new poem, a "panoramic" poem of a kind I'm not very proficient at (*vide Sex: oils*) but like.' L in 1981 (*FR*, 50–1): 'They [*Oils* and *Dry-Point*] were written in the late forties: Kingsley [Amis] called the first one my Sanders of the River poem – that was the first one, whooping it up – and I was so dashed that I dropped it.'
 1 *God in a thicket*: As in Exodus 3: 2–4 (the burning bush). 1–4 Booth (1992), 102, detects an echo of George Herbert's *Prayer (I)*. This would apply to the syntax and rhythm of successive noun phrases and to the mention of God: 'Prayer the Churches banquet, Angels age, | Gods breath in man returning to his birth, | The soul in paraphrase, heart in pilgrimage, | The Christian plummet sounding heav'n and earth'. **12** Booth (1992), 104, notes the 'ecstatic Hopkinesque eruption of "struck oil"'. Cf. Hopkins, *God's Grandeur*, 2–3: 'shook foil' rhymed with 'oil'.

'Who called love conquering'

DATE AND TEXT
Wkbk 2 (1/2/17) contains three pages of drafts of the whole poem after '2-6-50' dated '17 July [1950]' at the end. Revised as poem XV in *XX Poems* (copy-text). Reprinted in *CP* (1988), 45, with the comma missing at the end of l. 10.

L to MJ, 22 Oct. 1954 (Bodl. MS Eng. c. 7409/82): 'I thought that only one, namely XV, had gone quite dead.'

    1 Cf. the Latin proverb *'Amor vincit omnia'* ('love conquers all'), originally 'Omnia vincit Amor' in Virgil, *Eclogues*, x. 69.

Arrival

DATE AND TEXT
Wkbk 2 contains six and a half pages of drafts of stanzas 1 and 2 between '28 / x / 50' and '4 / xi / 50' (1/2/22), and three pages of drafts of the whole poem except for the title between '4 / xi / 50' and '28 / 11/ 50' (1/2/25). Revised as poem VI in *XX Poems*. Reprinted in *CP* (1988), 51.

'Since the majority of me'

DATE AND TEXT
Wkbk 2 contains: two pages of drafts, principally of stanza 1 (though one draft has two additional stanzas) between '4 / xi / 50' and '28 / 11 / 50' (1/2/27); and two pages of drafts of the whole poem dated '5 xii 50' at the end, and a further draft of stanza 3 dated '6 xii 50' at the end (1/2/31). Revised as poem VII in *XX Poems*. Reprinted in *CP* (1988), 50.

1, 2 *majority*: In conventional grammar, a 'count noun' (applicable only to countable entities), so 'most' would be expected instead of 'the majority' here. The word is the first of several associated with politics: *Debating . . . Divide . . . unopposed . . . return*.
9 Cf. 'the silent majority': 'the mass of people whose views remain unexpressed, esp. in political contexts; those who are usu. overlooked because of their moderation': *OED*, silent 7.

March Past

DATE AND TEXT
L to MJ, 23 May 1951 (Bodl. MS Eng. c. 7405/63): 'haven't written anything for ages, except a bad sonnet & a bad unfinished poem about a march on Sunday afternoon'. *Wkbk* 2 (1/2/41) contains five pages of drafts of all but the last stanza after '19. iii. 51', dated '25 / 5 / 51' at the end. Half a page of drafts of the last stanza immediately follow, and the next date in *Wkbk* 2 is '12 June 1951', twelve pages away. The title at this stage was 'Sunday parade'. There is a t.s. with holograph corrections in pencil (Hull DPL 1/2/52). A t.s. of the poem is included in a letter dated 15 Oct. 1951 to MJ (Bodl. MS Eng. c. 7406/50): copy-text. The title 'March past' has been regularised to 'March Past' in the present edition. Published in *CP* (1988), 55, from the earlier t.s.

VARIANTS (from Hull DPL 1/2/52)
Title A The march past ['A march' is in t.s., the rest in pencil.]
14–15 Pure marchings, pure apparations, | Honeycombs of heroic separations, [with 'marchings' underlined and alts. 'congress?' and 'meetings?' suggested in the margin; and with arrows suggesting a reversal of the two lines]
21 (But unsupported broke, and were not mended) –
22 for such things] because it for such things [cancelled by typing through]
23 exhumable] disturbable exhumable

L to MJ, 15 Oct. 1951 (Bodl. MS Eng. c. 7406/48), with the poem: 'As for my poems I have 3 only written since the collection [i.e. *XX Poems*]. None is good, but to prove it I send one [. . .] I know it's quite all right as far as it goes but its fault is in not going far enough*', '*having just endured typing it I'm not so sure.'
    Title L saw Orange parades in Belfast, though as James Booth, Booth (2000), 200, remarks, the poem is 'without a single Orange, or Irish reference'. A letter to MJ dated 12 July 1951 (Bodl. MS Eng. c. 7405/111–13) stresses the ugliness, slovenliness, tawdriness and hypocrisy of an Orange Order march past. Another, of 13 July 1953 (Bodl. MS Eng. c. 7408/38), refers to 'the enormous drab march'. 14 Steve Clark and James Booth, Booth (2000), 168, 201, note the parallel repetition of 'pure' in *Essential Beauty*, 18–19. ·

Marriages

DATE AND TEXT
Wkbk 2 (1/2/43) contains six and a half pages of drafts of the whole poem after '25 / 5 / 51', dated '12 June 1951' at the end. The copy-text is Hull DPL 1/2/61, a t.s. with corrections and additions in pencil, dated '12 June 1951' in L's hand. The title is in pencil. Published by AT in Hartley (1988), 46–7, and in *CP* (1988), 63–4.

VARIANTS (from Hull DPL 1/2/61)
10 old] ~~a~~ old
17 Scarecrows of] ~~With motheaten~~ Scarecrows of

'To put one brick upon another'

DATE AND TEXT
?1951. Hull DPL 2/3/36 (t.s.). Published in *CP* (1988), 58.

Maturity

DATE AND TEXT
?1951 Hull DPL 2/3/16 (t.s. with holograph corrections, 'stet' and 'start' being in ink): copy-text. In l. 2 'I shall have' is cancelled, then reinstated by dots under it and 'stet' in the margin. Published in *CP* (1988), 62, with 'stationary' (l. 1) in roman, though in the t.s. it is underlined to signal italic.

VARIANTS (from Hull DPL 2/3/16)
1 A *stationary* sense] ~~A sense of standing still~~ A *stationary* sense
2 I shall have] ~~I shall have It will be~~ stet
4 start] ~~come~~ start
the] ~~a~~ the
7 And this must be] ~~This now, then, is But~~ And this must ~~then now~~ be
life] life~~?~~

'You think yourself no end of fun'

DATE AND TEXT
Included in a letter to MJ dated 20 Feb. 1952 (Bodl. MS Eng. c. 7407/28). L tells MJ he has found an alternative kind of Valentine

card: 'the insulting sort – very cruel really – to be sent anonymously to people you *don't* like. Each bore a picture, in the vulgar postcard style, & a rhyme, the point of wch in the last line was emphasised by heavy type, e.g. (this is more or less fictitious) [poem].' Previously unpublished.

'Somewhere on the Isle of Mull'

DATE AND TEXT
Written on the inside back cover of *Wkbk* 4 (1/4/39) and dated '1952'.

2 *Dreiser*: There is no reason to think L is referring to the American novelist Theodore Dreiser.

'When she came on, you couldn't keep your seat'

DATE AND TEXT
There are three pages of drafts in *Wkbk* 3 (1/3/5) after '24 Jan. 1953': a draft of ll. 1–11 with the title 'He hears that his beloved has become engaged', dated '29 1 53'; two further drafts, one nearly complete, one complete but untitled dated '2-2-53' at the end, with a further version of stanza 2 immediately after it. The copy-text is Hull DPL 2/3/23 (t.s. with holograph corrections in pencil). Above the t.s. text, L writes 'For C.G.B.', but there is no title. Underlinings, signalling italics, in ll. 12 and 14 are in pencil, and the poem is numbered VII. Published in *CP* (1988), 66, with the title from *Wkbk* 3 and a completion date of 29 Jan. 1953.

VARIANTS (from Hull DPL 2/3/23)
4 how we went ha ha ha!] { the crowd went ha ha ha } – how we/!
[Dash cancelled before 'how we']
11 (I used mine to sit tight)] without which I sat which I used to sit I used mine to sit tight
13 but] and but

[Dedication] Geoff Bradshaw, to whom WA became engaged at the end of 1952: WA interviewed in *AL*, 1 (Apr. 1996), 13. She reports L's reaction to her engagement: 'I feel as if someone had handed me a new MS by D. H. Lawrence and I'd left it sitting on my desk till after Christmas, only to find it gone': *AL*, 12 (Oct. 2001), 28. She and Bradshaw married in 1954. On WA, see notes on *Lines on a*

Young Lady's Photograph Album. [**Title**] Reminiscent of several grandiose titles in Yeats's *The Wind among the Reeds* (1899), e.g. *He Bids his Beloved be at Peace, He Gives his Beloved Certain Rhymes, He Hears the Cry of the Sedge.* Perhaps this is why L removed it. **3** *Tup-heavy*: weighty as a ram; cf. 'top-heavy'.

'At thirty-one, when some are rich'

DATE AND TEXT
Wkbk 3 (1/3/9, 11, 13) contains thirteen pages of drafts of the whole (unfinished) poem between '18. 8. 53' and '18. 9. 53'. The copy-text is Hull DPL 2/3/18 (t.s., with a correction in l. 24, rescinded by a row of dots under the corrected word, in holograph). At the end of the text, in t.s.: 'unfinished'. Published in *CP* (1988), 69–70, with a colon for the semicolon at the end of l. 22.

VARIANTS (from Hull DPL 2/3/18)
24 wise] ~~wise smart~~ wise

George H. Gilpin, Booth (2000), 76, locates the poem at the end of L's affair with PS. **25** *kinetic*: dynamic, full of energy.

Mother, Summer, I

DATE AND TEXT
Wkbk 3 (1/3/10, 13, 16) contains three pages of drafts after '18. 8. 53', the final (complete) one dated '5 / x / 53' at the end. The copy-text is Hull DPL 2/3/22 (t.s. with holograph corrections). In l. 14 L leaves a gap between 'That' and 'me', and writes 'cant' for the cancelled 'can't'. In l. 16, he reinstates the cancelled 'An autumn' by 'stet'. Published in *CP* (1988), 68, with 'summer' in the title regularised to 'Summer', as in the present edition.

VARIANTS (from Hull DPL 2/3/22)
14 ~~I can't confront, and so I wait await~~ That   me, anxiously I await
~~but facing me~~ I cant confront: I must await
16 ~~An autumn Autumnals~~ An autumn

1 L to JBS, 11 May 1948 (Hull DP 174/2/174): 'my poor mother, she doesn't like thunderstorms'. To MJ, 20 July 1955 (Bodl. MS Eng. c. 7411/109), when he is at his mother's house: 'a storm grumbled round all night, sheet lightning flashing from time to time rather prettily [. . .] Mother hated it of course.' To MJ, 4 Aug.1960 (Bodl. MS Eng. c. 7421/110): 'mother was in a low mood because of real and imagined thunderstorms'. 4 *grape-dark*: Cf. *Livings II*, 11–12: 'sky builds | Grape-dark'; *Light, Clouds, Dwelling-places*, 1: 'grape-dark sky'.

Autumn

DATE AND TEXT
L to WA, 7 Oct. 1953 (*SL*, 214): 'Shall just lay this aside for an hour or so as I have a poem on hand [. . .] Did quite a bit of poem, a loose, somewhat rhetorical effort: not about you this time – about nature.' AT's guess ('Probably "Autumn"') in *SL*, 214 n. is correct. *Wkbk* 3 (1/3/17) contains six pages of a complete draft after '5 / x / 53', dated '10 October '53' at the end and immediately followed by another draft of the first five stanzas on a single page before '13. x. 53'. L to WA, 28 Oct. 1953 (Bodl. MS Res. c. 616): 'I've been busy with poems. I'm thinking of trying Ludovic Kennedy with 3 poems recently written – your album, autumn, & one written the other night about, oh dear, well, how-we-automatically-change-an-event-in-our-minds-until-it's-no-existence-except-in-nightmares. Don't suppose anything will come of the venture.' (Ludovic Kennedy, 1919–2009, British journalist and broadcaster, from 1953 edited and introduced the radio series *First Reading* on the BBC Third Programme. L and KA were among the writers he presented.) The third poem mentioned by L became *Whatever Happened?* in *TLD*.

Hull DPL 2/3/21 (t.s. with holograph corrections) is the copy-text. Below the text L writes 'bwbwbw'. Published in *CP* (1988), 75.

VARIANTS (from Hull DPL 2/3/21)
1 air] ~~wind~~ air
13 night skies] ~~sky stars at night~~ night skies
14 their] ~~its~~ their
16 Like] Like ~~As~~
20 door, mantle the fat flame,] door ~~and light a farthing dip set the~~ mantle the fat flame,
21 once more alone] ~~alone once more~~ once more alone

L to MJ, 27 Sept. 1956 (*SL*, 266): 'Autumn, autumn! It comes quickly in these parts. I wish that poem I once wrote hadn't been such a flop: I long to do *The Seasons*, though I never can write set pieces. It would be my great ambition, like the 4 *quartets*. But I know I never shall [. . .] I doubt if it would *interest* me enough to get finished, & it wd be hard to avoid being corny – typing up various ideas with each season, like *Ulysses* (autumn – dissolution – middle age – resignation – twilight of W. civilisation, etc.).'

17–18 Reminiscent of Eliot, *The Love Song of J. Alfred Prufrock*, 15 ('The yellow fog'), 23, 26, etc. ('And indeed there will be time', 'There will be time, there will be time'), *Rhapsody on Windy Night*, 8, 14–16, etc. (street lamps), as Osborne (2008), 57, hints.

Best Society

DATE AND TEXT
Wkbk 3 (1/3/19) contains five and a half pages of drafts of four stanzas and an additional fifth between '13. x. 53' and '22. x. 53'. The copy-text is Hull DPL 2/3/17: t.s., with a title, a comma after 'Then' in l. 9, and a quotation from Wordsworth ('Prelude II, 298, 'solitude more active even than "best society"') in holograph. At the end of the text, in t.s.: 'unfinished'. Published in *CP* (1988), 56–7, with the date '1951?' and without a note on its being unfinished (though such notes are provided elsewhere).

L to MJ, 24 July 1952 (Bodl. MS Eng. c. 7407/65): 'Seriously, I think it is a *grave fault* in life that so much time is wasted in social matters, because it not only takes up time when you might be doing individual private things, but it prevents you storing up the psychic energy that can then be released to create art or whatever it is.' To MJ, 10 Aug. 1968 (Bodl. MS Eng. c. 7437/117): 'Alone, I am placid, industrious, inventive, amiable. In company, I am locked in a rictus of rage and irritation.'

Title John Carey, Booth (2000), 63, notes Milton, *Paradise Lost*, 9. 249: 'For solitude sometimes is best society' (Adam riskily conceding Eve's right to solitude). **1** Carey also notes 1 Cor. 13: 11: 'When I was a child . . . I thought as a child'. **1–8** Osborne (2008), 55, acknowledging L's friend Ted Tarling, cites Sassoon, *The Heart's Journey*, xi. [1–3]: '*When I'm alone*' . . . | As though to be alone were nothing strange. | '*When I was young*,' he said; '*when I was young*.' **22** Cf. *Vers de Société*, 24: '*Virtue is social.*' **26** *The gas-fire breathes*: As in *Vers de Société*, 5, to which see the note. **31–2** L to MJ, 5 Dec. 1950 (Bodl. MS Eng. c. 7404/18): 'silence is nearly a necessity: that blessed state in which very slowly one's mind can emerge from its shell like a tender snail'. To WA, 22 Aug. 1953 (Bodl. MS Res. c. 616): 'some grow lumpish & sodden alone (they tell me), I become fine-spun & shimmering'.

Unfinished Poem

DATE AND TEXT
Wkbk 2 (1/2/47) contains eight pages of drafts of the first six stanzas after '22 / 3 [1951]', L's error for '22 / 8'. *Wkbk* 3 (1/3/2) contains five pages of drafts of all ten stanzas before '22. 1. 53' (1/3/2), and half a page of drafts of stanza 1 between '24. x. 53' and '26. x. 53' (1/3/21). Hull DPL 2/3/20 is a t.s. with holograph annotations and two corrections, one of a typing error. At the top, L writes: 'nb find that remark by ?Freud "When a girl says she fears death, I know she fears love".' Below the text: '(unfinished)'. Hull DPL 2/3/38, a t.s., signed in t.s. 'Philip Larkin', is the copy-text. Published in *CP* (1988), 60–1, with 'threshhold' corrected to 'threshold' in l. 36, as in the present edition.

VARIANTS (from Hull DPL 2/3/20)
Title [No title]
15 his] ~~the~~ his

10 *seeks and will always find*: 'Seek, and ye shall find' (Matt. 7: 7; Luke 11: 9). Cf. *Letter to a Friend about Girls*, 17. 16 *immortal memory*: The phrase is strongly associated with the speech commemorating Robert Burns at Burns Suppers. 24 *making the fig*: inserting the thumb between two fingers as a gesture of contempt. 27 *Paring my nails*: John Osborne, Booth (2000), 148, invokes James Joyce, *Portrait of the Artist as a Young Man*, ch. 5: 'The artist, like the God of creation, remains behind or beyond or above his handiwork, invisible, refined out of existence, indifferent, paring his fingernails.'

Hospital Visits

DATE AND TEXT
Wkbk 3 (1/3/23) contains five and a half pages of drafts of the whole poem after '26. x. 53', dated '4 xi 53' at the end. Hull DPL 2/3/15 (t.s. with holograph corrections) is the copy-text. Line 25 originally

read 'They had her back once again'. L cancelled 'back once' and wrote 'in' to the right. Also to the right is written 'She must come in again'. It is not possible to ascertain which version is the latest one, but the cancellation and 'in' are written more heavily than the alternative version of the whole line, and therefore, as was done in *CP* (1988), 77, the present edition prints 'They had her in again'.

VARIANTS (from Hull DPL 2/3/15)
3 screens] ~~a screen~~ screens
8 was] ~~they~~ was
9 Just] ~~It was~~ Just
15 Thereafter] ~~Therefore~~ Thereafter
21 Watched] ~~She saw~~ Watched
22 Winter] ~~When w~~Winter
23 When he] When ~~H~~he
25 They had her ~~back once~~ again She must come in again   in

Autobiography at an Air-Station

DATE AND TEXT
Wkbk 3 (1/3/25) contains a complete draft on one page after '4 xi 53', dated '6. xii. 53' at the end. Four days later, L sent a version in a letter to PS (*SL*, 219–20). Hull DPL 2/3/14 is a t.s. with a MS correction, and it constitutes a revision of the text: copy-text. Published in *CP* (1988), 78, with L's misspelling 'Stupified' in l. 12 corrected.

VARIANTS
7 Perhaps] Try to *Letter to PS*
12 Stupefied] Hypnotised *Letter to PS*; ~~Hypnotised~~ Stupified *Hull t.s.*
13 Begins to ebb outside] Outside begins to ebb *Letter to PS*
14 Now it's failed.] Has it failed? *Letter to PS*

Title *Air-Station*. Superseded by 'airport', as in *The Building*, 9.
14 *Assumption*: supposition; but also reception into heaven of the Virgin Mary, which was declared official Catholic dogma by Pope Pius XII in 1950. L to PS, 10 Dec. 1953 (*SL*, 220): 'If the reader doesn't twig that I'm using *assumption* in the religious sense (and I don't see why he should, though I think it's quite funny when you see it) then of course it loses what little point it has.' Nevertheless L draws attention to the religious sense by using a capital 'A'.

Negative Indicative

Wkbk 3 (1/3/29) contains a one-page draft, complete except for a
title, after '6. xii. 53', dated '28 xii 53' at the end, and, immediately
after it, another complete draft with the title '<u>Never</u>' before '29
xii 53' (three pages later). Hull DPL 2/3/13 (t.s. with title and
corrections in holograph) is the copy-text. L writes 'unfinished?'
on the t.s. Published in *CP* (1988), 79.

VARIANTS (from Hull DPL 2/3/13)
14 first] ~~evening~~ first
15 a] ~~the~~ a
17 Alive] ~~Alight~~ Alive

Title In grammar, a negative indicative mood of the verb would be
used to state that something is not a fact (e.g. 'he is not here').

Love ('Not love you? Dear, I'd pay ten quid for you')

Wkbk 3 (1/3/32) contains a single page bearing three complete
drafts, dated '31 Dec '53', '31. xii. 53' and '8. 1. 54' respectively.
The first bears the title '<u>To Miss A. W. Arnott</u>'. On Winifred Arnott,
see the notes on *Lines on a Young Lady's Photograph Album*. The
copy-text is Hull DPL 2/3/10 (t.s.). Some cancelled words in l. 2 are
reinstated by dots underneath them. Quoted in *CP* (1988), xxi.

VARIANTS (from the t.s.)
2 ~~and~~ and five ~~more~~ when I ~~got~~ ~~get~~ got

1 Cf. the opening of Walter de la Mare's *Not Yet*: '"Not love me?
Even yet"'. *quid*: pounds (colloq.).

Marriage

8–27 Jan. 1954. Hull DPL 2/3/11 (t.s.), immediately following the
previous verse and preceding *Midwinter Waking*. Quoted in *CP*
(1988), xxii.

2 Cf. Eliot, *Fragment of an Agon*, 49: '*Two live as one*'.

Midwinter Waking

DATE AND TEXT
Wkbk 3 (1/3/39) contains a page of drafts after '23 Jan 1954',
including a complete draft with the title '<u>January</u>' dated '27. 1 . 54'
at the end. The copy-text is Hull DPL 2/3/12 (t.s.). Published in
CP (1988), 87. As was done in *CP*, 'waking' in the title has been
regularised to 'Waking' in the present edition.

'Those who give all for love, or art, or duty'

DATE AND TEXT
The four lines are dated '13. 3. 54' in *Wkbk 3* (1/3/41), and are
misidentified in the Hull catalogue as part of the drafts of *Success
Story*. Though they are a draft, a final version with no uncancelled
alternative readings is discernible. Previously unpublished.

Gathering Wood

DATE AND TEXT
Wkbk 3 (1/3/44) contains three and a half pages of drafts after
'16. 3. 54', including a complete draft dated '23. 3. 54', a revised
draft of stanzas 2 and 3 dated '24 / 3 / 54', and a second complete
draft dated '25 / 3 / 54'. The copy-text is Hull DPL 2/3/9 (t.s. with
holograph corrections). The t.s. bears a title and two versions of the
poem, one below the other. As was done in *CP* (1988), 91, in the
present edition the second version is printed and the title is retained.
In l. 7 of the first version, L inserts a caret, and writes 'back' in the
margin as the word to be inserted, and then cancels the word. In
l. 11, he indicates that the words 'still' and 'short' are to be reversed.

VARIANTS (from Hull DPL 2/3/9)
4 coverts] ~~thickets~~ coverts *1st version*
7 ~~To be carried~~ Carrying them home ~~back~~ *1st version*
9 Soon] ~~Now~~ Soon *2nd version*
haze] ~~glaze~~ haze *1st version*
11 short, still] ~~still, short~~ short, still *1st version*

L to MJ, 22 Sept. 1958 (Bodl. MS Eng. c. 7418/108): 'I still think
"Now air-frosts haze snow-thickened shires" to be as good a verse

as I dyd euer pen [. . .] what a beautiful verse, nay poem, it is!'
Quoting ll. 9–10 (again with 'Now' for 'Soon') in a letter to MJ
dated 7 Jan. 1960 (Bodl. MS Eng. c. 7420/130), he exclaims: 'Oh,
if I could always write like that!' In another dated 16 Nov. 1965
(Bodl. MS Eng. c. 7431/83), he declares of ll. 9–12: 'And how I love
that quatrain – one of the best, & certainly the most individual, I
ever managed. It has realism & ecstasy, all in 14 words – 4, 3, 4,
3, so simple. You mustn't lose it, dear. Anway, it was very like it on
Sunday. Now crossed legs faze Beer-thickened eyes.'

11–12 John Osborne, Booth (2000), 147, notes that the short
double exclamation is a favourite mannerism of Rimbaud. See
Absences, 10; *Sad Steps*, 11–12; *The Card-Players*, 14.

'Long roots moor summer to our side of earth'

DATE AND TEXT
Wkbk 3 (1/3/52) contains four pages of drafts of stanzas 1 and 2
after '26 5 54'. *Wkbk* 4 (1/4/2) contains half a page of drafts of six
or seven lines (including the first and the last two) before the date
'10 June 1954' at the top of the next page, which bears a complete
draft dated '14 June '54' at the end. Below the latter date is a second
draft of stanza 3. Hull DPL 2/3/7 (t.s. with holograph corrections) is
the copy-text. L has written 'June 12 1954' on it: this was the date
when WA married Geoff Bradshaw in London. She had told L the
date of her marriage by 29 Apr. 1954, when L told PS (*SL*, 227).
Published in *CP* (1988), 96, with a completion date of 12 June (from
the t.s.). However, the t.s. contains revisions to the *Wkbk* text, and
must have been produced after 14 June.

VARIANTS (from Hull DPL 2/3/7)
 5 upward] upwards
11 I] ~~we~~ I
12 Myself] ~~Ourselves~~ Myself

3 Cf. *The Trees*, 9, 12: 'Yet still the unresting castles thresh', 'Begin
afresh, afresh, afresh'; 'The poet has a straight face', 108: 'the castle
of leaves'.

'What have I done to be thirty-two?'

DATE AND TEXT
Included in a letter to MJ dated 10 Aug. 1954 (Bodl. MS Eng. c. 7408/120) and in another of the same date to Arthur Terry (*SL*, 228; copy-text).

VARIANTS (from the letter to MJ)
5 Yet] And

L in the letter to Terry: 'For my birthday I composed the following poem: *not* for the *Spectator* [. . .] A perfect description of how I, feel, anyway.' L's birthday was on 9 Aug.

3 *screw*: (slang) earnings (*OED*, sb.¹ 20). As in *Money*, 11.

'Is your field sunny?'

DATE AND TEXT
Wkbk 4 (1/4/7) contains a single draft after '28 / 7 / 54' (four pages before), dated '27. 8. 54' at the end. It has no uncancelled alternative readings, and brings the text to the state of the copy-text, Bodl. MS Eng. c. 7555/88, an undated greetings card sent to MJ in which L wrote the poem. Previously unpublished.

The poem is written in terms characteristic of L's relationship with MJ: see 'Her birthday always has', 'My name it is Benjamin Bunny', and notes.

Boars Hill

DATE AND TEXT
Inscribed to 'P. M. S.' [Patricia Strang]: 'From P. L. after delightful visit, Sept. '54'. Written by L on a copy of the first edn. of Betjeman's *A Few Late Chrysanthemums* (1954). Published in catalogue 1433 (2009) of Maggs Brothers Ltd. with a comma missing before the dash at the end of l. 1, L's error 'see' silently corrected to 'seen' in l. 7, and 'Kimansky' for 'Komansky' (l. 7).

The poem is an affectionate parody of Betjeman.

Title Boars Hill is a select residential area just south of Oxford. PS had gone to live there during a separation from her husband

Colin Strang. Her affair with L had ended in 1953 after she and her husband had moved to Newcastle, though she and L remained friends. Betjeman mentions Boars Hill in *Myfanwy at Oxford*, 32. **4** *the Ashmolean*: Oxford museum, originally opened in 1683. **6** *Heals*: Heal & Sons Ltd., London furniture store since 1810. **11** *the Matthew Arnold air*: Arnold's poem *The Scholar-Gipsy* is set around Oxford. It opens with the shepherd being called 'from the hill', and 'the eye travels down to Oxford's towers' (l. 30), as it would from Boars Hill.

Christmas

DATE AND TEXT

L typed it on a Christmas card to MJ, and added the inscription 'A rhyme and a present, with all love, *From* Philip *To* Monica for Christmas 1954': Bodl. MS Eng. c. 7410/22 = *LTM*, 135, where the verse is reproduced in facsimile. He told her that both it and another verse 'came "straight off"': letter dated 9 May 1955 (Bodl. MS Eng. c. 7411/15).

The poem accords with L's tender representations of MJ as a rabbit, which permeate his correspondence with her.

A Sense of Shape

DATE AND TEXT

Wkbk 4 (1/4/11) contains four and a half pages of drafts of the whole (but unfinished) poem between '10 October 1954' (nine pages before) and '13 / 5 / 55' (four pages later). The latest version from the last of the drafts is printed in *LTM*, 134, though with a comma instead of the full stop at the end of l. 2 (which it then had), 'shapes' for 'shape's' and 'What decides' for 'That's what it decides' in l. 4, and 'safe in the loop, | Bright in the star' not enclosed in parentheses in ll. 11–12. The copy-text is a t.s. included in a letter to MJ dated 3 June 1955: Bodl. MS Eng. c. 7411/48.

L in the letter: 'I believe our lives <u>are</u> affected much more by early chance ("Hap") than by consideration and reason. This is what I had tried to express in the poem that came to nothing, <u>A sense of shape</u>' [. . .] I stopped it because of its mechanical quality, but it's smart enough, don't you think? (No, I don't, I think it's rotten. Sunday.)'

Long Sight in Age

DATE AND TEXT

Wkbk 4 (1/4/16) contains: after '13 / 6 / 55', three pages of drafts of the whole poem, dated '20 / 6 / 55' at the end; and, on the next page, a further draft of ll. 1–5. The text published in *CP* (1988), 105, is taken from the draft just above the date, which has no uncancelled alternative readings, but may, as AT acknowledged, be unfinished. The *CP* text has 'last' for 'lost' (l. 5), 'Wrinkling' for 'Wincing' (l. 9), 'waves' for 'vanes' (l. 10), and no comma after 'away' (l. 9).

Counting

DATE AND TEXT

Wkbk 4 (1/4/23) contains a unique draft of the whole poem after '11 / 9 / 55'. The next date in the *Wkbk* is '15 / 2 / 56', twenty pages away. Published in *CP* (1988), 108.

'Back to this dreary dump'

DATE AND TEXT

Included in a letter dated 26 Sept. 1955 to MJ (Bodl. MS Eng. c. 7412/38 = *LTM*, 182).

L in the letter: '– This verse sprang almost unthought-of from my head as the train ran into Hull just before midday. I'm sure no subsequent verse could keep up the high standard. *Pigs* & *digs* rhyme, of course, likewise *work* & *shirk*, & *Hull* & *dull*, but triple rhymes are difficult. Anyway, it gives an indication of how I'm feeling.'

   1 L to RC, 24 July 1955 (*SL*, 245): 'Hull. It's a frightful dump.'

'The local snivels through the fields'

DATE AND TEXT

L included it in a letter to MJ dated 27 Sept. 1956 (*SL*, 265), and
stated: 'This was the parody of myself I wrote for the group I
mentioned earlier, so you see my mind has been running on these
lines' (*SL*, 266). AT in *SL*, 265 n.: 'It evidently dates from 1951, or
possibly 1952, although this letter makes it sound recent.' AT dated
it '1951?' in *CP* (1988), 59, on the basis, he told Zachary Leader, of
the position of Hull DPL 2/3/6 (t.s.) in the folder of L's 'Unpublished
Poems': Amis, *Letters*, 477 n. But the poems preceding it in DPL
2/3/6 date from 9 Jan. 1959, 31 Dec. 1958, 5 Nov. 1958, 18 Oct.
1958 and before 14 May 1957, and it is immediately followed by
poems dating from 12 June 1954, 24 Apr. 1954, 25 Mar. 1954, 27
Jan. 1954, 29 Dec. 1953 and after 10 Dec. 1953. There is therefore
no strict chronological sequence, but also nothing that would
indicate that the poem dates from 1951. L to MJ, 18 Sept. 1956
(Bodl. MS Eng. c. 7414/68): 'Kingsley & I knocked out a bunch of
feeble parodies of "the movement" in Swansea, & he thinks he can
get Spender to print them in *Encounter* [. . .] they're so feeble I don't
think they'll ever achieve print.' It is not known who wrote which,
except the seventh (by L). L made a visit to KA in Swansea that
began on 18 August 1956: Amis, *Letters*, 471, 475. On 27 Aug. L
wrote a letter of apology to Vernon Watkins for not getting in touch
with him during the visit (*SL*, 264). I date the poem, and the other
parodies, from 18 to 27 August 1956, therefore.

The copy-text is Hull DPL 2/3/6 (t.s.): this is the version L himself
preserved. The collection of parodies was entitled 'ALL ABOARD
THE GRAVY TRAIN: | OR, MOVEMENTS AMONG THE
YOUNGER POETS | by RON CAIN': Amis, *Letters*, 1141. They
were turned down by Stephen Spender (*Encounter*) and by John
Lehmann (*London Magazine*): Zachary Leader in Amis, *Letters*, 6,
7. Published in *CP* (1988), 59.

All eight parodies were published by Zachary Leader, in the *TLS*,
5066 (5 May 2000), 14, and in Amis, *Letters*, 1141–5, from the t.s.
texts in Amis's letter of 27 Dec. 1956 to L in the Bodleian Library.

VARIANTS

[**Title**] Poetry of Comings Back *Letter from KA, 27 Dec. 1956*
4 Baby-sized] Baby-size *27 Sept. 1956 letter*
8 Should after fourteen days] Of fourteen days should thus *27 Sept.
1956 letter*

'The Movement' is a supposed grouping of 1950s writers originally identified in an article, 'In The Movement', by J. D. Scott, in *The Spectator*, 1 Oct. 1954. Those who have been taken to be members of the group include L, KA, RC, Donald Davie (1922–85), D. J. Enright (1920–2002), Thom Gunn (1929–2004), Elizabeth Jennings (1926–2001) and John Wain (1925–94). Among the characteristics attributed to the group have been scepticism, irony, anti-romanticism, robust commonsense, and philistinism. 'MOVEMENTS' in the title reduces the idea to a literal sense, and each of the parodies relates to a train journey.

L to MJ, 27 Sept. 1956 (*SL*, 266): 'It has an air of the train from Rabbithampton, to my *ears*. (Incidentally I *know* that country people wouldn't *buy* plums, especially in the next town, but I was too lazy to alter it all.) I sit between fat lop-eared does | Whose weekly day excursion yields | Three-decker novels, garden hoes [. . .] That would be a nice picture to draw, wouldn't it?'

1 *local*: local train.

Getting Somewhere

DATE AND TEXT
The first parody, of 'K+NGSLEY AM+S', in *All Aboard the Gravy Train*, dating from after 18 Aug. 1956. See the notes on the previous poem.

5 *Three-Cornered Hat*: 1919 ballet with music by Manuel de Falla. 6 *Caff*: vulgar or jocular slang for 'café'.

To Hart Crane

DATE AND TEXT
The second parody, of 'R+BERT C+NQUEST', in *All Aboard the Gravy Train*, dating from after 18 Aug. 1956. See the notes on 'The local snivels through the fields'.

Title American poet Hart Crane (1899–1932). 'The Death of Hart Crane' was published in Conquest's *Poems* (1955). 1 *victrola*: record-player (1906 onwards). 2 *Hudson*: river that flows through eastern New York. 3 *Bell-bottomed*: Bell-bottomed trousers, as worn by sailors and as part of naval uniform. 5 *Lucifer's*: Satan's. 7 *the El*: Chicago's rapid transit system (1892 onwards).

11 *the Mexique Bay*: Referred to in this way in Marvell's
Bermudas, 36.

A Midland Syllogism

DATE AND TEXT

The third parody, of 'D+NALD D+VIE', in *All Aboard the Gravy
Train*, dating from after 18 Aug. 1956. See the notes on 'The local
snivels through the fields'.

2 *Peeping . . . Tom*: A 'peeping Tom' is a furtive voyeur. 6 Cf.
Tennyson, *In Memoriam*, cxxxvi. 155–6: 'And one far-off
divine event, | To which the whole creation moves.' 9 *George
Whitefield*: itinerant revivalist preacher (1714–70). Davie's parents
were Baptists, and he aligned himself for a time with English
nonconformism. 11–12 *gorgon . . . hair*: in Greek myth, the
Gorgons were terrifying female creatures with snaky hair and a gaze
that turned those who met it to stone.

Outcome of a Conversation

DATE AND TEXT

The fourth parody, of 'D. J. ENR+GHT', in *All Aboard the Gravy
Train*, dating from after 18 Aug. 1956. See the notes on 'The local
snivels through the fields'.

1–6 Enright, an academic as well as a poet, was Visiting Professor at
Konan University, Japan, 1953–6. 7 *Austin*: British motor company
founded in 1905. 9 Keats in a letter of 27 Feb. 1818 to John Taylor:
'if Poetry comes not as naturally as leaves to a tree it had better not
come at all'.

The Wild Ones

DATE AND TEXT

The fifth parody, of 'TH+M G+NN', in *All Aboard the Gravy Train*,
dating from after 18 Aug. 1956. See the notes on 'The local snivels
through the fields'.

The parody reflects Gunn's homosexuality.

7 *Argos*: Greek city in the Peloponnese. 9 *Patroclus*: son of Menoetius, comrade of Achilles. 10 *Achilles*: Greek hero of the Trojan War in the *Iliad*.

Travellers

DATE AND TEXT
The sixth parody, of 'EL+ZABETH J+NNINGS', in *All Aboard the Gravy Train*, dating from after 18 Aug. 1956.

See the notes on 'The local snivels through the fields'.

Behind Time

DATE AND TEXT
The eighth and final parody, of 'J+HN W+IN', in *All Aboard the Gravy Train*, dating from after 18 Aug. 1956.

See the notes on 'The local snivels through the fields'.
   The parody highlights the influence on Wain (1925–94) in the 1950s of the poems of Empson (1906–84), especially in the three-line stanza and the aphoristic manner.
   1 *Bradshaw*: railway timetable (from 1839 onwards), named after its publisher George Bradshaw (1801–53).

'You'll do anything for money'

DATE AND TEXT
Included in a letter to RC dated 29 Nov. 1956. Published in *SL*, 270.

L in the letter: 'Another editor (mad millionairess) wants a poem on Hungarian children. My God! [poem] Think that's worth £1. 1. 0? Ah you're too kind.'

To +++++ ++++++ and Others

DATE AND TEXT
Two versions are included in a letter to MJ dated 4 Dec. 1956 (Bodl. MS Eng. c. 7415/14, 17). L also included it in a letter to RC

dated 5 Dec. 1956 (*SL*, 271): copy-text. In a letter to MJ dated 30 Sept. 1967 (Bodl. MS Eng. c. 7435/155), L describes it as 'a triolet composed by myself & Kingsley many years ago'.

VARIANTS (from the letter of 4 Dec. 1956)
Title [No title]
3 You're allowed to, you know: *1st version*
5–[10] With a *Poem* (For Trevor) | Or *Pan*, or whatever? | We'll all shout bravo | If you make a good show; | ~~So just you g~~ Go on, have a go, | If you're so bloody clever . . . *1st version*

Before the first version L tells MJ he would finish his 'little *rondeau* or whatever they're called' if he 'knew the form'. Before the second version, he remarks: 'I finished my little villanelle, or whatever it's called: it is now quite strict in form.' The poem is written in response to the attack in *Encounter* by David Wright and others on the anthology *New Lines* (ed. RC, with contributions by L). L in the letter to RC: 'God what puking riff-raff turned up to root for Wright, what? I felt inclined to turn a little Dobsonish verse.' L writes in the manner of Austin Dobson (1840–1921).

'Get Kingsley Amis to sleep with your wife'

DATE AND TEXT
Included in a letter to MJ dated 29 Jan. 1958 (Bodl. MS Eng. c. 7417/98). Published in *LTM*, 235.

L in the letter: 'I see "W." John Morgan is interviewing Kingsley next Saturday – [couplet], haw haw.'

'Oh who is this feeling my prick?'

DATE AND TEXT
George and Jean Hartley told L they had accepted Thom Gunn's poem *The Feel of Hands* for publication in *Listen*, 2. 4 (spring 1958). 'Does it go like this?' L asked, delivering his spoof immediately. Published by Jean Hartley in *AL*, 13 (Apr. 2002), 7.

1 Gunn, l. 16: 'I do not know whose hands they are.' 2 'Tom, Dick, and Harry' is a phrase meaning random representatives of the populace.

'Her birthday always has'

DATE AND TEXT
Hull DPL 1/2/58, part of a page torn from *Wkbk* 4 or *Wkbk* 5,
bears a complete draft. The final version is written on a birthday
card to MJ, with the postmark 6 May 1958 on the envelope (Bodl.
MS Eng. c. 7418/29). On the front of the card is a picture of rabbits
having an outdoor picnic, with 'tea laid on the grass'. Previously
unpublished.

Throughout his correspondence with MJ, L affectionately regards
her as a rabbit, and frequently includes drawings of rabbits. See '"Is
your field sunny?"' and the two poems after this one.

'My name it is Benjamin Bunny'

DATE AND TEXT
By 3 Nov. 1958, when it accompanied L's drawing of a rabbit
gathering twigs, captioned 'Earth fills his lap with treasures of her
own': Bodl. MS Eng. c. 7419/3. Cf. Wordsworth, *Ode: Intimations
of Immortality from Recollections of Early Childhood*, 77: 'Earth
fills her lap with pleasures of her own'. Previously unpublished.

Immediately after the verse: '(*Oh yes! he gathers & sells them for
money* – ghostly rabbit chorus. My dear! Who w^d heed my talk of
rabbits but you? I think my rhyme better than BP's, if the truth be
known.)' Beatrix Potter (1866–1943) published two collections of
verses: *Appley Dapply's Nursery Rhymes* (1917) and *Cecily Parsley's
Nursery Rhymes* (1922).

   1 *Benjamin Bunny*: character in Beatrix Potter's tales of rabbits
such as *The Tale of Peter Rabbit* (1902) and *The Tale of Benjamin
Bunny* (1904). Cousin of Peter Rabbit.

'Snow has covered up our track'

DATE AND TEXT
The draft in *Wkbk* 5 (1/5/9) is dated '14 / xii / 58' and has no
uncancelled alternative versions. A missing quotation mark at the
end of l. 4 has been supplied. Previously unpublished.

Far Out

DATE AND TEXT
The four pages of drafts in *Wkbk 5* (1 /5/14) are: a first draft after
'8. i. 59' of stanza 1 and an additional stanza, dated '9. 1. 59' at
the end; and two and a half pages of a second complete draft after
'18. 1. 59' dated '1: 2. 59' at the end. L included the poem (based on
the first draft) in a letter dated 11 Jan. 1959 to MJ (Bodl. MS Eng. c.
7419/48). There are two t.s. versions: Hull DPL 2/3/1, and Hull DPL
2/3/40. The latter is the copy-text. It is loosely inserted at the front
of a bound file of 'Unpublished poems, 1948– ', and it is signed, in
t.s., 'Philip Larkin'. Published in *CP* (1988), 120.

L prefaces the verse in the Bodl. MS: 'I tried to write a short poem
about the stars as observed on my midnight returns. It is not much
good, nor even finished, but as it has a faint rabbity air I transcribe
it.' To the right of the verse, he writes: 'no, this is awful, really –
worse than E. Jennings. Tripe, tripe, tripe, tripe, tripe.'

VARIANTS
Title [No title] *Bodl. MS or Hull DPL 2/3/1*
1–3 Walking at night, I stare | Beyond the bright cartoons | At darker
spaces, where *Bodl. MS, Hull DPL 2/3/1*
4–8 The big nailed brilliances | Guide or amuse by name. | Faint
dusty swarms like these | Can never do the same, | Yet me they
always please. *Bodl. MS*
me] me [*alt. some?*] *Hull DPL 2/3/1*
9–12 [Not represented in *Bodl. MS or Hull DPL 2/3/1*]

'Not to worry, Len's having a dip'

DATE AND TEXT
Included in a letter to MJ dated 16 Feb. 1959: Bodl. MS Eng. c.
7419/72. Previously unpublished.

L in the letter: 'Yes (as you'd say) I expect everyone thinks it's all
right about national figures, *but I don't*. If I wrote a *Phone*, it w^d
start something like [verse]. Below the verse, L remarks: 'M'm, not
bad. Scene in a ~~pavilion~~ cricket café, of course.'
   1 *Len's*: The famous English Test cricketer Len Hutton (1916–
90). **2** *char*: tea (slang).

'Let there be an empty space where *Rabbit* used to stand'

DATE AND TEXT

Included in a letter to MJ dated 21 Feb. 1959 (Bodl. MS Eng. c. 7419/74). Previously unpublished.

1 *Rabbit*: MJ. 2 *Fraser*: G[eorge] S[utherland] Fraser (1915–80), Scottish poet, critic and academic, who was at the University of Leicester, 1959–79, and was therefore MJ's colleague.

'Let the classroom dais be empty where the rabbit used to thump'

DATE AND TEXT

Included in a letter to MJ dated 11 Mar. 1959 (Bodl. MS Eng. c. 7419/90). Previously unpublished.

L in the letter: 'I hope you are working to rule.'

1 *the rabbit*: MJ. 2 *Fraser*: G. S. Fraser. See the note on 'Let there be an empty space where *Rabbit* used to stand'. *niners*: classes at 9 a.m.

'They are all gone into the world of light'

DATE AND TEXT

Included in a letter to RC dated 13 Aug. 1959 (*SL*, 307).

L to MJ, 29 Apr. 1963 (Bodl. MS Eng. c. 7426/77): 'They tell me Davie has "got" Colchester – ogh ogh. They are all gone into the world of light.'

1 The opening line of poem by Henry Vaughan (1620–95), which rhymes 'light' with 'bright'. L refers to the poem in a letter dated 2 Oct. 1942 to Michael Hamburger: 'Philip Larkin: A Retrospect', *PN Review*, 14. 4 (Dec. 1987), 72. 2 *Kingsley*: KA had been appointed Visiting Fellow in Creative Writing at Princeton University, 1958–9. *John*: novelist, poet and critic John Wain (1925–94). *Bob*: Robert ('Bob') Conquest had been appointed a Fellow at the University of Buffalo, 1959–60.

Homeward, rabbit, homeward go

DATE AND TEXT
Included in a letter to MJ dated 19 Aug. 1959 (Bodl. MS Eng. c. 7420/24). L had been listening to Handel's *Apollo and Dafne* and imagining rabbit scenarios for the music: 'Now the final sad rabbit-across-the-snow section is being played.' The verse is accompanied by a drawing, for which see *LTM*, 254, where it was first published. A full stop has been added at the end of the verse.

3 Cf. Eliot, *Preludes*, I, 1: 'The winter evening settles down'.

'"Living for others," (others say) "is best"'

DATE AND TEXT
The lines are dated '14. 9. 59' in *Wkbk 5* (1/5/22). They are not part of a larger poem, and though they are a draft there are no uncancelled alternative readings. Previously unpublished.

'A *Lecturer* in drip-dry shirt arrayed'

DATE AND TEXT
L tells MJ in a letter dated 7 Oct. 1959 that he has begun writing the poem, and quotes ll. 1–4 and two additional lines (Bodl. MS Eng. c. 7420/60 = *LTM*, 259). At this stage he had 'a mind to work it up into a satiric dialogue'. Hull DPL (2) 1/5/2: holograph MS, much corrected. In l. 1, L's 'drip dry' has been changed in the present edition to 'drip-dry' (he writes 'drip-dry' in the letter.) Previously unpublished.

VARIANTS
1–2 A Lecturer ~~There was a~~ A *Lecturer* ~~with expenses paid~~ in drip-dry shirt arrayed |
To teach creative writing ~~in the States~~ Rode with us, his expenses newly paid *Hull MS, 1st version* [Both lines subsequently cancelled.]
2 his] ~~his with~~ his *Hull MS*
fully] ~~safely~~ fully *Hull MS, 2nd version*; nicely *Bodl. MS*
4 ~~Armed with a First in som~~ (Plus a few summer schools and lecture dates).
Additional lines ~~Though pushing forty~~ He had the keenest nose ~~from here to Texas~~ | ~~For ambiguities and complexes~~ *Hull MS*;

Where'er he went, it was his common caper | To steal some sheets
of headed letter-paper *Bodl. MS*
5 ~~For in his life time he'd bandied~~ Literature students ~~heard~~ knew
his critics' *argot Hull MS*
7 ~~And always had~~ For ~~bed and board well he knew how to get~~ he
was good at getting fees and perks *Hull MS*
8 Mythologising] ~~By~~ Mythologising *Hull MS*
10 ~~Providing each with~~ Each had ~~its~~ a its pattern and ~~its own~~ a new
dilemma, *Hull MS*
12 ~~No-one should~~ must read things ~~on their own~~ by himself ~~again~~
Hull MS, 1st version
No-one should] ~~No-one sho You must not~~ No-one ~~must~~ should *Hull
MS, 2nd version*
13 ~~And he knew lots of several people~~ Further, he had some cronies
on the Third *Hull MS*
14 Who'd squeeze] ~~Who squeezed~~ Who'd squeeze *Hull MS*

1–2 The lecturer is introduced as though he is one of the pilgrims
in the *General Prologue* to Chaucer's *The Canterbury Tales*. L in
the letter to MJ of 7 Oct. 1959: 'I have decided that G.S.F. [see
the note on 'Let there be an empty space where *Rabbit* used to
stand', 2] & his kind are THE MODERN PARDONER – &
my Protestant soul revolts at the self-interposition of this mangy
crew between the simple reader & the Word.' 1 *drip-dry*: made
of material that will not wrinkle when hung up to dry; from
1953. 2 *His expenses fully paid*: Cf. *Naturally the Foundation will
Bear your Expenses*. 9 Novels by George Eliot, Conrad, Dickens,
and Austen. 13 *the Third*: as in *Naturally the Foundation will
Bear your Expenses*, 8 (to which see note). 14 *Brecht*: German
dramatist Bertolt Brecht (1898–1956). *Wᵐ Byrd*: English composer
William Byrd (1539/40–1623). 15 *Yeats*: W. B. Yeats (1865–
1939). 16 *Wordsworth's Daffodil*: As in Wordsworth's poem
'I wandered lonely as a cloud', which is about daffodils (plural).

Letter to a Friend about Girls

DATE AND TEXT .
In *Wkbk* 4 (1/4/37) there are just over seven pages of drafts below
the title, between '16 / x / 57' and '16 / 3 / 58'. The text at this stage
only slightly resembles the final poem. *Wkbk* 5 (1/5/25) contains
thirteen and a half pages of drafts of the whole poem between

'6. xi [1959]' and '17. 1. 60'. L tells MJ in a letter dated 1 Dec. 1959 (Bodl. MS Eng. c. 7420/97) that he has been 'hacking at a satirical poem called *Letter to a friend about girls*, wch has been in my mind for some time. It's not going very brilliantly.' L to AT, 29 Jan. 1978 (*SL*, 577): '*Letter* was written in 1959, if you are interested – *Well, finished then. Begun 1957*.' To AT, 19 Mar. 1970 (*SL*, 428): 'I have had the enclosed poem knocking around for ten years now, and every so often I take it out, alter it slightly, and try to bring myself to send it off somewhere, but I am always held back by the oppressive thought that it really isn't any good.' There are six t.s. versions: Hull DPL 2/3/43; DPL 1/7/58, loosely inserted at the back of *Wkbk 7*; DPL 1/7/63, which has holograph corrections in pencil, loosely inserted at the back of *Wkbk 7*; DPL 1/7/79, loosely inserted at the back of *Wkbk 7*; DPL 1/8/36, loosely inserted at the front of *Wkbk 8* and inscribed 'For Anthony, not the friend in this case but in all others, with admiration & respect – Horatio Larkin'; and DPL 1/8/39, loosely inserted at the front of *Wkbk 8*. Hull DPL 2/3/43 is the earliest, followed by 1/7/63; then by 1/7/58 and 1/8/39, which are identical; then by 1/8/36 and 1/7/79, which are identical. The version sent to AT with the 1970 letter is the latest, and is the copy-text. Published in *CP* (1988), 122–3.

VARIANTS

2 I see how I've been losing] I've found out why they're different *DPL 2/3/43*
the] this *DPL 2/3/43, DPL 1/7/63, DPL 1/7/58, DPL 1/8/39*
3 a different gauge] another kind *DPL 2/3/43*; a different race <u>kind</u> *DPL 1/7/63*; a different <u>kind</u> *DPL 1/7/58, DPL 1/8/39*
4 and] then *DPL 2/3/43*
8 Before, I couldn't credit] Now I can understand how *DPL 2/3/43*
9–10 Constantly waddle home hung with success | While plans of mine start nothing from the covers, *DPL 2/3/43*
10 though they're from alien] ~~that rise~~ though they're from different *DPL 1/7/63*
alien] different *DPL 1/7/58, DPL 1/8/39*
21 accepted slang] a shorthand sign *DPL 2/3/43*
22 But, in return, won't you acknowledge mine? *DPL 2/3/43*
23 They have] This is *DPL 2/3/43*
27 Some of them go quite] The prettier can go *DPL 2/3/43*
29 so not worth considering] means you don't respect them *DPL 2/3/43*
31 Till] And *DPL 2/3/43*

34 start] touched *DPL* 2/3/43
35 there, don't mind] don't regard *DPL* 2/3/43
36 happier] happy *DPL* 2/3/43; ~~happy~~ happier *DPL* 1/7/63
37 strange we never] funny we don't *DPL* 2/3/43
39 One day perhaps I'll] And yet I'd like to *DPL* 2/3/43
40 What makes you be] How is it you're *DPL* 2/3/43; ~~As well how you're~~ Just how you are *DPL* 1/7/63
40–1 [No gap] *DPL* 2/3/43, *DPL* 1/7/63, *DPL* 1/7/58, *DPL* 1/8/39
41 Are there more things in Heaven and earth, Horatio? *DPL* 2/3/43
Horatio.] Horatio? *DPL* 1/7/58, *DPL* 1/8/39

L to JE, 28 Nov. 1959 (*SL*, 311): 'I've just been looking at my *Letter to a Friend* & I don't feel happy about it – the whole idea is too complicated a trap to spring, and the actual stanza form & rhyme scheme is dull and unhelpful. It won't reveal anything [. . .] except my inability to write poetry.' To AT, 19 Mar. 1970 (*SL*, 428–9): 'what it was *meant* to do was to postulate a situation where, in the eyes of the author, his friend got all the straightforward easy girls and he got all the neurotic difficult ones, leaving the reader to see that in fact the girls were all the same and simply responded to the way they were treated. In other words, the difference was in the friends and not in the girls. The last line originally ran "– One of those 'more things', could it be, Horatio?", making it a letter from Hamlet to Horatio: to make it a letter from Horatio to Hamlet may make better or worse sense, according to whether you think Horatio was a nicer chap than Hamlet or not. Certainly (presumably) Hamlet was a more neurotic chap than Horatio [. . .] if I am going to print it I really must do so soon, as the *moeurs* it embodies are getting awfully old-fashioned!' L to AT, 29 Jan. 1978 (*SL*, 576–7): 'I read [the poem] with great interest, not having seen it for some years. My reaction was that in the first place it wasn't at all funny: very sad and true; in the second, that the "joke" was either too obvious or too subtle to be seen; thirdly, that it could do with a bit of polishing up. But fourthly, I'm afraid, that it would hurt too many feelings for me to publish it. If it were a simply marvellous poem, perhaps I might be callous, but it's not sufficiently good to be worth causing pain [. . .] We'll have to leave it until the posthumous volume'.

Title Osborne (2008), 171, notes a precedent in *Letters to a Friend* (1937) by Winifred Holtby (an author with strong Hull connections): her correspondence with another woman is conducted as being between 'Rosalind' and 'Celia' from *As You Like It*. He also notes Byron's *Epistle to a Friend*, which 'similarly involves a male narrator explaining that it is his unhappy love life that prevents him from partaking in his male addressee's cheeriness'. Zachary Leader rightly states that the 'friend' is at least partly based on KA, on the strength of l. 13, which recalls a letter from KA to L dated 24 Sept. 1956 in which he reveals having an affair with a woman whose husband always attends home fixtures of the Swansea and District Rugby Football Club: Amis, *Letters*, 480, 1061 n. KA to L, 9 Nov. 1957 (Amis, *Letters*, 516): 'Letter to a friend about girls sounds an absolutely fucking marvellous idea. I longt pongt long to see an instalment. But don't get me wrong (though I suppose it needn't be "me" in the poem); what I mean is I am no Don J at all, really.' KA to RC, 6 Dec. 1986 (Amis, *Letters*, 1040): 'Friend could be you or me but probably no one chap.' This is why L tells AT in the letter of 29 Jan. 1978 that to publish it would hurt too many feelings. **16** *Described on Sundays only*: in popular tabloid newspapers which deal in scandal. L to JE, 21 Oct. 1957 (*SL*, 280): 'My Sunday morning consists of plodding across Pearson Park, past the children's playground, & then on the other side I buy 4 Sunday papers of steep scurrility & vanish into a drab premises called the Queen's Hotel.' **17** *seek to find*: 'Seek, and ye shall find' (Matt. 7: 7; Luke 11: 9). Cf. *Unfinished Poem*, 10. **35** *saeva indignatio*: savage indignation, intense anger at human folly. As Osborne (2008), 172, notes, it is from Jonathan Swift's epitaph *ubi saeva indignatio ulterius cor lacerare nequit* ('where savage indignation can tear his heart no more'). **41** *Hamlet*, 1. 5. 168–9: 'There are more things in heaven and earth, Horatio, | Than are dreamt of in your philosophy'.

'None of the books have time'

DATE AND TEXT
In *Wkbk 5* (1/5/26) the page on which the entire poem is written is dated '17. 1. 60' (with '7' written through '6') at the top, and the date at the top of the next page, which bears another version of ll. 1–2 is '18. 1 [1960]'. Included, unrevised, in a letter to AT dated 29 Jan. 1978 (*SL*, 577–8). Published in *CP* (1988), 124. *SL* prints a full stop at the end of l. 2; *CP*, a comma. A full stop is correct.

7–8 L to MJ, 23 Apr. 1967 (Bodl. MS Eng. c. 7434/126): 'I think it is funny the way my idea of happiness is to be listening, part-drunk, to jazz.' 8 L to MJ, 3 May 1955 (Bodl. MS Eng. c. 7410/120): 'An' cigarettes for further orders.' Osborne (2008), 57, cites Flann

O'Brien's *At Swim-Two-Birds* (a Larkin favourite): 'There will be whisky and porter for further orders': Penguin edn. [1975], 35.

Goodnight World

DATE AND TEXT
Written to accompany a drawing by Bridget Egerton, 7 Mar. 1960: AT in *SL*, viii. The handwritten poem is reproduced on the back endpaper of *SL*. I regularise 'Good night' to 'Goodnight' in the title.

'Great baying groans burst from my lips'

DATE AND TEXT
The couplet appears in *Wkbk 5* (1/5/31) on a page dated '30 / 3 [1960]' at the top, in the middle of elaborate drafts of *Faith Healing*. Slightly misquoted by L in a letter of 29 Jan. 1978 to AT (*SL*, 577, where it is wrongly ascribed to *Wkbk 8*). I supply a full stop at the end.

'A sit-on-the-fence old gull'

DATE AND TEXT
Written on a p.c. to MJ postmarked 22 Nov. 1960 (Bodl. MS Eng. c. 7422/46). The p.c. bears a photograph of a great black-backed gull. In a letter to MJ dated 27 Nov. 1960 (Bodl. MS Eng. c. 7422/50), L confesses he still has the rhythm in his head and offers two sets of two additional lines: 'A give-great-offence old gull | An arms-for-defence old gull' and 'A down with the blacks old gull, A get off our backs old gull'. Previously unpublished.

The rhythm and metre are from Gilbert and Sullivan's *Patience*.

'BJ's the man in charge'

DATE AND TEXT
Included in a letter to MJ dated 12 Oct. 1961 (Bodl. MS Eng. c. 7423/122). Previously unpublished.

L announces that he has added a line to the first two. After the lines he writes '[Like all the others].'

1 Sir Brynmor Jones was Vice-Chancellor of the University of Hull, 1956–72, when L was Librarian.

'Hotter shorter days arrive, like happiness'

DATE AND TEXT
Wkbk 6 (1/6/12) contains two pages of drafts after '9. 10. 61', dated '13. 10. 61' at the end. The lines are included in the present edition on grounds that they exist in a text with no uncancelled alternative versions and they may constitute a poem (a sonnet). A full stop has been added at the end. Published in *Metre* (Autumn 2001), 6, with a comma at the end of l. 9, 'No one' for 'No-one' (l. 13), and 'its' for 'it' (l. 14).

'And now the leaves suddenly lose strength'

DATE AND TEXT
Wkbk 6 (1/6/12) contains three pages of drafts of the whole poem between '25. x. 61' and '3 xi 61'. Despite the heavy drafting, a version without uncancelled alternative versions is discernible. In l. 12, L has not altered the capital at the beginning of 'Gentleman', but the reading 'Frockcoated gentleman' is clearly meant. Published from *Wkbk 6* in *CP* (1988), 139, with 'windows' for 'window' (l. 3, where L has cancelled the final 's'), 'buses' for ''buses' (l. 6), a full stop instead of the dash after 'morning' (l. 8), and a comma missing after 'squares' (l. 10). Thereafter, AT prints the syntactically awkward 'And no matter where goes down, | The sallow lapsing drift in fields | Or squares behind hoardings, all men hesitate'. However, 'goes down' does not belong to the end of l. 8 but to the latter half of l . 9: 'goes' is not aligned with l. 8, but slightly below it, and 'goes down' supersedes the cancelled wordings 'is seen', 'happens' and 'occurs' in l. 9; 'down' supersedes the cancelled 'by' and 'past'; and 'in' supersedes the cancelled 'through'. The lines should therefore read: 'And no matter where | The sallow lapsing drift goes down, in fields | Or squares, behind hoardings, all men hesitate'.

4 *rubricate*: coloured (or, if a verb, colour) red. 13 *villein*: (in feudal system) peasant, country labourer.

January

DATE AND TEXT
Wkbk 6 (1/6/15) contains a page and a half bearing two drafts, the second of the whole poem, between '7. 1. 62' and '13. 1. 62'. Above the first draft are three underlined phrases: '<u>Why people do things</u>', '<u>Look at that silly old sod</u>', and, below, in the centre of the line before the poem, '<u>January</u>'. 'Look at that silly old sod' occurs in drafts of *The Old Fools*, and 'Why people do things' also does not relate to this poem. However, 'January' plausibly does, and this, the position of the word, and the composition date, suggest that it is a title. Published without a title in *CP* (1988), 142, from the complete draft, which contains no uncancelled alternative readings.

6 *ectoplasm*: viscous substance supposed to emanate from the body of a spiritualistic medium, and to develop into a human form or face.

'Sir George Grouse to Sir Wm Gull'

DATE AND TEXT
Included in a letter to MJ dated 13 Jan. 1962 (Bodl. MS Eng. c. 7424/62). Previously unpublished.

After the lines, L writes: '[Here the *Briddes* do daunce *Grotesquely*.]' He sometimes jokingly signs himself 'William Gull' in letters to MJ. Another verse with the same opening line is dated 31 Jan. 1962: see below.

'Sir George Grouse to Sir Wm Gull' [second version]

DATE AND TEXT
Included in a letter to MJ dated 31 Jan. 1962 (Bodl. MS Eng. c. 7424/79). Previously unpublished.

After the lines L writes: '[here the Briddes doe wagge Th^r Heddes groteskly.]' See the notes on the other poem with the same opening line dated 13 Jan. 1962 (above). L had been to see *A Taste of Honey* at the local cinema: 'was pleased to find many of the University queueing in the rain as I emerged. I walked down the line with the general demeanour of Sir Wm Gull.'

'Chaps who live in California'

DATE AND TEXT
Included in a letter to MJ dated 7 Mar. 1962 (Bodl. MS Eng. c. 7424/100). Previously unpublished.

L in the letter: 'I've got the new Isherwood – quite appalling.' L is referring to the novel *Down There on a Visit* by Christopher Isherwood (1904–86), who had moved from Britain to Hollywood, California, in 1939. The couplet is followed by 'as Bob might say': 'Bob' is Robert Conquest (b. 1917), among whose numerous and varied accomplishments are virtuosic limericks: see *A Garden of Erses. Limericks by Jeff Chaucer*. Introduction by Robert Conquest (2010).

'Praise God from whom all blessings flow'

DATE AND TEXT
Included in a letter to MJ dated 16 Sept. 1962 (Bodl. MS Eng. c. 7425/49). Previously unpublished.

Sitting working on a poem, L introduces the lines: 'Merciful quiet from below: if they had one of their fiddling sessions on, "I couldn't do it."'

The lines are a parody of the opening of the last verse, often sung as the doxology, of the hymn 'Awake, my soul, and with the sun', by Thomas Ken: 'Praise God, from Whom all blessings flow; | Praise Him, all creatures here below.'

'Sitting across the aisle'

DATE AND TEXT
Included in a letter to RC dated 21 Sept. 1962 (SL, 346). It is written continuously, with slant lines marking the lines of verse.

L in the letter: 'Off to Aberystwyth now for a Conference – the Evans country.' The lines parody KA's 'The Evans Country' poems.

1, 4 *Prestatyn | satin*: L uses the rhyme in *Sunny Prestatyn*, which dates from 16–20 Oct. 1962. 5 Cf. Eliot, *The Waste Land*, II A *Game of Chess*, 1: 'The Chair she sat in . . .' Cf. Leigh Hunt 'Jenny kissed me when we met', 2, 'Jumping from the chair she sat in' (with 'rise' later too).

Long Last

DATE AND TEXT
Wkbk 6 contains five pages of drafts of the whole poem between
'13. 1. 63' and '3. 2. 63' (1/6/27): L to MJ, 19 Jan. 1963 (Bodl. MS
Eng. c. 7426/14): 'Am currently doing one arising from the death of
my mother's friend before Christmas'. It also contains one and a half
pages of drafts of the last stanza between '3. 3. 63' and '5. 3. 63'
(1/6/29), and a final draft of the last stanza dated '18. 3. 63'
(1/6/31). Hull DPL 1/2/59 is a t.s. loosely inserted at the back of
Wkbk 2. Hull DPL 1/6/45 is a t.s. loosely inserted at the front of
Wkbk 6 and is the copy-text. Published by AT in Hartley (1988), 48,
and in *CP* (1988), 151.

VARIANTS (from DPL 1/2/59)
14 remember] remembered
21 What] How
do] spend
22 hunt] hunting

'Castle, Park, Dean and Hook'

DATE AND TEXT
?July 1963. The context of the verse is the planning of the second
stage of the Brynmor Jones Library. L wrote to JE about this in a
letter dated 17 July 1963: *SL*, 356. Published in Brennan (2002), 105.

1 The architects for the building, 'a change of architects not entirely
favoured by Philip', according to Campbell (68).   4 A variant of the
phrase 'All my eye and Betty Martin', meaning 'Nonsense!': *OED*,
Betty Martin, from 1781. Sir Leslie Martin (1908–99), Head of the
School of Architecture at the University of Hull before the war, had
been Professor of Architecture at the University of Cambridge since
1956, and was chief consultant for the library plans.

'I would I were where Russell plays'

DATE AND TEXT
Wkbk 2 (1/2/48) contains a version of the lines and two additional
lines on a third of a page after 22 Aug. 1951. Included in a letter
dated 13 Oct. 1964 to MJ (Bodl. MS Eng. c. 7429/10 = *LTM*, 342):
copy-text. L immediately after the lines: 'as I used to say'.

L had got tickets for a concert: 'Condon won't be calling the key, of course, but Russell will certainly be playing.' On Russell and Condon, see the notes on 'And did you once see Russell plain?' In a 1968 review, L remarks: 'how good Pee Wee was in his Condon days': *AWJ*, 219.

1 Cf. the ballad *Helen of Kirkconnel*, 1: 'I would I were where Helen lies'. L's verse has the same rhyme scheme as the ballad and is metrically similar.

Laboratory Monkeys

DATE AND TEXT

Wkbk 7 (1/7/6) contains four pages of drafts of the whole poem except for the title between '12. 2. 65' and '24. 2. 65'. Hull DPL 1/7/76 is a t.s. with an alternative title in pencil and the dates 'begun 12. 2. 65 | finished 24. 2. 65' in pencil in what looks to be L's hand. L does not cancel the title 'Laboratory Monkeys', however. He included a t.s. with a letter to MJ begun on 23 Feb. 1965 (Bodl. MS Eng. c. 7429/134). Published in *CP* (1988), 160, with 'Ape Experiment Room' as the title. The Bodleian t.s. is the copy-text in the present edition. The title 'Laboratory Monkeys' accords more accurately with L's account of what prompted the poem (monkeys rather than apes); and it accords better too with what is described in ll. 13–16. L's slight misalignment of the first line, which characterises both DPL 1/7/76 and the text sent to MJ, has been regularised.

VARIANTS (from DPL 1/7/76)
Title Laboratory Monkeys Ape Experiment Room

L to MJ, 24 Feb. 1965: 'I thought you might like to see this – I don't know who else will, as it isn't really publishable [. . .] it was inspired by the photo on *The Listener* cover a week or so ago of a rhesus monkey & her baby monkey [. . .] It carried that complete & utter condemnation of the human race monkeys seem to be able to convey. It was accompanied by accounts of fatuous American experiments of taking baby monkeys away from their mothers & noting that they are unhappy.' The experiments were conducted from the mid-1950s through the mid-1960s by Dr Harry Harlow, Professor of Psychology and Director of the Primate Research Laboratory at the University of Wisconsin: see G. L. Kriewald's article in *AL*, 28 (Oct. 2009), 30–1, for further details.

'O wha will o'er the downs with me'

DATE AND TEXT
Included in a letter to MJ dated 23 Apr. 1965 (Bodl. MS Eng. c. 7430/29 = *LTM*, 347).

L in the letter: 'Are there no ballads now?'

4 *The University of Strathclyde*: Scottish university given a royal charter in 1964 as the UK's first technological university.

'Welcome 1966!'

DATE AND TEXT
Included in a letter to MJ dated 2 Jan. 1966 (Bodl. MS Eng. c. 7432/21). Previously unpublished.

L inadvertently wrote 'fewer pricks' in l. 2, and signed it 'Kathleen Raine'. He then cancelled the signature and remarked: '(sorry, this is mixed up – *more* pricks & sign it E J Howard, say)'. L refers to poet and scholar Kathleen Raine (1908–2003) and to novelist Elizabeth Jane Howard (b. 1923), who was KA's wife, 1965–83.

'Lowell, Lowell, Lowell, Lowell'

DATE AND TEXT
Included in a letter to RC dated 5 Mar. 1966 (*SL*, 382): copy-text. A slightly different version is included in a letter to MJ dated 31 July 1964 (Bodl. MS Eng. c. 7428/94).

VARIANTS
2 he] that *Bodl. MS*

1 *Lowell*: American poet Robert Lowell (1917–77), who was a candidate for the Oxford Professorship of Poetry. L in the letter to RC: 'I didn't of course, vote, but if I had I'd have voted for Blunden – who was a faint amount of good once, not like old R. L. who's never looked like being a single iota of good in all his born days.' AT notes (*SL*, 382) that Edmund Blunden (1896–1974) was elected on 5 Feb. 1966, by 477 votes to 241.

'Scratch on the scratch pad'

DATE AND TEXT
Wkbk 7 (1/7/13) contains a page of two drafts after '20. 5. 66', the second of which contains no uncancelled alternative readings and bears the date '19. 7. 66' at the end. The second draft is the source of the text published in *CP* (1988), 164, where the editor, AT, queried whether it might be unfinished. The verse is included in the present edition as possibly being finished.

'Then the students cursing and grumbling'

DATE AND TEXT
Included in a letter to MJ dated 19 Nov. 1966 (Bodl. MS Eng. c. 7434/68). Previously unpublished.

L prefaces the lines with the remark 'This is a gruelling time'. He parodies ll. 11–16 of Eliot's *Journey of the Magi*, a poem he included in *OBTCEV*.

'Fill up the glasses, since we're here for life'

DATE AND TEXT
Included in a letter to JE dated 7 Dec. 1966 (Bodl. MS Eng. c. 7454/130), in which L tells her of his attending two drunken dinners in Hull. Below the verse, he writes '© The Philip Larkin Co.' Previously unpublished.

2, 4 *Dr Gamme*. Probably a nickname: no person of this name is traceable in the archives of Hull University.

'Here's a health to the Squire'

DATE AND TEXT
Written in ink in a Christmas card to MJ (Bodl. MS Eng. c. 7454/133). The envelope is postmarked 19 Dec. 1966. Previously unpublished.

L prefaces the lines: 'Best wishes for a rural Christmas'.
  1 A traditional toast, commonly found in hunting songs.

The Dance

Wkbk 6 (1/6/32) contains thirty-eight pages of drafts of the
unfinished poem after '30 / 6 / 63', with the final page dated
'12. 5. 64' at the top. The last four and a half pages bear drafts
of additional lines not found in the t.s. version, Hull DPL 2/3/44,
and they come to a stop with a draft of eight lines with only one
revision, but without a full stop at the end. *Wkbk* 7 (1/7/16)
contains half a page of drafts of three and a half lines (cancelled)
and a further six lines between '13. 1. 67' and '30 1 67'; these
represent a continuation of the drafting of the additional lines, but
they end inconclusively after six lines. On the next page is a line and
a half ('Knowing you will be there, I dress | In cold May evening
light') between '30 1 67' and '1. 2. 67'. In *CP* (1988), 154–8, the t.s.
version was printed, and it was noted that the poem was unfinished.
The eight lines from the penultimate draft were printed in Tolley
(1997), 111; by Chris Lamb in *AL*, 21 (Summer 2006), 12; and by
James Booth in *AL*, 23 (Apr. 2007), 24. None of these accounts
mentions the later draft of six of the eight lines in *Wkbk* 7. The
present edition prints the t.s. version supplemented by the latest
draft of the additional lines from *Wkbk* 7, which are identical to the
penultimate draft in all but the last three lines, and records the last
three lines from the penultimate draft among the variants below.
This provides the completest record of the poem, which remains
unfinished no matter which version is printed.

Harry Chambers, visiting L in Sept. 1963, recalls him 'confessing
to having got into difficulties with a poem about dancing': Thwaite
(1982), 62. In the summer of 1973 L gave MB a copy of the poem
inscribed 'unfinished poem called "The Dance" given to Maeve by
Philip long afterwards with undimmed memories': Motion (1993),
423; Brennan (2002), 59, where it is noted that the copy does
not include any additional lines. In the Hull archives there is an
audiotape of L reading the poem to strict tempo dance-band music.
He includes the additional lines: Brennan (2002), 59; *AL*, 14 (Oct.
2002), 25.

Title [No title] *Hull DPL 2/3/44*
49 look] ~~cling~~ look *Hull DPL 2/3/44*
50 door] ~~open~~ door *Hull DPL 2/3/44*
Additional lines Of too-explicit music, till | I see for the first time as
something whole | What earlier seemed safely divisible

L to MJ, 30 May 1951 (Bodl. MS Eng. c. 7405/75): 'Dances are my bane. I *hate* them, because I *can't* dance.' To MJ, 18 June 1951 (date as postmark), Bodl. MS Eng. c. 7405/93: 'As for *going to dances*, they are purgatory to me. "I don't dance, I don't dance," I mumble, till the sentence seems to assume grotesque humiliating symbolism.' To MJ, 12 May 1958 (Bodl. MS Eng. c. 7418/38): 'I hate dances really, all the standing & talk that I can't catch & non-food [. . .] Was it a dinner-suit do? I don't like mine.' Brennan (2002), 33: L 'only once patronised a mid-term hop, an experience he found emotionally threatening and commemorated in the unfinished, bitter-sweet poem "The Dance"'. L kept the admission ticket, dated 10 May 1963: loc. cit. MB recalls that it was a University Senior Common Room function, and that L described the poem as 'a great obstacle in my creative life': *AL*, 14 (Oct. 2002), 18.

1 *Drink, sex and jazz*: Lieutenant Archer in ch. 3 of KA's novel *My Enemy's Enemy* (1955) anticipates post-war London being full of 'girls and drinks and jazz'. Janice Rossen views the phrase as a 'modernised version of the traditional elements of revelry, "Wine, women, and song"': 1989, in Regan (1997), 154. 46–7 MB notes that L was not a very good dancer: Salwak (1989), 33. 'Philip repeatedly said I was the only person he could, or dare, dance with': Brennan (2002), 30. 'I taught him to dance – passably well – in the privacy of his flat': Brennan (2002), 43. 123 *Which*: See the note on *Vers de Société*, 11.

'High o'er the fence leaps Soldier Jim'

DATE AND TEXT
Included in a letter to MJ dated 23 July 1967 (Bodl. MS Eng. c. 7435/76). Previously unpublished.

L in the letter is discussing a visit to Shropshire. Immediately before the couplet he remarks: 'There'll hardly be enough time to get that Housman feeling.' L ascribes the lines to '*Gems from the Poets*'. Housman (1859–1936), who was homosexual in orientation, had his first volume of poems, *A Shropshire Lad*, published in 1896. His poems frequently have military subjects.

'In Xanadu did Kubla Khan'

DATE AND TEXT
?1967. Brenda Moon became L's deputy at the Brynmor Jones
Library in 1967, and she notes that in that year stage 2 of the
building was rising to the west of the first building: *AL*, 8 (Oct.
1999), 8. Published in Brennan (2002), 105. Donald Campbell,
who republished the verse in *AL*, 20 (Autumn 2005), 69, recalls
that meetings to discuss stage 2 of the library were lengthy, and that
Brenda Moon would wheel in a huge trolley crammed with the files,
many of which were filled with papers from the University Grants
Committee (UGC), whose nitpicking frustrated L.

1–2 The opening lines of Coleridge's *Kubla Khan*.

'At the sign of The Old Farting Arse'

DATE AND TEXT
The first five lines are included in a letter to MJ dated 27 Oct. 1968
(Bodl. MS Eng. c. 7438/30). The second five, in a letter to MJ dated
7 Nov. 1968 (Bodl. MS Eng. c. 7438/40). In the latter he announces:
'I've continued *At the Sign* [. . .] This is the second half of the first
verse.' In a letter to MJ dated 10 Nov. 1968 (Bodl. MS Eng. c.
7438/44), he says: 'In my little song, substitute "we say" for the
second "we think".' In the present edition ll. 8–9 have been indented
to match ll. 3–4, and 'the' in l. 10 has been converted to match 'The'
in l. 1. Previously unpublished.

L prefacing the verse in the letter: 'Good leader in the *Express* today.
Enoch for premier, Nabarro for Home Secretary. I shan't pander to
'em, shall wait till the morning paper to see how far International
Communism has succeeded in causing disorder here. I hope T. Ali
gets clobbered. Rotten shower.' L refers to British Conservative
politician Enoch Powell (1912–98), who was sacked from the
government in 1968 for his 'Rivers of Blood' speech warning of the
alleged dangers of mass immigration; and to Gerald Nabarro (1913–
73), a flamboyant Conservative who supported Powell's position.
On Tariq Ali, see below. Under the verse L writes: '(*Tune*: Old Apple
Tree)'.
    Title Cf. Austin Dobson, *At the Sign of the Lyre* (1885). **1** In
the letter, L illustrates the verse with a pub sign displaying a farting
arse. **4** *Hair*: 1967 American musical, hippie and anti-Vietnam-

war, featuring drugs and nudity. **5** *Ali's*: Tariq Ali's. See the note on 'I dreamed I saw a commie rally', 2. Bodl. MS Eng. c. 7438/33 is a press cutting of a photograph of Tariq Ali at a political rally. L has added captions: 'I'm a bloody fool who wants his arse kicking' and 'I'm an Indian bastard trying to spread communism'. *Khyber Pass*: Cockney rhyming slang for 'arse'. The Khyber Pass links Pakistan and Afghanistan. **6** *Mao*: Mao Zedong (1893–1976), Leader of the People's Republic of China, 1949–76. **7** *Jackie's*: Jacqueline Kennedy (1929–94), wife of John F. Kennedy (1953–63), First Lady (1961–3), and wife of tycoon Aristotle Onassis (1968–75). **8** *Younger's*: Scottish brewer William Younger's beer. (Younger's and McEwan's merged in 1931, but 'Younger's' remained a brand name.) **9** L in the letter: 'I like the sudden eager passionate assertion about Younger's.'

'After drinking Glenfiddich'

DATE AND TEXT
Included in a letter to MJ dated 24 Nov. 1968 (Bodl. MS Eng. c. 7438/58). Previously unpublished.

L prefaces the verse: 'I bought some Glenfiddich yesterday, to anticipate budget prices, and after drinking some found myself murmuring [verse]'.
    1 *Glenfiddich*: single malt Scotch whisky. **2** A drunken version of the saying 'Good riddance to bad rubbish'.

'Morning, noon & bloody night'

DATE AND TEXT
Included in a letter to MJ dated 27 Nov. 1968 (Bodl. MS Eng. c. 7438/62 = *LTM*, 394). The last line is typed without separation of the words, and this is reproduced. (It was not done so in *LTM*.) A full stop has been added at the end.

L in the letter: 'Nice to be a *pawet*, ya knaw, an express ya *feelins*. Eh? The last line should be *screamed* in a paroxysm of rage.' **5** *kick the bucket*: slang for 'die'.

'The world's great age begins anew'

DATE AND TEXT

Included in a letter to MJ dated 8 Dec. 1968 (Bodl. MS Eng. c. 7438/70). Previously unpublished.

L in the letter: 'Last night I finished my December piece & records of the year, thank God. Isn't it odd, I was able to end (it will be the end of the book) with mention of the 2nd ed. of a book the 1st ed of wch I devoted my opening pagagraph to in 1961!'

1 The opening line of a poem by Shelley. 2 Yeats, *Sailing to Byzantium*, 19; 'perne in a gyre', meaning spool in a spiral or circle, as in a spinning wheel. The image relates to Yeats's cyclical view of history. 4 *pull your wire*: (slang) masturbate.

'See the Pope of Ulster stand'

DATE AND TEXT

3 Feb. 1969, when it was included in a t.s. letter to the Revd A. H. R. Quinn of the University of Keele: Hull DPL (2) 1/5/3. Previously unpublished.

L was awarded an honorary D.Litt. by Queen's University, Belfast, in the summer of 1969. He acknowledges to the Revd Quinn that it was 'extremely kind and flattering of Queen's to honour me in this way', but expresses the hope that 'it won't involve writing an ode to the Reverend Ian Paisley'. He introduces the verse in the letter by remarking 'As a matter of fact, I have a little quatrain in mind which might do', and after it he comments 'Nice, don't you think? I had better make sure of getting my Doctorate first, though.'

1 *Pope of Ulster*: the Reverend Ian Paisley (b. 1936), veteran Northern Ireland Protestant, Orangeman and politician. L to Peter du Sautoy, 7 Jan. 1969 (*SL*, 410): 'Tell Charles I will stand him a gin and Paisley when I next see him (gin and bitter orange).' 2 *shillelagh*: club, usually of oak or blackthorn; originally made in Shillelagh, Co. Wicklow, Ireland. 3 *the Border*: Between Northern Ireland and the Republic of Ireland. From 1956 to 1962 the Irish Republican Army conducted the 'Border Campaign' of guerrilla warfare designed to overthrow Northern Ireland and establish a united Ireland. 4 A parody of 'Father, Son, and Holy Spirit'. *Orange Order*: Fraternal Protestant organisation, chiefly based in Northern Ireland and Scotland, named after the Dutch-

born William of Orange (King William III of England, William II of Scotland), whose forces defeated the Catholic army of James VII & II at the Battle of the Boyne on 12 July (New Style) 1690.

'I dreamed I saw a commie rally'

DATE AND TEXT

6 Apr. 1969. Included in letters to RC (*SL*, 413–14) and John Norton-Smith dated 7 and 8 Apr. 1969. L in the latter: 'This reminds me of a quatrain I compos'd upon *Easter Day*'. Previously unpublished in full.

2 *Tariq Ali*: b. 1943, British-Pakistani political commentator and activist. Active in the New Left in the 1960s, in 1968 he joined the Trotskyist International Marxist Group. In a letter to MJ dated 21 Mar. 1968 (Bodl. MS Eng. c. 7436/118), L describes him as '"Chairman of the Ad Hoc Committee" for stirring up civil strife'. 3 *Vanessa Redgrave*: b. 1937, British actress, socialist and political activist. CBE, 1967. L to MJ, 1 May 1969 (Bodl. MS Eng. c. 7439/43): '*Vanessa Redgrave* (didn't see her – I'd like to have seen if she was wearing her CBE), heap bad medicine. Traitorous cow.' To KA, 25 June 1975 (Huntington MS AMS 353-393): 'Many thanks for writing so kindly about the CBE. It's a great thrill, I can tell you, to be on a level with John Dankworth and Vanessa Redgrave.' John Dankworth (1927–2010), English jazz composer and soloist, was created CBE in 1974. In 1959 he had chaired the Stars Campaign for Inter-Racial Friendship.

Holiday

DATE AND TEXT

Wkbk 6 (1/6/22) contains four pages of drafts of the whole poem except for the title between '14. 9. 62' and '21. ix. 62'. Hull DPL 1/6/44 is a t.s. with MS alterations loosely inserted at the front of *Wkbk 6*. Included in a letter to MJ dated 3 Dec. 1969 (Bodl. MS Eng. c. 7440/64 = *LTM*, [404]), where it is reproduced in facsimile: copy-text. L in the letter (Bodl. MS Eng. c. 7440/62): 'I found the poem about our Alnmouth holiday, & enclose a copy – it isn't a good poem, far from it, hence it's never been published. I expect you remember where it all was – different places, of course.' The text sent to MJ is identical to DPL 1/6/44, a t.s. with the title and revisions to l. 7 in ink. The poem is placed according to the date on which this revised version was sent. Published in *Metre* (Autumn 2001), 7, from the final *Wkbk* draft (sixteen lines long, with different wording in places, and with no title).

VARIANTS
Title [Added to Hull and Bodl. t.s. in ink]
7 ~~Inland a~~A
inland] [Added to Hull and Bodl. t.s. in ink]

Some details in the poem are reworked in *To the Sea*: cf. l. 6 ('The sea collapses, freshly') and *To the Sea*, 7 ('The small hushed waves' repeated fresh collapse'); the ship immobile on the horizon (ll. 13–15) and *To the Sea*, 9 ('A white steamer stuck in the afternoon'); l. 13 ('in the horizon'), and *To the Sea*, 5 ('under the low horizon').
   14–16 Cf. Auden, 'Seen when the night is silent', 6–8: 'The tiny steamer in the bay . . . You have gone away.'

'The polyp comes & goes'

DATE AND TEXT
Included in a letter to MJ dated by L '?6 Apr. 1970' (Bodl. MS Eng. c. 7441/17). Previously unpublished.

L to MB, 10 July 1969, referring to a polyp in his right nostril: 'My dreary old nose is giving me gyp': *AL*, 3 (Apr. 1997), 13.
   After the lines in the letter to MJ, L writes '(Wordsworth)'. He parodies Wordsworth's *Ode: Intimations of Immortality from Recollections of Early Childhood*, 10–11: 'The Rainbow comes and goes, | And lovely is the Rose'.

How to Win the Next Election

DATE AND TEXT
The first verse is included in a letter to MJ dated 5 Apr. 1966 (Bodl. MS Eng. c. 7432/116), untitled; repeated, with title, in a letter to RC dated 19 June 1970 (*SL*, 432); and without the title and with other, minor differences, in a letter to Colin Gunner dated 19 Nov. 1973 (*SL*, 493). The present edition prints the 1970 text of the first verse and the second verse as included in a letter to MJ dated 21 Dec. 1966 (Bodl. MS Eng. c. 7434/9), where L announces that he

has 'thought up a second verse for our "Election Song". *Wkbk 7* (1/7/38) contains a version of the first verse and three additional lines ('Back law and order, | Cut students' grants, | Defend the Border') between '8 / 5/ 70' and '1. 6. 70'.

L in the letter of 5 Apr. 1966: '(Tune: *Rockabye Baby.*)' After the second verse he suggests: '(chorus) Commies, Commies, etc.'.

Title On 18 June 1970 the Conservatives under Edward Heath defeated Harold Wilson's Labour Party in the General Election. L in 1970 introducing the lines: 'Remember my song, How to Win the Next Election?' **2** *cat*: cat o' nine tails (whip used for punishment by flogging).

'The flag you fly for us is furled'

DATE AND TEXT
Included in a letter to MJ dated 27 Aug. 1970 (Bodl. MS Eng. c. 7441/104a). In an earlier letter dated 22 Aug. 1970 (Bodl. MS Eng. c. 7441/101), L included a version of ll. 3–4: 'two lines from my projected poem *To the Six Counties, or, Balls to Mary Holland*'. (Journalist Mary Holland, 1935–2004, interviewed him in *Queen* magazine, 25 May 1966. She specialised in writing about Northern Ireland.) Published in Motion (1993), 410, with 'done' for 'dumb' (l. 2).

VARIANTS
3 have not] never *Letter of 22 Aug. 1970*

L immediately after the lines in the letter of 27 Aug.: 'Ogh ogh. Some time. Maybe next year.'

The Manciple's Tale

DATE AND TEXT
Included in a letter to MJ dated 17 Sept. 1970 (Bodl. MS Eng. c. 7441/121). The title and ll. 1–4 are in ink, the rest in pencil. AT prints ll. 1–4 in *LTM*, 412. Otherwise unpublished.

L had just discovered that his accommodation as a Visiting Fellow of All Souls College, Oxford (Beechwood House, Iffley) did not have a garage for his car, and that heat was supplied only by an electric wall fire in the main room and ran off the only large plug. Such matters were dealt with by the manciple of the college, and L had been advised to see him.

VARIANTS (from the MS)
8 Lat hit be so] ~~So lat hem be~~ Lat hit be so
9 *withouten*] *without* ~~anen~~

Title As in Chaucer's *The Canterbury Tales*, which the poem imitates.

'Sod the lower classes'

DATE AND TEXT
Included in a letter to MJ dated 9 Dec. 1970 (Bodl. MS Eng. c. 7442/55). Previously unpublished.

L in the letter: 'I repeat to myself "*We're fighting the Unions*" and a warm glow spreads through me – well, metaphorically, any way.' The verse follows, and, below it, '(Tune: *Keep the home*, etc)', referring to the wartime song 'Keep the home fires burning'.

Poem about Oxford

DATE AND TEXT
L wrote the poem for MJ on the flyleaf of a 1970 reprint of John Betjeman's *An Oxford University Chest* (1938), which he gave to her at Christmas 1970, as Motion (1993), 405, records. The copy is now in the Hull History Centre, Hull. A photocopy of a draft is inserted in *Michaelmas Term at St Bride's* (Hull DPL (2) 1/13b/24–5): *TAWG*, 205 n. Published in *CP* (1988), 179.

1 L went up to St John's College, Oxford, in Oct. 1940 and graduated in July 1943. MJ was at St Hugh's College at the same time. Both read English and took first-class degrees, but had no contact until Sept. 1946. 2 *blacked-out*: With all lights extinguished or obscured, as a precaution against air raids. *butterless*: 'Life in college was austere [. . .] Because of Ministry of Food regulations, the town could offer little in the way of luxurious eating and drinking': L in the introduction to *Jill* (*RW*, 17). James Booth, *AL*, 10 (Oct. 2000), 13, notes a parallel in L's *Story I* (Hull DPL (2) 1/1/12),

which dates from Jan.–July 1941: 'Owing to the war, there was no bread and butter, of course.' **3** 'I didn't approve of Oxford and I don't want to go back there. It crushes the spirit in a more subtle way than I had imagined possible. I hardly wrote a line during my stay there, except in vacations, although I acquired a certain first-hand knowledge of people and what it is like to be implicated with them': L, quoted in Motion (1993), 105. **6** *la politesse*: politeness (with deprecatory connotation). **8** Hull and Leicester, where L and MJ lived and worked. **11** *Girton*: women's college in Cambridge University. **12** *King's*: King's College, Cambridge. **14** *Bodley*: the Bodleian Library, Oxford. *dark blue*: Oxford University's official sporting colour. **15** *the Boat Race*: the annual rowing race on the Thames between Oxford and Cambridge Universities. **17** *cake-queues*: 'It became a routine after ordering one's books in Bodley after breakfast to go and look for a cake or cigarette queue': L's introduction to *Jill* (*RW*, 17). **22** *Black Papers*: pamphlets on education which were opposed to what they viewed as the excesses of progressive education. **23** *Fleae*: John Donne's poem *The Flea*, in which a flea sucks the blood of a man and a woman and the man uses this fact in an attempt to persuade her to have sex with him. L's spelling is not found in any text of the poem. An attempted archaism?

Light, Clouds, Dwelling-places

DATE AND TEXT

The copy-text is DPL 1/7/77, a t.s. with holograph corrections in pencil, inserted at the back of *Wkbk 7*. Conrad James, who published it in *AL*, 21 (2006), 4, rightly claimed that the fact that L brought the text to this stage indicates that he was considering it as a valid poem. *Wkbk 6* contains: sixteen and a half pages of drafts after '17. 1. 62', with '24. 3. 62' at the top of the last page, and a possible title 'Under a cloud' on a page dated '14. 4. 62' at the top (1/6/16, wrongly identified in the Hull catalogue); a page and a half of drafts after '13. 5. 62', with the second page dated '23. 5. 62' at the top (1/6/19, again wrongly identified in the Hull catalogue). *Wkbk 7* (1/7/24, 25) contains: two and a half pages of drafts between '17. 10. 67' and '20. 1. 68' (1/7/24, 25); five pages of drafts after '9. 8. 70', with the last page dated '1. 2. 71' at the top. Though, as is shown below, there are details that L included in *The Building*, L rethought that poem entirely (see the note on its text). The text in *AL*, 21, is correct in all but two details: the title is given as 'Clouds, Dwelling-places, Light', and the last two lines are printed as part of the main body of the text. The title was originally 'Clouds, Dwelling-places, Lives', and L wrote 'Light' above 'Clouds', and cancelled 'Lives'. The position of 'Light' suggests that it is either an addition to the title, or an alternative not to 'Lives' but to 'Clouds'. There can be no certainty about this, however. The former seems more likely, on grounds that all three elements – light, clouds and dwelling-places – are present in the poem. Accordingly, *Light, Clouds, Dwelling-places*. As for the last two lines: both in the *Wkbk* drafts and in the t.s., a gap separates them from the main body of the text. In the *Wkbk* drafts, additional lines follow these two, but in the t.s. version they conclude the text.

VARIANTS (from DPL 1/7/77)
24 separately] ~~differently~~ separately
25 stale] ~~the~~ in stale
26 Hollow] ~~Interiors Abodes Hutches~~ Hollows ~~humid~~
27 prayer] ~~hymn~~ prayer
distempered] ~~infested~~ distempered
28 [Comma cancelled after 'cinemas'.]

1 *grape-dark sky*: Cf. *Mother, Summer, I*, 4: 'grape-dark clouds'; *Livings II*, 11–12: 'sky builds | Grape-dark'. **2–4** *illuminated . . . high . . . comb*: Cf . *The Building*, 1–2: 'Higher . . . lucent comb'. **3** *Humped*: Cf. *Livings II*, 19: 'humped inns'. **15** *terraced houses*: As in *The Large Cool Store*, 6. Cf. *The Building*, 41: 'terraced streets'. **16** *Goal-chalked*: Cf. *The Building*, 42: 'Where kids chalk games'. **19–20** Cf. *The Building*, 3–4: 'All round it close-ribbed streets rise and fall | Like a great sigh out of the last century.' **29** Cf. *Spring Warning*, 18: 'On his serious errand riding to the gorge'.

'I have started to say'

DATE AND TEXT
Wkbk 7 (1/7/46) contains a page and a half bearing two drafts, the second of the whole poem, after '7. 10 [1971]', with '8. 10 [1971]' at the top of the second page. The next date in the *Wkbk* is '11 / 10' at the top of the next page. Hull DPL 1/7/80 is a t.s. with holograph corrections in pencil, inserted loosely at the back of *Wkbk* 7. This is the copy-text: it contains no uncancelled alternative versions. Published in *CP* (1988), 185.

VARIANTS (from DPL 1/7/80)
9 ~~What's~~ All that's left to happen ~~now~~
11–12 ~~The order they'll come in~~ | ~~Is all I have to learn.~~ *1st version*
Their order, and their manner, | ~~Is life's interest now.~~ Remains to be
learnt. *2nd version*

'When the lead says goonight to the copper'

DATE AND TEXT
26 Oct. 1971, in a letter to Colin Gunner: Hull DP 179/3 (*SL*, 450).
In the letter the lines are written continuously but with a capital
marking the beginning of each line and a comma at the end of the
first three.

2 *Sheppard*: school contemporary of L. 3 In a letter to Gunner of 7
Feb. 1978 (Hull DP 179/18), L recalls Hardy, the Chemistry master,
shouting 'Shepherd! Bring me a spatula-full of graphite!'

'Sherry does more than Bovril can'

DATE AND TEXT
Written at the top of a letter to MJ dated 31 Oct. 1971 (Bodl. MS
Eng. c. 7443/111). Previously unpublished.

In the letter L confesses to having a hangover and thinks 'Perhaps
some Bovril or something w^d be a good thing.' Later (fo. 113), he
remarks: 'Groogh. The Bovril doesn't seem to have done much to
settle my stomach [. . .] Will sherry go with Bovril? It's going to try.'
    1–2 Cf. Housman, *A Shropshire Lad* LXII 21–2: 'And malt does
more than Milton can | To justify God's ways to man.' 1 *Bovril*:
thick salty meat extract diluted with hot water to drink.

'This was Mr Bleaney's bungalow'

DATE AND TEXT
Included in a letter to AT dated 30 Dec. 1973 (*SL*, 496).

L introducing the poem in the letter: 'The only house-prospect I have
is a kennel on a bypass past wch tankers thunder, *making ornaments
move*. Oh God. Stand by for a resurrection of Bleaney.'

1 Cf. *Mr Bleaney*, 1. 4 *old Toad*: Cf. *Toads Revisited*, 35.

'It's plain that Marleen and Patricia would'

DATE AND TEXT
Included in a letter to AT dated 26 Apr. 1974 (*SL*, 504).

2 *Christopher Isherwood*: 1904–86; novelist; gay. 3 *The Buffs*:
the Royal East Kent Regiment (till 1961). 4 *The Green Howards*:
Yorkshire regiment (till 2006). *Green Cuffs*: a familiar term for an
imaginary regiment. 5 *Her Majesty's Household Militia*: the British
Household Cavalry.

'Have a little more'

DATE AND TEXT
Written in a Christmas card to JE in 1974 (Bodl. MS Eng. c.
7457/105). Previously unpublished.

'When first we faced, and touching showed'

DATE AND TEXT
Wkbk 8 (1/8/23) contains a page and a half of drafts of the first
two stanzas and two lines from a third after '18. 12. 75', with the
last draft on a page dated '20. 12. 75' at the top. Hull DPL 1/8/48
is a t.s. inserted loosely at the back of *Wkbk 8*, bearing the date '20
/ 12/ 75' in what looks to be L's hand. L wrote the poem in a Kate
Greenaway Valentine's Day card, and sent it to Betty Mackereth on
30 Dec. 1975. Published in *CP* (1988), 205.

1 *faced*: Identifying the woman as L's secretary, Betty Mackereth,
James Booth observes, first, that L had seen her face every working
day for more than eighteen years before they finally 'faced', and,
second, that she was considerably taller than either MB or MJ,
and so could 'face' L in a way which they could not: Booth (2005),
105. L began an affair with her in the spring and summer of 1975:
Motion (1993), 450. 13–18 MB, Brennan (2002), 66, comments
that the final stanza 'sharply resembled Philip's actual words to
me on that February evening in 1961 when we embraced for the
first time'. However, James Booth, Booth (2005), 105, judges

that 'Though it clearly calls on memories of earlier encounters, the specific context of the poem is Larkin's new and different relationship with his secretary, Betty Mackereth.' See also *Dear Jake* (next) and 'We met at the end of the party'.

Dear Jake

DATE AND TEXT
T.s., with a handwritten comma after 'get' (l. 13), included with a letter to Betty Mackereth postmarked 23 Jan. 1976. It was revealed by her in Oct. 2010, and broadcast on BBC1 television on 12 Dec. 2010. See the notes above on 'When first we faced, and touching showed'.

Title Addressed to his imagined biographer Jake Balokowsky: see *Posterity* and notes. **2, 12** *singular*: In a note copied to me in an e-mail message, James Booth records that the related word 'singularity' occurs only once in L's poetry, in *Marriages*, 19. **3** *four lives*: those of the three women with whom L had relationships (Betty Mackereth, Maeve Brennan, Monica Jones), and L's own. **5** *one already mentioned*: Betty Mackereth. **11** *UP*: University Press.

'Be my Valentine this Monday'

DATE AND TEXT
Booth (2005), 203: 'Written in black ballpoint in a Valentine's Day card showing a grinning alligator and the legend "See you later alligator!", continuing inside "You mouth-watering morsel! Happy Valentine", after which Larkin has written "& love!" Philip left the card on Betty's desk on Saturday 14 February 1976 (addressed "Personal / Secretary to the Librarian / Brynmor Jones Library"), before departing for Oxford. She found it on her arrival at work on Monday 16 February.' Betty is Betty Mackereth: see the notes on 'When first we faced, and touching showed'. The first stanza was printed in the *Evening Standard* on 22 Oct. 2002, and the entire poem was published in Booth (2005), 203. Booth also records (202) that pencil drafts of the poem appear between the dates 7 and 21 Feb. 1976 in a manuscript notebook of L's that went to Maggs Bros. Ltd.

'Morning at last: there in the snow'

DATE AND TEXT
Wkbk 8 (1/8/25) contains a draft of the first stanza on a page dated
'1. 2. 76' at the top. According to MB, 'written a few weeks later'
than a visit she paid to L in Jan. 1976: Brennan (2002), 67. The
copy-text is Hull DPL 1/8/49, a t.s. with holograph corrections in
l. 7, bearing the date '1 / 2/ 76' in what looks to be L's hand, inserted
loosely at the back of *Wkbk 8*. Booth (2005), 202, records, however,
that pencil drafts appear between the dates 7 and 21 Feb. 1976 in a
manuscript notebook of L's that went to Maggs Bros. Ltd. Published
in *CP* (1988), 206.

VARIANTS (from DPL 1/8/49)
7 But when they] ~~Though~~ But when they ~~will~~

MB recounts how L told her he had looked out of an upstairs
window in 105 Newland Park and seen MB's footprints in the snow
following her visit the previous evening: Brennan (2002), 67; *AL*, 16
(Oct. 2003), 20. However, Booth (2005), 106, notes that L's drafts
of the poem are closer to those associated with Betty Mackereth, to
whom L gave a typed copy. On Betty Mackereth, see the notes above
on 'When first we faced and touching showed'.
  1–2 Cf. Blake, 'My Spectre round me night & day', 9–10: 'thy
footsteps in the snow | Wheresoever they come and go' (with 'rain'
in l. 11 of Blake's poem and in l. 7 of L's, and shared mentions of
morning and night). 2 *small blunt footprints*: L had remarked to
MB that her boots made her feet seem 'short and stubby': loc. cit.

'We met at the end of the party'

DATE AND TEXT
L sent it, written in black ink, with a letter to Betty Mackereth
on 22 Feb. 1976 from All Souls College, Oxford, where he was
spending a weekend. Booth (2005), 202, records that pencil drafts
appear between the dates 7 and 21 February 1976 in a manuscript
notebook of L's that went to Maggs Bros. Ltd. The first stanza was
printed in the *Evening Standard* on 22 Oct. 2002. Published in full
in *AL*, 14 (Oct. 2002), 4. See the notes above on 'When first we
faced, and touching showed'.

'Once more upon the village green'

DATE AND TEXT
Bodl. MS Eng. c. 7447/5 is a damaged p.c. bearing a postmark not completely on the card, which is also stamped 'HUMBER BRIDGE For Completion 1977'. 28 M[ar./ay] 197[?6]. The card is one of the rabbit cards by Racey Helps that L often sent to MJ. The verse is written in L's hand. In l. 5, though 'run' would make good sense in a cricket context, the word is definitely 'bun'. Previously unpublished.

'I want to see them starving'

DATE AND TEXT
Included in a letter to RC dated 26 May 1976 (*SL*, 541–2).

L introducing the lines in the letter: 'The latest campaign is for "the right to work", i.e. the right to get £70 a week for doing bugger all. It's led me to begin a hymn.' L quotes the first four lines of what he calls his 'dreary little hymn' in a letter to KA dated 10 Feb. 1979 (*SL*, 595), and again in a letter to Colin Gunner dated 30 July 1980 (Hull DP 179/19).

'Davie, Davie'

DATE AND TEXT
15 Jan. 1974, when L included it in a letter to AT (*SL*, 499–500); then, revised, in a letter of 1 Dec. 1976 to KA (Huntington MS AMS 323-393). The latter is the copy-text. It was printed in Motion (1993), 433, with the wrong format, 'in' missing from l. 6, and 'Chair' for 'chair' in l. 7; and in Amis, *Letters*, 822. KA tells RC he is going to suggest an alternative ending: 'But it's got you a chair, which, let's be fair, | Was the most that you had in view.'

VARIANTS (from the 1974 letter)
5 style] sense
7 [Written as 2 lines]
8 And a billet in Frogland too.

The poem is based upon the music-hall song *Daisy Bell*, 9–14 ('Daisy, Daisy, give me your answer do'). KA recalls in a letter dated 6 Dec. 1976 to RC (Amis, *Letters*, 821) that L sang him the lines in Wheeler's restaurant when the two last met. **1** *Davie*: Poet and critic Donald Davie (1922–95). **2** Davie had written a hostile review of L's *OBTCEV* in *The Listener*, 29 Mar. 1973, and a prickly correspondence ensued in the periodical's columns. L on Davie earlier in a letter to MJ dated 26 July 1957 (Bodl. MS Eng. c. 7416/80): 'I'm getting a bit tired of Davie & his book-fuddled pontificating. He's so wrong. He's like a chap who thinks you'll improve the quality of manure by feeding your animals on manure in the first place.' **7** Davie was Palmer Professor in Humanities at Stanford University, California, 1974–8. **8** L immediately comments, ' Last line might be improved'. In the 1974 text L refers to the fact that Davie spent much time in France.

'Well, I must arise and go now, and go to Innisfree'

DATE AND TEXT

13 Jan. 1977, when it was included in a letter to KA (Huntington MS AMS 323-393). In the letter, L does not write the lines as verse, but signals verse by beginning 'where' with a capital. Previously unpublished.

1 Yeats, *The Lake Isle of Innisfree*, 1: 'I will arise and go now, and go to Innisfree'.

'After Healey's trading figures'

DATE AND TEXT

Included in a letter to AT dated 9 Feb. 1977 (*SL*, 557).

L in the letter: 'But I'm afraid my only recent verse (from an unwritten Jubilee poem to HM) is [poem]. Shall I add five or six verses to that for you? "You" in the poem is HM, of course. Perhaps that needs making a bit clearer. "What a treat to turn to you", perhaps. If one does turn to HM. She hasn't come across with that grace & favour house yet.' ('HM' is 'Her Majesty'.)

1 *Healey's*: Denis Healey (b. 1917) had been Chancellor of the Exchequer in the Labour government since 1974. **2** *Wilson's squalid crew*: the Labour government under Prime Minister Harold Wilson (1916–95), who had stood down as leader on 5 Apr. 1976.

'California, here I come'

DATE AND TEXT
Included in a letter to RC dated 11 Apr. 1977 (*SL*, 561). L first
thought of it in a letter to MJ dated 13 June 1967 (Bodl. MS Eng.
c. 7435/51): 'Davie's off to California next year again. Couldn't
we do a parody of *California here I come*? California, here I come,
Watching out for drink and bum. Can you contribute?' 'Davie' is the
poet and critic Donald Davie: see 'Davie, Davie'.

L introducing the lines in the letter to RC: 'Sing Davie my song
about California'. 1 *California, here I come*: Opening of the popular
song recorded in 1924 by Al Jolson.

'The little lives of earth and form'

DATE AND TEXT
Hull DPL 1/8/52 is a holograph draft with no uncancelled
alternative versions, dated '6. 5. 77' in L's hand, and loosely inserted
at the back of *Wkbk 8*. Written for MJ in *Thorburn's Mammals*
(1974): see *CP*, 319 n. Published in *CP* (1988), 207. L's 'forme' (l. 1)
and 'sett' (l. 6) have been corrected to to 'form' and 'set', as in *CP*.

VARIANTS (from DPL 1/8/52)
  1 earth] ~~sett~~ earth
  form] ~~earth sett~~ forme
  6 den] ~~hole~~ den
  hole] ~~den~~ hole
  7 identity] ~~is something that~~ identity
  9 Will link] ~~But That~~ Will links
  constantly] ~~centrally~~ constantly
  10 rock] ~~soil~~ rock

1 *form*: the nest or lair in which a hare crouches (*OED*, sb. 21
a.) 6 *set*: the earth or burrow of a badger (*OED*, sb.¹ 32). 11–12 Cf.
Auden, *Family Ghosts*, 7, 9: 'It is your face I see . . . Filtered through
roots of the effacing grass.'

Administration

Wkbk 7 (1/7/8) contains two drafts of the poem, the first cancelled and the second without uncancelled alternative readings, on the lower half of a page dated '3. 3. 65' at the top. The next page is dated '6. 3. [1965]' at the top. L cancelled the titles '<u>Time & Motion Study</u>' and '<u>Staff Management</u>' in favour of '<u>Administration</u>' at the beginning of the first draft. The second draft is the source of the version published in *CP* (1988), 161. L produced a revised version in a letter to KA dated 13 Apr. 1976 (Huntington MS AMS 323-393; *SL*, 538) when KA was collecting material for his *New Oxford Book of Light Verse*, and his latest version in a letter to Gavin Ewart dated 25 May 1977 (Hull DP 163/25): 'Years ago I wrote a Gavin Ewart poem: [writes out *Administration*] Unpublished, & let it stay so! I'd get shagged.' The latest version is the copy-text.

VARIANTS

1 As day by day shrewd] Day by day your *Wkbk, 1965*; As ~~day by day~~ daily my shrewd *1976 letter*

L to KA, 18 June 1976 (*SL*, 543): 'Actually I shall probably chicken out on "Administration". I don't think I could meet the eyes of my staff if it were printed, much less the Vice-Chancellor (no longer my beloved Brynmor, but a tough nut who was in Churchill's wartime cabinet office). Anyway it's not really very funny.' 3 *pull their socks up*: make an effort, try harder.

'Haymakers and reapers by Stubbs'

DATE AND TEXT

Included in a letter to JE dated 12 Nov. 1977 (Bodl. MS Eng. c. 7458/44). In l. 3 L wrote 'top hatted' before inserting 'plume- ?' above it. The latter is chosen as representing his latest thoughts. Previously unpublished.

VARIANTS (from the MS)
3 plume-] top plume-

L in the letter: 'You may think that this Conspectus of world art does it less than justice, but vogue la galère. Note *even*: it costs me a lot to say that.' JE had been Assistant Keeper of the Tate Gallery's British Collection since 1974, and one of the exhibitions (with catalogues) she organised was of the work of George Stubbs, in 1984. She had written to L on 2 Oct. 1977 (Bodl. MS Eng. c. 7458/41): 'Meanwhile Stubbs's *Haymakers* and *Reapers* dominate my life at the Tate.'

1 'Haymakers' and 'Reapers' are two pastoral paintings done in 1785 by English painter George Stubbs (1724–1806). 5 See *The Card-Players*.

'The sky split apart in malice'

DATE AND TEXT
Included in a letter to CM dated 2 Mar. 1978 (*SL*, 581). L and Ted Hughes (1930–98) had been commissioned to write verses in celebration of the Queen's Silver Jubilee in 1978, to be inscribed on a stone monument in Queen Square, London. L's verse was *1952–1977*, which he includes in the letter to CM, before remarking 'I'm sure Ted will do better' and giving this parody of Hughes's *Crow* (1970).

'Thought you might welcome a dekko'

DATE AND TEXT
Written on a p.c. to JE dated 7 Apr. 1978 (Bodl. MS Eng. c. 7458/48). On the front is a reproduction of El Greco's 'Lady in a Fur Wrap'. Previously unpublished.

1 *dekko*: look (slang). 2 El Greco (1541–1614) was to become notable for the elongated forms in his paintings.

'Walt Whitman'

DATE AND TEXT
10 Apr. 1978, when it was included in a p.c. to KA (Huntington MS, AMS 353-393). L writes the text as four lines separated by slant lines, and leaves the fourth line as an ellipsis. He signs off as 'young bum. I Philip'. Previously unpublished.

From early on, readers have detected homoerotic feelings in Whitman's *Leaves of Grass* (various edns. from 1855 onwards). 2 *titman*: a fancier of women's breasts (slang); not in *OED*.

'If I could talk, I'd be a worthless prof'

DATE AND TEXT
SL, 588: letter to RC, 17 Aug. 1978.

The view of academics in the poem is consistent with that in
Naturally the Foundation will Bear Your Expenses and 'A *Lecturer*
in drip-dry shirt arrayed'.

    4 *old toad*: See *Toads* and *Toads Revisited*. L seems to be referring
here to his hardworking self. *Frank Kermode*: British literary scholar
and critic (1919–2010).

'The daily things we do'

DATE AND TEXT
Feb. 1979. Written by L for his Deputy Librarian Brenda Moon in
the library keepsake containing 'New eyes each year' (*AL*, 8 [Oct.
1999], 11). Published in *CP* (1988), 213.

L told Brenda Moon that he thought it a 'nice little verse', and that
'memory' in l. 8 meant 'memorial': *AL* 8, (Oct. 1999), 11.

'New brooms sweep clean'

DATE AND TEXT
Feb. 1979. Written in Betty Mackereth's copy of the library keepsake
containing 'New eyes each year', and published by her in *AL*, 25
(Apr. 2008), 13.

1 Proverbial. **3** Cf. Henry F. Lyte's hymn *Abide with Me*, 7: 'Change
and decay in all around I see'. **8** She had been his secretary since
May 1957.

Love Again

DATE AND TEXT
Wkbk 8 contains: a page and a half of drafts of the first two stanzas
and the first two lines of the third after '7. 8. 75', with the last draft
on a page dated '16. 12. 75' at the top (1/8/22); a half-page of drafts
of the same portion of the text on a page dated '22. 3. 76' at the top;
a page of drafts of the same portion of the text dated '17. 12. 77'

at the top (1/8/28); and four pages of drafts of the whole poem
between '15. 8. 78' and the completion date '20 / 9 / 79' (1/8/30).
Hull DPL 1/8/46 is a t.s. with holograph corrections, loosely inserted
at the end of *Wkbk 8*. It bears two dates, which look to be in L's
hand: '25 / 10 / 78' and '20 / 9 / 79'. The first of these confirms
what the text and corrections indicate: that it represents the poem
at the stage reached in the *Wkbk* on that date, with some further
thoughts on the ending. The copy-text comprises: stanzas 1 and 2
from DPL 1/8/46, and stanza 3 from the eighth (final) version of the
stanza dated '20 / 9 / 79', which contain no uncancelled alternative
versions. Published in *CP* (1988), 161.

VARIANTS (from DPL 1/8/46):
16 ~~There would have to have been a great difference~~ *1st version*
Perhaps it needs ~~greed, or~~ other violence [*alt.* veins of violence] |
Than ~~ownership~~ Other than ~~fruitless~~ end-stopped ecstasy. to bring
rewards *2nd version*
~~Love teaches is the Through love we learn our difference~~ *3rd version*
Love teaches ~~doubt, and~~ depth of difference. *4th version*
17 ~~A long way back; and~~ ['even then,' above caret] ~~the rewards~~ *1st
version*
the decades harden its rewards: *2nd version*
18 ~~Might not have meant much personally~~ *1st version*

L to MB, 7 Aug. 1975: 'I wish you hadn't gone away just when you
did: I miss you. A fearful boiling night was diversified by two dreams
about you, both "losing dreams" – you going off with someone
else – wch was all very silly, for how can one lose what one does
not possess?': Brennan (2002), 67–8. On 17 Aug. 1978 (*SL*, 588),
L told RC that he had been 'tinkering about tonight with a poem
abandoned years ago' and quoted ll. 7–8 ('poignant lines [. . .] which
seem rather good to me, though it's hard to recover the mood').
L to C. B. Cox, 22 Dec. 1983 (*SL*, 705): 'I am afraid there is little
hope for the poem. For one thing, it is intensely personal, with four-
letter words for further orders, and not the sort of thing the sturdy
burghers of Manchester would wish to read; for another, it broke
off at a point at which I was silly enough to ask myself a question,
with three lines in which to answer it. Well, of course, anyone who
asks a question by definition doesn't know the answer, and I am no
exception. So there we are.'
   Title Booth (2005), 102, cites the jazz lyric 'I'm falling in love
again' (by Frederick Hollander and Sammy Lerner). He also notes

the end of a letter to KA of 8 Jan. 1946 in which L, confessing crudely a desire to have sex with his girlfriend Ruth Bowman's friend Jane Exall, remarks: 'I know how tiresome all this is & I wish it "didn't have to" happen. Love again. (Don't look like that.)': *TAWG*, xix n. 28. 1 *wanking*: masturbating (slang). OED's earliest example is from 1950. L to Patsy Murphy, 18 Oct. 1955 (*SL*, 253): 'Hope love in a cottage goes better than Keats supposed – better than wanking in digs, anyway.' (L alludes to Keats, 'Love in a hut, with water and a crust, | Is – Love forgive us! – cinders, ashes, dust'.) When Jean Hartley once asked L what his cupboard full of pornography was *for*, 'he replied (somewhat embarrassed), "to wank to, or with, or at"': Motion, 222. 7 *cunt*: 'these words are part of the palette. You use them when you want to shock. I don't think I've ever shocked for the sake of shocking': L in 1981 (*FR*, 61). 13–14 John Carey, Booth (2000), 65, catches an echo of Yeats, *Among School Children*, 61–3: 'O chestnut-tree . . . O body swayed to music'. 16 Auden, *A. E. Housman*, 7–8: 'his private lust | Something to do with violence and the poor.' Noted by Grevel Lindop in *Housman Society Journal*, 20 (1994), 26–7. Lindop also notes (27, 29) that L quotes another line from Auden's poem in the review of Richard Perceval Graves's biography of Housman published in *The Guardian*, 1 Nov. 1979 (*RW*, 263–5), which is shortly after the time L was bringing his poem to completion.

'After eating in honour of Chichele'

DATE AND TEXT
14 Dec. 1979, in a letter to BP (Bodl. MS Pym 152/51; *SL*, 611). As in *SL*, L's lower case 'a' in 'after' has been changed to a capital, in the interests of preserving the couplet as verse. In the MS the lines are written continuously.

1 L tells BP that he had come down from Hull to Oxford for an All Souls Chichele dinner. Henry Chichele (1364–1443) was Archbishop of Canterbury and the founder of All Souls College, Oxford, where L had been a Visiting Fellow, 1970–1, working on *OBTCEV*. 2 *bichele*: L to MJ, 16 Sept. 1970 (Bodl. MS Eng. c. 7441/126) on the fellows of All Souls: 'they seem a bitchy lot'.

'Apples on a Christmas tree!'

DATE AND TEXT
Written on a Christmas card sent to Betty Mackereth in the late
1970s or early 1980s. Published in facsimile in *AL*, 20 (Autumn
2005), 90, with a note by James Booth. The card depicts a
Christmas tree laden with apples that look like tomatoes: *AL*, 20
(Autumn 2005), 91.

'The one thing I'd say about A. Thwaite'

DATE AND TEXT
Included in a letter to RC dated 7 Feb.1980 (*SL*, 615). The text is
written continuously in the letter, with slant lines marking the lines
of verse.

1 *A. Thwaite*: Anthony Thwaite (b. 1930), poet, editor of *Larkin
at Sixty* (1982), *CP* (1988, 2003), *SL* (1992), *FR* (2001) and *LTM*
(2010). 2 *Braithwaite*: Poet, and historian of Caribbean culture,
Edward Kamau Brathwaite (b. 1930), with the surname misspelt,
as AT notes (*SL*, 615), for the sake of the rhyme. 4 *Parnassus*:
mountain in central Greece, anciently revered as the home of Apollo
and the Muses. 5 *Douglas Dunn*: b. 1942. Scots poet, and friend of
L, under whom he worked at the Brynmor Jones Library, University
of Hull.

The View

DATE AND TEXT
Wkbk 8 contains lines that relate only loosely to the final poem on
a page dated '29. 3. 72' at the top (1/8/6) and five more lines on
a page dated '14 / 8 / 72' at the top. Hull DPL 1/8/45, a t.s. with
holograph corrections in pencil and, in the last two lines, in ink,
loosely inserted at the beginning of *Wkbk 8*, is clearly a version of
the final poem, and is later than the *Wkbk* drafts. L contributed the
poem to a volume of handwritten poems compiled to mark AT's
fiftieth birthday: this is the copy-text. L sent the poem with a letter
to Ann Thwaite dated 9 Feb. 1980. The birthday was on 23 June
1980. On the volume, see Zachary Leader's note in Amis, *Letters*,
887. Published in *CP* (1988), 195.

Title The View ~~from Fifty~~
  4 to] and
  5 led me to] ends upon
 12 What's left is drear] ~~The rest~~ mounts sheer. ~~falls~~
 14 view that] ~~see it~~ view that
 15 final. And] final, ~~a~~And

L in 1972 (*FR*, 92): 'Really one should ignore one's fiftieth birthday.
As anyone over fifty will tell you, it's no age at all. All the same it is
rather sobering to realize one has lived longer than Arnold of Rugby
or Porson, the eighteenth-century Professor of Greek. It's hard not
to look back and wonder why one hasn't done more or forward
and wonder what . . . what if anything, you'll do in the future. I
seem to have spent my life waiting for poems to turn up [. . .] As
regards the future, I doubt if writers get better after they're fifty
and I don't suppose I shall be any exception.' L refers to Thomas
Arnold (1795–1842), Headmaster of Rugby School (1828–41), and
to Richard Porson (1759–1808), who held the Regius Professorship
of Greek at Cambridge, 1792–1808. L to KA, 11 Aug. 1972 (*SL*,
462): 'I feel rather dead and buried at the moment, poetically, but
I hope one day to rise again [. . .] Funny being fifty, isn't it. I keep
seeing obits of chaps who've passed over "suddenly, aged 55",
"after a short illness, 56", "after a long illness bravely borne, aged
57" – and add ten years on, what's ten years? [. . .] No, it doesn't
bear thinking about [. . .] I begin to think that, give me another ten
or twenty years, I'm just on the verge of seeing how life ought to be
lived. I'll be just about ready then.' L to JE, 16 Aug. 1972 (*SL*, 463):
'Well, it is an elder of the tribe that writes to you now. If the days
of our life are three score years and ten, I've had 5/7ths of mine.
Isn't that dreadful? And I've done nothing.' To WA, 15 Aug. 1973
(*SL*, 488): 'life begins at forty AND ENDS AT FIFTY, or so I fancy'.
To BP, 22 Jan. 1975: 'Already I find it incredible to be over 50 and
"nothing done", as I feel': *SL*, 520. To WA, 21 Aug. 1976 (Bodl. MS
Res. c. 616): 'I found 50 a great watershed; things seemed to close
down and leave nothing but shortening lines and the prospect of age
and death and remorse & all that.' This view is confirmed by MB
in Salwak (1989), 35. To AT, 6 June 1980, on his fiftieth birthday
(*SL*, 624): 'Of course it *is* hell, and gets worse in my experience.
My poem wasn't really serious, as some of the rhymes suggest, apart
from meaning what it said.' To AT, 14 Oct. 1980 (*SL*, 630): 'How're
you liking being fifty? Rotten decade for me, like the twenties.'

The verse form is that of Housman's *A Shropshire Lad* VII, XXI, XXIX and *Last Poems* XXXIX.

6 *snowcaps*: *OED* records only one example, from 1871: 'polar snow-caps'. 12 *Search me*: A characteristic Larkin response. To MJ, 20 Dec. 1955 (Bodl. MS Eng. c. 7412/111): 'Search me. O Lord.' To MJ, 12 Oct. 1957 (Bodl. MS Eng. c. 7417/6): 'Why write a note to you when I shall see you tomorrow? "Search me" – '. To MJ, 3 Nov. 1959 (Bodl. MS Eng. c. 7420/77): 'Tonight I am back in the treadmill, the mouse-wheel. Why? Search me.' To JE, 14 Dec. 1974 (*SL*, 516): 'As Randolph Turpin said when they asked him why he didn't get off the ropes when Sugar Ray was hitting him, "Search me."' To AT, 19 June 1975 (*SL*, 527): 'Why don't we all do everything? Search me.' To Julian Barnes, 25 Oct. 1984 (*SL*, 721): 'Search me, O Lord, as someone says', referring to Ps. 139: 23: 'Search me, O God'. 13 R. J. C. Watt, *A Concordance to the Poetry of Philip Larkin* (1995), viii, notes Hopkins, *The Wreck of the Deutschland*, 13. 8: 'unchilding unfathering deeps'. *Unchilded*: not merely 'childless', but 'deprived of children' (*OED*); so, too, 'unwifed', for which *OED* records only one example, from 1834, with the different sense 'not made a wife'. L to MJ, 3 May 1955 (Bodl. MS Eng. c. 7411/7): 'I have no house no wife no child no car no motor mower no holidays planned for Sweden or Italy [. . .] I dread being one who *only* at 50 gains what everyone else has had since they were 25.' To Norman Iles, 4 July 1972: '& of course I haven't any biblical things such as wife, children, house, land, cattle, sheep etc.': *SL*, 460.

'All work & no wassail'

DATE AND TEXT
Included in a letter to JE dated 29 Nov. 1980 (Bodl. MS Eng. c. 7459/52; *SL*, 631).

L in the letter: 'Have now reascended the wagon: honestly, I think my system is *rejecting alcohol*, wch is very convenient but rather dreary. [couplet] – I suppose that doesn't rhyme. May not even be grammar.' (*SL* mistranscribes: 'good grammar'.)

1 *wassail*: revelry, carousal.

'Good for You, Gavin'

DATE AND TEXT
Wkbk 8 (1/8/34) contains two and a half pages of drafts of the whole poem after '20. 11. 79'. Published in a letter from Gavin Ewart in *The Observer*, (29 Dec. 1985), 16, who reports that the poem was among those secretly collected by his wife for his sixty-fifth birthday, which was on 4 Feb. 1981. The *Wkbk* drafts have 'Tea-chests' twice and 'Teachests' once in l. 6, and with 'attic'd' this makes sense: 'Teachers' in *The Observer* text is a misprint, reproduced in *CP* (1988) and corrected in the rev. edn., 1990. The copy-text is Hull DPL 1/8/44, a photocopy of the holograph MS signed 'Philip Larkin' and dated '26 Nov. '81'. The punctuation at the end of l. 2 should be a semicolon, not a comma as in *CP* (1988), 216.

Title *Gavin*: the poet Gavin Ewart (1916–95), noted for light verse. L, reviewing KA's *The New Oxford Book of Light Verse* in 1978 (*FR*, 295): 'I should have liked a lot more Gavin Ewart'. L in 1979 thought Ewart 'extraordinarily funny' (*RW*, 53), and on 6 June 1980 (*SL*, 623), gave his opinion that *The Collected Ewart 1933–1980* was 'a fat solid fairground of a book'. In 1982 he hailed 'this astonishing unstoppable talent' and welcomed 'the advent, or perhaps I should say the irruption [of] the most remarkable phenomenon in the English poetic scene during the last ten years': *FR*, 321, 320. **10** *keeping your eye on the ball*: remaining alert (*OED*, ball 18). **11** *Glenlivet*: single malt Scotch whisky. L to Colin Gunner, 26 Dec. 1984: 'Awoke in no very good shape this morning, possibly through imbibing some 20-year-old Glenlivet that tasted like liquid Christmas pudding but was I suppose quite potent': Hull DP 179/30.

'Beware the travelogue, my son'

DATE AND TEXT
Included in a letter to Andrew Motion dated 24 Mar. 1981 (*SL*, 645), where it is written continuously but with capitals signalling the beginnings of lines.

L in the letter: 'What's this *India* poem? [poem] Pardon these ramblings: just jealousy, of course.' L is referring to Motion's *Independence* (1981).

The lines imitate Carroll's *Jabberwocky*: 'Beware the Jabberwock, my son! | The jaws that bite, the claws that catch! | Beware the Jubjub bird, and shun | The frumious Bandersnatch!'

3 *Kirkup*: poet, translator and travel writer James Kirkup (1918–2009), who left England in 1956 to live and work abroad, especially in Japan, where he spent thirty years.

'"When one door shuts, another opens." Cock!'

DATE AND TEXT
Included in a letter to JE dated 20 Sept. 1981 (*SL*, 658).

L in the letter: 'What happens then I don't know! A fatalist w^d say the way will be shown, but I've never found that. [couplet]'.

1 Proverbial.

'The chances are certainly slim'

DATE AND TEXT
Included in a letter to Gavin Ewart dated 2 Mar. 1982 (*SL*, 665).

2 *Barbara Pym*: English novelist (1913–80). L admired her work, and corresponded with her. 5 L in the letter, immediately after the limerick: 'but with what authority I don't know: OED refers to "queme" – "snug, closefitting, protected against the wind" etc. but no "obsc." sense. How strange. Do you know the word?' *quim*: a woman's genitals (British vulgar slang).

1982

DATE AND TEXT
21 July 1982. Written on a p.c. sent to MJ bearing the postmark 21 July 1982 (Bodl. MS Eng. c. 7445/54). Hull DPL 1/8/51 is a holograph draft dated '21 July 1982', loosely inserted at the back of *Wkbk 8*. The lines are headed '1982', both on the draft dated '21 July 1982' at the end, and on the version sent to MJ: this therefore looks to be a title. Published in *CP* (1988), 219, without the title.

VARIANTS (from DPL 1/8/51)
2 white] ~~faint~~ white

3 ~~Then grow to At midday you Middays that~~ By midday you meet
5 Whatever] ~~All that~~ Whatever
6 Now] ~~Is n~~Now

L jokingly signs himself 'Ted' (i.e. Ted Hughes) on the p.c., on the front of which is depicted the occupation of the month (July) and the associated sign of the zodiac (Leo) from the Calendar in a Book of Hours illuminated in France for the English market by the Fastolf Master, *c.*1440–50. Half of the card shows corn being reaped, and, beyond, a green field with yellow flowers; the other half shows Leo, the lion.

'My feet are clay, my brains are sodden'

DATE AND TEXT
Included in a letter to Harry Fairhurst dated 10 Nov. 1982 (*SL*, 681).

AT's note in *SL*, 681: 'In a paper he had circulated among Yorkshire librarians, L had allowed the term "K", denoting a thousand, to appear. Fairhurst, at that time Librarian of the University of York, had challenged L light-heartedly on this "modernism".' After the poem L signs himself 'Penitently, | Philip'.

'This collection of various scraps'

DATE AND TEXT
Included in a letter to RC dated 30 Oct. 1983 (*SL*, 703). In the letter the text is written continuously, with slant lines marking the lines of verse.

1 L's *RW* was published on 21 Nov. 3 *Priestley*: novelist, broadcaster and dramatist J. B. Priestley (1894–1984). 5 *old Bob*: RC.

'Outside, a dog barks'

DATE AND TEXT
Included in a letter to RC dated 30 Oct. 1983 (*SL*, 704), with line-divisions marked by slant lines.

L in the letter: 'Another load of crap from this Vikram Seth character, known to you I believe. Quite pleasant stuff, but fails to grip. Comes of being an Oriental, I suspect. [verse] Not my cup of tea.' Indian poet Vikram Seth's first collection of poems was the privately published *Mappings* (1980). He sent L a copy, and though in private L was disparaging, he gave him encouragement.

3 *Wang-Lei's*: By analogy with 'Wang-Wei', eighth-century Chinese poet. *Wang*: vulgar slang for penis (after 'prick', cueing the Lei/lay pun).

'Last night we put the clocks on'

DATE AND TEXT
Included in a letter to Gavin Ewart dated 27 Mar. 1984 (*SL*, 709). The clocks had been put forward an hour on the previous Saturday.

L in the letter: 'On Sunday I found myself saying [poem] – well, whether I am an hour younger, and if so why can't we do it on a larger scale. Well, I should be older, I suppose, but let's put the clocks back. Anyway, where is that hour? I could have done a lot with it. Never mind.'

Bun's Outing

DATE AND TEXT
Christmas 1984. The poem is pasted on to a Christmas and New Year greetings card (Bodl. MS Eng. c. 7445/93). Below the poem L writes '© Philip Larkin 1984'. Reproduced in facsimile in *LTM*, 445.

Title 'Bun' is L's pet name for MJ. 8 Cf. Ralph Hodgson's poem *Stupidity Street*, printed on p. 311 of *The Oxford Book of Death*, ed. D. J. Enright (1983). L reviewed the volume on 24 Apr. 1983 (*FR*, 345–7).

'After reading the works of MacCaig'

DATE AND TEXT
Included in a letter to RC dated 10 Oct. 1985 (*SL*, 754), with the beginnings of lines signalled by capitals.

L in the letter, immediately before the lines: 'There's no real news here: the eccentric Craig Raine is running Faber poetry, and to my mind indulging some pretty fearful talents. But there is no poetry nowadays. No one has any ear. I'm labouring through the collected N. MacCaig at present.' The lines follow. After them, L remarks: 'it does, you know': he is registering the fact that Raine's 'Martian' poetry, which cultivates representing the world as though seen for the first time, shares that characteristic with MacCaig's.

1 The *Collected Poems* of Norman MacCaig (1910–96) had just been published. 5 *Raine (Craig)*: poet and critic Craig Raine (b. 1944), as distinct from poet and scholar Raine (Kathleen), 1908–2003.

UNDATED
OR APPROXIMATELY DATED POEMS

'There was an old fellow of Kaber'

DATE AND TEXT
Published in Thwaite (1982), 46, where CM says 'written years
before' 'I hope games like tossing the caber', published in 1977.

CM in Thwaite (1982), 46–7: 'The somewhat obscure third and
fourth lines Philip explained as "fillers" to be replaced more
specifically as occasion demanded. For example: When they said
"Meet Ted Hughes", | He replied, "I refuse", or When they said,
"Meet Thom Gunn", | He cried, "God, I must run", and so on.'
   CM reports that the verse, the 'First Faber Limerick', was inspired
'by his chance passing through a village in North Yorkshire called
Kaber, which, he realized, provided the perfect rhyme. (I have a
photograph of him draped glumly over the name-board.)': Thwaite
(1982), 46.
   5 *Charles*: Charles Monteith of Faber & Faber. *love your
neighbour*: Lev. 19: 18, Matt. 22: 39, Mark 12: 31. *neighbour*: Poets
Ted Hughes and Thom Gunn were also published by Faber & Faber.

The Way We Live Now

DATE AND TEXT
KA, *Memoirs* (1991), 60, introducing the poem: 'I remember, from
one of the lost letters of probably the Fifties, a poem that shows
him to have had a talent for light verse comparable with Bob
Conquest's, though different in approach and, to our loss, not so
often exercised.'

5 *bogs*: (slang) toilets.

'What is booze for?'

TEXT
Written on an undated Christmas card sent to Kenneth Hibbert, identified as L's 'friend, insurance adviser and fellow member of the Hull Literary Club' by Zachary Leader, who published the poem, L's self-parody of *Days*, in Amis, *Letters*, 1040.

'When the night is hoar'

TEXT
Bodl. MS Eng. c. 7446/97: a small card bearing two 'rabbit' verses numbered 'i.' and 'ii.', with illustrations, in L's hand. This is the first. Previously unpublished.

'On the shortest day'

TEXT
See the notes on the previous poem. This is the second poem on the card. Previously unpublished.

'Roses, roses all the way?'

TEXT
Bodl. MS Eng. c. 7446/117: a gift card depicting roses on the front, with L's handwritten verse inside. Previously unpublished.

'No power cuts here –'

TEXT
Bodl. MS Eng. c. 7553: Written by L inside a Christmas card sent to MJ. Previously unpublished.

'Those long thin steeds'

TEXT
Bodl. MS Eng. c. 7554/81: a birthday card sent to MJ. The front shows 'Priam winning the Gold Cup at Goodwood in 1831'. L's verse is written in ink on the verso and signed ' P.A.L.' Published

by Christopher Fletcher in *The Sunday Times*, 11 May 2008. The horses in the picture are galloping at full stretch in front of an ornate grandstand. In the background, trees and downs are visible. The card and poem are reproduced in *LTM*, [xii]–[xiii].

'Though there's less at wch to purr'

TEXT
Bodl. MS Eng. c. 7555/55: a Valentine's Day card sent to MJ bearing L's handwritten verse in ink. Previously unpublished.

VARIANTS (from the MS)
3 In] ~~You iIn~~
4 You're] ~~Are~~

'Snow on Valentine's Day!'

TEXT
Bodl. MS Eng. c. 7555/60: a Valentine's Day card sent to MJ bearing L's handwritten verse in ink. Previously unpublished.

APPENDICES

This is an account of the contents of the eleven typescript booklets prepared by Larkin before publication of *The North Ship* in July 1945. The account in Tolley (2005), 349–54, is full of errors: the earliest collection is not *The Happiest Day* but *The Happiest Days*; the title of the poem *Young Woman Blues* should be *Young Woman's Blues*; the opening line 'Turning from these obscene verses to the stars' should not contain 'these'; the date of *Further Poems* is June, not July, 1940, and its subtitle is not 'Nine poems of depression' but 'Nine poems of depression and dismay'; the opening line 'When night puts twenty veils' should be 'When the night puts twenty veils'; the punctuation in the middle of the opening line of *Midsummer Night, 1940* should be a semicolon, not a colon; the first line of *Chorus from a Masque* is not 'You took our advice' but 'You take our advice'; 'From windows at sundown' (p. 353) should be 'From the window at sundown'; 'Guests are numerous; for the far arid strand' should be 'Quests are numerous; for the far acid strand'; for 'Evening, and I, were young' read 'Evening, and I, young'; 'After Dinner Remarks' should be 'After-Dinner Remarks', and 'after dinner' in 'Further after dinner remarks' should be 'afterdinner' (p. 351); 'growing up' should be 'growing-up' (p. 353); and the sailors in 'Sailors brought back strange stories of those birds' brought back stories of 'lands', not 'birds'. Tolley gives first lines after titles, but not for the poems in *Sugar and Spice*. This is a comparatively minor omission, however: he does not provide bibliographical references to the MS sources, or note L's numbering of poems within collections.

Unless it is stated otherwise, the footnotes in the following bibliographical description are all editorial, not authorial. Titles of poems have been italicised and regularised.

[First Collection, untitled]

HULL DPL 2/1/1

This contains seven poems composed between 8 June and 19 September 1939. Several other poems mentioned were removed by L from the collection. The 'modern writer' mentioned in the first paragraph has not been identified.

L's Preface to the collection:

It is a debatable point, whether writing about oneself is a more exquisite pleasure than talking about oneself. But the fact that oneself is a subject of the most absorbing interest cannot be disputed by any man, whether he prefer the immediate applause of the conversation, or the more delicate delight of 'long-range confession', as a modern writer puts it.

An illusion that I and my affairs are of some interest, then, is a main motive in this collection of what have become known as the 'Stanley Poems'. But, I flatter myself, it is not the sole one. It is also interesting to note the development in poetic style (and, perhaps, ability) as revealed in the poems, and also – and this, to me, is the most interesting – the attitude towards the subject.

Let us take the poetic style first. It is a source of constant wonder to me that the first poem was written when it was. It is one of the few perfect sonnets I have ever come across. A sense of the most delicate irony pervades all; the 'splintered' thirteenth line is done so well that it is incredible that it was conceived and written offhand in one night. Looking at the original manuscript, I note that lines 1, 7, 8, 9, 12, 13,[1] and 14 went in as they stood without correction.

With the second poem, however, we return to more familiar ground. The emotion is trite, the verse sloppy, with an almost unbearable swing into the good old iambic pentameter for the big finish. The influence of 'Ecclesiastes' is obvious in both matter and style.

I used to think 'The Ships at Mylae' not ineffective. I now think it no better than the others. The effect of 'Ecclesiastes' had worn off, and I returned to the familiar pseudo-Keats babble in which that unforgettably bad poem 'Apollo and Hyacinthus' was written.

'Alvis Victrix' is a vain attempt to regain the touch of the first poem. In almost every department it is inferior.

'Stanley en Musique' was, I suppose, the first authentic Stanley poem. The metre has helped to gain the ironic tone, and its restraint is more than welcome after the preceding outpourings. It also marks my first ventures into the obscure (under the influence of Eliot) and I think it not too incompetent. In the next poem (written almost exactly two months afterwards) consciousness of what I was doing spoilt it, and the lengthening of the last lines

[1] Not '15', as stated in Tolley (2005), 357.

of the stanzas induce sentimentality where emotion was desired. 'Erotic Play' is back again in the Eliot metre, more obscure, but as sentimental; while the next poem, in the same metre, is definitely on the way to an ironic pornography.

'Stanley Folâtre'[2] is much more important. Two points distinguish it from the previous poems: the metre, which was entirely original, and the vocabulary and treatment, which was decidedly Auden. The attitude will be mentioned later. Also, I think it to be a model of the elementary 'compressed force' I admire so much. This style steadily increases from this point, but the slobber style had several strong kicks to give yet, including the 'Masque', which is not printed here, and other poems, which are.

'Stanley Gothique' is not important: the technique is, perhaps, unequal to the thought. 'Their seed-time past', on the other hand, is one of the last of the slobber poems. Actually it was the epilogue spoken by the Chorus in the masque, 'Behind the Façade' (a fantastic mixture of slobber and the Auden–Isherwood style).

Passing over the nursery rhyme, the next piece is a curious combination of the slobber and the Auden styles; the stanza is brazenly filched from Auden, but the language is Audenized slobber, and falls vainly.

The remaining poems show a rather easier compromise between the instinctive slobber and the desired 'compressed' styles. The use in these of dissonance is also noticeable, and stanzas are invented with more freedom than[3] before, although I am never above plagiarising a rhyme-scheme or metre if it suits the poems I want to write. I regard the presence of 75 single-syllable words in a poem of 84 words ('Take your tomorrow'), as being something of a technical achievement.[4]

Turning to the attitude towards the subject, I find myself less at ease. But it may be noted that the emotional attitude does change quite considerably during the space of time in which these poems were written. I will attempt to divide them up.

(1) Plain admiration. (This includes the first four poems.)
(2) Admiration and amusement. The inherent irony of poems I and IV resolved into a cynical amusement of V as the conception of the character 'Stanley' emerged. As

2 One of the poems, like 'Stanley Gothique' below, that L took out.
3 L types 'that' by mistake.
4 L types 'acheivement'.

> 'eyes in which I learn
> That I am glad to look, return
> My glances every day'[5]

there was no need at that time to think of themes of death, parting, dust & roses, etc.

(3) Ashes to ashes. This, represented by 'Stanley et la glace', grew into maturity in the immediate post-summer holiday period, when the 'eyes in which I learn that I am glad to look' by no means returned my glances every day. It grew into the Parting theme, strongly stressed by the latter poems of the book, when the war started and I knew that school, even when it did start, would be Stanley-less.

(4) Character. Contemporary with the last two attitudes, a serious conception of the character of 'Stanley' appeared. Stanley was the lord of life, the instinctive barbarian, the magnificent savage. 'Stanley Folâtre'[6] puts this point very clearly, where the connection between the 'frolicking' Stanley and early heroes is indicated. 'Erotic Play', again, gives the conception of Stanley as one who can enjoy his 'scattered time'.

(5) Cooler admiration: the future. The final emotion is a return of the early, unqualified love in a less unbridled form, as well as a calmer contemplation of the future (although 'Promise' gives a ghastly vision of what may come). The poems are less noisy, more skilful, yet 'May the passing moon delight . . .' is, in emotion, only a return to 'The Days of thy Youth', with a dash of 'The Ships at Mylae'. The final poem, 'Take Your Tomorrow', is a fusion of love, resignation at parting, the serious Stanley, and the past. Possibly it is the best of them all.

Not all the Stanley poems are included here. Some have been excluded on grounds of inferiority of verse, others, of emotion. Nor are the poems addressed to other (and inferior) Stanleys included.

CONTENTS

---

5 Auden, *A Summer Night* [early version], 25–7: *The English Auden*, ed. Edward Mendelson (1977), 137.
6 L typed 'folâtre'.

The Ships at Mylae: 'You are not happy here. Not here'
Alvis Victrix: 'What is this voluptuous monster, painted red'
Stanley en Musique: 'The dull whole of the drawing room'
Stanley et la Glace: 'Three pennies gain a twisted whorl'
Erotic Play: 'Your summer will sing of this'.

One O'Clock Jump

HULL DPL 2/2
All that survives of this collection is the title-page, with the title in
t.s. and the MS inscription 'Philip Larkin, October 1939'. The title is
that of the famous hit by the Count Basie Orchestra.

The Village of the Heart

HULL DPL 2/1/2.
'12 poems by | philip larkin'.

The poems are numbered, and the Prologue and Epilogue bring the
total number to fourteen. The date '1940' is typed on the title-page,
and L has added 'March 28th' by hand. Also on the title-page, L
quotes 'To settle in this village of the heart | My darling, can you bear
it?' and identifies the author as W. H. Auden.

CONTENTS
Prologue: 'Such is our springtime, sprawling its sprouting'
   I 'Standing on love's farther shores'
   II 'The hills in their recumbent postures'
   III 'Falling of these early flowers'
   IV 'So you have been, despite parental ban'
   V 'Through darkness of sowing'
   VI 'Praise to the higher organisms!'
   VII 'Prince, fortune is accepted among these rooms'
   VIII '(from James Hogg) Lock the door, Lariston, lock it, I say to
       you'
   IX 'Nothing significant was really said'
   X 'Turning from obscene verses to the stars'
   XI 'Autumn sees the sun low in the sky'
   XII 'The cycles hiss on the road away from the factory'
Epilogue: 'Will hoped-for rains'.

Further Poems

HULL DPL 2/1/3

'Further Poems. | Nine poems of depression and dismay. | Philip Larkin.'

L seems to have counted the 'Two Sonnets' as one item. The poem typed as Epigraph brings the total number of poems to eleven. The date 'June, 1940' is written by L in ink on the bottom right corner of the title-page.

CONTENTS

[As Epigraph]: 'For who will deny'
After Dinner Remarks: 'A good meal can somewhat repair'
Two Sonnets:
I *The Conscript*: 'So he evolved a saving fiction as'
II *The Conscientious Objector*: 'This was the first fruit of his new
  resolve – '
Further Afterdinner Remarks: 'I never was much of a one for beauty'
Poem: 'Still beauty'
Remark: 'Seconds of tangled love and art'
Sonnet: 'But we must build our walls, for what we are'
Historical Fact: 'Shelley | Had a belly'
Midsummer Night 1940: 'The sun falls behind Wales; the town and
  hills'
'But as to the real truth, who knows? The earth.'

Poems August 1940

HULL DPL 2/1/4

On the front cover of the small booklet are written 'poems' and 'August 1940'. 'August 1940' is typed again below the heading 'FOREWORD', and the Foreword is signed 'Philip Larkin' in pencil. L counts the two versions of 'As a War in Years of Peace' as two items (there is no poem VIII).

L's Foreword:

This collection of poems was made with no deliberation at all, many poems being printed within a few days of their being written. In consequence, there is much work that is silly, private, careless or just ordinarily bad here. Poems number III, IV, VI, IX, and X are included only to fill up space, not because they are of value.

The keynotes of this collection are Carelessness (=Spontaneity) and Platitudinousness (=Simplicity). The qualities in parentheses are what I aimed at. On the other hand, I like most of the poems here except the ones named above.

CONTENTS

Chosen Poems

HULL DPL 2/1/5

On the front cover is typed 'chosen poems 1941', and on the title-page 'Chosen Poems. | by | Philip Larkin.' and the date 'april 1941'. On the next page is the dedication 'To J. B. S.', and on the facing page a quotation from Auden: 'For now the moulding images of growth . . . The stoves and resignations of the frozen plains'. Following this: 'One copy of this edition | has been printed, of which none is ['are' corrected by hand to 'is'] for sale. This is number: 1 [number written in by hand].

L's Foreword:

This selection was made from a total mass of about twice as many poems, covering approximately a period of three years (1938–41). They are printed roughly in chronological order, and are generally speaking the original text as it was left at the time.

They are thus selected because as every poet should *like* his poems (not necessarily think them good), I like those I have included enough to want them collected together. Also, I regard the changes that are shown throughout in style as being of interest to the psychologist, if not to the literary critic. They exemplify, to my mind, the natural and to some extent inevitable ossification of a 'boyish gift' with the passing of time, shown by the gradual disappearance of spontaneous verse forms and natural energy, and the accompanying depersonalization which characterizes the later poems. These latter (still speaking from the standpoint of the psychologist) are nearer the poems of a novelist than the poems of a poet.[7]

As for their literary interest, I think that almost any single line by Auden would be worth more than the whole lot put together. The course of ossification, in fact, is concurrent with the gradually increasing traces of the Auden manner (and is possibly the cause of it) until towards the end the poems are to be judged solely by comparison with the Auden of 'Look, Stranger!'. Certainly they are not very similar, but Auden's ease and vividness were the qualities I most wished to gain.

The earlier poems, on the other hand, show very little influence at all. Actually I have omitted all extremely early ones,[8] but they, apart from a little superficial Keats, have no mannerisms. For this reason, perhaps, I think them comparatively successful, and have included five poems from the first selection of poems I ever made.

The significance of the whole collection, however, is uncertain. Obviously the poems are not all of equal merit. Some I included because I liked them wholly; some, because I like one or two lines in them, or because I liked the emotion expressed. Some were written with practically no corrections or consideration, others

7 Against this L has written 'You hope.'
8 L's footnote: 'including a Shakespearean sonnet which began:

"In any garden full of scented blooms
    There will be one rose, most surpassing fair,
O'ertopping every other by its plumes,
    To Summer's crown of glory certain heir . . ."'

were carefully premeditated and worked out. But in any case, they will always be of interest to myself, who wrote them, for whom they were written, and for whom this selection is primarily intended.

April, 1941.
Warwick.

CONTENTS

He was safe' [from *PAug40*]

Seven Poems

HULL DPL 2/1/6

The collection in fact contains eight poems, owing to the addition of the last (unnumbered) poem.

L's prefatory note:

Another collection, ranging in time from the last one (April, 1941) to the end of the year. Surprisingly little produced: I suspect some is lost or not to hand.

    Same faults: too much Auden, and all that implies.

        P. A. L.

        Warwick,

        January, 1942.

CONTENTS

The Seventh Collection

HULL DPL 2/1/7

'the seventh collection | being | poems | by| philip larkin | July 1942.'

L's prefatory note:

This collection covers the period from April to July the tenth of this year, with the exception of poems II and IV, written in 1940 and 1941 respectively.

Warwick, July 1942.

CONTENTS

Sugar and Spice

BODLEIAN MS ENG. C. 2356; HULL DPL (2) 1/11

A Sheaf of Poems by Brunette Coleman.

The title-page bears the nursery rhyme:

What are little boys made of, made of?
What are little boys made of?
Snaps and snails, and puppy-dogs' tails;
And that's what little boys are made of, made of.

What are little girls made of, made of?

What are little girls made of?
Sugar and spice, and all that's nice;
And that's what little girls are made of, made of.
    (Rhyme taught to children.)

After this is the date '– September 1943 –'

    L's preface:

These poems were all written in the August and September of this
year, and I make no apology for presenting a collection of what
may seem 'trivia' in these disturbed times. I feel that now more
than ever a firm grasp on the essentials of life is needed.
    The two poems with titles in the French language are suggested,
of course, by their namesakes by François[9] Villon and Charles
Baudelaire, but they are not, of course, 'renderings' in any sense.
In my opinion they are improvements.
    Finally, I dedicate this slim volume to all my sister-writers, with
the exception of Margaret Kennedy, who wrote in *The Constant
Nymph*: 'English schoolgirls are not interesting.'
        Brunette Coleman, 1943.[10]

CONTENTS
The False Friend: 'It's no good standing there and looking haughty'
Bliss: 'In the pocket of my blazer'
Femmes Damnées: 'The fire is ash: the early morning sun'
Ballade des Dames du Temps Jadis: 'Tell me, into what far lands'
Holidays: 'Let's go to Stratford-on-Avon, and see a play!'
The School in August: 'The cloakroom pegs are empty now'
Fourth Former Loquitur: 'A group of us have flattened the long
    grass' [appended in MS in Hull DPL (2) 1/11; not represented in
    Bodl. MS Eng. c. 2356].

9 I have added a cedilla to 'Francois'.
10 Blanche Coleman (1910–2008) was the leader of an all-female British jazz band
which was famous in the 1940s. Motion (1993), 86, 101, notes L's adaptation of the
name.

II DATES OF COMPOSITION

This table is designed to give a sense of what Larkin was working on at a given time, and to record something of the relation of published to unpublished poems. When two dates are given, the first represents the earliest point of composition and the second the latest. In some cases the second date is that of final publication, though a poem may have been substantially drafted before then; Larkin usually made revisions (adding titles, for instance) before publication. Sometimes the dates give an indication of the points between which a poem was composed; sometimes, they represent the precise points of starting and completion. More detailed information is supplied in the notes on individual poems in the commentary.

1936
'Who's that guy hanging on a rail?'

1938
Coventria (early)
Winter Nocturne (?summer). Publ. Dec.
Fragment from May Publ. Dec.

1938–9
Thought Somewhere in France 1917 (?winter)
'What the half-open door said to the empty room . . .'

1939
Summer Nocturne Publ. Apr.
Butterflies (spring/summer)
A Meeting – Et Seq. (2) (spring/summer)
The Ships at Mylae (8 July)
Alvis Victrix (12 July)
Stanley en Musique (15 July)
Founder's Day (summer, *c.*23 July)
Collected Fragments (summer)
'The sun was battling to close our eyes' (before 9 Aug.)
Chorus from a Masque (Aug.)
Stanley et la Glace (14 Sept.)
Erotic Play (19 Sept.)
The Days of thy Youth (25 June–9 Sept.)

Street Lamps Publ. Sept.
(À un ami qui aime.) (Sept.–Oct.)
'The grinding halt of plant, and clicking stiles' (Sept.–Oct.)
'Smash all the mirrors in your home' (Sept.–Oct.)
'Watch, my dear, the darkness now' (Sept.–Oct.)
'Has all History rolled to bring us here?' (Sept.–Oct.)
'In a second I knew it was your voice speaking' (Sept.–Oct.)
(A Study in Light and Dark) (Sept.–Oct.)
'Within, a voice said: Cry!' (Sept.–Oct.)
'What is the difference between December and January?' (Sept.–
  Oct.)
To a Friend's Acquaintance (Sept.–Oct.)
To a Friend (Sept.–Oct.)
A Farewell (Sept.–Oct.)
Young Woman's Blues (Sept.–Oct.)
'Lie there, my tumbled thoughts' (Sept.–Oct)
'Now the shadows that fall from the hills' (Sept.– Oct.)
'The pistol now again is raised' (Sept.–Oct.)
'Autumn has caught us in our summer wear' (late)
Evensong (?late)
'This is one of those whiteghosted mornings'
'We see the spring breaking across rough stone'
'Why did I dream of you last night?'

1940
'The cycles hiss on the road away from the factory' (8 Feb.)
'So you have been, despite paternal ban' (16 Mar.)
'Through darkness of sowing' (18 Mar.)
'Falling of these early flowers' (Sept.–Oct. 1939–28 Mar. 1940)
'Praise to the higher organisms!' (Sept.–Oct. 1939–28 Mar. 1940)
'(from James Hogg) | Lock the door, Lariston, lock it, I say to you'
  (Sept.–Oct. 1939–28 Mar. 1940)
'Turning from obscene verses to the stars' (Sept.–Oct. 1939–28 Mar.
  1940)
'Autumn sees the sun low in the sky' (Sept.–Oct. 1939–28 Mar.
  1940)
Prologue (before 28 Mar.)
'Standing on love's farther shores' (before 28 Mar.)
Epilogue (before 28 Mar.)
Remark (10 Apr.)
Long Jump (21 Apr.)
Spring Warning Publ. Apr.

'Quests are numerous; for the far acid strand' (4 May)
'For the mind to betray' (10 June)
'For who will deny' (10 June)
Poem ('Still beauty') (12 June)
Midsummer Night, 1940 (c.24 June)
Two Sonnets I The Conscript II The Conscientious Objector (before July)
Further Afterdinner Remarks (before July)
Historical Fact: (before July)
'But as to the real truth, who knows? The earth' (before July)
'It is late: the moon regards the city' (by 23 Aug.)
'A birthday, yes, a day without rain' (by 23 Aug.)
'Art is not clever' (before Sept.)
'O today is everywhere' (before Sept.)
Creative Joy (before Sept.)
'The spaniel on the tennis court' (before Sept.)
Schoolmaster (before Sept.)
'When we broke up, I walked alone' (before Sept.)
'From the window at sundown' (before Sept.)
'You've only one life and you'd better not lose it' (before Sept.)
'The question of poetry, of course' (before Sept.)
Rupert Brooke (before Sept.)
Postscript | On Imitating Auden (before Sept.)
'The earliest machine was simple' (autumn)
Last Will and Testament Publ. Sept.
'Mr A. J. Wilton' (late Nov.)
'There's a high percentage of bastards' (19 Dec.)
Christmas 1940 (19 Dec.)
Ghosts (by 20 Dec.)
Poem ('Walking on summer grass beneath the trees') (?late)
Prayer of a Plum (?1940)
'A bird sings at the garden's end' (?1940)
'I should be glad to be in at the death' (?1940)
Chant (?1940)
Hard Lines, or Mean Old W. H. Thomas Blues (?1940)

1941
'O won't it be just posh' (5 Feb.)
'Having grown up in shade of Church and State' (8 June 1939–30 Apr. 1941)
'When the night puts twenty veils' (before Sept. 1939–30 Apr. 1941)
'Nothing significant was really said' (18 Mar. 1940–30 Apr. 1941)

'Prince, fortune is accepted among these rooms' (before 28 Mar.
    1940–30 Apr. 1941)
'The hills in their recumbent postures' (before 28 Mar. 1940–30 Apr.
    1941)
'At once he realised that the thrilling night' (?before 10 June 1940–
    30 Apr. 1941)
After-Dinner Remarks (before July 1940–30 Apr. 1941)
Ultimatum (before July 1940–30 Apr. 1941). Publ. 28 Nov. 1940.
'Unexpectedly the scene attained' (before Sept. 1940–30 Apr. 1941)
'There are moments like music, minutes' (before Sept. 1940–30 Apr.
    1941)
'Could wish to lose hands' (before Sept. 1940–30 Apr. 1941)
Story (Oct. 1940–Apr. 1941). Publ. 13 Feb. 1941.
'There is no language of destruction for' (?late 1940–30 Apr. 1941)
'Out in the lane I pause: the night' (18–19 Dec. 1940–30 Apr. 1941)
New Year Poem (31 Dec. 1940–30 Apr. 1941)
'Evening, and I, young' (by 30 Apr.)
'Stranger, do not linger' (by 30 Apr.)
The Poet's Last Poem (by 30 Apr.)
'The world in its flowing is various; as tides' (by 30 Apr.)
'Time and Space were only their disguises' (by 30 Apr.)
'The house on the edge of the serious wood' (by 30 Apr.)
'Out of this came danger' (by 30 Apr.)
The Dead City: A Vision (?by 30 Apr.)
A Writer (before Apr.–8 May). Publ. 8 May.
'At school, the acquaintance' (by 21 May)
'The wind at creep of dawn' (by 15 June)
'Those who are born to rot, decay' (?Oct.)
Observation (Apr.–22 Nov.) Publ. 22 Nov.
'O what ails thee, bloody sod' (4 Dec.)
'After the casual growing-up' (before 21 May–31 Dec. 1941)
May Weather (before 5 June–31 Dec. 1941). Publ. 5 June 1941
'There behind the intricate carving' (15 June–31 Dec. 1941)
'Sailors brought back strange stories of those lands' (Apr.–18 Nov.–
    31 Dec. 1941)
Dances in Doggerel (Apr.–Dec.–31 Dec. 1941)
Lines after Blake (Apr.–Dec.–31 Dec. 1941)

1942
Disintegration Publ. Feb. 1942
'I don't like March' (by 7 Mar.)
'The doublehanded kiss and the brainwet hatred' (Mar.)

'A day has fallen past' (Apr.)
'If days were matches I would strike the lot' (Apr.)
'I walk at random through the evening park' (Apr.)
'At the flicker of a letter' (?late Nov. 1940–10 July 1942)
'Where should we lie, green heart' (Apr.–10 July)
'I am the latest son' (Apr.–10 July)
'This triumph ended in the curtained head' (Apr.–10 July)
'The sun swings near the earth' (Apr.–10 July)
Leave (Apr.–10 July)
'As the pool hits the diver, or the white cloud' (Apr.–10 July)
'Flesh to flesh was loving from the start' (Apr.–10 July)
July Miniatures (Apr.–10 July)
'Blind through the shouting sun' (Apr.–10 July)
The Returning (Apr.–10 July)
Now (?mid-1942)
'The poet has a straight face' (23 Apr. 1940–9 Aug. 1942)
To James Sutton | *Poem* (by 17 Aug.)
'Llandovery' (14 July–20 Aug. 1942)
Fuel Form Blues (by 20 Aug. 1942)
Poem ('I met an idiot at a bend in the lane') (20 Aug.)
'The canal stands through the fields; another' (23–28 Aug. 1942)
Planes Passing (?1940–?31 Aug. 1942)
'As a war in years of peace' (Aug. 1940–15 Sept. 1942)
A Member of the 1922 Class Looks to the Future (?late)
A Member of the 1922 Class Reads the 1942 Newspapers (?late)
A Democrat to Others (?late)
'After a particularly good game of rugger' (by 8 Nov.)
Poem ('The camera of the eye') (*c*.Dec.)

1943
'(from the back) | We're Middleton Murry & Somerset Maugham'
    (by 2 Jan.)
Mythological Introduction Publ. Mar., and 12 June.
Songs of Innocence and Inexperience (Oct. 1940–June 1943)
'If approached by Sir Cyril Norwood' (Oct. 1940–June 1943)
A Stone Church Damaged by a Bomb Publ. 12 June.
Letters (?June)
Blues (12 July)
'The – er – university of Stockholm – er –' (28 July)
The False Friend (Aug.–13 Sept.)
Bliss (Aug.–13 Sept.)
Ballade des Dames du Temps Jadis (Aug.–13 Sept.)

Holidays (Aug.–13 Sept.)

The School in August (Aug.–13 Sept.)

Femmes Damnées (Aug.–13 Sept.). Publ. 1978.

Fourth Former Loquitur (?Aug.–Sept.)

'I would give all I possess' (early Oct.)

'Sent you a letter, but it had to go by boat' (by 25 Oct.)

'The wind that blows from Morpeth' (8 Nov.)

Address to Life, by a Young Man Seeking a Career (before Sept. 1940–postscript, 29 Nov. 1943)

'What ant crawls behind the picture?' (?1943)

'Someone stole a march on the composer' (?1943)

'Did you hear his prayer, God?' (?1943)

Leap Year (?1943)

'Some large man had a pendulous eyeball' (?1943)

1943–4

End (?1943–4)

On Poetry (?1943–4)

Inscription on a Clockface (?1943–4)

'Wall up the day in words' (?1943–4)

'Kick up the fire, and let the flames break loose' (?1943–4). Publ. in *TNS*.

'Morning has spread again' (?1943–4). Publ. Feb. 1945, then in *TNS*.

'To write one song, I said' (?1943–4). Publ. in *TNS*.

'This is the first thing' (?1943–4). Publ. in *TNS*.

'There is snow in the sky'

'If I saw the sky in flames'

'When this face was younger'

'Honour William Yeats for this success'

Poem ('Summer extravagances shrink:')

1944

'If I wrote like D. H. Lawrence, I wouldn't need to drink no beer' (12 Mar.)

Poem ('Last night, by a restless bed') (15 Apr.)

Girl Saying Goodbye (by 21 Apr.)

'Mary Cox in tennis shorts' (1 July)

'Small paths lead away' (29 Aug.)

'Sheaves under the moon in ghostly fruitfulness' (6 Oct.)

[*Crewe*] (by 3 Nov.)

'Why should I be out walking' (2–9 Nov.)

'We are the night-shite shifters shifting the shite by night and
  shouting' (10 Dec.)

1945
'Snow has brought the winter to my door' (8 Jan.)
To S. L. (8–13 Jan.)
'Because the images would not fit' (13–14 Jan.)
'Days like a handful of grey pearls' (14–16 Jan.)
'Numberless blades of grass' (16–19 Jan.)
'Draw close around you' (5–14 Feb.)
'I have despatched so many words' (25–6 Feb.)
'Where was this silence learned' (27 Feb.)
'So through that unripe day you bore your head' (Aug. 1942–28
  Feb. 1945). Publ. Feb. 1945, then in *TNS*.
'All catches alight' (by 21 Apr. 1944–28 Feb. 1945). Publ. Feb.
  1945, then in *TNS*.
'The moon is full tonight' (1943–4–28 Feb. 1945). Publ. Feb., then
  in *TNS*.
'The bottle is drunk out by one' (?1943–4–28 Feb. 1945). Publ.
  Feb., then in *TNS*.
'Love, we must part now, do not let it be' (?1943–4–28 Feb. 1945).
  Publ. Feb., then in *TNS*.
'Ride with me down into the spring' (1–16 Mar.)
'Safely evening behind the window' (16 Mar.–11 Apr.)
Song with a Spoken Refrain (10 June)
'Happiness is a flame' (25 June–2 July)
'Lie with me, though the night return outside' (2 July)
'When trees are quiet, there will be no more weeping' (22–4 July)
Conscript (5 June 1941–31 July 1945). Publ. Oct.–Nov. 1941,
  then, revised, in *TNS*. 'This was your place of birth' (publ. 28 Feb.
  1942–31 July 1945). Publ., revised, in *TNS*
'I dreamed of an out-thrust arm of land' (Mar. 1943–31 July 1945).
  Publ. Mar. 1943 and June 1945, then, revised, in *TNS*.
Winter (?1943–4–31 July 1945). Publ. in *TNS*.
'Like the train's beat' (?1943–4–31 July 1945). Publ. in *TNS*.
'I put my mouth' (?1943–4–31 July 1945). Publ. 28 Feb. 1945, then,
  revised, in *TNS*.
'The horns of the morning' (?1943–4–31 July 1945). Publ. Feb.
  1945, then, revised, in *TNS*.
The Dancer (?1943–4–31 July 1945). Publ. in *TNS*.
Ugly Sister (?1943–4–31 July 1945). Publ. in *TNS*.

'If hands could free you, heart' (?1943–4–31 July 1945). Publ. in
   TNS.
'Is it for now or for always' (?1943–4–31 July 1945). Publ. in TNS.
'Pour away that youth' (?1943–4–31 July 1945). Publ. in TNS.
Dawn (?1943–4–31 July 1945). Publ. in TNS.
Nursery Tale (Aug. 1944–31 July 1945). Publ. in TNS.
'If grief could burn out' (5 Oct. 1944–31 July 1945). Publ. in TNS.
The North Ship. Legend (6 Oct. 1944–31 July 1945). Publ. in TNS.
'Within the dream you said' (by 8 Oct. 1944–31 July 1945). Publ. in
   TNS.
Night-Music (8 Oct. 1944–31 July 1945). Publ. in TNS.
'Climbing the hill within the deafening wind' (12 Oct. 1944–31 July
   1945). Publ. in TNS.
The North Ship. 65°N (23 Oct. 1944–31 July 1945). Publ. in TNS.
The North Ship. 75°N Blizzard (27 Oct. 1944–31 July 1945). Publ.
   in TNS.
The North Ship. Above 80°N (29 Oct. 1944–31 July 1945). Publ. in
   TNS.
The North Ship. 70°N Fortunetelling (31 Oct. 1944–31 July 1945).
   Publ. in TNS.
'The dead are lost, unravelled; but if a voice' (20–3 Aug.)
'Lift through the breaking day' (23–7 Aug.)
'Past days of gales' (7–17 Oct.)
'The cry I would hear' (17–24 Oct.)
'Who whistled for the wind, that it should break' (14–15 Dec.)

1946
'Sky tumbles, the sea' (23 Feb.–26 Apr.)
'Sting in the shell' (15 May)
'A stick's-point, drawn' (30 May–3 June)
'There is no clearer speaking' (12 June)
Plymouth (10 June 1945–25 June 1946). Publ. May 1946.
'THE MAYOR OF BRISTOL WAS DRINKING GIN' (17 July)
Beggars (19 Jan. 1945–6 Oct. 1946)
'When the tide draws out' (27 Aug. 1945–6 Oct. 1946)
Blues Shouter (5 Oct.–8 Nov.)
'That girl is lame: look at my rough' (8–13 Nov.)
'Voices round a light' (15 Nov.–17 Dec.)

1947
Laforgue (11 Jan.)
'And did you once see Russell plain?' (11 Jan.)
'From this day forward, may you find'

1948

'Heaviest of flowers, the head' (?1943–4–early 1948). Publ. in *TNS*. Revised in *ITGOL*.

Winter (?1943–4–early 1948). Publ. in *TNS*. Revised in *ITGOL*.

'One man walking a deserted platform' (by 5 Oct. 1944–early 1948). Publ. in *TNS*. Revised in *ITGOL*.

'Within the dream you said' (5 Oct. 1944–early 1948). Publ. in *TNS*. Revised in *ITGOL*.

Night-Music (5 Oct. 1944–early 1948). Publ. in *TNS*. Revised in *ITGOL*.

'Coming at last to night's most thankful springs' (27 Feb. 1945–early 1948).

Portrait (7 Oct. 1945–early 1948). Publ. May 1946. Revised in *ITGOL*.

Deep Analysis (15 Dec. 1945–early 1948)

'Come then to prayers' (13 May 1946–early 1948)

'And the wave sings because it is moving' (14 May 1946–early 1948)

Two Guitar Pieces (14 May 1946–early 1948)

Träumerei (26 Sept. 1946–early 1948)

To A Very Slow Air (28 Sept. 1946–early 1948)

'At the chiming of light upon sleep' (29 Sept. 1946–early 1948)

'Many famous feet have trod' (4 Oct. 1946–early 1948)

Thaw (17 Dec. 1946–early 1948)

'An April Sunday brings the snow' (4 Apr.)

'And yet – but after death there's no "and yet"' (Apr.)

1949

'I am washed upon a rock' (18 Mar.)

Neurotics (18 Mar.–13 May)

On Being Twenty-six (18 Mar.–13 May)

'Sinking like sediment through the day' (13 May)

'In our family' (13 May)

To Failure (17–18 May)

Epigram on an Academic Marriage (19 May)

My Home (?May)

1950

Compline (12 Feb.)

How to Sleep (8–10 Mar.)

The Literary World (17–20 Mar.)

Strangers (19–23 May)

'Under a splendid chestnut tree' (28 May–17 July)

'Westminster's crown has gained a special jewel' (28 Nov.)

'Teevan touched pitch: the pitch was very wild' (18 Dec.)
The Spirit Wooed (?1950)

1951
To My Wife (6 Feb.–19 Mar.)
The Dedicated (18 Sept. 1946–27 Apr. 1951). Publ. privately 27
  Apr. (*XX Poems*).
Wedding-Wind (26 Sept. 1946–27 Apr. 1951). Publ. privately 27
  Apr. (*XX Poems*), then in *TLD*.
'Waiting for breakfast while she brushed her hair' (15 Dec. 1947–27
  Apr. 1951). Publ. privately 27 Apr. (*XX Poems*), then in July 1956,
  then in *TNS* (Sept. 1966).
Modesties (18 Mar. 1949–27 Apr. 1951). Publ. privately 27 Apr.
  (*XX Poems*), then in autumn 1958.
At Grass (?Dec. 1949–27 Apr. 1951). Publ. privately 27 Apr.
  (*XX Poems*), then Mar. 1954, then in *TLD*.
Oils (12 Mar. 1950–27 Apr. 1951). Publ. privately 27 Apr. (*XX
  Poems*).
Spring (20 Mar. 1950–27 Apr. 1951). Publ. privately 27 Apr.
  (*XX Poems*), then in *TLD*.
Wants (28 May 1950–27 Apr. 1951). Publ. privately 27 Apr.
  (*XX Poems*), then in *TLD*.
'Who called love conquering' (2 June 1950–27 Apr. 1951).
  Publ. privately 27 Apr. (*XX Poems*).
Arrival (28 Oct. 1950–27 Apr. 1951). Publ. privately 27 Apr.
  (*XX Poems*).
'Since the majority of me' (4 Nov. 1950–27 Apr. 1951).
  Publ. privately 27 Apr.
March Past (19 Mar.–*c*.25 May)
Marriages (25 May–12 June)
'To put one brick upon another' (?1951)
Maturity (?1951)

1952
'You think yourself no end of fun' (20 Feb.)
'Somewhere on the Isle of Mull'

1953
'When she came on you couldn't keep your seat' (24 Jan.–Feb.)
'At thirty-one, when some are rich' (18 Aug.–19 Sept.)
Wires (4 Nov. 1950–2 Oct. 1953). Publ. 2 Oct. 1953, then in *TLD*.
Mother, Summer, I (18 Aug.–5 Oct.)
Autumn (5–13 Oct.)

Best Society (13–22 Oct.)
Unfinished Poem (22 Aug. 1951–26 Oct. 1953)
Hospital Visits (26 Oct.–4 Nov.)
Autobiography at an Air-Station (4 Nov.–c.10 Dec.)
Negative Indicative (6–29 Dec.)

1954
Love ('Not love you? Dear, I'd pay ten quid for you') (31 Dec.
  1953–8 Jan. 1954)
Marriage (8–27 Jan.)
Midwinter Waking (23–7 Jan.)
Fiction and the Reading Public (13 May 1949–31 Jan. 1954). Publ.
  Jan. 1954.
Latest Face (10 Jan. 1951–5 Mar. 1954). Publ. privately 27 Apr.
  1951 (*XX Poems*), then, revised, 5 Mar. 1954, then in *TLD*.
'Those who give all for love, or art, or duty' (13 Mar.)
Gathering Wood (16–25 Mar.)
If, My Darling (20 May 1950–31 Mar. 1954). Publ. privately 27
  Apr. 1951 (*XX Poems*), then, revised, in Mar. 1954, then in *TLD*.
Arrivals, Departures (22 Jan. 1953–31 Mar. 1954). Publ. Mar. 1954,
  autumn 1955, and in *TLD*.
Lines on a Young Lady's Photograph Album (17 Aug. 1953–31 Mar.
  1954). Publ. Mar. 1954, then in *TLD*.
Whatever Happened? (24 Oct. 1953–31 Mar. 1954). Publ. Mar.
  1954, then in *TLD*.
Triple Time (12 June 1951–30 Apr. 1954). Publ. 28 Jan. and 30 Apr.
  1954, then in *TLD*.
'Long roots moor summer to our side of earth' (26 May–14 June)
Skin (13 Mar.–2 July). Publ. 2 July, then in *TLD*.
Age (24 May–2 July). Publ. 2 July, then in *TLD*.
'What have I done to be thirty-two?' (by 10 Aug.)
'Is your field sunny?' (28 July–27 Aug.)
Boars Hill (Sept.)
Christmas (Christmas)

1955
A Sense of Shape (10 Oct. 1954–13 May 1955)
Long Sight in Age (13–20 June)
Mr Bleaney (13 May–8 Sept.). Publ. 8 Sept., then in *TWW*.
The Importance of Elsewhere (27 May–8 Sept.). Publ. 8 Sept., then
  in *TWW*.
Counting (c.11 Sept.)
'Back to this dreary dump' (26 Sept.)

Going (15 Dec. 1945–24 Nov. 1955). Publ. privately 27 Apr. 1951
(*XX Poems*), then, revised, in *TLD*.

Deceptions (20 Feb. 1950–24 Nov. 1955). Publ. privately 27 Apr.
1951 (*XX Poems*), then, revised, in *TLD*.

Coming (25 Feb. 1950–24 Nov. 1955). Publ. privately 27 Apr. 1951
(*XX Poems*), then, revised, in *TLD*.

Dry-Point (12 Mar. 1950–24 Nov. 1955). Publ. privately 27 Apr.
1951 (*XX Poems*), in summer 1954, then, revised, in *TLD*.

No Road (5 Aug. 1950–24 Nov. 1955). Publ. privately 27 Apr. 1951
(*XX Poems*), in summer 1955, then, revised, in *TLD*.

Absences (4 Nov. 1950–24 Nov. 1955). Publ. in *TLD*.

Next, Please (1 Jan. 1951–24 Nov. 1955). Publ. privately 27 Apr.
1951 (*XX Poems*), in spring 1955, then, revised, in *TLD*.

Myxomatosis (15 Nov. 1953–24 Nov. 1955). Publ. 26 Nov. 1954,
then, revised, in *TLD*.

Reasons for Attendance (28 Dec. 1953–24 Nov. 1955). Publ. in
TLD.

I Remember, I Remember (8 Jan. 1954–24 Nov. 1955). Publ.
autumn 1955, then, revised, in *TLD*.

Born Yesterday (17 Jan. 1954–24 Nov. 1955). Publ. 30 July 1954,
then, revised, in *TLD*.

Poetry of Departures (20 Jan. 1954–24 Nov. 1955). Publ. 10 June
and winter 1954, on 8 Sept. 1955, then, revised, in *TLD*.

Toads (13 Mar. 1954–24 Nov. 1955). Publ. summer 1954, then,
revised, in *TLD*.

Church Going (24 Apr. 1954–24 Nov. 1955). Publ. 18 Nov. 1955,
then, revised, in *TLD*.

Places, Loved Ones (27 Aug. 1954–24 Nov. 1955). Publ. 7 Jan.
1955, then, revised, in *TLD*.

Maiden Name (14 Nov. 1954–24 Nov. 1955). Publ. in *TLD*.

1956

Ignorance (21 Aug. 1955–summer 1956). Publ. summer, then in
TWW.

'The local snivels through the fields' (18–27 Aug.)

Getting Somewhere (18–27 Aug.)

To Hart Crane (18–27 Aug.)

A Midland Syllogism (18–27 Aug.)

Outcome of a Conversation (18–27 Aug.)

The Wild Ones (18–27 Aug.)

Travellers (18–27 Aug.)

Behind Time (18–27 Aug.)

'You'll do anything for money' (29 Nov.)
For Sidney Bechet (6 Dec. 1953–30 Nov. 1956). Publ. Nov., then in
  TWW.

To +++++ ++++++ and others (4–5 Dec.)

1957
Pigeons (27 Dec. 1955–30 Jan. 1957). Publ. Jan. 1957.
Tops (22 Sept. 1953–spring 1957). Publ. spring 1957.
Days (6 Feb. 1951–summer/autumn 1957). Publ. summer–autumn,
  then in *TWW*.
Success Story (27 Jan. 1954–winter 1957/8). Publ. Feb. 1957, then,
  revised, winter 1957/8.

1958
'Get Kingsley Amis to sleep with your wife' (29 Jan.)
'Oh who is this feeling my prick?' (spring)
'Her birthday always has' (by 6 May)
'My name it is Benjamin Bunny' (by 3 Nov.)
'Snow has covered up our track' (14 Dec.)

1959
Far Out (8 Jan.–1 Feb.)
'Not to worry, Len's having a dip' (16 Feb.)
'Let there be an empty space where *Rabbit* used to stand' (21 Feb.)
'Let the classroom dais be empty where the rabbit used to thump'
  (11 Mar.)
Home is so Sad (29 Dec. 1958–18 June 1959). Publ. 18 June, then in
  TWW.
The Whitsun Weddings (14 May 1957–30 June 1959). Publ. 30
  June, then in *TWW*.
'They are all gone into the world of light' (13 Aug.)
'Homeward, rabbit, homeward go' (19 Aug.)
'"Living for others," (others say) "is best"' (14 Sept.)
'A *Lecturer* in drip-dry shirt arrayed' (*c.*7 Oct.)
Letter to a Friend about Girls (16 Oct. 1957–31 Dec. 1959)

1960
'None of the books have time' (17–18 Jan.)
Goodnight World (7 Mar.)
'Great baying groans burst from my lips' (30 Mar.)
Faith Healing (19 Mar.–21 July). Publ. 21 July, then in *TWW*.
MCMXIV (17 Oct. 1956–10 Oct. 1960). Publ. 10 Oct., then in
  TWW.
'A sit-on-the-fence old gull' (by 22 Nov.)

A Study of Reading Habits (19 Aug.–winter). Publ. winter, then in *TWW.*

1961
Naturally the Foundation will Bear Your Expenses (14 Nov. 1960–11 Feb. 1961). Publ. July 1961, then in *TWW.*
Ambulances (29 Nov. 1960–30 Apr. 1961). Publ. Apr., then in *TWW.*
'BJ's the man in charge' (12 Oct.)
'Hotter shorter days arrive, like happiness' (9–13 Oct.)
'And now the leaves suddenly lose strength' (25 Oct.–3 Nov.)
Breadfruit (19 Nov.). Publ., revised, winter 1961.

1962
January (7–13 Jan.)
'Sir George Grouse to Sir Wm Gull' (13 Jan.)
Broadcast (5 Nov. 1961–25 Jan. 1962). Publ. 25 Jan., then in *TWW.*
'Sir George Grouse to Sir Wm Gull' [second version] (31 Jan.)
Nothing to be Said (18 Oct. 1961–28 Feb. 1962). Publ. Feb., then in *TWW.*
'Chaps who live in California' (7 Mar.)
'Praise God from whom all blessings flow' (16 Sept.)
'Sitting across the aisle' (21 Sept.)
Send No Money (27 Sept. 1960–18 Nov. 1962). Publ. 18 Nov., then in *TWW.*
Toads Revisited (21 Sept.–23 Nov.). Publ. 23 Nov., then in *TWW.*

1963
Long Last (13 Jan.–18 Mar.)
Dockery and Son (13 May 1962–11 Apr. 1963). Publ. 11 Apr., then in *TWW.*
'Castle Park Dean and Hook' (?July)
Take One Home for the Kiddies (6 Apr. 1954–5 Dec. 1963). Publ. 5 Dec., then in *TWW.*
As Bad as a Mile (4 Feb. 1960–12 Dec. 1963). Publ. 28 Mar. 1960, then, revised, on 12 Dec. 1963, then in *TWW.*

1964
Love Songs in Age (2 Feb. 1953–28 Feb. 1964). Publ. in *TWW.*
Water (5 Apr. 1954–28 Feb. 1964). Publ. summer–autumn 1957, then, revised, in *TWW.*
Reference Back (20 June 1955–28 Feb. 1964). Publ. autumn 1955 and summer 1958, then, revised, in *TWW.*

An Arundel Tomb (11 Sept. 1955–28 Feb. 1964). Publ. May 1956,
  Easter 1957 and again in 1957, then, revised, in *TWW*.
First Sight (20 Feb. 1956–28 Feb. 1964). Publ. 13 July 1956, then,
  revised, in *TWW*.
Self's the Man (5 Nov. 1958–28 Feb. 1964). Publ. in *TWW*.
Talking in Bed (5 June 1959–28 Feb. 1964). Publ. winter 1960,
  then, revised, in *TWW*.
Afternoons (30 Aug. 1959–28 Feb. 1964). Publ. spring 1960, then,
  revised, in *TWW*.
The Large Cool Store (16 May 1961–28 Feb. 1964). Publ. 14 July
  1961, then, revised, in *TWW*.
Here (6 Sept. 1961–28 Feb. 1964). Publ. 24 Nov. 1961, then,
  revised, in *TWW*.
Wild Oats (10 May 1962–28 Feb. 1964). Publ. Feb. 1963, then,
  revised, in *TWW*.
Essential Beauty (28 May 1962–28 Feb. 1964). Publ. 5 Oct. 1962,
  then, revised, in *TWW*.
Sunny Prestatyn (16 Oct. 1962–28 Feb. 1964). Publ. Jan. 1963,
  then, revised, in *TWW*.
'I would I were where Russell plays' (22 Aug. 1951–13 Oct. 1964)

1965
Laboratory Monkeys (12–24 Feb.)
'O wha will o'er the downs with me' (23 Apr.)

1966
'Welcome 1966!' (2 Jan.)
'Lowell, Lowell, Lowell, Lowell' (5 Mar.)
'Scratch on the scratch pad' (20 May–19 July)
'Then the students cursing and grumbling' (19 Nov.)
'Fill up the glasses, since we're here for life' (7 Dec.)
'Here's a health to the Squire' (by 19 Dec.)
Love ('The difficult part of love') (7 Nov. 1962–after summer 1966).
  Publ. summer 1966.

1967
The Dance (30 June 1963–1 Feb. 1967)
'High o'er the fence leaps Soldier Jim' (23 July)
How Distant (20 Nov. 1965–26 Oct. 1967). Publ. 26 Oct. 1967,
  then in *HW*.
Sympathy in White Major (4 Aug. 1966–30 Dec. 1967). Publ. Dec.
  1967, then in *HW*.
'In Xanadu did Kubla Khan' (?1967)

1968

The Trees (9 Apr. 1967–17 May 1968). Publ. 17 May 1968, then in HW.

High Windows (3 Mar. 1965–spring–summer 1968). Publ. spring–summer 1968, then in HW.

Sad Steps (7 Mar.–28 June). Publ. 28 June, then in HW.

Posterity (24 Apr.–28 June). Publ. 28 June, then in HW.

Friday Night in the Royal Station Hotel (25 Apr. 1966–autumn 1968). Publ. 7 Jan. 1967, then, revised, in autumn 1968, then in HW.

'At the sign of The Old Farting Arse' (27 Oct.–10 Nov.)

'After drinking Glenfiddich' (24 Nov.)

'Morning, noon & bloody night' (27 Nov.)

'The world's great age begins anew' (8 Dec.)

1969

Homage to a Government (31 Jan. 1968–15 Jan. 1969). Publ. 19 Jan. 1969, then in HW.

'See the Pope of Ulster stand' (3 Feb.)

'When the Russian tanks roll westward' (18 Mar.). Publ. 1969.

'I dreamed I saw a commie rally' (6 Apr.)

Holiday (14 Sept. 1962–3 Dec. 1969)

1970

Annus Mirabilis (16 June 1967–31 Jan. 1970). Publ. Feb. 1968, then, revised, in Jan. 1970, then in HW.

To the Sea (14 Sept. 1969–31 Jan. 1970). Publ. Jan. 1970, then in HW.

'When Coote roared: "Mitchell, what about this jazz?"' (Feb.). Publ. 1982.

'The polyp comes & goes' (?6 Apr.)

How to Win the Next Election (5 Apr. 1966–19 June 1970)

'The flag you fly for us is furled' (22–27 Aug.)

How (10 Apr.–autumn). Publ. autumn 1970.

The Manciple's Tale (17 Sept.)

The Card-Players (3 May–31 Oct.). Publ. Oct., then in HW.

Dublinesque (1 June–31 Oct.). Publ. Oct., then in HW.

'Sod the lower classes' (9 Dec.)

Poem about Oxford (?1943–Christmas 1970)

1971

Light, Clouds, Dwelling-places (17 Jan. 1962–1 Feb. 1971)

Vers de Société (4 Nov. 1964–18 June 1971). Publ. 18 June 1971, then in HW.

Cut Grass (2 June–29 July). Publ. 29 July, then in *HW*.

Forget What Did (30 Jan. 1967–19 Aug. 1971). Publ. in *HW*.

This Be The Verse (14 Apr.–31 Aug.). Publ. Aug., then in *HW*.

'I have started to say' (7–11 Oct.)

'When the lead says goonight to the copper' (26 Oct.)

'Sherry does more than Bovril can' (31 Oct.)

1972

Livings I (19 Sept. 1971–28 Feb. 1972). Publ. Feb. 1972, then in *HW*.

Livings II (16 Oct. 1971–28 Feb. 1972). Publ. Feb. 1972, then in *HW*.

Livings III (23 Nov. 1971–28 Feb. 1972). Publ. Feb. 1972, then in *HW*.

The Building (17 Jan. 1962–17 Mar. 1972). Publ. 17 Mar. 1972, then in *HW*.

Heads in the Women's Ward (6 Mar.–31 May). Publ. May 1972.

The Explosion (7 Dec. 1969–17 Aug. 1972). Publ. 17 Aug. 1972, then in *HW*.

1973

The Old Fools (12 Aug. 1972–1 Feb. 1973). Publ. 1 Feb. 1973, then in *HW*.

Continuing to Live (18 Apr. 1954–5 Oct. 1973). Publ. 5 Oct. 1973.

Money (11 Feb. 1973–autumn–winter 1973/4). Publ. autumn/winter 1973/4, then in *HW*.

'This was Mr Bleaney's bungalow' (30 Dec.)

1974

'It's plain that Marleen and Patricia would' (26 Apr.)

Solar (6 Oct. 1964–3 June 1974). Publ. 25 May 1966, then, revised, in *HW*.

Going, Going (10 Jan. 1972–3 June 1974). Publ., censored, 24 May 1972, reprinted 4 June 1972, then, revised, in *HW*.

Show Saturday (13 Oct. 1973–3 June 1974). Publ. Feb. 1974, then, revised, in *HW*.

The Life with a Hole in it (7 Aug.–Christmas). Publ. Christmas 1974.

'Have a little more' (Christmas)

1975

Bridge for the Living (28 Jan.–15 Dec.). Performed with music 11 Apr. 1981. Published 1981.

'When first we faced, and touching showed' (18–20 Dec.)

1976
Dear Jake (by 23 Jan.)
'Be my Valentine this Monday' (7–14 Feb.)
'Morning at last: there in the snow' (1–21 Feb.)
'We met at the end of the party' (7–22 Feb.)
'Once more upon the village green' (28 Mar. or May)
'I want to see them starving' (26 May)
'Davie, Davie' (15 Jan. 1974–1 Dec. 1976)

1977
'Well, I must arise and go now, and go to Innisfree' (13 Jan.)
'After Healey's trading figures' (9 Feb.)
'California, here I come' (11 Apr.)
'The little lives of earth and form' (6 May)
Administration (3 Mar. 1965–25 May 1977)
'Haymakers and reapers by Stubbs' (12 Nov.)
'I hope games like tossing the caber' Publ. Nov.
Aubade (11 Apr. 1974–23 Dec. 1977). Publ. 23 Dec.

1978
'The sky split apart in malice' (2 Mar.)
1952–1977 (27 Feb.–2 Mar.). Publ. 23 June.
'Thought you might welcome a dekko' (7 Apr.)
'Walt Whitman' (10 Apr.)
'If I could talk, I'd be a worthless prof' (17 Aug.)

1979
'The daily things we do' (Feb.)
'New brooms sweep clean' (Feb.)
'New eyes each year' (8–9 Mar.). Publ. 9 Mar.
The Mower (12 June–autumn). Publ. autumn.
Love Again (7 Aug. 1975–20 Sept. 1979)
'After eating in honour of Chichele' (14 Dec.)
'Apples on a Christmas tree!' (?Christmas)

1980
'The one thing I'd say about A. Thwaite' (7 Feb.)
The View (29 Mar. 1972–9 Feb. 1980)
'All work & no wassail' (29 Nov.)

1981
'Good for you, Gavin' (20 Nov. 1979–4 Feb. 1981)
'Beware the travelogue, my son' (24 Mar.)
'"When one door shuts, another opens." Cock!' (20 Sept.)

1982
'The chances are certainly slim' (2 Mar.)
1982 (21 July)
'Dear CHARLES, My Muse, asleep or dead' (by 24 Aug.). Publ.
  1982.
'My feet are clay, my brains are sodden' (10 Nov.)

1983
'By day, a lifted study-storehouse' (before 26 Oct.). Publ. 26 Oct.
'This collection of various scraps' (30 Oct.)
'Outside, a dog barks' (30 Oct.)

1984
Party Politics Publ. Jan.
'Last night we put the clocks on' (27 Mar.)
Bun's Outing (Christmas)

1985
'After reading the works of MacCaig' (10 Oct.)

Undated or Approximately Dated Poems
'There was an old fellow of Kaber'. Before 1977. Publ. 1982.
The Way we Live Now
'What is booze for?'
'When the night is hoar'
'On the shortest day'
'Roses, roses all the way?'
'No power cuts here – '
'Those long thin steeds'
'Though there's less at wch to purr'
'Snow on Valentine's Day!'

How to Win the Next Election, 311, 643–4
'How we behave, I find increasingly', 290
'Hurrying to catch my Comet', 52

'I am a ripe plum on a sunny wall', 172
'I am a woman lying on a leaf', 256–7
'I am the latest son', 203–4, 554
'I am washed upon a rock', 266, 593
'I deal with farmers, things like dips and feed', 77
'I don't like March!', 200, 552
'I dreamed I saw a commie rally', 310, 642
'I dreamed of an out-thrust arm of land', 16
'I feared these present years', 267–8
'I have despatched so many words', 245, 579
'I have started to say', 314, 647–8
'I hear you are at sea, and at once', 215
'I hope games like tossing the caber', 114, 494
'I looked for a pearl', 130
'I met an idiot at a bend in the lane', 216
'I never remember holding a full drink', 121
'I never was much of a one for beauty', 158–9
'I put my mouth', 11
I Remember, I Remember, 41–2, 382–3
'I saw it smell; I heard it stink', 235
'I saw three ships go sailing by', 21
'I see a girl dragged by the wrists', 15–16
'I should be glad to be in at the death', 174, 538–9
'I squeezed up the last stair to the room in the roof', 284–5
'I think I read, or have been told', 145
'I thought it would last my time –', 82–3
'I walk at random through the evening park', 202, 553
'I want to see them starving', 317, 652
'I will climb thirty steps to my room', 14
'I work all day, and get half-drunk at night', 115–16
'I would give all I possess', 231, 569
'I would I were where Russell plays', 304, 633–4
'I wrote these letters through a year', 225
'If approached by Sir Cyril Norwood', 225, 565
'If days were matches I would strike the lot', 201, 553
'If grief could burn out', 14
'If hands could free you, heart', 17
'If I could talk, I'd be a worthless prof', 319, 657

Myxomatosis, 37, 374–5